BANKING AND SECURITY LAW IN IRELAND

BANKING AND SECURITY LAW IN IRELAND

by

William Johnston

MA, Solicitor,
Partner, Arthur Cox

Butterworths

Ireland	Butterworth (Ireland) Ltd, 26 Upper Ormond Quay, DUBLIN 7
United Kingdom	Butterworths a Division of Reed Elsevier (UK) Ltd, Halsbury House, 35 Chancery Lane, LONDON WC2A 1EL and 4 Hill Street, EDINBURGH EH2 3JZ
Australia	Butterworths Pty Ltd, SYDNEY, MELBOURNE, BRISBANE, ADELAIDE, PERTH, CANBERRA and HOBART
Canada	Butterworths Canada Ltd, TORONTO and VANCOUVER
India	Butterworths India, NEW DELHI, India
Malaysia	Malayan Law Journal Sdn Bhd, KUALA LUMPUR
New Zealand	Butterworths of New Zealand Ltd, WELLINGTON and AUCKLAND
Puerto Rico	Butterworths of Puerto Rico Inc, SAN JUAN
Singapore	Reed Elsevier (Singapore) Ltd, SINGAPORE
South Africa	Butterworths Legal Publishers (Pty) Ltd, DURBAN
USA	Michie, CHARLOTTESVILLE, Virginia

© Butterworths 1998

A CIP Catalogue record for this book is available from the British Library.

ISBN 1 85475 8705

9 781854 758705

Printed in Ireland by Sciprint Ltd, Shannon.

scattered through the volumes of the Irish statutes are laws which though not exclusively dealing with the relationship of banker and customer (the Sale of Goods and Supply of Services Act, 1980, the Consumer Credit Act, 1995, the Family Home Protection Act, 1976, the Agricultural Credit Act 1978, for example) directly affect some aspect of it. In addition there is a considerable body of Irish case law (not all of it reported) on the subject and on the related law of securities. And there are EU directives which relate to banking law which have been implemented in this country by Irish regulations. The body of law relating to banking and securities, as the size of this volume eloquently testifies, is considerable and a considerable portion of it is Irish law. English text-books are therefore of only limited value to the practitioner and the need for an up to date and discrete text book on the subject has been a very real one. This need has been splendidly satisfied by Mr Johnston's work.

His task has not been a simple one. Take, for example, the law relating to fixed charges over book debts (a form of security which financial institutions frequently seek). The law on this subject has been developed by a number of Irish decisions (In *re Lakeglen Construction* [1980] IR 347; In *re Keenan Brothers* [1985] IR 347, In *re AH Masser Ltd* [1986] IR 455, In *re Wogan's (Drogheda) Ltd* [1993] 1 IR 157, In *re Holidair Ltd* [1994] 1 IR 417) and a careful exposition of the law required that these cases be analysed and explained. The distinction between book debts and the proceeds of book debts was one which was adverted by Walsh J in *Keenan Brothers* and as this distinction was fully explored in a later case in England (In *re New Bullas Trading* [1993] BCLC 1389 and [1994] BCLC 485) these developments called for consideration, as did the impact of EU law on charges on book debts. Having examined the case law on the subject and helpfully summarised it, the author then undertook what he rightly termed "the daunting prospect" of suggesting how a debenture might be drafted which would (a) ensure that the bank's charge over book debts might obtain priority over its customer's preferential creditors in the event of its insolvency and (b) meet the customer's requirement that the charge would not restrict the manner in which its business was carried on. But the author's task did not end there. The Oireachtas, in s 115 of the Finance Act, 1986 stepped in to restore the Revenue's priority in the event of the liquidation of a company which had executed a valid fixed charge over book debts, and this section was later amended by s 174 of the Finance Act, 1995. Both sections are carefully examined and the report of the Government Task Force on Small Businesses which recommended the repeal of the earlier legislation (because the level of finance to industry had been reduced following the drop in the securities available to banks following the enactment of the 1986 Act) is quoted.

Another example of the careful consideration given to the complexities of the subject matter of this work is to be found in the author's treatment of the law relating to the granting of security to banks over deposits held with them by their customer. This involved a review of recent Irish case law, the effect of the Companies (Amendment) Act, 1990 (as construed in *Re Atlantic Magnetics Ltd* [1993] 2 IR 561) and a recent decision of the House of Lords in *Re Bank of Credit and Commerce International SA (No 8)* [1997] 2 All ER 449. On this subject, as in many others dealt with in this work the benefit of an author with wide practical experience is clearly to be seen. For the author is able to suggest how the practical problems he has identified may be overcome, and provide precedents for doing so. Indeed, one of the strengths of this book are the forms and precedents which are made available to practitioners on a whole range of transactions involved in the banker/customer relationship (for example, the statutory declarations which may be required in cases in which the Family Law Acts apply, the forms of undertakings relating to title deeds and of certificates of title most recently approved by the Law Society). These forms and precedents may be available elsewhere but their accessibility in this volume practitioners will welcome.

A significant development in court procedures (and one not generally appreciated outside the Four Courts) has been the practice of the filing, in cases in which contentious legal issues arise, of written legal submissions by counsel which are supplemented by oral argument - a practice which is helpful for judges but, more importantly, appreciably reduces the length of court hearings. It used to be thought that text books by living authors should not be quoted in court (apparently on the curious ground that living authors might change their minds). Old traditions die hard and whilst written submissions frequently refer to the cases analysed in text books there seems to be a reluctance to refer to the text itself. The facts of reported cases and the reasons for the decisions which are recorded in them frequently require careful reading but the summary given by reliable authors is frequently a good starting point for a legal argument. Whether this view becomes generally acceptable or not, I venture to think that this work will be widely used in court in cases in which issues of banking and security law fall for consideration (either with or without express acknowledgement) and that its influence on the future development of that law will be considerable.

Declan Costello

Judge of the High Court from May 1977

Acting-President and later President of the High Court, October 1991 to December 1997.

Preface

60 years' ago, in 1938 Ireland's first President, Douglas Hyde, took office. But of more importance economically, 1938 was the year in which the Commission of Inquiry into Banking, Currency and Credit reported. The Report, running to over 600 pages, lead ultimately to the enactment of the first Central Bank Act and the establishment of the Central Bank of Ireland.

Banking, however, did not develop significantly until 40 years' ago, in 1958, when Ireland, a predominately agricultural country, suffered a poor harvest. That harvest offered the banks, at the time, the opportunity to extend credit, an opportunity which they took and so started the resurgence in Irish banking business. On the industrial front, that year marked the opening up of the customs free zone at Shannon Airport, and indeed, the commencement of the first Irish transatlantic air service. On the banking front that year saw the acquisition of Hibernian Bank by Bank of Ireland which marked the beginning of the consolidation and amalgamation of banks in Ireland. On the economic front, that year saw Ireland's first Programme for Economic Expansion and on the legal front the submission of the Report of the Company Law Reform Committee, chaired by Arthur Cox, incorporating its recommendations for the reform and up-dating of company law; this lead ultimately to the Companies Act, 1963. Since then, Ireland's economy has grown steadily and with it the development of banking and the provision of security for financing.

25 years' ago, in 1973, Ireland joined the European Economic Community thereby creating new markets for its exports; that year also saw a change of government and with it a dynamic new Foreign Affairs Minister, Garret FitzGerald, as well as the election of a new President, Erskine Childers, who rejuvenated the spirit of the Nation. As an economics student, in that year I travelled in a bus across Europe through the Iron Curtain, which divided Europe at the time, and entered Poland in darkness amidst a spectacular thunder storm. It was the turning point in my life as my meeting with maritime economics graduate Helena Andryca in Gdynia Harbour Authority and our subsequent marriage two years' later in Gdansk meant it was time to consider a more certain path of remuneration than that of an economics journalist, as had been recommended by my tutor in Trinity College Dublin; thus, with the support of Helena, I turned to the law.

Although my grandfathers George Johnston and John Cunningham, my father Robert and my brother Paul have written books on philosophy, medicine, taxation and engineering respectively, from the length of time it has taken to produce this work it would be a surprise if either of my patient and understanding sons George and Anthony were to follow in such footsteps.

In completing this work I would like to thank first Butterworth Ireland, not only for their faith in asking me to write this book, but also for their subsequent infinite patience in acknowledging that my principal task is that of looking after the interests of clients of Arthur Cox, whether they be banks or borrowers, in their day to day business. I would like to thank former Butterworth's employees Larry Ennis and Finola O'Sullivan who started me on the process of this work, as well as Therese Carrick who saw me through the middle ground. In the more recent years the general manager Gerard Coakley and legal editor Louise Leavy not only gave me the final necessary encouragement but organised and helped in the completion of this work in a very relaxed but professional manner. I am very much obliged to Julitta Clancy for preparing the index and laying it out in such a helpful manner - an essential ingredient in a book for any practitioner.

I am grateful to a number of my partners in Arthur Cox namely, Grainne Hennessy, Caroline Devlin, Isabel Foley and Carl O'Sullivan each of whom gave their time freely in pointing out improvements which were made to the script. I am grateful also to my colleague Ultan Shannon for his time and attention to detail.

I am particularly grateful to Tom Courtney, solicitor, author of *The Law of Private Companies* not only for the considerable time he spent in reading over half the manuscript and for his forthright and very helpful comments, but also for his enthusiasm and consistent vigorous support all of which contributed immeasurably to the completion of the work. Professor John Wylie and Brendan Hyland, solicitor (Roscrea and Kilkenny), each read a draft of a chapter and provided useful pointers.

Each chapter of this work has undergone several drafts. Not only has my secretary, Deirdre Walker, typed every word, but she has sorted innumerable jigsaw puzzles of words which few would have put up with. Her ability to read my writing, at times even better than I can, has proved to be invaluable. The laborious task undertaken with enthusiasm and competence greatly facilitated the completion of the book and is much appreciated.

25 years' ago a young gentleman became the Attorney General of Ireland before subsequently serving on the High Court Bench for over twenty years. The number of his judgments in this work are a testimony to both his service and his impact on the law. Mr Justice Costello was the obvious choice to prepare a foreword for this work. I am very grateful for the trouble he has taken to read the work and of course very honoured by his foreword.

One of Mr Justice Costello's early class-mates in Dublin was Meeda Cunningham, my mother - a person who gave her best in everything she did. It may be useful at times for bankers and lawyers, in their professional work, to remember her motto - "up to standard, not down to cost".

As the *Irish Times* indicated in an editorial commenting on the initiation of the Consumer Credit Bill in 1994, "credit is the blood of industry". Usually security is required to be provided for that credit. There are many facets to banking and the taking of security all of which have become more complex through a myriad of legislation and judicial authorities. This book attempts to give for the first time to persons interested, whether professionally or otherwise, an understanding of the law relating to banking and security in Ireland and its practical application.

However, the book is not a substitute for professional legal advice in any particular transaction. While care has been taken in the preparation and completion of this work, no responsibility is undertaken by me or by the publisher, in respect of any transaction which may be based, partly or wholly, on information set out in this publication.

Although there are a few references to 1998 developments, the book states the law as I see it as of 1st January 1998.

William Johnston
Dublin
Easter Day, 1998

Contents

Chapter 3   Banker's Duty of Secrecy

Chapter 4   Bank Accounts

Chapter 5   Cheques

Chapter 6   Payments by Bankers

Chapter 7   Facility Letters

Chapter 8   Avoidance of Security by Undue Influence

Chapter 10 Mortgages and Charges of Land

Chapter 11 Mortgages and Fixed Charges of Chattels

Chapter 12 Pledges and Trust Receipts

Chapter 13 Floating Charges

Chapter 14 Security over Debts

Chapter 15 Security over Deposits

Chapter 18 Compliance

Table of Statutes

Constitution of Ireland

Statutory Instruments

Table of Cases

B

1

D

E

F

G

H

I

L

M

O

Q

R

S

T

U

Y

Z

Chapter 1

The Relationship of Banker and Customer

WHO IS A BANKER OR BANK

Common Law Definition

> "By custom we call a man a banker who has an open shop, with proper
> counters, servants, and books for receiving other people's money, in order to
> keep it safe, and return it upon demand; and when any man has opened such a
> shop we call him a banker, without inquiring whether any man has given him
> money to keep".

[1.01] This description of a banker, made in the House of Commons over 250
years ago,[1] may still be regarded as generally applicable to-day.

[1.02] Subsequently, at the beginning of this century the Irish Court of Appeal
held in *Re Shields' Estate*[2] that a business which received moneys in exchange
for promissory notes and deposit receipts and lent out moneys on promissory
notes or otherwise was the business of a banker. Holmes LJ stated, "the real
business of the banker is to obtain deposits of money which he may use for his
own profit by lending it out again."[3] This decision was supported in Australia in
*The Commissioners of the State Savings Bank of Victoria v Permewan, Wright
& Co Ltd.*[4] However, more recently Lord Denning pointed out that if this were
still the law it would mean the building societies were all banks and that "money
is now paid and received by cheque to such an extent that no person can be
considered a banker unless he handles cheques as freely as cash."[5]
In the same decision of the English Court of Appeal, Harman LJ noted that[6] "the
collection of cheques is in English practice, at any rate in recent times, an
additional requirement" and Diplock LJ added,[7] "Definitions and dicta in cases

---

1. In 1746 by Mr Joseph Danvers, see FR Ryder, 'The Business of Banking (Practical Aspects of
   the Legal Definition)' - Gilbart Lectures on Banking 1970; it seems though at that time banking
   in Ireland was used primarily to enable landlords to transfer rents from the provinces to Dublin
   or from Dublin to London, see Ollerenshaw, *Banking in Nineteenth Century Ireland* (1987)
   p 4.
2. [1901] 1 IR 172.
3. *Ibid* at 207.
4. (1915) 19 CLR 457.
5. In *United Dominions Trust Ltd v Kirkwood* [1966] 1 All ER 968 at 975; [1966] 2 WLR 1083 at
   1091.
6. *Ibid* 982 and 1101 respectively.
7. *Ibid* at 986 and 1107 respectively.

before the First World War, before cheques became the common method of payment, must I think be approached with caution."

However, in 1955 one of the great writers on banking law wrote:[8]

> "... a banker, in the modern sense of the word, may be defined as one whose principal function is the borrowing of money from some at a low rate of interest (or, indeed, in the case of current accounts today, without payment of interest) for the purpose of employing such money profitably, by investing it in securities, by making advances and by discounting bills. The essential feature, therefore, of a banker is the borrowing from some in order to lend to others".

Furthermore, the Irish Court of Appeal's decision in *Re Shields' Estate*[9] has been applied since the Second World War in *Commercial Banking Co Ltd v Hartigan*[10] where it was held that a company which had no current accounts and did not operate on cheques drawn by customers was nevertheless *bona fide* carrying on the business of banking.

The suggestion made by the English Court of Appeal that a banker must handle cheques to be regarded as a banker is surely erroneous as Isaacs J pointed out in the High Court of Australia:[11] "bankers are not bound by law to open current accounts. They may confine themselves, if they wish, to what are known as deposit accounts."

[1.03] One of the better, if non-legalistic, descriptions of the nature of banking may be found in Isaacs J's judgment in the High Court of Australia where he said:[12]

> "The essential characteristics of the business of banking ... may be described as the collection of money by receiving deposits upon loan, repayable when and as expressly or impliedly agreed upon, and the utilisation of the money so collected by lending it again in such sums as are required. These are the essential functions of a bank as an instrument of society. It is, in effect, a financial reservoir receiving streams of currency in every direction, and from which they issue outflowing streams where and as required to sustain and fructify or assist commercial, industrial or other enterprises or adventures."

The difficulty of defining what a bank is can be seen from the Report of the Company Law Committee in England under the chairmanship of Lord Jenkins.[13]

[8.] Milnes Holden, *The History of Negotiable Instruments in English Law* (1955) p 204.
[9.] [1901] 1 IR 172.
[10.] (1952) 86 ILTR 109; see also Lord Goddard's judgment in *R v Industrial Disputes Tribunal* [1954] 2 All ER 730.
[11.] *The Commissioners of the State Savings Bank of Victoria v Permewan, Wright & Co Ltd* (1915) 19 CLR 457 at 471.
[12.] *Ibid* at 470-471.
[13.] Cmnd 1749.

The Board of Trade had requested the Committee to define "bank" or "banking business" in their Report. The Committee's considered response was, "We do not think it would be possible."[14]

Statutory Definition

"Bankers are a privileged class. They are exempt from the vexatious restrictions which are imposed on other moneylenders. They are an exclusive circle to which entry is limited. It is important that we should know what these privileges are; for we shall see that Parliament, when granting them, has never defined who is a banker."[15]

[1.04] There are many statutes which describe or refer to a bank, banker or banking business.[16] However the principal statutes applicable to banking are the Central Bank Acts, 1942 to 1997. The Central Bank Act, 1971 provides that a person may not, unless he obtains a banking licence from and maintains a stipulated deposit with, the Central Bank of Ireland (or is otherwise exempted), in or outside the State, carry on banking business or hold himself out or represent himself as a banker or as carrying on banking business or on behalf of any other person accept deposits or other repayable funds from the public.[17]

[1.05] Those persons specifically exempted include the Central Bank of Ireland, the central banks in the other States that are members of the European Union, ACC Bank plc, ICC Bank plc, the Post Office Savings Bank, a trustee savings bank certified under the Trustee Savings Banks Acts, building societies, industrial and provident societies, friendly societies, credit unions or the managers or trustees under a unit trust or collective investment scheme in respect of the carrying on of the business of the scheme.[18] The Minister for Finance may add or delete some of the persons from the foregoing list.[19] The Central Bank Act 1971 further provides that the Central Bank may exempt a person from holding a banking licence if in the opinion of the Central Bank the

---

[14.] *Ibid* at para 405; for further analysis of the common law meaning of "bank" or "banking business" see the historical outline given by Lord Denning MR and Diplock LJ in *United Dominions Trust Ltd v Kirkwood* [1966] 1 All ER 968; [1966] 2 WLR 1083; the judgment of Ross J, although reversed by the Irish Court of Appeal in *Re Shields' Estate* [1901] 1 IR 172 includes a brief description of the historical development of banking in Ireland.

[15.] Lord Denning MR in *United Dominions Trust Ltd v Kirkwood* [1966] 1 All ER 968 at 972.

[16.] Such as the Bankers' Books Evidence Act, 1879 (s 9), as amended by the Disclosure of Certain Information for Taxation and Other Purposes Act, 1996, (s 13), the Bills of Exchange Act, 1882 (s 2) as amended by the Building Societies Act, 1989 (s 126(2)), the Industrial and Provident Societies Act, 1893 (s 19), the Cheques Act, 1959, the Insurance (Amendment) Act, 1978 (s 2), the Building Societies Act, 1989 (s 2).

[17.] Section 7 (as amended by the Central Bank Act, 1997, s 70).

[18.] Section 7(4)(a) (as amended by s 30 of the Central Bank Act, 1989).

[19.] Section 7(4)(b) (as amended by s 31 of the Central Bank Act, 1989).

person does not in fact carry on or propose to carry on banking business and does not otherwise hold himself out or represent himself as a banker or as carrying on banking business.[20] In practice, the Central Bank will not permit a body of persons to carry on business with the word bank in its name unless that body has a banking licence.[21]

[1.06] Banking business is defined by the Central Bank Act, 1971[22] as meaning;

    (a) the business of accepting, on own account, sums of money from the public in the form of deposits or other repayable funds whether or not involving the issue of securities or other obligations, howsoever described, or

    (b) the business aforesaid and any other business normally carried on by a bank, which may include the granting of credits on own account.

The specific statutory exclusions from the foregoing definition include:

    (i) deposits with a trader from persons employed by him in his trading business or from his customers in the normal course of his trading business and deposits or instalments in respect of the letting, leasing or selling of goods under a hire-purchase agreement or a leasing agreement, or a credit sale agreement, or

        .....

    (vi) a sum or sums of money accepted by a person where it can be shown that -

        (I) no part of the business activities of the person so accepting or of any other person is financed wholly or substantially out of those funds, and

        (II) such funds are, in the normal course of business, accepted on a casual or incidental basis only.

[1.07] In recognising that the definition is somewhat wide the legislation provides[23] that, subject to such conditions (if any) as it may consider appropriate, the Central Bank:

    may exempt any person or any class or classes of person from the requirement to hold a licence in respect of the issuing of any category or categories of securities or other obligations, howsoever described, where -

---

[20.] Section 8(1) (as amended by s 31 of the Central Bank Act, 1989).

[21.] Section 21 of the Companies Act 1963 prohibits a company from being registered by a name which in the opinion of the Minister for Enterprise, Trade and Employment "is undesirable". It may be possible to carry on business other than banking business through a name in a foreign language the English translation of which includes the word bank.

[22.] Section 2 (as amended by s 70 of the Central Bank Act, 1997).

[23.] Central Bank Act, 1971 s 8(2)(a) (as amended by s 70 of the Central Bank Act, 1997).

(i) the requirements would arise only out of the issuing of such securities or other obligations to which the definition of "banking business" relates; and

(ii) the [Central] Bank is of the opinion that the exemption would not conflict with the orderly and proper regulation of banking.

The Central Bank has utilised this exemption on three occasions to permit the issue of commercial paper.[24]

The initial widening of the definition of banking business by the Central Bank Act 1989 to its present format was done so as, "to secure greater protection for the public from unauthorised deposit taking and to conform with definitions of banking in EC Directives."[25] The greater protection being that a person whose business comes within the definition would be obliged to comply with the Central Bank's licensing requirements.

The Central Bank is now empowered to seek an injunction to prohibit the continuance by any person of any banking business or of such person holding himself out as a banker.[26]

[1.08] The Second EC Banking Directive gave mutual recognition in the provision of banking services between members of the European Union. This was implemented in Ireland on 1 January 1993 pursuant to the European Communities (Licensing and Supervision of Credit Institutions) Regulations, 1992.[27] Under these Regulations a credit institution authorised and supervised by the competent authority of another Member State may carry on banking business within Ireland by establishing a branch or by any other means provided that the business is in accordance with the authorisation of the credit institution in the home Member State.[28]

Furthermore, a financial institution which is a subsidiary of a credit institution, or which is a jointly owned subsidiary of two or more credit institutions, may carry on banking business within Ireland by establishing a branch subject to complying with conditions specified in the Regulations.

WHO IS A CUSTOMER OF A BANK

"There must be some sort of account, either a deposit or a current account or some similar relation, to make a man a customer of a banker."

[1.09] These are the words of Lord Davey in his judgment in *Great Western Railway Co v London and County Banking Co Ltd*.[29] In that case, Mr Huggins had cashed cheques received to his order at the London and County Banking Co Ltd over the course of many years. However, Mr Huggins had no account with

---

24. 31 October 1989, 16 November 1990 and 20 February 1998; see further para **[7.78]**.
25. Explanatory and Financial Memorandum to the Central Bank Bill, 1988.
26. Central Bank Act, 1997 s 74.
27. SI 395/1992.
28. Reg 20.
29. [1901] AC 414 at 420.

the bank and accordingly the House of Lords held he was not a customer of the bank. This case established that a course of dealing alone will not be sufficient to make a person a customer of a bank.

On the other hand, once a bank has opened, or agreed to open, an account for a person,[30] or as soon as a bank accepts instructions from a person,[31] that person becomes a customer without the need to establish any course of dealing. It has been said that the most ordinary meaning of a customer is "a person who keeps an account at the bank".[32] Thus, a person may be regarded as a customer of a bank either as soon as he opens an account with the bank or as soon as the bank accepts instructions from the person, but not when he requests a bank simply to cash a cheque.[33]

CONTRACTUAL RELATIONSHIP

"Banking law is not a separate body of law, though, like innumerable other activities, it has statutory provisions dealing exclusively with it, and, being a distinctive and important activity, text-books dealing separately with it. Those aspects of law with which we are at present concerned are aspects of the general law of contract applicable to banking. The principles of that law of contract applicable to banking are the principles of the general law of contract."[34]

Offer and Acceptance

[1.10] Thus, the basic relationship between a banker and customer arises under contract[35] and is that of debtor and creditor.[36] The judgment of Lord Cottenham

---

30. *Ladbroke and Co v Todd* (1914) 30 TLR 433; *Commissioners of Taxation v English, Scottish and Australian Bank Ltd* [1920] AC 683 (Privy Council); *Warren Metals Ltd v Colonial Catering Co Ltd* [1975] 1 NZLR 273.

31. *Woods v Martins Bank Ltd* [1958] 3 All ER 166; [1958] 1 WLR 1018.

32. Bankes LJ in *Importers Company Ltd v Westminster Bank Ltd* [1927] 2 KB 297.

33. For a fuller treatment of what is a customer see *Paget's Law of Banking* (11th ed, 1996) pp 106-109; see also Weerasooria, *Banking Law and the Financial System in Australia* (2nd ed, 1988) pp 241-246.

34. Ungoed-Thomas J in *Selangor United Rubber Estates Ltd v Cradock (No 3)* [1968] 1 WLR 1555 at 1607.

35. *Paget's Law of Banking* (11th ed, 1996) p 110, Milnes Holden, *The Law and Practice of Banking* (5th ed, 1991) Ch 2, Penn, Shea and Arora, *The Law Relating to Domestic Banking* (1987) para 30.1; "in the ordinary case of banker and customer their relations depend either entirely or mainly upon an implied contract" - *per* Mocatta J in *Burnett v Westminster Bank Ltd* [1965] 3 All ER 81 at 85.

36. See *Sleech's Case (Devaynes v Noble)* (1816) Cas in Ch 531 at 558; Lord Finlay in *London Joint Stock Bank Ltd v Macmillan and Arthur* [1918] AC 777 at 789; Ronan LJ and O'Connor LJ in *Reade v The Royal Bank of Ireland Ltd* [1922] 2 IR 22 at 24 and 26 respectively; Lord Atkinson in *Westminster Bank Ltd v Hilton* (1926) 43 TLR 124 at 126; Kennedy CJ in *Kinlan v The Ulster Bank Ltd* [1928] IR 171 at 181; Lord Goddard CJ in *R v Davenport* [1954] 1 All ER 602 at 603; McMullin J in *Balmoral Supermarket Ltd v Bank of New Zealand* [1974] 2 NZLR 155 at 156; May LJ in *Lipkin Gorman v Karpnale Ltd* [1992] 4 All ER 409 at 418; Rose LJ in *Re Bank of Credit and Commerce International SA (No 8)* [1996] 2 BCLC 254 at 263.

LC in *Foley v Hill*[37]sets out the position. He said:[38]

> "The money placed in the custody of a banker is, to all intents and purposes, the money of the banker, to do with it as he pleases; he is guilty of no breach of trust in employing it; he is not answerable to the principal if he puts it into jeopardy, if he engages in a hazardous speculation; he is not bound to keep it, or deal with it, as the property of his principal; but he is of course answerable for the amount, because he has contracted, having received that money, to repay to the principal, when demanded, a sum equivalent to that paid into his hands ... the banker is not an agent, or factor, but he is a debtor."

[1.11] Following that decision the nature of the relationship was set out clearly by Atkin LJ in *Joachimson v Swiss Bank Corp*[39] where he said:[40]

> "... there is only one contract made between the bank and its customer. The terms of that contract involve obligations on both sides and require careful statement. They appear upon consideration to include the following provisions:

> (1) The bank undertakes to receive money and to collect bills for its customer's account.[41]

> (2) The proceeds so received are not to be held in trust for the customer, but the bank borrows the proceeds and undertakes to repay them.

> (3) The promise to repay is to repay at the branch of the bank where the account is kept, and during banking hours.[42]

> (4) It includes a promise to repay any part of the amount due against the written order of the customer addressed to the bank at the branch, and as such written orders may be outstanding in the ordinary course of business for two or three days, it is a term of the contract that the bank will not cease to do business with the customer except upon reasonable notice.

> (5) The customer on his part undertakes to exercise reasonable care in executing his written orders so as not to mislead the bank or to facilitate forgery.

[37.] (1848) 2 HLC 28.

[38.] *Ibid* at 36; applied by Ronan LJ in *Reade v The Royal Bank of Ireland Ltd* [1922] 2 IR 22 at 24.

[39.] [1921] 3 KB 110; the principles of which were approved by the Supreme Court in *Kinlan v Ulster Bank Ltd* [1928] IR 171 (Kennedy CJ at 181, Murnaghan J at 193); the Privy Council regarded it as "the classic analysis" of the contractual relationship, see *Tai Hing Cotton Mill Ltd v Liu Chong Hing Bank Ltd* [1985] 2 All ER 947.

[40.] *Ibid* at 127; the numbering in the quotation is inserted by the author; for an analysis of this statement see Ungoed-Thomas J in *Selangor United Rubber Estates Ltd v Cradock (No 3)* [1968] 1 WLR 1555 at 1594.

[41.] The collection of bills includes the collection of dividend warrants, see McCarthy J in *Schioler v Westminster Bank Ltd* [1970] 3 All ER 177 at 182.

[42.] See also *Clare & Co v Dresdner Bank* [1915] 2 KB 576 where the plaintiff who had an account at the Berlin branch of the defendants was not entitled to demand payment from the London branch.

(6) ... it is necessarily a term of such contract that the bank is not liable to pay the customer the full amount of his balance until he demands payment from the bank at the branch at which the current account is kept."[43]

[1.12] As with all contractual relationships, the first point to note is that there must be offer and acceptance. A useful example is the case of *Balmoral Supermarket Ltd v Bank of New Zealand.*[44] The plaintiff's employee entered the defendant's bank premises and placed cash on the counter. The bank clerk counted some of the cash and put the counted cash aside. During the count the bank was robbed and the uncounted cash on the counter was taken. The Supreme Court of New Zealand held that the bank had not accepted the uncounted cash and accordingly the loss was that of the bank's customer.

Consideration

[1.13] The third essential ingredient for contracts not under seal is consideration. An oral contract, or a written contract executed under hand, will be unenforceable unless the obligation contained in the contract is given for consideration.[45] A financing company learnt this lesson the hard way in *The Commodity Broking Co Ltd v Meehan.*[46] In that case the defendant, the owner of Pistola Investments Ltd which owed Stg£36,000 to the plaintiff, acknowledged that the company was insolvent. The defendant refused to sign a guarantee of the indebtedness but agreed to pay Stg£1,000 a month. After receiving two payments the plaintiff received no further moneys and accordingly sued the defendant for the balance of the debt claiming that as a result of the defendant's agreement he had refrained from suing the company and had thus given consideration. Barron J found that the agreement was an indemnity rather than a guarantee but that there was no implied or express request by the defendant for the plaintiff not to sue the company - "its reason for not doing so was not the defendant's promise to pay, but the realisation that it would be a fruitless exercise"[47] - no consideration was given for the defendant's promise. Accordingly, the plaintiff's claim was dismissed.

[1.14] This case can be contrasted with that of *Fullerton v Provincial Bank of Ireland*[48] where the House of Lords held that the forbearance by the bank from

---

[43.] "As a general rule the contract between a bank and its customer is governed by the law of the place where the account is kept, in the absence of agreement to the contrary" - Staughten J in *Libyan Arab Foreign Bank v Bankers Trust Co* [1988] 1 ILTR 259 at 270.

[44.] [1974] 2 NZLR 155.

[45.] See generally Clark, *Contract Law in Ireland* (3rd ed, 1992) Ch 2; Chesire, Fifoot & Furmston's *Law of Contract* (13th ed, 1996) Ch 4.

[46.] [1985] IR 12.

[47.] *Ibid* at 21.

[48.] [1903] AC 309.

demanding immediate repayment of the overdraft was consideration for the customer's agreement to deposit title deeds as security for the overdraft although the agreement was made after the debt had been incurred. Lord Macnaghten stated:[49]

> "it is not necessary that there should be an arrangement for forbearance for any definite or particular time. It is quite enough if you can infer from the surrounding circumstances that there was an implied request for forbearance for a time, and that forbearance for a reasonable time was in fact extended to the person who asked for it."

Banks and their advisers should not be complacent as to the courts ability to imply forbearance. In *Provincial Bank of Ireland Ltd v Donnell*[50] Andrews LJ stated in the Northern Ireland Court of Appeal: "one ought to be slow in implying consideration in favour of the Bank, whose document this is."[51]

[1.15] It should be noted however that forbearance, to be sufficient consideration, must in reality be forbearance from something it would not otherwise have had. In *Blanford & Houdret Ltd v Bray Travel Holdings Ltd & Hopkins*[52] Gannon J held that a guarantee given by the second defendant for the first defendant's debts was unenforceable as the consideration was past[53] - the promise by the plaintiff in return for the guarantee to forebear from exercising his right to withhold future services from the first defendant was a right the plaintiff had in any event once the first defendant's payments were in arrears.

Implied Terms

[1.16] Every contract involving a service entered into by a bank in the course of its business shall, unless properly excluded, have terms implied into the contract that:[54]

   (i)   the bank has the necessary skill to render the service,

   (ii) the bank will supply the service with due skill, care and diligence, and

   (iii) where materials are used (such as computers), they will be sound and reasonably fit for the purpose for which they are required.

---

49. *Ibid* at 313.
50. [1934] NI 33; see para **[9.03]** below.
51. *Ibid* at 44.
52. High Court, unrep, 11 November 1983, Gannon J,.
53. Past consideration is no consideration - see Clark, *Contract Law in Ireland* (3rd ed, 1992) p 47, Chesire, Fifoot and Furmston's *Law of Contract* (13th ed, 1996) p 76.
54. Sale of Goods and Supply of Services Act, 1980 s 39 (the fourth implied term that where goods are supplied under the contract they will be of merchantable quality would rarely apply to a banking contract).

Accordingly, any breach of these terms (where not excluded) gives rise to an action for damages for loss suffered arising out of such breach.[55]

[1.17] These implied terms may be excluded or varied by an express term of the contract or by the course of dealing between the parties (or by usage if the usage is such as to bind parties to the contract).[56] If these implied terms are to be excluded, all implied terms, not just statutory, should be excluded as "a bank has a duty under its contract with its customer to exercise 'reasonable care and skill' in carrying out its part with regard to operations within its contract with its customer."[57]
However, where the customer of the bank "deals as consumer", the bank must show that the express exclusion is (1) "fair and reasonable" and (2) has been specifically brought to the customer's attention.[58] A customer will be deemed to "deal as consumer" provided first, he neither makes the contract in the course of a business nor holds himself out as doing so, secondly, the bank makes the contract in the course of a business and thirdly, the services supplied pursuant to the contract are of a type ordinarily supplied for private use.[59]

[1.18] Additional remedies are given to persons who enter into a contract for the supply of a service as a result of a misrepresentation being made to that person.[60] Where the contract contains a clause excluding or restricting a liability or remedy for misrepresentation such exclusion or restriction is unenforceable unless it is shown to be "fair and reasonable".[61]

[1.19] The Sale of Goods and Supply of Services Act, 1980 provides[62] that where a question arises as to whether a term is fair and reasonable "regard shall be had to the criteria set out in the Schedule in deciding it." The first paragraph of the Schedule states that:

> In determining .... if a term is fair and reasonable the test is that it shall be a fair and reasonable one to be included having regard to the circumstances which

---

55. See Clark, *Contract Law in Ireland* (3rd ed, 1992) Ch 19; Chesire Fifoot & Furmston's *Law of Contract* (13th ed, 1996) Ch 21.
56. Sale of Goods and Supply of Services Act, 1980, s 40(1).
57. Ungoed-Thomas J in *Selangor United Rubber Estates Ltd v Cradock (No 3)* [1968] 1 WLR 1555 at 1608.
58. Sale of Goods and Supply of Services Act, 1980, s 40(1).
59. Sale of Goods and Supply of Services Act, 1980, s 3(1); see *Re O'Callaghan v Hamilton Leasing (Ireland) Ltd* [1984] ILRM 146 where McWilliam J held that a person does not deal as consumer where he purchases goods for the purpose of his business (even where such goods are not to be resold); see also *Cunningham v Woodchester Investments Ltd*, High Court, unrep, 16 November 1984, McWilliam J.
60. Sale of Goods and Supply of Services Act, 1980, ss 43-45.
61. *Ibid* s 46.
62. Section 2.

were, or ought reasonably to have been, known to or in contemplation of the parties when the contract was made."

The second paragraph states:[63]

> Regard is to be had in particular to any of the following which appear to be relevant:
>
> (a) the strength of the bargaining positions of the parties relative to each other, taking into account (among other things) alternative means by which the customer's requirements could have been met;
>
> (b) whether the customer received an inducement to agree to the term, or in accepting it had an opportunity of entering into a similar contract with other persons, but without having to accept a similar term;
>
> (c) whether the customer knew or ought reasonably to have known of the existence and extent of the term (having regard, among other things, to any custom of the trade and any previous course of dealing between the parties);
>
> (d) where the term excludes or restricts any relevant liability if some condition is not complied with, whether it was reasonable at the time of the contract to expect that compliance with that condition would be practicable.

Exemption Clauses

[1.20] It might be noted though, that even where the recipient of the service is not dealing as consumer, reasonable notice of exemption clauses should be given prior to the contract being concluded.[64] Failure to do so may prevent the bank from relying upon them. In *Western Meats Ltd v National Ice and Cold Storage Co Ltd and Nordic Cold Storage Ltd*[65] Barrington J held that "a businessman, offering a specialist service, but accepting no responsibility for it, must bring home clearly to the party dealing with him that he accepts no such responsibility".[66] In that case, although the court held that the parties were competent to have exclusion clauses, the failure to bring to the attention of the recipient of the service the clause excluding damage due to negligence or any other cause whatsoever prevented the supplier from being able to rely on the clause.

[1.21] Although the Supreme Court has held that an exclusion clause may not be relied upon where there has been breach of a fundamental term of the contract,[67]

---

63. There is a fifth factor not relevant to a banker-customer relationship.
64. For further reading on exemption clauses and their application see Clark, *Contract Law in Ireland* (3rd ed, 1992) Ch 7.
65. [1982] ILRM 99.
66. *Ibid* at 102.
67. *Clayton Love & Sons (Dublin) v British & Irish Steampacket Co Ltd* (1970) 104 ILTR 157.

there is some doubt as to whether this decision would be followed again in the Supreme Court.[68] The principal English authority[69] which states that exclusion clauses which are clear and unambiguous should be given effect to has received judicial approval in Ireland.[70] However, bankers should note that no matter how clear the exemption clause, a court may find that it is ineffective if it is used to exclude the consequences of breach of a fundamental term.[71]

Illegal Contracts

[1.22] Banks and other persons who lend money should note that money lent for an illegal purpose is irrecoverable.[72] In *Anthony v Shea*[73] the Circuit Court held that money knowingly lent for the purpose of gaming was irrecoverable.

Similarly where the lender of money exceeds its statutory restriction on lending, loans made exceeding such limits may not be recovered by lawful action. In *Irvine v Teague*[74] the plaintiff exceeded its statutory power of being permitted to lend £10 to a borrower. It was held that the loan being contrary to statute could not be recovered and the mortgage given as security could not be enforced. There may however, be circumstances where an unauthorised loan is not necessarily illegal and irrecoverable.[75]

MISTAKE

"Whenever a man of full age and understanding, who can read and write, signs a legal document which is put before him for signature - by which I mean a document which, it is apparent on the face of it, is intended to have legal consequences - then, if he does not take the trouble to read it but signs it as it is, relying on the word of another as to its character or contents or effect, he

---

68. See Clark, *Contract Law in Ireland* (3rd ed, 1992), pp 149-151.
69. House of Lords' decision in *Photo Production Ltd v Securicor Transport Ltd* [1980] 1 All ER 556; see also the subsequent House of Lords' decisions in *Ailsa Craig Fishing Co Ltd v Malvern Fishing Co Ltd* [1983] 1 All ER 101 and *George Mitchell (Chesterhall) Ltd v Finney Lock Seeds Ltd* [1983] 2 All ER 737.
70. *Western Meats Ltd v National Ice and Cold Storage Co Ltd and Nordic Cold Storage Ltd* [1982] ILRM 99 at 101.
71. Either by the application of *Clayton Love & Sons (Dublin) Ltd v British & Irish Steampacket Co Ltd* (1970) 104 ILTR 157 or if applicable by finding the exclusion clause is not fair and reasonable.
72. See Furmston in 'Illegality and Banking Transactions' - Butterworths Banking & Financial Law Review 1987 p 152 - "Essentially the answer must depend on BANKER'S knowledge, actual or imputed, of the illegal purpose of the loan ... It seems clear ... that if BANKER has no reason to suspect CUSTOMER'S improper purpose, he can recover, and that if he actually knows it he cannot".
73. (1951) 86 ILTR 29.
74. (1898) 32 ILTR 109.
75. See *The Treasurer of the Enniskillen Loan Fund Society v Green* [1898] 2 IR 103 and *Lindsay v Maguire* [1899] 2 IR 554.

cannot be heard to say that it is not his document. By his conduct in signing it he has represented, to all those into whose hands it may come, that it is his document; and once they act on it as being his document, he cannot go back on it, and say that it was a nullity from the beginning."[76]

[1.23] This statement of principle by Lord Denning MR was considered by Lord Pearson to be "not only a clear and concise formulation but also a valuable guide to the right decision to be given by a court in any ordinary case."[77]

[1.24] The courts, however, may give relief to a person who without being negligent, signs an agreement with another and subsequently claims he understood the agreement to be something incorporating very different rights and obligations. This claim is known as a claim of *non est factum*.[78] In *Bank of Ireland v McManamy*[79] the defendants signed a guarantee of a co-operative society's indebtedness to the bank. At the time of signing the guarantee they believed it to be a receipt for manure received from the co-operative or in some cases a receipt for milk supplied to the co-operative (at the initial trial the jury found that the guarantee was signed by the defendants without negligence on their part). The court held that the defendants were not bound by the guarantee and in so doing applied the principle set by Byles J in *Foster v McKinnon*,[80] namely that:[81]

"It seems plain, on principle and on authority, that, if a blind man, or a man who cannot read, or who for some reason (not implying negligence) forbears to read, has a written contract falsely read over to him, the reader misreading to such a degree that the written contract is of a nature altogether different from the contract pretended to be read from the paper which the blind or illiterate man afterwards signs; then, at least if there be no negligence, the signature so obtained is of no force. And it is invalid not merely on the ground of fraud, where fraud exists, but on the ground that the mind of the signer did not accompany the signature; in other words, that he never intended to sign, and therefore in contemplation of law never did sign, the contract to which his name is appended."

Cherry LCJ explained in *Bank of Ireland v McManamy*[82] that:

"where a party signs a document under a fundamental mistake as to its nature and character, and that mistake is not due to negligence on his part, he is not bound by his signature, upon the ground that there is, in reality, no contract at

---

[76.] Lord Denning MR in *Gallie v Lee* [1969] 1 All ER 1062 at 1072.
[77.] *Saunders v Anglia Building Society* [1970] 3 All ER 961 at 978.
[78.] The English translation of which is "it is not his deed".
[79.] [1916] 2 IR 161.
[80.] (1869) LR 4 CP 704 - see Chesire, Fifoot & Furmston's *Law of Contract* (13th ed, 1996) p 268.
[81.] (1869) LR 4 CP 704 at 711.
[82.] [1916] 2 IR 161 at 173.

all binding on his part ... The principle of the cases is not, however, that fraud vitiates consent, but rather that there is an entire absence of consent. That the mind of the party who signs under a fundamental error does not go with the act of signing, and that there is consequently no contract at all in fact."

[1.25] More recently, in England the House of Lords, while acknowledging the essential features of the doctrine contained in the above quoted decision in *Foster v McKinnon*,[83] has shown that the plea of *non est factum* should be kept within narrow limits. In *Saunders v Anglia Building Society*[84] a widow who intended to give her house to a nephew subject to a right of residence in her favour signed a deed transferring the house to a third party who subsequently mortgaged the house to a building society. At the time of signing, the widow was unable to read the deed due to her broken glasses but had been informed by the third party that it transferred the house to her nephew in accordance with her wishes. The House of Lords affirmed the Court of Appeal's decision[85] which held that as the essential character of the document which the widow intended to execute was such as to divest herself of her property by transferring it to another so that the transferee could deal with the property and raise money on it, the deed was not totally different in character than that which she intended to sign and accordingly the plea of *non est factum* failed.

[1.26] The legal position on *non est factum* may be summarised by Mocatta J's interpretation[86] of the House of Lords' decision[87] namely:

"That case decided that

(a) there is a heavy burden of proof on the person who seeks to invoke the remedy;

(b) there must be a radical or fundamental difference between what the defendant signed and what he thought he had signed; and

(c) the defendant must prove he acted carefully."

Signing Incomplete Forms

[1.27] The subsequent decision in *United Dominions Trust Ltd v Western*[88] is a reminder of the dangers of signing blank forms. In that case the defendant agreed to purchase a car; the car dealer produced a form which the defendant signed leaving the dealer to fill in the blanks. The dealer inserted higher figures

---

83. (1869) LR 4 CP 704; see Lord Pearson in *Saunders v Anglia Building Society* [1970] 3 All ER 961 at 980.
84. [1970] 3 All ER 961.
85. *Gallie v Lee* [1969] 1 All ER 1062.
86. In *Credit Lyonnais v PT Barnard & Associates Ltd* [1976] ILTR 557 at 559.
87. In *Saunders v Anglia Building Society* [1970] 3 All ER 961.
88. [1975] 3 All ER 1017.

than agreed. The plaintiff finance company accepted the transaction in good faith and sent the defendant a copy of the agreement. The defendant made no complaint and following his default he then claimed there was no valid contract as the document did not represent his true intention and thus the consensus *ad idem* necessary to constitute a contract was absent. The English Court of Appeal held that the signatory was under a duty of care in completing the document and that as he had failed to discharge the onus of showing he acted carefully the contract was binding. Megaw LJ quoted[89] Lord Wilberforce's words in *Saunders v Anglia Building Society*:[90]

> "a person who signs a document, and parts with it so that it may come into other hands, has a responsibility, that of the normal one of prudence, to take care what he signs, which, if neglected, prevents him from denying his liability under the document according to its tenor."

Thus, if reasonable care is not exercised the plea of *non est factum* will not be upheld.[91]

[1.28] This scenario was put simply by Lord Pearson in *Saunders v Anglia Building Society*[92] when he said:

> "Suppose that the very busy managing director of a large company has a pile of documents to be signed in a few minutes before his next meeting, and his secretary has arranged them for maximum speed with only the spaces for signature exposed, and he "signs them blind", as the saying is, not reading them or even looking at them. He may be exercising a wise economy of his time and energy ... Such conduct is not negligence in any ordinary sense of the word. But the person who signs documents in this way ought to be held bound by them, and ought not to be entitled to avoid liability so as to shift the burden of loss on to an innocent third party. The whole object of having documents signed by him is that he makes them his documents and takes responsibility for them. He takes the chance of a fraudulent substitution. I think that the right view of such a case is that the person who signs intends to sign the documents placed before him, whatever they may be, and so there is no basis on which he could successfully plead *non est factum*."

---

89. *Saunders v Anglia Building Society* [1970] 3 All ER 961 at 973.
90. *Ibid.*
91. See also *Credit Lyonnais v PT Barnard & Associates Ltd* [1976] ILTR 557 (bills of exchange drawn in French accepted); *Avon Finance Co Ltd v Bridger* [1985] 2 All ER 281 (son procured parents to execute second legal charge over their house - parents failed to exercise reasonable care).
92. [1970] 3 All ER 961 at 980; quoted with approval by Scarman LJ in *United Dominions Trust Ltd v Western* [1975] 3 All ER 1017 at 1023.

REGULATION OF CONSUMER CREDIT

[1.29] In more recent times attention has been focused on protecting individuals borrowing money while acting outside the course of their business, trade or profession.[93] The Director of Consumer Affairs is empowered to:[94]

(a) keep under general review practices in relation to any obligations under the Act,

(b) carry out investigations of any such practices where he considers it to be in the public interest; in this regard he has wide powers to require information from any person whom he considers could have relevant information,[95]

(c) request persons in carrying out such practices, which are likely to be contrary to statutory obligations, to discontinue such practices,

(d) institute proceedings (after consultation with the Central Bank) for orders to restrain persons from engaging in such practices,

(e) investigate complaints concerning breaches of the Act, and

(f) publish Codes of Practice in order "to secure transparency and fairness" in relation to consumer agreements.

The Director is empowered also to provide information or advice to consumers concerning consumer credit agreements, in particular on obligations imposed on creditors under the Consumer Credit Act, 1995.[96] He is required to produce an annual report which is made available to the public.[97]

THE OMBUDSMAN FOR THE CREDIT INSTITUTIONS

[1.30] In 1990, the principal credit institutions established arrangements for an independent adjudicator to receive complaints from individuals in relation to services provided to them by the participating credit institutions.[98] The services of the adjudicator, known as the Ombudsman for the Credit Institutions is paid for by the participating credit institutions and is provided free of charge to individuals with complaints. An individual will be required in the first instance to lodge his complaint with the relevant credit institution. Only if such

---

[93] Consumer Credit Act, 1995; see paras **[7.09]**-**[7.17]** and **[10.74]**-**[10.84]**; the European Communities (Unfair Terms in Consumer Contracts) Regulations, 1995 (SI 27/1995); see paras **[18.01]**-**[18.05]**.

[94] Consumer Credit Act, 1995, s 4(1).

[95] *Ibid* s 5.

[96] *Ibid* s 4(2).

[97] *Ibid* s 4(3).

[98] The first, and only, adjudicator appointed is Mr Gerard Murphy BL. He was re-appointed for a second five year term in 1995.

complaint has not been dealt with satisfactorily within six months of it being lodged, may the individual present his complaint to the Ombudsman (the complaint must be made within six months of the non-resolution with the credit institution). The function of the Ombudsman is to try and procure a settlement of the dispute between the credit institution and the customer. If he fails to do so, he may make a decision on the dispute, stating his reasons for the decision.

His decision is binding on the credit institution provided the individual accepts the decision. An individual who does not accept the Ombudsman's decision will have the alternative remedy of seeking redress in the courts, but obviously, initially at least, at the cost of the individual.

With effect from 1 October 1994 the persons who may bring a complaint have been extended to limited liability companies having an annual turnover of up to IR£250,000.

[1.31] An award against a credit institution cannot exceed IR£25,000.[99] The Terms of Reference for the Ombudsman issued in October 1990 provide:[100]

> "No award shall be of a greater amount than in the opinion of the Ombudsman is appropriate to compensate the applicant for loss, damage or inconvenience suffered by him by reason of the acts or omissions of the credit institution against which the award is made. Additionally, or in the alternative, an award may direct the credit institution named in the complaint to take or desist from taking such steps as the Ombudsman may specify".

When making his recommendation or award, the Ombudsman, who is not bound by his previous decisions, is required to:[101]

(a) observe any applicable rule of law or relevant judicial authority (including but not limited to any such rule or authority concerning the legal effect of the express or implied terms of any contract between the applicant and any credit institution named in the complaint);

(b) have regard to the rules, if any, required by law to be made by the credit institution named in the complaint;

(c) have regard to general principles of good business practice and any relevant code of practice applicable to the subject matter of the complaint;

(d) have regard to any advertisement or promotional literature issued by the credit institution named in the complaint; and

(e) act impartially and fairly in all the circumstances.

[99.] Subject to inflationary increase.
[100.] Para 12.
[101.] Terms of Reference (1990) para 14.

[1.32] The Ombudsman is not empowered to consider a complaint relating to (1) the "commercial judgment" of the credit institution in decisions about lending or security, (2) general interest rate policies of a credit institution, or (3) a general practice or policy of a credit institution which does not breach a duty or obligation owed by it. [102]

The Ombudsman will not consider the complaint unless he is satisfied that the complaint is neither frivolous nor vexatious and involves one of the following:[103]

    (i)   a breach of obligations of a credit institution under any contract;

    (ii)   unfair treatment;

    (iii)   maladministration.

The complainant will be required to give a written waiver in respect of any duty of confidentiality owed to it by the credit institution, the subject of the complaint.

[1.33] If a credit institution wishes to avoid having the matter decided by the Ombudsman because it considers that the point of issue has important consequences for it or raises an important or novel point of law it must notify the complainant (before the complaint is made to the Ombudsman) that it requires such issue or point of law to be determined by a court. It must then notify the Ombudsman in writing. If the Ombudsman considers this concern to be "reasonable (but not otherwise)",[104] he shall not consider the complaint.

[1.34] The Ombudsman is required to issue an annual report containing a general review of his activities for the year of the report.[105] In his first report,[106] the Ombudsman reiterated his role (as outlined in the Terms of Reference):

> "From time to time I am asked to comment publicly on some aspect of the practice or policy of the credit institutions. Although not precluded by my Terms of Reference from doing this, I have taken the view that it is inappropriate for me to do so. I see it as my chief, if not sole function to consider such complaints as come to me, to investigate each one, and where a settlement is not arrived at, to arbitrate in the particular dispute between the parties in each case, so as to achieve what I consider to be justice between them. I do not feel that I have any supervisory or regulatory role to play in relation to the conduct of banking or building society business."

However, the seven annual reports issued to date have clearly set out trends in

---

[102.] *Ibid* para 16.
[103.] *Ibid* para 18(1).
[104.] *Ibid* para 20.
[105.] *Ibid* para 27.
[106.] Annual Report 1991.

complaints with a view no doubt to pointing out to the credit institutions the areas of their practice which need to be re-considered. For instance in his second report, the Ombudsman indicated, "that the high proportion of complaints about lending arises from a failure of communication between the lending institution and the borrower during the negotiating phase."

This approach has proved highly effective for despite extending the scheme to small companies and despite the increasing number of transactions by the public with credit institutions, the number of complaints brought to the Ombudsman fell from 1073 in 1993 to 1033 in 1997. The use of the Ombudsman has had obvious benefits to the customer in that the average length of time for the Ombudsman to bring about a result has been three and a half months compared with, what the Ombudsman indicated, a period of up to two years in finalising a case brought before the Circuit Court.[107] While any party is free to retain professional legal advice in its dealings with the Ombudsman, the Ombudsman has no power to award costs and thus legal costs must be absorbed by the instructing party.

BANKS' CHARTER AND CODES OF BEST PRACTICE

[1.35] The Irish Bankers' Federation has issued a Charter for Small Business Customers[108] and a Charter for Personal Customers.[109] The Charter for Small Business Customers seeks "to promote good banking practice by formalising standards of conduct which member banks agree to observe". The Charter indicates that the Ombudsman for the Credit Institutions "will use it in adjudicating on complaints" received from eligible small business customers. The Charter for Personal Customers echoes the same sentiments concerning standards of good practice and account being taken of the terms of the Charter by the Ombudsman for the Credit Institutions. Members of the Irish Bankers' Federation have adopted the Code of Best Practice of the European Banking Industry on card-based payment systems.[110]

[107.] Annual Report 1995.

[108.] October 1995.

[109.] September 1997.

[110.] Copies of the Charters and Code are available from the Irish Bankers' Federation, Nassau House, Nassau Street, Dublin 2.

Chapter 2

Holding Items for Safe Custody

[2.01] Banks, as part of their services, may offer customers the facility of holding customers' valuables for safe custody. These valuables may take any form but would be principally share certificates, bonds, title deeds, jewellery, coins and wills. The holding of such items is governed by the contract under which they are held and the law of bailment.[1] Unless otherwise agreed, it appears that items deposited for safe keeping with a bank should be held at the branch at which the items are deposited.[2]

IDENTITY OF CUSTOMER

[2.02] Nowadays a banker taking custody of items for safe keeping will do so following signature by its customer of a short agreement specifying the terms under which the banker holds the items.[3] Before taking items for safe custody, the bank must establish the identity of the customer.[4] The Guidance Notes[5] issued for use by banks and building societies states:[6]

> "Particular precautions need to be taken in relation to requests to hold boxes, parcels and sealed envelopes in safe custody. Where such facilities are made available to non-account holders, the identification procedures set out in these Guidance Notes should be followed."

EXPRESS CONTRACTUAL OBLIGATIONS AND EXCLUSIONS

[2.03] The extent of the duties and obligations of a bank holding items for safe custody may, subject to contrary statutory requirements,[7] be limited by the

---

1. For a fuller treatment of bailment see Bell, *Modern Law of Personal Property in England and Ireland* (1989) Butterworths pp 86-135.
2. See Weerasooria, *Banking Law and the Financial System in Australia* (2nd ed) Butterworths paras 27.31 and 31.16.
3. The form of receipt suggested by the Central Association of Bankers in 1896 did not incorporate any exclusion clause - 1 LDAB 231.
4. See paras **[4.02]-[4.12]**.
5. See para **[4.02]**.
6. Paragraph 76.
7. Particularly in the case of bailors who are individuals acting outside the course of their business, see below, the Sale of Goods and Supply of Services Act, 1980 and the European Communities (Unfair Terms in Consumer Contracts) Regulations, 1995.

express contractual provisions under which the items are deposited with the bank.[8] Thus, for example, in *British Road Services Ltd v Arthur V Crutchley & Co Ltd*[9] a bailee agreed to store whisky and included in its terms of contract a clause limiting liability to £800 per ton. Following the theft of the whisky due to the bailee's negligence, the bailee's liability was limited to £800 per ton.

[2.04] The terms of the agreement will simply acknowledge receipt by the bank of the goods and re-delivery on production of the agreement. The following is a suggested form of agreement between the bank and its customer where items are deposited with the bank for safe keeping:

"[Bank Letterhead]

[Addressed to Customer - name of customer, address, date]

Dear Sir/Madam,

We acknowledge receipt this day of the under-mentioned items which we are holding for your account subject to the terms and conditions specified below:

[List of items]

[Optional requirement for bank] Fee of IR£ ___. per month or part month payable in advance on the first day (or the first day in which we are open for business) of each month.

It should be noted that while we retain the foregoing items for your account we shall not be liable for their loss or damage caused by thieves, fire, explosion, war, riot, lightning, impact, earthquake, aircraft, floods, storm, civil commotion or any other cause whatsoever.

Furthermore, we shall not be liable for any loss that may be incurred by bills, bonds, notes or coupons not being duly presented when due. In the event that you wish us to undertake such a task we should be notified in writing of your request whereupon we shall indicate the terms upon which such service may be provided by us.

The foregoing exclusions of liability shall not apply where we or our employees or agents are found to be negligent or to have acted with wilful misconduct or fraud.

The contractual rights which you enjoy by virtue of section 39 of the Sale of Goods and Supply of Services Act, 1980 are in no way prejudiced by the foregoing otherwise than is permitted under section 40 of the said Act.

---

8. Although see the contrary assertion by the Central Association of Bankers (1896) 1 LDAB 230 namely, "While in the opinion of Counsel it is possible for a banker by special contract made with his customer at the time of the deposit to contract himself out of his liability, the opinion of your Committee is that this would be generally impossible in practice and, where not impossible, inadvisable; and that the liability can only be guarded against by precautions taken by the banker".
9. [1968] 1 All ER 811.

In view of our restricted liability, you are strongly advised to obtain insurance cover on all the foregoing articles deposited with us.

The items are returnable to you upon your written request signed in the form as this agreement is signed by you.

Yours faithfully,

[Branch manager]

I, the undersigned, have this day lodged the foregoing items with your bank for safe custody upon the above terms and conditions. I acknowledge that the above terms and conditions have been specifically drawn to my attention and are understood by me.

[Signature of customer]"

It should be noted that the European Communities (Unfair Terms in Consumer Contracts) Regulations, 1995[10] will apply to such an agreement when executed with a consumer.[11] Accordingly, any unfair term in the agreement will not be binding on a customer who is a consumer.[12]

[2.05] The English Court of Appeal considered an all-embracing exclusion clause in *J Spurling Ltd v Bradshaw*[13] where barrels of orange juice held for storage were found to be damaged. The Court found that although the storer was found to be negligent, he was protected by the exemption clause. However, Denning LJ sounded a warning note to bailees when he said:[14]

"If the clause is taken literally, it is wide enough to exempt the company from any obligation to redeliver the goods. It would mean that if the managing director sold the orange juice to somebody else ... the company would not be liable ... If the clause went to those lengths, it would be very unreasonable and might for that reason be invalid ... but I do not think that this clause is to be construed as widely as that. These exempting clauses are nowadays all held to be subject to the overriding proviso that they only avail to exempt a party when he is carrying out his contract, not when he is deviating from it or is guilty of a breach which goes to the root of it ...

The essence of a contract by a warehouseman is that he will store the goods in the contractual place and deliver them on demand to the bailor or his order. If he stores them in a different place, or if he consumes or destroys them instead of storing them, or if he sells them, or delivers them without excuse to somebody else, he is guilty of a breach which goes to the root of the contract and he cannot rely on the exempting clause. But if he should happen to damage

---

10. SI 27/1995, see Ch 18.
11. A natural person who is acting for purposes which are outside his business (SI 27/1995, reg 2).
12. SI 27/1995, reg 6.
13. [1956] 1 WLR 461.
14. *Ibid* at 465.

them by some momentary piece of inadvertence, then he is able to rely on the exempting clause: because negligence by itself without more, is not a breach which goes to the root of the contract."

The foregoing is certainly comfort for bankers (who hold items for safe custody under contracts with exemption clauses[15]) in defending a claim where the items are damaged without their wilful default. However, the depositor can draw comfort from the subsequent passage of Denning LJ's judgment where he stated:[16]

"Another thing to remember about these exempting clauses is that in the ordinary way the burden is on the bailee to bring himself within the exemption. A bailor, by pleading and presenting his case properly, can always put on the bailee the burden of proof. In the case of non-delivery, for instance, all he need plead is the contract and a failure to deliver on demand. That puts on the bailee the burden of proving either loss without his fault ... or, if it was due to his fault, it was a fault from which he is excused by the exempting clause ... But where the only charge made in the pleadings - or the only reasonable inference on the facts - is that the damage was due to negligence and nothing more, then the bailee can rely on the exempting clause without more ado."

FUNDAMENTAL BREACH

[2.06] The difficulty for a banker to escape liability, even with the benefit of an exclusion clause, where he cannot deliver the goods can be seen from the decision in *Woolmer v Delmer Price Ltd.*[17] A fur coat was stored under a contract, one of the terms of which stated "All goods left at customer's risk". The court held that, although the exemption clause excluded liability for loss by negligence whilst the goods remained with the bailees, if the bailees fail to adduce satisfactory evidence as to how the loss occurred and if it could have occurred in a way not covered by the exemption clause, such as delivery to a sub-contractor, the exemption clause could not apply, "because there would have been a fundamental breach in dealing with the goods otherwise than as authorised by the contract."[18]

[2.07] More recently in a case where a carpet disappeared without explanation and the bailee sought to rely on a limitation clause,[19] Lord Denning explained

---

[15.] Provided the exemption clause fulfils the requirements of the Sale of Goods and Supply of Services Act, 1980 and in the case of consumers, the European Communities (Unfair Terms in Consumer Contracts) Regulations, 1995.
[16.] [1956] 1 WLR 461 at 466.
[17.] [1955] 1 All ER 377.
[18.] *Ibid per* McNair J at 379.
[19.] *Levison v Patent Steam Carpet Cleaning Co Ltd* [1978] QB 69.

clearly the nature of the burden of proof which the bailee must discharge in order to rely on a limitation or exemption clause:[20]

"... in a contract of bailment, when a bailee seeks to escape liability on the ground that he was not negligent or that he was excused by an exception or limitation clause, then he must show what happened to the goods. He must prove all the circumstances known to him in which the loss or damage occurred. If it appears that the goods were lost or damaged without any negligence on his part, then, of course, he is not liable. If it appears that they were lost or damaged by a slight breach - not going to the root of the contract - he may be protected by the exemption or limitation clause. But, if he leaves the cause of loss or damage undiscovered and unexplained - then I think he is liable: because it is then quite likely that the goods were stolen by one of his servants; or delivered by a servant to the wrong address; or damaged by reckless or wilful misconduct; all of which the offending servant will conceal and not make known to his employer. Such conduct would be a fundamental breach against which the exemption or limitation clause will not protect him."

[2.08] There are limits as to what will constitute a fundamental breach. In *John Carter (Fine Worsteds) Ltd v Hanson Haulage (Leeds) Ltd,*[21] the judge at first instance precluded the defendants from relying on a limitation clause because of their negligence in failing to make enquiries of an employee's former employers. The Court of Appeal though held by a majority that the limitation clause could be relied upon as such negligence was not a fundamental breach:

"a fundamental breach disentitling a party from relying upon an exemption clause occurs if an act amounting to a complete departure from the contract is done which can be imputed to the contracting party himself as opposed to an act for which the contracting party is vicariously responsible as having been committed by one of his servants."[22]

An exclusion (or exemption) clause though, in contrast to a limitation clause, will not apply to such a loss unless the exclusion clause is sufficiently wide so as to specifically cover the misappropriation by the bailee's employee.[23]

[2.09] A banker who passes the items to another for safe keeping without the customer's agreement will have fundamentally breached its contract of bailment and thereby lose the benefit of exemption clauses under that contract. In *Edwards v Newland & Co; E Burchett Ltd,*[24] the bailee, unknown to the bailor,

---

[20.] *Ibid* at 82.

[21.] [1965] 2 QB 495.

[22.] *Ibid per* Davies LJ at 524.

[23.] See the English Court of Appeal's unanimous decision in *Williams v The Curzon Syndicate (Ltd)* (1919) 35 TLR 475.

[24.] [1950] 2 KB 534.

sub-contracted for furniture to be held by a third party. Part of the furniture disappeared following the bombing of the sub-contractor's premises. The bailee was liable to make good the loss to the bailor. Somervell LJ said:[25]

> "... a man who has undertaken to be a bailee for storage and who never in fact acts as such a bailee, but gets somebody else to take possession of the goods, seems to me to be in breach of his contract *ab initio*".

The reasoning put forward in the same court by Denning LJ[26] is difficult to argue with:

> "If the contractor employs a sub-contractor, he does it at his own risk because, if the goods are lost whilst in the hands of the sub-contractor, the contractor cannot say that they would have been lost in any event. He, by breaking his contract, has prevented any evidence as to what would have happened if he had fulfilled it personally."

[2.10] The same principle applies where goods are stored at a different place to that agreed as happened in *Lilley v Doubleday*:[27]

> "if a bailee elects to deal with the property entrusted to him in a way not authorised by the bailor, he takes upon himself the risks of so doing, except where the risk is independent of his acts and inherent in the property itself."[28]

IMPLIED TERMS AND EXCLUSIONS

[2.11] The contracts under which items for safe custody are governed have implied into them[29] the following terms:[30]

    (i)   that the banker has the necessary skill to render the service of holding items for safe custody,

    (ii)   that the banker will give the service with due skill, care and diligence, and

    (iii)   that where materials are used, such as a strongroom, locks and locking devices, they will be sound and reasonably fit for the purpose for which they are required.

These implied terms may be excluded or varied by an express term of the contract or by the course of dealing between the parties or by usage.[31]

[25.] *Ibid* at 538.

[26.] *Ibid* at 542.

[27.] (1881) 7 QBD 510.

[28.] *Ibid* per Grove J at 511; see also *Bontex Knitting Works Ltd v St John's Garage* (1943) 60 TLR 44 and (1944) 60 TLR 253.

[29.] Except where properly excluded under s 40 of the Sale of Goods and Supply of Services Act, 1980.

[30.] As specified by s 39 of the Sale of Goods and Supply of Services Act, 1980.

[31.] Sale of Goods and Supply of Services Act, 1980, s 40(1).

[2.12] However, where the customer "deals as consumer it must be shown that the express term is fair and reasonable and has been specifically brought to his attention."[32] Where a banker acts as bailee, the customer will be dealing "as consumer" where he neither makes the contract in the course of a business nor holds himself out as doing so and the goods are of a type ordinarily used for private use, such as jewellery worn by the customer.[33] In considering whether a term is fair and reasonable "the test is that it shall be a fair and reasonable one to be included having regard to the circumstances which were, or ought reasonably to have been, known to or in contemplation of the parties when the contract was made"[34] and regard shall be given in particular to any of the following criteria which appear to be relevant:[35]

1. The strength of the bargaining positions of the parties relative to each other, taking into account (among other things) alternative means by which the customer's requirements could have been met;

2. Whether the customer received an inducement to agree to the terms, or in accepting it had an opportunity of entering into a similar contract with other bankers, but without having to accept a similar term;

3. Whether the customer knew or ought reasonably to have known of the existence and extent of the term (having regard, among other things, to banking practice and any previous course of dealing between the parties);

4. Where the term excludes or restricts any relevant liability if some condition is not complied with, whether it was reasonable at the time of the contract to expect that compliance with that condition would be practicable.

It should be noted though, that a term which is considered fair and reasonable pursuant to the Sale of Goods and Supply of Services Act, 1980 may still be considered to be an unfair term within the meaning of the European Communities (Unfair Terms in Consumer Contracts) Regulations 1995.[36]

[2.13] Furthermore, it is an offence for a bank to provide a document incorporating an exclusion clause otherwise than under s 40 of the Sale of Goods and Supply of Services Act, 1980.[37] It is also an offence for a bank to

---

32. *Ibid.*
33. Sale of Goods and Supply of Services Act, 1980, s 3(1); see also *O'Callaghan v Hamilton Leasing (Ireland) Ltd* [1984] ILRM 146.
34. The Schedule to the Sale of Goods and Supply of Services Act, 1980 as incorporated by s 2(3).
35. *Ibid.*
36. SI 27/1995, see Ch 18.
37. Sale of Goods and Supply of Services Act, 1980, s 41(2).

provide a document to a customer limiting the customer's rights unless the statement of limitation is accompanied by a clear and conspicuous declaration that the contractual rights which the customer enjoys by virtue of s 39 of the Sale of Goods of Supply of Services Act, 1980 are in no way prejudiced by the relevant statement.[38]

CUSTODIAL AGREEMENTS

[2.14] Bankers and financial institutions have in recent years increasingly acted as custodians, principally for corporate customers. Large corporate bodies which carry on treasury activities under which they manage their debt often require a custodian to hold bonds, certificates and instruments as well as to carry out other duties in respect of the customer's investments. Invariably, the customer will enter into a contract with the custodian setting out the terms under which the custodian will hold the items deposited with it and carry out any ancillary functions with regard to such items. This contract is known as a Custodial Agreement. The principal features of a Custodial Agreement are:

1. The appointment of the bank as custodian of the company's portfolio such as bonds, monies, debentures, debt instruments, treasury bills, certificates of deposit and commercial paper;

2. The custodian is permitted to employ sub-custodians, usually from a panel approved by the company;

3. The duty of the custodian to hold the certificates, bills and bonds in safe keeping for the company's account and on the company's behalf;

4. The duty of the custodian to act on and deliver securities in accordance with the company's written instructions;

5. Permission to register securities in the name of the custodian;

6. Agreement that the custodian shall open and maintain a bank account in the name of the company for receipt of payment of monies earned on the securities;

7. Agreement for the custodian to collect on behalf of the company the monies and interest earned on the company's securities, including the detaching and submission of coupons for the collection of interest;

8. Where the custodian is not a bank there should be provision for the custodian to appoint a bank as its agent (without relieving the custodian of any liability);

9. Authorisation for the custodian to deposit the company's securities in a recognised clearing system on certain conditions such as keeping the company's securities separate from other securities held by the custodian and detailing the terms on which transactions will be paid for and recorded;

[38.] *Ibid* s 41(4).

10. The requirement for the custodian to maintain records and keep books of account in relation to the securities, and the provision of independent audited accounts.

The custodial agreement should provide that the custodian will be indemnified by the company in respect of all costs and liabilities incurred in carrying out its custodial duties.

The agreement should cover also the termination of the custodian's appointment by the company on usually 90 days notice or earlier termination in the event of default or insolvency by the custodian. Finally, the agreement should have a confidentiality clause, a notice clause, a governing law clause[39] and submission to jurisdiction of the High Court of Ireland (or other courts).[40]

DEGREE OF CARE REQUIRED BY BANKER

[2.15] A banker may take custody of goods for safe keeping for a fee or gratuitously. Even where a banker does take goods gratuitously, the bailment of such goods may nonetheless be regarded as a bailment for reward since the bank is likely to offer such services with a view to retaining the customer for other services for which a fee would be charged.[41] The distinction, however, is probably irrelevant, for as Lord Salmon stated:[42]

---

[39] See further paras **[7.62]**-**[7.66]**.

[40] See further paras **[7.67]**-**[7.71]**.

[41] See *Chitty on Contracts* (26th ed) para 2659; *Paget's Law of Banking* (11th ed) p 132; Tyree, *Banking Law in Australia* (2nd ed) para 4.59; see also Lord Salmon where he said by way of *obiter* in *Port Swettenham Authority v T W Wu & Co (M) Sdn Bhd* [1978] 3 All ER 337 at 340:

"... a bank, which offers its customers, in the ordinary course of business, the service of looking after goods deposited with it, can hardly be described as a gratuitous bailee. The bank must realise that were it to refuse a customer such a service it would probably lose the customer who would have no difficulty in finding another bank which would be happy to render the service which is normally offered by banks to their customers";

The contrary but probably out-dated view was made by the Central Association of Bankers in their 1896 report as cited in 1 LDAB 230 namely, "The better opinion seems to be that when a banker takes charge of a locked box supposed to contain valuables (...), he would be held to be a gratuitous bailee."

This view is supported by Halsbury's *Laws of England* 4th ed. However, a judicial decision on the point is awaited - see editorial note to *Houghland v RR Low (Luxury Coaches) Ltd* 8 LDAB 52.

[42] In *Port Swettenham Authority v TW Wu & Co (M) Sdn Bhd* [1978] 3 All ER 337 at 340; see also Sachs LJ in *British Road Services Ltd v Arthur V Crutchley & Co Ltd* [1968] 1 All ER 811 at 822:

"one of the reasons stems from the fact that normally it is only the bailee who knows what care was being taken of the goods, and another from the number of temptations to which a bailee may succumb;"

although for a contrary view in respect of gratuitous bailments see the English Court of Appeal's judgments in *Bullen v The Swan Electric Engraving Co* (1907) 23 TLR 258.

"The onus is always on the bailee, whether he be a bailee for reward or a gratuitous bailee, to prove that the loss of any goods bailed to him was not caused by any fault of his or of any of his servants or agents to whom he entrusted the goods for safe keeping."

[2.16] The context of that statement is particularly relevant for bankers who take items for safe custody from customers without charging a fee for the service. In that case *(Port Swettenham Authority v TW Wu & Co (M) Sdn Bhd)*[43] a port authority kept cargo in a shed in accordance with normal practice prior to its delivery to the consignee or to a warehouse. No fees were charged for the service as it was part of the overall service provided by the port authority and effectively it was covered by the inward cargo charges. The Privy Council rejected the port authority's submission that in the case of a gratuitous bailment the onus of proving that the loss of goods bailed was caused by the negligence or misconduct of the bailee rests on the bailor.[44]

[2.17] It could be said that the current approach of the courts to the degree of care required by a bailee has emanated from the English Court of Appeal's decision in *Houghland v RR Low (Luxury Coaches) Ltd*.[45] In that case the plaintiff deposited her suitcase with a coach driver who put it into the boot for transport. Following the breakdown of the coach, the passengers and luggage were transferred to a second coach. However, the removal of the luggage from the first coach was not supervised. The plaintiff's suitcase could not be found on arrival. Although it was accepted that the defendants were only gratuitous bailees, the Court of Appeal considered "that the standard of care required in a case of bailment ... is the standard of the circumstances demanded by that particular case"[46] and "that once the bailment has been established, and once the failure of the bailee to hand over the articles in question has been proved, there is a *prima facie* case, and the plaintiff is entitled to recover, unless the defendant can establish to the satisfaction of the court a defence."[47] The Court held that in the circumstances it was for the defendants to adduce evidence to rebut a presumption of negligence, they had failed to do so and the plaintiff was entitled to damages.

[2.18] This approach was applied more recently in Ireland in *Sheehy v Faughnan*.[48] The plaintiff left his mare in the defendant's stud farm, 16 days

---

43. [1978] 3 All ER 337.
44. Supported by *Giblin v McMullen* (1868) 21 LT 214 of which Lord Salmon stated, "Their Lordships however gravely doubt whether that case was correctly decided."
45. [1962] 2 All ER 159; [1962] 2 WLR 1015.
46. *Ibid* per Ormerod LJ at 161 and 1017 respectively.
47. *Ibid* per Ormerod LJ at 161 and 1018 respectively.
48. [1991] 1 IR 424.

later the plaintiff telephoned to enquire about his mare and was informed that she had died 12 days previously. Barr J stated that *Houghland v RR Low (Luxury Coaches) Ltd*[49] and certain earlier decisions "establish that there is an onus on the bailee to show that he was not in breach of his duty to take care and that, if he was, that breach was not the cause of the loss." In applying this principle Barr J upheld the Circuit Court's award of damages to the plaintiff as the defendant had failed to prove what caused the death of the mare. Furthermore, the defendant could not establish that what caused her death happened notwithstanding all reasonable care on his part since, by failing to notify the plaintiff promptly of the mare's death, the exact cause of death remained unknown (no pathological examination of the mare having been carried out).

[2.19] Similarly, in *Roche v Cork, Blackrock, and Passage Railway Company*[50] the defendants were liable for the theft of £10 from a bag deposited in the defendant's cloakroom as the defendant had not discharged the onus of giving an explanation for the loss and therefore the proper inference to be drawn was that the loss resulted from their negligence.

[2.20] The burden of proof remains no less onerous even where clearly an outside or third party has destroyed the bailed goods.[51] In *Keenan v McCreedy*[52] when the plaintiff sought compensation for bailed goods which were destroyed by fire, the bailee's counsel sought a direction that the plaintiff had not proved any negligence. Sheehy J in the Circuit Court ruled that once the plaintiff had proved that there was a bailment for reward and the non-return of the goods (at the end of the bailment), the onus of proof shifted to the defendant to show that he had not been guilty of any negligence. The judge was not satisfied that the appropriate precautions had been taken particularly in view of the defendant's experience that fire was likely. Accordingly, the plaintiff was awarded damages.

[2.21] Similarly in a case before the High Court of Australia[53] wool, which was retained by a broker following its sale, was destroyed by fire. The court held that the broker retaining the wool was a bailee with duties analogous to those of a bailee for reward and that the broker, by failing to have adequate fencing to keep intruders out, had failed to show that it had taken reasonable precautions to keep the wool safe.

[49.] [1962] 2 All ER 159; [1962] 2 WLR 1015.

[50.] (1889) 24 LR Ir 250.

[51.] See for example *Henry v Sanderson* (1972) 106 ILTR 12 where the defendant was liable for negligence where bailed equipment were stolen from the back seat of a car which was locked, the equipment was covered by a rug, the car was parked for ten minutes under a street lamp in a busy street in Dublin.

[52.] [1953-54] Ir Jur R 74.

[53.] *Pitt Son & Badgery Ltd v Proulefco SA* [1984] 153 CLR 644.

[2.22] The test to be considered in these cases is whether or not the system of protection was adequate. In *British Road Services Ltd v Arthur V Crutchley & Co Ltd*[54] Lord Pearson stated:[55]

> "... the defendants' system of protection, though useful so far as it went, was not proved to be adequate in relation to the special risks involved in the nature and conduct of the defendants' business ... Nor was it proved that the inadequacy of the system was not a cause of the theft ... The defendants failed to discharge their burden of proving that the loss was not caused by any negligence on their part."

BANKER'S LIABILITY AS INSURER

[2.23] A bailee of goods is not an insurer of them while he holds the goods during the agreed tenor of the bailment. Thus, if the goods are stolen without default on the bailee's part the bailee will not be liable.[56] But, if the bailee fails to give the bailor notice of the theft he may be liable in negligence as the onus will be on him to prove that if he had given prompt notice of the theft the goods would still not have been recovered.[57]

[2.24] However, if the bailee fails to deliver the bailed goods to the bailor when requested to do so, it appears the bailee thereupon becomes an insurer of them. In *Mitchell v Ealing London Borough Council*[58] the defendants, who were storing the plaintiff's furniture gratuitously, failed to meet the plaintiff's husband at the appointed time to hand over the furniture. By the time a new appointment had been arranged the furniture had disappeared through no fault of the defendants. The court held that from the time the defendants failed to meet at the appointed time, they held the furniture at their peril and were insurers of it; accordingly they were liable for its loss.

In giving judgment for the plaintiff, the court applied the decision of *Shaw & Co v Symmons & Sons*[59] where the court held that the bailee was liable for the bailor's loss by failing to deliver books within a reasonable time requested - the books were subsequently destroyed by fire when in the bailee's possession. The court, however, considered the failure to deliver within a reasonable time as being a breach of contract and did not go so far as to hold that the bailee was an insurer of the books.

---

54. [1968] 1 All ER 811.
55. *Ibid* at 819.
56. *Coldman v Hill* [1918-19] All ER Rep 434; [1919] 1 KB 443.
57. *Ibid.*
58. [1979] QB 1.
59. [1917] 1 KB 799.

BANKER'S LIABILITY FOR EMPLOYEES

[2.25] As a general rule, where an employee carries out an act within the course of his employment, his employer will be liable to a third party who suffers foreseeable loss as a result of the employee's act or omission.[60]

[2.26] The question arises as to whether a fraudulent action by an employee can be considered as an act coming within the course of his employment, as clearly it is not an act either sanctioned or within the scope of the employee's authority to conduct. However, any escape of liability on this ground was unanimously rebutted by the House of Lords in *Lloyd v Grace, Smith & Co.*[61] In that case the court found a solicitor liable to compensate a client whose lands were fraudulently transferred by the solicitor's managing clerk who had had authority to receive deeds for the solicitor and carry out sales on the solicitor's behalf. The critical factor is whether the act comes within the type of work held out by the employer which the employee is entitled and authorised to do. In his judgment in the House of Lords, Lord Shaw put the point by quoting from Lord Herschell LC in *Thorne v Heard*,[62] namely:[63]

> "It appears to me perfectly clear that in order to charge any person with a fraud which has not been personally committed by him the agent who has committed the fraud must have committed it while acting within the scope of his authority, while doing something and purporting to do something on behalf of the principal. If the person is doing something within the scope of his authority and purporting to do it for his principal, although in doing it he commits a wrong which his principal neither sanctioned nor intended, the principal may be liable. But if the person, although he has been employed as agent, is not, in the transaction which is the wrongful act, acting for, or purporting to be acting for, the principal, it seems to me impossible to treat that as a fraud of the principal."

[2.27] That decision was applied in *Uxbridge Permanent Benefit Building Society v Pickard*[64] where a solicitor's managing clerk obtained £500 from the plaintiff by producing a fictitious deed. The English Court of Appeal held that although the clerk's fraud involved forgery his employer was nonetheless liable

---

[60.] For an interesting brief discussion on bankers' vicarious liability in respect of safe custody services, see Weerasooria, *Banking Law and the Financial System in Australia* (2nd ed) para 27.3; for further and more detailed treatment of vicarious liability see McMahon & Binchy, *Irish Law of Torts* (2nd ed) pp 748-768; see also *Bontex Knitting Works Ltd v St John's Garage* (1943) 60 TLR 44 and 253.

[61.] [1911-13] All ER Rep 51; [1912] AC 716.

[62.] [1895] AC 495 at 502.

[63.] [1911-13] All ER Rep 51 at 62; curiously this passage from Lord Shaw's judgment is omitted from the report of the decision [1912] AC 716.

[64.] [1939] 2 All ER 344; see also its application in *United Africa Company Ltd v Saka Owoade* [1955] AC 130.

as the clerk had acted within his ostensible authority. The court acknowledged that it was not within the clerk's actual authority to commit a fraud but it was within his ostensible authority to perform acts involving the preparation and delivery of title documents. "So long as he is acting within the scope of that class of act, his employer is bound, whether the clerk is acting for his own purposes or for those of his employer".[65]

[2.28] Ostensible authority arose in the context of the bailor's ostensible authority in *Morgan v Smith*.[66] In that case the owner's agent left a lorry with a garage proprietor for repair. The agent then, with the knowledge of the proprietor, lent it to the proprietor's employee who damaged it. The proprietor was held liable for the damage - Budd J held that it was not within the agent's ostensible authority to lend the lorry to a third party; the proprietor by permitting the lorry to be used by an unauthorised person did not take reasonable care of the lorry and was liable for the damage flowing naturally from his default. Decisions involving liability for a bailee often arise where the bailee's employee or employees fraudulently remove the bailed items as happened with the disappearance of items from a shed in Port Swettenham, Malaysia. In giving the Privy Council's advice, Lord Salmon said:[67]

> "When a bailee puts goods which have been bailed to him in the care of his servants for safe custody, there can be no doubt that the bailee is responsible if the goods are lost through any failure of those servants to take proper care of the goods. The heresy that any dishonest act on the part of a servant employed to take care of the goods is necessarily outside the scope of his employment, and that the master cannot be liable for the dishonest act unless done for his benefit or with his privity, was exorcised by *Lloyd v Grace, Smith & Co* (1912). It was on the basis of this heresy that *Cheshire v Bailey* (1905) 1 B 237 laid down the startling proposition of law that a master who was under a duty to guard another's goods was liable if the servant he sent to perform the duty for him performed it so negligently as to enable thieves to steal the goods, but was not liable if that servant joined with the thieves in the very theft. This proposition is clearly contrary to principle and common sense, and to the law."

[2.29] The Irish High Court followed *Lloyd v Grace Smith & Co*[68] and chose specifically not to follow *Cheshire v Bailey*.[69] In *Johnson & Johnson (Ireland) Ltd v CP Security Ltd*[70] the defendant was engaged to provide a security service to the plaintiff. An employee of the defendant while he was carrying out his

---

[65.] *Ibid* at 348 *per* Sir Wilfred Greene MR.
[66.] [1953-54] Ir Jur R 70.
[67.] *Port Swettenham Authority v TW Wu & Co (M) Sdn Bhd* [1978] 3 All ER 337 at 341.
[68.] [1911-13] All ER Rep 51; [1912] AC 716.
[69.] [1905] 1 KB 237.
[70.] [1986] ILRM 559.

delegated duty to guard the plaintiff's premises opened the premises to enable third parties to remove some of the plaintiff's products. The plaintiff recovered damages from the defendant despite the court being satisfied that the defendant had carried out proper enquiries into the employee's background, working history and reliability without receiving any evidence of dishonesty and despite the defendant's previous suggestion to withdraw the employee from the premises following earlier suspicions raised by the plaintiff. Egan J quoted [71] and effectively adopted the position as stated by Lord Denning:[72]

> "If you go through the cases on this difficult subject, you will find that in the ultimate analysis they depend on the nature of the duty owed by the master towards the person whose goods have been lost or damaged. If the master is under a duty to use due care to keep goods safely and protect them from theft or depredation, he cannot get rid of his responsibility by delegating his duty to another. If he entrusts the duty to his servant, he is answerable for the way in which the servant conducts himself therein. No matter whether the servant be negligent, fraudulent, or dishonest, the master is liable. But not when he is under no such duty."

[2.30] An example of an employer being liable for his employee's theft where items were bailed not for value but for convenience can be seen from *Mullins v Laird*.[73] In that case a customer of a hairdresser in Grafton Street, Dublin, handed two diamond earrings to an employee of the hairdresser while she had her hair washed. The earrings disappeared and the hairdresser was liable for the loss.

BANKER'S LIABILITY FOR AGENTS

[2.31] A person may deposit items for safe custody with a bank (or other institution) with or without the knowledge and agreement that the items will be left by the bank with a third party whose duty it will be to safeguard the items. The extent of the bailee's liability for the third party's loss of the items was considered by the High Court in *McElwee v McDonald*.[74] Kenny J stated:[75]

> "When an article is entrusted to a bailee ... and the bailee, with or without the consent of the owner, engages an independent contractor ... and this is not a breach of the contract, the bailee is liable for any damage to the article unless the bailee establishes that the independent contractor and he were not negligent

---

71. *Ibid* at 562.
72. In *Morris v CW Martin & Sons Ltd* [1965] 2 All ER 725 at 730.
73. (1916) 50 ILTR 7.
74. [1969] IR 437.
75. *Ibid* at 439; Kenny J drew support from the English Court of Appeal's judgments in *British Road Services Ltd v Arthur V Crutchley & Co Ltd* [1968] 1 All ER 811.

or unless the owner has agreed that the bailee is not to be liable for the carelessness of the sub-contractor."

[2.32] Kenny J's exclusion is somewhat wider than the decision of the President of the Circuit Court in *Morgan v Maurer & Son*[76] where the Court held that although it was reasonable for the bailee to send a watch to his agent, the onus rested on the bailee to prove he had the bailor's permission to do so. As he had not discharged that onus he was liable when the watch disappeared after it had been sent back by the agent by registered post. Thus, strict liability attached to the bailee by parting with possession without permission, notwithstanding that the loss did not result from any negligence by the bailee or his agent.[77]

[2.33] The interaction of exemption clauses, sub-bailment and vicarious liability for employees arose in *Morris v CW Martin & Sons Ltd*.[78] That case is somewhat analogous to a customer depositing certificates or other valuables with a bank, being informed by the bank that it does not have safe keeping facilities but that its parent will hold the items and ultimately the items disappearing through theft by an employee of the parent. In that case, when the plaintiff sent her fur to a furrier for cleaning, she agreed that the fur could be cleaned by the defendant. The furrier arranged for the fur to be cleaned by the defendant on the usual trade conditions which provided *inter alia* that goods belonging to customers were held at the customer's risk and the defendant could not be responsible for any loss or damage however caused except by reason of negligence. Following the theft of the fur by the defendant's employee, the English Court of Appeal considered whether the defendant could escape liability by virtue of the exemption clause notwithstanding that the owner of the fur had not been a party to the contract to the sub-bailment. The Court held that, since the plaintiff had consented to the sub-bailment she was bound by the conditions but, the conditions were insufficiently wide to exempt the defendant as the plaintiff was not the defendant's customer, the furrier was. Accordingly, applying the decision of *Lloyd v Grace, Smith & Co*,[79] the defendant was responsible for his employee's theft and was liable to the plaintiff for breach of duty as bailee notwithstanding the absence of privity of contract between the plaintiff and defendant.

---

76. [1964] Ir Jur R 31.
77. See also *Lilley v Doubleday* (1881) 7 QBD 510 and *Edwards v Newland & Co; E, Burchett Ltd* [1950] 2 KB 534 discussed in paras **[2.09]-[2.10]** above.
78. [1965] 2 All ER 725.
79. [1911-13] All ER Rep 51; [1912] AC 716.

Appointment of Sub-Custodians in the IFSC

[2.34] In its role as a supervisory authority for operations in the International Financial Services Centre,[80] the Central Bank of Ireland has issued a memorandum in relation to the standard of care which must be exercised in relation to the appointment and subsequent supervision/monitoring of sub-custodians to the effect that care and diligence must be exercised in choosing and appointing a third party as a safe keeping agent so as to ensure that the third party has and maintains the expertise, competence and standing appropriate to discharge the responsibilities concerned. Furthermore, an appropriate level of supervision is required to be maintained over the safe keeping agent and appropriate enquiries should be made from time to time to confirm that the obligations of the agent continue to be competently discharged. The Central Bank has indicated that this is the minimum standard of care expected in custodial agreements.

The Central Bank has indicated also that on the basis of legal advice which it has retained once a person "has demonstrably exercised the level of care and diligence in the appointment and subsequent supervision/monitoring of its agents, in the context of the market in which the sub-custodian is operating, it is unlikely to be found liable by the courts for losses arising in respect of the actions or inaction of such agent".[81]

BANKER'S LIABILITY FOR CONVERSION

> "One of the common law duties owed by a bailee of goods to his bailor is not to convert them, ie, not to do intentionally in relation to the goods an act inconsistent with the bailor's right of property therein ... This duty, which is common to all bailments ... is independent of and additional to the other common law duty of a bailee for reward to take reasonable care of his bailor's goods".[82]

[2.35] This common law duty applies to the banker even where unknown to the banker his employees or agents convert the bailed goods while in the course of their employment.[83]

[2.36] A point to watch for all bankers is the liability for conversion which would arise if the items deposited with the bank for safe custody are mistakenly delivered to a person other than the owner of the items. In *Langtry v The Union Bank of London*[84] the plaintiff's jewels, which had been deposited with the bank

---

[80.] Central Bank Act 1989, ss 89-96A.
[81.] Issued by the Securities and Exchanges Supervision Department, June 1997.
[82.] Diplock LJ in *Morris v CW Martin & Sons Ltd* [1965] 2 All ER 725 at 735.
[83.] As in *Morris v CW Martin & Sons Ltd* [1965] 2 All ER 735 and as in *United Africa Company Ltd v Saka Owoade* [1955] AC 130.
[84.] (1896) 1 LDAB 229.

for safe custody, were delivered to an unauthorised person on foot of a forged order. Following settlement of the case, the Journal of the Institute of Bankers published a memorandum setting out the terms of a report, of a sub-committee of the Central Association of Bankers, adopted by the Association. The report states *inter alia*:[85]

> "It is necessary to distinguish between cases in which valuables are by mistake delivered to the wrong person, (as in Mrs Langtry's case), and cases in which they are destroyed, lost, stolen, or fraudulently abstracted, whether by an offer of the bank or by some other person.
> The best legal opinion appears to be that in the former case the question of the negligence of a bailee does not arise; that the case is one of wrongful conversion of the goods, and that the bank is liable for this wrongful conversion apart from any question of negligence."

Where items which have been deposited for safe custody with a bank are subsequently held and retained by a third party, the bank being in possession at the time of the conversion is entitled to damages for conversion.[86] However once the bailor settles its claim for damages (against a third party) arising out of loss or damage to a chattel, the bailee cannot take a separate action to recover damages.[87]

BANKER'S LIABILITY WHERE TITLE CONTESTED

[2.37] The facts of *Langtry v The Union Bank of London*[88] are a reminder of the consequences for a bank in releasing the items deposited for safe custody to the wrong person. A quandary arises when a third party indicates to the bank that the owner of the items is not the bailor but a third party as, "the bailee has no better title than the bailor, and, consequently, if a person entitled as against a bailor to the property claims it, the bailee has no defence against him."[89] If the bank refuses possession to the owner, the owner may institute proceedings against the bank for detinue. If the bank hands over possession it runs the risk of the bailor instituting proceedings for conversion.

[2.38] In *Clayton v Le Roy*[90] the defendant was the bailee of a watch which had been purchased by the bailor. The defendant who was aware that the watch had

---

85. 1 LDAB 230.
86. *Midland Bank Ltd v Eastcheap Dried Fruit Company* [1962] 1 LLR 359; see also the reference at 362 to Sir Richard Henn Collins MR in *The Winkfield* [1902] P 42 at 60:
    "The chattel that has been converted or damaged is deemed to be the chattel of the possessor and of no other."
87. *O'Sullivan v Williams* (1992) *The Independent*, 20 March 1992.
88. (1896) 1 LDAB 229.
89. Blackburn J in *Biddle v Bond* (1865) 6 B & S 225 at 231.
90. [1911] 2 KB 1031.

been stolen, wrote to the owner and the bailor notifying them of the position and inquiring as to their wishes The owner did not reply but sent a solicitor's clerk to demand the return of the watch on his behalf. On the bailee's refusal the clerk immediately served a summons for detinue. The English Court of Appeal held that as there was no indication on the bailee's part of a wrongful intention to withhold the watch from its owner, the owner had no cause of action.

[2.39] The courts however require the bailee to act promptly to ascertain the true owner. In *Poole v Burns*[91] an auctioneer was found liable in detinue for retaining a horse, the ownership of which was in dispute, for five weeks pending the result of police investigations. The court held that the horse should have been retained only for a reasonable time and the auctioneer had failed to do everything possible to expedite the release of the horse. This Circuit Court decision appears unduly harsh - bankers, however, should take notice of its implications.

[2.40] The correct course for a bank to follow when faced with rival claims is to instigate interpleader proceedings.[92] This can be seen from the decision in *EE McCurdy Ltd (in liq) v Postmaster-General*.[93] The New Zealand postal authorities received rival claims to certain parcels. The Postmaster-General issued an interpleader summons calling on the rival claimants to appear and to obtain an adjudication in respect of their claims. The plaintiff on being successful in the first action then instituted proceedings against the Postmaster-General for unlawful detention. The New Zealand Supreme Court held that the action should be struck out as there had been no refusal to deliver the goods, the defendants were ready and willing to deliver them to the lawful owner and had promptly taken the proper course to have the rival claims determined by the court.

[2.41] However, the courts should not be used to avoid delivery to the true owner. In *Ranson v Platt*[94] the bailee when faced with rival claims from husband and wife refused delivery except upon a magistrate's order. However, application for such an order was made only with the knowledge of the bailee and the husband. No notice of the wife's claim was given to the magistrate. Following an order for delivery to the husband, the bailed goods were so delivered. The English Court of Appeal held that the bailee had failed to fulfil

---

91. [1944] Ir Jur R 20.
92. See McMahon & Binchy, *Irish Law of Torts* (2nd ed) p 539; "a bailee who forbears to adopt that mode of proceeding and makes himself a party by retaining the goods for the bailor, must stand or fall by his title" - Lord Tenterden CJ in *Wilson v Anderton* (1830) 1 B & Ad 450 at 456.
93. [1959] NZLR 553.
94. [1911] 2 KB 291.

his obligations as a bailee and could not rely for protection upon the magistrate's order.

> "It is the duty of a bailee to take care of the goods bailed to him, and, if a hostile claim is made to them, to see that the bailor's property is properly defended, or at any rate to give notice to him, if possible, of proceedings hostile to his title. In the present case the bailee allowed the bailor to remain in ignorance of the fact that a hostile claim had been made ..."[95]

JOINT BAILORS

[2.42] Where items are deposited by persons jointly, unless otherwise agreed with the depositors, the items should be returned to them jointly or handed over to a third party on the joint instructions of the depositors. If a bank hands over the items on the instructions of only one of the depositors, the other depositor(s) may have a right of action against the bank. Care needs to be taken in the pleadings as can be seen from *Brandon v Scott*.[96] In that case goods were deposited with the defendant on the terms that they would not be handed over without the instructions of the three depositors. Subsequently, one of the depositors received the goods without the joint instructions. All three depositors brought an action against the defendant. The court held that the claim failed as the depositor who had received the goods was precluded from suing for what he himself had procured and therefore could not maintain an action with others. The possibility of proceedings against a bank in this position was adverted to by Lord Campbell CJ in his judgment:[97]

> "As, in fact, one of the plaintiffs has got the goods the question arises whether he can sue the defendants for giving them to himself. It would be contrary to all principle, and the cases cited clearly show that it would be contrary to all decisions, if he could. I do not think an action at law could be maintained against bankers in this position more than against others; but it is not to be supposed they could therefore with impunity deliver up to one securities deposited with them to hold for several. I think in such a case they would stand in the relation of trustees for all the joint bailors; and there would be a clear remedy in equity for the breach of trust in delivering the joint property to one only of the *cestui que trusts*."

BANKER'S LIEN

> "There is no question that, by the law merchant, a banker has a lien for his general balance on securities deposited with him. I consider this as part of the established law of the country, and that the Courts will take notice of it."[98]

---

95. *Ibid per* Fletcher Moulton LJ at 305.
96. (1857) 7 El & Bl 234.
97. *Ibid* at 236.
98. Lord Lyndhurst in *Brandao v Barnett* (1846) 12 Ch & Fin 787 at 810.

[2.43] The general rule that a banker has a lien on items deposited with it to cover monies due to it by the depositor is subject to the over-riding duty of a bailee to a bailor as under bailment, "the general rule is that one who has received property from another as his bailee, agent or servant must restore or account for that property to him from whom he received it."[99]

[2.44] Thus, in *Leese v Martin & Co*[100] boxes containing securities which had been deposited with a bank for safe custody were held not to be subject to any banker's lien - the keys to the boxes were kept by the depositor and the bank had no notice of the contents of the boxes. This decision followed the earlier decision of *Brandao v Barnett*[101] where the facts were somewhat similar although in that case the bankers actually handled the bills deposited for the purposes of collecting interest. Lord Campbell acknowledged that bankers have a general lien on securities deposited with them but that this is subject to circumstances showing an implied contract inconsistent with a lien, such as in that case where the bills had been deposited in boxes the key to which was retained by the depositor.

[99.] Hall V-C in *Leese v Martin & Co* [1861-73] All ER Rep 912 at 915.
[100.] [1861-73] All ER Rep 912.
[101.] (1846) 12 Ch & Fin 787.

Chapter 3

Banker's Duty of Secrecy

"It is not possible to frame any exhaustive definition of the duty".[1]

[3.01] The starting point in considering the banker's duty of secrecy is the English Court of Appeal's decision in *Tournier v National Provincial and Union Bank of England*.[2] The principal judgment was delivered by Bankes LJ who considered that the bank's duty of secrecy was a legal one arising out of contract. The customer's credit worthiness can depend to a large extent on its banker complying with the duty of secrecy.[3] Accordingly, confidentiality is an implied term in a contract between a banker and its customer.[4] This duty, however, is not absolute[5] but qualified.[6] Bankes LJ stated:[7]

"the qualifications can be classified under four heads:[8]

    (a) where disclosure is under compulsion by law;

    (b) where there is a duty to the public to disclose;

    (c) where the interests of the bank require disclosure;

    (d) where the disclosure is made by the express or implied consent of the customer."

As to the limits of the duty, Bankes LJ stated:

"the duty does not cease the moment a customer closes his account. Information gained during the currency of the account remains confidential unless released in circumstances bringing the case within one of the classes of qualification I have already referred to ... the confidence is not confined to the

---

1. *Per* Bankes LJ in *Tournier v National Provincial and Union Bank of England* [1924] 1 KB 461 at 472.

2. [1924] 1 KB 461.

3. See 3 LDAB 311.

4. For questions as to the extent of the duty, see Goode, *The Banker's Duty of Confidentiality* (1989) JBL 269.

5. Penn, Shea and Arora consider the duty is not absolute in the sense that it is subject to a duty of reasonable care, 'The Law Relating to Domestic Banking' Vol 1 (1987) para 4.02.

6. "It is common case that the customary and contractual right of a client to confidentiality from his banker ... is and always has been subject to a very wide range of exceptions", Murphy J in *Chestvale Properties Ltd and Hoddle Investments Ltd v Glackin* [1993] 3 IR 35 at 45; [1992] ILRM 221 at 229.

7. *Tournier v National Provincial and Union Bank of England* [1924] 1 KB 461 at 473.

8. See also, Donnelly, 'The Erosion of the Banker's Duty of Secrecy' (1996) CLP 226.

actual state of the customer's account. It extends to information derived from
the account itself."

The principal qualification in practice to the banker's duty of secrecy is where
disclosure is required by law, for as Diplock LJ stated:[9]

"The contractual duty of confidence, generally implied though sometimes
expressed, ... between banker and customer ... is subject to, and overridden by,
the duty of any party to that contract to comply with the law of the land."

SUPERVISORY REQUIREMENTS

[3.02] Article 12 of the First Banking Directive[10] as amended by Article 16 of
the Second Banking Directive[11] anticipates the need not only for regulators to
"be bound by the obligation of professional secrecy" but also that confidential
information may need to be disclosed in criminal law cases and in civil or
commercial proceedings.[12]

[3.03] Every officer and employee of the Central Bank of Ireland is precluded
from disclosing any information concerning the business of any person or body
which comes to his knowledge by virtue of his office or employment (unless
such disclosure is to enable the Central Bank to carry out its functions)[13]. Each
officer and employee at the time of his appointment is required to acknowledge
that he has been informed and understands his secrecy obligations.[14] The
implications of, and rationale for, the secrecy obligations of the Central Bank's
officers and employees were highlighted by O'Hanlon J in *Cully v Northern
Bank Finance Corporation Ltd*[15] when he upheld the objections of the Central
Bank to disclosing information following the service of a subpoena. He stated:[16]

"... the provisions of s 31 of the Central Bank Act 1942 [now replaced by
s 16(3) of the 1989 Act], give rise to a claim of privilege on grounds of public
policy from disclosure of any information of the type referred to in the oath of
secrecy. Section 6(1) of the same Act provides that in relation to part, at least of
the functions and duties of the Central Bank 'the constant and predominant aim
shall be the welfare of the people as a whole'. This gives some indication for

9. In *Parry Jones v The Law Society* [1968] 1 All ER 177 at 180.
10. First Council Directive 77/780/EEC of 12 December 1977.
11. Second Council Directive 89/646/EEC of 15 December 1989.
12. For further consideration of the application of the Banking Directives to bank secrecy see
Dassesse, Isaacs and Penn, *EC Banking Law* (2nd ed) Ch 17.
13. Central Bank Act, 1989, s 16(1); under the Official Secrets Act, 1963 to the extent that the
information which an officer or employee has is "official information", the officer or employee
may not communicate such information to any other person unless duly authorised to do so.
14. Central Bank Act, 1989, s 16(3).
15. [1984] ILRM 683.
16. *Ibid* at 685.

the justification for granting an exceptional degree of protection to the confidentiality of the bank's transactions, as a matter of public interest."

These non-disclosure requirements have been made subject to a number of exceptions.[17]

Officers and employees of banks will generally be required to acknowledge in their contract or terms of employment their secrecy obligations. This procedure serves to draw the attention of the officer or employee to his obligations, which in any event at common law include a duty not to disclose, whether before or after termination of employment, information received in confidence in the course of employment (save where disclosure is required in the public interest).[18]

[3.04] Statutory exceptions to the prohibition of disclosure, include:[19]

    (a) disclosure required by a court in criminal proceedings,

    (b) disclosure made with the consent of the person to whom the information relates and of the person from whom the information was obtained,

    (c) disclosure to the principal where the Central Bank is acting as agent, and

    (d) disclosure where the Central Bank considers it necessary for the common good made to a person charged with the supervision of financial institutions.

An example of the third exception can be seen from the court's decisions in *Desmond and Dedeir v Glackin, The Minister for Industry and Commerce of Ireland and The Attorney General.*[20] In that case Glackin was appointed by the Minister for Industry and Commerce as an inspector for the purpose of investigating the affairs of two companies. The inspector requested the Minister to obtain information from the Central Bank through the Minister for Finance concerning transactions of a related company. The Central Bank had relevant information arising out of its duties under the Exchange Control Act, 1954. It was held in the High Court, and affirmed by the Supreme Court, that (1) as the Central Bank was acting as agent of the Minister for Finance in relation to its

---

17. European Communities (Licensing and Supervision of Credit Institutions) Regulations, 1992 SI 395/1992, Reg 19; European Communities (Consolidated Supervision of Credit Institutions) Regulations, 1992 (SI 396/1992) Reg 7; European Communities (Deposit Guarantee Schemes) Regulations, 1995 SI 168/1995, Reg 28; Investment Intermediaries Act, 1995 s 49(2).
18. See *Initial Services Ltd v Putterill* [1967] 3 All ER 145.
19. See s 16(2) of the Central Bank Act, 1989 as amended by the Stock Exchange Act, 1995 s 50 and the Investment Intermediaries Act, 1995 s 49(1).
20. [1993] 3 IR 67.

functions under the Exchange Control Act, 1954 it was bound to divulge the relevant information to its principal, the Minister for Finance, (2) the Minister for Finance was not bound by any duty of confidence under the Central Bank Act, 1989 and (3) the public interest required all the information which the inspector needed for the purposes of his investigation to be made available to him, and that there was no countervailing public interest of equal or near equal weight in denying the inspector access to the information emanating from the Central Bank.

The public interest requirement referred to in the judgments and indeed the fourth "common good" exception may mean that even where the Central Bank is acting as principal and not agent, as it does in its supervisory and licensing functions, it should disclose information to an inspector.[21]

[3.05] Each bank in the State is required to provide the Central Bank with "such information and returns" concerning its business as the Central Bank may specify from time to time (or request in writing) (being information and returns which the Central Bank considers to be necessary for the performance of its statutory functions).[22]

The statutory function of the Central Bank includes the licensing and supervision of banks.[23] Accordingly, a bank must comply with a request to provide information to the Central Bank, even where the bank's customer has obtained an injunction restraining disclosure.[24] For as Hirst J put it, since the legislation governing the functions of the Bank of England:[25]

> "overrode the duty of confidence, it must also override *inter partes* orders made on that basis, otherwise the Bank could not properly discharge its public duty of supervision".[26]

MONEY LAUNDERING[27]

[3.06] Every bank and building society,[28] including their directors, employees and officers is required to report to the Garda Sióchána where they "suspect"

---

21. See further paras **[3.31]-[3.36]** below.
22. Central Bank Act, 1971, s 18 as amended by the Central Bank Act, 1989, s 37.
23. See Part II, Central Bank Act, 1971.
24. See *A v B Bank* [1992] 1 All ER 778.
25. In the case in question it was the Banking Act 1987 governing the functions of the Bank of England.
26. *A v B Bank* [1992] 1 All ER 778 at 788.
27. For further reading see Reid, 'Cleaning up the Financial System: Money Laundering and the Criminal Justice Act, 1994: A New Regime for Banks' (1994) CLP 279; Haynes, 'Money Laundering and Changes in International Banking Regulation' [1993] 11 JIBL 454.
28. And the other bodies specified in the Criminal Justice Act, 1994, s 32(1).

that a money laundering offence[29] in relation to the business of that bank, building society or other body has been or is being committed.[30] A banker's difficulty in deciding whether to make a disclosure and run the risk of breaching its duty of confidentiality where there turns out to have been no offence is helped by the statutory provision that disclosure made in good faith in the course of making the report is not regarded as a breach of statutory or common law duty of confidentiality.[31]

A bank (its directors, officers and employees) which discloses to its customer that it has made a report to the Garda Siochána in respect of funds in its customer's account will commit an offence if such disclosure "is likely to prejudice any investigation arising from the report into whether an offence has been committed".[32] Thus, a bank is required to inform on its customer without alerting its customer to the fact of its disclosure. Guidance notes issued to the credit institutions require banks to designate an officer at management level with responsibility for the bank's obligations in relation to money laundering and to provide continuing training programmes for their employees. The role of the money laundering officer is set out in the guidance notes.[33]

A money laundering offence will be committed if a bank or other person handles funds "knowing or believing" that the funds wholly or partly, directly or indirectly represent "proceeds of drug trafficking or other criminal activity".[34] This applies also where such person, or a director, officer or employee thereof, thinks that the funds were "probably, or probably represented, such proceeds."[35] Any advice or assistance in relation to such funds is also a money laundering offence.[36]

LEGAL PROCEEDINGS

[3.07] The Bankers' Books Evidence Act, 1879 provides that:[37]

> On the application of any party to a legal proceeding a court or judge may order that such party be at liberty to inspect and take copies of any entries in a banker's book for any of the purposes of such proceedings.

[29.] See Criminal Justice Act, 1994, s 31.
[30.] *Ibid* s 57(1).
[31.] *Ibid* s 57(7).
[32.] Criminal Justice Act, 1994, s 58(2).
[33.] Issued with the approval of the Money Laundering Steering Committee, April 1995, rr 94-98.
[34.] Criminal Justice Act, 1994, s 31(3).
[35.] *Ibid* s 31(8).
[36.] *Ibid* s 31(5) and (6).
[37.] Section 7, first sentence.

The expression "banker's book", "includes any records used in the ordinary business of a bank" including microfilm, magnetic tape and other records in any non-legible form capable of being reproduced in a permanent legible form.[38] The expression "used in the ordinary business of the bank" does not mean that the book must be in use each day but a book which was used and is now kept for reference purposes.[39] It should be noted that the meaning of "bankers' book" as defined is not all inclusive and although amended by statute as recently as 1989[40] it may include any record in a bank however recorded provided it is done so in the ordinary business of the bank.[41] The words of Bridge LJ should be borne in mind namely:[42]

> "The Bankers' Books Evidence Act ... must be construed ... in relation to the practice of bankers as we now understand it. So construing the definition of 'bankers' books' and the phrase 'an entry in a banker's book', it seems to me that clearly both phrases are apt to include any form of permanent record kept by the bank of transactions relating to the bank's business, made by any of the methods which modern technology makes available."

[3.08] In New Zealand a manager's diary has been held to be a banker's book.[43] However, it has been held that letters contained in a correspondence file in a bank are not banker's books.[44] This of course raises the question as to whether microfilm which contains records of letters (for storage purposes) would be excluded notwithstanding the specific statutory inclusion of microfilm. It would be somewhat illogical if a microfilm record of a letter is a 'banker's book' but the letter itself or a copy is not. This conundrum remains to be reconciled by the courts. It seems therefore that what is required is an entry in a book; thus cheques and paying-in slips retained by a bank are not "banker's books".[45] The words of McGregor J in the Supreme Court of New Zealand are a useful guide:[46]

---

38. See s 9 of the Bankers' Books Evidence Act, 1879 as amended by s 2 of the Bankers' Books Evidence (Amendment) Act, 1959 and s 131(d) of the Central Bank Act, 1989; the narrow meaning of 'bankers' books' as applied by Murphy J in *JB O'C v PCD and A Bank* [1985] IR 265 at 273; [1985] ILRM 123 at 129 would be overtaken by the expanded definition of s 131(d) in the subsequently enacted Central Bank Act, 1989.
39. See *The Asylum for Idiots v Handysides* (1906) 22 TLR 573.
40. Central Bank Act, 1989, s 131.
41. See also the definition of "books" in the Finance Act, 1983 as applying to financial institutions.
42. In *Barker v Wilson* [1980] 2 All ER 81 at 83.
43. See *The Queen v William Bacon and Co Ltd* [1969] NZLR 228.
44. See *R v Dadson* (1983) 77 Cr App Rep 91.
45. *Williams v Williams; Tucker v Williams* [1987] 3 All ER 257; but see the contrary comments of Caulfield J in *Barker v Wilson* [1980] 2 All ER 81 at 83.
46. In *The Queen v William Bacon and Company Ltd* [1969] NZLR 228 at 229.

"A copy of an entry cannot be received in evidence unless it is first proved that the book was at the time of the making of the entry one of the ordinary books of the bank, and that the entry was made in the usual and ordinary course of business, and that the book is in the custody and control of the bank."

[3.09] The courts have adopted a cautious approach in permitting this Act to be used. In *L'Amie v Wilson*[47] Andrews J stated:[48]

"Such caution is requisite, even when the inspection applied for is of the account of a party to the action; but when the account is that of a third party, still greater caution is necessary; and before granting an inspection of a third party's account, the Court or Judge, ought to be satisfied that there are good grounds for believing that there are entries in the account material to some issue to be tried in the action, and which would be evidence at the trial for the party applying for the inspection."

In *Staunton v Counihan*[49] Dixon J began his judgment by saying:[50]

"The jurisdiction to order inspection of entries in a banking account conferred by section 7 of the Bankers' Books Evidence Act, 1879, must be exercised with extreme caution even where it is the account of a party to the action."

This cautious approach seems consistent with that applying in England:

"In civil proceedings the courts have set their face against s 7 of the 1879 Act being used as a kind of searching inquiry or fishing expedition beyond the ordinary rules of discovery."[51]

Lord Widgery CJ said in *Williams v Summerfield*:[52]

"... one must I think recognise that an order under s 7 can be a very serious interference with the liberty of the subject. It can be a gross invasion of privacy; it is an order which clearly must only be made after the most careful thought and on the clearest grounds."

[3.10] In *South Staffordshire Tramways Company v Ebbsmith*[53] it was held that the jurisdiction to order inspection of entries in bankers' books under s 7 ought to be exercised in conformity with the general law as to discovery, by which a party to an action is entitled to refuse discovery of entries prior to the trial of the action which he swears to be irrelevant. In that case, the defendant stated on affidavit that entries in his bank account were irrelevant to the matters in dispute

---

[47.] [1907] 2 IR 130.
[48.] *Ibid* at 132.
[49.] (1957) 92 ILTR 32.
[50.] *Ibid* at 33.
[51.] *Encyclopedia of Banking Law* C (93), Butterworths; these in fact were the words used by Lord Widgery CJ in *Williams v Summerfield* [1972] 2 All ER 1334.
[52.] [1972] 2 All ER 1334 at 1338.
[53.] [1895] 2 QB 669.

and the court decided that an order for inspection of those entries before the trial ought not to be made under the Act.

In criminal proceedings Lord Widgery CJ laid down certain guidelines which should be followed by the courts in considering whether an inspection should be ordered pursuant to s 7. He stated:[54]

> "... in criminal proceedings, justices should warn themselves of the importance of the steps which they are taking in making an order under s 7; should always recognise the care with which the jurisdiction should be exercised; should take into account amongst other things whether there is other evidence in the possession of the prosecution to support the charge; or whether the application under s 7 is a fishing expedition in the hope of finding some material on which the charge can be hung".

It should be noted though that the Bankers' Books Evidence Acts and the meaning of a banker's book do not limit the power of a court to order discovery or inspection of an item which may not be a banker's book.[55]

[3.11] An example of the constraints of the application of s 7 can be seen from the decision in *Staunton v Counihan*.[56] In that case, the plaintiff sued the defendant as guarantor of a debt of £12,000 incurred by a company owned by the defendant's son who was a co-guarantor. The plaintiff applied to inspect the company's account in a Dublin bank for the purpose of proving that the debt existed. In refusing the application, Dixon J approached the principles of the legislation on two grounds:[57]

(1) "The jurisdiction was intended really to extend only to accounts which were in form and substance those of a party to the action."[58]

(2) "The entries must be material to some issue in the action and, if they are so, must be admissible in evidence on behalf of the applicant."[59]

---

54. [1972] 2 All ER 1334 at 1338.
55. See *Larkins v National Union of Mineworkers and Bank of Ireland Finance Ltd* [1985] IR 671 and in particular the remarks of Barrington J at 695-6.
56. (1957) 92 ILTR 32.
57. These two grounds were applied by Carroll J in granting an order for inspection of bank accounts in Dublin, see *Chemical Bank v McCormack* [1983] ILRM 350 (where the order was not granted for foreign accounts).
58. (1957) 92 ILTR 32 at 33 applying *Pollock v Garle* [1898] 1 Ch 1; however in *R v Grossman* [1981] Crim LR 396 the English Court of Appeal considered the wording of the statute (ie the definition of "legal proceeding" in s 10) "is wide enough to cover the account not only of a party to the proceedings ... but also an account of other persons with the bank" *per* Lord Denning MR. In the same decision Oliver LJ stated, "So far as the question of jurisdiction is concerned, although it was not treated at first as entirely clear that s 7 of the Bankers' Books Evidence Act enabled an order to be made in relation to an account of a person not a party to any proceedings, it has now been clearly established for many years that the section does enable such order to be made."

Dixon J found, on the first issue, that the account was not in any sense in form and substance the defendant's account, nor was it so closely connected with her that it could be regarded really as her account in another name and, on the second issue the plaintiff's proof does not essentially depend on the entries in the company's bank account and therefore at this stage the entries were not clearly and necessarily admissible in evidence.

[3.12] An essential feature of an order under s 7 is that it should be limited in time.[60] In *R v Marlborough Street Magistrates' Court Metropolitan Stipendiary Magistrate, ex p Simpson*[61] orders for inspection under s 7 were quashed on the grounds that they were not limited in time. Lord Widgery CJ, delivering the principal judgment of the Court, quoted from his judgment in *Williams v Summerfield*[62] where he stated that justices should approach s 7 applications:

> "alive to the requirement of not making the order extend beyond the true purposes of the charge before them, and ... limit the period of the disclosure of the bank account to a period which is strictly relevant to the charge before them."

[3.13] Where a bank is not a party to proceedings, notice of an application for inspection need not be served on the bank.[63] In England the courts have criticised the practice of making orders *ex parte* in respect of the accounts of third parties.[64]

BANKS WITH FOREIGN OFFICES

[3.14] As already indicated, s 7 applies to records used in the ordinary business of a bank. Any bank which holds a banking licence from the Central Bank comes within the ambit of the Act.[65] However, it has been decided that the records or other entries in a "banker's book" should not apply to the books of a

---

59. *Ibid* at 33-34; see also *L'Amie v Wilson* [1907] 2 IR 130.
60. The period of time can be extensive such as 1920 to 1928 as in *Ironmonger & Co v Dyne* (1929) 44 TLR 579.
61. (1980) 70 Cr App R 291.
62. [1972] 2 All ER 1334 at 1338.
63. In *Staunton v Counihan* (1957) 92 ILTR 32, Dixon J considered notice on the party whose account was to be inspected was sufficient; in *Larkins v National Union of Mineworkers and Bank of Ireland Finance Ltd* [1985] IR 671 an order for inspection was granted *ex parte*; but in *L'Amie v Wilson* [1907] 2 IR 130 Andrews J thought notice of the application should be given.
64. See Lord Widgery CJ in *R v Marlborough Street Magistrates' Court Metropolitan Stipendiary Magistrate ex p Simpson* (1980) 70 Cr App R 291 at 294; Shaw LJ and Oliver LJ in *R v Grossman* [1981] Crim LR 396.
65. Bankers' Books Evidence Act, 1879, s 9 (as amended by s 2 of the Bankers' Books Evidence (Amendment) Act, 1959).

foreign branch of a licensed bank.[66] In *Chemical Bank v McCormack*[67] Carroll J held:[68]

> "There are no clear words in the 1879 Act or the amending 1959 Act which would support the interpretation of an intention to have extra territorial effect ...
>
> *R v Grossman* appears to be authority for the making of an order addressed to AIB as a company incorporated within the jurisdiction to make available for inspection in this country the account of the defendant .... in the Park Avenue branch of the bank in New York.
>
> However, even if it is, I do not propose to make such an order in case there would be a conflict of jurisdiction, which should be avoided in the interest of the comity of courts."

In fact in *R v Grossman*[69] the Inland Revenue had sought details of moneys in a Manx bank, which held a numbered account at a branch of an English bank in the Isle of Man. Savings and Investment Bank obtained an injunction in the Isle of Man restraining the English bank from disclosing details of the numbered account. The English Court of Appeal held that although in criminal matters an order could be made under s 7 of the Bankers' Books Evidence Act, 1879 for an inspection of the bank account, as the English bank's branch in the Isle of Man was subject to Manx law and regulations it was to be considered as a different entity from its headquarters branch in London and thus it should be considered as a foreign bank and therefore not subject to the Court's jurisdiction.

FOREIGN BANKS WITH IRISH OFFICES

[3.15] It would seem that a bank with its head office outside Ireland would not be subject to the jurisdiction of the Irish courts so far as producing records which were kept outside the jurisdiction of Ireland, but only such records kept in Ireland relating to the bank's branch.[70] In *MacKinnon v Donaldson Lufkin & Jenrette Securities Corp*[71] the plaintiff obtained an order in England under s 7 of the 1879 Act for an inspection and the production of copies of entries in the New York branch of Citibank (a New York bank) relating to the defendant's account. The plaintiff also obtained a subpoena requiring production by the bank of all documents wherever held concerning the defendant's account with the bank. The plaintiff contended that since the bank was registered in England (as a bank)

---

66. Consistent with this approach is the non-application of deposit interest retention tax to the payment of interest earned on deposits made with a foreign branch of a bank resident in the State, see further paras **[3.23]-[3.27]** below.
67. [1983] ILRM 350.
68. *Ibid* at 353.
69. [1981] Crim LR 396.
70. This is consistent also with the approach of applying deposit interest retention tax to deposits made with an Irish branch of a bank not resident in the State (Finance Act, 1986 Chapter IV).
71. [1986] 1 All ER 653.

and had submitted to the jurisdiction of the English court it should obey the subpoena. On this contention Hoffmann J stated:[72]

"... this argument confuses personal jurisdiction (ie who can be brought before the court) with subject matter jurisdiction (ie to what extent can the court claim to regulate the conduct of those persons). It does not follow from the fact that a person is within the jurisdiction and liable to be served with process that there is no territorial limit to the matters on which the court may properly apply its own rules or the things which it can order such a person to do."

The court held that:

1. It was an established principle that a State should refrain from demanding obedience to its sovereign authority on the part of foreigners in respect of their conduct outside the jurisdiction;

2. A subpoena or order under the 1879 Act was not the enforcement of a private right but was an exercise of sovereign authority to assist in the administration of justice;

3. Accordingly the court would not impose on a foreign bank (which was not a party to the proceedings) any requirement to produce documents which were outside the court's jurisdiction and concerned business outside the court's jurisdiction;

4. In the case of a bank the court would have particular regard to the principle of the sovereignty of others because documents in the custody of a bank concerned not only their business but also that of their customers and they owed their customers a duty of confidence regulated by the law of the country where the account is kept.

Accordingly, the order and the subpoena were discharged.

The court did however state that there may be exceptional circumstances such as in *London and County Securities v Caplan*[73] where the English Court of Appeal ordered an English bank to procure from its foreign banking subsidiaries documents in order to trace assets which had been embezzled.

DISCLOSURE REQUIRED BY THE REVENUE COMMISSIONERS

Reasonable Grounds for Disclosure

[3.16] A bank "may"[74] be required to disclose details of a customer's account with it by the High Court on the application of an inspector or other duly

---

[72.] *Ibid* at 657.

[73.] Court of Appeal, unrep, 26 May 1978.

[74.] "The use of the word "may" in [the section] is clearly designed to confer a discretion upon the Court as to whether or not in any particular case the order sought should be granted" per Murphy J in *JBO'C v PCD and A Bank* [1985] IR 265 at 269; [1985] ILRM 123 at 125.

authorised officer of the Revenue Commissioners.[75] The High Court must be "satisfied that there are reasonable grounds for making the application."[76] The grounds on which an application may arise are set out in s 908(2) of the Taxes Consolidation Act, 1997 which states:

> Where:
>
> > (a) a person who, for the purposes of tax, has been duly required by an inspector to deliver a statement of the profits or gains arising to him from any trade or profession or to deliver to the inspector a return of income, fails to deliver that statement or that return to the inspector, or
> >
> > (b) the inspector is not satisfied with such a statement or return so delivered,
>
> an authorised officer may, if he is of the opinion that that person maintains or maintained an account or accounts, the existence of which has not been disclosed to the Revenue Commissioners, with a financial institution or that there is likely to be information in the books of that institution indicating that the said statement of profits or gains or the said return of income is false to a material extent, apply to a judge for an order requiring that financial institution to furnish the authorised officer-
>
> > (i) with such particulars of all accounts maintained by that person, either solely or jointly with any other person or persons, in that institution during a period not exceeding ten years immediately preceding the date of application, and
> >
> > (ii) with such information as may be specified in the order relating to the financial transactions of that person, being information recorded in the books of that institution which would be material in determining the correctness of the statement of profits or gains or the return of income delivered by that person or, in the event of failure to deliver such statement or return, would be material in determining the liability of that person to tax.

The Act also enables the High Court to prohibit any transfer or dealing with any assets or moneys in the custody of the financial institution at the time the order is made.[77]

[3.17] In the first reported decision on the section,[78] Murphy J stated: "Undoubtedly any order made under the section would involve an invasion of the traditional bond of confidentiality between a banker and his customer."[79]

[75.] Taxes Consolidation Act, 1997, s 908.

[76.] *Ibid* s908(3).

[77.] *Ibid* s 908(4).

[78.] Prior to the Taxes Consolidation Act, 1997 it was s 18 of the Finance Act 1983 as amended by s 10 of the Disclosure of Certain Information for Taxation and Other Purposes Act, 1996.

[79.] *Re JBO'C v PCD and A Bank* [1985] IR 265 at 269; [1985] ILRM 123 at 125.

In the Supreme Court in the same case Finlay CJ stated:[80]

> "Section 18 can be summarised with regard to its purpose and effect as giving to the High Court wide and entirely novel powers of forcing a bank to reveal the affairs of a customer and in addition, under certain circumstances, vests in the High Court a discretion to freeze the bank account of a taxpayer."

It should be noted that where neither of the conditions stated in paragraphs (a) and (b) of s 908(2) are satisfied, the court will not make an order requiring disclosure. In *JO'C v PCD and A Bank*,[81] although it was established that the taxpayer had failed to make returns of income for over ten years, had failed to keep proper accounting records, had mislaid his banking records and had been very unco-operative with the Revenue authorities, the Supreme Court unanimously upheld Murphy J's refusal to order disclosure. The refusal was upheld on the grounds that the section must be construed as containing a precondition that the taxpayer has been required to deliver a statement of profits or gains or a return of income and that such requirement applies both in the case of a failure to deliver and to the delivery of a statement or return with which the inspector of taxes is not satisfied.

[3.18] However, disclosure was granted under (the forerunner to) s 908 in *Liston v GO'C and AO'C*.[82] In that case, an inspector of taxes in the investigation branch of the Revenue Commissioners, formed the view that the tax payers maintained an account or accounts at specified branches of AIB plc and Bank of Ireland and that the books of both banks were likely to contain information regarding the tax payers' financial affairs leading to the conclusion that returns of income made by them were false. Following an *ex parte* application by the inspector of taxes, an order was made by the High Court (pursuant to s 908) requiring the banks to furnish the inspector of taxes with particulars of all accounts held by the tax payers at specified branches during a two year period, as well as details of all lodgments and withdrawals into or out of the accounts for that period and any mandates or other instructions relating to the operation of the accounts.

The High Court's decision was upheld by the Supreme Court. In giving the judgment of the Court,[83] Keane J explained the scope of s 908:[84]

> "the role of the inspector under the section is a purely investigative one. His belief that the information which he seeks from the bank will indicate that there have been significant omissions from the taxpayers' return of income may

---

[80.] *Ibid* at 277 and at 132 respectively.
[81.] *Ibid*.
[82.] [1996] 1 IR 501.
[83.] O'Flaherty J and Murphy J concurring with the judgment of Keane J.
[84.] [1996] 1 IR 501 at 511.

prove to be erroneous. The clear object of the provision is, however, to enable the Revenue Commissioners to obtain information of this nature in order to ensure that all taxpayers pay the tax which by law they are required to pay. That object would be seriously frustrated if an onus was imposed on the applicant to satisfy the court that the information sought would in fact disclose that false returns had been made. However, an order made under the section seriously abridges the right of confidentiality which every person dealing with a bank enjoys and it is for that reason that the Oireachtas not merely stipulated that the inspector must have reasonable grounds for his belief but provided the additional and valuable safeguard that a High Court Judge must be satisfied that such reasonable grounds exist before the institution concerned can be required to furnish the information sought."

Transfer of Assets Abroad

[3.19] A further head under which the Revenue Commissioners may require disclosure arises under s 808 of the Taxes Consolidation Act, 1997.[85] Under this section the Revenue Commissioners may require any person to furnish such particulars as they think necessary in connection with the transfer of assets abroad by persons ordinarily resident in the State. However, the banker-customer confidentiality relationship is respected by the exclusion of a bank from such disclosure requirement of "any particulars of any ordinary banking transactions between the bank and a customer carried out in the ordinary course of banking business".[86] Whether a transaction is one carried out in the ordinary course of banking business will depend upon the ordinary business of "that type of banking institution" and not whether it is in the ordinary course of banking business generally.[87]

[3.20] In considering the application of s 808(4) of the Taxes Consolidation Act, 1997 it is relevant to review the judgment of Megarry J in *Royal Bank of Canada v Inland Revenue Commissioners*.[88] That case involved the application of s 414(5) of the English Income Tax Act 1952, the relevant portion of which is identical to s 808(4). In the course of his judgment Megarry J stated:[89]

"Questions as to the ambit of the term 'ordinary banking transactions' are not made easier by the circumstances that at least on some views there are many different types of bank ...
A transaction that to one type of bank may be ordinary may to another type be exceptional ...

[85.] Formerly s 59 of the Finance Act, 1974.
[86.] Taxes Consolidation Act, 1997, s 808(4).
[87.] See McWilliam J in *The Royal Trust Co (Ireland) Ltd and Whelan v The Revenue Commissioners* [1982] ILRM 459 at 464.
[88.] [1972] 1 All ER 225.
[89.] *Ibid* at 235.

I certainly do not accept that every transaction lawfully carried out by a bank is a 'banking transaction'. Furthermore, even if they were 'banking transactions' I cannot regard them as being 'ordinary' banking transactions. I do not think it is for counsel for the commissioners to establish that they were 'unusual' or 'extra-ordinary' or whatever is the appropriate antithesis to 'ordinary'; it is for counsel for the bank to show that they were 'ordinary'. ... nothing will suffice him save a sufficient demonstration of ordinariness."

[3.21] This approach was applied by McWilliam J in *The Royal Trust Company (Ireland) Ltd and Whelan v The Revenue Commissioners*[90] where he held that one type of transaction came within the exclusion but that the second type did not, "as there has not been what Megarry J described as 'sufficient demonstration of ordinariness' with regard to them."[91]

[3.22] Section 890 of the Taxes Consolidation Act, 1997[92] requires every person in receipt of money belonging to a chargeable person to prepare and deliver, when required to do so (by an inspector of taxes), a list in a prescribed form containing (a) a statement as to the money, (b) the name and address of every person to whom it belongs and (c) a declaration whether such person is, *inter alia* of full age, or resident in the State. The equivalent section in England[93] was considered in *AG v National Provincial Bank Ltd*[94] where Rowlatt J held that the section applied to a bank which held a mortgage or pledge of stock in relation to the interest earned on that stock and held for the account of the mortgagor or pledgor being the chargeable person in the case in point.

Deposit Interest Retention Tax

[3.23] Banks are obliged, when required to do so by an inspector of taxes,[95] to disclose to the inspector declarations made by (1) depositors not ordinarily resident in the State concerning the beneficial ownership of such deposit,[96] (2) depositors who have taken out special savings accounts,[97] (3) depositors being companies within the charge to corporation tax or being a pension scheme,[98] or (4) deposits which form part of the income of a body of persons or trusts treated by the Revenue Commissioners as being established for charitable purposes only.[99]

---

90. [1982] ILRM 459.
91. *Ibid* at 465.
92. Formerly s 176 of the Income Tax Act, 1967.
93. Income Tax Act, 1918, s 103(1).
94. (1928) 44 TLR 701.
95. Taxes Consolidation Act, 1997, s 263.
96. *Ibid.*
97. *Ibid* s 264(2).
98. *Ibid* s 265(1)(c).
99. *Ibid* s 266(1)(c).

Chapter IV of the Finance Act, 1986 introduced a concept commonly referred to as DIRT (Deposit Interest Retention Tax).[100] Under s 257 of the Taxes Consolidation Act, 1997 that Act a bank when making a payment of interest in respect of a deposit is required to "deduct out of the amount of the payment the appropriate tax in relation to the payment".[101] The bank is required to make a return to the Collector-General of the relevant interest paid by it and of the appropriate tax in relation to the payment of that interest[102] (but it is not required that such return contain details of the recipients of the interest payments). To escape the deduction of tax from interest on deposits the beneficial owner will have details of its deposit disclosed to the inspector of taxes if it comes within one of the following categories.

[3.24] Where the beneficial entitlement to interest on a deposit is held by a person who is not ordinarily resident in the State, tax is not to be deducted by the bank on the interest payable provided the person making the declaration declares, in such form as is prescribed or authorised by the Revenue Commissioners, that the person who is beneficially entitled to the interest is not ordinarily resident in the State.[103] The declaration will include details of the name of the person, the address of his principal place of residence and the name of the country in which he is ordinarily resident.[104] The declaration must be kept by the bank for the longer of six years, or three years after the deposit is repaid.[105] The bank is required to make the declaration available to the inspector of taxes as and when required by the inspector of taxes.[106]

[3.25] A deposit account may be designated by the bank holding the deposit as a "special savings account"[107] provided that the depositor is an individual beneficially entitled to the interest, of full age, does not hold another special savings account and the account is not for an amount greater than £50,000.[108] The individual must make a declaration in such form as may be prescribed or authorised by the Revenue Commissioners.[109] The declaration must include

---

[100.] Now re-enacted under the Taxes Consolidation Act, 1997, s 256 and subsequent sections. For a fuller treatment of this topic see Judge *Irish Income Tax* (1997-98 ed) Butterworths para 2.4.

[101.] There are a number of exceptions to this - see the definition of relevant deposit in s 256(1) of the Taxes Consolidation Act, 1997.

[102.] Taxes Consolidation Act, 1997, s 258(2).

[103.] *Ibid* s 263(1).

[104.] *Ibid* s 263(1)(d).

[105.] *Ibid* s 263(2)(a)(i).

[106.] *Ibid* s 263(2)(a)(ii).

[107.] "Special savings accounts" were introduced in 1992 in anticipation of the abolition of exchange controls.

[108.] Taxes Consolidation Act, 1997, s 264(1) covers additional requirements for joint accounts.

[109.] *Ibid* s 264(2)(b).

details of the name and address of the individual beneficially entitled to the interest. An advantage for the depositor of such accounts is that the interest earned will not be subject to any further tax after the deduction of a reduced rate of tax by the holder of the deposit.[110] However, the bank is required to keep such declarations and make them available to the inspector of taxes as required by him.[111]

[3.26] Deduction of deposit interest retention tax is not required in respect of interest on a deposit (made with a bank) which is beneficially owned by a company within the charge to corporation tax or a pension scheme and a declaration is made to that effect in such form as the Revenue Commissioners may prescribe or authorise containing the beneficial owner's name, address and tax reference number as well as such information as the Revenue Commissioners may reasonably require.[112] Such declarations must be kept by the bank and made available to the inspector of taxes as and when required by him.[113]

[3.27] Similarly, deduction of deposit interest retention tax is not required where a declaration is made that the interest on the deposit:

    (i)   (I) forms part of the income of a body of persons or trust which is treated by the Revenue Commissioners as a body or trust established for charitable purposes only, or

            (II) is, according to the rules or regulations established by statute, charter, decree, deed of trust or will, applicable to charitable purposes only and is so treated by the Revenue Commissioners, and

    (ii) will be applied to charitable purposes only.[114]

The declaration must contain the name and address of each person entitled to interest on the account[115] and such information as the Revenue Commissioners may reasonably require.[116] Such declarations must be kept by the bank and made available to the inspector of taxes as and when required by him.[117]

Tax Arrears

[3.28] A bank may be required to disclose to the Revenue Commissioners the amount standing to the credit of its customer in the event of the bank being

---

110. *Ibid* s 264(4).
111. *Ibid* s 264(3).
112. *Ibid* s 265B(1).
113. *Ibid* s 265B(2).
114. *Ibid* s 266(1)(c).
115. *Ibid* s 266(1)(d).
116. *Ibid* s 266(1)(f).
117. *Ibid* s 266(2).

informed by the Revenue Commissioners that the customer is in arrears of its tax payments. A bank will be obliged to make a disclosure where it has received written notification from the Revenue Commissioners that the bank's customer has defaulted, and not made good the default, "in paying, remitting, or accounting for, any tax, interest on unpaid tax, or penalty to the Revenue Commissioners."[118]

The written notification, referred to in the section as "the notice of attachment" should direct the bank:

(1) to deliver to the Revenue Commissioners within 10 days a written return specifying

　　(i) whether any debt is due by the bank to its customer and

　　(ii) the amount of the debt, or where the debt is equal to or greater than the notified tax arrears, the amount of the so notified tax arrears, and

(2) to pay to the Revenue Commissioners the lower of the amount of the debt or the amount of tax arrears notified.[119]

[3.29] Where the deposit is held in the bank by more than one party for their joint benefit, the bank must on receipt of the notice of attachment notify both depositors of relevant details including details of tax arrears of the relevant depositor. The notice which the bank gives to the depositors should inform the depositors of the notice of attachment and that the deposit is deemed to be held for the benefit of the depositors equally unless evidence to the contrary is produced to the satisfaction of the bank within 10 days.[120] Unless such evidence is produced the bank is required to pay to the Revenue Commissioners the amount of the deposit deemed to be held by the defaulting taxpayer (or, if lower, the amount stated in the notice of attachment).[121] It can be seen that this requirement imposes on the bank a duty to disclose to one of its customers the fact that another customer has tax arrears of a specified amount. In addition, it imposes on the bank the obligation of deciding whether evidence which may be produced to it that the deposit is not held equally is satisfactory.[122]

Once a notice of attachment has been delivered to a bank, the bank is precluded from paying moneys to the depositor except to the extent that such moneys will not reduce the deposit below the amount specified in the notice.[123] The

---

118. *Ibid* s 1002.
119. *Ibid* s 1002(2)(a)(iii).
120. *Ibid* s 1002(2)(c).
121. *Ibid*.
122. The potential dilemma for the bank is highlighted in Breslin, 'Revenue Power to attach Debts under section 73 Finance Act, 1988: Implications for Credit Institutions' (1995) CLP 167.
123. Taxes Consolidation Act, 1997, s 1002(6).

legislation is silent as to whether a bank is still required to comply with an attachment notice where a security interest whether by way of assignment or charge is created over the deposit in favour of the bank itself or a third party.[124]

[3.30] In *Orange v The Revenue Commissioners*[125] the applicant sought to challenge the constitutionality of s 73 on the grounds that the attachment notice constituted an unfair attack on his property rights.[126]
Geoghegan J held that:[127]

> "... the applicant had a property right in the debt owing to him ... That property right was a chose in action. The [Revenue Commissioners] had no proprietary right, whether by way of charge or otherwise, to that debt or any part of it. In my view, the notice procedure under section 73 ... constitutes an attack on the applicant's property rights."

However he found:[128]

> "An attack on property rights is not unjust by reason of some theoretical argument; it can only be unjust in all the surrounding circumstances of the particular case."

On the facts, he found that the Revenue Commissioners had been reasonable in their previous treatment and arrangements with the defaulting taxpayer. He concluded though that a suitable amendment to the legislation might be considered and that while he would not envisage any circumstances under which the section would be declared unconstitutional, "conceivably there might be cases where the actual service of the notice under the section amounted to an unconstitutional exercise of the Revenue Commissioners' powers."[129]

COMPANY INVESTIGATIONS

[3.31] In certain circumstances[130] a company may have an inspector appointed to it to investigate its affairs[131] or to investigate and report on its membership[132]. Subject to the court's approval, an inspector appointed to investigate the affairs of a company may investigate also the affairs of any other body corporate which is related to such company.[133]

[124.] See further paras **[15.29]**-**[15.34]**.

[125.] [1995] 1 IR 517; see also para **[15.34]**.

[126.] Section 73 of the Finance Act, 1988 was re-enacted as s 1002 of the Taxes Consolidation Act, 1997.

[127.] [1995] 1 IR 517 at 521.

[128.] *Ibid* at 524.

[129.] *Ibid*.

[130.] Companies Act, 1990, ss 7, 8 and 14.

[131.] *Ibid* ss 7 and 8 (on 30 March 1998 inspectors were appointed to National Irish Bank Ltd).

[132.] *Ibid* s 14.

[133.] *Ibid* s 9.

[3.32] The Companies Act, 1990[134] requires all officers and agents of a body corporate whose affairs are being investigated to produce to an inspector all books and documents relating to the body corporate. Section 10(2) provides:

> If the inspectors consider that a person other than an officer or agent of the company or other body corporate is or may be in possession of any information concerning its affairs, they may require that person to produce to them any books or documents in his custody or power relating to the company or other body corporate, to attend before them and otherwise to give them all assistance in connection with the investigation which he is reasonably able to give; and it shall be the duty of that person to comply with the requirement.

[3.33] The problem that this statutory provision poses for banks was highlighted in the correspondence leading up to the application of *Chestvale Properties Ltd, Hoddle Investments Ltd v Glackin and Ansbacher Bankers Ltd, Noel Smyth and Partners and the AG.*[135] Following the request to the bank from the inspector to deliver certain documents relating to the applicants, the applicants' solicitors wrote to the bank's solicitors stating:[136]

> "If your client [the bank] now complies with the demands and it is subsequently deemed that your client [the bank] was not obliged to do so then our clients [the applicants] would have an appropriate remedy."

That case involved an unsuccessful application that the order sought was unconstitutional on the grounds that the section contravened the personal property rights of citizens.[137]

[3.34] The unenviable predicament for bankers was highlighted a month later by Murphy J in *Chestvale Properties Ltd & Hoddle Investments Ltd v Glackin*[138] when he said:[139]

> "Obviously the bank and the solicitor are in an awkward position; if they neglect to produce books or documents which should properly have been produced they expose themselves to the risk of penalties which might be imposed on them for contempt of court. On the other had if they hand over books or records which do not fall within the terms of the Act they may be liable to their clients for damages for breach of contract."

The impact of this predicament was felt by the bank a month later in *Re Chestvale Properties Ltd and Hoddle Investments Ltd, Glackin v Trustee*

[134.] Section 10(1).
[135.] [1993] 3 IR 35; [1992] ILRM 221.
[136.] *Ibid* at 42 and at 226 respectively.
[137.] Article 40 s 3 sub-s 2 of the Constitution of Ireland.
[138.] High Court, unrep, 10 March 1992.
[139.] *Ibid* page 2.

Savings Bank and McInerney.[140] When the bank was requested by the inspector to supply documents it contended that without their customer's consent, or a High Court order, they could not comply with the inspector's request without breaching the duty of confidentiality which it owed to its customer. The court held that not only did the bank have to supply the documents but also to pay the inspector his costs of the hearing.

[3.35] When considering s 10(2) of the Companies Act, 1990 the words of Costello J in *Re Chestvale Properties Ltd and Hoddle Investments Ltd*[141] should be heeded. He stated:[142]

> "It seems to me that the bank has misunderstood its statutory duty ... It is a duty to give assistance if requested to do so under s 10, sub-s 2 of the Act of 1990. It is not permitted to refuse assistance, because of a contractual arrangement with a customer which may have involved a term of confidentiality.
> The Oireachtas has made perfectly clear, to my mind, what people ... are required to do. They are required to assist the inspector. They are not entitled to obstruct him and they must observe his requests. They are not entitled to ask their customer whether or not the customer objects. Whatever contractual arrangement there has been between the bank and the customer has been clearly over-ridden by the provisions put into this section by the Oireachtas and the manner in which it should comply with the request has been made clear by Mr Justice Murphy. They are to give assistance to the inspector when requested to do so".

[3.36] The reference by Costello J to Murphy J was a reference to his decision in *Chestvale Properties Ltd & Hoddle Investments Ltd v Glackin.*[143] Murphy J indicated in the course of his judgment that under s 10 of the Companies Act, 1990 there are two classes of obligation imposed on agents or former agents of a company whose affairs are being investigated namely:

> "first of all an obligation to produce books and documents and secondly an obligation to attend and give *viva voce* evidence ... those words 'all assistance in connection with the investigation' illuminate fully the nature of the obligation imposed upon an addressee with regard to not merely information but also to the production of books and records. In my view the nature of the obligation which is imposed upon officers or agents can indeed be expressed in terms comparable to that of the obligation imposed upon a person of whom discovery is sought ... All the persons to whom the demand is addressed can do is to produce books and records which in their honest opinion may be of assistance to the inspector".

---

140. [1993] 3 IR 55.
141. *Ibid.*
142. *Ibid* at 62.
143. High Court, unrep, 10 March 1992 Murphy J.

CONSUMER AFFAIRS

[3.37] An authorised officer, appointed by the Minister for Enterprise, Trade and Employment or by the Director of Consumer Affairs, may for the purpose of obtaining information to enable the Director of Consumer Affairs to carry out his functions under the European Communities (Unfair Terms in Consumer Contracts) Regulations, 1995:[144]

    (a) at all reasonable times enter premises at which any business or any activity in connection with a business is carried on ...

    (b) require any person who carries on such business or activity and any person employed in connection therewith to produce to the authorised officer any books, documents or records relating to such business or activity which are in that person's power or control and to give the officer information in regard to any entries in any books, documents and records,

    (c) inspect and take copies from such books, documents and records,

    (d) require any such person to give to the authorised officer any information the officer may require in regard to the persons carrying on such business or activity...

    (e) require any such person to give to the officer any other information which the officer may reasonably require in regard to such business or activity.

These powers are certainly intrusive, but it should be borne in mind that they are only to enable the Director of Consumer Affairs to carry out his functions under the Regulations and therefore should not in the normal course involve opening accounts to the officer, but rather procedures adopted by banks or financial institutions in its dealings with consumer customers generally.

DISCOVERY

> "In order to enable justice to be done ... it is a very important part of the court's armoury to be able to order discovery".[145]

[3.38] A court will order a bank to open its books to facilitate the tracing of money which has been obtained by fraud.[146] In *Bankers Trust Co v Shapiro*[147] the English Court of Appeal made an order for discovery against Discount Bank (Overseas) Ltd to enable the plaintiff to follow the proceeds of money which had been obtained from it by means of forged cheques presented by the first two

---

[144.] Pursuant to reg 10 of the European Communities (Unfair Terms in Consumer Contracts) Regulations, 1995 (SI 27/1995).

[145.] Lord Denning MR in *Bankers Trust Co v Shapiro* [1980] 3 All ER 353 at 357.

[146.] In *Re Hallett's Estate* (1879) 13 Ch D 696; *A v C* [1980] 2 All ER 347.

[147.] [1980] 3 All ER 353.

defendants who were outside the jurisdiction. In granting the order for discovery Lord Denning MR set out guidelines for the making of such an order. He said:[148]

> "It is a strong thing to order a bank to disclose the state of its customer's account and the documents and correspondence relating to it. It should only be done when there is a good ground for thinking the money in the bank is the plaintiff's money, as for instance when the customer has got the money by fraud, or other wrongdoing, and paid it into his account at the bank. The plaintiff, who has been defrauded, has a right in equity to follow the money. ... So the court, in order to give effect to equity, will be prepared in a proper case to make an order on the bank for their discovery. The plaintiff must of course give an undertaking in damages to the bank and must pay all and any expenses to which the bank is put in making the discovery; and the documents, once seen, must be used solely for the purpose of following and tracing the money, and not for any other purpose."

The order for discovery made was the disclosure of balances in the accounts of the first and second defendants with the bank and copies of all correspondence between the first two defendants and the bank, all cheques drawn on their accounts and all debit vouchers, transfer applications and orders and internal memoranda relating to the accounts of the first two defendants.

[3.39] Where a Mareva injunction is granted and the assets the subject of the injunction include moneys in a bank account the court may, if it decides that the plaintiff is entitled to discovery of the balance in the account, exercise its powers under s 7 of the Bankers' Books Evidence Act, 1879 to order that the plaintiff may inspect and take copies of entries in the bankers' books.[149] To do otherwise would prevent the mareva injunction from being effective.[150]

SUBPOENA

> "A document must be produced to the Court if a subpoena be served upon a person who has it."[151]

[3.40] A bank which is compelled by subpoena to produce bank statements to a court will not breach its contractual duty of secrecy by doing so without obtaining the customer's consent.[152] However, although the bank is under no duty to inform its customer of the subpoena it should use its best endeavours to do so.[153] This of course may pose problems for a bank in deciding whether or not

---

[148.] *Ibid* at 357.

[149.] *A v C* [1980] 2 All ER 347.

[150.] *Ibid per* Goff J at 352.

[151.] *Per* Darling J in *The King v Daye* [1908] 2 KB 333 where it was held that a sealed packet may be a "document".

[152.] See *Robertson v Canadian Imperial Bank of Commerce* [1995] 1 All ER 824.

[153.] *Ibid.*

it should inform its customer as it may be, entitled for its own protection or, compelled by public duty[154] to refrain from informing its customer.[155]

SEQUESTRATION OF BANK DEPOSITS

[3.41] The effect which a sequestration order has on a bank's duty of confidentiality and on the bank's obligations with regard to its customer's deposits was outlined by Sir John Donaldson in *Eckman v Midland Bank Ltd*[156] where he stated:[157]

> "The problem only arises when, as the banks admit in the present case, the contemnor's title is clear and the property is without doubt liable to sequestration. The authorities seem to establish the following propositions:
>
> (1)   A writ of sequestration does not create a charge on the contemnor's property (*Re Pollard, ex p Pollard*).
>
> (2)   The collusive creation of a mortgage with a view to preventing the enforcement of sequestration is ineffective (*Ward v Booth*).
>
> (3)   A writ of sequestration affects possession not title. Accordingly, money paid into court for the credit of a sequestration account under authority of the writ is available to the contemnor's creditors, but it is otherwise if pursuant to a specific order of the court the money is paid out or paid into court for the general credit of an action (*Re Pollard*).
>
> (4)   If a third party pays or transfers money or property to sequestrators on their demand, he is protected from claims by the contemnor.
>
> (5)   No court has ever declared that a third party should pay money or transfer property to the sequestrator without also making a specific order to that effect.
>
> (6)   In one case (*Re Pollard, Pollard v Pollard*) Joyce J took the view that he had no power on motion to order the payment of a sum equal to the money which had been paid to the contemnor by the third party after notice of the writ of sequestration and in breach of an undertaking given to the sequestrators, but it seems from a report of subsequent proceedings that his order to pay over the money remaining in the hands of the third party was without prejudice to the sequestrators' rights to take further proceedings against the third party."
>
> "Counsel for the banks has asked that we define the duty of banks and other third parties in relation to their dealings with a contemnor's property following the issue of writs of sequestration. We do not think that we can do this exhaustively, but in our judgment it at least extends to the following:

[154.] See para **[3.41]** below.

[155.] See the remarks of Lord Nolan in *Robertson v Canadian Imperial Bank of Commerce* [1995] 1 All ER 824 at 830.

[156.] [1973] 1 All ER 609.

[157.] *Ibid* at 615.

(1) The third party is completely unaffected unless and until he knows of the issue of the writ of sequestration.

(2) The only duty which arises out of mere knowledge that a writ of sequestration has been issued is a duty to refuse to take any action the object of which is known by the third party to be the frustration of the object of the writ. Thus, in the absence of express instructions from the sequestrators banks can continue to honour cheques and stockbrokers can sell securities on the authority of the contemnor, unless they know that the transactions are exceptional and designed to obstruct or prevent the sequestration. If they have any doubts they can protect themselves by reporting the facts to the sequestrators.

(3) A demand by sequestrators for disclosure of property held for account of the contemnor not only may but must be answered promptly, fully and accurately. The duty of disclosure extends to revealing, on request, that no such property is held, or, if it has been but is no longer held, when, in what manner and to whom it was disposed of. If there is doubt as to the contemnor's title or the property is or may be subject to a charge, the full facts must be given to the sequestrators, who are as much entitled to the information as is the contemnor.

(4) If sequestrators require the transfer of possession of property which is or may be held for account of the contemnor or (which is the same) that the property be held to their order, the requirement must be strictly complied with unless (a) someone other than the contemnor has or may have an interest in the property, eg the bank itself has a charge on securities possession of which is demanded by the sequestrators or money is held on the joint account of the contemnor and others or there is notice of a trust in favour of others; or (b) there is doubt whether the property is liable to sequestration; in these exceptional cases it is the duty of the third party to explain the reasons for its failure to comply with the sequestrators' demand in order that the sequestrators may decide whether or not to seek a specific order from the court."

[3.42] In that case, the Amalgamated Union of Engineering Workers refused to pay a court fine following which a sequestration order was made which required the union's bankers to disclose amounts held on deposit with banks by the Union. The banks contended that while the order entitled them to give the information sought, it did not compel them to do so. The court held however that a sequestration order required the bank to disclose details of the depositor's accounts.

Not Applicable for Enforcement of Foreign Penal Law

[3.43] The courts though will not enforce a foreign sequestration order on the grounds that the courts will not be used to enforce a penal law of a foreign State.[158] The reason for this approach is that the courts are not competent to arbitrate on the justice or injustice of the penal laws of foreign States.[159] An

---

[158.] *Buchanan Ltd v McVey* [1954] IR 89 as applied in *Larkins v National Union of Mineworkers and Bank of Ireland Finance Ltd* [1985] IR 671.

example of the application of these principles arose in the case of *Larkins v National Union of Mineworkers and Bank of Ireland Finance Ltd*[160] which attracted much publicity at the time.[161] English courts appointed the first four plaintiffs sequestrators following the failure of the first defendant (the union) to pay a fine. The sequestrators sought an interim order from the High Court claiming that the union had transferred funds of approximately £8,000,000 from its account in the United Kingdom to bank accounts with the second defendant (the bank). The sequestrators claimed possession of the funds and they needed to establish the whereabouts of the funds with a view to preventing them from leaving the Irish jurisdiction. Barrington J made an interim order providing *inter alia* that:

1. The union and the bank and their servants and agents and "any bank or financial institution" within the Irish jurisdiction be restrained from disposing of or otherwise dealing in any manner with any monies held to the union's account;

2. The bank (or any financial institution or bank in Ireland served with notice of the order) produce for inspection "the bankers' books including correspondence or computer printouts from electronic recordings" relating to any account of the union held by the bank.

At the trial of the action (where it was held that the sequestrators were not entitled to the funds on deposit on the grounds that the court would not enforce a penal law or process of a foreign State[162]), Barrington J gave his reasons for his "very far reaching order":[163]

"In the normal course a freezing order would have been sufficient to maintain the status quo and there would have been no justification for making an inspection order such as this, *ex parte*. The necessity for the *ex parte* order arose from the fear that portion of the funds had already been transferred to other financial institutions in Ireland, the identity of which was unknown to the sequestrators."[164]

Funds of an Unlawful Organisation

[3.44] Under the Offences Against the State (Amendment) Act, 1985 a bank is required on receipt of a document, "purporting to be signed by the Minister for

---

[159.] See the interpretation of Kingsmill Moore J's judgment in *Buchanan Ltd v McVey* [1954] IR 89 by Barrington J in *Larkins v National Union of Mineworkers and Bank of Ireland Finance Ltd* [1985] IR 671 at 683.

[160.] [1985] IR 671.

[161.] The principal officers of the union concerned, who were trustees of its funds, were Arthur Scargill (president), Michael McGahey (vice president) and Ernest Heathfield (secretary).

[162.] Barrington J accepted the proposition that "the process, whether civil or criminal and whether coercive or punitive in purpose, is essentially penal in effect" - *Ibid* at 688.

[163.] *Ibid* at 695.

[164.] As it transpired funds had been transferred not to other financial institutions in Ireland but to banks in New York, Luxembourg and Switzerland.

Justice," which states that in the opinion of the Minister moneys described in the document and held by the bank are the property of an unlawful organisation, to pay the moneys so specified into the High Court.[165] This statutory requirement runs for periods of three months and if not renewed lapses until renewed.[166] The consequences of a bank failing to comply with such a requirement are a fine of up to £100,000 and fines and/or imprisonment for directors or officers of the bank including the manager or other official of a branch of the bank.[167]

As well as the bank being required to pay moneys into the High Court, it may be required by the court:

> "to produce and prove to the court all or specified documents that are relevant to the payment of the moneys or part of them into or out of the bank or to the opening, maintenance, operation or closing of any account at the bank in respect of the moneys or part of them."[168]

Statutory protection is given to a bank which complies with a requirement under s 2 of the Act.[169]

A person claiming to be the owner of such moneys paid into the High Court may within six months apply to the Court seeking an order that the moneys be returned with interest. The Court will make the order if it is satisfied that the applicant is the owner of the moneys and the moneys do not belong to an unlawful organisation.

[3.45] In *Clancy and McCarthy v Ireland and the Attorney General*[170] the plaintiffs claimed that they had been unconstitutionally deprived of their moneys, following the transfer of in excess of £1.75 million by Bank of Ireland to the High Court pursuant to an order from the Minister for Justice. Barrington J held that the Act amounted to a permissible delimitation of property rights in the interests of the common good. Furthermore, while the Act provided for the freezing of a bank account and the payment of funds from the account to the High Court without notice to the account holder, the Act entitled the account holder to claim the funds in the High Court and thus it did not confiscate the funds nor deprive the account holder of a fair hearing.[171]

---

[165] Section 2(1)(a).

[166] Offences Against the State (Amendment) Act, 1985 s 2(1)(c).

[167] *Ibid* s 7.

[168] *Ibid* s 5(3).

[169] *Ibid* s 6.

[170] [1989] ILRM 670.

[171] Nonetheless the onus of proof is on the account holder to establish his title.

PROSECUTION OF CRIMINAL OFFENCES

Winding-up of Company

[3.46] Under s 299(2) of the Companies Act, 1963 if it appears to the liquidator in the course of a voluntary winding-up that any past or present officer or member of the company has been guilty of any offence in relation to the company for which he is criminally liable, he shall report the matter to the Attorney General. In the event of a liquidator not making such a report, a person interested in the winding up may apply to the court seeking a court direction for such a report to be made.[172] Following such report, if the Attorney General institutes proceedings, it is the duty of every past and present banker to the company "to give all assistance in connection with the prosecution which he is reasonably able to give."[173]

In the case of a compulsory court winding-up, any criminal proceedings are taken by the Director of Public Prosecutions[174] but in this instance there is no requirement for a banker to give such assistance.

This is a clear instance of failure by the draftsman to follow through on his amendments as prior to the amendment of s 299(1) of the Companies Act, 1963 there was such a requirement. The effect of the amendment introduced by s 143 of the Companies Act, 1990 whereby the Attorney General was replaced by the Director of Public Prosecutions has meant that the statutory requirement for a banker to assist such proceedings has been removed.

Insider Dealing

[3.47] Where it appears to the stock exchange that a person has committed an offence under Part V of the Companies Act, 1990, the exchange must make a report to the Director of Public Prosecutions. If the Director issues proceedings following such report it is the duty of every person who appears to the Director to have relevant information "to give all assistance in connection with the prosecution which he or they are reasonably able to give."[175] In applying the principles outlined by Costello J in *Re Chestvale Properties Ltd and Hoddle Investments Ltd, Glackin v Trustee Savings Bank and McInerney*[176] a bank would be required to disclose details of such accounts as are required by the Director of Public Prosecutions in the course of his proceedings for unlawful dealing.

---

172. Companies Act, 1963, s 299(3).
173. *Ibid* s 299(4).
174. *Ibid* s 299(1).
175. Companies Act, 1990, s 115(4).
176. [1993] 3 IR 55 at 62 see para **[3.34]** above.

Application of Garda Síochána

[3.48] The legislature has endeavoured to assist the Garda Síochána in bringing to justice persons who may have committed a criminal offence by permitting them access to documentation held in a bank. Section 7A(1) of the Bankers' Books Evidence Act, 1879 as inserted by the Central Bank Act, 1989[177] and as expanded by the Disclosure of Certain Information for Taxation and Other Purposes Act, 1996,[178] provides:

> If, on an application made by a member of the Garda Siochana not below the rank of Surperintendent, a court or a judge is satisfied that there are reasonable grounds for believing -
>
> (a) that an indictable offence has been committed; and
>
> (b) that there is material in the possession of a bank specified in the application which is likely to be of substantial value (whether by itself or together with other material) to the investigation of the offence;
>
> a court or judge may make an order that the applicant or another member of the Garda Síochána designated by him be at liberty to inspect and take copies of any entries in a banker's book, or inspect and take copies of any documentation[179] associated with or relating to an entry in such book, for the purposes of investigation of the offence.

Obligations of Bank

[3.49] In *Barclays Bank plc v Taylor; Trustee Savings Bank of Wales and Border Counties v Taylor*[180] it was held that as responsibility for granting an access order rests with the judge, there is no implied obligation on the part of the bank to contest the application unless the bank knows something relevant which is not apparent on the face of the application. The English Court of Appeal held also not only that there was no implied obligation on the part of the bank to inform its customer of the application but as there is a public interest in assisting police in the investigation of a crime, if the bank had informed its customer of the application it would have hindered the police inquiries.

[3.50] Guidelines to be followed in the prosecution of criminal offences may be seen from the judgment of Lord Widgery CJ in *Williams v Summerfield*.[181]

[177.] Section 131.

[178.] Section 14.

[179.] "Documentation" is deemed to include "information kept on microfilm, magnetic tape or in ay non-legible form (by use of electronics or otherwise) which is capable of being reproduced in a permanent legible form" (Banker's Books Evidence, Act 1879, s 7A(2)(b) as inserted by the Disclosure of Certain Information for Taxation and Other Purposes Act, 1996, s 14).

[180.] [1989] 3 All ER 563.

[181.] [1972] 2 All ER 1334; see para **[3.10]** above.

DUTY TO THE PUBLIC TO DISCLOSE

[3.51] The second qualification to the bank's duty of secrecy referred to by Bankes LJ in *Tournier v National Provincial and Union Bank of England*[182] is where there is a duty to the public to disclose. There has been a dearth of precedent or case law to illustrate this principle until the Supreme Court's decision in *National Irish Bank Limited and National Irish Bank Financial Services Limited v Radio Telefís Éireann.*[183] In that case, the defendants sought to publish information showing that certain named customers of the plaintiffs had, at the suggestion of the plaintiffs, used their moneys on deposit (with the plaintiffs) for the purpose of investing in an Isle of Man company, Clerical Medical Insurance, the result of which the defendants alleged, enabled the return on such moneys to evade tax which would otherwise have been payable on the deposit accounts. Although it was not proved that the customers intended to evade tax and the plaintiffs denied it was the intention of the scheme to evade tax, the Supreme Court held by a 3-2 majority that the defendants could disclose to the public at large the information which they possessed including the names of individual customers (albeit at the risk of a claim for defamation from the customers).

The principle of this exception to the duty of secrecy was set out clearly by Lynch J in his majority judgment[184] where he said:[185]

> "There is no doubt that there exists a duty and a right of confidentiality between banker and customer as also exists in many other relationships such as for example doctor and patient and lawyer and client. This duty of confidentiality extends to third parties into whose hands confidential information may come and such third parties can be injuncted to prohibit the disclosure of such confidential information. There is a public interest in the maintenance of such confidentiality for the benefit of society at large. On the other hand there is also a public interest in defeating wrong doing and where the publication of confidential information may be of assistance in defeating wrong doing then the public interest in such publication may outweigh the public interest in the maintenance of confidentiality."

In applying the principle in the case Lynch J held:[186]

> "... the allegation which [the defendants] make is of serious tax evasion and this is a matter of genuine interest and importance to the general public and especially the vast majority who are law abiding tax payers and I am satisfied

---

182. [1924] 1 KB; see para **[3.01]** above.
183. Supreme Court, unrep, 20 March 1998.
184. O'Flaherty J and Barrington J concurred with his judgment.
185. At p15 of the transcript.
186. At p16 of the transcript.

that it is in the public interest that the general public should be given this information".

The lack of proof by the defendants of any wrongdoing, but simply an allegation of wrongdoing, made the majority decision somewhat surprising.[187] In his judgment Keane J, with whom Hamilton CJ concurred, pointed out that the details of the scheme were already the subject of inquiries by the Revenue Commissioners and the Central Bank. Keane J stated:[188]

> "The authorities ... made it clear that where someone is in possession of confidential information establishing that serious misconduct has taken place or is contemplated, the courts should not prevent disclosure to persons who have a proper interest in receiving the information. RTE accordingly, should not be restrained in this case from disclosing to the Revenue Commissioners the confidential information in their possession which, they say, establishes that this scheme has been availed of in order to evade the payment of tax."

This approach should, it is submitted, have been sufficient to satisfy the public interest. However, there is no denying that there is a high degree of public curiosity as to other persons' financial affairs. It seems, therefore, according to the Supreme Court, that disclosure to the public at large is in the public interest not just where there is wrongdoing but where there is a suspicion of wrongdoing.[189]

[187.] But in its editorial of 21 March 1998 *The Irish Times* stated, "Perhaps we should not be unduly surprised. The Supreme Court has a proud and distinguished record of affirming individual rights and liberties", no mention being made of the rights of customers to have their affairs kept confidential.

[188.] At p 15 of the transcript.

[189.] This runs contrary to the position as stated in Paget's *Law of Banking* (11th ed, 1996) Butterworths p 122.

Chapter 4

Bank Accounts

OPENING A BANK ACCOUNT

[4.01] When opening a bank account, the banker is required to "take reasonable measures to establish the identity" of its new customer.[1] Where the banker believes that the customer is acting for a third party, the banker must carry out the same "reasonable measures" to identify the third party.[2] The banker is then required to retain "for use as evidence in any investigation into money laundering:[3]

(a) in the case of the identification of a customer or proposed customer, a copy of all materials used to identify the person concerned for a period of at least 5 years after the relationship with the person has ended;[4]

(b) in the case of transactions, the original documents or copies admissible in legal proceedings relating to the relevant transaction for a period of at least 5 years following the execution of the transaction."

[4.02] In April 1995 a sub-committee[5] of the Money Laundering Steering Committee issued Guidance Notes for use by banks and building societies.[6] The Guidance Notes indicate[7] that the identification procedures set out in the Notes "are good industry practice" and are "the measures to establish identity that might reasonably be expected of credit institutions with effect from 2 May 1995". Accordingly, a bank which complies with such procedures may be

---

[1]   Criminal Justice Act, 1994, s 32(3).
[2]   *Ibid* s 32(5).
[3]   *Ibid* s 32(9); The Guidance Notes (referred to below) indicate (at Para 78) "that this obligation applies even if the person identified does not become a customer or the proposed transaction is not actually effected".
[4]   That is the closing of an account or the commencement of proceedings to recover debts on insolvency (see Para 80 of the Guidance Notes (referred to below)).
[5]   Comprising of representatives from the Central Bank of Ireland, the Irish Bankers Federation and the Irish Mortgage & Savings Association.
[6]   Separate Guidance Notes have been issued for other bodies including other financial institutions supervised by the Central Bank.
[7]   Paragraph 28.

deemed to have taken "reasonable measures" within the meaning of the Criminal Justice Act. These procedures include:[8]

1. Wherever possible, there should be face to face contact with the prospective customer,[9]

2. ... it is necessary that the current permanent address supplied by the person be separately verified.[10]

3. Where there is a requirement to establish the identity of a prospective customer, business should not proceed until satisfactory evidence of identity has been established. In exceptional cases, a credit institution may accept the application for account opening and a payment from the customer immediately subject to satisfactory establishment of identity as soon as is reasonably practicable ... In no circumstances should transactions be permitted on an account before the customer's identity has been established and this should be made clear to the customer.[11]

[4.03] The rules as to the establishment of the identity of Irish resident personal customers are as follows:[12]

(i) The true name of the prospective customer and his/her/its correct permanent Irish address, including postal code when applicable should be provided by the customer; in addition, the date of birth should normally be supplied.

(ii) The true name used should be verified by reference to a document obtained from a reputable source which bears a photograph and signature. Whenever possible a current valid full passport should be requested and reference numbers and other relevant details recorded ...

(iii) In addition to the name verification, ... the current permanent address should also be verified. Some of the best means of verifying are:

- checking the Electoral Register ...,

- requesting sight of a recent utility bill, bank or building society statement (originals),

- checking a local telephone directory or available street directory.

(iv) In respect of joint accounts, the names of all account holders, not just the first named, should be established and the addresses of each verified.

---

8. Separate procedures apply where business is conducted by post, telephone or electronically.
9. Paragraph 30.
10. Paragraph 31.
11. Paragraph 34.
12. Paragraph 45.

(v) An introduction from a respected customer, personally known to a member of management in the branch or office in the credit institution concerned, may assist in the verification of the name and address of a person for whom a credit institution proposes to provide a service. In such a situation, details of the introduction should be recorded on the customer file and signed by the member of management concerned.

[4.04] In the case of students and young people, these rules are:

(a) When opening accounts for students and young people, the normal identification procedures set out in paragraph 45 should be followed save in exceptional circumstances. In situations where it is not possible to obtain verification of identity directly from the prospective customer it should be obtained from another source such as the home address of the parent(s) or by enquiries from the college or university.[13]

(b) Under normal circumstances a minor would be introduced to the bank or building society by a family member or guardian who has an existing relationship with the credit institution concerned and such introduction may be relied upon as satisfactorily establishing identity.[14]

[4.05] With regard to partnerships:[15]

In cases where a formal partnership arrangement exists, a mandate from the partnership authorising the opening of an account and conferring authority on those who will operate it should be obtained. In the case of partnerships, the identity of at least two partners and of all those authorised to operate the account should be established in accordance with paragraph 45.

[4.06] In the case of Irish incorporated bodies, to establish identity a credit institution should obtain:[16]

(i) the original or certified copy of the Certificate of Incorporation or the Certificate to Trade;

(ii) Memorandum and Articles of Association;

(iii) a list of directors' names, occupations, residential and business addresses and date of birth;

(iv) properly authorised mandate of the directors to open an account and conferring authority on those who will operate it.

[4.07] The Guidance Notes also stipulate that it may be prudent to carry out a search in the Companies Registration Office to confirm the date of incorporation and the list of directors correspond to those provided. The Notes go on to

---

13. Paragraph 52.
14. Paragraph 53.
15. Paragraph 60.
16. Paragraph 67.

provide that where a majority of the directors are not known to the credit institution the following additional procedures should be carried out:[17]

(i) the identity of at least two directors and all persons authorised to operate the account from time to time should be established ...

(ii) a list of names and addresses of shareholders holding 10 per cent or more of the issued share capital of the company should be obtained from the company and in the case of individual shareholders their occupations and dates of birth should also be obtained.

It is also recommended to carry out a search in the Companies Registration Office to corroborate the list of shareholders. Proof of beneficial ownership of a 25 per cent corporate shareholder is advised. If adequate information is not forthcoming, the Guidance Notes do not recommend a cessation of dealings with the customer but simply that "the credit institution should pay particular attention to business relations and transactions with that corporate customer".

Banker's Liability for Failure to Identify

[4.08] It should be noted that a banker may be liable, not only under the money laundering legislation, but also to third parties at common law for failure to take reasonable precautions in establishing the identity of a new customer.[18] In *Ladbroke and Co v Todd*[19] a thief stole a cheque in favour of a Mr Jobson crossed "account of payee". The thief took the cheque to the defendant bank, represented himself as Mr Jobson and asked that the cheque be cleared at once so that he could draw on it straightaway. In an action against the bank, for recovery of the amount paid, the bank pleaded that it received payment for a customer "in good faith and without negligence" and thus was entitled to the protection of the Bills of Exchange Act, 1882.[20] The court held that although the bank had received the payment in good faith for a customer, the bank was not protected by the Act as it had not taken reasonable precautions to safeguard the interests of persons who might be the true owners of the cheque.

[4.09] In *Nu-Stilo Footwear Ltd v Lloyds Bank Ltd*[21] Sellers J stated:[22]

"The immunity of the bank depends on whether, in the matters in question, they acted according to the standards of the reasonable and prudent banker in regard to the precautions taken in opening the new account in question."

---

17. Paragraph 69.
18. *Hampstead Guardians v Barclays Bank Ltd* (1923) 39 TLR 229.
19. (1914) 30 TLR 433.
20. Section 82.
21. (1956) 7 LDAB 121.
22. *Ibid* at 122.

That case exemplified the difficulties which a bank can face when opening a new account. Mr Montague worked as an accountant in the plaintiff's company. He approached the defendant bank using the name Mr Baier indicating he was a freelance agent and wished to open an account. He gave the name of Mr Montague (ie himself) as his referee. On the same day the bank telephoned Mr Montague who gave a very satisfactory reference and gave the name of his bankers. Mr Montague's bankers confirmed that Mr Montague, being an accountant in the plaintiff company, was an established customer and a suitable person to give a reference. The court found that the defendant bank had acted without negligence in opening the account.[23]

[4.10] In *Marfani & Co Ltd v Midland Bank Ltd*[24] Diplock LJ said:[25]

> "What facts ought to be known to the banker, ie, what inquiries he should make, and what facts are sufficient to cause him reasonably to suspect that the customer is not the true owner, must depend on current banking practice, and change as that practice changes. Cases decided thirty years ago, when the use by the general public of banking facilities was much less widespread, may not be a reliable guide to what the duty of a careful banker, in relation to inquiries and as to facts which should give rise to suspicion, is today."

Accordingly, future decisions involving the appropriate standard of care to be exercised by a banker in opening an account are likely to be made by reference to the Guidance Notes, at least for accounts opened since 2 May 1995, rather than by reference to standards set by courts in particular circumstances over decades.

[4.11] It would be prudent also for bankers to enquire as to the potential customer's employers, not so much from the identification viewpoint but so as to be better able to detect a fraud should the employer's cheques be endorsed in favour of the customer and lodged to the credit of the customer's account.[26]

[4.12] In drawing up internal rules for identification for use by a bank, bankers should ensure that such rules are complied with in practice. Accordingly, there is little point in preparing excessively cautious rules if they are not implemented

---

23. The bank however was held liable on eight of the nine charges as the second cheque was a third party cheque endorsed for an amount in excess of what a freelance agent would have earned and uncovering the fraud of this cheque would have prevented the subsequent cheques being cashed.
24. [1968] 2 All ER 573.
25. *Ibid* at 579.
26. See *Bissell v Fox Brothers & Co* (1885) 53 LT 193; *Harding v London Joint Stock Bank (Ltd)* (1914) 3 LDAB 81; *AL Underwood, Ltd v Bank of Liverpool and Martins Ltd* [1924] 1 KB 775; *Lloyds Bank Ltd v The Chartered Bank of India, Australia and China* [1929] 1 KB 40; *Lloyds Bank Ltd v EB Savory and Co* [1933] AC 201.

in practice. Bankers should heed the words of Lawrence LJ in *Lloyds Bank Ltd v EB Savory and Co*:[27]

> "The fact that a breach of the rules had been committed did not necessarily prove that the bank had acted negligently, as the rule which had been broken might have been made from excessive caution; but in most cases it would furnish a strong *prima facie* ground for holding that the bank had not acted without negligence."

CAPACITY AND AUTHORITY

Minors

[4.13] An individual, aged 18 years or older, being of sound mind is capable of opening a bank account. A minor, that is an unmarried person under the age of 18 years,[28] has the capacity to open an account but is subject to certain protections which would render it unwise for a bank to offer a minor a current account. However, a deposit account would not be inappropriate.

[4.14] Apart from contracts for necessaries or beneficial contracts of service, a contract with a minor is voidable by a minor - the contract will not bind him unless he affirms it within a reasonable time of attaining majority age.[29] Furthermore, the Infants Relief Act 1874 provides[30] that:

> All contracts ... entered into by infants[31] for the repayment of money lent or to be lent ... shall be absolutely void.

A loan to a minor, being void, cannot be ratified by the minor on attaining the age of majority.[32] Nor is a minor liable to honour a cheque drawn by him.[33] Bankers should ensure that they obtain appropriate verification of a young customer's age whether by means of a passport or birth certificate. For if a banker lends money to a minor upon the minor's misrepresentation that he was of majority age, the banker will be unable to recover the loan.[34]

[27.] [1932] 2 KB 122 at 138.
[28.] Age of Majority Act, 1985, s 2.
[29.] See Clark, *Contract Law in Ireland* (3rd ed) Sweet & Maxwell, p 359.
[30.] Section 1.
[31.] Now known as minors (Age of Majority Act, 1985, s 3).
[32.] See also the Betting and Loans (Infants) Act 1892, s 5.
[33.] *Re Soltykoff* [1891] 1 QB 413 at 415 (per Lord Esher MR); *Hutley v Peacock* (1913) 30 TLR 42.
[34.] *R Leslie Ltd v Sheill* [1914] 3 KB 607.

Partnerships

[4.15] Partnership accounts are opened in the name of all the partners or in the name of the firm by which the partnership is known. In the latter case in particular the bank should obtain a copy of the partnership agreement. A partnership exists where two or more persons carry on business with a view of profit.[35] Under the Partnership Act, 1890:[36]

> Every partner in a firm is liable jointly with the other partners, ... for all debts and obligations of the firm incurred while he is a partner; and after his death his estate is also severally liable ... for such debts and obligations ... but subject ... to the prior payment of his separate debts.

To get round the limitation of recovery from a partner in the event of his bankruptcy (which is subject to payment of his other debts), a partnership bank mandate will typically provide for joint and several liability for monies borrowed from the bank. The bank will not then have to await recovery subsequent to other creditors of the partners, unless its return on its loan to the partnership varies depending upon the profit or loss of the partnership.[37]

A mandate should be signed by all the partners, or alternatively where it is clear under a partnership agreement (furnished to the bank) that certain partners have authority to open banks accounts and operate them, it would be sufficient for a bank to act on a mandate opened by such partners on behalf of the firm. The mandate should provide clearly whether all or certain specified partners have authority to draw cheques on the partnership account.

FORM OF MANDATE

[4.16] Each bank has its own standard form of mandate.[38] The mandate is a request by a customer and his authorisation of the bank to do certain things such as:

(i)   to open an account in the customer's name,

(ii)   to carry out requests for withdrawal, whether by direct debit, a cash withdrawal or when a cheque drawn by the customer is presented by a collecting bank for payment,

(iii)   to countermand payment of cheques on request, and

(iv)   to credit moneys lodged to the account.

---

[35]. Partnership Act 1890, s 1(1).

[36]. Section 9.

[37]. In which event the bank will be deemed to be a partner of the partnership and on the bankruptcy of a partner will have its claim subordinated to other creditors of the partner (Partnership Act 1890, s 3).

[38]. For further reading see Milnes Holden, *The Law and Practice of Banking* (5th ed) Vol 1, paras 11-67-11-82.

More recently, the mandate often contains an authorisation to act on telephone or facsimile instructions or other means of telephonic or electronic communication, but such authorisation usually contains an indemnity from the customer to the bank indemnifying the bank for any losses or liabilities incurred from acting on such instructions, purporting to be given by the account holder, where the bank *bona fide* believed the instructions were given by the account holder.

[4.17] In the case of joint accounts the mandate will contain clear instructions as to whether either of the account holders can make a withdrawal or whether both must sign. Sometimes it may provide that any one holder is authorised up to a certain monetary limit on any one day but beyond that limit both holders must sign.

JOINT ACCOUNTS

[4.18] The concept of joint accounts is very different today to what it was forty years ago. Now such an account is typically a current account held in the joint names of husband and wife, both of whom typically would be employed, with the authority of either to draw funds usually by way of cheque or cash withdrawal from the account. Forty years ago a joint account was more typically a deposit account or deposit receipt. The latter form of account was described by Johnston J in the following manner:[39]

> "This form of investment is favoured by the Irish banks, who find it useful and profitable to be entrusted with the small sums that the farmers in large numbers are able to place in their hands, whilst the latter find it convenient to be able to get their money back without any delay and with the addition of a trifle of interest; but, after the experience of a quarter of a century in the Irish courts, I am able to say that the system leads to a great amount of litigation."

The judicial approach to the first type of account may be best illustrated by Vaisey J's decision nearly fifty years ago where he stated:[40]

> "In my view a husband's earnings or salary, where the spouses have a common purse, and pool their resources, are earnings made on behalf of both ... the money which goes into the pool becomes joint property".

This approach was subsequently applied in the English Court of Appeal.[41]

[4.19] Under a joint mandate the bank agrees with each of the account holders the terms under which funds may be withdrawn by cash or by cheque. Thus,

---

[39.] In *Murray v Murray and Scanlon* [1939] IR 317 at 321.
[40.] In *Jones v Maynard* [1951] Ch 572 at 575.
[41.] *Rimmer v Rimmer* [1953] 1 QB 63.

each account holder has a right of action against the bank where it fails to honour the terms of the mandate.[42]

Death of One Account Holder

[4.20] A joint account opened in the name of two or more persons will have the effect that on the death of one the remaining party or parties to the account will continue to hold the monies in such account. In other words the estate of the deceased account holder will acquire no rights to the account.[43] This was decided in the Circuit Court over ninety years ago in *Diver v McCrea*.[44] But a year earlier the Court of Appeal decided otherwise in *O'Flaherty v Browne*.[45] Subsequently the Supreme Court[46] upheld the Court of Appeal's decision and in doing so specifically disapproved of the Circuit Court's decision.[47] However, the Supreme Court have now overruled their earlier decision and thus the Circuit Court judgment has been vindicated. The case of *Lynch v Burke and Allied Irish Banks plc*[48] was similar in its facts to that of *Diver v McCrea*.[49] In the former case an aunt opened a joint deposit account in her name and in the name of her niece. Both signed the account opening form but all monies deposited were those of the aunt; on her death the Supreme Court unanimously held that the monies in the account belonged to the niece. O'Flaherty J stated:[50]

> "The monies on deposit with the bank represent a debt or chose in action. Since Frances McFadden and Moira Burke contracted jointly with the bank it would seem right that the bank should be liable to both - in accordance with the terms of the contract. There was sufficient mutuality of interest between Frances McFadden and Moira Burke to justify this assessment of the legal situation."

Even in the absence of a signature by all the account holders, and thus the absence of privity of contract between the bank and those account holders who have not signed the mandate, the courts will give effect to the clear intention of the account holders. In *Murray v Murray and Scanlon*[51] the High Court held that

---

[42]. *Jackson v White and Midland Bank Ltd* [1967] 2 LLR 68 (unless such account holder is estopped by its own forgery).

[43]. Subject to any contrary intention clearly expressed.

[44]. (1908) 42 ILTR 249.

[45]. [1907] 2 IR 416.

[46]. *Owens v Greene* [1932] IR 225.

[47]. *Ibid* at 238 per Kennedy CJ and at 251 *per* FitzGibbon J.

[48]. [1995] 2 IR 159; [1996] 1 ILRM 114.

[49]. (1908) 42 ILTR 249 which involved an uncle and nephew who resided together (although the nephew did not sign the bank mandate); see also *Young v Sealey* [1949] Ch 278.

[50]. [1995] 2 IR 159 at 163; [1996] 1 ILRM 114 at 118; all four other Supreme Court judges agreed with O'Flaherty J's judgment.

[51]. [1939] IR 317.

the benefit of a deposit account opened in the name of the donor and his nephew and niece passed to the nephew and niece on the donor's death.

COMBINATION AND SET-OFF

[4.21] Where a bank is owed money by a customer but also holds money from that customer, there are three methods by which the bank may use the money it holds or otherwise owes to the customer in reducing the level of its customer's indebtedness to it. Assuming the bank has no security in the nature of a mortgage, charge or other encumbrance the customer's indebtedness to the bank may be reduced by (1) the banker's right of combination of accounts,[52] (2) contractual set-off between the banker and its customer[53], and (3) the exercise of set-off rights upon the customer's bankruptcy or insolvency.[54]

Banker's Right of Combination

[4.22] At common law a bank has a right to combine accounts of similar nature held by a customer.[55] This was put simply by Lord Kilbrandon in *National Westminster Bank Ltd v Halesowen Presswork and Assemblies Ltd*[56] when he stated:[57]

> "In the ordinary case, and in the absence of any agreement expressing or necessarily implying the contrary, where a customer has two current accounts, the bank is entitled to utilise the credit balance on one account to cover a debit on the other ... The bank, however, cannot combine accounts where one of the accounts is a loan account and the other is a current account."

[4.23] The banker's right of combination extends to the same type of account which the customer may have at the bank, whether or not at the same branch.[58] This was confirmed in *Barclays Bank Ltd v Okenarhe*[59] where Mocatta J stated:[60]

[52.] See para **[4.22]**; sometimes referred to a banker's general right by set-off or even the banker's lien.
[53.] See para **[15.15]**.
[54.] See para **[4.29]** below.
[55.] For further reading see Penn, Shea & Arora, *The Law Relating to Domestic Banking* Vol 1 (1987) Sweet & Maxwell, paras 13.31-13.36; *Paget's Law of Banking* (11th ed) Butterworths, pp 529-537.
[56.] [1972] 1 All ER 641.
[57.] *Ibid* at 661.
[58.] *Garnett v McKewan* (1872) 27 LT 560.
[59.] [1966] 2 LLR 87.
[60.] *Ibid* at 95.

"As regards the case in which the customer has separate running current accounts at each of two branches of a bank, it is plain that the general principle is that the bank is entitled to combine the two accounts".

Different types of account cannot be combined such as a current account and a loan account or a current account and a deposit account.[61] With regard to the former, a bank cannot suddenly close an account and combine the accounts without reasonable notice to the customer.[62] With regard to the latter, there may be some flexibility as a suspense account may be combined with a deposit account.[63] This right of combination does not apply to any account held for a specific purpose.[64] Nor does it extend to accounts which are held by a customer acting in different capacities[65] unless that fact is not known by the bank.[66] The extent of the level of enquiry necessary by a bank and whether certain facts might constitute notice was set out by Lord Herschell LC:[67]

"It cannot, I think, be questioned that under ordinary circumstances a person, be he banker or other, who takes money from his debtor in discharge of a debt is not bound to inquire into the manner in which the person so paying the debt acquired the money with which he pays it. However that money may have been acquired by the person making the payment, the person taking that payment is entitled to retain it in discharge of the debt which is due to him ... I cannot assent to the proposition that even if a person receiving money knows that such money has been received by the person paying it to him on account of other persons, that of itself is sufficient to prevent the payment being a good payment and properly discharging the debt due to the person who receives the money. No doubt if the person receiving the money has reason to believe that the payment is being made in fraud of a third person, and that the person making the payment is handing over in discharge of his debt money which he has no right to hand over, then the person taking such payment would not be entitled to retain the money, upon ordinary principles."

As for any imputed knowledge concerning stockbroker accounts, Lord Herschell LC stated:[68]

... if, because an account is opened with bankers by a stockbroker, they are bound to inquire into the source from which he receives any money which he pays in, it would be wholly impossible that business could be carried on, and I know of no principle or authority which establishes such a proposition."

[61.] *Re EJ Morel (1934) Ltd* [1962] 1 Ch 21.
[62.] See *Buckingham v The London and Midland Bank Ltd* (1895) 12 TLR 70.
[63.] *Freaney v The Governor and Company of the Bank of Ireland* [1975] IR 376.
[64.] *WP Greenhalgh & Sons v Union Bank of Manchester* [1924] 2 KB 153.
[65.] *Barclays·Bank Ltd v Quistclose Investments Ltd* [1970] AC 567.
[66.] *JR Thomson v Clydesdale Bank Ltd* [1893] AC 282; *Union Bank of Australia Ltd v Murray-Aynsley* [1898] AC 693.
[67.] In *JR Thomson v Clydesdale Bank Ltd* [1893] AC 282 at 287.
[68.] *Ibid* at 289.

[4.24] In *Clark v Ulster Bank Ltd*,[69] a solicitor opened a second account with his bankers for the purpose of depositing clients' moneys but in doing so he did not indicate to the bank the purpose of the account. The Court held that the bank was entitled to combine the accounts when the first account went into debit. In delivering the judgment of the Supreme Court in *The Governor and Company of the Bank of Ireland v Martin and Martin* [70] Fitzgibbon J stated:[71]

> "Of course there is authority for the proposition that where a customer has two or more current accounts, even in different branches of the same bank, the banker, in the absence of any special contract, may apply a credit balance on one account to feed the debit balance upon another, and that if one account be overdrawn the banker is not bound to honour cheques drawn upon a second account which happens to be in credit, if that credit balance is less than the deficit upon the first: *Garnett v McKewan*. But this decision, if it be sound law, applies only to current accounts, and even as regards them, is subject to any arrangement to the contrary with the customer: *Greenhalgh & Sons v Union Bank of Manchester*, and we have not been referred to any case in which it has been decided or even suggested that a banker may of his own motion transfer a customer's money, lodged on a deposit account to that customer's current account in order to discharge an overdraft thereon."

The Court explained in *Clark v Ulster Bank Ltd*[72] that when a bank acquires notice that one of the accounts kept by a customer is a trust account it may nevertheless exercise any right of set-off to which it may then be entitled having regard to the state of the accounts at the time of acquiring such notice.

[4.25] The banker's right of combination is subject to agreement to the contrary. Thus, where the bank agrees to rely exclusively on certain security for the repayment of money, it will have effectively excluded its right of combination.[73] Bankers should be mindful also of the decision in *Re Johnson & Co Ltd*.[74] In that case the company asked its bankers to close its overdraft account, which had a deficit secured by a guarantee from one of the shareholders, and to open a new account with a view to having an orderly winding down of the company. Following the company's liquidation the bank sought to combine or set off the two accounts. The court held that there was a special arrangement which

---

[69.] [1950] NI 132.
[70.] [1937] IR 189.
[71.] *Ibid* at 202.
[72.] [1950] NI 132, on the authority of *Roxburghe v Cox* (1881) 17 Ch D 520 and *Union Bank of Australia Ltd v Murray-Aynsley* [1898] AC 693.
[73.] *Barrington v The Governor and Company of the Bank of Ireland* High Court, unrep, 26 January 1993, Costello J.
[74.] [1902] 1 IR 439.

prevented the bank exercising its ordinary right of setting off one account of a customer against another.

[4.26] The customer has no right to combine unless the bank agrees otherwise. The lack of reciprocity shown to the customer was explained by Mocatta J:[75]

> "That limitation on the customer's rights, in other words, the inability of the customer without specific agreement to combine two accounts, is explained as necessary for business efficacy. It would make the task of a banker impossible if each branch was expected to know the state of a customer's account at every other branch".

Whether this principle applies today, over thirty years since that judgment, must be questionable in the light of a bank's ability to ascertain readily from its computer records the state of a customer's account at different branches of the bank.

[4.27] However, there may be circumstances where the banker is obliged to combine, such as prior to realising any security held for the overdrawn or loan account.[76]

[4.28] A banker may not combine accounts unless the amounts in such accounts are presently due and payable, for as indicated in *Jeffryes v Agra and Masterman's Bank*:[77] "you cannot retain a sum of money which is actually due against a sum of money which is only becoming due at a future time".

Thus actual indebtedness may not be combined with contingent indebtedness.

SET-OFF ON CUSTOMER'S INSOLVENCY

[4.29] Upon an individual's bankruptcy or the liquidation of a company,[78] proof of the insolvent's debts is undertaken by reference to the First Schedule to the Bankruptcy Act, 1988.[79] Paragraph 17(1) of that Schedule states:

---

75. In [1966] 2 LLR 87 at 95.
76. See *Mutton v Peat* [1900] 2 Ch 79.
77. (1866) LR 2 Eq 674 at 680 *per* Sir Page Wood VC.
78. The Companies Act, 1963, s 284 incorporates the bankruptcy rules in the winding up of a company; see also Kenny J in *Re Tailteam Freight Services Ltd (in liq)*; *Freaney v The Governor and Company of the Bank of Ireland* [1975] IR 376 at 38; Henchy J in *Re Euro Travel Ltd Dempsey v Bank of Ireland* Supreme Court, unrep, 6 December 1985 p 8; Carroll J in *Re Irish Shipping Ltd* [1986] ILRM 518 at 519; Costello J in *Re McCairns (PMPA) plc* [1989] ILRM 501 at 510 and Blayney J in *Re Baltimore Boatyard Company Ltd* [1991] ILRM 817 at 822 and also in *Re Frederick Inns Ltd* [1994] 1 ILRM 387 at 400.
79. Pursuant to the Bankruptcy Act, 1988, s 76.

> Where there are mutual credits or debts as between a bankrupt and any person
> claiming as a creditor, one debt or demand may be set off against the other and
> only the balance found owing shall be recoverable on one side or the other.[80]

In the absence of any agreement to the contrary, as soon as a company passes a
resolution for its winding up, its bank is entitled to consolidate the company's
accounts with it and to exercise its right of set off.[81] Effectively, moneys held by
a person in a bank account at the time of his/its bankruptcy/liquidation may be
used by the bank as a security to be set against what the person owes the bank.[82]
It should be noted that unlike its English equivalent[83] the claims "may be set off"
rather than "shall be set off". Thus in Ireland a bank is not obliged to set off.[84]
Moneys which have been paid into a company's bank account by mistake
cannot be used to set off the company's liabilities to the bank.[85]

It should be noted that where a bank makes facilities available to its customer
and stipulates in its facility letter that security for the facilities will be limited to
stipulated security such as a charge on land or a charge on shares, the bank will
have effectively waived its right to security over a bank account. Accordingly, it
will be precluded from exercising its right of set off.[86]

Mutuality

[4.30] For set off to be permitted upon a company's insolvency there must be
mutuality of debts so as to come within para 17 of the First Schedule to the
Bankruptcy Act, 1988. It is difficult to find authority as to the meaning of
"mutual" in this context. What is helpful though is the Australian High Court

---

[80.] It might be noted that in England and Wales under rule 4.90 of the Insolvency Rules 1986
sums due from one party to another in respect of mutual dealings *shall* be set off; the
mandatory provision has applied in England and Wales since the Bankruptcy Act, 1869,
s 39.

[81.] *National Westminster Bank Ltd v Halesowen Presswork and Assemblies Ltd* [1972] 1 All
ER 641; *Re Tailteam Freight Services Ltd (in liq)*; *Freaney v The Governor and Company
of the Bank of Ireland* [1975] IR 376.

[82.] *Re McCairns (PMPA) plc* [1989] ILRM 501; see also Lord Hoffmann in *Stein v Blake*
[1995] 2 All ER 961 at 964; for further reading see *Paget's Law of Banking* (11th ed)
Butterworths pp 540-546.

[83.] Rule 4.90 of the Insolvency Rules 1986.

[84.] Thus the reader should not rely on English case law on this point notwithstanding Lynch,
Marshall & O'Ferrall, *Corporate Insolvency and Rescue* (1996) Butterworths para 7.38.

[85.] *Re Irish Shipping Ltd* [1986] ILRM 518.

[86.] See *Barrington v The Governor and Company of the Bank of Ireland*, High Court, unrep,
26 January 1993, Costello J; although in this case the plaintiff was not bankrupt, the
banker's waiver could affect its entitlement under para 17(1).

decision in *Gye v McIntyre*[87] in which the Court stated,[88] by reference to the equivalent Australian section:[89]

> "the word 'mutual' conveys the notion of reciprocity rather than that of correspondence. It does not mean 'identical' or 'the same'. So understood, there are three aspects of the section's requirement of mutuality. The first is that the credits, the debts, or the claims arising from other dealings be between the same persons. The second is that the benefit or burden of them lie in the same interests. In determining whether credits, debts or claims arising from other dealings are between the same persons and in the same interests, it is the equitable or beneficial interests of the parties which must be considered ... The third requirement of mutuality is that the credits, debts or claims arising from other dealings must be commensurable for the purposes of set-off under the section. That means that they must ultimately sound in money."

[4.31] The two claims or debts being set off must be claims or debts in the same right.[90] An example of claims in different rights can be seen from the facts of the decision in *The Incorporated Law Society of Ireland v O'Connor.*[91] O'Connor dissipated £164,000 of his clients' moneys. The Law Society re-imbursed the clients out of its Compensation Fund, recovered £94,000 from O'Connor and claimed the balance of £70,000. Their claim arose pursuant to a right of subrogation.[92] O'Connor claimed a right of set-off against monies owed to him by the Law Society.

The Law Society claimed that no set-off could arise because of lack of mutuality between the two claims - the Law Society was not claiming in its own right but by virtue of being subrograted to the rights of O'Connor's claims. Murphy J agreed with the Society and on appeal the Supreme Court unanimously upheld the High Court's decision.

[4.32] Moneys may be debited from an insolvent's account after the date of winding up if such moneys were owing but not due on the date of winding up. In *Re Ashmark Ltd (in liq), Jackson v Allied Irish Banks, plc*[93] Lardner J held that

---

[87.] (1991) 171 CLR 609.

[88.] *Ibid* at 623.

[89.] The Bankruptcy Act, 1966, s 86 provides for set-off "where there have been mutual credits, mutual debts or other mutual dealings".

[90.] *Continental Irish Meat Ltd v The Minister for Agriculture* [1983] ILRM 503; *Clover Meats Ltd v The Minister for Agriculture* [1991] 2 IR 299; *Re Frederick Inns Ltd, The Rendezvous Ltd, The Graduate Ltd, Motels Ltd* [1994] 1 ILRM 387.

[91.] High Court, unrep 24 June 1994, Murphy J and Supreme Court, unrep, 25 November 1994.

[92.] Standing in the shoes of O'Connor's clients by virtue of the Solicitors (Amendment) Act, 1960, s 21(8).

[93.] [1994] 3 IR 460.

interest and fees which had accrued on an overdraft account could be set off after the liquidator was appointed as against moneys which the bank owed the company on the company's current account. Lardner J rejected the liquidator's contention that the payment, post liquidation of interest and fees which had not become due and payable prior to liquidation was a disposition of property contrary to the Companies Act, 1963 s 218. Lardner J followed the approach of Buckley LJ (in *Halesowen Presswork and Assemblies Ltd v National Westminster Bank Ltd*[94]) by indicating the correct principle was one of combination rather than set-off. Buckley LJ had stated:[95]

> "Where the relationship of banker and customer is a single relationship ... albeit embodied in a number of accounts, the situation is not ... a set off situation which postulates mutual but independent obligations between the two parties. It is an accounting situation in which the existence and amount of the parties liability to the other can only be ascertained by discovering the ultimate balance of their mutual dealings."

Lardner J held:[96]

> "At any time the amount of each party's liability to the other could only be ascertained by discovering the ultimate balance of their mutual dealings. Where interest has been accruing on a daily basis as in the present case which is a liability of Ashmark to the bank and at the same time, the bank owes a debt in respect of Ashmark's current account credit balance to Ashmark, it is not in my judgment correct to treat the ascertainment of the ultimate balance as a disposition of property by Ashmark on that date (or a disposition of a thing in action) within s 218 of the Companies Act, 1963. It seems to me properly considered as an account situation in which the existence and amount of the bank's liability in respect of the current account to Ashmark can only be ascertained by discovering the ultimate balance of their mutual dealings."

[4.33] Moneys in a bank account are moneys owed by the bank to the customer who has placed the money with the bank or to the named customer in the account where moneys have been lodged by a third party for the account of the customer. A bank may issue a receipt for such a deposit. As to the transfer of title to moneys evidenced by a deposit receipt, Ross J indicated that the law is as follows:[97]

> "If the owner directs a new deposit receipt to be taken out in the names of other persons, there is a resulting trust in favour of the owner, and the other persons are merely trustees for him. The onus is upon the other persons to show that the

---

94. [1970] 3 All ER 473.
95. *Ibid* at 488.
96. [1994] 3 IR 460 at 464.
97. In *McEneaney v Shevlin* [1912] 1 IR 32 at 36.

beneficial interest also was intended to pass to them. If, however, the owner stands in loco parentis to these other persons, the onus is the other way, and an advancement is presumed. It is, however, open to the persons in respect of whom the owner does not occupy the relationship indicated by the phrase in *loco parentis* to prove by contemporaneous declaration, or by other evidence, that the beneficial interest was intended to pass. All that is required is the surrender of the deposit receipt and the reception by the owner of the new deposit receipt in the names of the other parties, or in the names of the owner and other parties. No further writing is necessary. The requisition form is not a legal necessity. It is important to the bank as an authority for the issue of the new deposit receipt."

In answer to the contention that a written assignment is necessary to transfer title pursuant to the Supreme Court of Judicature (Ireland) Act, 1877[98] Ross J held:[99]

"No written assignment was or is now required. When we go to the root of the whole matter, I think the reason is plain enough. The money lies in the hands of the bank, a debt to the owner; the terms of the contract under which it is held are set out in the deposit receipt. The deposit receipt is not, like a promissory note, a negotiable instrument, and does not pass by endorsement. When it is handed in and a new deposit receipt taken out, it is not strictly an assignment at all. It is a novation or new contract between the bank and the depositor. When the request is orally made by the depositor, and the new deposit receipt is issued to him in the names of the persons nominated by him, the transaction is complete."

THE RULE IN *CLAYTON'S CASE*

[4.34] The question sometimes arises following the payment of moneys by a customer to his account as to what debt or portion of a debt (due by the customer) that payment discharges. This is particularly relevant where a banker has security for a customer's indebtedness and then receives notice that another banker has taken security from the same customer. In the absence of contrary agreement between the bankers, the rule in *Clayton's Case* will operate so that future payments made by the customer to the first banker will reduce the customer's indebtedness that is secured; any further advances to the customer by the first banker will not have the benefit of the security until the indebtedness to the second banker is discharged. The rule was explained in the following manner by Lord Shaw of Dunfermline:[100]

[98.] Section 28(6).

[99.] In *McEneaney v Shevlin* [1912] 1 IR 32 at 37; the plaintiff's appeal was dismissed [1912] 1 IR 278.

[100.] In *Deeley v Lloyds Bank Ltd* [1912] AC 756 at 783.

"After notice to the bank of a second mortgage by the customer, the debit is struck at the date of notice, and in the ordinary case, that is to say, where an account is merely continued without alteration, or where no specific appropriation of fresh payments is made, such payments are credited to the earliest items on the debit side of the account, and continue so to be credited until the balance secured under the first mortgage is extinguished."

This principle arose from one of the cases brought under the action of *Devaynes v Noble*.[101] Devaynes was a partner in a banking partnership and the question arose, following his death, whether his estate was liable to a number of customers, the banking partnership having become insolvent. One of the accounts was that of Mr Clayton.

The Master of the Rolls explained the operation of a bank account as follows:[102]

"... this is the case of a banking account, where all the sums paid in form one blended fund, the parts of which no longer have any distinct existence. Neither banker nor customer ever thinks of saying, this draft is to be placed to the account of the £500 paid in on Monday, and this other to the account of the £500 paid in on Tuesday. There is a fund of £1,000 to draw upon, and that is enough. In such a case, there is no room for any other appropriation than that which arises from the order in which the receipts and payments take place, and are carried into the account. Presumably, it is the sum first paid in, that is first drawn out. It is the first item on the debit side of the account, that is discharged or reduced, by the first item on the credit side. The appropriation is made by the very act of setting the two items against each other. Upon that principle all accounts current are settled, and particularly cash accounts."

[4.35] The Master of the Rolls indicated that specific agreement to the contrary can be allowed:

"If the usual course of dealing was, for any reason, to be inverted, it was surely incumbent on the creditor to signify that such was his intention. He should either have said to the bankers, - "Leave this balance altogether out of the running account between us", - or - "Always enter your payments as made on the credit of your latest receipts, so as that the oldest balance may be the last paid". Instead of this, he receives the account drawn out, as one unbroken running account."

Accordingly, it is common to provide in any security document that in the event the mortgagee/chargee receives notice of a subsequent encumbrance the customer's account will be ruled off and any subsequent advances by the banker will be made under a new account secured against cash or other form of security. This mechanism (and its implementation) will protect the effectiveness of the

---

[101.] Michaelmas Term 1815 (1816) Cases in Chancery 529.
[102.] *Ibid* at 608.

security for the debt as it stands at the date of receipt of notice of the second security.

[4.36] It is important to realise that the rule in *Clayton's Case* means that even if a banker has sanctioned a facility of up to a specified amount, and at the time it receives notice of a second indebtedness to another banker, the first banker has priority only to the amount outstanding to it at the time of notice, not the amount of its agreed facility.[103] However, the banker who has taken the first mortgage is not obliged to make further advances following receipt of notice of a second mortgage even if the banker has a committed facility to the mortgagor which has not been fully utilised.[104] This is because the further advances will no longer be secured by a first mortgage and therefore the customer will not be able to comply with the terms of its facility from the banker.

If a customer wishes to utilise advances up to its committed facility from the first banker as well as avail of advances from a second banker, the customer should ensure the agreement of both banks, as the rule in *Clayton's Case* can be dispensed with by agreement.[105] The first banker should ensure, prior to making any further advances or honouring any further cheques, that the second banker agrees that the first banker's security will have priority, over the second banker's for further revolving facilities (such as an overdraft) up to the amount of the first banker's agreed commitment to the customer.

APPROPRIATION OF PAYMENTS

[4.37] While the rule in *Clayton's Case* is usually associated with the priorities of securities, it is in fact a rule as to the appropriation of payments.[106] The customer has the right when making a payment to its banker to indicate to which account it should be credited,[107] otherwise the banker can appropriate as it wishes. In the absence of any specific intention the parties are presumed to have intended that the earliest credits to the account should be applied to the earliest debits to the account.[108]

[4.38] The importance for a customer to give clear written instructions so that there can be no doubt as to his intention can be seen from *Hennerty v The Governor and Company of the Bank of Ireland*.[109] In that case, a customer

[103.] See *Hopkinson v Rolt* (1861) 5 LT 90; *Re the Estate of Henry A Keogh* [1895] 1 IR 201; *West v Williams* [1899] 1 Ch 132; *Deeley v Lloyds Bank Ltd* [1912] AC 756.
[104.] See *West v Williams* [1899] 1 Ch 132 *per* Lindley MR at 143 and Chitty LJ at 146.
[105.] *Deeley v Lloyds Bank Ltd* [1912] AC 756 at 771 *per* Lord Atkinson.
[106.] See *Paget's Law of Banking* (11th ed) Ch 14; for a very clear treatment see Milnes Holden, *The Law and Practice of Banking* Vol 1 (5th ed) para 2-73 to 2-98.
[107.] *Kinnaird v Webster* (1878) 10 Ch D 139 at 145 *per* Bacon VC.
[108.] *Re the Estate of Chute and Kelly* [1914] 1 IR 180 at 185 *per* Ross J.
[109.] High Court, unrep, 5 July 1988 and 26 May 1989, O'Hanlon J.

lodged £20,000 with the defendant bankers who credited it against the customer's overdraft rather than its subsidiary's loan which carried a higher rate of interest. The bank confirmed this by letter. Although the customer contended that, he had made it clear the sums were to be credited against the loan and had telephoned the bank manager following receipt of his letter, O'Hanlon J held that as a matter of probability the banker's evidence was correct and not the customer's.

Consumer Loans

[4.39] The rule in *Clayton's Case* has been varied with respect to consumer loans (other than housing loans[110]). It is now provided by statute[111] that a consumer may appropriate as he sees fit (which he could do prior to the enactment) but where no appropriation has been made by the consumer "the payment shall be appropriated by the credit ... towards the agreements in proportion to the amounts due under the agreements".

It should be noted though that this provisions applies where the banker has two or more agreements (including facility letters) with the customer. If the customer opens more than one account under the same agreement, this provision will not be applicable. The usual practice though would be for a customer to sign a separate mandate in respect of each account; each mandate is an agreement in itself as between the banker and the customer.

[110.] Consumer Credit Act, 1995, s 44(3).
[111.] *Ibid* s 44(1) (subject to variations for hire purchase agreements).

Chapter 5

Cheques

1. FORM OF CHEQUES

Definition

[5.01] A cheque[1] may be defined as an unconditional order addressed to a banker, signed by the person giving it, requiring the banker to pay on demand a sum certain in money to or to the order of a specified person or to bearer.[2] Judicially it has been described as:[3]

> "... a revocable mandate by the customer to his bank which authorises the bank, as his agent, to make payment out of the moneys standing to the credit of his account or which the bank is willing to advance to him".

Thus a cheque is used as a means by which a person can settle his debt with his creditor.[4] The stamp duty[5] and bank charges[6] applicable to cheques combined with other means of payment such as credit cards may result in a diminishing use of cheques as a means for payment,[7] although the increasing number of

---

1.   Its spelling in the United States of America as "check" appears to be the original correct spelling as used in the English language in England - see Milnes Holden, *The History of Negotiable Instruments in English Law* (1955) p 209.

2.   Bills of Exchange Act, 1882, ss 73 and 3(1); for a more detailed breakdown of the definition see *Paget's Law of Banking* (11th ed, 1996) pp 236-238) see also O'Connor, *The Law and Practice in Ireland Relating to Cheques and Analogous Instruments* (1993) Ch II.

3.   Millett J in *Re Charge Card Services Ltd* [1987] BCLC 17 at 31.

4.   Bills of exchange, of which a cheque is a form, seem to have originated in Lombardy, Italy - see Milnes Holden, *The History of Negotiable Instruments in English Law* (1955); for the development of cheques with goldsmiths acting as bankers see Milnes Holden, *The Law and Practice of Banking* Vol 1 (5th ed) paras 2-4; see also O'Kelly, 'Old Limerick Private Bankers' (1946) 1 Journal of the Old Limerick Society 5 where the correlation between merchants and bankers is outlined in the development of the *Bank of Limerick* (Maunsell's Bank) and the *Limerick Bank* (Roche's Bank).

5.   Seven pence on each cheque - see Stamp Act, 1891, s 1 and First Schedule (as amended).

6.   These are variable; such charges seem to have been levied first in 1793 - see Hall, *History of the Bank of Ireland* (1949) Hodges, Figgis and Co Ltd, p 52.

7.   See *The Sunday Times* 14 August 1994 5.1:
     "with millions of people turning their backs on this time-consuming method of payment and switching to plastic, the chequebook's days are surely numbered. But with so much fun to be had with the old format, it will be a shame when they disappear altogether. Paying by cheque can be a wonderful way to get revenge, as one can be written on just about anything as long as all relevant details are included. Poll-Tax staff at Circencester received a cheque from one protestor written on a banana which they had to put in the fridge to stop it rotting before being cashed. Fellow objectors paid with cheques written on, among other things, a 50lb stone slab, an old sock and a rotting fish".

persons having bank accounts means that it has become a more widely practised means of payment.

[5.02] In considering the rights and obligations of parties to a cheque it may be useful to examine a form of cheque in order to facilitate a clear understanding of a cheque.

Limerick Bank	30th December 1997
Pay Donall Cunningham	or order
One hundred pounds	[IR£100-]
[7p Stamp]	Patricia Wolf
000094 123456	78901234

In this example, Limerick Bank is the addressee known as the drawee;[8] 30 December 1997 is the date of the cheque; Donall Cunningham is the specified person namely the payee; the reference to "or order" after the payee's name indicates that the payee may endorse the cheque (by signing his name on the reverse side) in favour of a third party - Donall Cunningham then becomes the endorser and the third party becomes the endorsee; the "sum certain in money" is specified in words and figures (where there is a discrepancy between the amount stated in words and figures the sum payable is the amount stated in words);[9] Patricia Wolf is the person signing the cheque and giving it, namely the drawer; stamp duty of seven pence is pre-printed and paid.[10] The three numbers at the foot of the cheque represent respectively cheque number 94 of the drawer, the drawee's sorting code and the drawer's bank account number with the drawee.[11]

On Demand

[5.03] It need not be specified on the cheque that it is payable on demand, as a cheque in which no time for payment is expressed is deemed to be payable on demand[12] (other than a post-dated cheque which is not payable prior to the date of the cheque[13]).

[8.] This derives from the early clearing house days in England where a bank collecting payment on a cheque for its customer would deposit the cheque in the paying bank's drawer in the clearing house - see Milnes Holden, *The History of Negotiable Instruments in English Law* (1955) p 230.
[9.] Bills of Exchange Act, 1882, s 9(2).
[10.] See fn 5 above.
[11.] These three numbers together with the amount of the cheque represent "the essential features of the cheque" - Bills of Exchange Act, 1882, s 45A(1).
[12.] Bills of Exchange Act, 1882, s 10(1).
[13.] See para **[5.06]** below.

To or to the Order of a Specified Person or to Bearer

[5.04] A cheque may be made payable to more than one person jointly, to one of a number of persons or to the holder of an office.[14] Where it is made payable to a fictitious or non-existing person it is treated as being payable to bearer.[15]

[5.05] A request on a cheque to pay "cash" means that the cheque is not a cheque within the meaning of that word under the Bills of Exchange Act, 1882 as it is not payable to or to the order of a specified person or to bearer.[16] Accordingly, a bank may refuse to honour such cheque. However, a number of provisions of the Cheques Act, 1959[17] protect a banker in honouring such a cheque; in practice therefore such orders are treated as cheques.

In *North and South Insurance Corp Ltd v National Provincial Bank Ltd*[18] a cheque was made payable to "cash or order". Branson J stated:[19]

> "... the words 'or to the order of a specified person' mean that in order to constitute a document a bill of exchange [or cheque] it must contain an order directing the person on whom it is drawn to pay to a specified person ... 'Cash' cannot be described as a 'specified person'."

He continued:[20]

> "'Cash' is not a payee, and the document was not drawn to pay any person at all. The document is not payable either to a specified person or to bearer, and it therefore fails to satisfy s 7 of the Bills of Exchange Act, 1882, in what is an essential part of a bill of exchange.[21] To come within s 7 of the Act of 1882, there must be a payee, and this document has no payee. ... I am driven to look at the words of the document and give them the construction which the parties who brought the document into being apparently intended. ... It says, 'Pay cash or order'. It cannot have been intended that 'cash', which is a purely impersonal collection of letters, should endorse this draft. That being so, I think the four words 'Pay cash or order' cannot be read so as to give any sensible meaning to the whole four, and the result is that the printed words 'or order' must be disregarded, and we have a direction to pay cash - by necessary implication, to pay it to the bearer of the document."

[14.] Bills of Exchange Act, 1882, s 7(2).

[15.] *Ibid* s 7(3).

[16.] *Ibid* s 3(2).

[17.] Sections 1(2)(a) and 4(2)(b).

[18.] [1936] 1 KB 328.

[19.] *Ibid* at 333.

[20.] *Ibid* at 335.

[21.] This was followed in *Cole v Milsome* [1951] 1 All ER 311 where it was held that the words, 'pay cash or order' meant the document was not a cheque.

Accordingly, it was held that the bank had authority to pay the cheque as instructed.

This decision was supported and applied by the English Court of Appeal in *Orbit Mining & Trading Co Ltd v Westminster Bank Ltd*[22] where it was held that cheques which had the word "Cash" inserted between the printed words "Pay" "or order" were not cheques within the meaning of the Bills of Exchange Act, 1882. Nevertheless, the paying bank was protected as the cheques were documents issued by a customer of a banker which were intended to enable a person to obtain payment from that banker of the sum mentioned on the document.[23] In this context a person "means any person, and does not require a named person: therefore, 'cash' is good enough."[24]

In practice, banks issue cheque books with the words "Pay" followed by a blank (for insertion of the payee's name), followed by "or order". Thus the insertion of the words "Cash" between "Pay" and "or order" is simply a request by the drawer to his banker to pay cash for the amount stated on the cheque.

Date of Cheque

[5.06] A cheque is not invalid by reason of its being undated.[25] However, notwithstanding this, it is the practice of banks not to honour cheques which are undated; such practice has been supported by the courts.[26] A banker on whom a cheque is drawn may insert the date himself.[27]

A cheque is not invalid by reason of its being ante-dated, post-dated[28] or dated on a Sunday.[29] *Milnes Holden*[30] has pointed out three reasons why a banker should not pay on a post-dated cheque prior to its date; these are:

> "(a) if he pays it and then dishonours other cheques which would otherwise have been paid he will be liable to his customer for damages to his credit,

---

[22.] [1962] 3 All ER 565.
[23.] Cheques Act, 1957, s 4(2)(b); these provisions give protection to a banker in Ireland by virtue of s 4(2)(b) of the Cheques Act, 1959.
[24.] *Per* Harman LJ in *Orbit Mining & Trading Co Ltd v Westminster Bank Ltd* [1962] 3 All ER 565 at 577.
[25.] Bills of Exchange Act, 1882 s 3(4)(a).
[26.] See *Griffiths v Dalton* [1940] 2 KB 264.
[27.] Bills of Exchange Act, 1882, s 20(1) - for the practice of paying and collecting bankers see further O'Connor, *The Law and Practice in Ireland Relating to Cheques and Analogous Instruments* (1993) paras 3.7-3.8.
[28.] However as a post-dated cheque is not payable on demand it is strictly speaking not a cheque although it is a bill of exchange.
[29.] Bills of Exchange Act, 1882, s 13(2).
[30.] *The Law and Practice of Banking* Vol 1 (5th ed, 1991) para 7-16.

(b) even if he re-credits his customer's account with the amount of the post-dated cheque and holds the cheque until the arrival of its due date, the customer may become bankrupt in the meantime; and

(c) in any event, the customer may countermand payment of the cheque before its due date."

It is the practice of bankers to refuse payment of a cheque which has on its face a date six months or more prior to the date of its presentment.[31]

2. CHEQUE SIGNATORY

Liability of the Person giving a Cheque

[5.07] The capacity of a person giving a cheque to incur liability on the cheque "is co-extensive with capacity to contract".[32]

[5.08] Unless precluded by its crossing,[33] the payee (that is, the person to whose order the cheque is made) may endorse the cheque in favour of a third party or generally by putting his signature on the reverse of the cheque. The person giving the cheque incurs a liability to the holder of the cheque (that is the payee or other endorser who has paid on foot of the cheque) for the amount stated on the cheque.[34] The liability arises when the cheque is presented for payment to the addressee (known as the drawee). This liability may be avoided if the appropriate procedure for dishonour is not implemented within the required time period.[35]

[5.09] The drawer or endorser of a cheque may make a stipulation on the cheque negating or limiting liability to the holder.[36] A typical example is where an endorser inserts the words "*sans recours*"[37] after his endorsing signature - in other words, the holder cannot seek recompense from the endorser in the event that the cheque is dishonoured but only from a prior endorser or the drawer (as the case may be).

[31.] See O'Connor, *The Law and Practice in Ireland Relating to Cheques and Analogous Instruments* (1993) para 3.17.

[32.] Bills of Exchange Act, 1882 s 22(1); for cheques drawn by minors, lunatics and intoxicated persons see O'Connor, *op cit*, paras 4.16-4.32.

[33.] See para **[5.49]** below.

[34.] Bills of Exchange Act, 1882 s 55(1)(a) imposes liability on the drawer of a cheque and s 55(2)(a) imposes liability on an endorser of a cheque.

[35.] For further reading see O'Connor, *The Law and Practice in Ireland Relating to Cheques and Analogous Instruments* (1993) Ch IX.

[36.] Bills of Exchange Act, 1882, s 16(1).

[37.] See *Wakefield v Alexander and Co and Chaproniere and Co* (1901) 17 TLR 217.

Signature

[5.10] As a general rule, a person does not incur liability on a cheque unless he has signed it.[38] Accordingly, a signature which is forged or placed on a cheque without the authority of the person whose signature it purports to be is inoperative.[39]

[5.11] However, a person who signs a cheque in a trade or assumed name is liable thereon as if he had signed it in his own name; furthermore the signature of the name of a firm is equivalent to the signature by the person so signing of the names of all persons liable as partners in that firm.[40] The signature of a partner in a firm imposes personal liability on that partner and indeed all partners of the firm (unless the partner has not authority to sign and the recipient of the cheque knew of such lack of authority).[41]

[5.12] A person's signature may be written on the cheque "by some other person by or under his authority".[42] A person when signing a cheque who describes himself as an agent or representative will not be exempt from liability on the cheque unless he indicates the name of the person (principal) for whom he is signing.[43] Where a person does sign as agent and adds words such as "for", "on behalf of", "per pro", the holder is put on notice that the agent is acting within authority from the principal and the principal then is only bound to the holder if the agent acted within the terms of such authority.[44]

[5.13] A person who is under an obligation to endorse a bill in a representative capacity may do so in such terms as to negative personal liability.[45]

Signature on behalf of Company

[5.14] A company is deemed to have given a cheque if it is given in its name by a person acting under the authority of the company.[46] A person derives authority from a company to draw company cheques usually from a resolution of its board of directors.[47] However, even where an officer of a company does not have

---

[38] Bills of Exchange Act, 1882, s 23.
[39] *Ibid* s 24.
[40] *Ibid* s 23.
[41] Partnership Act, 1890, s 5; *Ringham v Hackett* (1980) 124 Sol J 221; *Central Motors (Birmingham) Ltd v PA and SN Wadsworth* 10 LDAB 207.
[42] Bills of Exchange Act, 1882, s 91(1).
[43] *Ibid* s 26(1).
[44] *Ibid* s 25; for further discussion on this see *Paget's Law of Banking* (11th ed, 1996) pp 391-393.
[45] Bills of Exchange Act, 1882, s 31(5).
[46] Companies Act, 1963, s 39.
[47] As provided in the company's articles of association - see Companies Act, 1963 First Schedule Table A, Part I, reg 88.

authority to sign a cheque on behalf of the company, the company may be bound by his signature.[48] In *Dey v Pullinger Engineering Co Ltd*[49] it was held that as the managing director of the drawer could have been authorised under the drawer's articles of association, a holder was entitled to assume that he had authority and was not bound to enquire into the internal management of the company or to prove an actual authority. Thus, a person duly authorised by a company who signs his name to a cheque below or above the company's printed name on the cheque does not incur personal liability for the amount of the cheque.[50]

[5.15] It should be noted that an officer of a company or any person on behalf of the company who signs, or authorises to be signed on behalf of the company, a cheque where the company's name is not mentioned correctly may be liable to a fine and may be personally liable to the holder of the cheque for its amount unless it is paid by the company.[51]

[5.16] Examples of personal liability for a director signing a company cheque include:[52]

(i) where the account number of the company is printed but not its name;[53]

(ii) where the word "limited" is omitted from the printed name of a limited company.[54]

[5.17] Abbreviations and misspelling may not give rise to personal liability such as:

(i) Co instead of company;[55]

(ii) Primkeen Limited instead of Primekeen Limited;[56]

[48.] But there are limitations to this, particularly where the officer's signature has not been for the benefit of the company as in *AL Underwood Ltd v The Bank of Liverpool and Martins Ltd* [1924] 1 KB 775, *Alexander Stewart & Son of Dundee Ltd v Westminster Bank Ltd* (1926) 4 LDAB 40 (director drawing against company cheques endorsed by him); see also *Kreditbank Kassel GmbH v Schenkers Ltd* [1927] 1 KB 826, and *B Liggett (Liverpool) Ltd v Barclays Bank Ltd* [1928] 1 KB 48.

[49.] (1920) 37 TLR 10.

[50.] See *Bondina Ltd v Rollaway Shower Blinds Ltd* [1986] BCLC 177; see also (1982) 4 ILT 182 and (1987) 8 Co Law 29.

[51.] Companies Act, 1963, s 114(4); the fine is not to exceed £250.

[52.] For a discussion of earlier decisions see Wright, 'What's in a Company Name?' (1983) 3 Co Law 156.

[53.] *Rafsanjan Pistachio Producers Co-operative v Reiss* [1990] BCLC 352.

[54.] *British Airways Board v Parish* [1979] 2 LLR 361; discussion (1979) JBL 215; *Blum v OCP Repartition SA* [1988] BCLC 170; *Lindholst & Co A/S v Fowler* [1988] BCLC 166.

[55.] *Banque de l'Indochine et de Suez v Euroseas Group Finance Co Ltd* [1981] 3 All ER 198.

[56.] *Jenice Ltd v Dan* [1993] BCLC 1349.

However, personal liability arose where:

1. "LR Agencies Ltd" was printed for "L & R Agencies Ltd".[57]
2. "R & G Associates Ltd" was printed for "R & G Associates (London) Ltd".[58]

[5.18] However where the plaintiff is responsible for the misdescription he will be estopped from obtaining recompense from the signatory.[59]

[5.19] In distinguishing these cases, particularly in trying to ascertain whether personal liability is likely to attach to a director where there is an error in the name of the company, it may be useful to consider the judgment of R Titteridge QC where he distinguished the misspelling of "Primekeen"[60] and the omission of "&" between L and R.[61] He said: [62]

> "There is, in my judgment, in principle, a distinction to be drawn between a misdescription which may mislead (although authority clearly shows that it does not have to) and a spelling or typographical error which in the circumstances of a particular case cannot possibly mislead.
>
> ... a mis-spelling, by the omission of a letter in the middle of a word, is not to be equated with the omission of a whole word ...
>
> ... a strict construction has to be given to the statutory provision, but a strict construction does not require any court to reach a nonsensical conclusion ...
>
> ... in truth, no ordinary person, looking at what has happened in this case, would say, in the words of the section, that the company's name is not mentioned. It is mentioned and it is mis-spelt and, as I have observed, in circumstances that do not lead to any of the vices against which the statutory provisions were directed."

Signature by Facsimile

[5.20] Where an individual gives a cheque it seems possible for his signature to be done in facsimile,[63] but it is less clear whether this applies to a company.[64]

[57.] *Hendon v Adelman* (1973) 117 Sol Jo 631.
[58.] *Barber & Nichols v R & G Associates (London) Ltd* (1983) 9 LDAB 65.
[59.] *Durham Fancy Goods Ltd v Michael Jackson (Fancy Goods) Ltd* [1968] 2 All ER 987; discussed (1969) JBL 45.
[60.] In *Jenice Ltd v Dan* [1993] BCLC 1349.
[61.] In *Hendon v Adelman* (1973) 117 Sol Jo 631.
[62.] *Jenice Ltd v Dan* [1993] BCLC 1349 at 1352 and at 1356.
[63.] See *Goodman v J Eban Ltd* [1954] 1 QB 550 and *Jenkins v Gaisford and Thring* (1863) 3 Sw & T 93.
[64.] See Denning LJ in *Lazarus Estates Ltd v Beasley* [1956] 1 QB 702 at 710 (although Denning LJ gave a dissenting judgment in *Goodman v J Eban Ltd*), but in *McDonald v Twiname Ltd* [1953] 2 All ER 589 Sir R Evershed MR stated (at 594): "A limited company can sign a document by means of some duly authorised pserson putting its printed signature to it or impressing the printed name of the company on it. That will suffice as a proper execution except in cases where the common seal must be affixed".

In *Bennett v Brumfitt*[65] Sir William Bovill stated:

> "The ordinary mode of affixing a signature to a document is not by the hand alone, but by the hand coupled with some instrument, such as a pen or pencil. I see no distinction between using a pen or a pencil and using a stamp, where the impression is put upon the paper by the proper hand of the party signing. In each case it is the personal act of the party, and to all intents and purposes a signing of the document by him."

In the same case Wills J stated:

> "The using of a stamp is only a compendious way of writing the party's name."

In giving the majority decision in *Goodman v J Eban Ltd*[66] Evershed MR stated:[67]

> "In my judgment, therefore, it must be taken as established, from the citations which I have made, that where an Act of Parliament requires that any particular document be 'signed' by a person, then, *prima facie*, the requirement of the Act is satisfied if the person himself places upon the document an engraved representation of his signature by means of a rubber stamp. Indeed, if reference is made to the Shorter Oxford English Dictionary, it will be found that the primary meaning of the verb 'to sign' is not confined to actual writing with a pen or pencil. The word in origin appears to have related to marking with the sign of the cross. But the later meanings include '(2) To place some distinguishing mark upon (a thing or person)' and '(4) To attest or confirm by adding one's signature'; to affix 'one's name to a document etc)'. It follows, then, I think, that the essential requirement of signing is the affixing in some way, whether by writing with a pen or pencil or by otherwise impressing upon the document, one's name or 'signature' so as personally to authenticate the document."

The judge noted that the stamp had been placed by the person himself and stated also that a "typed or printed representation" of his name "would not appear to carry the same warrant of authenticity."

[5.21] The use of a rubber stamp with a facsimile signature facilitates a person with access to the stamp to present cheques with a forged signature.[68] In practice, to mitigate any concern about accepting cheques with facsimile signatures a bank should take an indemnity from the drawer to cover itself for payments made against facsimile signatures.[69]

---

[65]. (1867) LR 3 CP 28.

[66]. [1954] 1 QB 550.

[67]. *Ibid* at 557.

[68]. See for example *Kepitigalla Rubber Estates Ltd v National Bank of India Ltd* [1909] 2 KB 1010.

[69]. See Anu Arora, *Annotation of Bills of Exchange Act, 1882*, p 14 (1987, Lloyd's of London Press Ltd); O'Connor, *The Law and Practice in Ireland Relating to Cheques and Analogous Instruments* (1993) para 4.39.

3. Paying Banker's Duties

Current Account

> "The relation of banker and customer in respect of a current account rests upon a special contract ... The due and unfailing performance of that contract on the part of the banker is, as he knows, vital to the ordinary daily life of his customers in our modern social organisation. The customer relies on his credit balance being at his instant call for innumerable purposes - commercial, domestic, social - constantly pressing upon him. The banker knows that if the credit balance is withheld from the customer when he demands payment, inevitably the customer must immediately procure an equivalent amount of money from some other source - probably by borrowing at interest. But the customer may fail to obtain a loan, or the delay may be such that injurious consequences naturally flow from the banker's default - a judgment may be marked against the customer, he may be evicted, his goods may be taken in execution, he may lose the benefit of a valuable contract, in a variety of ways he may suffer grievous loss and damage as the direct result of the banker's refusing him payment of his credit balance on his demand.[70]

[5.22] The relationship between a banker and his customer is grounded on contract.[71] A customer who opens an account with a bank signs a bank mandate form,[72] a document in which the customer requests the bank to honour requests for withdrawal of moneys from the customer's account with the bank (provided there are sufficient funds belonging to the customer deposited with the bank to meet the cheques drawn or in the absence of a sufficiency of funds the bank has agreed the customer may overdraw and provided the amount drawn on the cheque, when paid, will not cause any limit on the agreed overdraft to be exceeded). The drawer's instruction in a cheque to the bank on which a cheque is drawn is the mandate or authority granted to the paying bank by its customer to honour a cheque and deduct the amount of the cheque from the customer's account with the bank.[73]

As with all contracts, the terms of the agreement cannot be varied unilaterally by one party without bringing the variation to the other party's notice and obtaining the agreement or consent to such variation. In *Burnett v Westminster Bank Ltd*[74] a notice was printed on the cover of a cheque book to the effect that cheques in the book could be drawn only on the account printed on the cheques. The court held that the notice was inadequate to affect the pre-existing contractual

---

[70.] Kennedy CJ in *Kinlan v Ulster Bank Ltd* [1928] IR 171 at 185.
[71.] See paras **[1.10]-[1.19]**.
[72.] See para **[4.16]**.
[73.] See *Chalmers & Guest on Bills of Exchange, Cheques and Promissory Notes* (14th ed) p 616-7.
[74.] [1965] 3 All ER 81.

relationship between the bank and its customer and that the bank had failed to give sufficient notice to its customer of the restricted use of the cheques.

Duty to Honour Cheques

[5.23] There is an implied term (unless otherwise varied) in the banker-customer relationship that the banker will repay money (lodged to the customer's account with it) on demand (whether by cheque or other order) made during banking hours at the branch of the bank at which the account is standing[75] - "the bank is bound to honour his [customer's] cheques only at that branch where he keeps his account and it is entitled to refuse to pay at any other branch".[76] This implied term is limited to the extent that there are funds in the customer's account to meet the liability of cheques presented to the bank or the bank have agreed otherwise that the customer may overdraw on its account to a specified limit[77] (and the honouring of a cheque does not cause that limit to be exceeded). To use the words of O'Hanlon J:[78]

> "A banker is bound to pay cheques drawn on him by a customer in legal form provided he has in his hands at the time sufficient and available funds for the purpose, or provided the cheques are within the limits of an agreed overdraft. He must either pay cheques or refund payment at once, a request to re-present amounts to dishonour."[79]

The duty of a bank to pay or dishonour a cheque on demand does not mean "'on the spot', but within such time as is reasonable" and what is reasonable depends upon practice and the facts of the case in question.[80]

A paying bank is obliged to honour a cheque drawn on it, where it has been correctly made out and signed and presented by the drawer to the payee in conjunction with a bank card. Essentially the bank undertakes directly with the payee in such circumstances to honour cheques drawn to the value of the card.[81]

---

[75] See Kennedy CJ in *Kinlan v Ulster Bank Ltd* [1928] IR 171 at 181; see also Atkin LJ in *Joachimson v Swiss Bank Corp* [1921] 3 KB 110 at 127, see para **[1.11]** above.

[76] McLoughlin J in *The Governor and Company of the Bank of Ireland v Hussey* [1965] IR 46 at 54.

[77] The facility granted by a bank to its customer to enable it to overdraw is known as an overdraft facility.

[78] In *TE Potterton Ltd v Northern Bank Ltd* [1993] 1 IR 413 at 420; [1993] ILRM 225 at 230 (where he adopted Halsbury's statement at para 163 4th ed, Vol 3 - (the law report stated Vol 2)).

[79] See also Henchy J in *Dublin Port and Docks Board v The Governor and Company of the Bank of Ireland* [1976] IR 118 at 135.

[80] As stated by Lavery J in *The Royal Bank of Ireland Ltd v O'Rourke* [1962] IR 159 at 178 and cited by Murphy J in *Brennan v The Governor and Company of the Bank of Ireland* High Court, unrep, 23 May 1985 at p 12 and by O'Hanlon J in *Towey v Ulster Bank Ltd* (1987) ILRM 142 at 150.

[81] See Millett J in *Re Charge Card Services Ltd* [1987] BCLC 17 at 31.

As for dishonour, Kennedy CJ stated in 1922 that:[82]

> "... it has long been settled law that if a banker wrongfully dishonours the cheque of a customer who is a trader, the customer is entitled to substantial, and not merely nominal, damages, without proof of special damage".

However, a customer who is a non-trader would not be entitled to recover substantial damages for breach of contract for the wrongful dishonour of his cheque, unless he can prove special damage.[83] But, a customer will be entitled to damages where he can prove gross malice.[84]

[5.24] The principal although inconclusive decision for a non-trader is that of the Supreme Court in *Pyke v The Hibernian Bank Ltd.*[85] In that case the paying bank returned three cheques of its customer, one marked "Refer to Drawer, Present Again" and the other two it marked "Refer to Drawer". The customer had an overdraft facility with the bank and the honouring of the cheques would not have caused the limit on the facility to be breached.

The customer brought an action against the bank for damages for breach of contract and libel claiming that the words "Refer to Drawer" contained innuendos against his character. The trial judge withdrew the question of innuendo from the jury but nonetheless the jury awarded damages against the bank for libel and nominal damages for breach of contract. The Supreme Court (with four judges sitting) divided equally on the question of libel so the High Court's award stood.[86]

In his judgment Maguire CJ, in accepting the view of Scrutton LJ in *Flach v London and Southern Western Bank Ltd*,[87] stated:[88]

> "as to the meaning of the words, 'Refer to Drawer'. These are words carefully chosen by banks with the object of saying that they were not paying at the moment, leaving it to the drawee[89] of the cheque to go back to the drawer for an explanation of their action. I am unable to construe the words as reflecting on the solvency, honesty, or good faith of the drawer of the cheque. I can not

---

[82.] In *Kinlan v Ulster Bank Ltd* [1928] IR 171 at 181.
[83.] See *Gibbons v Westminster Bank Ltd* [1939] 3 All ER 577.
[84.] See *Grealy v Bank of Nova Scotia* High Court, unrep March 1972 Pringle J, Supreme Court, unrep, 11 April 1975, ILSI Gazette (1975) Vol 69 p 150.
[85.] [1950] IR 195; for a discussion of this decision and earlier English decisions see *Banker and Customer* (1950) XVI Ir Jur 37.
[86.] In the Supreme Court Black J (who held the words not to be libellous) said, "In my opinion it would be equitable that a gentleman in the plaintiff's position should recover substantial damages for breach of contract by the dishonour of his cheques in this case."
[87.] 31 TLR 334.
[88.] [1950] IR 195 at 201.
[89.] The judge should have stated payee rather than drawee.

extract from them a meaning which exposes the drawer of the cheque to hatred, contempt, or ridicule in the eyes of right-thinking men.

The words, 'Present again', which were endorsed by the Bank on one of the cheques, mean that the Bank is not paying at the moment, but may pay later.
It seems to me that these words are equally incapable of a defamatory meaning."

However, O'Byrne J in his judgment pointed out that the decision of *Flach v London and Southern Western Bank Ltd*,[90] relied on by the Chief Justice was inappropriate, as in that case the circumstances were such that the bank were under no obligation to pay the cheque. In considering whether the words "Refer to Drawer" were capable of a defamatory meaning, O'Byrne J stated:[91]

"The matter is of general importance owing to the widespread use of cheques at the present day, in payment of accounts. Where a bank has funds belonging to a customer, it is, to the extent of such funds, the debtor of the customer and is, to the same extent, legally bound to honour cheques drawn upon it by the customer. Bearing this in mind, what is the inference to be drawn by reasonable men from the dishonouring of a cheque? It seems to me that one or other of two alternative views at once emerges - either (a) that there are no funds to meet the cheque or (b) that the order for payment contained in the cheque has been countermanded since the cheque was given to the payee and, presumably, consideration was obtained therefor. Either of these views seems to me to be reasonably capable of a defamatory meaning *quoad* the drawer of the cheque as implying (a) that he is insolvent or (b) that he is guilty of a want of good faith towards the payee of the cheque."

O'Byrne J considered that if the trial judge was satisfied that the words were reasonably capable of a defamatory meaning he was bound to leave the case to the jury to decide whether the words were defamatory.[92]

[5.25] The fact that the jury found that the words marked on the cheque "Refer to Drawer", "Present Again" and "Refer to Drawer" when it had been agreed that funds would be available to meet the cheques, to be defamatory seems conclusive that such words are defamatory in such circumstances (notwithstanding the split decision of the Supreme Court[93]).[94] This is supported also by *Grealy v Bank of Nova Scotia*[95] where the jury found the words "Refer to

---

[90.] 31 TLR 334.
[91.] [1950] IR 195 at 204.
[92.] Geoghegan J agreed with O'Byrne J's judgment ([1950] IR 201).
[93.] Ironically, Black J who found the words not to be defamatory opened his judgment by saying "... in view of the seeming conflict between the highest authorities. ... I think it would serve the Bar and the public to settle these questions once for all" [1950] IR 195 at 207).
[94.] See also O'Connor, *The Law and Practice in Ireland Relating to Cheques and Analogous Instruments* para (1993) paras 10.11 and 10.12.

Drawer" defamatory. The bank's appeal to the Supreme Court was unsuccessful.[96] The doubts expressed in England[97] in the earlier part of this century as to whether "Refer to Drawer" could be defamatory seem now to be resolved also by the jury's decision in *Jayson v Midland Bank Ltd*[98] where the jury found that the effect of the words "Refer to Drawer" was to lower the drawer's reputation in the minds of right-thinking people.

[5.26] A cheque returned marked with the words "not sufficient" when at the time of presentment there were sufficient funds in the account to meet the cheque is libellous.[99]

[5.27] The words "present again" marked on a cheque when there were funds in the account to meet it were held by the Supreme Court of Auckland to be reasonably capable of a defamatory meaning. In *Baker v Australian and New Zealand Bank Ltd*,[100] the Supreme Court of Auckland held that (1) as the customer was not a trader she was entitled to only nominal, and not substantial, damages for the bank's breach of contract in returning three cheques to the payee marked "present again" (unless she could prove actual damage suffered) and (2) the words "present again" were reasonably capable of a defamatory meaning as they intimated that the drawer had defaulted in her legal and ethical obligation to provide funds for the immediate payment of the cheques.

[5.28] The words "account closed" marked on a dishonoured cheque may also be defamatory as giving rise to the implication that the drawer of the cheque cannot be trusted in his business dealings (offering a payment by cheque on an account with no funds).[101]

[5.29] The Supreme Court's decision in *Kinlan v Ulster Bank Ltd*[102] appears to have decided that defamation does not arise where a bank refuses to make a payment to its customer as there is no third party involved.[103] In that case, the Supreme Court (by a majority) allowed an appeal by the bank against an award of damages and granted only nominal damages where the bank refused to honour cheques drawn by the customer in his favour on his account

---

[95.] Before Pringle J, March 1972, see ILSI Gazette (1975) Vol 69 p 150.

[96.] Supreme Court, unrep, 11 April 1975.

[97.] *Flach v London and South Western Bank Ltd* 31 LTR 334.

[98.] [1968] 1 LLR 409.

[99.] *Davidson v Barclays Bank Ltd* [1940] 1 All ER 316.

[100.] [1958] NZLR 907.

[101.] See *Russell v Bank of America National Trust and Savings Association* (1977) 9 LDAB 44.

[102.] [1928] IR 171.

[103.] If other customers in the bank hear a refusal by the bank to honour a request for payment there may be grounds for damages for libel (which was not pleaded in *Kinlan v Ulster Bank Ltd*).

notwithstanding the fact that sufficient funds were in the customer's account to meet the cheques.

Duty not to Pay without Authority

"... the law is clear that a bank owes a contractual duty to a customer to exercise reasonable care and skill in paying a cheque drawn on that customer's account ... and that the exercise of that reasonable care and skill includes in appropriate circumstances making inquiry of the customer as to the propriety of the cheque before paying it."[104]

[5.30] A bank may deduct money from its customer's account only where it has the appropriate authority to do so. The terms of such authority are usually set out in pre-printed bank mandate forms signed by the customer at the time an account is opened. Failure to exercise reasonable care and skill in checking the authorised signatories can result in the bank being obliged to re-credit the account with the amount withdrawn.[105]

[5.31] However, where a bank honours cheques drawn in a manner not in compliance with the customer's mandate to it, the bank may nonetheless be able to debit the customer's account with the amount of the cheque where the cheque payment has been made to discharge the customer's indebtedness to its trade creditors in respect of goods supplied to the customer.[106] In *B Liggett (Liverpool) Ltd v Barclays Bank Ltd*[107] Wright J, in applying equitable principles, stated:[108]

"The equitable principle has been applied beyond question over and over again to cases where an agent not having the authority of his principal has borrowed money as on behalf of his principal. Under those circumstances at common law the principal cannot be sued and cannot be made to repay the amount so borrowed, but in equity it has been held that to the extent that the amount so borrowed has been applied in payment of the debts of the principal, the quasi lender is entitled to recover from the quasi borrower."

The court held that even where a cheque was drawn and paid by the banker, without proper authority, from a credit balance to discharge a debt of the drawer, the bank could still deduct the payment from the account because the customer

---

[104] Hutton J in *Prescott Meat Company Ltd v Northern Bank Ltd* [1981] NI 150 at 158; it should be borne in mind though in considering the reference to "making inquiry" that Hutton J was very influenced in his judgment by the much criticised decisions in *Selangor United Rubber Estates Ltd v Crodock (No 3)* [1968] 2 All ER 1073 and *Karak Rubber Co Ltd v Burden (No 2)* [1972] 1 All ER 1210 see para **[6.27]**.

[105] See *Prescott Meat Co Ltd v Northern Bank Ltd* [1981] NI 150 where the principal shareholder of the customer signed a cheque without authorisation.

[106] See further *Paget's Law of Banking* (11th ed, 1996) p 341.

[107] [1928] 1 KB 48.

[108] *Ibid* at 60.

is really no worse off as a result of the discharge of its legal liability to the payee.

[5.32] It has been suggested that a banker has authority to pay cheques only if presented to it during public banking hours;[109] the answer to this is unclear. However, banks "are entitled within a reasonable business margin of their advertised time for closing to deal with a cheque ... to pay it".[110]

Revocation of Banker's Authority

[5.33] The duty and authority of a banker to pay a cheque drawn on him by his customer are determined by (1) countermand of payment; or (2) notice of the customer's death.[111]

[5.34] Although a bank is under a duty to honour cheques at the branch at which the customer keeps his account,[112] common law precedent seems to indicate that a customer who sends a countermand of payment to his branch may nonetheless have to reimburse the bank for the amount of the cheque should another branch, without knowledge of the revocation, honour the cheque.[113] This seems hard to justify as a customer cannot be expected to notify all branches of a bank and nowadays, with on-line information available at each branch, it may be doubtful whether this precedent will be followed. Indeed in such circumstances the High Court[114] refused to extend the list of exceptions to the "well-established principle that the head office of a bank and all its branches constitute only one corporation or firm and that each branch is a separate agency of a common principal."[115]

[5.35] No particular form is required in order to revoke the banker's authority to honour cheques. Thus a written notification, received by the bank prior to honouring the cheque, along the following lines should suffice - "Stop my cheque number xxxx drawn for xxx signed xxx."[116] In *Reade v The Royal Bank of Ireland Ltd*[117] countermand was given by way of telegram; the (Irish) Court of

---

[109.] LC Mather in *Banker and Customer Relationship and the Accounts of Personal Customers* (5th ed, 1979) p 123.
[110.] So held by Lord Hewart in *Baines v National Provincial Bank Ltd* (1927) 137 LT 631.
[111.] Bills of Exchange Act, 1882, s 75.
[112.] See para **[5.23]** above.
[113.] *London Provincial and South-Western Bank (Ltd) v Buszard* (1918) 35 TLR 142, adopted by *Paget's Law of Banking* (11th ed) p 335; see also Mocatta J in *Burnett v Westminster Bank Ltd* [1965] 3 All ER 81 at 86; the statement in *Chalmers and Guest on Bills of Exchange, Cheques and Promissory Notes* (14th ed) p 619 that, "the customer need notify only the branch of the bank on which the cheque was drawn" is not supported by any authority.
[114.] In the *Governor and Company of the Bank of Ireland v Hussey* [1965] IR 46.
[115.] *Ibid* at 51 per McLaughlin J.
[116.] Held to be sufficient in *Reade v The Royal Bank of Ireland Ltd* [1922] 2 IR 22.
[117.] [1922] 2 IR 22.

Appeal had no difficulty in accepting this as being proper notification. This is in contrast to the English Court of Appeal which indicated that a bank is not bound to accept an unauthenticated telegram as sufficient authority to stop a cheque.[118] A banker is faced with a difficulty here[119] - if it receives notification of countermand of authority, and subsequently honours a cheque, it may be liable to reimburse its customer with the amount of the cheque which the banker has paid.[120] On the other hand, if it refuses payment of a cheque and it transpires that the customer had not revoked the banker's authority to pay, the bank is leaving itself open to a suit for defamation from its customer whose reputation may have been tarnished by the stopping of the cheque.[121] A practical way of resolving this difficulty for a banker has been suggested by *LC Mather* as follows:[122]

> "Having regard to the need for prompt action by the drawer to stop payment either upon receipt of notice that the payee has lost a cheque or on finding fault with the goods delivered against the cheque, it is natural that for speed resort may be had to the telephone or telegram to advise the Bank. The authority of instructions over the telephone may be verified to some extent by discussion with the caller, but a telegram can be despatched by anyone and can be verified only by independent enquiry. In both cases, therefore, the instructions require immediate confirmation in writing and, if the cheque is presented for payment in the meantime, it should be returned with an answer which clearly explains the position. For example, the reply 'payment countermanded by telephone or telegram (as the case may be) and postponed pending confirmation' adequately protects the position."

An alternative practical suggestion is for the paying bank to write on the cheque, pending confirmation of countermand - "Payment postponed pending confirmation of drawer's instructions".[123]

[5.36] It has been held in English Court of Appeal that countermand is not effective until the notice is read by an employee of the bank and that receipt by the bank of a notification but not read is not notification.[124] This decision, over-ruling decisions of two lower courts, seems difficult to justify; if it were to be

---

118. *Curtice v London City and Midland Bank Ltd* [1908] 1 KB 293.
119. "It must always be remembered that a bank can be sued just as much for failing to honour a cheque as for cashing a cheque that has been stopped" - Viscount Dunedin in *Westminster Bank Ltd v Hilton* (1926) 43 TLR 124.
120. As in *Reade v The Royal Bank of Ireland Ltd* [1922] 2 IR 22.
121. See paras **[5.23]-[5.29]** above.
122. In *Banker and Customer Relationship and the Accounts of Personal Customers* (5th ed, 1979) p 118.
123. See O'Connor, *The Law and Practice in Ireland Relating to Cheques and Analogous Instruments* (1993) para 10.27.
124. *Curtice v London City and Midland Bank Ltd* [1908] 1 KB 293.

adopted in Ireland the customer should have grounds for recovery in negligence or for money had and received.

[5.37] It is essential that the notice of revocation is clear and unambiguous. In *Westminster Bank Ltd v Hilton*[125] the customer notified his banker by telegram - "Stop payment of cheque 117283 amount of £8 1s 6d to Poate". The bank paid a cheque numbered 117285 for this amount to Poate. The customer sought recovery from the bank (as he meant to stop cheque 117285 but the other details were correct). The House of Lords allowed the bank's appeal - "There can be only one cheque bearing a printed number; there may be many cheques in favour of the same drawee and for the same amount".[126]

The court approached the case on the basis of principal and agent and the requirement for clear instructions by the principal to his agent. Lord Atkinson stated in his judgment: [127]

> "It is well established that the normal relation between a banker and his customer is that of debtor and creditor, but it is equally well established that quoad the drawing and payment of the customer's cheques as against money of the customer's in the banker's hands, the relation is that of principal and agent. The cheque is an order of the principal's addressed to the agent to pay out of the principal's money in the agent's hands the amount of the cheque to the payee thereof. Difficulty arises when, as in this case, the principal's order to his agent is ambiguous in character capable of conveying a command bearing different or inconsistent meanings. A question of this kind arose in the case of *Ireland v Livingston* (LR 5 HL 396) ... where Lord Chelmsford said:
>
> > 'Now, it appears to me that if a principal gives an order to an agent in such uncertain terms as to be susceptible of two different meanings, and the agent *bona fide* adopts one of them and acts upon it, it is not competent to the principal to repudiate the act as unauthorised because he meant the order to be read in the other sense of which it is equally capable. It is a fair answer to such an attempt to disown the agent's authority, to tell the principal that the departure from his intention was occasioned by his own fault, and that he should have given his order in clear and unambiguous terms'."

[5.38] Following clear notification that a cheque is to be stopped, the paying banker should return the cheque to the collecting banker (or payee, if presented by the payee). When returning the cheque, care is needed in the language of the paying banker so as to avoid any suggestion that the drawer has inadequate funds to meet the cheque.[128] Accordingly, the safest wording to be marked on

---

125. (1926) 43 TLR 124.
126. *Ibid per* Viscount Dunedin at 126.
127. *Ibid*.
128. Thereby giving rise to an action for defamation, see paras **[5.23]-[5.29]** above.

the cheque would appear to be "payment countermanded by the drawer".[129] A cheque which has been stopped, following the countermand by the drawer of the cheque to the paying bank, will be deemed to be a dishonour of the cheque by non-payment,[130] thereby giving rise to a cause of action by the payee against the drawer.[131]

[5.39] *Richardson's Guide to Negotiable Instruments*[132] indicates that in addition to the events set out in s 75 of the Bills of Exchange Act 1882[133] a bank's authority to pay is terminated on:[134]

(a) Receiving notice of the insanity of the customer;[135]or

(b) Receiving notice of an act of bankruptcy by the customer; or

(c) Receiving notice of a receiving order in bankruptcy against the customer; or

(d) Receiving notice of the commencement of winding-up, if the customer is a company; or

(e) On closure of the bank; or

(f) An assignment of balance by the customer; or

(g) Receiving notice of a breach of trust (e.g., if it appears fairly certain that the cheque in question, drawn by a trustee, is a withdrawal of money to be used otherwise than for the purpose of the trust);[136] or

(h) Receiving notice of defect in the presenter's title - this must obviously entail refusal to pay since a bank must pay in good faith; or

(i) Receiving notice of a court order affecting the relevant account; [137]

[5.40] Insanity does not need to be certified. In *The Governor and Company of the Bank of Ireland v Hussey*[138] the bank received notification from solicitors

---

129. See LC Mather, *Banker and Customer Relationship and the Accounts of Personal Customers* (5th ed, 1979) p 124.

130. *Gaynor v McDyer and Hurley* [1968] IR 295 applying ss 50(2)(c)(5) and 47(1) of the Bills of Exchange Act, 1882 and overruling *Kenneally v Lyons* [1958] Ir Jur Rep 54.

131. Bills of Exchange Act, 1882, s 47(2).

132. (8th ed) Butterworths.

133. See para **[5.33]** above.

134. Richardson's *Guide to Negotiable Instruments* (8th ed) para 16.13; see further *Chalmers and Guest on Bills of Exchange, Cheques and Promissory Notes* (14th ed) pp 623-631.

135. See para **[5.40]** below; for a fuller treatment of countermand of authority by reason of insanity see O'Connor, *The Law and Practice in Ireland Relating to Cheques and Analogous Instruments* (1993) paras 10.39 to 10.40.

136. See *Midland Bank Ltd v Reckitt* [1933] AC 1.

137. For countermand of authority upon notification of a garnishee order or an injunction, including a Mareva injunction, see O'Connor, *The Law and Practice in Ireland Relating to Cheques and Analogous Instruments* (1993) paras 10.51-10.60.

138. [1965] IR 46.

113

that a doctor having examined the customer indicated the customer "was by reason of his mental condition incapable of transacting business or of looking after his business affairs". This notification was sufficient as to be a countermand of authority to the branch to honour cheques. McLaughlin J stated:[139]

> "I think that I must recognise the modern tendency not to stigmatise a person as lunatic or insane and it seems to me that a person who is stated to be incapable of managing his business affairs by reason of his mental condition is, while in that condition, suffering from the same mental incapacity as a person who has been certified as insane."

Crossing a Cheque

> "A crossing is a direction to the paying bank to pay the money generally to a bank, or to a particular bank, as the case may be, and when this has been done the whole purpose of the crossing has been served".[140]

[5.41] A cheque may be crossed[141] in order to minimise the risk that payment may be obtained in respect of it by a person other than the payee or endorsee.[142]

[5.42] A cheque is crossed generally where it bears across its face:

> "(a) The words "and company" or any abbreviation thereof between two parallel transverse lines, either with or without the words "not negotiable"; or
>
> (b) Two parallel transverse lines simply, either with or without the words "not negotiable"".[143]

A cheque may be crossed generally by either the drawer[144] or the holder.[145] The holder may also add the words "not negotiable" to a cheque which has been crossed generally.[146]

[5.43] A special crossing is "where a cheque bears across its face an addition of the name of a banker, either with or without the words "not negotiable", that

---

[139.] *Ibid* at 51.

[140.] Bigham J in *Akrokerri (Atlantic) Mines Ltd v Economic Bank* [1904] 2 KB 465 at 472.

[141.] For illustrations of crossings see O'Connor, *The Law and Practice in Ireland Relating to Cheques and Analogous Instruments* (1993) paras 7.3 and 7.4.

[142.] "Crossings were originally developed as an administrative convenience, but are now directed at increasing the security of the cheque as a means of payment" - *Banking Services: Law and Practice Report by the Review Committee* (1989) Cm 622 para 7.12; for further reading see Donnelly, 'Cheque Fraud: Modern Treatment and Future Trends' (1997) CLP 216.

[143.] Bills of Exchange Act, 1882, s 76(1).

[144.] *Ibid* s 77(1).

[145.] *Ibid* s 77(2).

[146.] *Ibid* s 77(4).

addition constitutes a crossing and the cheque is crossed specially and to that banker".[147]

[5.44] Section 80 of the Bills of Exchange Act, 1882 provides that:

> Where the banker, on whom a crossed cheque is drawn, in good faith[148] and without negligence pays it, if crossed generally, to a banker ... the banker paying the cheque shall ... be entitled to the same rights and be placed in the same position as if payment of the cheque had been made to the true owner thereof.

[5.45] Where the paying banker and the collecting banker are the same, whether it be different branches or not, payment of the crossed cheque by the paying banker through crediting the payee/endorsee's account will be payment to a banker within the meaning of s 80.[149]

Cheque Crossed "Not Negotiable"

> "... it is very important that everyone should know that people who take a cheque which is marked "not negotiable" and treat it as a negotiable security must recognise the fact that if they do so they take the risk of the person for whom they negotiate it having no title to it."[150]

[5.46] The crossing of a cheque with the words "not negotiable" does not add anything to the duties of the paying bank, or indeed collecting bank, other than the fact that it is a crossed cheque and the paying banker can avail of the defence open to paying on a crossed cheque provided it has paid it to a banker.[151] The significance of the words "not negotiable" when added to a crossing is set out in s 81 of the Bills of Exchange Act, 1882 which states:

> Where a person takes a crossed cheque which bears on it the words 'not negotiable', he shall not have and shall not be capable of giving a better title to the cheque than that which the person from whom he took it had.

[5.47] The effect of such a crossing therefore, is that a subsequent holder of the cheque cannot have a better title to it than the payee or any prior holder.[152] Thus, if the cheque is obtained fraudulently a holder which had given value for it will not be able to enforce payment on it or indeed an innocent person who had given value for the cheque and received payment thereunder may be obliged to

---

[147.] *Ibid* s 76(2).

[148.] "A thing is deemed to be done in good faith, within the meaning of this Act, where it is in fact done honestly, whether it be done negligently or not" - Bills of Exchange Act, 1882, s 90.

[149.] See *Chalmers and Guest on Bills of Exchange, Cheques and Promissory Notes* (14th ed) p 651.

[150.] Earl of Halsbury LC in *The Great Western Railway Company v The London and County Banking Company Ltd* [1901] AC 414.

[151.] See para **[5.44]** above.

[152.] See further para **[5.85]** below.

reimburse the true owner. In *Wilson & Meeson v Pickering*[153] a partner in the plaintiff firm signed on behalf of the firm a blank cheque crossed "not negotiable" and instructed his secretary to complete the cheque payable to the Inland Revenue for £2. His secretary completed it in favour of the defendant for £54 and handed it to the defendant in discharge of a debt due by the secretary. The defendant took the cheque in good faith and cashed it. The firm sought to recover £54 from the defendant. The Court of Appeal held that the cheque came within s 81 of the Bills of Exchange Act, 1882 and thus the defendant had no better title to it than the secretary and accordingly the firm were entitled to recover £54 from the defendant.

[5.48] In *The Great Western Railway Co v The London and County Banking Co Ltd*,[154] Lord Brampton stated:[155]

> "The object of s 81 is obvious. It is to afford to the drawer or the holder (s 77) of a cheque who is desirous of transmitting it to another person as much protection as can reasonably be afforded to it against dishonesty or accidental miscarriage in the course of its transit, if he will only take the precaution to cross it, with the addition of the words 'not negotiable', so as to make it difficult to get such cheque so crossed cashed until it reaches its destination."

Accordingly, it is unwise for a person to accept an endorsement of a cheque which has been crossed "not negotiable" unless such person is fully satisfied as to the title of the payee and any subsequent endorsee.[156] For the drawer of a cheque, such a crossing may be useful where the cheque is being drawn for payment in advance for goods or services so that, in the absence of delivery of the goods and services, payment of the cheque may be countermanded without the drawer being liable on the cheque itself.[157] Drafts issued by banks usually contain such a crossing.

"Non-transferable" Cheques

[5.49] A cheque, whether crossed or not, may have on its face words to the effect that it is non-transferable.[158] This means that the cheque is a non-negotiable instrument.[159] Thus, the payee cannot endorse it but can receive payment itself. The words "non-transferable" are not essential, but simply a clear intention stated on the cheque as to its non-transferability such as "Pay

---

153. [1946] 1 All ER 394.
154. [1901] AC 414.
155. *Ibid* at 422.
156. *Shield Life Insurance Co Ltd and O'Callaghan v Ulster Bank Ltd* [1995] 3 IR 225; see para **[5.85]** below.
157. Assuming the cheque has not already been honoured.
158. Bills of Exchange Act, 1882, s 8(1).
159. *Ibid*.

Donall Cunningham only". [160] This is the drawer's direction to the paying bank who is thus mandated to pay the named payee only. Standard cheque book forms issued by banks contain the printed words on each cheque "Pay ... or order". The reference "or order" anticipates that the payee may endorse the cheque to another. As paying bankers have a certain protection when paying endorsed cheques,[161] banks do not encourage non-transferability. To avoid a contradiction on the face of a cheque, the words "or order" should be deleted by the drawer if the drawer intends the cheque to be non-transferable.

Payment of Endorsed Cheques

[5.50] A banker on whom a cheque (crossed or uncrossed) is drawn which pays out on such a cheque will be deemed to have paid in due course when it pays "in good faith and in the ordinary course of business" even though the payee's indorsement or a subsequent indorsement was made without authority.[162] Thus a banker must show that it paid not only "in good faith" (that is, it paid honestly whether or not it was negligent)[163] but also that it paid "in the ordinary course of business".

[5.51] There is limited authority as to what constitutes payment "in the ordinary course of business". First, the appropriate steps should be taken by the paying banker to examine the cheque;[164] secondly, payment should be made within the bank's advertised opening hours or "within a reasonable margin" of its advertised closing time;[165] and thirdly, it is probable that it includes payment of cheques across the counter to a bank's customer at a branch other than where the customer keeps his account.[166] Payment though of a crossed cheque contrary to its crossing would not be payment in the ordinary course of business.[167] It seems unclear whether a bank could be deemed to be acting "in the ordinary course of business" where it has acted negligently.[168]

[160.] See further examples in Richardson's *Guide to Negotiable Instruments* (8th ed) para 14.15.
[161.] Bills of Exchange Act, 1882, s 60.
[162.] *Ibid.*
[163.] *Ibid* s 90.
[164.] As suggested by Milnes Holden, *The Law and Practice of Banking* Vol 1 (5th ed, 1991) para 7-66.
[165.] See *Baines v National Provincial Bank Ltd* (1927) 137 LT 631 referred to at para **[5.32]** above.
[166.] As suggested by Chorley & Smart, *Leading Cases in the Law of Banking* (6th ed) p 148 and by Penn, Shea & Arora, *The Law Relating to Domestic Banking* (1987) Vol 1 para (1987) 18.124, but questioned by *Paget's Law of Banking* (11th ed) p 384.
[167.] See *Chalmers and Guest on Bills of Exchange, Cheques and Promissory Notes* (14th ed) p 519.
[168.] See the contrasting judgments in *Carpenters' Co v British Mutual Banking Co Ltd* [1937] 3 All ER 811.

[5.52] The protection granted to a paying banker by s 60[169] does not apply to cheques which have not been indorsed or which have been irregularly endorsed. Protection is nonetheless given to paying bankers in respect of such cheques by the Cheques Act, 1959, s 1(1) of which provides:

> Where a banker in good faith and in the ordinary course of business pays a cheque drawn on him which is not indorsed or is irregularly indorsed, he does not in doing so, incur any liability by reason only of the absence of, or irregularity in indorsement, and he is deemed to have paid it in due course.

Notwithstanding this statutory provision bankers still adopt a practice of requiring a cheque which is presented for payment across the counter to be endorsed.[170] Such an endorsement though may be considered to be a receipt for payment rather than an endorsement of a negotiation of the cheque.[171]

4. FORGED CHEQUES

Paying Banker's Liability

> "A cheque with the signature of a customer forged is not the customer's mandate or order to pay. With regard to that cheque it does not fall within the relation of banker and customer. If the bank honours such a document not proceeding from its customer, it cannot make the customer answerable for the signature and issue of a document which he did not sign or issue; the banker paying accordingly has paid without authority and cannot charge the payment against a person who was a stranger to the transaction."[172]

[5.53] These words are a stark reminder to all bankers that where the signature on a cheque is forged[173] the honouring of such a cheque by a banker will result in the banker not being able to debit his customer's account or, where he has done so, in re-crediting the account with the amount so debited.[174]

[169.] Bills of Exchange Act, 1882.

[170.] See O'Connor, *The Law and Practice in Ireland Relating to Cheques and Analogous Instruments* (1993) para 8.11.

[171.] See *Chalmers and Guest on Bills of Exchange, Cheques and Promissory Notes* (14th ed) pp 515, 520.

[172.] Lord Shaw of Dunfermline in *London Joint Stock Bank Ltd v Macmillan and Arthur* [1918] AC 777 at 823; see also Kerr J in *National Westminster Bank Ltd v Barclays Bank International Ltd* [1974] 3 All ER 834 at 844 - "The principle is simply that a banker cannot debit his customer's account on the basis of a forged signature, since he has in that event no mandate from the customer for doing so".

[173.] A forgery is "the making of a false document in order that it may be used as genuine" - Forgery Act, 1913, s 1.

[174.] The same principle applies to a forged withdrawal mandate see *Ma Chiu Chong v The Chase Manhattan Bank NA and Ma Wai Kong Eugene* [1993] 1 JIBL N9 where the plaintiffs were reimbursed by the bank following the withdrawal of US$2 million by their son (an employee of the bank).

Customer's Duty[175]

"A customer of a bank owes a duty to the bank in drawing a cheque to take reasonable and ordinary precautions against forgery, and if as the natural and direct result of the neglect of those precautions the amount of the cheque is increased by forgery, the customer must bear the loss as between himself and the banker". [176]

[5.54] A banker-customer relationship imposes duties on both parties. A customer's negligence in the manner of drawing a cheque will permit the banker to avoid having to reimburse the customer's account with the amount of the forged cheque paid by the bank in good faith, if the payment of the forgery is a "natural and uninterrupted sequence"[177] from the breach of duty. The loss will thus fall on the customer and not on the banker. However, notwithstanding a customer's carelessness, a paying banker may nonetheless remain liable for the loss but with a reduction in damages due to the customer's contributory negligence.[178] Customers would do well to remember the words of Lord Shaw of Dunfermline:[179]

"That duty is so to fill up his cheque as that when it leaves his hands a signed document it shall be properly and fully filled up, so that tampering with its contents or filling in a sum different from what the customer meant it to cover shall be prevented.

... this is the sole ratio of the blank cheque decisions. The customer in such cases is bound to accept the responsibility for whatever the contents of the cheque may be, if he has allowed a cheque to pass out of his hands blank."

[5.55] Where the customer's delay in notifying its bank of forgeries results in the bank incurring loss, which it might not have incurred had the forgery been notified promptly, the customer will be estopped from asserting that the cheques are forgeries and therefore will not be able to prevent its account being deducted with the amount of the cheques. In *Greenwood v Martins Bank Ltd*[180] the plaintiff's wife repeatedly forged her husband's signature; the plaintiff became aware of the forgeries, but was persuaded by his wife not to disclose them; when he decided to disclose them his wife committed suicide. The plaintiff sought to recover from the bank the amount paid on foot of the forged cheques. The court held that the failure of the plaintiff to disclose the forgeries when he became aware of them prevented the bank from suing the plaintiff's wife, as following

---

[175.] See also Gill, 'The Duties of a Customer to his Bank' (1986) 4 ILT 47.

[176.] Head-note in *London Joint Stock Bank Ltd v Macmillan and Arthur* [1918] AC 777.

[177.] Lord Parmoor in *London Joint Stock Bank Ltd v Macmillan and Arthur* [1918] AC 777 at 834.

[178.] See *Lumsden & Co v London Trustee Savings Bank* [1971] 1 LLR 114.

[179.] In *London Joint Stock Bank Ltd v Macmillan and Arthur* [1918] AC 777 at 826.

[180.] [1932] 1 KB 371.

her death no action could be taken against her or her husband for her wrongs; the plaintiff was thus estopped from asserting that the cheques were forgeries.

[5.56] It should be noted though that "it is not every breach of duty, or every carelessness, which will be found an estoppel".[181] The breach must be in the transaction itself and be the proximate cause of leading the other party into that mistake. In giving the leading judgment in the Court of Appeal in *Greenwood v Martins Bank Ltd*[182] Scrutton LJ concluded [183] that:

> "while the carelessness of the Bank was a proximate cause of the Bank's loss in paying the forged cheques, it was not the proximate cause of the Bank losing its right of action against the forger. This was caused by the failure of the husband to inform the bank of the forgery till his wife was dead and the cause of action was lost."

[5.57] Thus, it should be noted that the customer's carelessness must be in the transaction itself. In *Lewes Sanitary Steam Laundry Co Ltd v Barclay & Co Ltd*[184] the customer's company secretary forged a large number of cheques. The bank alleged that the corporate customer had been negligent in failing to scrutinise its account and in appointing a secretary who had been previously guilty of forgery. The court nonetheless held the bank liable to reimburse the moneys deducted with the forged cheques as the customer's negligence was not in the transaction itself.

[5.58] A customer whose cheques are forged following the loss of his cheque book may be comforted by Parke B's statement in *Bank of Ireland v Evans' Trustees*:[185]

> "If a man should lose his cheque book, or neglect to lock the desk in which it is kept, and a servant or stranger should take it up, it is impossible in our opinion to contend that a banker paying his forged cheque would be entitled to charge his customer with that payment".

[5.59] Furthermore, in *Kepitigalla Rubber Estates Ltd v National Bank of India Ltd*[186] Bray J indicated that he could find no authority for the proposition that a customer must, in the course of carrying on his business, take reasonable precautions to prevent his servants from forging his signature, or, if the customer be a company, the directors must take reasonable precautions to prevent the company's servants from forging their signatures.

---

181. *Ibid per* Scrutton LJ at 381.
182. [1932] 1 KB 371.
183. *Ibid* at 384.
184. (1906) 95 LT 444.
185. (1855) 5 HLC 389 at 410.
186. [1909] 2 KB 1010.

Checking Bank Statements

[5.60] While a customer is under a duty to inform his banker of unauthorised payments from his account once he becomes aware of such payments, he is not under a duty to check his bank statements.[187] In *Tai Hing Cotton Mill Ltd v Liu Chong Hing Bank Ltd*,[188] the bank agreed to send its customer, a Hong Kong textile manufacturer, periodic statements which were deemed to be confirmed unless the customer notified the bank of any error within a certain time period. An employee of the customer presented forged cheques to the bank who honoured such cheques. The Court of Appeal of Hong Kong held that the customer was estopped by its own negligence from challenging the correctness of the bank statements. However, the Privy Council overruled the Appeal Court's decision and held that:[189]

> "The customer's duty in relation to forged cheques is ... twofold: he must exercise due care in drawing his cheques so as not to facilitate fraud or forgery and he must inform his bank at once of any unauthorised cheques of which he becomes aware."

Rule 13 of the bank's rules and regulations which governed the operation of its customers' accounts stated:

> "A statement of the customer's account will be rendered once a month. Customers are desired:(1) to examine all entries in the statement of account and to report at once to the bank any error found therein, (2) to return the confirmation slip duly signed. In the absence of any objection to the statement within seven days after its receipt by the customer, the account shall be deemed to have been confirmed."

No confirmation slips were sent to the customer and the customer never sent any confirmation or acknowledgment to the bank.

The Privy Council were quite clear that Rule 13 was insufficient to bind the customer - they held:[190]

> "If banks wish to impose on their customers an express obligation to examine their monthly statements and to make those statements, in the absence of query, unchallengeable by the customer after expiry of a time limit, the burden of the obligation and of the sanction imposed must be brought home to the customer ...

---

[187] See *Chatterton v London & County Banking Co Ltd* (1891) 10 LDAB 560 and *Kepitigalla Rubber Estates Ltd v National Bank of India Ltd* [1909] 2 KB 1010.

[188] [1985] 2 All ER 947.

[189] *Ibid* at 958.

[190] *Ibid* at 959 "the court was not leaning over backwards to be helpful to the bank in its view of the duties of the customer to the bank" - Fidler Nov 1986 1 FLR 29.

It must be borne in mind that, ... the true nature of the obligations of the customer to his bank where there is no express agreement is limited to the *Macmillan* and *Greenwood* duties. Clear and unambiguous provision is needed if the banks are to introduce into the contract a binding obligation on the customer who does not query his bank statement to accept the statement as accurately setting out the debit items in the accounts."

[5.61] It appears, however, that where a customer does check his bank statement and fails to notify his bank that cheques have been drawn in breach of his mandate, the customer will be estopped from claiming repayment as he will be deemed to have represented that the cheques were validly drawn (the bank thereby being deprived of the possibility of recovering the sums drawn from the fraudster).[191]

Assessing Liability for Loss

[5.62] The first problem for a banker/customer and their respective lawyers when a cheque has been forged and paid by the banker, without detecting the forged signature, will be to ascertain whether the customer was careless, and if so, whether the carelessness was such as to give rise to him being unable to require the banker to put him in funds for the amount paid.

The principal guidance may be obtained from the House of Lords decision prior to the Treaty[192] in *London Joint Stock Bank Ltd v Macmillan and Arthur.*[193] In that case a clerk in a firm had a cheque signed by a partner with the amount in words left blank with 2.0.0 in figures. There was a sufficient gap either side of the 2 to enable him to insert 1 prior to the 2 and 0 after it. He wrote in one hundred and twenty pounds and disappeared with the money. The House of Lords unanimously overruled the Court of Appeal and held that:

1. The firm had been guilty of a breach of the special duty arising from the relation of banker and customer to take care in the mode of drawing the cheque;

2. The alteration in the amount of the cheque was the direct result of that breach of duty;

3. The bank was therefore entitled to debit the firm's account with the full amount of the cheque.

Appropriate guidelines can be gleaned from the Finlay LC's judgment:[194]

[191.] See *London Intercontinental Trust Ltd v Barclays Bank Ltd* [1980] 1 Lloyds Rep 241.
[192.] *The Articles of Agreement for a Treaty between Great Britain and Ireland* (6th December 1921).
[193.] [1918] AC 777.
[194.] *Ibid* at 789.

"The relation between banker and customer is that of debtor and creditor, with a superadded obligation on the part of the banker to honour the customer's cheques if the account is in credit. A cheque drawn by a customer is in point of law a mandate to the banker to pay the amount according to the tenor of the cheque. It is beyond dispute that the customer is bound to exercise reasonable care in drawing the cheque to prevent the banker being misled. If he draws the cheque in a manner which facilitates fraud, he is guilty of a breach of duty as between himself and the banker, and he will be responsible to the banker for any loss sustained by the banker as a natural and direct consequence of this breach of duty ...

As the customer and the banker are under a contractual relation in this matter, it appears obvious that in drawing a cheque the customer is bound to take usual and reasonable precautions to prevent forgery ... If the cheque is drawn in such a way as to facilitate or almost to invite an increase in the amount by forgery if the cheque should get into the hands of a dishonest person, forgery is not a remote but a very natural consequence of negligence of this description ...

The duty which the customer owes to the bank is to draw the cheques with reasonable care to prevent forgery, and if, owing to neglect of this duty, forgery takes place, the customer is liable to the bank for the loss ...

Of course the negligence must be in the transaction itself, that is, in the manner in which the cheque is drawn. It would be no defence to the bankers, if the forgery had been that of a clerk of a customer, that the latter had taken the clerk into his service without sufficient inquiry as to his character ...

... in the case of banker and customer, the manner in which the cheque is to be filled up is entirely in the hands of the customer, and if he leaves unusual blank spaces which facilitate forgery,... there is negligence as between him and the banker ...

If the customer chooses to dispense with ordinary precautions because he has complete faith in his clerk's honesty, he cannot claim to throw upon the banker the loss which results. ... it is a very simple thing in drawing a cheque to take reasonable and ordinary precautions against forgery. If owing to the neglect of such precautions it is put into the power of any dishonest person to increase the amount by forgery, the customer must bear the loss as between himself and the banker. ... further it is well-settled law that if a customer signs a cheque in blank and leaves it to a clerk or other person to fill it up, he is bound by the instrument as filled up by his agent ...."

[5.63] In drawing a cheque where a gap is left between the words "Pay" and the name of the payee which facilitates the insertion of another name or initials, the drawer may have his damages reduced by virtue of his contributory negligence.[195] However, it appears that a customer who leaves gaps between the name of the payee and the words "or order" is not negligent.[196]

[5.64] A possible defence for a bank which has honoured a forged cheque is estoppel. An example of the application of this principle can be seen from the facts of *Brown v Westminster Bank Ltd.*[197] In that case an 86 year old widow sued the bank for honouring cheques forged by her servants. However, for some years successive bank managers had their suspicions and brought to the plaintiff's attention their suspicions - the widow had stated that she was satisfied that her statement of account was correct. The court held that the widow was estopped from denying her representations and debarred from setting up true facts as to cheques already forged and as to future cheques forged in a similar manner; the bank had acted to their detriment in paying the cheques as a result of the widow's statement and her silence. In considering the application of estoppel, Roskill J applied the words of Lord Tomlin when he upheld the Court of Appeal's decision in *Greenwood v Martins Bank Ltd*[198] where he said:[199]

> "The essential factors giving rise to an estoppel are I think:
>
> 1. A representation or conduct amounting to a representation intended to induce a course of conduct on the part of the person to whom the representation is made.
>
> 2. An act or omission resulting from the representation, whether actual or by conduct, by the person to whom the representation is made.
>
> 3. Detriment to such person as a consequence of the act or omission.
>
> Mere silence cannot amount to a representation, but when there is a duty to disclose deliberate silence may become significant and amount to a representation."

Roskill J held that each of the three principles of estoppel applied to the facts of the *Brown* case.

Recovery of Forged Cheque Payment

[5.65] A paying banker who has honoured a forged cheque may be in a position to recover payment on the grounds that it made the payment on mistake of fact. In *National Westminster Bank Ltd v Barclays Bank International Ltd*[200] the paying bank having honoured a cheque which had been forged skilfully was able to recover payment from the payee on the grounds of mistake of fact

---

[195.] See *Lumsden & Co v London Trustee Savings Bank* [1971] 1 LLR 114.

[196.] See *Slingsby v District Bank Ltd* [1932] 1 KB 544.

[197.] [1964] 2 LLR 187.

[198.] [1933] AC 51.

[199.] *Ibid* at 57.

[200.] [1974] 3 All ER 834; see also para **[6.11]**.

notwithstanding that the payee had acted to his detriment in reliance on the payment having been made. However, the moneys were still in the payee's account with the collecting bank and it seems if the moneys had been disbursed recovery would not have been possible.

5. TRAVELLERS' CHEQUES

Duty of Care by Customer

[5.66] A travellers' cheque is not at the time it is issued to a customer a cheque within the meaning of the Cheques Act, 1959.[201] It is however a safer method for persons travelling to have disposable purchasing power without the necessity and greater risk of carrying cash. However, as it is common for the customer to sign his name initially on the cheques, before signing again at the time of encashment, they are more readily open to being fraudulently used for the enrichment of the thief. Accordingly, banks or other issuers of travellers' cheques are more vigilant in requiring a strict contractual duty of care on the part of the customer than is otherwise applied for cheques.

[5.67] In *Braithwaite v Thomas Cook Travellers Cheques Ltd*[202] the customer purchased £50,000 worth of travellers' cheques on condition that he "properly safeguarded each cheque against loss or theft". He placed the cheques in a transparent plastic bag and fell asleep in a London Underground train (following a drinking session with friends), during which time the bag was stolen. The court held that the onus of proof was on the customer to show that he had "properly safeguarded" the cheques and that his conduct contributed to the loss and was causative of it. Accordingly, he could not claim against the defendant for the cheques cashed.

[5.68] The absence of a clear contractual obligation to safeguard travellers' cheques will expose the issuer of such cheques to liability for his loss even where the loss of the cheques has arisen from the customer's negligence. This is the effect of the decision in *Elawadi v Bank of Credit and Commerce International SA*.[203] In that case, the customer having purchased £50,000 worth of travellers cheques left them in a plastic bag on the back seat of his unlocked and unattended car overnight. Hutchison J stated:[204]

[201.] See further *Chitty on Contracts* (26th ed) paras 2841-2850; Milnes Holden, *The Law and Practice of Banking* Vol 1 (5th ed, 1991) paras 4-11-4-11B.

[202.] [1989] 1 All ER 235.

[203.] [1989] 1 All ER 242.

[204.] *Ibid* at 247.

> "It seems to me that it is an inescapable conclusion that, in his dealing with these cheques, he [the customer] was guilty of the most serious negligence and it was that singular want of care that led to their being stolen."

He held nevertheless that there was either an express or implied term that the bank would give the customer a refund and that there was no implied term precluding the customer recovering "where the loss of the cheques had resulted from his want of care or recklessness."

6. COLLECTING BANKER'S DUTIES

Duties of a Collecting Banker

> "The duties of a collecting banker are to present cheques drawn upon another branch or on another bank for payment as promptly as possible and to credit the person who has lodged the cheque with the proceeds when they are received."[205]

[5.69] It can be seen from the foregoing quotation that the term "collecting banker" denotes a bank which collects payment of cheques lodged with it drawn in favour of its customer.[206] It seems clear that the collecting bank's duty is not only to present cheques for payment to the paying banker promptly but to take whatever further steps may be proper to obtain payment for his customer.[207]

[5.70] The framework within which a cheque collected by a bank is presented for payment by that collecting bank on behalf of the payee, its customer, to the drawer's bank, the paying bank is encompassed in the Bills of Exchange Act, 1882.

Section 45(2) deals with the presentation of a cheque:

> Where the bill is payable on demand, ... presentation must be made within a reasonable time after its issue in order to render the drawer liable ... In determining what is a reasonable time, regard shall be had to the nature of the bill, the usage of trade with regard to similar bills, and the facts of the particular case.

[205.] Kenny J in *Dublin Port and Docks Board v The Governor and Company of the Bank of Ireland* [1976] IR 118 at 142; cited also by O'Hanlon J in *Towey v Ulster Bank Ltd* [1987] ILRM 142 at 150.

[206.] For further consideration of the role of the collecting banker see O'Connor, *The Law and Practice in Ireland Relating to Cheques and Analogous Instruments* (1993) Ch XI.

[207.] See the remarks of Murphy J in *Brennan v The Governor and Company of the Bank of Ireland* High Court, unrep, 23 May 1985 pp 11-13 cited by O'Hanlon J in *Towey v Ulster Bank Ltd* [1987] ILRM 142 at 152; see also Lavery J in *The Royal Bank of Ireland Ltd v O'Rourke* [1962] IR 159 at 178.

It has become the accepted practice for cheques to be presented for payment through the clearing system.[208] In *Brennan v The Governor and Company of the Bank of Ireland*[209] Murphy J said:[210]

"... the clearing house system ... originated as an informal meeting place where the messengers concerned exchanged cheques and settled the difference between the total exchanged. It is now well settled law that the engagement by a customer of a bank to carry out financial transactions on his behalf impliedly authorises the bank to adopt the established commercial usage. That usage includes resort to the clearing house system."[211]

The presentation of a cheque by a collecting bank to a paying bank follows from sub-s (3) of s 45:

Presentation must be made by the holder or by some person authorised to receive payment on his behalf ... either to the person designated by the bill as payer, or to some person authorised to pay or refuse payment on his behalf if with the exercise of reasonable diligence such person can there be found.

Accordingly, the handing over of a cheque by the collecting bank to the paying bank in a clearing house is a presentation for payment and the paying bank then has a duty to honour or dishonour it.[212]

On the question of presenting cheques promptly, cheques should be presented to the paying bank by the collecting bank no later than the day following receipt.[213] More recently, the transmission of information through electronic means has been recognised by the additional rules as to the presentation of cheques which apply by virtue of s 45A of the Bills of Exchange Act, 1882.[214]

[5.71] A collecting bank's principal concern when collecting a cheque, on behalf of its customer, is to ensure that the cheque is owned by its customer and not by a third party.[215] By collecting a cheque which is not the property of its

---

[208] For a detailed analysis of the clearing procedure and the application of s 45 of the Bills of Exchange Act, 1882 to it see Bingham J in *Barclays Bank plc v Bank of England* [1985] 1 All ER 385.

[209] High Court, unrep, 23 May 1985.

[210] *Ibid* at p 22.

[211] The reference by Murphy J to "an informal meeting place" was no doubt reference to the early practice in London of meeting on street corners and subsequently in a public house - see Holden, *History of Negotiable Instruments in English Law* (1955) pp 214-215; however in Ireland the first clearing system seems to have been operated in the Bank of Ireland's premises at College Green - see Hall, *History of the Bank of Ireland* (1949) p 212-213.

[212] See Lavery J in *The Royal Bank of Ireland Ltd v O'Rourke* [1962] IR 159 at 177.

[213] See Lavery J, *ibid* at 176 applying *Hare v Henty* 10 CBNS 65.

[214] As introduced by s 132(1)(c) of the Central Bank Act, 1989.

[215] A cheque drawn by a company in favour of a fictitious person and endorsed to the collecting bank's customer is the property of the drawer - see *Carpenters' Co v British Mutual Banking Co Ltd* [1937] 3 All ER 811.

customer the bank is running the risk of the true owner, or the person entitled to immediate possession,[216] of the cheque seeking recovery from the bank in damages for conversion or for money had and received.[217] The potential liability and predicament for a banker have been clearly stated by Diplock LJ when giving judgment in the English Court of Appeal;[218] he said:[219]

> "A banker's business, of its very nature, exposes him daily to this peril. His contract with his customer requires him to accept possession of cheques delivered to him by his customer, to present them for payment to the banks on which the cheques are drawn, to receive payment of them and to credit the amount thereof to his own customer's account, either on receipt of the cheques themselves from the customer, or on receipt of actual payment of the cheques from the banks on which they are drawn. If the customer is not entitled to the cheque which he delivers to his banker for collection, the banker, however innocent and careful he might have been, would at common law be liable to the true owner of the cheque for the amount of which he receives payment, either as damages for conversion or under the cognate cause of action, based historically on assumpsit, for money had and received."

[5.72] Although the concept of conversion[220] connotes the taking of a chattel, it applies to a collecting bank by treating the cheque as a chattel and the money received under the cheque as being the value of the converted chattel.[221] The measure of damages for conversion of a cheque is its face value.[222]

[5.73] At the time the Bills of Exchange Act was enacted in 1882 it was considered appropriate to give the collecting bank some protection. This protection was given by s 82 of that Act which provided that if the collecting bank acted "in good faith and without negligence" in the collection of a cheque which was crossed generally or specifically to itself, the banker would not incur liability to the cheque's true owner by virtue of having collected the cheque. The protection given to a bank was effectively widened in the replacement of this section by the Cheques Act, 1959, s 4(1)[223] of which states:

[216.] See McNair J in *Marquess of Bute v Barclays Bank Ltd* [1954] 3 All ER 365.
[217.] See *Bavins, Jim and Sims v The London and South Western Bank* [1900] 1 QB 270; *Marquess of Bute v Barclays Bank Ltd* [1954] 3 All ER 365.
[218.] In *Marfani & Co Ltd v Midland Bank Ltd* [1968] 2 All ER 573.
[219.] *Ibid* at 578.
[220.] For a further explanation of conversion as applying to cheques see Richardson's *Guide to Negotiable Instruments* (8th ed) para 14.4.
[221.] See explanation of Scrutton LJ in *Lloyds Bank Ltd v The Chartered Bank of India, Australia and China* [1929] 1 KB 40 at 55.
[222.] *Morison v London County and Westminster Bank Ltd* [1914] 3 KB 356; *Carpenters' Co v British Mutual Banking Co Ltd* [1937] 3 All ER 811.
[223.] In conjunction with s 4(2)(a).

Where a banker, in good faith and without negligence, -

(a) receives payment for a customer of [a cheque]; or

(b) having credited a customer's account with the amount of such [cheque], receives payment thereof for himself;

and the customer has no title, or a defective title, to the [cheque] the banker does not incur any liability to the true owner of the [cheque] by reason only of having received payment thereof.

The protection is given also in respect of cheques made payable to "cash".[224]

Thus to obtain protection the banker needs to act in good faith and without negligence and to receive payment for a customer[225] (or credit a customer's account or receive payment for itself).

Collecting Banker Must Act "In Good Faith"

[5.74] Although the Bills of Exchange Act, 1882 provides that,[226] "A thing is deemed to be done in good faith ... where it is in fact done honestly, whether it is done negligently or not," a collecting banker should be mindful of the words of Lord Herschell in *The London Joint Stock Bank v Simmons*:[227]

> "... regard to the facts of which the taker of [negotiable] instruments had notice is most material in considering whether he took in good faith. If there be anything which excites the suspicion that there is something wrong in the transaction, the taker of the instrument is not acting in good faith if he shuts his eyes to the facts presented to him and puts the suspicions aside without further inquiry."

Collecting Banker Must Collect "Without Negligence"

[5.75] A banker, acting in good faith, who collects on a cheque for its customer[228] and credits its customer's account will be able to escape liability, for having received, where its customer was not entitled to the cheque if it acted "without negligence". The onus is on the banker to prove that it acted without negligence.[229] Conversion of a cheque following non-compliance with the collecting bank's internal regulations will not necessarily mean that the bank has been negligent (as the regulation may be excessively cautious), but it will be "a

---

[224.] See *Orbit Mining and Trading Co Ltd v Westminster Bank Ltd* [1962] 3 All ER 565; see para **[5.05]** above.

[225.] As to the meaning of "customer" see para **[1.09]**.

[226.] Section 90.

[227.] [1892] AC 201 at 221.

[228.] For what constitutes a "customer" see para **[1.09]**.

[229.] See Lord Wright in *Lloyds Bank Ltd v EB Savory and Co* [1933] AC 201 at 233; Diplock LJ in *Marfani & Co Ltd v Midland Bank Ltd* [1968] 2 All ER 573 and 581; Hutton J in *Prescott Meat Company Ltd v Northern Bank Ltd* [1981] NI 150 at 168.

strong *prima facie* ground for holding that the bank had not acted without negligence."[230]

There is a line of authority to the effect that a collecting banker will be deemed to have acted without negligence where it has followed the current or usual practice of bankers in collecting cheques. The principal common law decisions on the test of negligence for a collecting banker have come from the courts in London - in the Court of Appeal,[231] "this is to be judged by the practice of careful bankers", in the Privy Council,[232] "it must be the standard to be derived from the ordinary practice of bankers", and in the House of Lords,[233] "The standard by which the absence, or otherwise, of negligence is to be determined must be ascertained by reference to the practice of reasonable men carrying on the business of bankers."

[5.76] A stricter approach was applied in *EB Savory and Co v Lloyds Bank Ltd*[234] by Lawrence LJ when he stated in his Court of Appeal judgment:[235]

"In my opinion, bankers who have disregarded their statutory duty towards the true owner of the cheques collected by them for a customer cannot, when challenged by the true owner, successfully plead that they have acted without negligence in his case because for a long time they and other bankers have acted in disregard of their statutory duty in other cases. To allow such a plea would be to hold that if a negligent act were repeated sufficiently often, it would cease to be negligent and become careful."

In the House of Lords in the same case Lord Wright stated:[236]

"It is argued that ... a bank is not negligent if it takes all precautions usually taken by bankers. I do not accept that latter proposition as true in cases where the ordinary practice of bankers fails in making due provision for a risk fully known to those experienced in the business of banking".

This approach would mean that if a collecting bank follows the usual and common practice of bankers it should not be regarded as having acted without negligence if the practice had an inherent defect, resulting in the conversion of the cheque, which ought to have been obvious to any person giving the matter due consideration.[237] It should not be forgotten that the collecting banker is

[230.] See Lawrence LJ in *EB Savory and Co v Lloyds Bank Ltd* [1932] 2 KB 122 at 138.
[231.] Diplock LJ in *Marfani & Co Ltd v Midland Bank Ltd* [1968] 2 All ER 573 at 581.
[232.] Lord Dunedin in *Commissioners of Taxation v English, Scottish and Australian Bank Ltd* [1920] AC 683 at 689.
[233.] Lord Warrington in *Lloyds Bank Ltd v EB Savory and Co* [1933] AC 201 at 221.
[234.] [1932] 2 KB 122.
[235.] *Ibid* at 144.
[236.] *Lloyds Bank Ltd v EB Savory and Co* [1933] AC 201 at 232.
[237.] See *Roche and Roche v Pielow and Pielow* [1985] IR 232.

supplying a service and accordingly is obliged to carry out that service "with due skill, care and diligence".[238] The situations where a collecting banker would be deemed not to have acted without negligence are numerous and varied.[239]

[5.77] In practice, a bank relies on the protection given to it by s 4 of the Cheques Act, 1959 where, having collected for its customer a cheque belonging to a third party, its customer withdraws the proceeds and moves out of the jurisdiction or becomes otherwise inaccessible. To minimise this risk, a banker, before opening an account for a prospective customer, will endeavour to satisfy itself that its prospective account holder is trustworthy. It will do this either by obtaining references from the prospective customer's employer or previous banker or as a result of an introduction by another trustworthy customer. [240]

[5.78] The importance for a banker to obtain a reference prior to collecting monies for a new customer can be seen from Lord Wright's judgment in the House of Lords in *Lloyds Bank Ltd v EB Savory and Co* when he said:[241]

> "There may ... be relevant negligence in connection with the opening of the customer's account by the banker. It is now recognised to be the usual practice of bankers not to open an account for a customer without obtaining a reference and without inquiry as to the customer's standing; a failure to do so at the opening of the account might well prevent the banker from establishing his defence [under s 4] if a cheque were converted subsequently in the history of the account."

Clearly references obtained by a banker should be checked with the source of the reference. Failure to check references opens up the possibility of the prospective customer writing his own reference as happened in *Nu-Stilo Footwear Ltd v Lloyds Bank Ltd.*[242]

[5.79] A banker who obtains a reference in respect of a prospective customer may nonetheless be unable to show that it acted without negligence if it did not also enquire as to the prospective customer's employer.[243] In the principal House of Lords' judgment in *Lloyds Bank Ltd v EB Savory and Co*[244] Lord Wright stated:[245]

---

238. See Sale of Goods and Supply of Services Act, 1980, s 39.
239. See further para **[5.79]**; see also a helpful list in para 11.94 of O'Connor, *The Law and Practice in Ireland relating to Cheques and Analogous Instruments* (1993).
240. See further O'Connor, *op cit*, para 11.53.
241. [1933] AC 201 at 231.
242. (1956) 7 LDAB 121 see para **[4.09]**; see also *Guardians of St John, Hampstead v Barclays Bank Ltd* 39 TLR 229.
243. See *Lloyds Bank Ltd v EB Savory and Co* [1933] AC 201.
244. [1933] AC 201.
245. *Ibid* at 233.

".... a reference or introduction merely speaks to the general reputation of the man: knowledge of who are his employers is aimed at an entirely different purpose, that is to arm the Bank against the known, even if problematical, risk: it is unfortunately common knowledge that persons of respectability, well introduced, may still commit frauds."

The "risk" to which Lord Wright referred is the danger that the bank's customer may present to his banker for collection cheques drawn in favour of his employer but fraudulently endorsed in his favour or indeed his employer's cheques drawn fraudulently in his favour. Examples of such occurrences resulting in successful claims against the collecting banker for failing to act without negligence are prolific.[246] Bankers have suffered also where a director has lodged company cheques to his own account[247] and where a partner has lodged partnership cheques to his own account.[248]

[5.80] The hard approach adopted by Lawrence LJ and Lord Wright[249] in the case of *Lloyds Bank Ltd v EB Savory and Co*[250] has been softened by two English Court of Appeal decisions in the 1960s. In *Orbit Mining & Trading Co Ltd v Westminster Bank Ltd*[251] where a director used company cheques for his own purposes the English Court of Appeal allowed an appeal by the bank in holding that they had discharged the onus of proving that they had acted without negligence as it was the practice of banks to pay on cheques drawn in a certain manner.[252] Harman LJ quoted Lord Dunedin in *Commissioners of Taxation v English, Scottish and Australian Bank*:[253]

"It is not a question of negligence in opening the account, though the circumstances connected with the opening of an account may shed light on the question of whether there was negligence in collecting a cheque."[254]

---

246. See *Bissell & Co v Fox Brothers & Co* 53 LTR 193; *Morison v London County and Westminster Bank Ltd* [1914] 3 KB 356; *Harding v London Joint Stock Bank Ltd* (1914) 3 LDAB 81; *Lloyds Bank Ltd v The Chartered Bank of India, Australia and China* [1929] 1 KB 40; *Lloyds Bank Ltd v EB Savory and Co* [1933] AC 201; *Carpenters' Co v British Mutual Banking Co Ltd* [1937] 3 All ER 811; *Nu-Stilo Footwear Ltd v Lloyds Bank Ltd* (1956) 7 LDAB 121.

247. See *AL Underwood, Ltd v The Bank of Liverpool and Martins Ltd* [1924] 1 KB 775.

248. See *Baker v Barclays Bank Ltd* [1955] 2 All ER 571 (where it was held that the bank manager had not made sufficient enquiry).

249. See para **[5.76]** above.

250. [1933] AC 201.

251. [1962] 3 All ER 565.

252. Pay cash or order on a crossed cheque.

253. [1920] AC 683 at 688.

254. This passage used by Harman LJ has been described as "inconsistent with the other authorities and cannot be implicitly relied upon" - see editorial note of Sir John Paget in 3 LDAB at 82.

Harman LJ went on to state that,[255] "It cannot at any rate be the duty of the bank continually to keep itself up to date as to the identity of a customer's employer." However, in view of the more recent concern applicable to moneylaundering and the necessity for prospective customers to produce identification in opening bank accounts,[256] a bank is likely to face a stiff task in discharging the onus of proving that it acted without negligence if an account is opened without appropriate enquiries having been made and satisfactory answers verified.

[5.81] In *Marfani & Co Ltd v Midland Bank Ltd*[257] references were given at the time an account was opened, one referee indicating that he had known the prospective customer "for some time" which if enquiries had been made would have resulted in the disclosure that "for some time" meant one month. It was held that the bank was protected by s 4 of the English Cheques Act 1957 (identical to s 4 of the Cheques Act, 1959) as the bank had acted in accordance with the current practice of bankers and thereby discharged the onus of proving they acted without negligence. Diplock LJ stated that,[258] "this court should be hesitant before condemning as negligent a practice generally adopted by those engaged in banking business."

[5.82] More recently, the approach in *Marfani & Co Ltd v Midland Bank Ltd*[259] was adopted in *Shield Life Insurance Co Ltd and O'Callaghan v Ulster Bank Ltd*.[260] The President of the High Court held that the true owner of a cheque, which has been credited to another account, is entitled to damages for conversion against the collecting bank unless the collecting bank can establish that "it took reasonable care that its customer's title to the cheque was not defective." In elaborating on the test to be applied, Costello P indicated: [261]

> "What facts are sufficient to cause a bank reasonably to suspect that its customer is not the true owner of the cheque depends on current banking practice. All the circumstances surrounding the transaction including past circumstances may be relevant.
>
> Each case must ultimately depend on its own facts. But there may be special circumstances in a case which affect the banker's duty of care to which the banker should pay particular regard. Those special circumstances may include, as in this case, a situation in which a customer maintains two accounts, an office account and a clients' account, and in which it is clear that the customer is holding money in an account as a trustee. Previous movements in and out of

---

[255.] [1962] 3 All ER 565 at 579.
[256.] See paras **[4.01]-[4.07]**.
[257.] [1968] 2 All ER 573.
[258.] *Ibid* at 581.
[259.] [1968] 2 All ER 573.
[260.] [1995] 3 IR 225.
[261.] *Ibid* at 238.

that account by the customer which may suggest that it is not being operated in a manner consistent with the customer's duty as a trustee may be relevant in considering the bank's duty in relation to the payment into a clients' account of a cheque which has been irregularly indorsed."

Collection of Cheque Crossed "Account Payee"

[5.83] The crossing of a cheque "account payee", "account payee only" or "account of payee" is done by the drawer of the cheque to ensure that (subject to any contrary instructions) it is credited only to the payee's account;[262] as such it is a direction from the drawer to the collecting bank that the proceeds of the cheque are to be credited to the payee's account with the collecting bank.[263] The duty imposed on the collecting bank by the drawer's crossing in the foregoing manner is to ensure that the payee is not defrauded.[264] Thus, unless there are particular circumstances which would justify a contrary decision,[265] a bank may not be deemed to have collected a cheque without negligence[266] where it credits the proceeds of a cheque to an account contrary to the specific direction of the drawer.[267] Confirmation of this can be seen from the Privy Council's advice in *Universal Guarantee Pty Ltd v National Bank of Australasia Ltd*[268] where it was indicated that:[269]

> "The addition of the words "a/c payee" or "a/c payee only" ... operate as a warning to the collecting bank that if it pays the proceeds of the cheque to some other account it is put on inquiry and it may be in difficulty in relying on any defence under ... the Act in an action against it for conversion of the cheque."

[5.84] This could raise a problem for a person without a bank account who receives a cheque crossed "account payee". A suggested solution to this difficulty was indicated by Atkin LJ as follows:[270]

---

262. For the background to, and further treatment of, this crossing see O'Connor, *The Law and Practice in Ireland Relating to Cheques and Analogous Instruments* (1993) para 11.77-11.81.

263. See the judgment of Channell J in *Bevan v The National Bank Ltd* 23 TLR 65; see also Bigham J in *Akrokerri (Atlantic) Mines Ltd v Economic Bank* [1904] 2 KB 465 at 472.

264. See *Kenton v Barclays Bank Ltd* (1977) referred to by Chorley & Smart in *Leading Cases in the Law of Banking* (6th ed) p 186-7.

265. As in *Bevan v The National Bank Ltd* 23 TLR 65 where Wade had been regarded as the only partner in *Malcolm Wade and Co*.

266. And thus be unable to rely on the protection given to collecting banks by s 4 of the Cheques Act, 1959.

267. See *House Property Company of London Ltd v The London County and Westminster Bank Ltd* 31 TLR 479.

268. [1965] 2 All ER 98.

269. *Ibid* at 102.

270. In *Importers Company Ltd v Westminster Bank Ltd* [1927] 2 KB 297 at 309.

"... cheques are occasionally drawn marked "Account payee" and sent to a person who has no banking account. I do not agree that those cheques are of no value to that person. I see no reason why such a person should not request some one who has a banking account to present and get the cheque cleared for him. I agree that there is a duty upon the bank which takes a cheque in those circumstances to see that, in fact, they are collecting the money for the account of the payee, and that the proceeds, when received, will go to the payee."

Collection of Cheque Crossed "Not Negotiable"

[5.85] As already indicated, a person taking a crossed cheque marked "not negotiable" cannot have a better title to the cheque than the person from whom he took it.[271] The question may arise whether a bank which collects for its customer a cheque marked "not negotiable" is liable in negligence to the true owner (not being its customer). This question was addressed by Costello P in *Shield Life Insurance Co Ltd and O'Callaghan v Ulster Bank Ltd*[272] where he held:[273]

"The acceptance from a person other than the payee of a crossed non-negotiable cheque without making enquiries is not in itself conclusive evidence of negligence on the part of a banker should the payee have been defrauded. It is, however, a matter to be taken into consideration together with all the other relevant circumstances when deciding whether the banker was guilty of breach of duty to the true owner."

Contributory Negligence

[5.86] The established English cases indicate that when a person seeks recovery from a collecting bank for the bank's conversion of the person's cheque, any negligence on the part of the claimant, such as failure to supervise an employee, will not affect his claim against the bank. In Northern Ireland it has been held[274] that the liability of a bank for failing to exercise reasonable care and skill in paying a cheque could not be reduced through any contributory negligence on the part of its customer as the bank's duty was a contractual duty and the doctrine of contributory negligence did not apply to a breach of contract. However, in *Lumsden & Co v London Trustee Savings Bank*,[275] the plaintiff had its award reduced by ten per cent for its contributory negligence in the manner in which it drew cheques. With the exception of this case, the English approach has been that a bank which commits an act of conversion is fully liable for the loss

---

271. Bills of Exchange Act, 1882, s 81; see paras **[5.46]-[5.48]** above.
272. [1995] 3 IR 225.
273. *Ibid* at 242.
274. In *Prescott Meat Co Ltd v Northern Bank Ltd* [1981] NI 150.
275. [1971] 1 LLR 114.

suffered by the true owner notwithstanding any lack of care on the part of the owner giving rise to such loss.

[5.87] In Ireland the bank's defence of contributory negligence on the part of the owner may result in a diminution of any award. This is made possible through the Civil Liability Act, 1961,[276] s 34 of which states, *inter alia*:

> (1)   Where, in any action brought by one person in respect of a wrong committed by any other person, it is proved that the damage suffered by the plaintiff was caused partly by the negligence or want of care of the plaintiff or of one for whose acts he is responsible (in this Part called contributory negligence) and partly by the wrong of the defendant, the damages recoverable in respect of the said wrong shall be reduced by such amount as the court thinks just and equitable having regard to the degrees of fault of the plaintiff and defendant ...
>
> (2)(d) the plaintiff's failure to exercise reasonable care in the protection of his own property shall, except to the extent that the defendant has been unjustly enriched, be deemed to be contributory negligence in an action for conversion of the property.

The application of this section will obviously depend upon the facts of a case brought before the courts, but the reference in sub-s (1) to applying to "a wrong" seems to indicate that it would apply to all wrongs including a wrong, such as conversion, for which there was no defence on the grounds of lack of care on the part of the owner.[277] However, the Act will not assist a bank, in its defence, where it is unable to prove contributory negligence on the part of the plaintiff.[278]

[276.] No 41 of 1961.

[277.] See Lord Wright in *Lloyds Bank Ltd v EB Savory and Co* [1933] AC 201 at 229.

[278.] See *Shield Life Insurance Co Ltd and O'Callaghan v Ulster Bank Ltd* [1995] 3 IR 225 at 240.

Chapter 6

Payments by Bankers

1. Payments by Mistake

Mistaken Payments

"The general rule is usually stated to be that where money is paid under the influence of a mistake, and the mistake is one of fact, an action will lie to recover it back; but that to entitle the plaintiff to recover, the mistake upon which he has acted must be one of fact, not of law."[1]

[6.01] This statement however is just a starting point and any suggestion that it is simply a matter of distinguishing a mistake of fact from a mistake of law is shaken by Kenny J's opening remarks in the same Supreme Court decision (which was unanimous) as that containing the above quotation. In his judgment Kenny J, after reciting the facts, began by saying: "The aphorism 'money paid under a mistake of fact may be recovered but money paid under a mistake of law cannot' is grossly inadequate."[2]

[6.02] The common law development of money paid by mistake was reviewed by Budd J in *The National Bank Ltd v O'Connor and Bowmaker (Ireland) Ltd*.[3] Budd J referred first to *Kelly v Solari*[4] under which Parke B stated[5] the relevant law to be:

"that where money is paid to another under the influence of a mistake, that is, upon the supposition that a specific fact is true, which would entitle the other to the money, but which fact is untrue, and the money would not have been paid if it had been known to the payer that the fact was untrue, an action will lie to recover it back, and it is against conscience to retain it."

Thus, negligence on the part of the plaintiff does not preclude recovery. In considering the House of Lords' decision in *RE Jones Ltd v Waring and Gillow Ltd*[6] Budd J said:[7]

[1.] Griffin J in *Rogers v Louth County Council* [1981] IR 265 at 270; [1981] ILRM 144 at 146.
[2.] *Ibid* at 273 and 148 respectively.
[3.] (1969) 103 ILTR 73.
[4.] (1841) 9 M & W 54.
[5.] *Ibid* at 58.
[6.] [1926] AC 670.
[7.] (1969) 103 ILTR 73 at 93.

"The decision is on my understanding of it, an authority for the proposition that when payment is made to a person, because of a supposed obligation to pay someone, induced by the frauds of another, and because it is believed that payment to that person is appropriate and suitable or will discharge the supposed obligation, and there is no obligation, the money paid may be recovered as paid under a mistake of fact."

[6.03] It is not necessary however that the mistake should actually be "induced by the frauds of another" provided the mistake is one as to liability to pay. Budd J[8] deduces this from the decision in *Barclay and Co Ltd v Malcolm and Co.*[9] Although there is some doubt as to whether this decision is good law, at least in England,[10] it is nonetheless one which banks in particular should take note of in their daily practice. The facts of the case were that a Polish company instructed the Bank of Warsaw to pay the defendants £2,000. The bank telegraphed its London agents, the plaintiffs, to pay the defendants, which they did. The bank then sent a letter confirming the telegram. The plaintiffs made a further payment of £2,000 (having failed to notice the letter confirmed the earlier telegram). The Court held that as the mistake was not due to the defendants and as it was not a mistake with regard to the liability of one person to pay, the defendants should be permitted to keep the money. Accordingly, although there is some doubt as to whether this decision would be applied today,[11] banks when receiving letters of instructions to transfer funds should take care to see that such funds have not already been transferred on foot of earlier telexed or faxed instructions.

[6.04] According to Budd J,[12] the decision in *Morgan v Ashcroft*[13] "supports the view that a voluntary payment does not come within the class of cases where money can be recovered as paid under a mistake of fact." In that case, the plaintiff, a bookmaker, overpaid the defendant by £24. The Court of Appeal held that in order to succeed on a claim for money paid under a mistake of fact the mistake must be fundamental and that as the plaintiff would have been under no liability to make the payment which was in law only a voluntary payment; accordingly, the claim failed.

---

8. *Ibid* at 91.
9. (1925) 133 LT 512.
10. Goff J in *Barclays Bank Ltd v WJ Simms, Son & Cooke (Southern) Ltd* [1979] 3 All ER 522 at 534; [1980] 2 WLR 218 at 231 where Goff J pointed out that the decision was made subsequent to the Court of Appeal's but prior to the House of Lords' decisions in *RE Jones Ltd v Waring and Gillow Ltd* [1926] AC 670.
11. See Budd J in *The National Bank Ltd v O'Connor and Bowmaker (Ireland) Ltd* (1969) 103 ILTR 73; see also in *Re Irish Shipping Ltd (in liq)* [1986] ILRM 518.
12. (1969) 103 ILTR 73 at 91.
13. [1938] 1 KB 49.

[6.05] After reviewing the decided cases, Budd J acknowledged that it was not easy to reconcile the decisions and accordingly it was difficult to give a precise statement as to when money is recoverable. However, he considered it could be recovered in the following circumstances:[14]

> "First where it has been proved that it has been paid under a mistake of fact (it being necessary to show that the fact supposed to be true was untrue and that the money would not have been paid if it was known that the fact was untrue). It must be a fundamental mistake ...
>
> Secondly, it must be shown that the mistake was as to a fact, which if true, would make the payer either liable or under a duty to pay the money - the mistake has not to be shown to be a mistaken belief on the part of the payer that he was under a liability to pay the payee. It is sufficient if it be shown that the payer was under a mistaken belief that he was under an obligation to pay someone and that payment to the actual payee would be appropriate and would discharge the obligation."

[6.06] The facts of *The National Bank Ltd v O'Connor and Bowmaker (Ireland) Ltd*[15] were that the plaintiff's employee issued two bank drafts in the plaintiff's Tuam branch without consideration to the first defendant. The first defendant obtained value for the drafts in the plaintiff's Athlone branch in exchange for a further draft in favour of the second defendant. The plaintiff sought recovery of the money. Budd J held that the drafts were issued from the Tuam branch under a mistake of fact and without consideration being given for them and would not have been honoured by the Athlone branch unless in the belief that the bank was liable to pay them. This mistake of fact between the plaintiff and the first defendant was a mistake *inter partes* and of a fundamental nature; thus the plaintiff was entitled to recover as money paid under a mistake of fact.

[6.07] More recently in England, Goff J considered at length the decisions concerning money paid under a mistake of fact and concluded with the following principles:[16]

> "(1) If a person pays money to another under a mistake of fact which causes him to make the payment, he is *prima facie* entitled to recover it as money paid under a mistake of fact.
>
> (2) His claim may however fail if:
>
>> (a) the payer intends that the payee shall have the money at all

---

[14.] (1969) 103 ILTR 73 at 94 where he had particular regard to the House of Lords' decision in *RE Jones Ltd v Waring and Gillow Ltd* [1926] AC 670.

[15.] (1969) 103 ILTR 73.

[16.] *Barclays Bank Ltd v WJ Simms, Son & Cooke (Southern) Ltd* [1979] 3 All ER 522 at 535; [1980] 2 WLR 218 at 232; see also an analysis of this judgment in *Butterworths Banking & Financial Law Review 1987*, Ryder, 'Mistaken Payments by Banks' 61.

events, whether the fact be true or false, or is deemed in law so
to intend;

(b) the payment is made for good consideration, in particular if
the money is paid to discharge, and does discharge, a debt
owed to the payee (or a principal on whose behalf he is
authorised to receive the payment) by the payer or by a third
party by whom he is authorised to discharge the debt;

(c) the payee has changed his position in good faith, or is deemed
in law to have done so".

Honouring Countermanded Cheques

[6.08] In *Barclays Bank Ltd v WJ Simms, Son & Cooke (Southern) Ltd*[17] a
customer of the plaintiff drew a cheque in favour of a building company to settle
a debt. Following the appointment of a receiver to the building company, the
customer instructed the plaintiff to stop payment of the cheque. However, the
cheque was paid due to a mistake by one of the plaintiff's employees. The
plaintiff brought an action for recovery of the amount paid as money paid under
a mistake of fact. The Court held that:

(1) Where a person paid money to another under a mistake of fact which
caused him to make the payment, he was *prima facie* entitled to
recover it as money paid under a mistake of fact. His claim might
however fail if:

   (i) the payer had intended that the payee should have the money
at all events (irrespective of whether the fact was true or false)
or was deemed in law to have so intended,

   (ii) the payment had been made for good consideration, and in
particular if the money had been paid to discharge, and did
discharge, a debt owed to the payee by the payer or a third
party by whom he had been authorised to discharge the debt,
or

   (iii) the payee had changed his position in good faith or was
deemed in law to have done so.

However, his claim would not fail merely because the mistake had
not been "as between" the payer and the payee or because the mistake
had not induced the payer to believe that he was liable to pay the
money to the payee.

(2) Where a bank paid, under a mistake of fact, a cheque drawn on it by
one of its customers, it was *prima facie* entitled to recover payment

---

[17.] [1979] 3 All ER 522; [1980] 2 WLR 218.

from the payee if it had acted without mandate (for example if it had overlooked a notice of countermand given by a customer) unless the payee had changed his position in good faith or was deemed in law to have done so.

(3) The plaintiff was entitled to succeed because:

    (i)   their mistake in overlooking the drawer's instructions to stop payment of the cheque had caused them to pay the cheque,

    (ii)   they had acted without mandate since the drawer had countermanded payment, and so the payment was not effective to discharge the drawer's obligation on the cheque and as a result the payee had given no consideration for the payment, and

    (iii)   there was no evidence of any actual change of position on the part of either of the defendants (notice of dishonour was not required and so the payee was not deemed to have changed his position).

[6.09] In his judgment, Goff J posed the query[18] as to the circumstances in which a bank can recover payment from a payee of its customer's cheque on the ground that it was paid under a mistake of fact.

The first situation arises where the bank pays in the mistaken belief that there are sufficient funds or overdraft facilities to meet the cheque. The effect of the bank's payment of the cheque is that, it accepts the customer's request for overdraft facilities and the payment has the same legal consequences as if the payment had been made pursuant to previously agreed overdraft facilities; the payment is made within the bank's mandate, and in particular the bank is entitled to debit the customer's account, and the bank's payment discharges the customer's obligation to the payee on the cheque (because the bank has paid the cheque with the authority of the customer).

The second situation arises where the bank overlooks or ignores a notice of countermand from the customer who has drawn the cheque. The effect of the bank's payment is that as it is made outside the terms of the mandate the bank is unable to debit the customer's account. In addition the payment will not discharge the customer's obligation (if any) to the payee, as the bank has no authority to discharge such obligation. As the bank's payment is outside the terms of its mandate, the bank cannot recover the payment from its customer. However, the customer's debt to the payee is not discharged and, *"prima facie, the bank is entitled to recover the money from the payee, unless the payee has changed his position in good faith, or is deemed in law to have done so."*[19]

[18.] *Ibid* at 539 and 235 respectively.
[19.] *Ibid* at 540 and 237 respectively.

[6.10] The question then arises as to the circumstances in which the payee has a good defence to the bank's claim to recover the money paid under a mistake of fact. The early common law indicated that the payee, on receiving payment, is deprived of the opportunity of giving notice of dishonour at the time the amount becomes due and accordingly is deemed to have changed his position; he thus has a good defence to the bank's claim. However, as Goff J pointed out[20] this has no application where notice of dishonour is not required as in the case of a simple unendorsed cheque, payment of which is countermanded by the drawer.[21]

Payment of Forged Cheques

[6.11] Payment by a bank on foot of a forged cheque is payment outside the terms of its mandate[22] and is *prima facie* recoverable as being payment by reason of mistake of fact. In *National Westminster Bank Ltd v Barclays Bank International Ltd*[23] Kerr J held that the mere fact that a banker had honoured a cheque on which his customer's signature had been undetectably forged did not carry with it an implied representation by the banker to the payee that the signature was genuine and there was no bar on the banker's right to recover the money as having been paid under a mistake of fact. However, it should be noted in that case the first defendant (the collecting bank) had not parted with the proceeds of the forged cheque. If it had parted with the proceeds - in reliance on the cheque having been honoured - the plaintiff (the paying bank) would not have been able to recover because it would have met with the defence that the recipient had changed his position in good faith to his detriment.

An example of a recipient, of payment of an irregular bill, changing his position can be seen from *The London and River Plate Bank Ltd v The Bank of Liverpool Ltd*.[24] In that case, a bank in good faith paid moneys to a holder of a bill who took the money in good faith. It transpired that endorsements on the bill had been forged. The court held the money may not be recoverable if the recipient of the money has in the meantime altered his position. In so deciding Mathew J stated:[25]

> "The true principle is developed in the clearest possible form in the case of *Cocks v Masterson*[26] ... In *Cocks v Masterson* the simple rule was laid down in clear language for the first time that when a bill becomes due and is presented for payment the holder ought to know at once whether the bill is going to be

---

20. *Ibid* at 541 and 238 respectively.
21. Bills of Exchange Act, 1882, s 52(2)(c).
22. See para **[5.53]**.
23. [1974] 3 All ER 834; [1975] 2 WLR 12.
24. [1896] 1 QB 7.
25. *Ibid* at 11.
26. (1829) 9 B & C.

paid or not. If the mistake is discovered at once, it may be the money can be recovered back; but if it be not, and the money is paid in good faith, and is received in good faith, and there is an interval of time in which the position of the holder may be altered, the principle seems to apply that money once paid cannot be recovered back. That rule is obviously, as it seems to me, indispensable for the conduct of business ... It is one of the few rules of business which is perfectly clear and distinct at present and, as it seems to me, it is unimpeachable."

Tracing Mistaken Payments

[6.12] Moneys mistakenly paid into an account of another may be traced by the owner provided the moneys standing to the credit of the account are not reduced below the amount mistakenly paid in. In *Re Irish Shipping Ltd (in liq)*[27] the Korean Exchange Bank made a duplicate payment to Irish Shipping's account with Citibank NA. Payment was made four months prior to the date of Irish Shipping's winding up and was not discovered until a month after the winding up commenced. Carroll J held that Citibank NA could not exercise its right of set-off against the mistaken payments as first, where moneys are paid by mistake into a company's account, such moneys do not form part of the company's assets at the date of its liquidation and secondly, moneys paid by mistake must be regarded as being akin to lost property rather than trust property, and may be traced by the payer (in the absence of equitable estoppel).

Citibank NA had claimed that the duplicate payment was moneys to be held on trust for the payer but as Citibank NA had no notice of such trust, they should be entitled to treat the moneys as belonging to Irish Shipping and to set them off against moneys owing to them at the date of liquidation.[28] In deciding against Citibank NA, Carroll J followed the decision in *Chase Manhattan Bank NA v Israel-British Bank (London) Ltd.*[29] In that case it was held that the equitable right of tracing was available to recover a duplicate payment. Carroll J considered[30] that the law as between the liquidator of a company receiving a mistaken payment and the payer was correctly stated by Goulding J when he said:[31]

---

[27] [1986] ILRM 518.

[28] Supported by the House of Lords' decision in *Thomson v Clydesdale Bank Ltd* (1893) AC 282, and the Privy Council in *Union Bank of Australia Ltd v Murray-Aynsley* [1898] AC 693; and *Clark v Ulster Bank Ltd* [1950] NI 132.

[29] [1979] 3 All ER 1025; [1980] 2 WLR 202.

[30] *Re Irish Shipping Ltd (in liq)* [1986] ILRM 518 at 522.

[31] In *Chase Manhattan Bank NA v Israel-British Bank (London) Ltd* [1979] 3 All ER 1025 at 1033; [1980] 2 WLR 202 at 210.

"the assets (if any) in the defendant's hands properly representing the plaintiff's money at the commencement of the winding-up, did not belong to the defendant beneficially and never formed part of its property."

Carroll J pointed out[32] that the fallacy of Citibank's claim was that it tried to equate a constructive trust with an express trust where a beneficiary consciously places money at the disposal of a trustee who fails to notify the bank of the trust; that the funds belonged at all times to the Korean Exchange Bank and the only function which Irish Shipping Ltd had was to return the funds to their rightful owner.

[6.13] In *Re PMPA Insurance Co Ltd*[33] moneys payable by bank giro into the PMPA Insurance Company's account were mistakenly credited by the banker to the account of the Private Motorists Provident Society. Lynch J held that these moneys were held on trust for the Company by the Society which had no beneficial interest in the moneys: "the same applies to moneys paid by bankers overlooking the expiration of bankers' orders and therefore paid without any authority or consent of the owners of such moneys."[34]

Alteration of Customer's Position on Receipt of Mistaken Payment

[6.14] Problems arise as to conflicting claims where a person receives a payment mistakenly and subsequently disburses the mistaken payment. Where the customer is shown not to have been aware that the proceeds of the mistaken payment were not his property and where he has altered his position, he may successfully defend an action for recovery of the moneys.[35] In *Lloyds Bank Ltd v The Hon Cecily K Brooks*,[36] the plaintiff mistakenly paid additional amounts into Brooks's account with it and sought recovery. The defendant contended that as there was a relationship of banker and customer:

1. The plaintiff was under a duty to take reasonable care to ensure that the pass sheets delivered to her from time to time contained an accurate statement of her account;

2. By sending the defendant the pass sheets setting out these sums as credited to her they represented that they had received them on her behalf and for her use and formed part of her income; and

---

[32.] In *Re Irish Shipping Ltd (in liq)* [1986] ILRM 518 at 523.

[33.] [1986] ILRM 524.

[34.] *Ibid* at 527.

[35.] See the reference to the decision in *Cocks v Masterson* (1829) 9 B & C 902 by Mathew J in his judgment in *The London and River Plate Bank Ltd v The Bank of Liverpool Ltd* [1896] 1 QB 7 para **[6.11]** above.

[36.] (1950) 6 LDAB 161.

3. Relying on those representations contained in those pass sheets, the defendant had altered her position to her detriment in that she was led to believe that her income was greater than it was in fact and has spent more money than she otherwise would have done.

Having found that the payments were made under a mistake of fact and that the defendant was unaware that she was not entitled to such payments (which arose from a trust of which she was a beneficiary), Lynskey J stated:[37]

"(1) there was a duty on the bank to keep the defendant correctly informed as to the position of her account,

(2) there was a duty on the bank not to over-credit her statement of account, and

(3) there was a duty on the bank not to authorise her or induce her by faithful representations contained in her statement of account to draw money from her account to which she was not entitled."

The court found that the defendant, relying on the bank's representations, acted, through no fault of hers, to her detriment in spending the money and accordingly, the bank was unable to recover the mistaken payments.

Although the defendant was found in the circumstances not to be at fault in thinking she owned the mistaken payments, advisers to customers of banks might note Lynskey J's words:

"it is important that a man or a woman should know the state of their account and the state of their finances, and a wise man or a wise woman looks at that statement before they spend money."[38]

[6.15] Where a customer receives money mistakenly and spends it, he will be unable to resist recovery if it can be shown he would still have made an investment. In *United Overseas Bank v Jiwani*[39] two credit entries were made to the defendants' bank accounts (as a result of a bank clerk acting on foot of a telex instruction and again on the letter confirming the telex instruction). Mackenna J held that the customer must repay the bank the additional payment made in error unless he can show that the bank is estopped;[40] he laid down three conditions to be satisfied:[41]

1. The customer must show that either the bank was under a duty to give him accurate information about the state of the account and that in breach of this duty inaccurate information was given or that in some

37. *Ibid* at 169.
38. *Ibid*.
39. [1977] 1 All ER 733; [1976] 1 WLR 964.
40. See also *Platt v Casey's Drogheda Brewery Co* [1921] 1 IR 279.
41. [1977] 1 All ER 733 at 737 and [1976] 1 WLR 964 at 968 respectively.

other way a misrepresentation was made to the customer about the state of the account for which the bank is responsible;

2. The customer must show that this inaccurate information in fact misled him about the state of the account and caused him to believe that the bank was his debtor for a larger sum than was the case and to make the transfer in that mistaken belief; and

3. The customer must show that because of his mistaken belief he changed his position in a way which would make it inequitable to require him now to repay the money.

The customer was obliged to return the mistaken payments because he failed to satisfy the third test, unlike the customer in *Lloyds Bank Ltd v The Hon Cecily K Brooks*.[42]

Recovery of Money paid under Mistake of Law

[6.16] We have seen according to the Supreme Court that as a general rule money paid under a mistake of fact is recoverable but not money paid under a mistake of law.[43] Indeed in 1874 Whiteside CJ said:[44]

"it is quite clear that, as this money was paid under a mistake of law, and with knowledge of the facts, it cannot be recovered back by legal process, and it must be left to the high sense of morality of the gentlemen in Clare to do what may by them be considered right under the circumstances."

This approach was continued in *Casey v The Irish Sailors and Soldiers Land Trust*[45] where the Supreme Court held that rent paid by ex-servicemen, having been paid upon a mistaken view of the law, was irrecoverable.[46] Murnaghan J was unambiguous in the Supreme Court when he said:[47]

"It is ... well settled law that when money has been wrongfully paid under a mistake of law no action lies to recover the amount so paid ... the rule has been so long and so firmly established that it cannot be called into question."

---

42. (1950) 6 LDAB 161.
43. Para **[6.01]**; "there is no unanimity that money paid in mistake of law cannot be recovered" - Ryder in *Butterworths Banking & Financial Law Review 1987* at 72; see also Lord Abinger CB in *Kelly v Solari* (1841) 9 M & W 54 at 57 - "The safest rule ... is that if the party makes the payment with full knowledge of the facts, although under ignorance of the law, there being no fraud on the other side, he cannot recover it back."
44. In *O'Loghlen v O'Callaghan* (1874) IR 8 CL 116 at 121.
45. [1937] IR 208.
46. See also *Holt v Markham* [1923] 1 KB 504.
47. [1937] IR 208 at 221, 222.

The traditional distinction between the remedies for payment under a mistake of fact and a mistake of law has become greyer. Indeed according to *Penn, Shea* and *Arora*:[48]

> "The distinction between a mistake of fact and one of law is notoriously difficult (if not impossible) to make, and many have suggested that the distinction should be abolished. In our view, the present state of the law as shown in the cases is ridiculous and scandalous, and we make no attempt to bring order from chaos, since we believe it to be both impossible and pointless."

However, in *Dolan v Neligan*[49] Kenny J brought some light when he stated:[50]

> "The statement that money paid under a mistake of law cannot be recovered is, I think, an inaccurate simplification of a complex problem and, ... I am satisfied that money paid by one person because of a mistake of law can be recovered by him if the cause of the mistake were statements about the law made to him by the party receiving the money or if the parties were not on equal terms at the time when the payment was made."

[6.17] The payment of moneys by reason of mistake of law came to be considered by the Supreme Court in *Rogers v Louth CC*.[51] The claim concerned an overpayment to the defendants in redeeming an annuity under the Housing Act, 1966. The Court held that the payment was not made voluntarily and although the payment was made under mistake of law the defendants were primarily responsible for the mistake, the parties were not in *pari delicto*; in applying the principles of the Privy Council's advice in *Kiriri Cotton Co Ltd v Dewani*,[52] the plaintiff was entitled to recover the overpayment. The Supreme Court adopted the following passage from the Privy Council's advice:[53]

> "Nor is it correct to say that money paid under a mistake of law can never be recovered back. The true proposition is that money paid under a mistake of law, by itself and without more, cannot be recovered back. ... If there is something more in addition to a mistake of law - if there is something in the defendant's

[48] *The Law Relating to Domestic Banking* Vol 1 (1987) para 11.13.
[49] [1967] IR 247.
[50] *Ibid* at 259; Kenny J's decision was overruled by the Supreme Court on other grounds - "it is unnecessary to consider the other interesting aspects of the case relating to the conditions under which money paid by reason of a mistake of law or a mistake of fact may be recovered at common law" - Walsh J *ibid* at 276.
[51] [1981] IR 265; [1981] ILRM 144.
[52] [1960] 2 WLR 127.
[53] *Ibid* at 133; this passage was also approved by Kenny J in *Dolan v Neligan* [1967] IR 247 at 260, and by Hamilton J in *Dublin Corporation v The Provost, Fellows and Scholars of the College of the Holy and Undivided Trinity of Queen Elizabeth Near Dublin* [1985] ILRM 283 at 286.

conduct which shows that, of the two of them, he is the one primarily responsible for the mistake - then it may be recovered back. Thus, if as between the two of them the duty of observing the law is placed on the shoulders of the one rather than the other - it being imposed on him specially for the protection of the other - then they are not in *pari delicto* and the money can be recovered back ... Likewise, if the responsibility for the mistake lies more on the one than the other because he has misled the other when he ought to know better - then again they are not in *pari delicto* and the money can be recovered back."

Payment of moneys into court by insurance underwriters under a mistake of law induced by the fraudulent representations of the other party are recoverable.[54] But if an innocent party to the proceedings had received the money and "had spent it or used it irretrievably, the position might have been different".[55]

Money Laundering

[6.18] In recent times, transactions involving "money laundering" have been considered by the courts[56]. A description of the nature of money laundering can be seen from the facts of *Agip (Africa) Ltd v Jackson*.[57] The plaintiff, a Jersey registered company, held a US dollar account at Banque du Sud in Tunis. The plaintiff's accountant fraudulently altered the payee's name on the payment order of the plaintiff to that of Baker Oil. The bank in Tunis debited Agip's account with the amount on the payment order and Baker Oil's account with Lloyds Bank in London was credited (following its request to Citibank New York to debit Banque du Sud's account in New York and credit Lloyds in New York with the amount of the payment). The amount received by Baker Oil was subsequently transferred to Jackson & Co (of which the defendants were the partners) at Lloyds Bank. Subsequently, this amount was transferred to an account of Jackson & Co in the Isle of Man at the Isle of Man Bank Ltd. The defendants contended that the plaintiff had no title to sue as the relationship of banker and customer was that of debtor and creditor and it was the bank's money subsequently transferred not the plaintiff's. The English Court of Appeal held that the money was paid under a mistake of fact, that equity permitted tracing into a mixed fund, a fiduciary relationship existed between the plaintiff and its accountant and the defendants must have known that they were laundering money and were found to be liable as constructive trustees.

54. *Carey v WH Ryan Ltd, McMillan and Jervois* [1982] IR 179.
55. *Ibid* per Henchy J at 187.
56. For examples of money laundering, see Appendix C to the *Money Laundering Guidance Notes for Credit Institutions* (April 1995).
57. [1992] 4 All ER 451 (affirming the decision of Millett J [1992] 4 All ER 385).

2. FRAUDULENT PAYMENTS

"The general rule is that where a person purports to pay money directly to another, or to pay it to his credit, and that other has notice that the payment has been induced by fraud, the payee or would-be payee does not get any title to the money: see *Nelson v Larholt*.[58] If the money has reached the payee, then, while it is in his hands, he is a constructive trustee of it for the rightful owner who has been defrauded into paying it and the payee can be compelled to repay it. If it has not been paid to the payee, but remains in the hands of an intermediary who becomes aware of the fraud, then the intermediary becomes a constructive trustee of the money for the defrauded payer and can be ordered to return it to him."[59]

[6.19] In *Carey v WH Ryan Ltd, McMillan and Jervois*[60] insurance underwriters paid money into court arising out of an injury to the plaintiff while employed by the first named defendant. It transpired that the employer had misrepresented to the insurers the amount of wages being paid to its employees. As the level of premiums was based on the level of wages this misrepresentation vitiated the insurance policy. Accordingly, the moneys lodged by the insurance underwriters were recoverable, despite the plaintiff being blameless.

Onus of Proof for Recovery

[6.20] The Supreme Court's decision in *Banco Ambrosiano SpA v Ansbacher and Co Ltd*[61] clarified the degree of proof required for payments to be returned on the grounds of fraud. The plaintiffs alleged that moneys had been fraudulently misappropriated from them to the defendants. The President of the High Court's finding that the plaintiffs had failed to discharge the onus of proof that funds were fraudulently misappropriated was unanimously overruled by the full Supreme Court. The Supreme Court's decision on the standard of proof was given by Henchy J who said:[62]

"When fraud has to be proved in a criminal court as an element of an offence charged, it must of course be proved beyond a reasonable doubt, which is the prescribed degree of proof for every essential ingredient of a criminal charge. In the civil courts, while fraud is not recognised as a distinct tort or cause of action, it is well recognised as an element which, if proved in the appropriate manner, will vitiate the act or conduct which it induced or resulted in, so that the court will seek to undo the intended and actual effect of the fraud by

---

[58.] [1947] 2 All ER 751.
[59.] Henchy J in *Carey v WH Ryan Ltd, McMillan and Jervois* [1982] IR 179 at 185.
[60.] [1982] IR 179.
[61.] [1987] ILRM 669.
[62.] *Ibid* at 700.

awarding damages or making such order as it deems necessary for the purpose of doing justice in the circumstances.

What will constitute fraud in a civil action is not easy to state in advance, for fraud usually hides behind conduct which is disguised, devious and dishonest, so that it may assume an infinite variety of forms ...

The normal rule in a civil case is that the person on whom lies the onus of proving a particular averment is held to have discharged that onus if the court is satisfied on the balance of probabilities that the averment in question is correct ...

If, as has been suggested, the degree of proof of fraud in civil cases is higher than the balance of probabilities but not as high as to be (as is required in criminal cases) beyond reasonable doubt, it is difficult to see how that higher degree of proof is to be gauged or expressed. To require some such intermediately high degree of probability would, in my opinion, introduce a vague and uncertain element, just as if, for example, negligence were required to be proved in certain cases to the level of gross negligence ...

I am unable therefore to discern, in principle or in practice, any rational or cogent reason why fraud in civil cases should require a higher degree of proof than is required for the proof of other issues in civil claims."

The Court found that, the depositor had obtained the moneys through a series of transactions involving intentional deception in depriving Banco Ambrosiano of the funds, the depositor had no title to the funds deposited and, accordingly the deposit together with accrued interest were to be returned to Banco Ambrosiano SpA.

3. BANK'S LIABILITY AS CONSTRUCTIVE TRUSTEE

Paying Banker as Constructive Trustee

[6.21] A difficulty for a banker when collecting funds for its customer is that on occasion such funds may not belong to its customer and in subsequently paying away those funds, at the request of its customer - whether through honouring cheques or otherwise, the banker may become liable to the true owner of the funds. The liability for such a paying banker arises by means of a constructive trust.[63] Although moneys once paid into a bank account become the property of the bank,[64] the courts may nonetheless hold that the bank, notwithstanding its legal ownership of such moneys is liable to the true owner of the original funds should it allow such moneys, to be paid away. The concept of a constructive

---

[63.] Where the bank has been informed that the funds are to be applied for a specific purpose a resulting trust will arise - see *Barclays Bank Ltd v Quistclose Investments Ltd* [1968] 3 All ER 651, see para **[6.35]** below.

[64.] See *Lipkin Gorman v Karpnale Ltd* [1992] 4 All ER 409 per May LJ at 418.

trust was stated by Costello J in *HKN Invest OY and Wicaba Finland KY (PVT) v Incotrade PVT Ltd*[65] as follows:[66]

> "A constructive trust will arise when the circumstances render it inequitable for the legal owner of property to deny the title of another to it. It is a trust which comes into existence irrespective of the will of the parties and arises by operation of law. The principle is that where a person who holds property in circumstances which in equity and good conscience should be held or enjoyed by another he will be compelled to hold the property in trust for another."

[6.22] *Keane* in his book *Equity and the Law of Trusts in the Republic of Ireland*[67] divides constructive trusts into two categories - those where the constructive trustee is already a trustee and secondly where a constructive trust arises where there is no fiduciary relationship between the parties. *Keane*[68] breaks this second category down into four "principal categories" namely (i) the vendor of property, (ii) mortgages, (iii) mutual wills and (iv) strangers receiving or dealing with trust property. It is this last category under which banks may incur liability through receiving funds while unaware of their being tainted with fraud or dishonesty.[69]

Test of Knowledge

[6.23] The underlying points of principle whereby a bank can incur liability through being deemed to be a constructive trustee are highlighted in the English Court of Appeal's decision in *Polly Peck International plc v Nadir (No 2)*.[70] In that action the administrators of the plaintiff claimed *inter alia* that the fifth defendant, IBK, a Northern Cyprus bank was responsible for misapplying £142 million of the plaintiff's funds by enabling the funds to be paid out or applied otherwise than for the proper purposes of the plaintiff. £45 million of the moneys misapplied were transferred by IBK to the account of the fourth defendant, the Central Bank of Northern Cyprus. The administrators contended that either the Central Bank had actual knowledge that the funds were diverted from the plaintiff and had been improperly diverted or the circumstances of the case put the Central Bank on inquiry that this was so - they pleaded also that the Central Bank was a constructive trustee. The Court of Appeal held that:

---

65. [1993] 3 IR 152.
66. *Ibid* at 162.
67. (1988) Butterworths.
68. *Ibid* at para 13.07.
69. For further treatment of bankers as constructive trustees see *Paget's Law of Banking* (11th ed, 1996) pp 397-402, 428-434; Penn, Shea and Arora in *The Law Relating to Domestic Banking* Vol 1 (1987) Ch 10; and Shea, *Butterworths Banking & Financial Law Review 1987* pp 78-98.
70. [1992] 4 All ER 769.

1. Where liability as a constructive trustee was sought to be imposed on the basis that *the defendant had assisted in the misapplication of trust property,* something amounting to dishonesty or want of probity on the part of the defendant had to be shown and a stranger could not be made liable for knowing assistance in a fraudulent breach of trust unless knowledge of the fraudulent design could be imputed to him.

2. However, where liability was sought to be imposed on the basis that *the defendant had received and dealt in some way with trust property,* the misapplication of trust funds did not have to be fraudulent but it did have to be shown that the defendant had had knowledge, whether actual or constructive, that the funds were trust funds and that they were being misapplied.

The Court went on to decide that the Central Bank's knowledge that the plaintiff was, *via* IBK, exchanging substantial sums of sterling in London for Turkish lire in Northern Cyprus was not calculated to give the Central Bank cause to suspect improprieties and did not put it on enquiry as to whether there were improprieties.

The principal judgment of the Court was delivered by Scott LJ who stated:[71]

> "There is a general consensus of opinion that, if liability as constructive trustee is sought to be imposed, not on the basis that the defendant has received and dealt in some way with trust property (knowing receipt) but on the basis that the defendant has assisted in the misapplication of trust property (knowing assistance), 'something amounting to dishonesty or want of probity on the part of the defendant must be shown' (see per Vinelott J in *Eagle Trust plc v SBC Securities* [1992] 4 All ER 488 at 499). Vinelott J described as 'settled law' the proposition that 'a stranger cannot be made liable for knowing assistance in a fraudulent breach of trust unless knowledge of the fraudulent design can be imputed to him. ...' (at 499). I respectfully agree.
>
> Millett J, in the judgment below, treated the present case as one of 'knowing assistance' rather than 'knowing receipt'. In respect of the nine sterling transfers I think that is right. The Central Bank received the funds transferred not in its own right but as banker, and, as banker, credited the funds to IBK in Northern Cyprus. But in respect of the bulk of the transfers the case is, in my opinion, one of 'receipt' rather than, 'assistance'. The Central Bank was exchanging Turkish lire for sterling and became entitled to the sterling not as banker for IBK but in its own right. IBK became entitled to the Turkish lire.
>
> Liability as a constructive trustee in a 'knowing receipt' case does not require that the misapplication of the trust funds should be fraudulent. It does require that the defendant should have knowledge that the funds were trust funds and that they were being misapplied. Actual knowledge obviously will suffice. Mr

---

71. *Ibid* at 777.

Potts has submitted that it will suffice if the defendant can be shown to have had knowledge of facts which would have put an honest and reasonable man on inquiry, or, at least, if the defendant can be shown to have wilfully and recklessly failed to make such inquiries as an honest and reasonable man would have made (see categories (iii) and (v) of the categories of mental state identified by Peter Gibson J in *Baden's* case [1992] 4 All ER 161 at 235). I do not think there is any doubt that, if the latter of the two criteria can be established against the Central Bank, that will suffice."[72]

[6.24] The Court of Appeal's decision referred to the judgment of Vinelott J in *Eagle Trust plc v SBC Securities Ltd*,[73] where he held that a person would be liable only as a constructive trustee of money which he had received in payment of a commercial liability, and which had already passed through his hands, if it was possible to show that he knew that the money was misapplied trust money in the sense that he had:

(i)   actual knowledge of the breach of trust, or

(ii)   wilfully shut his eyes to the obvious, or

(iii) wilfully and recklessly failed to make the type of inquiries which an honest and reasonable man would have made.

He held that conversely, a person would not be liable merely because he had reason to suspect that there had been a breach of trust disentitling the trustee to make the payment. It had to be shown that the circumstances were such that knowledge that the payment was improper could be imputed to the recipient of the money, but, in the absence of any evidence or explanation by the recipient, knowledge of the breach of trust could be inferred if the circumstances were such that an honest and reasonable man would have inferred that the money was probably trust money and was being misapplied and either would not have accepted it or would have kept it separate until he had satisfied himself that the payer was entitled to use the funds in discharge of the liability.

[6.25] Millett J's judgment (affirmed by the English Court of Appeal) in *Agip (Africa) Ltd v Jackson*[74] set out the classifications of knowing receipt and knowing assistance categories of constructive trusts.[75] Millett J stated:[76]

---

[72] For a detailed dissertation on the imposition of liability for "knowing assistance" and "knowing receipt" see Clayton, 'Banks as Constructive Trustees - The English Position' [1993] 5 JIBL 191.

[73] [1992] 4 All ER 488.

[74] [1992] 4 All ER 385 (Millett J); [1992] 4 All ER 451 (C of A).

[75] For an earlier consideration see Vroegop, 'Constructive Trusteeship and the Bank' [1988] JBL 437.

[76] *Ibid* at 403; applied by Vinelott J in *Eagle Trust plc v SBC Securities Ltd* [1992] 4 All ER 488 at 494.

"*Knowing receipt* ... it is necessary to distinguish between two main classes of case under this heading.

The first is concerned with the person who receives for his own benefit trust property transferred to him in breach of trust. He is liable as a constructive trustee if he received it with notice, actual or constructive, that it was trust property and that the transfer to him was a breach of trust, or if he received it without such notice but subsequently discovered the facts. In either case he is liable to account for the property, in the first case as from the time he received the property and in the second as from the time he acquired notice.

The second and, in my judgment, distinct class of case is that of the person, usually an agent of the trustees, who receives the trust property lawfully and not his own benefit but who then either misappropriates it or otherwise deals with it in a manner which is inconsistent with the trust. He is liable to account as a constructive trustee if he received the trust property knowing it to be such ...

In either class of case it is immaterial whether the breach of trust was fraudulent or not. The essential feature of the first class is that the recipient must have received the property for his own use and benefit. This is why neither the paying nor the collecting bank can normally be brought within it. In paying or collecting money for a customer the bank acts only as his agent. It is otherwise, however, if the collecting bank uses the money to reduce or discharge the customer's overdraft. In doing so it receives the money for its own benefit.

Knowing assistance - a stranger to the trust will also be liable to account as a constructive trustee if he knowingly assists in the furtherance of a fraudulent and dishonest breach of trust. It is not necessary that the party sought to be made liable as a constructive trustee should have received any part of the trust property, but the breach of trust must have been fraudulent. The basis of the stranger's liability is not receipt of trust property but participation in a fraud."

[6.26] Liability for receiving and dealing with moneys as indicated in the decisions of *Polly Peck International plc v Nadir (No 2)*,[77] *Eagle Trust plc v SBC Securities Ltd*[78] and *Agip (Africa) Ltd v Jackson*[79] depends upon knowledge of the recipient. It is important to distinguish between knowledge and notice.[80] In *Re Montagu's Settlement Trusts, Duke of Manchester v National Westminster Bank Ltd*,[81] Sir Robert Megarry V-C stated:[82]

[77.] [1992] 4 All ER 769.

[78.] [1992] 4 All ER 488.

[79.] [1992] 4 All ER 451.

[80.] See also an earlier edition of *Paget's Law of Banking* (10th ed, 1989) p 236 - "Knowledge involves a degree of awareness and notice does not".

[81.] [1992] 4 All ER 308.

[82.] *Ibid* at 322.

"In the books and the authorities the word 'notice' is often used in place of the word 'knowledge', usually without any real explanation of its meaning. This seems to me to be a fertile source of confusion; for, whatever meaning the layman may attach to those words centuries of equity jurisprudence have attached a detailed and technical meaning to the term 'notice' without doing the same for 'knowledge'. The classification of 'notice' into actual notice, constructive notice and imputed notice has been developed in relation to the doctrine that a *bona fide* purchaser for value of a legal estate takes free from any equitable interests of which he has no notice ...

It seems to me that one must be very careful about applying to constructive trusts either the accepted concepts of notice or any analogy to them. In determining whether a constructive trust has been created, the fundamental question is whether the conscience of the recipient is bound in such a way as to justify equity in imposing a trust upon him."

[6.27] As to the degree of knowledge required to impose liability on a person as a constructive trustee in the knowing receipt category, the conclusion of Sir Robert Megarry's judgment[83] is instructive:

1. The basic question is whether the conscience of the recipient is sufficiently affected to justify the imposition of a constructive trust;

2. Whether a constructive trust arises depends primarily on the knowledge of the recipient and not on notice to him;

3. Knowledge is not confined to actual knowledge but includes actual knowledge that would have been acquired but for shutting one's eyes to the obvious or wilfully and recklessly failing to make such inquiries as a reasonable and honest man would make; for in such cases there is a want of probity which justifies imposing a constructive trust;

4. Carelessness will not normally amount to a want of probity;

5. A person is not to be taken to have knowledge of a fact that he once knew but has genuinely forgotten; the test is whether the knowledge continues to operate on that person's mind at the time in question;

6. 'Imputed knowledge' arises principally only in that a company is treated as having the knowledge that its directors and secretary have.

The degree of knowledge required to impose liability as outlined by Sir Robert Megarry V-C above is a higher degree of knowledge than the constructive knowledge test applied by Ungoed-Thomas J in *Selangor United Rubber Estates Ltd v Cradock (No 3)*[84] and by Brighton J in *Karak Rubber Co Ltd v Burden (No*

[83.] *Ibid* at 330.
[84.] [1968] 2 All ER 1073.

2).[85] These cases involved knowing assistance on the part of paying bankers. In the former case (applied in the latter) a paying banker was deemed to have knowledge where the circumstances were such that he should have made enquiry.[86] This constructive knowledge test, which was criticised by Sir Robert Megarry VC,[87] by *Paget* [88] and by *Penn, Shea* and *Arora*,[89] may be considered to be unduly onerous, although the courts in Ireland may adopt a more onerous test for bankers than the courts in England.[90]

[6.28] Prior to the reporting of the decisions in *Polly Peck International plc v Nadir (No 2)*,[91] *Eagle Trust plc v SBC Securities Ltd*,[92] *Agip (Africa) Ltd v Jackson*[93] and *Re Montagu's Settlement Trusts, Duke of Manchester v National Westminster Bank Ltd*[94] the Supreme Court decided that a recipient of trust funds must make good their loss as a result of having "constructive knowledge" of the breach.

In *Re Frederick Inns Ltd*[95] Motels Ltd and three of its subsidiaries made payments to the Revenue Commissioners in reduction of their tax liabilities and the tax liabilities of six other subsidiaries of Motels Ltd. The Supreme Court held that:

1. The memorandum of association of each of the companies making payments did not empower them to pay the debts of an associate company and thus the payments were *ultra vires*,

2. These *ultra vires* payments constituted a misapplication by the directors of the four companies (in breach of their fiduciary duties),

---

[85.] [1972] 1 All ER 1210.

[86.] In referring to these decisions at para 13.08-09 in *Equity and the Law of Trusts in the Republic of Ireland* (1988) Butterworths, Keane does not advert to any distinction between actual and constructive knowledge; in the *The Law and Practice in Ireland Relating to Cheques and Analogous Instruments*, O'Connor does not mention the former case but adverts to the latter in a footnote in conjunction with the decision in *Lipkin Gorman v Karpnale Ltd* [1992] 4 All ER 409 (fn 58 para 10.64); the English High Court decision in Karak though was criticised by the English Court of Appeal in Lipkin, see May LJ [1992] 4 All ER 409 at 421.

[87.] [1992] 4 All ER 308 at 325.

[88.] *Paget's Law of Banking* (10th ed, 1989) p 234.

[89.] *The Law Relating to Domestic Banking* Vol 1 (1987) para 10.09 - "It now seems reasonably clear ... that these cases should no longer be regarded as good law"; see also Butterworths, *Banking & Financial Law Review* 1987 p 87.

[90.] See Ch 8.

[91.] [1992] 4 All ER 769.

[92.] [1992] 4 All ER 488.

[93.] [1992] 4 All ER 385.

[94.] [1992] 4 All ER 308.

[95.] [1994] 1 ILRM 387.

3. When in receipt of these payments, the Revenue Commissioners had constructive knowledge of the breach of duty as the memoranda and articles of association were documents of public record; and

4. The payments on behalf of the six other subsidiaries were held by the Revenue Commissioners as constructive trustees and had to be re-paid to the liquidator of the payor companies.

The implications of this decision for bankers should not be overlooked. If a bank wishes to refinance its customer's indebtedness by lending to a subsidiary, parent or fellow subsidiary of the customer, so that the customer's indebtedness is repaid and the loan is now advanced to another company in the group, the question arises as to how this transaction is to be put in place. It could be argued that it should be done by way of inter-company loan but this may have adverse tax consequences and in the event of a subsequent liquidation within the preference period[96] the inter-company transaction may be upset as being a fraudulent preference. It may be appropriate to amend the memorandum and articles of association of the relevant company to permit the new borrower to discharge the previous borrower's indebtedness. In any event, as a result of the decision in *Re Frederick Inns Ltd*[97] the bank is likely to be fixed with knowledge of any lack of capacity on the part of its new customer.

[6.29] A limitation on the extent of knowledge to be imputed to a bank was laid down in the Northern Ireland courts in *Clark v Ulster Bank Ltd*.[98] In that case a solicitor who had an account with the bank opened a second account for the purpose of lodging clients' moneys. Notice of the purpose was not given to the bank who subsequently purported to exercise a right of set-off as between the two accounts. The court held that not only could the bank exercise the set-off but that when a bank does acquire notice that one of the accounts kept by a customer is a trust account it may nevertheless exercise any right of set-off to which it may then be entitled, having regard to the state of the accounts at the time of acquiring such notice.

In dismissing the contention that the bank knew that the second account was an account for clients' moneys, Black LJ stated:[99]

> "The mere fact that the customer's profession or business is such that it necessarily involves his having moneys belonging to other people from time to time in his hands, does not affect the banker with notice that any specific sum or sums paid in by the customer are trust moneys, nor does knowledge on the banker's part that the customer's practice is to pay moneys received by him on

---

[96.] Two years for connected persons - Companies Act, 1963, s 286 (as amended).
[97.] [1994] 1 ILRM 387.
[98.] [1950] NI LR 132.
[99.] *Ibid* at 135.

behalf of clients into his bank account, constitute such notice or put the banker on inquiry. He is entitled to treat the money passing through the account as the customer's own".

Test of Dishonesty rather than Knowledge

[6.30] Recently, the Privy Council decided that the criteria for establishing liability through ascertaining the degree of knowledge on the part of the person receiving misappropriated funds or assisting in the misappropriation of funds is best forgotten. The relevant knowledge requirement was first outlined in a judgment running to over 100 pages of the law reports by Peter Gibson J in *Baden v Societe Generale pour Favoriser le Developpement du Commerce et de l'Industrie en France SA.*[100] The decision of the Privy Council arose from the case of *Royal Brunei Airlines Sdn Bhd v Tan*[101] the facts of which were briefly as follows: Royal Brunei Airlines appointed BLT as its agent in the sale of aircraft tickets, the terms of which required BLT to hold moneys received from sales on trust for the Royal Brunei Airlines. BLT used the funds for its own business and when it became insolvent Royal Brunei Airlines sought recovery from BLT's managing director and controlling shareholder, Mr Tan.

The Privy Council considered that liability arises for a person assisting in a breach of trust only if he has been dishonest - that is "simply not acting as an honest person would in the circumstances"[102] and the test is not whether the person assisting the breach of trust acted knowingly. This test of knowledge was discarded on the grounds that it too often required a protracted consideration of the categories of knowledge.[103]

The Privy Council attempted to redefine the basis upon which a person might become liable for assisting in a breach of trust by discarding the test of knowledge which underpinned the earlier decisions.[104] However, it is submitted in reality the Privy Council's attempt to somehow simplify the approach to the assessment of liability as a constructive trustee may have the reverse effect. If a person assists in a breach of trust dishonestly he is surely doing so knowingly. In order to establish whether a person has been dishonest it must surely be

---

[100.] [1992] 4 All ER 161; [1983] BCLC 325.

[101.] [1995] 3 All ER 97.

[102.] *Ibid* at 105.

[103.] Prior to the Privy Council's decision *Paget* considered the "intriguing and complicated analysis" of knowledge as enunciated by Peter Gibson J "questionable" - *Paget's Law of Banking* (10th ed, 1989) p 235.

[104.] *Baden v Societe Generale pour Favoriser le Developpement du Commerce et de l'Industrie en France SA* [1992] 4 All ER 161; *Re Montagu's Settlement Trusts, Duke of Manchester v National Westminster Bank Ltd* [1992] 4 All ER 308; *Agip (Africa) Ltd v Jackson* [1992] 4 All ER 451; *Eagle Trust plc v SBC Securities Ltd* [1992] 4 All ER 488 and *Polly Peck International plc v Nadir (No 2)* [1992] 4 All ER 769.

necessary to show that the person acted in a manner which he knew not to be honest - it therefore requires a test of knowledge. Indeed, in the course of their advice to His Majesty The Sultan and Yang Di-Pertuan, the Privy Council stated:[105] ",.. for the most part dishonesty is to be equated with conscious impropriety.". While a test of "dishonesty" rather than "knowingly" might on the face of it seem simpler, the reality may be otherwise.[106]

Paying Banker's Liability Only for Breach of Contract

[6.31] The extent of a paying banker's liability as a constructive trustee was confined to certain parameters in the English Court of Appeal's decision in *Lipkin Gorman v Karpnale Ltd.*[107] In that case a partner in a firm of solicitors spent afternoons gambling at the expense of the client account at a local club (his fellow partners assuming he was out of the office on clients' business). The bank's branch manager was aware that the partner was cashing cheques at a gambling club and although he discussed it with the partner he did not pass on his concern to the other partners.[108] On discovering the fraud the firm claimed *inter alia* against the club as constructive trustee for knowing receipt of trust property and against the bank as constructive trustee for knowing assistance to a breach of trust.

The court, in allowing the bank's appeal, held that the bank would not be liable as a constructive trustee unless it was also liable for breach of contract, since the bank's contractual duty to pay cheques signed in accordance with its mandate required the bank to perform that duty without negligence and if there was no negligence on the part of the bank it could not be liable as a constructive trustee. Parker LJ stated:[109]

> "It is in my view clear that the bank could not have rendered itself liable as constructive trustee unless it was also liable for breach of contract and that if it was not liable for breach of contract it could not be liable as constructive trustee. This is because, stated in broad terms, the bank's duty to pay cheques signed in accordance with its mandate is subject to the qualification that it must be performed without negligence and that (i) negligence may exist where there is no question of the circumstances giving rise to a finding of constructive trusteeship, (ii) if there is no negligence I cannot envisage, at least in this case,

---

[105] [1995] 3 All ER 97 at 106.

[106] The legal correctness of the Privy Council's view that a test of liability is dishonesty was doubted by Berg in 'Constructive Trusts and Intermeddling - Liability of Third Parties' (1995) The Irish Centre for Commercial Law Studies.

[107] [1992] 4 All ER 409; aspects of the decision (other than the banker's liability) were appealed to the House of Lords, see [1992] 4 All ER 512.

[108] To have done so would have breached the banker's duty of confidentiality see para **[3.01]** above (although not to the extent that the cheques cashed were those of the firm).

[109] [1992] 4 All ER 409 at 437.

any facts which would found liability on the ground of constructive trusteeship."

In indicating the banker's duties should not be unrealistic he concluded:[110]

"If the solicitors' submissions were to be accepted, it would in my view place on banks a wholly unrealistic burden, for it would involve the manager of a bank which held a solicitors' client account and also the personal accounts of one or more of the partners, with power of signature on the client account, continually monitoring the personal and client accounts for signs that one of the partners might be abusing his signing powers."

Standard of Care Required by Paying Banker

[6.32] To ascertain the degree of vigilance required by a paying banker to avoid liability in carrying out an order for payment in accordance with its mandate consideration should be given to the court's judgments in *Barclays Bank plc v Quincecare Ltd*[111] and *Lipkin Gorman v Karpnale Ltd.*[112]

[6.33] In *Barclays Bank plc v Quincecare Ltd*[113] Stiller requested the bank for a loan of £400,000 to finance the purchase of four shops. The bank agreed subject to Stiller forming a company, the first defendant. Stiller requested the bank to transfer the bulk of the loan to a firm of solicitors who had acted for him previously and who he said were acting for the first defendant although they had not acted in the purchase of the four shops and knew nothing about the transaction. Following payment to the solicitors, the funds were subsequently transferred at Stiller's request to the United States. The bank sought recovery from, *inter alia* the company but the company contended that the bank had acted in breach of the implied duty of care in the customer/banker relationship because the circumstances of the transfer had been such that they would have raised questions in the mind of a reasonable banker as to whether the transaction was in fact truly authorised by the customer and for the customer's benefit thereby putting the banker under a duty of inquiry and that by making no enquiry the bank had been negligent. Steyn J held that the bank was entitled to judgment against the company, for at all material times the money transferred was in an ordinary current account and therefore no question of trust moneys was involved and no issue of knowing receipt arose nor any question of assisting a breach of trust since there was no want of probity on the part of the bank.

---

110. *Ibid* at 444.
111. [1992] 4 All ER 363.
112. [1992] 4 All ER 409.
113. [1992] 4 All ER 363.

In giving judgment for the bank, Steyn J indicated not only the nature of the paying banker's duty but the extent to which the banker must enquire to comply fully with that duty. He said:[114]

> "In my judgment it is an implied term of the contract between the bank and the customer that the bank will observe reasonable skill and care in and about executing the customer's orders ...
>
> Given that the bank owes a legal duty to exercise reasonable care in and about executing a customer's order to transfer money, it is nevertheless a duty which must generally speaking be subordinate to the bank's other conflicting contractual duties. *Ex hypothesi* one is considering a case where the bank received a valid and proper order which it is *prima facie* bound to execute promptly on pain of incurring liability for consequential loss to the customer. How are these conflicting duties to be reconciled in a case where the customer suffers loss because it is subsequently established that the order to transfer money was an act of misappropriation of money by the director or officer? If the bank executes the order knowing it to be dishonestly given, shutting its eyes to the obvious fact of the dishonesty, or acting recklessly in failing to make such inquiries as an honest and reasonable man would make, no problem arises: the bank will plainly be liable. But in real life such a stark situation seldom arises. The critical question is: what lesser state of knowledge on the part of the bank will oblige the bank to make inquiries as to the legitimacy of the order? In judging where the line is to be drawn there are countervailing policy considerations. The law should not impose too burdensome an obligation on bankers, which hampers the effective transacting of banking business unnecessarily. On the other hand, the law should guard against the facilitation of fraud, and exact a reasonable standard of care in order to combat fraud and to protect bank customers and innocent third parties. To hold that a bank is only liable when it has displayed a lack of probity would be much too restrictive an approach. On the other hand, to impose liability whenever speculation might suggest dishonesty would impose wholly impractical standards on bankers. In my judgment the sensible compromise, which strikes a fair balance between competing considerations, is simply to say that a banker must refrain from executing if and for so long as the banker is 'put on inquiry' in the sense that he has reasonable grounds (although not necessarily proof) for believing that the order is an attempt to misappropriate the funds of the company".

[6.34] The foregoing passage in Steyn J's judgment was approved and applied in the English Court of Appeal in *Lipkin Gorman v Karpnale Ltd*.[115] In outlining the paying banker's obligations May LJ stated:[116]

[114.] *Ibid* at 376.
[115.] [1992] 4 All ER 409.
[116.] *Ibid* at 421.

"The relationship between the parties is contractual. The principal obligation is upon the bank to honour its customers' cheques in accordance with its mandate on instructions. There is nothing in such a contract, express or implied, which could require a banker to consider the commercial wisdom or otherwise of the particular transaction. Nor is there normally any express term in the contract requiring the banker to exercise any degree of care in deciding whether to honour a customer's cheque which his instructions require him to pay. In my opinion any implied term requiring the banker to exercise care must be limited. To a substantial extent the banker's obligation under such a contract is largely automatic or mechanical. Presented with a cheque drawn in accordance with the terms of that contract, the banker must honour it save in what I would expect to be exceptional circumstances.

... an objective test had to be applied and ... accordingly there had to be some limits of the bank's entitlement to treat its mandate as absolute ... if a bank knows of facts which a reasonable bank manager would think were probably dishonest then enquiry would be appropriate.

For my part I would hesitate to try to lay down any detailed rules in this context. In the simple case of a current account in credit the basic obligation on the banker is to pay his customer's cheques in accordance with his mandate. Having in mind the vast numbers of cheques which are presented for payment every day in this country, whether over a bank counter or through the clearing bank, it is in my opinion only when the circumstances are such that any reasonable cashier would hesitate to pay a cheque at once and refer it to his or her superior, and when any reasonable superior would hesitate to authorise payment without inquiry, that a cheque should not be paid immediately upon presentation and such inquiry made. Further, it would I think be only in rare circumstances, and only when any reasonable bank manager would do the same, that a manager should instruct his staff to refer all or some of his customers' cheques to him before they are paid.

In this analysis I have respectively derived substantial assistance from the material parts of the judgment of Steyn J in *Barclays Bank plc v Quincecare Ltd* (1988) [1992] 4 All ER 363 esp at 375-377."

Receipt of Funds for a Specific Purpose

[6.35] Where moneys are advanced to a borrower for a specific purpose a trust is created in favour of the lender in respect of the moneys advanced which are not used for the designated purpose. In *Barclays Bank Ltd v Quistclose Investments Ltd*[117] Quistclose agreed to lend Rolls Razor Ltd £209,719 to enable Rolls Razor Ltd to pay a dividend. The bank was informed that the amount being lodged to the company's account with the bank was to be used only to meet the dividend.

[117.] [1968] 3 All ER 651; for a useful consideration of the principles of this decision see Clayton, 'Banks as Express and Resulting Trustees of Customers' Moneys' [1992] 5 JIBL 183.

Following the company's liquidation the bank sought to set-off the amount lodged against moneys owing by the company to the bank. The House of Lords held that the terms on which the loan was made were such as to impress on the money a trust in favour of Quistclose in the event that the dividend was not paid. On the question of notice that the moneys were to be used only for a specific purpose it was clear that the bank had notice. Lord Wilberforce indicated though that a mere request to put money into a separate account would not be sufficient to constitute notice.[118] Lord Reid indicated that a court would not be precluded from holding notice to be effective even if given after receipt of the moneys (assuming they had not been paid out).[119]

[6.36] There are no formal requirements to be complied with in order that moneys advanced be held on trust. In *Re Kayford Ltd*[120] deposits of the company's customers were placed into a separate bank account of the company. It was held that following the company's liquidation the moneys in the separate account belonged to the customers and not to the company (for distribution to creditors generally) notwithstanding that the bank received notice following the liquidation that the deposit was a trust account. Megarry J stated:[121]

> "... despite the loose ends ... I feel no doubt that the intention was that there should be a trust. There are no formal difficulties. The property concerned is pure personalty, and so writing, though desirable, is not an essential. There is no doubt about the so-called 'three certainties' of a trust. The subject matter to be held on trust is clear and so are the beneficial interests therein, as well as the beneficiaries. As for the requisite certainty of words, it is well settled that a trust can be created without using the words 'trust' or 'confidence' or the like; the question is whether in substance a sufficient intention to create a trust has been manifested."

[6.37] The principles of the House of Lords' decision were applied by the English Court of Appeal[122] when allowing a lender's appeal in *Re EVTR, Gilbert v Barber*.[123] The facts of the case were that Mr Barber lent £60,000 to the company to enable it to purchase new equipment. The company in fact paid out the moneys to persons who leased temporary equipment to the company. Following the appointment of a receiver to the company, the moneys were

---

[118.] *Ibid* at 656.
[119.] *Ibid* at 653.
[120.] [1975] 1 All ER 604.
[121.] *Ibid* at 606.
[122.] Also by Lord MacDermott in *Re McKeown* [1974] NI LR 226 see para **[6.38]** below and by Peter Gibson J in *Carreras Rothmans Ltd v Freeman Mathews Treasure Ltd* [1985] 1 All ER 155; [1984] BCLC 420.
[123.] [1987] BCLC 648; see also *Stanlake Holdings Ltd v Tropical Capital Investment Ltd* 24 May 1991 (FT Law Report).

refunded to the company in exchange for the equipment. In giving the principal judgment of the court, Dillon LJ held[124] that on *Quistclose* principles a resulting trust was created for the specific purpose of purchasing new equipment, that purpose failed as the company never acquired new equipment and accordingly the repayments made to the receiver were subject to the same trust as the original £60,000.

[6.38] In *Re McKeown*[125] a loan was made for a specific purpose and subject to a condition as to the proceeds from which it should be repaid. In that case a person lent money to a building contractor for the purpose of paying an arbitrator's costs and expenses on condition that the loan would be repaid out of the proceeds of the arbitrator's award. The Northern Ireland court applied the *Quistclose* decision and held that the arbitrator's fees and costs which had been awarded to the building contractor (subsequent to his bankruptcy) should be paid to the lender and not form part of the building contractor's assets.

[6.39] The usefulness of the *Quistclose* principle in corporate rescue restructuring can be seen from the decision in *Re Northern Developments (Holdings) Ltd.*[126] In that case 17 banks supported a company in difficulty by providing a fund in the parent's name for the express purpose of providing moneys for the company's unsecured creditors following the appointment of a receiver to the company. Sir Robert Megarry V-C held that there was a *Quistclose* type of trust attaching to the fund enforceable by the banks and by the company's creditors as against the parent.

4. Paying Banker's Liability to Payee

Duty of Paying Bank to Payee

"The general principle is that a payee named in a cheque has no right of action against the bank on which the cheque is drawn if the cheque is dishonoured."[127]

[6.40] When a paying bank is presented with a cheque drawn on it by its customer, its duty to pay or decline to pay, as the case may be, is in its capacity as paying banker to its customer. This general principle was applied in *Dublin*

[124.] *Ibid* at 650.

[125.] [1974] NILR 226.

[126.] High Court, unrep, 6 October 1978 as discussed by Peter Gibson J in *Carreras Rothmans Ltd v Freeman Mathews Treasure Ltd* [1984] BCLC 420 at 433.

[127.] Kenny J in *Dublin Port and Docks Board v The Governor and Company of the Bank of Ireland* [1976] IR 118 at 141; see also Kerr J in *National Westminster Bank Ltd v Barclays Bank International Ltd* [1974] 3 All ER 834 at 840 - "in deciding whether or not to honour a customer's cheque, at any rate when it is in proper form and the customer's signature appears to be genuine, a bank owes no duty of care to a payee."

Port and Docks Board v The Governor and Company of the Bank of Ireland[128] where the full Supreme Court unanimously held that the paying bank as paying bank owes no contractual duty to the payee of a cheque. In the principal judgment of the Court, Henchy J said:[129]

> "Under our law and our system of banking, when cheques drawn by a customer on a particular branch arrive in that branch from the central clearing house, the bank, in deciding whether to pay those cheques, acts entirely as a paying bank, and apart from statute, is bound only by the contract between it and the drawer of the cheque. I find no authority - judicial, text-book or otherwise - to support the proposition that in such circumstances the bank has a contractual duty to a payee of one of those cheques who happens to be a customer in another branch of the bank. The existence of such a contractual duty would run counter to both legal principle and sound banking practice. It would confuse and bring into possible conflict the paying and the collecting functions of the bank, it would make it impossible on occasion for the bank to act with the required propriety to both drawer and payee of a cheque, and also on occasion it would result in the unfair preferment of a payee who happened to be a customer in another branch of the bank over a payee who happened not to be a customer."

The general principle that a paying bank does not owe a duty to a payee of a cheque drawn on it arises under privity of contract. Although Griffin J stated:[130] "that a [paying] bank owes no duty of care to a payee", Henchy J was more careful in his concluding remarks by stating:[131]

> "For the purpose of this case it is sufficient to hold that the absence of a contractual duty owed to the plaintiffs, as payees of the cheque, by the defendants in the exercise of their functions as a paying bank in dealing with the cheques defeats the plaintiffs' claim for damages for negligence on the part of the defendants in carrying out their contractual obligations."

[6.41] On the question of the payee being entitled to damages for economic loss which the paying banker could have foreseen by refusing to honour a cheque, Kenny J stated:[132]

> "While foreseeability that one's action or inaction may cause personal injury or damage to property imposes liability, it does not create any liability for foreseen economic loss unless there is a special relationship between the parties as there was in *Hedley Byrne & Co Ltd v Heller & Partners Ltd* [1964] AC 465."

---

[128] [1976] IR 118.
[129] *Ibid* at 136.
[130] *Ibid* at 139.
[131] *Ibid* at 137; O'Higgins CJ and Parke J agreed with the judgments of Henchy J and Kenny J.
[132] *Ibid* at 141.

This raises the question as to when, if at all, a relationship of paying banker and payee comes within *Hedley Byrne & Co Ltd v Heller & Partners Ltd*. Such a relationship was held to arise in *TE Potterton Ltd v Northern Bank Ltd*.[133] In that case the words on a cheque were in ordinary script apart from the word "nine" which was in block. Although the paying bank had previously accepted such cheques it returned this cheque to the payee marked, "Refer to Drawer Present Again Alteration reqs drawer's conf." Ultimately payment was not received in respect of this cheque and the payee contended that if it had known of the drawer's difficulties it could have attempted to recover cattle at the time. O'Hanlon J held that:

1. While as a general rule a paying bank, on presentation of a cheque for payment, did not owe any duty to a payee of a cheque who was not its customer, that rule was subject to qualification where the paying bank embarked on a course of conduct for its own purposes which was calculated to deceive the payee in a manner which might result in financial loss to such payee, when there was no lawful justification for such action on the part of the bank.

2. The query raised by the bank about an alteration requiring confirmation had been a device to extricate it from having to dishonour the cheque and there could be no justification for the bank returning the cheque uncashed.

In granting damages to the plaintiff for economic loss O'Hanlon J considered Lord Reid's judgment in *Hedley Byrne & Co Ltd v Heller & Partners Ltd*,[134] he said:[135]

> "The question arises in every case where negligent misrepresentation or negligent misstatement is put forward as the cause of action, whether there existed between the parties some relationship based on contract, express or implied, or some other special relationship of the type referred to by Lord Reid which can give rise to liability in damages for economic loss attributable to the fact that the plaintiff acted on the faith of the representation made by the defendant ...

> Turning to the present case ... the defendant ... took it upon itself to communicate to the plaintiff its reason for refusing to honour the cheque at that point in time. In doing this I consider that it assumed an obligation to act honestly and carefully and not to deceive the plaintiff by putting forward a reason which was not the true reason, but was a spurious reason ...

---

[133] [1993] 1 IR 413; [1993] ILRM 225.
[134] [1964] AC 465.
[135] [1993] 1 IR 413 at 422.

This, in my opinion, brings the case within the four walls of the type of situation envisaged ... in *Hedley Byrne & Co Ltd v Heller & Partners Ltd.*

I hold that the defendant was in breach of the obligation which arose in the particular circumstances of this case to reply in a careful and honest manner once it took the course of indicating its reason for refusing payment on foot of the cheque, and that the plaintiff was thereby caused economic loss."

[6.42] It should be noted though that the honouring of a forged cheque by a paying banker is not a representation to the payee that the cheque is valid. If the payee has not discharged the proceeds of the cheque, it may be required to reimburse the paying bank for the amount of the invalid cheque which has been honoured.[136]

Cheque Cards - Banker's Liability to Payee

[6.43] It appears that where a person, such as a retailer, takes a cheque in good faith, such person will be able to obtain payment in respect of that cheque even where the signature is forged if, at the time the cheque was accepted, the payee was shown a cheque card and the details of the cheque card including the signature, matched that of the cheque.[137] The English Court of Appeal so decided by a majority in *First Sport Ltd v Barclays Bank plc*.[138] The retailer complied with all conditions of the cheque card including ascertaining that "the signature on the cheque agreed with the specimen on the card." The court held that when the retailer accepted the cheque which was supported by a cheque card and which complied with the conditions of the cheque card an independent contract was created between the retailer and the paying bank and such contract "is a separate and independent obligation which is not dependent in any way upon default of the customer".[139]

This decision underlines the importance of the wording in any set of conditions prepared by a bank and the bank's potential liability and thus loss, in the absence of clear language excluding liability. The decision is based very much on the conditions attaching to the cheque card, which were that the bank would pay up to £50 on a single personal cheque issued within the United Kingdom in respect of a single transaction during the validity period of the card, provided:

"(1) that no other cheque 'guaranteed' by a Barclays card was also used to settle the transaction;

---

136. See *National Westminster Bank Ltd v Barclays Bank International Ltd* [1974] 3 All ER 834; see para **[5.65]**.
137. On cheque cards see further *Chalmers & Guest on Bills of Exchange, Cheques and Promissory Notes* (14th ed) p 621-2.
138. [1993] 3 All ER 789.
139. *Ibid per* Evans LJ at 795.

(2) that the cheque was taken from a Barclays cheque book issued in the United Kingdom;

(3) that the signature on the cheque agreed with the specimen on the card;[140]

(4) that the signature on the cheque was written in the presence of the seller; and

(5) that the seller recorded the number of the card on the back of the cheque".

In the leading judgment of the Court of Appeal, Evans LJ stated:[141]

"The legal analysis in my judgment is as follows. The card conveys to the retailer, or to any other person to whom it is presented, an offer made by the bank which, if accepted, establishes contractual relations between them ... The bearer must have authority to convey the offer on behalf of the bank. The authorised signatory has actual authority to do this, even if this authority has been terminated, or is limited in any way, he will continue to have ostensible authority to convey the bank's offer on its behalf. If the bearer is some other person, even a thief, and provided the retailer had no reason to believe that he is not the authorised signatory and account holder, then in my judgment he too has ostensible authority to this limited extent. If the bank had intended to make it clear to the retailer that such a person would have no authority, actual or apparent, then the statement could have been worded to that effect. ... The retailer in my judgment is entitled to rely upon that statement, on its true construction, and if he complies with the conditions then the bank becomes bound by its undertaking to payees."

The contrary view as portrayed by Kennedy LJ in his dissenting judgment is the requirement that the card can be used only by the authorised signatory, that a "forged or unauthorised signature is wholly inoperative"[142] and that it has been held[143] a forged cheque is not a cheque but "a mere sham piece of paper"[144] (although Sir Thomas Bingham MR pointed out in his judgment supporting Evans LJ that this decision involved a dispute between a paying bank and a collecting bank). Leave to appeal to the House of Lords was granted.[145]

[140.] It is understood that this condition no longer applies to Barclays cheque cards where it is now stated that the cheque must be signed "by the person whose signature appears on the card" - see (1993) NLJ 430.

[141.] *Ibid* at 794.

[142.] Bills of Exchange Act, 1882, s 24.

[143.] In *National Westminster Bank Ltd v Barclays Bank International Ltd* [1974] 3 All ER 834.

[144.] *Ibid* at 836.

[145.] Although no report appears of any subsequent appeal.

In the House of Lords' decision in *Metropolitan Police Commissioner v Charles*[146] Lord Diplock stated:[147]

> "... the use of the cheque card ... gives to the payee a direct contractual right against the bank itself to payment on presentment, provided that the use of the card by the drawer to bind the bank to pay the cheque was within the actual or ostensible authority conferred on him by the bank.
>
> By exhibiting to the payee a cheque card containing the undertaking by the bank to honour cheques drawn in compliance with the conditions endorsed on the back, and drawing the cheque accordingly, the drawer represents to the payee that he has actual authority from the bank to make a contract with the payee on the bank's behalf that it will honour the cheque on presentment for payment."

[6.44] Accordingly, the issuing of a cheque card by a bank to its customer may give rise to a representation to a payee taking in good faith a cheque, supported by the cheque card, that the drawer of the cheque has the bank's authority to draw a cheque, in compliance with the conditions under which the card was issued (including the limit on the card), and that the cheque will be honoured by the bank.

5. PAYMENTS TO PERSONS OUTSIDE IRELAND

[6.45] The Central Bank's powers to restrict the transfer of funds outside Ireland pursuant to the Exchange Control Acts, 1954-1990 lapsed on 31 December 1992. These Acts were replaced by the Financial Transfers Act, 1992[148] whereby the Minister for Finance may restrict financial transfers between Ireland and other countries provided such restriction is made in conformity with the Treaties governing the European Communities.[149] Financial transfers are currently prohibited to residents of Iraq (or organisations consititued or incorporated under the law of Iraq)[150] and residents of Libya,[151] although in certain circumstances the Central Bank may grant permission to make a transfer.

---

[146] [1976] 3 All ER 112.

[147] *Ibid* at 114.

[148] In announcing this legislation the press statement issued by the Minister for Finance on 18 November 1992 indicated that without this Act "there would be a vacuum and it would not be possible to comply with international obligations".

[149] Financial Transfers Act, 1992, s 4.

[150] Financial Transfers (Iraq) Order, 1997 (SI 449/1997) pursuant to Council Regulation (EC) No 2465/96 of 17 December 1996).

[151] Financial Transfers (Libya) Order, 1993 (SI 410/1993) (giving effect to United Nations Security Council Regulation No 883 of 1993).

Chapter 7

Facility Letters

INTRODUCTION

[7.01] Since the enactment of the Consumer Credit Act, 1995 on 13 May 1996,[1] a person does not need a special licence or authority to lend money, save where such loan is being made to a consumer. Prior to that date lending was subject to the Moneylenders Acts 1900 to 1989 whereby a lender was required to have a moneylenders licence or come within one of the exemptions set out in the Moneylenders Act, 1900 (as amended).[2]

[7.02] A facility letter or loan agreement is a contract whereby one person, or a group of persons usually known as a syndicate, agree to lend money to another person or persons upon certain conditions.[3] It has been said that "there is no such thing as a standard international term loan agreement".[4] The same can be said for facility letters as each bank or lender tends to have its own standard or at least standard terms and conditions attached. The Consumer Credit Act, 1995 has endeavoured to standardise certain aspects of loan agreements or facility letters used by consumers[5] by requiring certain terms to be set out in a standard easy to understand manner.[6]

Clauses in a loan agreement may be classified into two categories. First, those setting out the commercial agreement between the lender and borrower, namely the amount and currency of the loan, when it may be drawn, when it is to be repaid, whether it may be prepaid and if so, in what denominations and what notice must be given, the rate of interest - this includes a base rate such as the

---

[1.] SI 121/1996.

[2.] Section 6 as amended by the Central Bank Act, 1989, s 136 and as exempted by Orders of Exemption of the Department of Industry and Commerce dated 31 July 1989 and 12 September 1989, the Moneylenders Act, 1900 (Section 6) (Exemptions) Order, 1992 SI 378/1992 and the Moneylenders Act, 1900 (Section 6(e)) Order, 1993 SI 167/1993.

[3.] For specimen loan agreements see Lingard, *Bank Security Documents* (3rd ed) Butterworths, para 5.11; Gabriel, *Legal Aspects of Syndicated Loans* (1986) Butterworths, Appendix 4; Penn, Shea & Arora, *The Law and Practice of International Banking* Vol 2 (1987) Sweet & Maxwell Ch 17.

[4.] Penn, Shea & Arora, *The Law and Practice of International Banking* Vol 2 (1987) (Sweet & Maxwell), para 6.01.

[5.] For the definition of consumer see para **[7.03]** below.

[6.] Consumer Credit Act, 1995, s 36 and the Consumer Credit Act, 1995 (Section 36) Regulations, 1996 (SI 128/1996).

three month Dublin Interbank Offered Rate plus any costs associated with making the loan (being costs imposed by a regulatory authority namely the Central Bank) such as reserve asset cost plus a margin, the rate where there has been a default in payment (known as default interest) together with an arrangement fee and a commitment fee. An arrangement fee is a fee to the lender for arranging the loan; a commitment fee is a fee for the lender committing itself to make moneys available but ceases to be chargeable in respect of such amounts of the approved loan which are advanced.

The second category of clauses are those which protect the lender such as representations and warranties of the borrower, the borrower's covenants, events of default, change in circumstances (namely, supervening illegality and increased costs), assignment clause and governing law and jurisdiction clause. The latter clauses generally provide that the law to govern the agreement and the courts which are to have jurisdiction are those of the lender's home State. It has been said that loan agreements have been weighted in favour of lenders to the detriment of the borrower.[7] The reason why loan agreements are so weighted is that once the loan has been advanced (which usually happens within days of signing the loan agreement[8]), all the risk falls on the lender - the borrower has the lender's money. In the case of governing law and jurisdiction, the lender will choose its home territory, not because the courts may lean in its favour (which is unlikely at least in the principal common law jurisdictions) but because the lender will be familiar with such law and courts and thus is less likely to be subject to unwelcome surprises.

Apart from consumer loans, a bank does not owe a duty of care in respect of the issue of a facility letter or loan agreement. Its duty of care is limited to the manner in which the account is administered and the execution of payment instructions.[9]

CONSUMER LENDING

[7.03] While freedom of contract still prevails in settling the terms of a loan agreement for a business,[10] the legislature has established certain requirements which must apply to loans made available to consumers namely, individuals acting outside their trade, business or profession when taking up the loan.[11]

---

7. "Generally, lenders have had it all their own way" - Mr Pat Rabbitte, Minister for Commerce, Science and Technology (The Irish Centre for Commercial Law Studies) 8 September 1995.
8. In consumer loans there is a ten day cooling off period to be observed whereby the loan may not be advanced, although the borrower may waive this period - Consumer Credit Act, 1995, s 50; see para [7.14] below.
9. See *Barclays Bank plc v Green and Challis* [1996] 4 JIBL N-82.
10. For further reading of the negotiation of loan agreements see Lingard, 'The Negotiation of Loan Agreements' (1995) CLP 27.
11. Consumer Credit Act, 1995, s 2(1).

Lending to a consumer is governed by rules both as to who may lend and the terms and format under which loans may be made available.[12]

Authorised Lender for Consumers

[7.04] The Consumer Credit Act, 1995 provides:[13]

(1) A person shall not engage in the business of moneylending on his own behalf unless -

    (a) he is the holder of a moneylender's licence, and

    (b) he maintains a business premises for that purpose which is not used as a residence by any person.

(2) A person shall not engage in the business of moneylending on behalf of a moneylender who is not the holder of a moneylender's licence.

The critical words here are "the business of moneylending".[14]

"Moneylending" is defined as meaning[15] "credit[16] supplied by a moneylender to a consumer on foot of a moneylending agreement".

"Moneylending agreement" is defined as meaning:

"a credit agreement[17] into which a moneylender enters, or offers to enter, with a consumer in which one or more of the following apply:

    (a) the agreement was concluded away from the business premises of the moneylender ...

    (b) any negotiations for, or in relation to the credit were conducted at a place other than the business premises of the moneylender ...,

    (c) repayments under the agreement will, or may, be paid by the consumer to the moneylender or his representative at any place other than the business premises of the moneylender ..., or

    (d) where the total cost of credit to the consumer under the agreement is in excess of an APR of 23 per cent, or such other rate as may be prescribed.

[12.] Consumer Credit Act, 1995 and the European Communities (Unfair Terms in Consumer Contracts) Regulations, 1995, SI 27/1995.

[13.] Section 98.

[14.] As to what is the meaning of carrying on a "business" see paras **[7.05]-[7.07]** below.

[15.] Consumer Credit Act, 1995, s 2(1).

[16.] "Credit" is defined as including "a deferred payment, cash loan, or other similar accommodation" (Consumer Credit Act, 1995, s 2(1) as amended by SI 277/1996).

[17.] "Credit agreement" is defined as meaning "an agreement whereby a creditor grants or promises to grant to a consumer a credit in the form of a deferred payment, a cash loan or other similar financial accommodation" (creditor is defined by reference to a credit agreement making the definitions here circular).

This definition raises the question as to whether a person may lend money to a consumer without any licence provided (1) the agreement is signed at the lender's place of business, (2) the negotiations for the conclusion of the agreement were concluded at the lender's place of business, (3) the repayments are made at the lender's place of business and (4) the interest rate is not in excess of an APR of 23 per cent. Some of these conditions may be impractical, particularly the third, but a person who can arrange his lending within that parameter can avoid the rigours which apply to the holder of a moneylender's licence.[18]

To complete the series of definitions, a "moneylender" is defined as meaning:

> a person who carries on the business of moneylending[19] or who advertises or announces himself or holds himself out in any way as carrying on that business.

It will be noticed that to be a moneylender, and thus to fall within the definition of a moneylending agreement which is subject to the requirements of a moneylender's licence, one must carry on the business of moneylending.[20] However, under the Act a "moneylender" is not deemed to include pawnbrokers, industrial and provident societies, friendly societies, "a credit institution", a supplier of money for the purchase, sale or hire of goods at an APR which is less than 23% or other prescribed rate, and "a mortgage lender". The latter is broadly speaking a credit institution which makes housing loans.[21]

A credit institution is defined as the holder of a banking licence, a bank licenced under EU regulations, a building society, trustee savings bank, ACC Bank plc, ICC Bank plc, ICC Investment Bank Ltd[22] as well as "such person or persons which may from time to time be prescribed". A number of financial institutions have been prescribed under the Consumer Credit Act, 1995 (section 2) (No 2) Regulations, 1996.[23] No exception is made for a person registered as a moneylender outside the State.[24]

[7.05] A question may often arise in practice as to whether a person (who is not exempt from the definition of moneylender), in making a once-off loan is carrying on a moneylending business. In *Cripps Warburg Ltd v Cologne Investment Co Ltd, Aran Friendly Society*[25] D'Arcy J held that a person who

---

[18.] Consumer Credit Act, 1995 ss 92-114.
[19.] The definitions are circular in that the definition of moneylending refers to credit supplied by a moneylender (Consumer Credit Act, 1995, s 2(1)).
[20.] This work does not deal with provisions relating to moneylending under Part VIII of the Consumer Credit Act, 1995.
[21.] Consumer Credit Act, 1995, s 2(1) as amended by SI 127/1996.
[22.] SI 127/1996.
[23.] SI 369/1996.
[24.] *The London Finance and Discount Company Ltd v Butler and Butler* [1929] IR 90.
[25.] [1980] IR 321.

made one isolated loan in Ireland was not deemed to be carrying on the business of moneylending in Ireland. This may be contrasted with the earlier decision of the highest court at the time where it was held in *Cornelius v Phillips*[26] that:[27]

"the respondent, in effecting a moneylending transaction with the appellant, was, in the ordinary sense, carrying on the moneylending business, and it is immaterial whether a single transaction or a number of transactions are involved."

The fact that this decision was not referred to in D'Arcy J's judgment must leave some doubt as to whether one transaction can be relied upon as not being sufficient to be carrying on a business.

[7.06] More recently in *The Minister for Industry and Commerce v Suicre Éireann cpt*[28] Lynch J, in relying upon D'Arcy J's judgment and *Halsbury's Laws of England*,[29] held that the ordinary meaning of the expression to carry on business "presupposes some sort of continuation of activity as contrasted with one or two isolated transactions."[30] But as with D'Arcy J, Lynch J made no reference to the 1918 House of Lords' decision[31] which held otherwise.

[7.07] There is less doubt that a business may be deemed to be carried on, even though only one transaction is effected, if it is intended to effect further transactions. The Court of Appeal's guidance in *Re Griffin*[32] might be noted:[33]

"Whether one or two transactions make a business depends upon the circumstances of each case. I take the test to be this: if an isolated transaction, which if repeated would be a transaction in business, is proved to have been undertaken with the intent that it should be the first of several transactions, that is, with the intent of carrying on a business, then it is a first transaction in an existing business. The business exists from the time of the commencement of that transaction with the intent that it should be one of a series".

[7.08] A person who does not have a moneylenders' licence or who is not otherwise exempt will be unable to enforce its moneylending contracts with a consumer.[34]

[26.] [1918] AC 199.
[27.] *Ibid* at 217 per Lord Parmoor.
[28.] [1992] 2 IR 215.
[29.] 4th ed Vol 7(1) para 22.
[30.] [1992] 2 IR 215 at 231.
[31.] *Cornelius v Phillips* [1918] AC 199.
[32.] (1890) 60 LJQB 235.
[33.] *Ibid* at 237 per Lord Esher MR.
[34.] Being contrary to the Consumer Credit Act, 1995, s 98(2); see also *The London Finance and Discount Company Ltd v Butler and Butler* [1929] IR 90.

Requirements of a Consumer Loan Agreement

[7.09] Lending to consumers has been transformed recently by the implementation of the Consumer Credit Act, 1995.[35] Prior to that, outside the moneylenders legislation, there was no legislation governing the lending of money to consumers, unlike the position in Northern Ireland under the Consumer Credit Act 1974. Only the Hire Purchase Acts of 1946 to 1980 regulated certain forms of credit but not loans. The impetus for change was brought from outside Ireland by the Council Directive of 22 December 1986 for the approximation of the laws, regulations and administrative provisions of the Member States covering consumer credit[36] as amended by Council Directive of 22 February 1990.[37]

[7.10] However, the first Directive was implemented in Ireland for a broader range of agreements than what was envisaged by the Council. The Irish legislation makes no distinction and applies to all consumer loans whether for £1 or £1 million. The Directive envisaged that such legislation would have no application to credit agreements involving amounts of less than 200 ECU or more than 20,000 ECU.[38] The rationale for such thresholds presumably is to avoid over-regulation for very small loans and that persons borrowing significant amounts should have the resources to retain their own independent advice. The absence of an upper threshold for large loans is a trap for the unwary.

[7.11] Before considering the provisions of the Consumer Credit Act, 1995 (which need to be complied with when a person makes a loan available to a consumer), it should be noted that the Act exempts certain types of loans, including loans made which attract no charge or rate of interest.[39] The most significant exemption from the Act is a credit agreement which is "in the form of an authentic act signed before a notary public or a judge".[40] Thus the execution of a facility letter or loan agreement by a consumer "in the form of an authentic act" before a notary public can avoid the application of the Act, not only as to the requirements for setting out appropriate repayment details on the face of the document[41] but also the restrictive termination provisions under

---

[35.] On 13 May 1996 - SI 121/1996.

[36.] 87/102/EEC.

[37.] 90/88/EEC. These directives are set out in the First Schedule to the Consumer Credit Act, 1995; it should be noted that s 2(7) of the Act provides that when a court is construing a provision of the Act it shall give to the Act, "a construction that will give effect to the Council Directive, and for this purpose a court shall have regard to the provisions of the Council Directive, including the preambles".

[38.] Article 2.1(f).

[39.] Consumer Credit Act, 1995, s 3(2).

[40.] *Ibid* s 3(2)(b).

[41.] Pursuant to the Consumer Credit Act, 1995, s 36 and the Consumer Credit Act, 1995 (Section 36) Regulation, 1996 (SI 128/1996).

s 54.[42] Indeed, it avoids the unwelcome consequences of unenforcement which arise pursuant to ss 38 and 140 of the Act. In practice this avoidance mechanism is sometimes used for large loans, well in excess of the Directive's upper threshold, but is not used generally for loans below £100,000. Views differ as to whether it may be used as there is no particular definition of "authentic act". However, clearly by its inclusion in the legislation, in conjunction with the interpretation provisions,[43] it is designed to be and can be used.

Advertising and Offering of Consumer Loans

> "From now on advertising for credit must be both informative and meaningful".[44]

[7.12] Every advertisement in which a person offers to provide or arrange credit to a consumer shall, if it mentions a rate of interest or cost of credit "contain a clear and prominent statement of the APR ... and no other rate of interest shall be included in the advertisement."[45]

An advertisement under which credit is offered, subject to conditions, security or restrictions must state the conditions, security or restrictions (as the case may be).[46]

Statutory Requirements of Consumer Loans

[7.13] Apart from housing loans which have their own particular requirements[47] and apart from "credit in the form of advances on a current account, or on credit card accounts,"[48] where a consumer borrows money a copy of the contract must be handed personally to the consumer immediately after it has been concluded or delivered to the consumer within 10 days.[49] The agreement must contain a statement as to the names and addresses of all the parties to the contract as well as "any costs or penalties to which the consumer may become liable for failure to comply with the terms of the agreement."[50] It is essential that these requirements be complied with as failure to do so will render the entire agreement, and any security given for the loan, unenforceable.[51]

[42.] See para **[7.54]** below.

[43.] Consumer Credit Act, 1995, s 2(7) see fn 37 above.

[44.] Mr Pat Rabbite, Minister for Commerce, Science and Technology, Irish Centre for Commercial Law Studies, 8 September, 1995.

[45.] Consumer Credit Act, 1995, s 21(1) as amended by the Consumer Credit Act, 1995 (Section 28) Regulations, 1996 SI 245/1996.

[46.] Consumer Credit Act, 1995, s 21(3), (4) and (6) respectively.

[47.] Pursuant to the Consumer Credit Act, 1995, ss 115-136 see paras **[10.74]-[10.84]**.

[48.] Consumer Credit Act, 1995, s 30(4).

[49.] *Ibid* s 30(1)(a).

[50.] *Ibid* s 30(3).

[51.] *Ibid* s 38.

[7.14] Save in the case of housing loans, credit by means of a credit account or an overdraft facility, a consumer may withdraw from his facility letter or loan agreement within 10 days of receiving it or a copy of it. This 10 day period is known as "the cooling-off period".[52] In order to withdraw, the consumer must give written notice to the lender.[53] This of course may create a problem for the lender, who will obviously not lend during the cooling-off period, as well as potentially creating a difficulty for the consumer who may wish to utilise the finance offered to him prior to the expiration of the cooling-off period. This difficulty is recognised in that s 50(2) provides that:

> A consumer may forego his right to a cooling-off period in any credit agreement by signing a statement to this effect separately from any other term of the agreement.[54]

This statement by which the consumer foregoes his right to a cooling-off period must state in a prominent position:[55]

> WARNING
>
> THIS WAIVER MEANS YOU ARE GIVING UP YOUR RIGHT TO A 10 DAY PERIOD TO RECONSIDER YOUR COMMITMENT TO THE AGREEMENT

The Act requires that the consumer loan agreement contain a statement that the consumer has a right to withdraw from the loan agreement by giving the lender notice within 10 days of receipt of the loan agreement and that the consumer may indicate he does not wish to exercise that right by signing the waiver; his signature to the waiver is required to be "separate from, and additional to, the consumer's signature in relation to any of the terms of the agreement".[56]

[7.15] A facility letter or loan agreement (other than in respect of advances on a current account (an overdraft facility)) is required to contain a statement of:[57]

    (a) the amount of the credit lent under the agreement,

    (b) the date the credit is to be advanced (if known),

    (c) the amount of each repayment instalment,

[52.] *Ibid* s 50.

[53.] *Ibid*.

[54.] The explanatory memorandum to the Bill may cause confusion as it indicates that the consumer may forego the cooling-off period by signing a waiver which is "separate to the agreement" rather than separate from any other term of the agreement. That seemed to reflect the initial thinking that a separate document would be needed as evidenced by the waiver notice to a cooling-off period which appeared in the Bill as passed by Dáil Éireann. A separate waiver document is not now required.

[55.] Consumer Credit Act, 1995, s 50(3).

[56.] *Ibid* s 30(2).

[57.] *Ibid* s 31(1).

(d) the rate of interest charged and the APR,[58]

(e) the conditions under which the APR may be changed,

(f) any charges not included in the calculation of the APR but which have to be paid by the borrower in certain given circumstances,

(g) the number of repayment instalments,

(h) the date, or the method of determining the date, upon which each repayment instalment is payable,

(i) the total amount payable in respect of the loan,

(j) the date of expiry of the loan,

(k) the means and the cost of any termination by the borrower of the agreement before the final repayment instalment.

The front page of a such an agreement must contain a notice in the following form:[59]

"IMPORTANT INFORMATION as at [date]

1. Amount of credit advanced £

2. Period of Agreement

3. Number of Repayment Instalments £

4. Amount of Each Instalment £

5. Total Amount Repayable £

6. Cost of this credit (5 minus 1) £

7. APR

NB YOU MAY WITHDRAW FROM THIS AGREEMENT AT ANY TIME WITHIN 10 DAYS OF RECEIVING THIS AGREEMENT OR A COPY OF IT."

It should be noted that the statutory format and requirements of consumer loan agreements may be amended by Ministerial order.[60] A lender who contravenes the statutory format and requirements commits an offence.[61] Furthermore, in the event that such requirements have not been complied with, the lender will be unable to enforce the loan agreement unless the court is satisfied that the non-

---

[58.] For the meaning of APR and the criteria for its calculation see the Consumer Credit Act, 1995 ss 9 and 10.

[59.] Consumer Credit Act, 1995, s 36 and the Consumer Credit Act, 1995 (Section 36) Regulations, 1996 (SI 128/1996).

[60.] *Ibid* s 37.

[61.] *Ibid* s 39 and s 12.

compliance[62] "was not deliberate and has not prejudiced the consumer, and that it would be just and equitable to dispense with the requirement."[63]

A person is not permitted to make a demand for payment of moneys arising under an agreement which is unenforceable.[64] Such person is precluded from invoking any collection proceedings.[65]

[7.16] A customer is entitled to prepay the loan prior to its maturity date (upon his giving written notice to the lender).[66] In making a prepayment the consumer is entitled to a reduction in the total cost of credit in accordance with a formula approved either by the Central Bank of Ireland or the Director of Consumer Affairs.[67]

Consumer Overdraft Facility

[7.17] In respect of an overdraft facility,[68] the facility letter should contain a statement of:[69]

    (a) the credit limit, if any, at the commencement of the agreement and any conditions in relation to any variation of the limit,[70]

    (b) the annual rate of interest and the charges applicable from the time the agreement is concluded and the conditions under which these may be amended, and

    (c) the procedure for determining the agreement.

The Act in fact provides that the consumer be informed "at the time, or before, an agreement is made".[71]

It further provides that this information "shall be confirmed by the creditor in writing to the consumer within 10 days of the making of the agreement".[72] Accordingly, a banker may agree orally with his customer as to the granting of an overdraft facility outlining to the customer the requirements set out in (a) to (c) above and then subsequent to the meeting send a letter to the customer setting out the same information.

[62.] The court has no discretion in the event of a failure to comply with the provisions of s 30, see para **[7.13]** above.

[63.] Consumer Credit Act, 1995, s 38.

[64.] *Ibid* s 49(1).

[65.] *Ibid* s 49(2).

[66.] *Ibid* s 52(1).

[67.] Which may be overridden by another formula or method prescribed by the Minister for Enterprise, Trade and Employment (s 52(2)).

[68.] Described in the Consumer Credit Act, 1995 also as "an advance on a current account" s 31(1) and s 35(1); different rules apply to an overdraft facility "tacitly accepted" - s 35(3).

[69.] Consumer Credit Act, 1995, s 35(1).

[70.] As amended by the Consumer Credit Act, 1995 (Section 37) Regulations, 1996 SI 129/1996.

[71.] Consumer Credit Act, s 35(1).

[72.] *Ibid* s 35(2).

The banker is required also to inform the consumer "of any change in the annual rate of interest or in the relevant charges at or before the time such change occurs".[73] This information "may be given in a statement of account[74] or in an advertisement published in a national newspaper published and circulating in the State".[75]

As with ordinary consumer loans, the failure of a banker to comply with the foregoing provisions may, apart from such failure being an offence,[76] prevent the banker from being able to enforce the terms of the agreement.[77]

COMMITMENT TO LEND

[7.18] A facility letter or loan agreement will set out the basis upon which the lender agrees to advance the loan. Usually in a syndicate each lender will agree to lend severally but not jointly - in other words lenders will not be obliged to lend any more than their share.[78] It is important to be clear in the language otherwise the commitment to lend could be construed as being joint, as pointed by Lord Halsbury when quoting from *Platt's* work on Covenants:[79]

> "No particular words are necessary to constitute a covenant of either kind (that is to say either joint or several). If two covenant generally for themselves, without any words of severance, or that they or one of them shall do such a thing, a joint charge is created; which shews the necessity of adding words of severalty where the covenantor's liability is to be confined to his own acts".

[7.19] A lender will be in breach of contract if it declines to lend prior to giving the borrower the opportunity to satisfy the conditions precedent within the stipulated time.[80] An exception to this would be where the drafting is such that the conditions precedent are conditions precedent to the coming into effect of any contract. This is rarely the position as in such event the lender will forego its arrangement fee. One of the principal conditions precedent is usually the completion of the security in a manner satisfactory to the lender and its advisers. Where the loan is being advanced to enable the borrower to purchase an asset over which the lender is to take security the advance of the loan will in fact

---

73. *Ibid s* 35(2).
74. This is likely to be impractical at or before the time such change occurs.
75. Consumer Credit Act, 1995, s 35(2).
76. *Ibid* ss 39 and 12.
77. *Ibid* s 38 - the agreement being unenforceable unless the court is satisfied that the failure to comply was not deliberate and has not prejudiced the consumer and it would be just and equitable to dispense with the requirement.
78. *Keightley v Watson* (1849) 3 Exch 716.
79. In *White v Tyndall* (1888) 13 App Cas 263 at 269.
80. *Smith v Butler* [1900] 1 QB 694.

happen immediately prior to the giving of security, albeit durir
the same meeting of the participants and their legal advisers.

No Specific Performance against Lender

[7.20] Although a lender is contractually bound to lend the agreed amount in the
agreed currency or currencies once the conditions precedent have been satisfied,
it seems that if the lender decides not to lend it cannot be forced to do so. In
delivering his judgment in *The South African Territories Ltd v Wallington*,[81]
Lord Macnaghten said simply:[82]

> "That specific performance of a contract to lend money cannot be enforced is
> so well established, and obviously so wholesome a rule, that it would be idle to
> say a word about it."

In delivering the majority judgment of the Privy Council in *Loan Investment
Corporation of Australasia v Bonner*,[83] Lord Pearson outlined the reasons why a
court will not order specific performance:[84]

> "A mere contract for the loan of money will not be specifically enforced ...
> There is an obvious objection in principle to granting specific performance of
> an unsecured loan. It would have a one-sided operation, creating a position of
> inequality. The borrower obtains immediately the whole advantage of the
> contract to him, namely the loan itself - a sum of money placed completely at
> his disposal. The lender on the other hand has to wait and hope for the payment
> of interest from time to time and for the eventual repayment of the capital. The
> Court has means of compelling a party to pay a sum of money if he is able to do
> so. But no writ of attachment or sequestration or other equitable process can
> compel the borrower to repay the loan, if when the time comes at the end of the
> period he has not enough assets to enable him to do so. This objection in
> principle may not prevail in exceptional cases".

Borrower's Right of Damages

[7.21] The borrower will of course have a right of action for damages for breach
of contract, the amount of damages being sufficient and no more than to
compensate the borrower for the foreseeable damage or loss to it arising from
the lender's breach.[85] Thus a borrower who has suffered no loss will receive no
damages.[86] As to the measure of damages, Bingham J clarified the position as
follows:[87]

---

81. [1898] AC 309.
82. *Ibid* at 318.
83. [1970] NZLR 724.
84. *Ibid* at 735.
85. *The South African Territories Ltd v Wallington* [1898] AC 309.
86. *Western Wagon and Property Company v West* [1892] 1 Ch 271.
87. In *Bahamas (Inagua) Sisal Plantation (Ltd) v Griffin* (1897) 14 TLR 139 at 140.

"It was not the amount of money which the defendant had promised to lend. It was only the difference between the rate of interest which the company had offered for the money and the rate which the company would have to pay in order to put it in the same position as if the defendant had performed his contract. But, in measuring the damages, it must be assumed that when the company applied elsewhere for an advance it still remained a company with ordinary credit. If, by reason of circumstances, the company had fallen into disrepute and bad financial odour, the defendant was not responsible for that."

However, there may be circumstances where a borrower can obtain substantial damages as a result of the lender declining to lend in breach of contract. In *The Manchester and Oldham Bank Ltd v WA Cook and Co*[88] Day J held:[89]

"The only other question is as to the damages. Now there was a contract and a breach of it, and I think Mr Cook is entitled to substantial damages, and not to the merely nominal damages which are usually given in the case of breaches of contracts to lend money, for the reason that usually if a man cannot get money in one quarter he can in another. But where special damage is the result of a breach of contract to lend money and a party is deprived of the opportunity of getting money elsewhere, as was the case here, the ordinary rule as to damages applies. Here the bank had express notice of the purpose for which the money was required ... it was by reason of the refusal of the bank to find the money that Cook was unable to complete his contract. In my judgment therefore the arbitrator has acted soundly in awarding to him substantial damages."

The measure of damages was explained in the concurring judgment of Smith J: "the damages should not be nominal, but should be the actual damage which Cook has sustained by not being able to carry out his contract."[90]

No specific Performance against Borrower

[7.22] Once the borrower has accepted the facility letter and agreed to borrow he will not be compelled to borrow. In *Rogers v Challis*[91] the defendant agreed to borrow from the plaintiff. Subsequently the defendant entered into negotiations with a third party on better terms. The court declined to order specific performance against the defendant.

Introduction of the Euro

[7.23] Currently, preparations are under way for the introduction of the Euro and in particular the transition to the Euro from the national currencies of those States which will adopt the Euro. It is already the law in Ireland that:[92]

---

[88]. (1883) 49 LTR 674.
[89]. *Ibid* at 678.
[90]. *Ibid* at 679.
[91]. (1859) 27 Beav 175.
[92]. Council Regulation (EC) No 1103/97 of 17 June 1997 on certain provisions relating to the introduction of the Euro, Article 3.

"The introduction of the Euro shall not have the effect of altering any term of a legal instrument or of discharging or excusing performance under any legal instrument, nor give a party the right unilaterally to alter or terminate such an instrument. This provision is subject to anything which parties may have agreed."

This applies to all loan agreements, facility letters, payment instruments, security documents and guarantees.[93] When Ireland adopts the Euro, reference in any loan agreement to any national currency should be as valid as if reference were made to the Euro unit according to the adopted conversion rates.[94]

INTEREST

[7.24] Interest is the cost to the borrower of having the use of the lender's money. The rate of interest may be fixed (commonly at the commencement of the loan) or more usually it is a variable rate. Typically interest will incorporate a margin, basically the lender's return, of anything from one half of one per cent per annum to four or five per cent per annum above DIBOR[95] (the Dublin Interbank Offered Rate) being the rate at which the lender can obtain deposits in the Dublin interbank market together with any reserve asset requirement of the Central Bank. The loan agreement will set out interest periods - these are typically three months but can vary between one and six months. Usually the period is a period selected by the borrower, but subject to the lender's agreement which is readily given, assuming it itself can fix rates for the relevant period (in other words, the lender can obtain deposits for the relevant period). Interest is typically payable in arrears on the final business day of each interest period, or each quarter where interest periods are in excess of three months.

In the case of large loans (with a variable rate of interest), the borrower will often enter into an interest rate exchange agreement with the lender fixing the rate of interest for a stipulated period, often for a shorter period than the loan, so that the position may be re-assessed later. These agreements are known as swaps[96] and contain complex provisions but have been largely standardised by lenders using the standard ISDA documents,[97] although each bank tends to have its own schedule of additional terms.

---

93. See definition of legal instruments in Article 1.
94. As provided for in Article 6.2 of a draft Council Regulation on the introduction of the Euro (No C236/8 OJ 2.8.97).
95. This is likely to be replaced by EURIBOR in the future.
96. For further reading on swaps see *Encyclopaedia of Banking Law* (Butterworths); Price & Henderson, *Currency & Interest Rate Swaps* (2nd ed) (Butterworths); for an earlier introduction to swaps see Penn, Shea & Arora, *The Law and Practice of International Banking* Vol 2 (1987) Sweet & Maxwell, Ch 11.
97. The 1992 Multicurrency - Cross Border Master Agreement of the International Swap Dealers Association, Inc.

Default Interest

[7.25] Most facility letters or loan agreements will stipulate that in the event the borrower fails to pay interest on the due date for payment, additional interest (known as default interest) will be payable over and above the agreed rate. This additional interest may vary from one half of one per cent to five per cent or more per annum. This raises the question as to whether this additional interest is liquidated damages and enforceable or a penalty and thus unenforceable.[98] Obviously the higher the rate the more likely that a court will construe it as a penalty.

The question came before the English courts in *Lordsvale Finance plc v Bank of Zambia*.[99] In that case the default interest was one per cent over and above the normal rate. The borrower contended that this was a penalty as its sole function was to ensure compliance and it was not a genuine pre-estimate of loss. Coleman J held that a provision for a prospective modest increase in the rate of default interest was not a penalty if it could be explained as commercially justifiable (which it was) provided the dominant purpose of the default interest was not to deter the other party from breach of contract. Coleman J indicated that previous authorities holding default interest as being a penalty appeared to be based on cases where the default interest acted retrospectively as well as prospectively from the date of default. He indicated that for default interest rates to be enforceable, the increased rate of interest must apply only from the date of default and the increase must be modest. He held that the increased rate, which was not a penalty, was simply an increase in the consideration for the loan as a result of the increased credit risk associated with a defaulting borrower.

An interesting feature of the decision is that it appeared to be motivated by a very understandable desire to avoid parties to international loan agreements choosing New York law as the governing law in preference to English law. The judge noted that New York courts give effect to provisions allowing default interest and thus English law should follow suit on the basis that New York and London are the centres of international banking. Notwithstanding the expanding presence, and contribution to Ireland's economy, of Dublin's International Financial Services Centre, Irish courts may favour a borrower[100] although it would be surprising if a default interest rate of one per cent acting prospectively from the date of default were to cause a difficulty in the courts of Ireland.

---

[98] For further reading as to the distinction see Chesire, Fifoot & Furmston's *Law of Contract* (13th ed) pp 634-639.
[99] [1996] 7 JIBL N-144.
[100] See McCarthy J in *Re Atlantic Magnetics Ltd* [1993] 2 IR 561 at 578-9.

Excessive Interest for Consumers

[7.26] The Consumer Credit Act, 1995 provides that[101] a consumer may apply to the Circuit Court for a declaration that "the total cost of credit provided for in any agreement is excessive."[102] However, this right of application does not apply to a loan made by a credit institution or a mortgage lender.[103] This carve out is presumably on the grounds that the charges of such institutions are regulated by the Central Bank.[104]

Upon an application being made to the Circuit Court, the Court may decide that the total cost of credit is excessive.[105] In doing so the court is required to have regard to all relevant factors including:[106]

(a) interest rates prevailing at the time the agreement was made or, where applicable, interest rates prevailing at any time during the currency of the agreement,

(b) the age, business competence and level of literacy and numeracy of the consumer,

(c) the degree of risk involved for the creditor and the security provided,

(d) the creditor's costs including the cost of collecting repayments, and

(e) the extent of competition for the type of credit concerned.

The one factor which seems out of place is (b) - it is certainly an encouragement for the lawyer representing the consumer to portray his client as being exceptionally naive and indeed stupid.[107]

The Director of Consumer Affairs is given a pivotal role in the assessment as to whether a charge is excessive as the Circuit Court may not make an order without giving the Director an opportunity to be heard.[108]

Where the court does decide that the total cost of credit is excessive:

"it may re-open the credit agreement so as to do justice between the parties and may ...

(a) relieve the consumer from payment of any sum in excess of the sum adjudged by the court to be fairly due in respect of such total cost of credit;

(b) set aside, either wholly or in part the agreement against the consumer;

---

101. Section 47(1).
102. See also the European Communities (Unfair Terms in Consumer Contracts) Regulations, 1995 (SI 27/1995) at paras **[18.01]-[18.05]** below.
103. Both as defined in the Consumer Credit Act, 1995, s 2(1).
104. Consumer Credit Act, 1995, s 47(4).
105. *Ibid* s 47(2).
106. *Ibid* s 47(3).
107. See Johnston, 'The New Regulatory Regime for the Provision of Consumer Credit' (The Irish Centre for Commercial Law Studies) 8 September 1995.
108. Consumer Credit Act, 1995, s 47(5).

(c) revise or alter the terms of the agreement; or

(d) order the repayment to the consumer of the whole or part of any sums paid.[109]

REPRESENTATIONS AND WARRANTIES

[7.27] A person will be willing to lend money on certain assumptions. Principally these assumptions are that the borrower has the capacity to borrow, has taken all appropriate action to authorise the borrowing and has obtained any relevant consent from a third party to enable it to enter into the loan agreement and become bound to its obligations thereunder. Effectively, these assumptions are made conditions of the loan agreement, as the borrower is required to represent and warrant the position on those matters to the lender.[110] One of the principal authorities on contract law[111] states, "A representation means a statement of fact, not a statement of intention or of opinion or of law." While the remedies for a misrepresentation are in law dependent upon whether the misrepresentation was made innocently, negligently or fraudulently[112] and while the remedy for breach of warranty may be different, in practice these technical differences are irrelevant as most facility letters/loan agreements will stipulate that a breach of representation or warranty will constitute an event of default entitling the lender to terminate its commitment to lend and call for the immediate repayment of the loan together with outstanding interest. Failure to repay will usually result in the enforcement of any security given for the loan. Accordingly, care must be taken by the borrower and its advisers as to the accuracy of the representations and warranties. Indeed the representations and warranties are meant to be a check-list for the borrower.

[7.28] In his work *The Law and Practice of International Finance,*[113] *Wood* suggests that representations and warranties would include:

1. Status - duly incorporated, validly existing and in good standing,[114]

2. Power and Authority - the borrower has the appropriate authority to enter into and perform the agreement, due authorisation has been given and the agreement has been validly executed,

---

[109] *Ibid* s 48(1).

[110] For an incisive analysis of representations and warranties in a loan agreement see Gabriel, *Legal Aspects of Syndicated Loans* (1986) Butterworths, Ch 4.

[111] Chesire, Fifoot & Furmston's *Law of Contract* (13th ed) Butterworths p 276.

[112] *Ibid* pp 291-306; see also Clark, *Contract Law in Ireland* (3rd ed) Sweet & Maxwell, Ch 11.

[113] (1980) Sweet & Maxwell para 10.5(3); listed also in *Sovereign Borrowers* (ed Kalderen and Siddiqi) (1984) Dag Hammaskjold Foundation and Butterworths, p 87.

[114] Although the term "in good standing" is an American concept, the Companies Registration Office have, on request, issued a letter of good standing (assuming the company's annual returns are filed up to date).

3. No Conflict - the execution and performance of the loan agreement will not contravene any law or regulation of the borrower or any agreement to which it is a party,

4. Legally binding and enforceable - "the loan agreement is the valid and legally binding obligation of the borrower enforceable in accordance with its terms",

5. Consents - all necessary governmental costs have been obtained,

6. Filings - no filings, recordings or registrations are necessary,

7. Financial Condition - the most recent audited accounts of the borrower show a true and fair view of the financial condition of the borrower and there has been no material adverse change since the date of the accounts,

8. Litigation - the borrower is not involved in any litigation, or to the best of the borrower's knowledge there are no proceedings pending against it, which may have a material adverse effect on the borrower's financial condition, and

9. Contracts - the borrower is not in default under any contracts to which it is a party.

It is this author's view that one or two of these warranties go too far. The purpose of the representations and warranties is to present the borrower in a clean state and to ensure the borrower does what is necessary within its rules and the law governing it, to enter into and be bound by the agreement. It is the duty of the lender and its advisers to ensure that the loan agreement, which invariably it has drafted, is valid and binding and, subject to the court's equitable discretion, enforceable in accordance with its terms. It is not for the borrower to warrant this nor indeed for its advisers to do so.[115] By so doing, it immediately creates a conflict of interest - how can the borrower's legal adviser in giving an opinion that a loan agreement is enforceable against its client subsequently act for its client in defending enforcement proceedings brought by the lender? It is the better practice for the borrower and certainly for its legal advisers not to give such comfort, although such practice may be difficult to uphold when dealing with the banks and lawyers in the United States of America who are unaccustomed to such practice. A similar point of principle arises with regard to filings - it is for the lender to put in place the agreement and any necessary registrations.

[115.] It does not form part of the representations and warranties of the sample loan agreement in Gabriel, *Legal Aspects of Syndicated Loans* (1986) Butterworths.

COVENANTS

[7.29] Covenants are contractual commitments of the borrower to carry out certain actions during the course of the loan facility, a breach of which will trigger an event of default.[116] *Murdoch's Dictionary of Irish Law*[117] describes a covenant as, "a clause, usually in a deed, which binds a party to do some act or to refrain from doing some act. No technical words are necessary to constitute a covenant."[118] Although it has been authoritatively stated that a covenant is an agreement under seal,[119] a court should give effect to it even where the loan agreement is not executed under seal.[120] In *Hayne v Cummings*[121] Willes J stated:[122]

> "It is urged that the word 'covenant' is inapplicable to anything but an instrument under seal. It is true that the word in strictness does not apply otherwise than to such agreements as are executed under the solemnity of a seal. But, in common parlance, it is applied to any agreement whether under seal or not."

The most important covenant is the borrower's agreement to repay the loan. In this regard, although it should be self-evident, a lender should ensure that the loan is made available to the persons covenanting to repay the loan (unless such a person is a guarantor).[123]

Some agreements may be negotiated along the lines that a borrower will covenant not to do something unless the prior written consent of the lender is obtained. In such instances the lender has an absolute right to withhold consent.[124] Some agreements may preclude certain action without such consent, but that such consent shall not be unreasonably withheld. Where consent is withheld in such circumstances it seems the onus of proof is on the borrower to show that it was withheld unreasonably and it is not for the lender to show it was justified in withholding consent.[125] When considering whether consent has been

---

[116.] See paras **[7.45]-[7.58]** below.

[117.] (2nd ed, 1993) Topaz Publications.

[118.] "No particular form of words is necessary to form a covenant: but, wherever the court can collect from the instrument an engagement on the one side to do or not to do something, it amounts to a covenant, whether it is in the recital or in any other part of the instrument", *The Great Northern Railway Co v Harrison* (1852) 12 CB 576 at 609, *per* Parke B.

[119.] *Halsbury's Laws of England* (4th ed) Vol 12 para 1539.

[120.] A facility letter will be executed invariably under hand.

[121.] (1864) 16 CBNS 421.

[122.] *Ibid* at 426.

[123.] This will avoid the consequences of what happened in *O'Keeffe v Russell and Allied Irish Banks plc* [1994] ILRM 137.

[124.] *Tredegar v Harwood* [1929] AC 72.

[125.] See Cozens-Hardy MR In *Shanly v Ward* (1913) 29 TLR 714 at 715; see also report of *British Gas Trading Ltd v Eastern Electricity plc* (CA) (1997) 18 Co Law 116 at 117.

unreasonably withheld it has been indicated that the covenant must be considered to ascertain its purpose when the parties contracted.[126]

Purpose of Loan

[7.30] The first covenant which the borrower usually gives, often in a separate clause to the covenants clause, is a commitment to use the proceeds of the loan in a certain manner. Although the bank is not obliged to ensure or enquire that the proceeds are used for the stated purpose,[127] in the event that the proceeds are used for a purpose which is outside the capacity of the company and the bank is aware of that, or deemed to be aware, the bank will be unable to recover the loan from the borrower.[128] Similarly, a loan used for a purpose (known to the lender) which is contrary to public policy will be void and irrecoverable.[129] Repayment of a loan made for a purpose which is prohibited by law will be unenforceable.[130] In the event that the loan is not used for the stated purpose as agreed by the borrower, the bank may be able to recover the funds by tracing.[131] Where the purpose has not been fulfilled, a liquidator of the borrower will be obliged to return the funds to the lender.[132] The leading decision on this point is that of *Barclays Bank Ltd v Quistclose Investments Ltd.*[133] In that case a loan was made to a company for the purpose of paying a dividend. The moneys were placed in the company's account with its bankers who were not the lenders. On the company's insolvency the bankers sought to combine the company's accounts. The House of Lords held that the purpose meant that the moneys advanced were not to become the company's property and when the purpose was not fulfilled the moneys had to be returned to the lender.

The facts in *Re EVTR Ltd, Gilbert v Barber*[134] were less straightforward. In that case money was lent to the company for the purpose of purchasing equipment. The court held that the trust attaching to the money terminated once the purpose was achieved and it was not revived when the purchase of the equipment subsequently fell through and part of the purchase price returned to the

---

[126.] See Roskill LJ in *West Layton Ltd v Ford* [1979] 1 QB 593 at 605.

[127.] *Re David Payne & Co Ltd, Young v David Payne & Co Ltd* [1904] 2 Ch 593 at 608, see para **[18.40]**.

[128.] *Re Introductions Ltd; Introductions Ltd v National Provincial Bank Ltd* [1969] 1 All ER 887 see para **[18.31]**.

[129.] *Foster v Driscoll* [1929] 1 KB 470.

[130.] *Regazzoni v KC Sethia* (1944) Ltd [1958] AC 301.

[131.] An equitable remedy which the courts may grant where they consider there is a fiduciary or quasi-fiduciary relationship between the claimant and the recipient of money, see *Re Diplock, Diplock v Wintle* [1948] 1 Ch 465 (the Court of Appeal's judgment runs to 89 pages of the Law Reports).

[132.] *Toovey v Milne* (1819) 2 B & Ald 683.

[133.] [1970] AC 567.

[134.] [1986] BCLC 523 and [1987] BCLC 648.

company. However, the Court of Appeal held otherwise, on the basis that the money was paid to the company for a specific purpose and that there was a resulting trust in favour of the payor if the purpose was not carried out. Thus once the moneys were returned to the company, those moneys were then held by the company on the basis of the original trust.

[7.31] Where the purpose of the loan is to enable a consumer to buy goods or obtain services and the lender and the supplier of the goods or services have a pre-existing agreement whereunder a loan is made available exclusively by that lender to customers of that supplier, for the acquisition of goods or services from that supplier and the customer obtains his loan pursuant to that pre-existing agreement, and the goods and services covered by the loan agreement are not supplied or are not in conformity with the contract for the supply of them, the consumer may seek compensation from the lender provided he has first sought compensation against the supplier and has failed to obtain satisfaction.[135]

Negative Pledge

[7.32] The second covenant, sometimes set out in a separate negative pledge clause, runs along the following lines:[136]

> "The borrower shall not create or permit to subsist[137] any mortgage, charge, pledge, assignment (by way of security), lien or encumbrance over any part of the borrower's undertaking, property, assets or revenues save for liens arising in the ordinary course of business."[138]

The purpose of this clause is to prevent the borrower from effectively transferring the benefit of its assets to another creditor thereby reducing the assets available to the lender in the event of the borrower's insolvency.

Occasionally a negative pledge clause may provide that in the event that security is created in favour of a third party similar security over the same assets is

---

[135.] Consumer Credit Act, 1995, s 42(2); for commentary on this section see Johnston, 'Preparing the Consumer Credit Industry for Implementation' (1995) The Irish Centre for Commercial Law Studies.

[136.] For a detailed analysis of a negative pledge see Harris, *Negative Pledge in Sovereign Borrowers* (eds Kalderen and Siddiqi) (1984) Dag Hammarskjold Foundation and Butterworths; Wood, *Law and Practice of International Finance* (1980) Sweet & Maxwell para 6.2; Gabriel, *Legal Aspects of Syndicated Loans* (1986) Butterworths pp 82-97.

[137.] An encumbrance may become effective, not from any direct creation on the part of the borrower but from some action which may result in an encumbrance, such as a judgment mortgage, taking effect, see *Croft v Lumley* [1843-60] All ER Rep 162.

[138.] In the High Court of Australia in *Downs Distributing Co Pty Ltd v Associated Blue Star Stores Pty Ltd* (1948) 76 CLR 463 at 477 Rich J described "ordinary course of business" as meaning that "the transaction must fall into place as part of the undistinguished common flow of business done, that it should form part of the ordinary course of business as carried on, calling for no remark and arising out of no special or particular situation"; applied by Taylor J in *Taylor v White* (1963-64) 110 CLR 129 at 154.

deemed to be created in favour of the bank. Whether such a clause is effective is open to question - at the very least registration will be required in the Companies Registration Office within 21 days of the deemed creation of the security[139] (the timing of which the lender may be unaware). It is also arguable that the clause itself will be unenforceable against a liquidator or a creditor in the event that particulars of it are not registered within 21 days of the execution of the facility letter/loan agreement, as an agreement to create a mortgage/charge is an equitable mortgage/charge and registrable.[140]

[7.33] A negative covenant may provide, particularly in a facility letter, that the borrower shall not borrow funds from any source without the bank's prior written consent. The purpose of such a clause is to prevent the borrower over-extending itself by borrowing further funds, incurring heavier indebtedness and becoming a more likely candidate for insolvency with a diminished return to the first lending bank. A question may arise as to whether such a clause could be deemed to be anti-competitive and unenforceable under competition law. In *Oakdale (Richmond) Ltd v National Westminster Bank plc*[141] such a clause was held not to be anti-competitive as the borrower is always free to pay off the bank (and thus discharge itself from the covenant) with money borrowed elsewhere. In giving his decision Chadwick J explained the rationale for such a clause:[142]

> "In assessing whether to lend ... it is likely to be highly material to evaluate at the time the decision is taken what other borrowing commitments the company has; that is to say it is necessary for the lender to understand the extent to which the company's continued trading is dependent on loan finance. A decision by the bank, made on the basis of material put before it at the time of that decision, would be undermined if the borrower was in a position to increase its borrowings without referring the matter back to the bank. A lender who lends on the basis that the borrower has no other borrowing commitments is concerned to ensure that he does not find, some six or 12 months later, that he is lending to a borrower who has incurred substantial other borrowing commitments."

[7.34] However, such a clause has proved to be unenforceable where the borrower comes under the protection of the court.[143] In *Re Holidair Ltd*[144] the borrowers covenanted in their debenture not "to borrow any monies whatsoever" without the prior written consent of the bank. The examiner appointed to the borrowers wished to borrow money to enable him to carry out

---

[139] Pursuant to the Companies Act, 1963, s 99.
[140] *Ibid.*
[141] [1996] BCC 919.
[142] *Ibid* at 930.
[143] Pursuant to the Companies (Amendment) Act, 1990.
[144] [1994] 1 ILRM 481.

his functions under the Companies (Amendment) Act, 1990. Costello J held[145] that the examiner must examine the company as he finds it and it would not be just and equitable to allow the examiner to breach the company's contracts without compensation. However, the Supreme Court unanimously allowed the examiner's appeal. In giving the judgment of the court on the point, Finlay CJ held that this covenant and the stated intention of the bank not to permit further borrowing "clearly constitutes a contract and conduct in pursuance of the contract which is likely to be to the detriment of the company".[146] Accordingly, the examiner was permitted to prevent the effects of the contract[147] and apply to the court to borrow moneys without the bank's consent.[148]

Financial Covenants

[7.35] The principal covenants are financial so that the borrower is obliged to operate within stipulated financial ratios which should ensure its profitability and indeed survival. The finance director of a corporate borrower should pay most attention to this aspect of the facility letter/loan agreement as a breach of these covenants will trigger an event of default, the likely calling in of the loan and the resultant possible insolvency of the corporate borrower. It is critical therefore that the borrower give such covenants which it can envisage being able to comply with.[149] Amongst these covenants will be a covenant typically to provide audited financial statements of the borrower within 90 days of the financial year end and quarterly management accounts within 30 days of the end each quarter.

LENDER'S OBLIGATION TO CONSUMER

Duty to Supply Information

[7.36] The Consumer Credit Act, 1995 introduced the concept of covenants by the lender in the case of loans made to consumers. During the term of a consumer loan agreement, the lender is required within 10 days of a written request from the consumer, to provide:[150]

---

145. High Court, unrep, 19 February 1994.
146. [1994] 1 ILRM 481 at 488.
147. Companies (Amendment) Act, 1990, s 7(5).
148. The effect of this decision means that contracts may subsequently be repudiated by an examiner; the Company Law Review Group in its *First Report* stated (at para 2.46) that section 7(5) "clearly undermines the reliability of contracts entered into with Irish companies and could pose serious consequences for the financing of Irish industry." Amending legislation was recommended.
149. For further reading on financial covenants see Wood, *Law and Practice of International Finance* (1980) Sweet & Maxwell para 6.6; for a sample financial covenants clause see Lingard, *Bank Security Documents* (3rd ed) Butterworths para 5.12.
150. Consumer Credit Act, 1995, s 43(1); this does not apply where a request has been made less than four weeks previously (s 43(4)).

a copy of the written agreement or a statement of -

(a) the amount paid,

(b) the amount, if any, due but unpaid, and the date and amount of each instalment that remains unpaid, and

(c) the total amount outstanding and the date and amount of each outstanding instalment,

under the agreement.

In making a request the consumer is required to provide a fee of £2.[151] This information requirement is in addition to the requirements under s 30 where the lender is obliged to supply the consumer with a copy of the agreement upon its completion. A lender should note that if it fails to comply with such a request for a period of 14 days (beyond the initial 10 day period), the lender shall, while the default continues, not be entitled to enforce the loan agreement or any security for the repayment of the loan.[152]

Restrictions on Written Communications

[7.37] A lender, when writing to a consumer, is prohibited from sending an envelope or other material with the name of the lender, or its logo, on the front or back cover.[153] Although the Bill as initiated enabled a return address to be printed on the envelope, only a PO Box number is permitted. The word "personal" or "private" may be printed on the envelope at the lender's discretion.[154] The Act specifically prohibits written communications to members of the consumer's family or his employer.[155]

A well known exception to the banker's duty of confidentiality is where the customer expressly consents to the disclosure of information.[156] Lenders are given specific authorisation, subject to the consumer's written consent, to communicate in writing to members of the consumer's family or another person designated by the consumer in respect of housing loans.[157] The absence of such a specific enabling provision with regard to non-housing loans indicates that the legislature did not intend that a consumer should have the right to consent to communications being sent to, for example, his parent, spouse or son/daughter. However, the provisions prohibiting exclusions from the Act[158] will not restrict

---

[151.] Or such other amount as the Minister may order (s 43(5), but no fee is necessary where information is supplied in connection with a moneylending agreement (s 43(6)).
[152.] Consumer Credit Act, 1995, s 43(3).
[153.] *Ibid s* 45(1).
[154.] This accords in any event with previous lending practice to have the word "private" on the envelope of every letter sent to a customer.
[155.] Consumer Credit Act, 1995, s 45(2).
[156.] See Ch 3.
[157.] Consumer Credit Act, 1995, s 45(3)(b).
[158.] *Ibid ss* 140 and 141.

the consumer consenting to disclosure to third parties unless the court takes the view that the prohibition on communication to a family member or lawyer is a "right". While a consumer's right cannot be excluded in any loan agreement,[159] this does not prevent a consumer unilaterally waiving such right.

Visits and Telephone Calls

[7.38] A bank or other person providing a consumer loan is precluded from contacting a consumer (without his consent) at his place of business.[160]
There is scope for some confusion here as a result of the draftman's reluctance to use a comma. A visit or telephone call to a consumer without his consent is prohibited, "at his place of employment or business unless the consumer resides at that place and all reasonable efforts to make contact with him have failed". It is unclear whether a consumer may be contacted at his place of employment only where he resides there and all reasonable efforts to contact him have failed, or whether the consumer may be contacted at his place of business where he resides elsewhere after all reasonable efforts to contact him have failed.
The reference to "all reasonable efforts" are likely to be subject to judicial consideration. Reasonable is a term which lacks clear definition but its meaning may vary depending upon the prevailing circumstances. Its lack of definition poses problems for persons advising on the application of the Act and the possible breach of it.
The drafting is clearer in the second part of the section, the effect of which permits a consumer to consent to a lender visiting or telephoning a consumer's employer or member of the consumer's family.[161] The consent must be given in writing separate from any other term of the consumer loan agreement.
The statutory prohibition on a creditor visiting or telephoning between the hours of 9pm on any week day[162] and 9am on the following day is restrictive. The manner in which the Act is drafted permits a consumer to be contacted at home on a Monday morning at any time prior to 9am.
The restrictions do not apply in the case of serving a document in connection with legal proceedings.[163]

CHANGE IN CIRCUMSTANCES

[7.39] A bank lends money on the basis of the current state of law and its interpretation. In the event that this changes, then the basis on which the bank is

---

[159] *Ibid* s 140(1).
[160] *Ibid* s 46.
[161] It is somewhat odd that the legislature enables a consumer to consent to oral communications to third parties but not to written communications (except in the case of housing loans).
[162] That is a day which is not a Sunday - Interpretation Act, 1937 Schedule, para 35.
[163] Consumer Credit Act, 1995, s 46.

prepared to lend or continue lending will change. Typically the risk of change in law or its interpretation will be borne by the borrower although usually the borrower will be given a right to pre-pay the loan in the event that it does not wish to borrow from the bank in question following the change in circumstances. This change in circumstances is broken down into three categories namely, (1) change in law, (2) increase in cost (to the bank), and (3) imposition of a tax, such as a withholding tax on the payment of interest to the bank.

(1) Change in Law

[7.40] If a bank makes a loan for a purpose which is unlawful it is likely to encounter difficulties in recovering the loan.[164] Accordingly, if, following the drawdown of the loan, the law changes so as to make the loan unlawful, or it is proposed that the law will so change, the bank will want the right to have the loan immediately repaid to it. Sometimes the parties will include a clause to the effect that in such circumstances the bank and the borrower will enter into negotiations in good faith with a view to finding an alternative lawful means of making the loan available to the borrower.[165] This will at least give the borrower comfort that the bank will endeavour to continue to provide facilities in the unlikely event that a change in law makes the loan unlawful.

(2) Increased Costs

[7.41] A bank funds a loan through raising the funds on the interbank market as well as paying the appropriate reserve assets costs (if any) to the Central Bank. For competitive reasons banks are reluctant to disclose the exact mechanism by which a loan is funded - this can cause some difficulty in the negotiation of an increased costs clause as, in the event that the operation of the clause is triggered, a borrower will wish to be satisfied that there has been an increased cost or lower rate of return to the bank than when the loan agreement was negotiated.[166] The clause will provide usually that any increase in the cost to the bank in making the loan whether through any change in applicable law, rule or regulation or in the interpretation thereof (whether or not having the force of law)[167] will be paid by the borrower. More comprehensive loan agreements will

---

[164.] For further reading on the consequences see Chesire, Fifoot & Furmston's, *Law of Contract* (13th ed) Butterworths Chs 11, 12 and 22; Clark, *Contract Law in Ireland* (3rd ed) Sweet & Maxwell, Chs 14, 15 and 20.

[165.] For further reading see Buchheit, 'How to Negotiate the Illegality Clause' (1994) IFLR (June) 24.

[166.] For further reading see Buchheit, 'How to Negotiate the Increased Costs Clause' (1993) IFLR (Apr) 30; Shea, 'Shifting the Goalposts' (1993) IFR 28 Aug.

[167.] The Revenue Commissioners may give an interpretation of a statutory provision the legality of which may be uncertain until tested in the courts.

cater for an increase in costs to the lender, a reduction in the rate of return for the lender on the loan (otherwise than by reference to tax on its overall income) or the imposition of any additional liability by way of a levy or otherwise on the lender. Although such clauses are relatively standard, the negotiation of them will depend somewhat on the significance of the borrower. Broadly speaking such clauses should be acceptable provided the borrower is not presented with a retrospective cost.

(3) Withholding Tax

[7.42] Interest which is payable by a borrower to a lender is the income which the lender earns for providing the loan to the borrower.[168] That income is subject to income or corporation tax in the hands of the lender.[169] The Taxes Consolidation Act, 1997 provides[170] that where any yearly interest[171] (charged with tax under Schedule D) is paid by a company[172] or by any person to another person whose usual place of abode is outside the State, then the person by or through whom the payment is made is obliged to deduct tax at the standard rate. There are a number of exceptions[173] including, interest paid in the State on an advance from a bank carrying on a *bona fide* business in the State,[174] and interest paid to a person whose usual place of abode is outside the State by a company in the course of carrying on an approved trading activity in the Shannon Airport Customs Area or in the International Financial Services Centre in Dublin.[175]

[7.43] Essentially the requirement for a borrower to withhold and deduct tax, in respect of interest payable to a non-resident lender, and then pay the tax to the Revenue Commissioners, is an ingenious way of one State taxing the income earned by an entity from another State. It is a form of protectionism against foreign financial institutions. However, this requirement effectively no longer applies in most instances as one of the exceptions is interest paid by a company which has been authorised by the Revenue Commissioners to pay interest without deduction of income tax.[176] In the case of payments outside the State,

---

[168]. Defined in the *Shorter Oxford English Dictionary* (3rd ed) as "money paid for the use of money lent (the principal), or for forbearance of a debt, according to a fixed ratio (rate per cent)".

[169]. For further reading see Judge, *Irish Income Tax (1997-98)* Butterworths para 2.306.

[170]. Section 264(2).

[171]. Interest payable on loans having an intended duration of not less than one year (Judge, *op cit* para 2.306).

[172]. Otherwise than when paid in a fiduciary or representative capacity to a person whose usual place of abode is in the State.

[173]. Taxes Consolidation Act, 1997, s 246(3).

[174]. *Ibid*, s 246(3)(a).

[175]. *Ibid* s 246(3)(c).

[176]. *Ibid* s 246(3)(d).

where the recipient is earning interest from a jurisdiction which
Double Tax Treaty with Ireland, the Revenue Commissione
appropriate authority, subject to completion of relevant documentation by the
payer and recipient of interest. Currently, Ireland has negotiated treaties with 29
countries. Lending from most of these jurisdictions should, subject to
compliance with the Revenue Commissioners' documentary requirements,
avoid the requirement to withhold tax. The recipient will then be subject to tax
on the interest earned in the normal course in its home jurisdiction.[177]

[7.44] Usually loan agreements provide that if withholding tax is required to be
deducted the borrower will pay the lender additional amounts sufficient to put
the lender in the same position as if no such deduction or withholding was
required - this is known as a grossing-up clause.[178] Some agreements provide for
an indemnity in addition to a grossing up clause to counteract the possibility that
through the mechanism of tax credits the lender may not be put in quite the same
position under a gross-up clause than if there had been no withholding.[179]
These clauses sometimes contain provisions that where the borrower is required
to gross up and the lender receives a tax credit and a benefit it would not
otherwise have received had the interest been paid gross in the normal course,
the lender will account to the borrower for that additional benefit. While lenders
will readily agree to such a provision, they will not agree to disclosing to the
borrower the exact mechanisms by which the benefit is arrived at - any lender
will be extremely reluctant to open its books to a borrower - indeed should it do
so, it would need to be careful to avoid a breach of the duty of confidentiality
which a bank owes to all its customers.[180]

EVENTS OF DEFAULT

[7.45] When negotiating the terms of a loan agreement much attention is spent
by both bankers and their corporate customers to the events of default clause.[181]
Borrowers pay attention as such clauses list the circumstances which may give
rise to early termination of the bank facilities - facilities which are the lifeblood
of the corporate borrower. A corporate borrower which incurs an event of
default is unlikely at that stage to be able to refinance with an alternative banker.

[177.] Not all Double Tax Treaties permit payment of interest without deduction (see eg, Australia,
Belgium, Canada, Israel, Italy, Japan, New Zealand, Poland and Portugal).
[178.] See Lingard, *Bank Security Documents* (3rd ed) para 5.11 Cl 7.01; Wood, *Law and Practice of
International Finance* (1980) Sweet & Maxwell para 12.5.
[179.] See Penn, Shea & Arora, *The Law & Practice of International Banking* Vol 2 (1987) Sweet &
Maxwell, para 5.07.
[180.] See para **[3.01]**.
[181.] For further reading see Penn, Shea & Arora, *The Law and Practice of International Banking*
Vol 2 (1987) Sweet & Maxwell, Ch 9; Youard in *Sovereign Borrowers* (eds Kalderen &
Siddiqi) (1984) Dag Hamnarksjold Foundation and Butterworths; Wood, *Law and Practice of
International Finance* (1980) Sweet & Maxwell, Ch 7; Clark and Taylor (1982) IFLR Sep
p 15; *Youard* [1986] JBL 276.

The alternative to liquidation, a period of court protection, or the appointment of a receiver, following the occurrence of an event of default, will be a further renegotiation with its banker on less favourable terms. In essence the events of default represent situations which must be avoided by the borrower at all times during the term of the facility.

On the other side for the banker, events of default represent the opportunity to recoup the advance or more likely renegotiate its repayment in the event of a serious deterioration in the borrower's financial position - it may represent an opportunity for the bank to recover its money before it is too late.

Although in practice default clauses are not categorised they may nonetheless be considered in three categories namely, payment default, non-payment default and potential default.

(1) Payment Default

[7.46] The two obvious instances of payment default are the failure to pay interest or other sum (such as fees) when due and secondly the failure to repay the principal when due. Sometimes grace periods are negotiated. However the borrower should be prepared to pay or repay amounts due on the stipulated days; grace periods for these events should be negotiated only for a technical administrative difficulty - occasionally moneys do not arrive even though seemingly transmitted.[182] The grace periods should obviously be reasonably tight such as two banking days, perhaps after notification to the borrower that the moneys have not been received.

[7.47] Unless a time of day is stipulated, payment may be received at any time up to midnight.[183] In *Afovos Shipping Co SA v Pagnan and Pagnan*[184] Lord Denning MR stated:[185]

> "It is suggested that in ordinary banking practice in London the telexes would only be received and processed on that day if they had been received by three o'clock within banking hours. The judge said that they might be processed in exceptional circumstances - on a special request - up until five o'clock when the banks close. But they would not be processed except in the most unusual

---

[182.] See *Afovos Shipping Co SA v Pagnan and Pagnan* [1982] 1 WLR 848 and [1983] 1 WLR 195 where an out of date entry in a telex directory resulted in a telex payment instruction being sent to a firm of sand suppliers instead of a bank.

[183.] *Startup v MacDonald* (1843) 6 Man & G 593 at 619; *Afovos Shipping Co SA v Pagnan and Pagnan* [1983] 1 WLR 195 at 201 *per* Lord Hailsham:

> "I take it to be a general principle of law not requiring authority that where a person under an obligation to do a particular act has to do it on or before a particular date he has the whole of that day to perform his duty".

[184.] [1982] 1 WLR 848.

[185.] *Ibid* at 853; (the Court of Appeal's decision was upheld by the House of Lords [1983] 1 WLR 195).

circumstances after five o'clock in the evening. Although that may be well understood to be normal banking practice, nevertheless it seems to me that the general rule of law applies that a default only occurs at midnight on the due date for payment".

Accordingly, if a bank is giving notice to the borrower of non-payment, it can only do so after the time due for payment namely the day following the day when payment is due. A notice given on the day it is due (unless due at a time of day prior to the time the notice is given) will be ineffective.[186]

[7.48] It is for the responsible officers of the corporate borrower to ensure that the payment dates can be met. They should not rely on the goodwill of the bank's officers, who themselves have to report to others on their performance. In any event, in future years new persons in the bank may become responsible for the account, people that the corporate officers have no relationship with, or indeed the loan may be sold to another bank. It would be as well for the corporate officer to bear in mind Lord Wilberforce's chilling words[187] - "there is only one kind of breach possible, namely to be late".

Although a payment made late is likely to be accepted by the bank, who will be glad to receive payment rather than embark on a uncertain, costly and time consuming course of recovery, there is no obligation on the bank to waive the default and accept payment - in other words late payment does not cure the default unless it is accepted by the bank.[188]

Any dispute as to whether payment was made or not can be resolved by applying the words of Megaw LJ:[189]

"Whatever mode of process is used, 'payment' is not achieved until the process has reached the stage that the creditor has received cash or that which he is prepared to treat as the equivalent of cash, or has a credit available on which, in the normal course of business or banking practice, he can draw, if he wishes, in the form of cash".

Thus, unless there is agreement to the contrary, payment is deemed to be made when it is available to the lender in cash.[190] For example, where a lender agrees that payment may be made by the borrower posting a cheque, the lender runs the risk of the cheque not arriving (as the post office is then deemed to be the agent of the payee).[191] However, where a course of dealing develops whereby a cheque

186. See *Afovos Shipping Co SA v Pagnan and Pagnan* [1982] 1 WLR 848 and [1983] 1 WLR 195.
187. In *Bunge Corporation v Tradax SA* [1981] 2 All ER 513 at 541.
188. *Mardorf Peach & Co Ltd v Attica Sea Carriers Corporation of Liberia, The Laconia* [1977] 1 All ER 545.
189. In *The Brimnes, Tenax Steamship Co Ltd v Owners of the Motor Vessel Brimnes* [1974] 3 All ER 88 at 110.
190. See *A/S Awilco v Fulvia SpA di Navgazione, The Chickuma* [1981] 1 All ER 652; *Baker v Lipton Ltd* (1899) 15 TLR 435.
191. *Warwicke v Noakes* (1791) Peake 98;

is sent in the post with a receipt form, the sending of the receipt form indicates that the parties agree that payment is not made until received by the payee.[192]

[7.49] The third category of payment default is what is known as the cross default clause namely, in the event that the borrower is unable to pay when due any indebtedness under any agreement with any person. This is a clause which will need very careful consideration by the borrower. A threshold amount may be negotiated to avoid the possibility that default in a small payment to another creditor triggers a collapse of the borrower's banking facilities.

(2) Non-payment Default

[7.50] The principal category here is the failure of the borrower to comply with any of the covenants in the loan agreement. It is often agreed that there will be some grace period - 28 days is generous, 14 is more sensible. The purpose of a grace period is to permit the borrower some time to rectify the breach of covenant in order to save itself. They should not give too much of a sense of comfort to the borrower bearing in mind that some covenants, particularly financial, may not be remediable within the stipulated grace period. A cross default will often apply here as well - the breach of another agreement.[193] A variation of this will be where another agreement is breached and as a result thereof the counter-party takes action - a cross acceleration clause. It is clearly preferable for a borrower to have cross acceleration rather than cross default.[194]

The second category is a breach of the representations and warranties of the borrower. As with covenants, the breach of some of these may not be remediable.

Other categories of default relate principally to insolvency, such as the appointment of an examiner, receiver or liquidator, the enforcement of security or the enforcement of a judgment, the inability to pay debts within the meaning of s 214 of the Companies Act, 1963, and the cessation of business. As well as similar events affecting a guarantor of the loan (or indeed subsidiaries), change in ownership without the lender's consent is usually a default - the lender having comfort from the owners and their track record when approving the loan - a change in owners is a change in the basis on which the loan was approved.[195] Similarly, default may be triggered by the disposal of a substantial or material part of the borrower's assets.

[192.] *Pennington v Crossley and Son* (1897) 77 LT 43.

[193.] See further Buckheit, 'How to Negotiate Cross Default Clauses' (1993) IFLR Aug p 27.

[194.] Gabriel, *Legal Aspects of Syndicated Loans* (1986) Butterworths p 114, argues there is no necessity for a cross default clause; the lender may not be aware of a cross default.

[195.] *Lingard*, 1995 CLP 27 suggests it may be a useful poison pill for a borrower to have to deter a hostile take-over - this seems doubtful as the acquirer is likely to have sufficient banking facilities available for the enlarged group.

[7.51] The most contentious default is a material adverse change in the final condition of the borrower. The difficulty here is that it can be subjective, particularly if it is stated to be in the bank's opinion. Where the clause is set out in an objective manner a question may arise as to what is or what constitutes a material adverse change. In *Levison v Farin*[196] the court held that a drop in the company's net asset value by 20% was a material adverse change. It must be said though, because of its ambiguity, a material adverse change clause is the clause a bank is least likely to utilise in order to call an event of default, as it may invite costly and protracted litigation.

(3) Potential Event of Default

[7.52] A clause which causes borrowers difficulty is one to the effect that an event happens which upon the expiration of time will or may constitute an event of default. The purpose of this clause for the lender is to trigger an event of default and repayment of principal before it may become too late to recover the moneys advanced. The borrower will need to consider the language with care so as to give it the flexibility of being in a position to rectify the event prior to the default being called by the bank.

Consequences of Default

[7.53] Most events of default clauses provide that upon the happening of any of the stipulated events the bank may terminate the facility and call for immediate payment of all moneys due to it. This is obviously preferable from the borrower's viewpoint than an automatic termination in the event of the happening of one of the events - it may indeed not be in the bank's interest to have automatic termination. It is even more useful for a borrower where a syndicate of banks are lending as it may take a day or two longer for a majority of the syndicate to terminate the facilities during which time the borrower may be able to persuade at least the agent or lead bank that an alternative course of action may be preferable for all parties and their respective interests.

In negotiating default clauses the borrower should bear in mind that it is not the bank's intention to have the loan repaid early to it, otherwise it would not have made the loan in the first place. The bank's intention is to earn an income out of the funds which it makes available to the borrower, that income being interest. It will hope that it will earn that interest over the duration of the loan. However, it needs to protect its investment and the events of default are designed to do that, in the hope that in the unexpected deterioration in the borrower's financial condition the bank will be able to recover its investment, although not the profit which it would otherwise have made.

---

196. [1978] 2 All ER 1149.

EVENTS OF DEFAULT IN CONSUMER LOAN AGREEMENTS

[7.54] One of the most adverse sections of the Consumer Credit Act, 1995 for lenders concerns the delay that a lender must impose on itself before calling in the loan following a default by the consumer. Lenders need to be absolutely meticulous in the preparation of paper work prior to the enforcement of consumer loan agreements. A lender who wishes to demand early payment of any sum (whether through an automatic early termination provision or otherwise), or to treat a right of the consumer to be determined, restricted or deferred must first serve on the consumer at least 10 days before it proposes to take any action, a notice specifying the following:[197]

    (i)   sufficient details of the agreement to identify it;

    (ii)   the name and address of the lender;

   (iii)   the name and address of the consumer;

   (iv)   the term of the agreement to be enforced; and

    (v)   a statement of the action the lender intends to take to enforce the term of the agreement, the manner and circumstances in which he intends to take such action and the date on or after which he intends to take such action.

The provisions of s 54 need to be considered carefully by a lender and its adviser involved in the preparation, and in particular the enforcement, of a consumer loan agreement. Not only does the Act stipulate certain procedures to be followed by a lender prior to demanding early payment or recovering possession,[198] it sets out further requirements to be complied with where there has been a breach of the agreement by a consumer.[199]

Where there has been a breach by a consumer of an agreement the lender cannot demand early payment, terminate the agreement, treat any right conferred on the consumer by the agreement as determined, restricted or deferred, or enforce security unless it has served on the consumer, not less than 10 days before it proposes to take any action, a notice specifying:[200]

    (i)   sufficient details of the agreement to identify it;

    (ii)   the name and address of the lender;

   (iii)   the name and address of the consumer;

   (iv)   the nature of the alleged breach;

[197.] Consumer Credit Act, 1995, s 54(1).

[198.] *Ibid.*

[199.] It may be worth considering to what extent an agreement can be framed so that a typical breach by a consumer may be constructed as not being a breach but simply an event giving rise to early payment or recovery, and thereby avoid the requirements of the second sub-section.

[200.] Consumer Credit Act, 1995, s 54(2).

(v) either:

  (a) if the breach is capable of remedy, what action is required to remedy it and the date by which the action must be taken (being not less than 21 days after the service of the notice); or

  (b) if the breach is not capable of remedy, the amount required to be paid in compensation for the breach and the date by which it must be paid (being not less than 21 days after the service of the notice); and

(vi) information about the consequences of failure to comply with the notice.[201]

To use the words of one commentator when considering the UK Consumer Credit Act,[202] "the adviser to the reluctant debtor here finds a fruitful pool in which to cast around".

[7.55] The Act further provides[203] that a consumer, having breached an agreement, who receives a notice setting out in detail the requirements of the Act, who then remedies the default up to 21 days after service of the notice, will have the benefit of receiving a clean record; the lender is required to treat the breach as not having occurred in any records maintained for information on the consumer's credit record. Fortunately, wiser counsel[204] prevailed and this is the only provision of the Act which was not implemented on 13 May 1996.[205]

[7.56] Some account has been taken of the possibility that a consumer, upon being given the 21 day grace period, may seek to remove his assets from the jurisdiction to evade a successful claim by the lender.[206] Thus the Act provides[207] that notwithstanding the foregoing, a lender may apply to a court of competent jurisdiction to have the provisions of s 54 dispensed with where the court is satisfied "that it would be just and equitable to do so". Whether in practice this additional sub-section may save the removal of assets from the lender's reach remains to be seen.

[7.57] Where for any reason the amount owed by a consumer under a loan agreement becomes payable before the agreed time for payment, the consumer is entitled to a reduction in the cost of the loan calculated in accordance with a

---

[201.] No guidelines are given as to how detailed such information should be.
[202.] FR Ryder, Gilbart Lectures on Banking 1978 - 'The Consumer Credit Act - The Present Stage with Reference to Banking'.
[203.] Consumer Credit Act, 1995, s 54(3).
[204.] See comments of Murphy, Banking and Community Law - ICEL 26 March 1994.
[205.] Consumer Credit Act, 1995 (Commencement) Order, 1996 SI 121/1996.
[206.] As pointed out by the March 1994 editorial in the Commercial Law Practitioner.
[207.] Consumer Credit Act, 1995, s 54(4).

formula approved by the Central Bank of Ireland or the Director of Consumer Affairs.[208]

[7.58] It should be noted that a lender is not permitted under any agreement with a consumer to:

(i) exclude or restrict any liability imposed on any person or any right conferred on a consumer, or

(ii) impose any further liability in addition to any liability imposed on a consumer ...

Under the Consumer Credit Act, 1995, any agreement containing such an exclusion, restriction or liability will be unenforceable.[209] This provision may catch a typical payment clause in a loan agreement precluding a right of set-off on the part of the consumer, on the grounds that it imposes an additional liability on the consumer.

ASSIGNMENT

[7.59] A loan agreement will usually contain an assignment clause under which the bank (or lender) may assign the benefit of the agreement and the loan to a third party, with a minimum of restriction.[210] A fairly concise and appropriate clause would read as follows:[211]

"(a) The borrower shall not assign or transfer all or any part of its rights, benefits and/or obligations under this agreement.

(b) The bank may, without the consent of the borrower, grant a participation in or make an assignment or transfer or otherwise dispose of the whole or any part or parts of its rights and benefits under this agreement.

(c) For the purpose of any such participation, assignment, transfer or disposal, the bank may disclose information about the borrower and the financial condition of the borrower as shall have been made available to the bank by the borrower or which is publicly available.

(d) The expression 'bank' wherever used in this agreement shall, to the extent of its interest for the time being herein, include every successor

---

[208.] Consumer Credit Act, 1995, s 53 which is subject to the right of the Minister for Enterprise, Trade and Employment to prescribe another method or formula; see also s 55 which provides for no unjust enrichment for a lender.

[209.] Consumer Credit Act, 1995, s 140. Section 141 prohibits the furnishing of a document which purports to exclude or restrict a liability imposed under the Act or any right conferred on a consumer by the Act.

[210.] "A contract which is assignable only by consent is not (unless there is some provision against the unreasonable withholding of consent) in strict language, assignable at all", per McCarthy J in *CB Percocke Land Co Ltd v Hamilton Milk Producers Co Ltd* [1963] NZLR 576 at 581.

[211.] For further reading on such clauses see Penn, Shea & Arora, *The Law and Practice of International Banking* Vol 2 (1987) Sweet & Maxwell, Ch 8.

> in title, participant, assignee, transferee or party to whom a disposal is made as aforesaid."

Typically, a borrower is precluded from assigning as the bank will have advanced the facility on the basis of the borrower's (or its guarantor's) creditworthiness.

From the borrower's viewpoint a concern with the right of a bank to assign, apart from the break in its relationship with the bank or lender who negotiated the facility, is the possibility that any such assignment or other disposal may result in a withholding tax[212] or increased cost[213] by virtue of the new bank or lender being located in a different jurisdiction. A protective clause might read as follows:

> "Notwithstanding any provisions to the contrary contained in this agreement, if the result of any participation, assignment, transfer or disposal by the bank of all or any part of its rights or obligations hereunder would, but for this paragraph, be to cause the borrower to become liable to pay any additional amount or amounts pursuant to this agreement which would not have been payable had not such participation, assignment, transfer or disposal occurred, then such additional amount or amounts shall not be payable or paid by the borrower and the same shall be paid by the assignee or transferee as the case may be."

[7.60] In the case of consumer loans, which are more rarely transferred, the assignee or transferee should note that the consumer is entitled to plead against it "any defence which was available to him against the original creditor including set-off".[214] In any event this principle applies to all transfers - hence the need for the transferee or assignee to obtain an indemnity or other comfort from the original bank.

[7.61] It should be noted that the transfer of obligations, whether by a bank or a borrower, will require the other party's approval; this is usually done in the form of a novation agreement.[215]

GOVERNING LAW[216]

Implied Choice of Law

[7.62] It is obviously of importance to the parties to the agreement as to certainty of terms and their interpretation; accordingly both parties should be clear as to

---

212. See para **[7.42]** above.

213. See para **[7.41]** above.

214. Consumer Credit Act, 1995, s 40 (which cannot be contracted out of - s 140).

215. For a form see *The Encylopaedia of Forms and Precedents* (Butterworths) 4th ed Vol 15.

216. For a detailed treatment of governing law issues see Wood, *Law and Practice of International Finance* (1980) Sweet & Maxwell Chs 1 and 2.

what law will govern the agreement. Where the governing law is not stated in the agreement it was considered as a general rule that the proper law was "the law which has the closest and most real connection with the contract and transaction."[217] This common law principle has now been statutorily applied by Article 4.1 of the Rome Convention[218] which provides that where the law has not been chosen, "the contract shall be governed by the law of the country with which it is most closely connected". A loan agreement concluded between an Irish incorporated lender or Irish branch of a foreign lender and an Irish incorporated borrower will have an implied term that the governing law of the agreement is that of Ireland, as that will be the law which is most closely connected with the agreement and the transaction.[219]

Express Choice of Law

[7.63] Most loan agreements are stated to be governed by the law of the place of business of the lender.[220] This is because the lender has or will have advanced the funds and it must have certainty and an understanding of the legal parameters within which it can obtain a return of the loan.[221] Lord Denning explained this practice in a different manner:[222]

"... in the absence of any express clause determining the proper law, the transaction should be governed by the law of the country of the lender. A borrower who comes from a foreign country seeking a loan must expect to conform to the laws of the country to which he comes: for otherwise he is unlikely to get the loan".

An express choice of law in a contract should be upheld in Ireland even where the agreement has no real connection with Ireland. In *Kutchera v Buckingham*

---

[217] Per D'Arcy J in *Cripps Warburg Ltd v Cologne Investment Company Ltd, Aran Friendly Society* [1980] IR 321 at 333; applying the Privy Council's decision in *Bonython v The Commonwealth of Australia* [1951] AC 201 *per* Lord Simonds at 219; see the Explanatory and Financial Memorandum to the Contractual Obligations (Applicable Law) Bill, 1990, para 10; see also *Re United Railways of Havana and Regla Warehouses Ltd* [1961] AC 1007 at 1068 *per* Lord Denning and at 1081 *per* Lord Morris of Borth-y-Gest; *Coast Lines Ltd v Hudiq & Veder Chartering NV* [1972] 2 QB 34 at 44 *per* Lord Denning MR and at 46 *per* Megaw LJ.

[218] Implemented into Irish law pursuant to the Contractual Obligations (Applicable Law) Act, 1991, s 2; for further reading on the Convention see Sainsbury, *The Incorporated Law Society of Ireland*; see also Hogan, *The Society of Young Solicitors* (1991).

[219] See Article 4.1 of the Rome Convention implemented by the Contractual Obligations (Applicable Law) Act, 1991, s 2(1).

[220] See *Cripps Warburg Ltd v Cologne Investment Co Ltd Aran Friendly Society* [1980] IR 321; *Northern Bank Ltd v Edwards* [1985] IR 284; [1986] ILRM 167.

[221] See further Buckheit, 'How to negotiate the Governing Law Clause' (1994) IFLR July p 33; see also Penn, Shea & Arora, *The Law and Practice of International Banking* Vol 2 (1987) Sweet & Maxwell Ch 1.

[222] In *Re United Railways of Havana and Regla Warehouses Ltd* [1961] AC 1007 at 1068.

International Holdings Ltd[223] the plaintiff, a South African resident, entered into an agreement through agents in the Bahamas to lend Canadian dollars to the defendant, a public company incorporated under the laws of Alberta, Canada. The loan agreement was stated to be governed by Irish law. Carroll J in the High Court held that the proper law of the contract was that of Alberta. However, the Supreme Court by a four to one majority held that a party which agrees that Irish law will govern a contract should not be permitted to evade the express contractual provision unless it can advance strong reasons to the contrary; accordingly Irish law applied to the agreement. McCarthy J indicated that as the parties had expressly agreed that Irish law applied to the contract there was no need to ascertain whether the contract had any connection with Ireland.[224] Although not mentioned in the Supreme Court judgments, support for its decision can be found in *Lloyd v Gilbert*,[225] and in *R v International Trustee for the protection of Bondholders AG*.[226] The Supreme Court's decision has been given statutory effect by virtue of the Contractual Obligations (Applicable Law) Act, 1991. This Act ratifies and adopts the EC Convention on the law applicable to contractual obligations of 19 June 1980 (known as the Rome Convention).[227] Article 3.1 of the Convention states:

> A contract shall be governed by the law chosen by the parties. The choice must be expressed or demonstrated with reasonable certainty by the terms of the contract or the circumstances of the case. By their choice the parties can select the law applicable to the whole or a part only of the contract.

[7.64] It is incorrect to state that an agreement shall be governed and construed in accordance with the laws of the Republic of Ireland, the correct name of the State being Ireland.[228]

[7.65] It may not be possible however to choose a foreign law to evade statutory provisions which would normally apply to the loan. In this regard the Consumer Credit Act, 1995 specifically precludes a lender from excluding or restricting any liability imposed on it under the Act by reference to any provision in the

---

[223.] [1988] IR 61.

[224.] *Ibid* at 68.

[225.] (1865) LR 1 QB 114 - "In determining a question between contracting parties, recourse must first be had to the language of the contract itself ... it is necessary to consider by what general law the parties intended that the transaction should be governed" *per* Wills J at 120.

[226.] [1937] AC 500 at 529 *per* Lord Atkin; see also *The Assuzione* [1954] 2 WLR 234 *per* Birkett LJ.

[227.] With effect from 1 January 1992, SI 303/1991.

[228.] Constitution of Ireland, Article 4; the name of the State "in the English language can be correctly described only as Ireland" per Walsh J in *Kutchera v Buckingham International Holdings Ltd* [1988] IR 61 at 67; [1988] ILRM 501 at 503.

loan agreement.[229] Furthermore, Article 5.2 of the Rome Convention stipulates that notwithstanding any express choice of law:

> a choice of law made by the parties shall not have the result of depriving the consumer of the protection afforded to him by the mandatory rules of the law of the country in which he has his habitual residence: - if in that country the conclusion of the contract was preceded by a specific invitation addressed to him or by advertising,[230] and he had taken in that country all the steps necessary on his part for the conclusion of the contract ...

Thus, the application of a foreign law in a loan agreement for a loan made to a consumer in Ireland will not be enforceable to the extent that it restricts or excludes any lender liability under the Consumer Credit Act, 1995.[231]

[7.66] Even where the governing law chosen is that of a State other than Ireland, the laws of Ireland will still apply to an Irish incorporated borrower with regard to its capacity to enter into the agreement,[232] the authority of its board to enter into and bind the borrower to the obligations under the agreement[233] and the insolvency laws which may apply to a borrower if it incurs financial difficulty and an examiner, receiver or liquidator is appointed to the borrower. Similarly, the application of withholding taxes will depend upon the laws of the jurisdiction of the borrower's tax residence.[234] Indeed in practice, many loan agreements governed by New York law specifically provide that the borrower's representations as to capacity and authority be governed by the local law of the borrower while all other clauses of the agreement are governed by New York law.

JURISDICTION

[7.67] The final clause in a loan agreement deals usually with jurisdiction namely, the courts which are to hear any disputes.[235] As with governing law, a jurisdiction clause is unnecessary where the lender and borrower are both incorporated in Ireland and the lender is advancing funds from an Irish place of

---

[229.] Section 140(a).

[230.] It would not be difficult for a consumer to claim that he entered the contract following an application for a loan made by him as a result of an advertisement he had seen or heard.

[231.] Section 140(b).

[232.] See *Kutchera v Buckingham International Holdings Ltd* [1988] IR 61 at 68; [1988] ILRM 501 at 504 for corporate capacity see paras **[18.30]-[18.34]** below.

[233.] *Ibid* paras **[18.45]-[18.58]** below.

[234.] See para **[7.42]** above.

[235.] For further reading see Wood, *Law and Practice of International Finance* (1980) Sweet & Maxwell, Ch 3; Penn, Shea & Arora, *The Law & Practice of International Banking* Vol 2 (1987) Sweet & Maxwell Ch 2.

business to the borrower's place of business in Ireland.[236] Where this does not apply, a jurisdiction clause should be specified under which the borrower expressly submits to the non-exclusive jurisdiction of the courts of Ireland. This will be given effect to by the courts of Ireland.[237] In *Kutchera v Buckingham International Holdings Ltd*[238] Walsh J held in the Supreme Court that:[239]

> "It is well established in a series of decisions, not merely in this jurisdiction but in the jurisdiction of other common law countries, that agreement by contract to submit to the jurisdiction of a foreign court is an unequivocal acceptance of the jurisdiction of that court, irrespective of whether the defendant fails to appear or fails to contest the case".

[7.68] This approach was more recently applied by the English Court of Appeal in *Continental Bank NA v Aeokos Cia Naviera SA*.[240] In that case, a US bank through its Athens branch granted loan facilities to Greek companies; the agreement provided that it was governed by English law and the companies irrevocably submitted to the jurisdiction of the English courts; the Greek companies took proceedings in Athens. The Court of Appeal held that:

1. On the proper construction of the jurisdiction clause the companies were clearly bound to submit all disputes relating to the loan facility to the English courts,

2. The parties to an exclusive jurisdiction agreement were presumed to have intended that all matters in dispute would be settled by the same court, and

3. Since there was a valid jurisdiction clause, Article 17 of the 1968 Convention,[241] which gave paramount effect to exclusive jurisdiction agreements, applied to deprive the courts of other contracting states of jurisdiction.

Where a party accepts jurisdiction of the courts of Ireland under the loan agreement, the proceedings may (with some exceptions) be brought against that party in the Irish courts notwithstanding that such party is not incorporated or resident in Ireland.

[7.69] The Jurisdiction of Courts and Enforcement of Judgments (European Communities) Act, 1988 implemented into Irish law the Convention on

---

[236.] See Articles 2 and 13 of the Brussels Convention, see para **[7.69]** below.

[237.] *International Altex Corporation v Lawler Creations Ltd* [1965] IR 264.

[238.] [1988] IR 61, [1988] ILRM 501.

[239.] *Ibid* at 69 and at 505 respectively.

[240.] [1994] 2 All ER 540.

[241.] *The Convention on Jurisdiction and the Enforcement of Judgments in Civil and Commercial Matters* (Brussels, 27 September 1968, EC 46 (1978)).

jurisdiction and the enforcement of judgments in civil and commercial matters signed at Brussels on 27 September 1968 ("the Brussels Convention").[242] A few of this Act's provisions were amended by the Jurisdiction of Courts and Enforcement of Judgments Act, 1993,[243] which implemented into Irish law the Convention on jurisdiction and the enforcement of judgments in civil and commercial matters signed at Lugano on 16 September 1988 ("the Lugano Convention").[244]

Article 2 of the Brussels Convention and the Lugano Convention ("the Conventions")[245] provide that, subject to certain exceptions, "persons domiciled in a Contracting State shall, whatever their nationality, be sued in the courts of that State". Article 5 provides that a person, domiciled in a Contracting State, being a party to a contract requiring performance in another Contracting State may be sued in respect of such performance in the courts of that other Contracting State. An individual is deemed to be domiciled in the State in which he is ordinarily resident.[246] A company is deemed to be domiciled in the State in which it has its "seat" namely the State in which it was incorporated or the State within which its central management and control is exercised.[247]

Consumers

[7.70] Special rules apply to certain contracts of consumers under the Conventions.[248] Such contracts include:[249]

[242.] Together with the Protocol on the interpretation of the 1968 Convention by the European Court, signed at Luxembourg on the 3 June 1971, the 1978 Accession Convention (Denmark, Ireland and the United Kingdom) and the 1982 Accession Convention (The Hellenic Republic); currently the Contracting States are Belgium, Denmark, France, Germany, Greece, Ireland, Italy, Luxembourg, Netherlands, Portugal, Spain, the United Kingdom and since 1997 Austria, Finland and Sweden.

[243.] Including the adoption of the 1989 Accession Convention (the Kingdom of Spain and the Portuguese Republic).

[244.] Currently the Contracting States are those States which are a party to the Brussels Convention as well as Iceland, Norway and Switzerland.

[245.] The terms of the Brussels Convention and the Lugano Convention are nearly identical - each being set out in Schedules to the Jurisdiction of Courts and Enforcement of Judgments Act, 1993.

[246.] Jurisdiction of Courts and Enforcement of Judgments (European Communities) Act, 1988, 5th Schedule, Part 1; see also *Deutsche Bank Aktiengesellschaft v Murtagh and Murtagh* [1995] 1 ILRM 381 where Costello J held that the words "ordinarily resident" had to be given their ordinary meaning in the light of the intention of the 1988 Act.

[247.] Jurisdiction of Courts and Enforcement of Judgments (European Communities) Act, 1988, 5th Sch Pt III.

[248.] For the purpose of the Conventions a "consumer" is a person who concludes a contract "for a purpose which can be regarded as being outside his trade or profession".

[249.] See Article 13.

a contract for a loan repayable by instalments, or for any other form of credit, made to finance the sale of goods, or ... a contract for the supply of services, and

(a) in the State of the consumer's domicile the conclusion of the contract was preceded by a specific invitation addressed to him or by advertising, and

(b) the consumer took in that State the steps necessary for the conclusion of the contract.

In the case of the foregoing contracts, Article 14 provides:

A consumer may bring proceedings against the other party to a contract either in the courts of the Contracting State in which that party is domiciled or in the courts of the Contracting State in which he is himself domiciled.

Proceedings may be brought against a consumer by the other party to the contract only in the courts of the Contracting State in which the consumer is domiciled.

These provisions cannot be contracted out of at the time the loan agreement is signed unless both consumer and lender at that time are domiciled or habitually resident in the same Contracting State and both parties agree to the jurisdiction of the courts of that State.[250]

Where a consumer enters into a contract with a party who is not domiciled in a Contracting State, but has a branch, agency or place of business in a Contracting State, that party will be deemed to be domiciled in the Contracting State where it has a branch, agency or place of business.[251]

Agreement as to Jurisdiction

[7.71] The Irish courts will have exclusive jurisdiction where one of the parties to a non-consumer loan agreement is domiciled in a Contracting State (to either of the Conventions and agrees with the other party or parties in the agreement, under the jurisdiction clause, that the courts of Ireland will have exclusive jurisdiction (which if not specified to be non-exclusive) to settle any dispute arising under the loan agreement.[252] Where the non-consumer loan agreement provides that for the benefit of the lender the courts of Ireland will have jurisdiction, the lender will retain the right to bring proceedings in any other court which has jurisdiction for the hearing of the action by virtue of the Conventions.[253]

---

[250] Article 15; a further exception permits the consumer to bring proceedings in courts other than those provided for in Article 13 or 14.

[251] Article 13.

[252] Article 17 (subject to Article 16).

[253] *Ibid.* For the application of the principles of Article 17 in Ireland, see the judgment of Keane J in *GPA Group plc v The Governor and Co of the Bank of Ireland and The European Organisation for the Safety of Air Navigation* [1992] 2 IR 408.

Where a party to a non-consumer loan agreement is domiciled outside a Contracting State and the agreement provides for a court of a non-Contracting State to have exclusive jurisdiction, an Irish court is unlikely to hear any dispute in relation to the agreement.[254] To be allowed to proceed the plaintiff will have to show that it is just and proper for the proceedings to continue in Ireland.[255]

COMMERCIAL PAPER

[7.72] In the early 1980s banks introduced a new type of facility known as a note issuance facility ("NIF"). As its name implies, this type of facility involved the customer issuing notes in exchange for cash. For the customer it was a cheaper method of raising finance than by way of loan from a bank as the amount advanced was not entered on the bank's balance sheet thereby avoiding a reserve asset cost. Accordingly, the interest or return which the customer was required to pay on the amount it received was lower than it otherwise would have been had reserve asset cost been charged. The banks took a commission on the notes placed, as well as a commission on any commitment to place notes as any notes not placed would be taken up by the banks themselves.

The purchaser of such notes obviously wanted to ensure that the note issuer would be in a position to pay interest and repay the principal amount of the funds on the maturity date. The NIFs arranged initially by banks were for semi-State companies and their commitments were guaranteed typically by the State.[256]

Subsequently, banks extended this type of facility to large corporate customers and guaranteed payment of the notes themselves. This type of facility, essentially the same as a NIF, came to be known as a "pro-note facility". The pro note facility was offered typically as an option to cash advance facilities. For the customer either choice resulted in cash being advanced to it but usually the availment of the pro note facility would result in a cheaper cost to the customer.

Avoidance of Deposit Interest Retention Tax

[7.73] In 1986 NIFs and pro-note facilities were given an added impetus by the introduction of a new tax known as deposit interest retention tax ("DIRT"). Under the Taxes Consolidation Act 1997[257] interest paid on all relevant deposits

---

[254.] *Law v Garrett* (1878) 8 Ch D 26; *Austrian Lloyd Steamship Co v Gresham Life Insurance Society Ltd* [1903] 1 KB 249; *Kirchner & Co v Gruban* [1909] 1 Ch 413; *Trendtex Trading Corporation v Credit Suisse* [1982] AC 679; *The Morviken* [1983] 1 Lloyd's Rep 1.

[255.] *Evans Marshall & Co Ltd v Bertola SA* [1973] 1 WLR 349; *Carvalho v Hull Blyth (Angola) Ltd* [1979] 1 WLR 1228; *Trendtex Trading Corporation v Credit Suisse* [1982] AC 679; but see Article 16.

[256.] The Minister for Finance is empowered to guarantee monies borrowed by several semi-State companies pursuant to the statutes applicable to such semi-State company.

[257.] Section 257.

made[258] by persons resident in Ireland with banks, building societies and certain other bodies[259] suffers a deduction of tax generally at the standard rate.[260] Accordingly, investors with funds available sought outlets for depositing funds without incurring DIRT.[261] Purchasing notes from corporations in exchange for providing them with funds avoided DIRT and yet as payment of the notes was guaranteed by banks, the note investment was as secure to the investor as a deposit directly with the bank.

There was initially though some doubt as to whether note facilities correctly avoided DIRT in that banks acted as intermediaries for their customers in taking funds used to purchase their customers' notes, and thus the receipt of funds by them might have been construed as a deposit.

Interest is defined in the 1986 Act as meaning:[262]

> any interest of money whether yearly or otherwise, including any amount whether or not described as interest paid in consideration of the making of a deposit.

Thus, where notes are sold on a discount basis,[263] which has become more common, the difference between the purchase price (for the note) and the maturity payment may properly be described as interest. Indeed, both interest and discount are chargeable with tax under Schedule D Case III of the Income Tax Act, 1967.[264]

A "deposit" is defined as:[265]

> a sum of money paid to a relevant deposit taker[266] on terms under which it will be repaid with or without interest and either on demand or at a time or in

---

[258.] Meaning all deposits other than certain exemptions stipulated in the definition of relevant deposit under the Taxes Consolidation Act 1997, s 256(1).

[259.] As set out in the definition of relevant deposit taker under the Taxes Consolidation Act 1997, s 256(1).

[260.] In 1986, 35 per cent; currently 26 subject to an exceptional rate of 15 per cent for special savings accounts (the former rate to be reduced to 24 per cent and the latter to be increased to 20 per cent with effect from 6 April 1998).

[261.] Although corporate investors within a charge to corporation tax in Ireland may avoid DIRT through completing other documentation provided by the Revenue Commissioners.

[262.] Taxes Consolidation Act 1997, s 256(1).

[263.] A typical formula would be a three month note of £100,000 would be purchased at a price of
$$£100,000 \text{ divided by } 1 + \frac{(I \times 90)}{36500}$$
where I equals the rate per cent per annum expressed as a number and not as a fraction at which the bank purchases a note or procures a purchase for a note.
An alternative formula is
$$£100,000 - (100,000 \text{ divided by } 1) + \frac{I \text{ (as a percentage)} \times 90}{365}$$

[264.] See Judge, *Irish Income Tax* (1997-98) (Butterworths) para 8.101.

[265.] Taxes Consolidation Act 1997, s 256(1).

[266.] Includes banks and building societies.

circumstances agreed by or on behalf of the person making the payment and the person to whom it is made.

It can be seen that where a bank offers an investor one of the bank's customer's notes and the investor purchases the note, the transferring of the purchase price by the investor to the bank appears to fall within the definition of deposit.

[7.74] However, provided funds pass as between the customer and the investor, albeit through the bank acting as intermediary or agent of the customer, DIRT should not be chargeable. But, where the bank retains part of the discount, there may be a risk that that part retained is properly subject to DIRT. Obviously the records should reflect the true nature of the transaction, namely, that the bank is simply a facilitator and that the receipt of moneys and repayment thereof appear only in the records of the bank's customer, even though such record is kept by the bank as the customer's agent.

The investor should also clearly be aware, as all sophisticated investors will be, that the bank is acting as agent and is not a principal in the transaction. It may be preferable, but not essential, that the investor knows the identity of the recipient of its investment. In practice, except in the case of semi-State bodies, the issuer of notes will not be known to the investor (who is relying on the bank's guarantee as security for repayment).

Interest on Notes issued by Semi-State Bodies

[7.75] An exemption from the requirement to withhold or deduct tax on the payment of interest[267] includes "interest on any securities in respect of which the Minister for Finance has given a direction under s 36 of the Taxes Consolidation Act, 1997".[268] Section 36 of the Taxes Consolidation Act, 1997[269] provides that, the Minister for Finance may direct that any securities[270] issued under his authority shall be deemed to be issued on the condition that interest on those securities shall be paid without deduction of tax.

As most semi-State bodies can borrow or raise money only with the consent or concurrence of the Minister for Finance, any notes issued by them with such consent or concurrence will be notes issued under the authority of the Minister for Finance. A direction must nevertheless be obtained from the Department of Finance. The issuer of notes and the intermediary, ie the bank selling the notes may be required to provide the Revenue Commissioners with the names and addresses of the person receiving the interest as well as certain details of the

---

[267.] See para [7.42] above.

[268.] Taxes Consolidation Act, 1997, s 246(3).

[269.] As applied by the Taxes Consolidation Act, 1997, s 38.

[270.] The term securities is not defined but is generally regarded as being sufficiently wide to include debentures or notes.

note itself.[271] Specific provision is made for the issue of securities (including notes) by certain named semi-State companies.[272]

Taking Funds from the Public

[7.76] Prior to the enactment of the Central Bank Act, 1989 banking business, the carrying on of which requires a licence from the Central Bank, was defined[273] as including "business which consists of - the business of accepting deposits payable on demand or on notice or at a fixed or determinable future date ..." (subject to certain exclusions).

The all important word "deposit" was not defined (in the Central Bank Act) but in other respects this definition would catch a person receiving funds for the issue of notes done on a regular basis. Indeed the definition of deposit in the Taxes Consolidation Act, 1997[274] would but for the reference of the money being paid to a "relevant deposit taker" in all respects catch the receipt of funds for the issuance of notes.

[7.77] Because of the uncertainty as well as "to secure greater protection for the public from unauthorised deposit taking and to conform with definitions of banking in EC Directives,"[275] the Central Bank Act, 1989 amended the definition of banking business to include: [276]

> the business of taking funds, other than deposits, from the public payable on demand or on notice or at a fixed or determinable future date (whether or not involving the issue of securities or other obligations, however described) (subject to certain exceptions).

This clearly included the receipt of money for notes issued to the public. Under the Central Bank Act, 1997[277] banking business now means (subject to certain exclusions):[278]

> (a) the business of accepting, on own account, sums of money from the public in the form of deposits or other repayable funds whether or not involving the issue of securities or other obligations, howsoever described, or

---

[271.] Taxes Consolidation Act, 1997, s 36(3).

[272.] *Ibid* s 37 (Aer Lingus Teoranta, Aer Rianta Teoranta, Bord Telecom Éireann plc, Irish Telecommunications Investments plc, ACC Bank plc, Electricity Supply Board, Ionrad Éireann, Bord Na Mona, Aerlinte Éireann Teoranta, Radio Telefis Éireann, ICC Bank plc and Bord Gais Éireann).

[273.] Central Bank Act, 1971, s 2.

[274.] Section 256.

[275.] See Explanatory Memorandum to the Central Bank Bill, 1988.

[276.] Section 29.

[277.] Implemented on 9 April 1997 by the Central Bank Act, 1997 (Commencement) Order, 1997 SI 150/1997.

[278.] Section 70(b).

(b) the business aforesaid and any other business normally carried on by a bank, which may include the granting of credits on own account.

[7.78] To enable the Central Bank to exempt certain categories from banking business and thereby the requirement to obtain a licence, the Central Bank Act 1989 amended s 8 of the Central Bank Act 1971 by providing that the Central Bank may exempt persons from the requirement to hold a licence where:[279]

(i) the requirement would arise solely out of the issuing of securities or other obligations to which the definition of 'banking business' relates, and

(ii) the [Central] Bank is of the opinion that the exemption would not conflict with the orderly and proper regulation of banking.

On 31 October 1989 the Central Bank announced that certain classes of persons are exempt from the requirement to hold a banking licence where the requirement would arise from the issue of commercial paper. Commercial paper are securities or other obligations to which the definition of banking business relates which have an original maturity of less than one year. A subsequent replacement notice of exemption was issued by the Central Bank on 16 November 1990. This has since been replaced by a notice of 16 February 1998.[280] These persons are, subject to certain compliance requirements:

I. Short Term Commercial Paper

(A) (i) a company or other body corporate (whether Irish registered or otherwise) or body created under Irish statute (statutory body), the latest audited accounts of which indicate that it has shareholders' funds (meaning paid-up share capital, capital reserves, revenue reserves and minority interests as disclosed in the most recent audited accounts of the company, or the appropriate equivalent for a statutory body) of at least £20 million or foreign currency equivalent, or

(ii) a company or other body corporate whose commercial paper is guaranteed by a parent, other company, or statutory body where the guarantor has shareholders' funds of at least £20 million or foreign currency equivalent;

(B) a company or other body corporate or statutory body whose commercial paper is guaranteed by an EC credit institution (as defined by the First Council Directive (77/780/EEC) of 12 December 1977 on the coordination of laws, regulations and administrative provisions relating to the taking up and pursuit of the business of credit institutions) or equivalent from an OECD member state;

[279.] Central Bank Act, 1971, s 8(2) as amended by the Central Bank Act, 1989, s 31, as further amended by the Central Bank Act, 1997, s 70(d).

[280.] Published in *Iris Oifigiúil* on 20 February 1998.

(C) any OECD member state, or the European Union, or a company or statutory body whose commercial paper is guaranteed by any OECD member state or by the European Union.

Commercial paper under any of the foregoing categories must be issued and transferable in minimum amounts of £100,000 or foreign currency equivalent.

II Asset-Based Commercial Paper

a company or other body corporate, whether Irish or otherwise, or a statutory body which issues commercial paper where:

1. at the time of issue, the commercial paper is backed by assets to at least 100 per cent of the value of the commercial paper issued;

2. at the time of issue, the commercial paper is rated to at least investment grade by one or more recognised rating agencies (based on the definitions set out in the Central Bank's implementation notes for credit institutions (BSD S 2/95 of 30 November 1995) of the EU Directive on the Capital Adequacy of Investment Firms and Credit Institutions; and

3. Commercial paper under this category must be issued and transferable in minimum amounts of £250,000 or foreign currency equivalent

Where commercial paper is issued (ie paper having a maturity of less than one year) under any of the foregoing categories, the following conditions must be complied with:

1. The issuer must notify the Central Bank as soon as it commences the activity stating the category under which it claims exemption from the requirement to hold a banking licence;

2. All commercial paper must identify the issuer by name and must carry the title "Commercial Paper".

3. It must be stated explicitly on the face of the commercial paper (and, where applicable, in the contract between investor and issuer) that it is issued in accordance with an exemption granted by the Central Bank under s 8(2) of the Central Bank Act, 1971, as inserted by s 31 of the Central Bank Act, 1989, as amended by s 70(d) of the Central Bank Act, 1997;

4. It must be stated explicitly on the face of the commercial paper (and, where applicable, in the contract between investor and issuer) that the investment does not have the status of a bank deposit, is not within the scope of the Deposit Protection Scheme operated by the Central Bank of Ireland and that the issuer is not regulated by the Central Bank of Ireland arising from the issue of commercial paper; and

5. Any issue of commercial paper which is guaranteed must carry a statement to the effect that it is guaranteed and identify the guarantor by name.

III Securities or other paper with an original maturity of one year or more

(i) a company or other body corporate, whether Irish or otherwise, or a statutory body which issues securities or other paper (with an original maturity of one year or more)

(ii) any OECD member state, or the European Union.

Private Offers

[7.79] It is arguable that this exemption is not needed for the pro note facility to operate, as this facility involves the offering and placing of notes privately. If notes are offered publicly then the prospectus requirements of the Companies Act, 1963 and subsequent regulations need to be complied with.[281] Prospectus is defined as meaning "any prospectus, notice, circular, advertisement or other invitation, offering to the public for subscription or purchase any debentures of a company".[282] Compliance with the prospectus requirements would make a pro note facility prohibitively expensive. Accordingly, in practice such facilities are private.

It is important to ensure obviously, that notes issued are done so pursuant to a private offering. To understand the distinction the relevant provisions of the Companies Act, 1963 need to be considered.

A company, to have the status of a private company, must prohibit in its articles of association "any invitation to the public to subscribe for any shares or debentures of the company."[283] A debenture is defined as including "debenture stock, bonds and any other securities of a company whether constituting a charge on the assets of the company or not".[284] It is generally accepted that a note falls within the definition of debenture. Thus a private company cannot issue notes to the public. Should it do so, apart from committing an offence,[285] the company's shareholders could become severally liable for the payment of its debts.[286]

Where a company agrees to allot or allots notes with a view to any of the notes being offered for sale to the public, "any document by which the offer for sale to the public is made" shall be deemed to be a prospectus.[287] Thus, in the case of a public company, it is important that if any notes are offered to the public the offer and acceptance are done by means of oral communication.

[281.] Companies Act, 1963, ss 43 to 57.

[282.] *Ibid s* 2(1).

[283.] *Ibid* s 33(1).

[284.] *Ibid* s 2(1).

[285.] Companies (Amendment) Act, 1983, s 21.

[286.] Companies Act, 1963, ss 34(1) and 36; unless the court is satisfied that the failure to comply with the prohibition "was accidental or due to inadvertence or to some other sufficient cause" (Companies Act, 1963, s 34(2)).

[287.] *Ibid* s 51(1).

The Companies Act, 1963 provides some illumination as to what may constitute a public offering of notes. First, public includes "any section of the public, whether selected as ... clients of the person issuing the prospectus or in any other manner."[288] However, the foregoing does not require an offer or invitation to be treated as made to the public:

> if it can properly be regarded, in all the circumstances, as not being calculated to result, directly or indirectly, in the ... debentures becoming available for subscription or purchase by persons other than those receiving the offer or invitation, or otherwise as being a domestic concern of the persons making and receiving it.[289]

The test is not who receives an offer (or invitation) but who may accept the offer (or invitation). In other words, the arrangement by which notes are sold must not be capable of constituting an offer for sale to the public and the terms under which the notes are sold must contain appropriate restrictions so as to avoid the offer being construed as a public one.

[7.80] A difficulty for arrangers has been the absence of clear statutory or even common law guidelines. One approach which has been adopted is for a list of potential purchasers to be agreed between the customer and the bank. It has generally been regarded in the market place that a maximum of 20 persons may be considered safe.

Additional safeguards adopted by some would be that not more than five potential offerees would be contacted on any one day and/or that only persons who expressed an interest in purchasing notes would receive an offer. A bank might ascertain independently of any particular transaction or facility by contacting potential offerees enquiring whether they would be interested in purchasing notes of customers (whose identity would not be disclosed at that stage).

Further safeguards include a covenant by the bank in the loan agreement or facility letter that the bank acting as agent for the customer in offering notes would indicate to the offeree that:

1. The invitation to purchase a note may be accepted only by the person to whom the invitation is made;

2. Notes would be issued only to persons acting on their own behalf and not as nominee for any other person;

3. The notes are not negotiable, transferable or renounceable;

[288.] *Ibid* s 61(1).
[289.] *Ibid* at s 61(2).

4. The customer issuing the notes and/or the bank are permitted to comply with any request by the Revenue Commissioners to furnish information regarding the holders or purchasers of any notes.

The first three restrictions are designed principally to avoid a secondary market for the customer's notes, as otherwise in the event of a secondary market arising it might be difficult to contend that the customer had arranged for a private issue of its notes.

[7.81] To avoid the prospectus requirements, the terms of the loan agreement/ facility letter under which notes are to be offered should specify that all or any invitations to purchase notes will be made orally and the acceptance will be oral; furthermore the bank will not circulate written details of any note, nor the note itself before or at the time of offering a note to any person. Accordingly, no invitation or offer should be made by any visible means of communication (whether it be by document, telex, facsimile, e-mail, internet or otherwise).[290] Furthermore, the terms of an oral offer should not be confirmed by such means. It is understood, in practice, a bank dealer would telephone an offeree and give the basic details such as identity of issuer, guarantor (if any), term of the note, principal amount, interest (whether through a discount arrangement or otherwise) and manner of payment. Whether the dealer would specify the conditions (1) to (4) above under which the offer is made is a question which only those who have bought or sold notes could answer.

It would be appropriate once a note has been sold by oral agreement for the dealer to send a written communication confirming the terms upon which the oral contract had been concluded. This communication would not be a contract but simply confirmation of the oral contract already concluded.

Company Records and Publicity

[7.82] Every company which issues a series of debentures each ranking *pari passu* is required to keep a register of the holders of such debentures and enter into the register the names and addresses of the debenture holders and the amount of debentures held by each holder.[291]

The register is required to be kept at the registered office of the issuing customer or at any other office of the customer at which the work of making it up is done.[292] As the bank arranges for the notes to be issued, the register would be kept by the bank for each particular customer at its office.

[290.] The Interpretation Act, 1937, s 36 provides that the word "writing" includes printing, type-writing, lithography, photography, and other modes of representing or producing words in visible form".

[291.] Companies Act, 1963, s 91(1).

[292.] *Ibid* s 91(2).

However, unless the register is kept at all times at the registered office of the issuing customer, notice of such register must be given to the registrar of companies.[293] To avoid the filing of such notice, and thereby giving publicity to the issue, the bank can notify the customer as and when its notes are sold and the customer can then enter the appropriate particulars in its own register.

[293.] *Ibid* s 91(3) and (4).

Chapter 8

Avoidance of Security by Undue Influence

UNDUE INFLUENCE

> "It is well settled that equity will set aside a contract where one party thereto has exercised undue influence over the other party as a result of which the latter has been induced to enter into an improvident transaction against his own interest."[1]

[8.01] One of the principal concerns for a banker in entering into a contract with a third party in respect of a customer's arrangements with the bank, is the possibility of the contract being set aside because of undue influence or misrepresentation. As a banker is often in a position of trust, it is essential that certain procedures are followed prior to completing any contract with a guarantor.

The Application of Undue Influence

[8.02] The underlying principles giving rise to undue influence may be ascertained from the judgments of Budd J in *Gregg v Kidd*[2] and of Costello J in *O'Flanagan v Ray-Ger Limited.*[3] Although the former case involved the transfer of property in consideration of affection, the principles may apply equally to a banker-customer relationship. The relevant principles from the High Court judgments for a banker and his adviser to note are:[4]

1. The courts will not confine the application of the principle to any stated form of relationship.[5]

2. It must be shown that either undue influence was exercised[6] or the

---

1. Barron J in *McGonigle v Black* High Court, unrep, 14 November 1988 p 9.
2. [1956] IR 183; see also Lord Scarman in *National Westminster Bank plc v Morgan* [1985] 1 All ER 821 at 829; [1985] 2 WLR 588 at 600.
3. High Court, unrep, 28 April 1983.
4. For an approach based on English decisions see Shea, 'Undue Influence and the Banker - Customer Relationship - A Review of Recent Cases' [1986] 1 JIBL 57; Wilkinson, 'Banks and the Relationship of Confidence' (1983) 133 NLJ 952.
5. [1956] IR 183 at 194; Costello J in *O'Flanagan v Ray-Ger Limited* High Court, unrep, 28 April 1983 at p 19; see also Fullagar J in *Blomley v Ryan* (1954-56) 99 CLR 362 at 405; Nourse LJ in *Goldsworthy v Brickell* [1987] 1 All ER 853 at 865.
6. The absence of which was the "fatal flaw" in *The Bank of Nova Scotia v Hogan and Hogan* [1996] 3 IR 239; [1997] 1 ILRM 407.

actual relations between the parties give rise to a presumption of influence.[7]

3. Where the relations between the bank and the guarantor or between the bank's customer and the guarantor are such as to raise a presumption that the bank or its customer had influence over the guarantor, the onus lies on the bank to establish that the guarantee was the spontaneous act of the guarantor acting in circumstances which enabled him to exercise an independent will and that the guarantee was the result of a free exercise of the guarantor's will.[8]

4. The presumption may be rebutted either by showing that the guarantor has had competent independent advice and acted of his own free will or in some other way.[9]

5. The most obvious way to prove that the guarantee was the result of the free exercise of independent will is to establish that the guarantee was made after the nature and effect of the transaction had been fully explained to the guarantor by some independent and qualified person so completely as to satisfy the court that the guarantor was acting independently of any influence from the bank or its customer and with a full understanding of what he was doing, and the advice relied on must be given with a knowledge of all relevant circumstances and must be such as a competent and honest adviser would give if acting solely in the interests of the guarantor.[10]

---

[7] Budd J referred only to the latter at [1956] IR 183 at 195; but Costello J at p 18 of his judgment in *O'Flanagan v Ray-Ger Limited* High Court, unrep, 28 April 1983, referred to both and was consistent with the English decisions which since *Allcard v Skinner* (1887) 36 Ch D 145 draw a distinction between cases where actual undue influence is proved and those where, due to the confidential relationship between the parties, undue influence is presumed and has to be rebutted - see further Slade LJ in *Bank of Credit and Commerce International SA v Aboody* [1989] 2 WLR 759 at 768-785.

[8] *Ibid* at 195-6, Budd J adopted the Privy Council's decision in *Inche Noriah v Shaik Allie Bin Omar* [1929] AC 127 at 133.

[9] *Ibid* at 196; see also MacKenzie J in *Leonard v Leonard* [1988] ILRM 245 at 246 - "the donor must be mentally able to understand her action, her will must be free and spontaneous, there must also be proper legal advice and the act itself must not be improvident"; see further Finlay J in *McCormack v Bennett* (1973) 107 ILTR 127 at 131; and 'Rebutting the Presumption of Undue Influence' Ir Jur (1955-56) Vol XXI-XXII 31; see also *Mahoney v Purcell* [1996] 3 All ER 61.

[10] *Ibid* at 196 and 202 where again Budd J expressly adopted the Privy Council's decision in *Inche Noriah v Shaik Allie Bin Omar* [1929] AC 127 at 135; see also *Leonard v Leonard* [1988] ILRM 245; see further Lynch J in *Noonan v O'Connell* High Court, unrep, 10 April 1987 p 7; see further TS McCann, 'The Setting Aside of Deeds and Gifts Inter Vivos obtained by the Exercise of Undue Influence' (1967) Ir Jur 205.

6. It is not necessary that the guarantor should actually follow the independent advice.[11]

Bank Customer's Surety

[8.03] Most of the decisions concerning the repudiation of a contract of guarantee by the guarantor involve a person seeking to set aside a security created in favour of a bank as a result of undue influence being applied to the guarantor or misrepresentation made to the guarantor, not by a bank over its customer but, by a bank or its customer over the guarantor.[12] This arises commonly where undue influence is exercised over, or a misrepresentation made to, a customer's wife.[13] Accordingly, the relationship between husband and wife needs to be understood for a banker and his adviser to assess the possibility of a document being set aside by reason of undue influence.

This relationship and its impact on the doctrine of undue influence is explained by the English Court of Appeal in *Midland Bank plc v Shephard*.[14] Neill LJ set out the following propositions in the judgment of the Court:[15]

1. The confidential relationship between husband and wife does not give rise by itself to a presumption of undue influence;[16]

---

11. *Ibid* at 202. Budd J expressly refused to follow the decision of Farwell J on this point in *Powell v Powell* [1900] 1 Ch 243. Budd J's decision is supported in Keane, *Equity and the Law of Trusts in the Republic of Ireland* (1988) Butterworths p 341. This must be correct as to use Keane's words it is, "illogical to take compliance with advice as a necessary proof of the exercise of an independent will. The decision, if it is to be genuinely independent, must remain that of the donor: one does not achieve that result by requiring that for the gift to be effective the donor must have in essence abdicated his right to make the decision in favour of the adviser"; see also Black J in *Provincial Bank of Ireland v McKeever* [1941] IR 471 at 484; see further *Leonard v Leonard* [1988] ILRM 245 where the transferor refused to include a revocation clause despite advice to have such a clause; but see Millett LJ in *Credit Lyonnais Bank Nederland NV v Burch* [1997] 1 All ER 144 at 156.
12. The effect on the bank in these circumstances is examined further by MacDonald, 'Undue Influence and Third Parties' (1990) JBL 469.
13. For example in *Bank of Credit and Commerce International SA v Aboody* [1989] 2 WLR 759.
14. [1988] 3 All ER 17; these propositions are consistent with the subsequent Court of Appeal decision in *Bank of Credit and Commerce International SA v Aboody* [1989] 2 WLR 759.
15. *Ibid* at 21-22.
16. Supported by the judgment of Dillon LJ in *Kingsnorth Trust Ltd v Bell* [1986] 1 All ER 423 at 427; [1986] 1 WLR 119 at 123 and by Lord Scarman *in National Westminster Bank plc v Morgan* [1985] 1 All ER 821 at 826; [1985] 2 WLR 588 at 596; see also Chesire, Fifoot & Furmston's *Law of Contract* (13th ed) p 327; more recently confirmed and applied by the Supreme Court in *The Bank of Nova Scotia v Hogan and Hogan* [1996] 3 IR 239; [1997] 1 ILRM 407; but see *Dunbar Bank plc v Nadeem* [1997] 2 All ER 253 where the wife (from Pakistan) was described by her son in evidence "as being a typical eastern housewife" who was never used to questioning her husband; in that case the court held that the relationship of trust and confidence was such as to give rise to a presumption of undue influence.

2. Even if the relationship between the parties gives rise to a presumption of undue influence, the transaction will not be set aside unless it was to the manifest disadvantage of the person influenced;[17]

3. The court should examine the facts to see whether the relevant transaction had been, or should be presumed to have been, procured by undue influence, and if so whether the transaction was so disadvantageous to the person seeking to set it aside as to be unfair;

4. The court will not enforce a transaction at the suit of a creditor if it can be shown that the creditor entrusted the task of obtaining the alleged debtor's signature to the relevant document to someone who was, to the knowledge of the creditor, in a position to influence the debtor and who procured the signature of the debtor by means of undue influence or by means of fraudulent misrepresentation.[18]

[8.04] In applying these propositions to the case in point Neill LJ indicated[19] that in order to establish the defence of undue influence it is necessary for the covenantor to prove that:

(i)   she was induced or must be presumed to have been induced to sign the covenant by the undue influence of her husband, or by his fraudulent misrepresentations or fraudulent concealment of material facts;

(ii) the contract into which she was induced to enter was manifestly disadvantageous to her; and

(iii) in the circumstances the acts of her husband are to be attributed to the bank.

The facts of *Midland Bank plc v Shephard*[20] were briefly that a husband's loan facility for business purposes was made available through an overdraft account held jointly by the husband and wife. The wife did not receive independent advice and she contended that her husband had acted as the bank's agent in procuring her signature and had exerted undue influence on her. After considering the propositions outlined above the Court of Appeal held there was no evidence that the husband had induced his wife to sign the mandate by exercising undue influence - what was signed was the standard joint account mandate signed by every customer who wished to operate a joint account.

---

17. See also Lord Scarman in *National Westminster Bank plc v Morgan* [1985] 1 All ER 821 at 827; [1985] 2 WLR 588 at 597.
18. See also Dillon LJ in *Kingsnorth Trust Ltd v Bell* [1986] 1 All ER 423 at 427; [1986] 1 WLR 119 at 123.
19. [1988] 3 All ER 17 at 22.
20. [1988] 3 All ER 17.

[8.05] Banks and their advisers should take particular note of the English Court of Appeal's decision in *Kingsnorth Trust Ltd v Bell*[21] where a man obtained a loan and took the mortgage over the family home to his wife for her signature. The wife signed the mortgage following the misrepresentation from her husband that it was to secure a loan made for the husband's business. In giving the decision of the Court, Dillon LJ stated:[22]

> "there is no presumption of law that a transaction between husband and wife for the husband's benefit was procured by undue influence on the part of the husband and there is no rule that such a transaction cannot be upheld unless the wife is shown to have had independent advice."

However, in setting aside the order for possession Dillon LJ in the Court of Appeal applied the decisions in *Turnbull & Co v Duval*[23] and *Chaplin & Co Ltd v Brammall*:[24]

> "which show that if a creditor, or potential creditor, of a husband desires to obtain, by way of security for the husband's indebtedness, a guarantee from his wife or a charge on property of his wife, and if the creditor entrusts to the husband himself the task of the obtaining the execution of the relevant document by the wife, then the creditor cannot enforce the guarantee or the security against the wife if it is established that the execution of the document by the wife was procured by undue influence by the husband and the wife had no independent advice."[25]

This passage was regarded by the Court of Appeal in the subsequent decision of *Bank of Credit and Commerce International SA v Aboody*[26] as being "the clearest statement of the principle."[27] As Dillon LJ explained:[28]

> "On the general law of principal and agent, the principal (the creditor) however personally innocent, who instructs an agent (the husband) to achieve a particular end (the signing of the document by the wife) is liable for any fraudulent misrepresentation made by the agent in achieving that end,

---

[21.] [1986] 1 All ER 423; [1986] 1 WLR 119.

[22.] [1986] 1 All ER 423 at 427; [1986] 1 WLR 119 at 123.

[23.] [1902] AC 429; this decision was considered to have laid "unsure foundations" of law - see Lord Browne-Wilkinson in *Barclays Bank plc v O'Brien* [1993] 4 All ER 417 at 425-428.

[24.] [1908] 1 KB 233.

[25.] [1986] 1 All ER 423 at 427; [1986] 1 WLR 119 at 123; see also *Northern Banking Company Ltd v Carpenter* [1931] IR 268, see para **[8.37]** below.

[26.] [1989] 2 WLR 759 per Slade LJ at 786.

[27.] The distinction made by the Court of Appeal *in Bank of Credit and Commerce International SA v Aboody* [1989] 2 WLR 859 at 788 was because, "the nature of the transactions - the guarantees of an overdraft of a company of which Mrs Aboody was herself a director and substantial shareholder - was not of a kind which should necessarily have alerted the bank to the possibility that undue influence might be exercised."

[28.] [1986] 1 All ER 423 at 427; [1986] 1 WLR 119 at 124.

including any continuing misrepresentation made earlier by the agent and not corrected."

Dillon LJ gave a lesson to persons taking security by stating:[29]

> "the moral is that where a creditor (or intending lender) desires the protection of a guarantee or charge on property from a third party other than the debtor and the circumstances are such that the debtor could be expected to have influence over that third party, the creditor ought for his own protection to insist that the third party has independent advice. That is the obvious means of avoiding the risk that the creditor will be held to have left it to the debtor to procure the execution of the relevant guarantee or security document by the third party."

[8.06] This principle can be seen also from the earlier decision in *Avon Finance Co Ltd v Bridger*[30] where a chartered accountant was held to be the finance company's agent in obtaining security, which he improperly explained, from his parents. The Court of Appeal held that the son's undue influence was attributable to the finance company who should have dealt directly with the parents.[31]

[8.07] However, in *Coldunell Ltd v Gallon*[32] where a son apparently intercepted letters to his parents advising them to obtain independent advice prior to executing a charge, the security was upheld notwithstanding the son's undue influence over his parents as it was considered the lender had not left the son to procure execution of the documents and accordingly the son had not in any way acted as the lender's agent. Oliver LJ considered that Dillon LJ went too far in *Kingsnorth Trust Ltd v Bell*[33] by requiring lenders to insist on the guarantor having independent advice. He stated:[34]

> "the fact is that no lender can ever be absolutely sure that a guarantor is not being subjected to pressure from the principal debtor, and to require him to do more than properly and fairly point out to the guarantor the desirability of obtaining independent advice, and to require the documents to be executed in the presence of a solicitor, is to put on commercial lenders a burden which would severely handicap the carrying out of what is, after all, an entirely

---

[29.] *Ibid* at 428 and 125 respectively.

[30.] [1985] 2 All ER 281; approved by *Barclays Bank plc v O'Brien* [1993] 4 All ER 417.

[31.] See also *Deutsche Bank AG v Ibrahim* [1992] 3 JIBL N-47 where a man's indebtedness to a bank was secured by the deposit of title deeds to properties owned by his daughters who received no independent advice and received no consideration or benefit for making the deposit; the bank were ordered to return the deeds.

[32.] [1986] 1 All ER 429; see note in *Insolvency Law & Practice* (1986) Vol 2 No. 1 p 26.

[33.] [1986] 1 All ER 423; [1986] 1 WLR 119.

[34.] [1986] 1 All ER 429 at 440.

common transaction of everyday occurrence for banks and other commercial lenders."[35]

Husband and Wife

[8.08] More recently in England there have been a series of decisions, nearly all involving a wife guaranteeing the business debts of her husband. The legal principles set out by these decisions accord remarkably closely with the principles enunciated over forty years ago by Budd J in *Gregg v Kidd*.[36] The most important of these decisions is that of the House of Lords in *Barclays Bank plc v O'Brien*.[37] In that case the bank lent money to a business secured by the guarantee of the principal shareholder, such guarantee being secured by a charge on the shareholder's home owned jointly by the shareholder and his wife, the defendant. When the bank sought possession of the home the defendant contended that her husband had put undue pressure on her to sign and had misrepresented to her that the charge secured £60,000 rather than £135,000. The bank obtained judgment but the Court of Appeal held that the charge was enforceable only to the extent of £60,000. The bank appealed to the House of Lords which held that the charge was unenforceable and should be set aside.

[8.09] Unusually for a House of Lords' decision only one judgment was delivered. The Lords, obviously mindful of the importance of the decision no doubt wished to avoid any blurring of the appropriate principles which might otherwise arise from a multiplicity of judgments, albeit leading to the same conclusion.[38] In the context of setting out the legal principles to be applied henceforth, Lord Browne-Wilkinson began by enunciating the basis on which such principles should be applied, namely:[39]

> "it is important to keep a sense of balance in approaching these cases. It is easy to allow sympathy for the wife who is threatened with the loss of her home at the suit of a rich bank to obscure an important public interest, viz the need to ensure that the wealth currently tied up in the matrimonial home does not become economically sterile. If the rights secured to wives by the law renders

---

35. See also *Butterworths Banking & Financial Law Review 1987*, pp 36-38 where the views expressed by Oliver LJ are preferred to those of Dillon LJ.
36. [1956] IR 183.
37. [1993] 4 All ER 417; the Supreme Court found this decision "both relevant and helpful" in *The Bank of Nova Scotia v Hogan and Hogan* [1996] 3 IR 239 at 246; [1997] 1 ILRM 407 at 413; for further analysis of this decision see Sanfey, 'Undue Influence and the "Tender Treatment" of Wives' (1994) 1 CLP 99 and Reid, 'Family Property and Sureties - Trouble for Lenders?' (1994) ILT 40.
38. "Your Lordships should seek to restate the law in a form which is principled, reflects the current requirements of society and providing as much certainty as possible" per Lord Browne-Wilkinson. *Ibid* at 428.
39. *Ibid* at 422.

vulnerable loans granted on the security of matrimonial homes, institutions will be unwilling to accept such security, thereby reducing the flow of loan capital to business enterprises. It is therefore essential that a law designed to protect the vulnerable does not render the matrimonial home unacceptable as security to financial institutions."

[8.10] Lord Browne-Wilkinson indicated that undue influence may be (1) actual or (2) presumed; it can be presumed where "there was a relationship of trust and confidence" between the person who exercised influence and the person over whom it was exercised. The judge indicated that this confidential relationship can be established as a matter of law (solicitor and client, medical advisor and patient) or "if the complainant proves the *de facto* existence of a relationship under which the complainant generally reposed trust and confidence in the wrongdoer". He explained that a wife who shows that she has relied on her husband in respect of all financial matters and does as he suggests, or who shows that she placed trust and confidence in her husband as to their financial affairs, will be able to raise the presumption of undue influence.[40] The judge indicated also that these principles would apply to all cases where there is an emotional relationship between co-habitees due to "the underlying risk of one co-habitee exploiting the emotional involvement and trust of the other".[41]

[8.11] Lord Browne-Wilkinson stated that the basis for the principles applicable to this area of the law is grounded on "the proper application of the doctrine of notice":[42]

> *Wife's rights*
>
> "A wife who has been induced to stand as a surety for her husband's debts by his undue influence, misrepresentation or some other legal wrong has an equity as against him to set aside that transaction. Under the ordinary principles of equity, her right to set aside that transaction will be enforceable against third parties (eg against a creditor) if either the husband was acting as a third party's agent or the third party had actual or constructive notice of the facts giving rise to her equity. Although there may be cases where, without artificiality, it can properly be held that the husband was acting as the agent of the creditor in procuring the wife to stand as surety, such cases will be of very rare occurrence.

[40.] See also the Supreme Court in *The Bank of Nova Scotia v Hogan and Hogan* [1996] 3 IR 239 at 248 (per Murphy J); [1997] 1 ILRM 407 at 414.

[41.] [1993] 4 All ER 417 at 431.

[42.] *Ibid* at 428; the quotations under the first two headings were adopted and applied by the Supreme Court in *The Bank of Nova Scotia v Hogan and Hogan* [1996] 3 IR 239 at 249; [1997] 1 ILRM 407 at 414.

Creditor on notice of wife's rights

The key to the problem is to identify the circumstances in which the creditor will be taken to have had notice of the wife's equity to set aside the transaction. The doctrine of notice lies at the heart of equity. Given that there are two innocent parties, each enjoying rights, the earlier right prevails against the later right if the acquirer of the later right knows of the earlier right (actual notice) or would have discovered it had he taken proper steps (constructive notice). In particular, if the party asserting that he takes free of the earlier rights of another knows of certain facts which put him on inquiry as to the possible existence of the rights of that other and he fails to make such enquiry or take such other steps as are reasonable to verify whether such earlier right does or does not exist, he will have constructive notice of the earlier right and take subject to it.[43] Therefore where a wife has agreed to stand surety for her husband's debts as a result of undue influence or misrepresentation, the creditor will take subject to the wife's equity to set aside the transaction if the circumstances are such as to put the creditor on inquiry as to the circumstances in which she agreed to stand surety.

Creditor put on enquiry

Therefore, in my judgment a creditor is put on inquiry when a wife offers to stand surety for her husband's debts by the combination of two factors: (a) the transaction is on its face not to the financial advantage of the wife; and (b) there is substantial risk in transactions of that kind that, in procuring the wife to act as surety, the husband has committed a legal or equitable wrong that entitles the wife to set aside the transaction.

Steps to be taken by creditor

It follows that, unless the creditor who is put on inquiry takes reasonable steps to satisfy himself that the wife's agreement to stand surety has been properly obtained, the creditor will have constructive notice of the wife's rights.

What, then are the reasonable steps which the creditor should take to ensure that it does not have constructive notice of the wife's rights, if any? Normally the reasonable steps necessary to avoid being fixed with constructive notice consist of making inquiry of the person who may have the earlier right (i.e. the wife) to see if whether such right is asserted. It is plainly impossible to require of banks and other financial institutions that they should inquire of one spouse whether he or she has been unduly influenced or misled by the other. But in my judgment the creditor, in order to avoid being fixed with constructive notice, can reasonably be expected to take steps to bring home to the wife the risk she is running by standing as surety and to advise her to take independent advice.

[43.] In Scotland it seems that a guarantee in favour of a bank will be set aside for undue influence only if the bank has actual notice of the undue influence rather than constructive notice (see *McNulty v Bank of Scotland* as discussed in Fallon, 'Undue Influence: A difference of emphasis' (1996) JIBFL 16).

For the future in my judgment a creditor will have satisfied these requirements if it insists that the wife attend a private meeting (in the absence of the husband) with a representative of the creditor at which she is told of the extent of her liability as surety, warned of the risk she is running and urged to take independent legal advice. If these steps are taken in my judgment the creditor will have taken such reasonable steps as are necessary to preclude a subsequent claim that it had constructive notice of the wife's rights.

In the context of suretyship, the wife will not have any right to disown her obligations just because subsequently she proves that she did not fully understand the transaction; she will, as in all other areas of her affairs, be bound by her obligations unless her husband has, by misrepresentation, undue influence or other wrong, committed an actionable wrong against her. In the normal case, a financial institution will be able to lend with confidence in reliance on the wife's surety obligation provided that it warns her (in the absence of the husband) of the amount of her potential liability and of the risk of standing surety and advises her to take independent advice."

Relationship of Trust Giving Rise to Presumption of Undue Influence

[8.12] A test as to whether the relationship (other than one between co-habitees) is such so as to give rise to a presumption of undue influence may be ascertained from the English Court of Appeal's decision in *Goldsworthy v Brickell*[44] which involved a sufficient degree of trust between neighbours. Nourse LJ stated:[45]

"the principle ... is that the degree of trust and confidence is such that the party in whom it is reposed, either because he is or has become an adviser of the other or because he has been entrusted with the management of his affairs or everyday needs or for some other reason, is in a position to influence him into effecting the transaction of which complaint is later made."

Young Persons

[8.13] The vulnerability of a young person and the need to provide appropriate protection to such person was recognised in *McMackin v Hibernian Bank*[46] where security granted by a daughter for her mother's indebtedness was set aside. Barton J declared lucidly the position applying to persons on reaching the age of majority when he said:[47]

"It is quite true that young persons (male or female) upon coming of age obtain capacity to sign notes and to execute mortgages, and that they may render themselves liable by so doing. But it is not correct to suppose that, as soon as the clock has struck the hour of technical legal emancipation, the young person

---

44. [1987] 1 All ER 853.
45. *Ibid* at 865.
46. [1905] 1 IR 296; see also *Whyte v Meade* (1840) 2 Ir Eq R 420.
47. *Ibid* at 304.

is discharged from all protection of the law. The law recognises that a young person, living with or under the influence of a parent, is likely to remain for some time under parental dominion, and is at an impressionable age, when gratitude, affection, and respect for a parent are fresh and strong, while knowledge and experience of the stress and struggle and varied obligations of human life have yet to be acquired. The law protects young persons under such circumstances and at such an age, not by curtailing their capacity to deal with others, but by binding the consciences of those who deal with them. A young person may pay or give security for a parent's or guardian's debt; and such a transaction will not be set aside if it can be shown to be a spontaneous act, carried out after real emancipation from control and influence, and with full knowledge of all material circumstances ... When the child is living with or under the control of the parent or guardian, such influence is presumed - and the burden of proof is thrown upon the person who has obtained the gift or security through the parent's influence to displace that presumption, eg by showing that the young person acted under independent professional advice. Such independent advice must be a reality, not a sham; it must be a shield for the young person, not a mere cloak to cover up the transaction."

Elderly Persons

[8.14] The first of the significant English decisions was that of the Court of Appeal in *Lloyds Bank Ltd v Bundy*.[48] This case involved an elderly farmer guaranteeing payment of an overdraft of his son's company and charging his house in support of the guarantee. The security was executed in the assistant's bank manager's office after the manager had indicated to the farmer the position of the company, although the farmer received no independent advice.

Sir Eric Sachs in his judgment pointed out that when the assistant bank manager was asking the farmer to sign the security, "the bank would derive benefit from the signature, that there was a conflict of interest as between the bank and the defendant, that the bank gave him advice, that he relied on that advice, and that the bank knew of the reliance".

The court set aside the guarantee and charge as the special relationship of confidence which existed between the bank and the farmer required the bank to see that the farmer was in a position to exercise an independent judgment. As the bank had failed in its fiduciary duty to see that the farmer obtained independent advice it would not be allowed to retain the benefit of the security.

[8.15] The Circuit Court's decision[49] in *Allied Irish Banks plc v English*[50] is consistent with this approach. In that case, the guarantee and charge taken by the bank from the borrower's parents was held to be unenforceable. The court held

---

48. [1974] 2 All ER 757; [1974] 3 WLR 501.
49. Judge Sheridan in the South Eastern Circuit.
50. (1993) ILT 208.

that where persons, particularly elderly persons, are induced to pledge their only assets without getting anything in return, it should be clearly brought to their attention by a suitable letter or memorandum as to precisely what the transaction involves and they should be told to seek legal advice subject to the fact that the matter can proceed if they refuse to take such legal advice.

Employees

[8.16] The courts will also intervene to grant relief to a guarantor who is an employee of the debtor, even though the guarantee may help keep the guarantor in employment by virtue of facilities being made available to the company which employs her. In *Credit Lyonnais Bank Nederland NV v Burch*[51] the English Court of Appeal considered such a guarantee by an employee as being one which "shocks the conscience of the court."[52]

Banker and Customer

[8.17] In *National Westminster Bank plc v Morgan*,[53] Lord Scarman in giving the judgment of the House of Lords said:[54]

"The wrongfulness of the transaction must ... be shown: it must be one in which an unfair advantage has been taken of another. The doctrine is not limited to transactions of gifts. A commercial relationship can become a relationship in which one party assumes a role of dominating influence[55] over the other ... a relationship of banker and customer may become one in which the banker acquires a dominating influence. If he does and a manifestly disadvantageous transaction is proved, there would then be room for the court to presume that it resulted from the exercise of undue influence."

[8.18] Lord Scarman went on to explain that, notwithstanding the interpretation by some of the Court of Appeal's decision in *Lloyds Bank Ltd v Bundy*,[56] the relationship between a banker and customer is not one which ordinarily gives rise to a presumption of undue influence[57] and, in the ordinary course of banking business a banker can explain the nature of a proposed transaction without laying himself open to a charge of undue influence.

---

51. [1997] 1 All ER 144.
52. *Ibid per* Millett LJ at 152.
53. [1985] 1 All ER 821; [1985] 2 WLR 588.
54. *Ibid* at 829 and 599 respectively; this passage was adopted by the Court of Appeal and applied in *Bank of Credit and Commerce International SA v Aboody* [1989] 2 WLR 759 at 771.
55. For a criticism on Lord Scarman's use of the words "dominating influence" see the Court of Appeal's judgments of Nourse LJ at 868, Parker LJ at 874 and Sir John Megaw at 877 in *Goldsworthy v Brickell* [1987] 1 All ER 853.
56. [1974] 3 All ER 757; [1974] 3 WLR 501.
57. See also Slade LJ in *Bank of Credit and Commerce International SA v Aboody* [1989] 2 WLR 759 at 768.

Actual Unduc Influence

[8.19] Where there has been actual undue influence, the English Court of Appeal held in *Bank of Credit and Commerce International SA v Aboody*[58] that a contract will not be set aside unless it is proved that the contract is manifestly disadvantageous to the person influenced.[59] In *Bank of Credit and Commerce International SA v Aboody*,[60] Mrs Aboody, a director and shareholder of the family company, guaranteed and charged her property as security for the company's borrowings. The court found that the husband had exercised undue influence over Mrs Aboody, the husband had acted as the bank's agent in obtaining her signature but that the transaction would not be set aside as it was not proved that it was manifestly disadvantageous to the wife.

As the giving of the security enabled the company of which Mrs Aboody was a director and shareholder to survive, the court held there was no manifest disadvantage and accordingly the guarantee and charge were not set aside.

It is unlikely the Irish courts would adopt the same principles, particularly as Mrs Aboody had the facts misrepresented to her by her husband (deemed to be acting as the bank's agent), had no independent advice and clearly did not exercise an independent judgment.[61]

[8.20] Subsequently, this decision was disapproved of by the House of Lords in *CIBC Mortgages plc v Pitt*.[62] Lord Browne-Wilkinson in giving the judgment of the court thought there was no logic in imposing a requirement of manifest disadvantage where actual influence has taken place. He said:[63]

> "Actual undue influence is a species of fraud. Like any other victim of fraud, a person who has been induced by undue influence to carry out a transaction which he did not freely and knowingly enter into is entitled to have that transaction set aside as of right.
>
> I therefore hold that a claimant who proves actual undue influence is not under the further burden of proving that the transaction induced by undue influence was manifestly disadvantageous he is entitled as of right to have it set aside."

---

58. [1989] 2 WLR 759.
59. See also note on *Woodstead Finance Ltd v Petrou & Anor* (1986) Court of Appeal, unrep in *Insolvency Law & Practice* (1986) Vol 2 No 4 p 129.
60. [1989] 2 WLR 759.
61. Mrs Aboody was born and educated in Baghdad, married at 17 without knowing English (becoming engaged to her husband on the day they met), had no business experience and although aged 30 when becoming a director and shareholder she was incapable of correctly drawing a cheque.
62. [1993] 4 All ER 433; see para **[8.27]** below.
63. *Ibid* at 439.

Relationship of Guarantor to Debtor

[8.21] The first point that needs to be addressed by a bank proposing to take a guarantee for its advance is whether or not the relationship between a debtor and the guarantor is one which gives rise to a presumption of undue influence. The reported decisions indicate that this may arise principally in the case of husband and wife where the wife has placed her trust and confidence in the husband or as Lord Browne-Wilkinson put it:[64]

> "the sexual and emotional ties between the parties provide a ready weapon for undue influence: a wife's true wishes can easily be overborne because of her fear of destroying or damaging the wider relationship between her and her husband if she opposes his wishes."

Bank on Enquiry

[8.22] In acknowledging that the risk of undue influence applies to all forms of cohabitation, Lord Browne-Wilkinson indicated that the same principle should apply to all cohibitees if, but only if, the bank is aware that the guarantor is living with the debtor.[65] This begs the question as to what enquiries a bank should make as to the relationship between the debtor and the guarantor.[66] No guidance has been given as to this conundrum. A bank or its solicitor who enquires as to the relationship may be perceived as being unduly inquisitive on a matter of great personal sensitivity to the debtor or guarantor. Yet a bank who fails to make such enquiry may be fixed with notice of the answer it would have received had it enquired. A bank's solicitor who fails to enquire on his client's behalf may run the risk of being held to be negligent and liable for the loss suffered by the bank should it subsequently transpire that the guarantor was a lover of the debtor at the time of the transaction.

[8.23] The English Court of Appeal has endeavoured to put a limit to the extent to which a bank should enquire, at least where there is no obvious relationship between the debtor and guarantor. In *Banco Exterior Internacional SA v Thomas*,[67] Mrs Dempsey, living in difficult financial circumstances, agreed to the suggestion made by a close personal friend Mr Mulcahy to receive an annual income from him in exchange for guaranteeing, and providing her house as security, for Mr Mulcahy's business loan. Mr Mulcahy's bank required Mrs Dempsey to take independent legal advice from a solicitor nominated by them, which she did. Her former solicitor, when handing over the title deeds to the

---

64. *Barclays Bank plc v O'Brien* [1993] 4 All ER 417 at 424.
65. *Ibid* at 431.
66. See also Johnston, 'Banking Contracts - the Influence of Spouses - editorial' (1993) JIBFL 523.
67. [1997] 1 All ER 46.

property, advised her not to proceed and informed the bank. Following her death, her executors sought to upset the transaction. The court of first instance upset the transaction but the Court of Appeal unanimously allowed the bank's appeal. The Court held that since a bank had no business inquiring into the personal relationship between those with whom it had dealings or as to their personal motives for wanting to help one another, it was not the bank's business to ask itself why Mrs Dempsey was willing to stand surety for Mr Mulcahy's indebtedness but merely to ensure that she knew what she was doing and wanted to do it, which she did, having received independent legal advice about the nature and effect of the transaction.[68]

[8.24] Once the relationship between the debtor and the guarantor is such as to put the bank on enquiry, a bank who fails to carry through its enquiry and follow up with appropriate action will do so at its peril. In *TSB Bank plc v Camfield*[69] two partners obtained an overdraft facility for their business. The facility was secured by a charge over their respective family homes. The bank stipulated that the wives should receive independent legal advice prior to signing the charge. The bank's solicitors confirmed to the bank that the wives would be separately advised, but they were not. The husband of the defendant misrepresented that the charge would secure only £15,000 whereas it secured an unlimited amount. The English Court of Appeal held that the charge should be set aside on the grounds that the bank was fixed with constructive notice of the husband's misrepresentation as it had failed to take reasonable steps to ensure that the wife understood the charge.

Although there was no indication in the report, it may be assumed that the bank would have a remedy in damages against its solicitors for failing to ensure that the wives were separately advised, as specifically requested by the bank.

[8.25] When the circumstances are such as to put the bank on enquiry, the bank should be conscious of the English Court of Appeal's decision in *Barclays Bank plc v Boulter*.[70] In that case, it was held that where a bank, as mortgagee of a property jointly owned by a husband and wife, brought proceedings for possession on the husband's default, and the wife alleged that her half share of the property was free of the bank's mortgage on the ground that her husband had induced her to sign the mortgage by misrepresentation, the burden was on the bank to plead and prove that it did not have constructive notice of the misrepresentation, and not on the wife to prove that it did.

[68.] "It was not the bank's business to ask itself why she was willing to do this. It was the bank's business to make sure that she knew what she was doing". *Ibid* at 55 per Sir Richard Scott VC.

[69.] [1995] 1 All ER 951.

[70.] [1997] 2 All ER 1002.

[8.26] A bank will not be put on enquiry if its solicitor, acting also for the borrower, is made aware of a fact from the borrower and such fact if known by the bank would put it on enquiry. In *Halifax Mortgage Services Ltd v Stepsky*[71] a solicitor acting for both borrower and lender was informed by the borrower that the loan would be used to settle business debts and not, as stated in the loan application, to purchase shares in the family business. The court held that in the absence of the borrower's consent to disclose the information to the lender, the solicitor's duty to the lender was to inform the lender that he could no longer act for the lender due to a conflict of interest. The solicitor was not free to pass on information which he had acquired in his capacity as solicitor for the borrower and accordingly the solicitor's knowledge of the true purpose of the loan could not be imputed on to the lender.

[8.27] A bank will not be put on enquiry where it makes a facility available to a husband and wife jointly and takes a mortgage/charge from them. The mere fact that there is a risk that one spouse will exercise undue influence over the other is not sufficient to put the bank on enquiry. This was decided by the House of Lords in *CIBC Mortgages plc v Pitt*.[72] In that case a husband and wife signed a loan application form for a loan of £150,000 to repay an existing mortgage and to purchase a holiday home. The husband and wife signed a charge over their home as security for the loan. The wife did not read what she had signed, did not receive separate advice and it was not suggested that she do so. The loan was credited to their joint account. After repaying the existing mortgagee the husband used the loan to purchase shares and not to purchase a holiday home. Although it was proved that the husband had exercised undue influence over the wife, the lender was not affected by such undue influence as the husband was not acting as its agent and it had no actual or constructive notice of undue influence. Only one judgment was delivered in the House of Lords - that of Lord Browne-Wilkinson. He agreed with the analysis of Peter Gibson LJ in the Court of Appeal namely:[73]

> "... equity does not presume undue influence in transactions between husband and wife. Further, *bona fide* purchasers for value without notice are recognised in equity as having a good defence to equitable claims. On principle, therefore, a creditor who is not on notice of any actual or likely undue influence in a transaction involving a husband and wife ought not to be affected by the exercise of undue influence by the husband."

In a warning to lenders to avoid delegating to one spouse the task of having the mortgage completed by both spouses, Peter Gibson LJ continued:

---

71. [1995] 4 All ER 656.
72. [1993] 4 All ER 433.
73. *Ibid* at 440.

"Of course if the creditor leaves it to the husband to procure the wife's participation in the transaction or otherwise makes the husband the creditor's agent, whether in a strict or some looser sense, then the creditor is affected by the acts of the agent and notice of undue influence by the husband can be imputed to the creditor."

In indicating the lengths to which a bank would need to go to ensure both spouses fully understood a transaction which was for their joint benefit, lengths to which he felt were unwarranted and counter-productive to doing business, Lord Browne-Wilkinson may in fact have inadvertently set out what a bank may now consider to be a prudent practice. He said:[74]

"If third parties were to be fixed with constructive notice of undue influence in relation to every transaction between husband and wife, such transactions would become almost impossible. On every purchase of a home in joint names, the building society or bank financing the purchase would have to insist on meeting the wife separately from her husband, advise her as to the nature of the transaction and recommend her to take legal advice separate from that of her husband. If that were not done, the financial institution would have to run the risk of a subsequent attempt by the wife to avoid her liabilities under the mortgage on the grounds of undue influence or misrepresentation. To establish the law in that sense would not benefit the average married couple and would discourage financial institutions from making the advance."

[8.28] A bank must be careful when advancing a joint facility to husband and wife on the security of property held jointly to ensure that the facility does not include any additional advance for one spouse. If the facility and security includes a loan to one spouse it is essential for the bank to ensure the non-borrowing spouse receives independent advice prior to executing the security. In *Dunbar Bank plc v Nadeem*[75] the bank advanced £260,000, £50,000 of which was to refinance Mr Nadeem's debts and £210,000 was for the acquisition of a larger house in the name of Mr and Mrs Nadeem. The court held that although there was no actual undue influence, the relationship of trust and confidence between the spouses was such as to give rise to a presumption of undue influence and the transaction was manifestly disadvantageous to the wife. The court held further that since the bank had constructive notice of that undue influence as it did not take any, let alone reasonable, steps to ascertain whether the wife understood what she was doing, the wife was entitled to have the charge set aside. However, the court was mindful that if the charge was set aside the wife would have received an inequitable benefit. Accordingly, the charge was

---

[74.] *Ibid* at 441; suggested also by Sanfey, 'Undue Influence and the "Tender Treatment" of Wives' (1994) CLP 99.

[75.] [1997] 2 All ER 253.

set aside as against the wife subject to the wife reimbursing the bank for half of the advance used for the property acquisition.

Independent Advice

"I do not mean to suggest that every transaction is saved by independent advice."[76]

[8.29] It should be noted that the provision of independent advice may not of itself rebut a presumption of undue influence. The approach of the court on this area may be seen from Black J's judgment in *Provincial Bank of Ireland v McKeever*[77] where he said:[78]

"Although independent advice is not a *sine qua non*, yet where it has been proved to have been given and rejected, there are indications in the decisions that proof of its having been given might alone be sufficient to rebut the presumption of undue influence. Nevertheless, the giving of such advice would not prove that the person to whom it was given fully understood it, and even if evidence were given (for instance of statements made by the advised person) showing that he did understand it, he might still have rejected it under the interested, or it might be, the well meant, perhaps even unconscious but none the less undue, influence of his trustee, parent, physician, solicitor, or religious superior. One cannot expect absolute disproof of undue influence. It is enough to establish a reasonable probability of the exercise of independent will founded upon adequate understanding ...

The courts have, I think, contemplated that the proof of independent advice having been given may in certain cases alone suffice. It seems to me that a combination of surrounding circumstances might furnish as good evidence, imperfect though it be, of the probability of an independent will as any independent legal advice. After all, a main object of such advice is to ensure that the party knows what he is doing. If the transaction is of so plain a character that it may fairly be believed that he did know what he was doing, that object is achieved without advice. Even the best independent advice, if not fully understood, might not achieve it."

[8.30] The absence of independent advice did not present a difficulty to Costello J in holding that there was no undue influence in the case of *Smyth v Smyth*.[79] He said:[80]

[76.] Lord Denning MR in *Lloyds Bank Ltd v Bundy* [1974] 3 All ER 757 at 765.
[77.] [1941] IR 471.
[78.] *Ibid* at 485.
[79.] High Court, unrep, 22 November 1978; but see Sir J Napier CS in *King v Anderson* (1874) IR 8 Eq 625 - "a court of equity requires adequate independent advice in all classes of transactions between parties in relation of confidence."
[80.] *Ibid* at p 24 where Costello J mentioned an example of the application of that principle in England namely, *Re Brocklehurst's Estate* [1977] 2 WLR 696.

"when the presumption of undue influence arises the absence of independent professional advice does not necessarily render the transaction invalid."

[8.31] In approving Sir Eric Sachs' judgment in *Lloyds Bank Ltd v Bundy*[81] Lord Scarman pointed out[82] that the duty of a bank, in the normal case where it takes a guarantee, is to explain to the guarantor the legal effect of the guarantee and the sums involved;[83] he said it is only where the bank advises on the transaction generally that a conflict of interest may arise as in *Lloyds Bank Ltd v Bundy*.[84] The distinction is obviously a fine one to be noted by bankers and their advisers in preparing guarantees for execution.

[8.32] The duty of a bank to explain the legal effect of the guarantee and the sums involved to a guarantor may not apply where the guarantor, even though not a customer, nonetheless has a commercial interest in the loan being guaranteed. In *O'Hara v Allied Irish Banks Ltd*[85] the guarantor was a director of the company obtaining an overdraft from the bank. The bank made no representations and explained nothing. Counsel for the guarantor adverted to Sir Eric Sachs' judgment in *Lloyds Bank Ltd v Bundy*[86] but Harman J held there was no duty of care owed by the bank.

[8.33] The absence of any legal obligation on a bank to ensure that a guarantor receives independent advice was the basis on which the English Court of Appeal decided in favour of the bank in *Bank of Baroda v Shah*.[87] In that case the English Court of Appeal unanimously allowed the bank's appeal to have its charge upheld notwithstanding the undue influence and misrepresentation exercised by a brother of one of the defendants. The court held that the bank was entitled to treat the return of the executed security by the debtor's solicitors as confirmation that the solicitors had been acting for the defendants. Dillon LJ stated:[88]

"[The bank] were entitled to assume that Shah & Burke would act honestly and would give proper advice to the defendants, if Shah & Burke were, as they represented, acting for the defendants."

[81.] [1974] 3 All ER 757; [1974] 3 WLR 501.

[82.] In *National Westminster Bank plc v Morgan* [1985] 1 All ER 821; [1985] 2 WLR 588.

[83.] For a suggested list of the appropriate details which require explanation see Penn, Shea and Arora, *The Law Relating to Domestic Banking* (1987) Sweet & Maxwell para 19.12.

[84.] [1974] 3 All ER 757; [1974] 3 WLR 501.

[85.] [1985] BCLC 52.

[86.] [1974] 3 All ER 757; [1974] 3 WLR 501.

[87.] [1988] 3 All ER 24; see also the remarks of the Privy Council in *MacKenzie v Royal Bank of Canada* [1934] AC 468.

[88.] *Ibid* at 29.

More recently the English Court of Appeal have twice approved and followed the judgment of Dillon LJ,[89]

[8.34] The safest course for the bank to adopt is obviously to ensure that the guarantor does take independent advice before giving the guarantee. Such a course of action should ensure that the guarantee will not be set aside by reason of undue influence or misrepresentation.[90]

In *Massey v Midland Bank plc*[91] Miss Massey was persuaded by her lover on his fraudulent misrepresentation to charge her house as security for an overdraft granted to her lover's business. The bank official indicated that the bank would require Miss Massey to be independently advised before completing the transaction. Miss Massey's lover arranged for her to be advised by his own solicitor, who explained the nature of the charge to her in the company of her lover. Miss Massey signed the charge which was returned to the bank by the solicitor who confirmed that he had explained the charge to Miss Massey. Miss Massey sought to have the charge set aside for undue influence and misrepresentation.

The English Court of Appeal's judgment was delivered by Steyn LJ who summarised the issues as follows:[92]

> "Taking the law enunciated, as opposed to the guidance offered in *Barclays Bank plc v O'Brien*, it is clear that two questions must be considered, namely (a) was the bank put on inquiry as to the circumstances in which Miss Massey agreed to provide the security and (b) if so, did the bank take reasonable steps to ensure that the agreement of Miss Massey to the charge was properly obtained".

The Court held that, although the bank had been put on inquiry by the circumstances in which Miss Massey had agreed to provide the security, it was entitled to believe that Miss Massey had received independent advice from the reputable firm of solicitors to whom it had sent the charge and to assume that the solicitor dealing with the matter would act honestly and give proper advice, and it was under no duty to inquire into what had transpired at the interview between Miss Massey and the solicitor by whom she was advised. Since the bank had taken reasonable steps to ensure that Miss Massey's agreement to grant the charge had been properly obtained and had received confirmation from the

---

89. In *Massey v Midland Bank plc* [1995] 1 All ER 929 at 935 and in *Banco Exterior Internacional v Mann* [1995] 1 All ER 936 at 944.
90. See Lord Brown-Wilkinson in *Barclays Bank plc v O'Brien* [1993] 4 All ER 417 at 430; in *Credit Lyonnais Bank Nederland NV v Burch* [1997] 1 All ER 144 where a guarantor's security was set aside notwithstanding that the guarantor had declined to take independent legal advice, despite being advised to do so by the bank's solicitors.
91. [1995] 1 All ER 929.
92. *Ibid* at 932.

solicitors that they had explained the charge to Miss Massey, it was not fixed with constructive notice of her lover's misrepresentation.

In indicating how far the bank should go, Steyn LJ stated:[93]

> "it is generally sufficient for the bank to avoid a finding of constructive notice if the bank urged the proposed surety to take independent advice from a solicitor. How far a solicitor should go in probing the matter, and in giving advice, is a matter for the solicitor's professional judgment and a matter between him and his client. The bank is not generally involved in the nature and extent of the solicitor's advice.

[8.35] This decision was followed by a majority of the English Court of Appeal in allowing the bank's appeal in *Banco Exterior Internacional SA v Mann*.[94] In that case, the bank's loan to a company controlled by the first defendant was secured over the family home. The bank's offer was conditional on the nature of the charge being explained to the wife by her solicitor and the solicitor certifying that he had done so. The husband passed the loan documents on to the company's solicitor who wrote to the wife explaining that the effect of the declaration she was being asked to sign was that she would thereby waive her rights in the matrimonial home in favour of the bank to the extent that it was owed any moneys by the company or to the extent of any collateral guarantees. The husband and wife later attended the solicitor's office where the wife signed the documents in the presence of the solicitor after he had explained the nature of the declaration, and the solicitor certified that he had done so.

The court held that where a bank made a loan to a company to be secured by a personal guarantee and a second charge over the matrimonial home of the guarantor and his wife, the bank was entitled to rely on the company's solicitor to give independent advice when advising the wife of the effect of a declaration waiving her rights in the matrimonial home in favour of the bank to the extent of the company's indebtedness or the amount recoverable under the guarantee, if the solicitor signed a certificate that he had done so. The test was how the transaction appeared to the bank, which was entitled to assume that the solicitor would regard it as his professional duty not merely to explain the nature and effect of the documents to the wife but also to advise her that if the worst happened she could lose her rights in the house and that it was for her to decide whether she was willing to take that risk or not; in delivering the leading judgment Morritt LJ stated:[95]

> "The essence of the matter is that the creditor should take reasonable steps to ensure in so far as he can that the undue influence of the husband is

---

[93.] *Ibid* at 934.
[94.] [1995] 1 All ER 936, see also *Barclays Bank plc v Thomson* [1997] 4 All ER 816.
[95.] *Ibid* at 943.

counteracted by enquiring that the wife is aware of the consequences to her of entering into the proposed transaction for the benefit of the husband".

The court decided that when the bank received back the form of declaration duly executed by the wife and duly certified by the company's solicitor there was nothing to fix it with constructive notice of any undue influence by the husband.

In a dissenting judgment Hobhouse LJ considered the bank should have advised the wife to take independent advice and that the bank had not taken steps "to ensure that the wife was signing the document as a result of the free exercise of her own will".[96] Bearing in mind that the High Court and the Court of Appeal collectively split 2-2, it is somewhat surprising that the Appeal Committee of the House of Lords subsequently refused leave to appeal.[97]

[8.36] The decision of Hobhouse LJ prevailed in the Court of Appeal in *Royal Bank of Scotland plc v Etridge*[98] where he managed to distinguish the case of *Banco Exterior Internacional* even though in both cases the bank relied on the borrower's solicitor to explain the nature of the guarantee and give advice to the wife executing the security. Unlike the *Banco Exterior Internacional* decision, this was the critical fact in *The Royal Bank of Scotland* where the court held that where a bank instructed a solicitor to act on its behalf for the purposes of discharging its duty of ensuring that a wife received independent advice in respect of her liabilities under a legal charge in its favour securing the debts of her husband, the bank was responsible for his discharge of that duty and would be fixed with constructive notice of any undue influence if he did not, notwithstanding the terms of any indorsement of the charge.

Hobhouse LJ stated:[99]

> "In the present case, the bank ... did not have the wife in, nor did they leave it entirely to the wife to take independent advice. They appointed their own agent to follow the course described by Lord Browne-Wilkinson. They appointed the solicitor to act as their own agent in this regard. Therefore, since they delegated their task to their own solicitor, they are responsible for his discharge of that duty. If he did not discharge it then they must accept that situation since they are in the same position as their agent. The only evidence is, at present, from the wife who says that he did not."

While it is difficult to reconcile these decisions, it is obviously safer for the bank to ensure that the chargor receives advice from a source independent of itself or in the case of a guarantee, the borrower.

---

96. *Ibid* at 948.
97. *Ibid* at 950.
98. [1997] 3 All ER 628.
99. *Ibid* at 634.

[8.37] In Ireland, as long ago as 1927 the High Court set aside a wife's security for her husband's debts on the grounds that the wife did not realise that she had deposited the title deeds with the bank as security rather than for safe custody. In *The Northern Banking Company Ltd v Carpenter*[100] the absence of independent advice proved critical for the bank. Prior to the taking of security in 1913 the bank's head office wrote to the local branch - "The security is open to the usual objection to taking a wife's security for her husband's account. She should have independent advice ie her own solicitor". Security was taken without independent advice being given to the wife after the husband indicated to the bank that his wife did not wish to take independent advice.

Delay by Guarantor

[8.38] Any delay by an aggrieved person in seeking to set aside a transaction by reason of undue influence may leave the aggrieved person without a remedy. In *JH v WJH*[101] Keane J held that:[102]

> "It is clear that once the influence has ceased, the person seeking to set aside the transaction on that must commence proceedings within a reasonable time or he or she will be taken to abide by the transaction and confirm it."

Duty of a Solicitor

[8.39] According to the principles laid down by Budd J,[103] a solicitor advising the guarantor should:

1. Apprise himself of the surrounding circumstances in so far as he reasonably can - if he does not do this he can never put himself in a position to advise his client fully and effectively;

2. Estimate in some reasonable degree the nature of the guarantor's incapacity;

3. Know how far his reasoning capacity was affected and how far he was capable of comprehending the manner in which the proposed transaction would affect his own interests and his future and to what extent he was competent to come to a rational decision;

4. Endeavour to discover whether his client was subject to the influence of the beneficiary of the guarantee or any third party and if so the extent of that influence;

[100.] [1931] IR 268 (the decision was upheld by the Supreme Court).
[101.] High Court, unrep, 20 December 1979.
[102.] *Ibid* p 30.
[103.] [1956] IR 183.

5. Make sure that the guarantor was capable of fully understanding the nature and results of a transaction such as that proposed;

6. Make sure that the guarantor did thoroughly understand what he was doing and how it would affect him; and

7. Consider very carefully whether the transaction was one for the guarantor's benefit.

ECONOMIC DURESS

[8.40] The concept of economic duress is difficult to establish and unlikely to overturn any arrangement entered into between commercial entities.[104] The recent English Court of Appeal decision in *CTN Cash and Carry Ltd v Gallaher Ltd*[105] will bring comfort to banks who press for payment lawfully due to them on the threat of discontinuing committed banking facilities and thus the survival of the debtor. In that case, the defendants demanded £17,000 which they thought was lawfully due to them by the plaintiffs on the threat of discontinuing credit facilities to the plaintiffs which would have had a material adverse effect on the plaintiffs' business. The court held that:

> "Although in certain circumstances a threat to perform a lawful act coupled with a demand for payment might amount to economic duress, it would be difficult, though not necessarily impossible, to maintain such a claim in the context of arm's length commercial dealings between two trading companies, especially where the party making the threat *bona fide* believed that its demand was valid. Any extension of the categories of duress to encompass "lawful act duress" in a commercial context in pursuit of bona fide claim would be a radical move with far-reaching implications and would introduce a substantial and undesirable element of uncertainty in the commercial bargaining process, in the sense that it would enable *bona fide* settled accounts to be reopened when parties to commercial dealings fell out. On the facts, the defendants were entitled in law to vary the terms on which they contracted with the plaintiffs by withdrawing credit facilities and they had made their demand for payment in good faith, genuinely and not unreasonably believing that they were owed the sum in question."

In *Shivas v Bank of New Zealand*[106] the High Court of New Zealand refused to upset the security given by the plaintiffs even though the bank had applied some degree of commercial pressure. The plaintiffs' two year delay in alleging duress was fatal to their claim.

[104.] For a discourse on duress see Clark, *Contract Law in Ireland* (3rd ed) Sweet & Maxwell Ch 12.
[105.] [1994] 4 All ER 714.
[106.] [1990] 2 NZLR 327.

UNCONSCIONABLE BARGAIN

[8.41] Where there has been no undue influence or misrepresentation[107] as to the effect of the documents, the courts may nonetheless set aside a transaction where they consider a person has been exploited. Examples of this tend to happen where a person transfers (or creates a mortgage over) property for a wholly inadequate return, such as was found in *Grealish v Murphy*.[108] As Fullager J said in *Blomley v Ryan*:[109]

> "inadequacy of consideration while never of itself a ground for resisting enforcement, will often be a specially important element in cases of this type. It may be important in either or both of two ways - firstly as supporting the inference that a position of disadvantage existed, and secondly as tending to show that an unfair use was made of the occasion."

[8.42] The courts are reluctant to define or set out in any detail what is meant by unconscionable bargain.[110] Perhaps the best description may be found in the High Court of Australia where Mason J said:[111]

> "'unconscionable conduct' is usually taken to refer to the class of case in which a party makes unconscientious use of his superior position or bargaining power to the detriment of a party who suffers from some special disability or is placed in some special situation of disadvantage ... Although unconscionable conduct in this narrow sense bears some resemblance to the doctrine of undue influence, there is a difference between the two. In the latter the will of the innocent party is not independent and voluntary because it is overborne. In the former the will of the innocent party, even if independent and voluntary, is the result of the disadvantageous position in which he is placed and of the other party unconscientiously taking advantage of that position."[112]

In *National Australia Bank Ltd v Garcia*,[113] the New South Wales Court of Appeal held that before relief can be granted against unconscionable conduct, there must be sufficient evidence to the creditor that the guarantor suffers from a special disability which prevents him or her from understanding the nature and effect of the transaction.

[107.] In the case of guarantees see paras **[9.70]** to **[9.74]**.
[108.] [1946] IR 35.
[109.] (1954-1956) 99 CLR 362 at 405.
[110.] See further Clark, *Contract Law in Ireland* (3rd ed) p 282.
[111.] In the *Commercial Bank of Australia Limited v Amadio* (1982-83) 151 CLR 447 at 461.
[112.] On the two concepts see also Doyle, 'Inequality of Position in Modern Irish Law' (1990) 8 ILT 282; this distinction is criticised in Phang, 'Undue Influence Methodoly, Sources and Influence' [1995] JBL 552.
[113.] [1996] 10 JIBL N-187.

If the guarantor is shown not to have fully understood the nature of the transaction nor to have had independent advice, the courts will not uphold the transaction where they consider it to be an improvident one.[114]

[8.43] Advice to the guarantor by an independent solicitor will go some way towards satisfying the court that the transaction resulted from the independent exercise of the covenantor's will.[115] However, this may not prevent the transaction from being set aside as in *Grealish v Murphy*[116] where the covenantor's solicitor was not fully familiar with all the material facts and had not given a complete explanation of the nature and effect of the deed. In addition the solicitor should realise limitations of the person he is advising - it is:[117]

> "a matter of high importance that [the covenantor's] advisers in this particular transaction should have been equipped to advise him with a just appreciation of his mental debility and his special need of protection. They were not so equipped and [the covenantor] did not get the circumspect advice and protection so necessary to him".

A transaction which appears to be improvident may nonetheless be upheld if the court is satisfied that the covenantor had independent advice from the solicitor of his choice and exercised his own independent judgment.[118] The courts will examine all the circumstances of a transaction so that even where the same solicitor acts for both parties in a sale,[119] the transaction may nonetheless be upheld.[120]

INEQUALITY OF BARGAINING POWER

[8.44] Although the courts will not stand over a transaction where a weaker member of society without proper advice parts with property without due compensation,[121] the courts have shown that they will not overturn a transaction

---

[114.] As in *Lydon v Coyne* [1946] Ir Jur R 64.
[115.] *Rae v Joyce* (1892) 29 LR Ir 500 at 514.
[116.] [1946] IR 35.
[117.] *Ibid* at 48 *per* Gavan Duffy J.
[118.] *McCormack v Bennett* 107 ILTR 127; see also the Master of the Rolls in *O'Connor v Foley* [1905] 1 IR 1 at 16 - "Mere improvidence will not necessarily vitiate a settlement or gift. But when, as here, you find not alone extreme improvidence, but the absence of knowledge of rights, extreme pressure, ignorance of law, poverty, influence ... and the absence of an effective legal advice, it is impossible to say that the parties to the contract were on a footing of equality, or that the dealing was such as this court could allow to stand."
[119.] "This is another example of the undesirability of one solicitor acting for both parties in a transaction of this kind." - McLoughlin J in *Haverty v Brooks* [1970] IR 214 at 218.
[120.] *Haverty v Brooks* [1970] IR 214.
[121.] *Slater v Nolan* (1876) IR 11 Eq 367; *Grealish v Murphy* [1946] IR 35; see also *O'Connor v Foley* [1905] 1 IR 1.

simply because two persons of unequal resources complete a transaction.[122] In
Kelly v Morrisroe[123] an old and infirm lady sold property without independent
professional advice from a solicitor or valuer. The Irish Court of Appeal overruled the High Court by upholding the transaction as the lady had received
advice from a prominent member of the town and the purchaser had discharged
the onus of showing that the transaction was a fair and honest one. In the Irish
Court of Appeal Sir James Campbell LC stated:[124]

> "The learned Judge does not say that this old lady was not capable of
> transacting business, but that she was eccentric in habits and mentally
> abnormal ... The Judge merely says that she was eccentric and not normal, but
> we have all had experience of eccentric old ladies - eccentric in habits and
> eccentric in dress, but as cute as possible in money matters, and quite well able
> to understand the value of money and transact business, yet not mentally
> normal."

[8.45] More recently, the legislature has sought to address the issue of inequality
of bargaining power through the enactment of the European Communities
(Unfair Terms in Consumer Contracts) Regulations, 1995[125] and the Consumer
Credit Act, 1995.[126]

[122.] "The common law does not recognise the doctrine of inequality of bargaining power in
commercial dealings" - per Steyn LJ in *CTN Cash and Carry Ltd v Gallaher Ltd* [1994] 4 All
ER 714 at 717; the approach of the courts is dealt with further in Doyle, 'Inequality of Position
in Modern Irish Law' (1990) 8 ILT 282; the approach of the Irish courts is more likely to be
along similar lines to the courts of Australia or Canada than the tighter approach applied in
England - see Chesire, Fifoot & Furmston's *Law of Contract* (13th ed) p 324.

[123.] (1919) 53 ILTR 145.

[124.] *Ibid* at 147.

[125.] SI 27/1995; see paras **[18.01]-[18.05]** below.

[126.] See Ch 7.

Chapter 9

Guarantees

NATURE OF A GUARANTEE

[9.01] Although often loosely described as a security and coming within the parameters of this book on banking and security law, as indeed in many books on bank security,[1] a guarantee[2] is not a security in the sense that it does not attach to any asset of the guarantor.[3] Nor does any record of a guarantee need to be recorded in a public register, whether under the Bills of Sale Acts, the Companies Acts[4] or otherwise. In essence, therefore, the potential exposure of a person pursuant to guarantees is not readily ascertainable.

A guarantee is not a security in the sense that a power "to secure the payment of money" in a company's memorandum of association will not be a sufficient power to enable it to give a guarantee.[5]

Nevertheless, guarantees play a very critical role in the provision of security for bank finance. A customer may not have sufficient assets of its own to satisfy a lender's requirement to have security which can be realised in the event of the customer's default in repayments due to the lender. Accordingly, a third party is brought into the transaction, this third party being the guarantor.

[1.] Lingard, *Bank Security Documents* (3rd ed); Milnes Holden, *The Law and Practice of Banking* Vol 2, *Securities for Bankers' Advances* (7th ed); Sheridan, *Rights in Security;* Mather, *Securities Acceptable to the Lending Banker* (4th ed) where a guarantee is described as "probably the simplest form of banking security, more easily obtained than any other and yet frequently most difficult to realise".

[2.] According to de Colyar in his *Treatise on the Law of Guarantees and of Principal and Surety* (3rd ed) (1897) p 2 guaranty [or guarantee] was the Norman-French version of warranty as Guillaume is to William; indeed nowadays a certificate of guarantee which often comes with the purchase of electrical equipment is in reality a warranty.

[3.] See also commentary by McCracken, *The Banker's Remedy of Set-off* (1993) Butterworths p 166.

[4.] Which requires the filing of particulars of charges and the filing of annual returns showing indebtedness in respect of mortgages and charges (which are required to be registered).

[5.] *Northern Bank Finance Corporation Ltd v Quinn and Achates Investment Co* [1979] ILRM 221; see further para **[18.35]**.

[9.02] In its simplest form[6] a guarantee may be described as a written agreement by a person[7] to answer for the debt of another.[8]

Earlier this decade, the Supreme Court of Canada set out the nature of a guarantee in terms which can be readily understood:[9]

> "A guarantee is generally a contract between a guarantor and a lender. The subject of a guarantee is a debt owed to the lender by a debtor. In the contract of guarantee, the guarantor agrees to repay the lender if the debtor defaults. The exact nature of the obligation owed by the guarantor to the lender depends on the construction of the contract of guarantee, but the liability of the guarantor is usually made coterminous with that of the principal debtor: Generally speaking, if the principal debt is void or unenforceable, the contract of guarantee will likewise be void or unenforceable".

As with any agreement, the rules and principles applicable to the law of contract apply to guarantees.[10]

CONSIDERATION

[9.03] Every contract which is not under seal requires consideration to render it enforceable.[11] An example of how a bank was caught on this point can be seen from the case of *Provincial Bank of Ireland Ltd v Donnell*.[12] The defendant signed a guarantee under hand in favour of the bank under which it was provided that in consideration of advances made or that might thereafter be made from time to time by the bank to her husband she guaranteed payment of life assurance premiums. No further advances were made (the bank admitting it

---

6. For forms of guarantees, see *The Encyclopaedia of Forms and Precedents* (5th ed) Butterworths Vol 17(2) in particular Forms 14 and 15; see also Rowlatt, *The Law of Principal and Surety* (4th ed) and Lingard, *Bank Security Documents* (3rd ed) Documents 3 and 4; for helpful explanations of guarantee clauses and the need for them see Milnes Holden, *The Law and Practice of Banking*, Vol 2 (7th ed) Ch 19 and *Paget's Law of Banking* (11th ed) pp 634-642.
7. In this publication such person is referred to as a guarantor, although often referred to by the courts (and therefore at times appearing herein) as a surety; it seems that strictly speaking a surety is a person who provides tangible security for another's debt - see Penn, Shea and Arora, *The Law Relating to Domestic Banking* Vol 1, para 20.01.
8. For a review of definitions set out in previously published works see Sir Wilfred Greene MR in *Re Conley ex p The Trustee v Barclays Bank Ltd* [1938] 3 All ER 127 at 130.
9. *Communities Economic Development Fund v Canadian Pickles Corp* (1992) 85 DLR (4th) 88 at 106.
10. "The law of guarantee is part of the law of contract" - *per* Lord Diplock in *Moschi v Lep Air Services Ltd* [1972] 2 All ER 393; for a comprehensive review of the nature and construction of guarantees see Richard Salter QC IBC UK Conferences Limited, 25 April 1996.
11. See para **[1.15]** above; Clark, *Contract Law in Ireland* (3rd ed) Ch 3; Chesire, Fifoot & Furmston's *Law of Contract* (13th ed) Ch 4.
12. [1934] NI 33; see para **[1.14]** above.

did not intend to make further advances) nor did the bank threaten to issue proceedings before the guarantee was signed. The Northern Ireland Court of Appeal held that there was no sufficient consideration to support the guarantee because, (a) as regards past advances the agreement could not be construed as a forbearance to sue; and (b) as regards future advances the agreement only amounted to an indication on the bank's part that they might make further advances to the debtor, but there was no agreement binding them to do so, and as no advance had in fact been made, the undertaking of the defendant failed for want of consideration. Despite this decision, a guarantee executed after the advance has already been made may not fail for want of consideration if it was a condition of the making of the advance that the guarantee would be provided.[13] If a specific amount is to be inserted in the guarantee as the consideration, that amount must be advanced; the guarantee will be unenforceable if a lower amount is actually advanced to the principal debtor.[14] To avoid being caught by such technicalities it is preferable as a matter of practice to have guarantees executed, whether by individuals or corporations, under seal.

[9.04] Every guarantee to be enforceable must be in writing or be evidenced in writing.[15] As a contract of guarantee (unless executed under seal) needs to have consideration, it would seem that the written contract or note, to comply with s 2 of the Statute of Frauds (Ireland) 1695, should contain a reference to the consideration.[16] This is supported by the decisions in *Saunders v Wakefield*[17] and *Cole v Dyer*[18] where the absence of a written statement as to the consideration rendered the guarantee in each case unenforceable. In the former case Holroyd J put it simply and clearly:[19]

> "In the present case, that which is reduced into writing is merely an engagement to pay the bill. Now, unless there be a consideration for that, no action lies upon such a promise. If a consideration is to be introduced, it may be either past or future, and must be proved by parol evidence. If that were allowed, all the danger which the Statute of Frauds was intended to prevent, would be again introduced."

[13.] See judgment of Murphy J at p 10 of Supreme Court decision in *First National Commercial Bank plc v Anglin*, 27 June 1996.

[14.] See *Burton v Gray* (1873) 8 Ch App 932.

[15.] See para **[9.06]** below.

[16.] Which must be sufficient see Clark, *Contract Law in Ireland* (3rd ed) p 41; Chesire, Fifoot & Furmston's *Law of Contract* (13th ed) p 82-113; see also Chitty LJ in *Sheers v Thimbleby and Son* (1897) LT 709 at 711.

[17.] (1821) 4 B & Ald 595.

[18.] (1831) 1 C & J 465.

[19.] (1821) 4 B & Ald 595 at 603.

[9.05] This pitfall was removed by s 3 of the Mercantile Law Amendment Act 1856 which stated that a guarantee would not be invalid "by reason only that the consideration of such promise does not appear in writing or by necessary inference from a written document."

In 1897 Chitty LJ highlighted the Statute of Frauds' requirement to specify consideration in guarantees:[20]

> "That Statute required that the whole contract should be evidenced by writing; that is, the parties by name or description, the consideration, the promise, and the subject-matter should all be shown with reasonable certainty. But since the Mercantile Law Amendment Act, it is not necessary that the consideration should appear in writing: it may be proved by parol evidence."

However, on 16 May 1983 the Oireachtas repealed the Mercantile Law Amendment Act 1856. This Act, along with many others, was perceived as having no current application in Ireland and was thus removed from law by the Statute Law Revision Act, 1983. It remains to be seen whether the courts will apply the early nineteenth century decisions and require the consideration to be stated in writing. Clearly since 1983 it is prudent to specify consideration in any guarantee executed under hand.

The uncertainty caused by the repeal of the Mercantile Law Amendment Act 1856 is an additional reason, over and above any doubts as to the sufficiency of consideration, as to why a guarantee should be executed under seal. It should be noted though, that non-fulfilment by the bank of any stated consideration will render a guarantee under seal unenforceable due to a breach of a condition precedent.[21] All may not be lost though if the guarantee is under hand and the guarantee indicates that the liability being guaranteed is a prospective one, rather than one already in existence which would necessitate forbearance.[22]

STATUTE OF FRAUDS (IRELAND) 1695[23]

[9.06] The first point to note is that although an oral guarantee may be valid it will be unenforceable[24] by virtue of the Statute of Frauds (Ireland) 1695,[25] s 2 of which provides that:

[20.] In *Sheers v Thumblely and Son* (1897) 76 LT 709 at 711.

[21.] See para **[9.83]** below.

[22.] See Marks & Moss, *Rowlatt on Principal and Surety* (4th ed) pp 35-36.

[23.] For a more detailed treatment of the applicability of the Statute of Frauds to guarantees see de Colyar, *A Treatise of the Law of Guarantees and of Principal & Surety* (3rd ed) Butterworths (1897) Ch I, II and III; Marks and Moss, *Rowlatt on Principal and Surety* (4th ed) Ch 3; Andrews and Millett, *Law of Guarantees* (2nd ed) (FT Law & Tax) Ch 3.

[24.] Unless evidenced by a note or memorandum signed by the guarantor.

[25.] For a brief historical background to the Statute of Frauds see Chesire, Fifoot & Furmston's *Law of Contract* (13th ed) pp 207-210.

no action shall be brought ... to charge the defendant upon any special promise
to answer for the debt, default or miscarriage of another person ... unless the
agreement upon which such action shall be brought, or some memorandum or
note thereof, shall be in writing, and signed by the party to be charged
therewith, or some other person thereunto by him lawfully authorised.

The principal purpose behind the requirement for a guarantee to be evidenced in
writing is to give protection to persons against whom it may be alleged that they
guaranteed the debts of another.[26] An example of the need for a creditor to
ensure that the guarantee is in written form and signed can be seen from the case
of *Deutsche Bank AG v Ibrahim*.[27] As security for an overdraft facility Ibrahim
arranged for the deeds of two flats owned by his daughters to be handed to the
bank. The court held that the deposit of the title deeds for the debt of another
was a guarantee, which was unenforceable under the Statute of Frauds in the
absence of a written note of the guarantee.

[9.07] Lawyers should note that an oral guarantee given by a lawyer in his
capacity as a lawyer (and thus as an officer of the court) can be enforceable. In
Re Greaves, Gent[28] the court indicated that:

"Even supposing the undertaking to be void by the Statute of Frauds, the court
may nevertheless exercise a summary jurisdiction over one of its own officers,
an attorney of the Court. The undertaking was given by the party in his
character of attorney, and in that character the Court may compel him to
perform it. An attorney is conusant of the law, and, if he gave an undertaking
which he must know to be void, he shall not be allowed to take advantage of his
own wrong, and say that the undertaking cannot be enforced."

Requirement of Guarantor's Signature

[9.08] In *Bank of Ireland v McCabe*,[29] the appellant gave the bank a guarantee in
respect of a particular transaction which was completed. When the company
sought a new advance and the branch bank manager mentioned security, the
appellant, who was the company's principal director, stated that "you have my
existing guarantee". The Supreme Court held that this statement could not be
taken as reviving the guarantee since it was not signed by the appellant.

[9.09] Notwithstanding the language of the statute as to signature, the courts
have held that a person may be bound where an unsigned note is delivered by

---

[26.] Where the guarantee itself is not in writing but only a note or memorandum thereof, such note
or memorandum to satisfy the Statute of Frauds must contain the relevant details of the
guarantee - *Page v Norfolk* (1894) 70 LTR 781.

[27.] [1992] 3 JIBL N-47.

[28.] (1827) 1 Cr & J 374; *Evans v Duncombe* (1831) 1 Cr & J 372.

[29.] Supreme Court, unrep, 19 December 1994; (1995) CLP 99.

the agreement of the person to be charged.[30] This is sometimes referred to as "the authenticated signature fiction".[31] The Supreme Court held in *Casey v Irish Intercontinental Bank Ltd*[32] that a letter typed on the auctioneers' headed notepaper but unsigned was held to be a sufficient note to satisfy the Statute of Frauds - the heading was deemed to be the signature of the auctioneer.[33] In *Deutsche Bank AG v Ibrahim*[34] the bank claimed that the memoranda sent by it to the daughters with the daughters' names on it was sufficient to satisfy the Statute of Frauds - the judge held though it would be wrong to infer approval from their silence.

[9.10] More recently, Lord Brandon of Oakbrook indicated, in giving the House of Lords judgment in *Elpis Maritime Co Ltd v Marti Chartering Co Inc (The Maria D)*,[35] that the Statute of Frauds prescribes two ways in which a guarantee may be enforceable,[36] namely:[37]

> "The first way is by having a written agreement signed by the party to be charged or his agent. The second way is by having a note or memorandum of the agreement similarly signed. In the latter case this agreement itself may be oral".

A person who appends his initials to a document may be deemed to have signed it.[38] A printed signature[39] or a signature in pencil[40] may be sufficient.

[9.11] The Statute of Frauds makes no requirement as to signature by the recipient of the guarantee. Nineteenth century case law confirms that the only signature necessary is that of the person against whom the agreement is to be enforced.[41]

---

30. *Evans v Hoare* [1892] 1 QB 593, *Leeman v Stocks* [1951] 1 All ER 1043.
31. For historical background see Quilliam J in *Bilsland v Terry* [1972] NZLR 43 at 49.
32. [1979] IR 364.
33. In giving the judgment of the Court, Kenny J stated at 368:
   "It seems to me that, in principle, when the party to be charged has written or dictated a document on or onto paper which has his name printed on it, he should be regarded as having adopted the printed name as his signature and so should be regarded as having signed the document."
34. [1992] 3 JIBL N-47.
35. [1991] 3 All ER 758.
36. Assuming other requirements are complied with such as, *inter alia*, capacity of the guarantor.
37. [1991] 3 All ER 758 at 762.
38. See *Chichester and Wife v Cobb* (1866) III BR 433.
39. *Schneider v Norris* (1814) 2 M & S 286; *Leeman v Stocks* [1951] 1 All ER 1043.
40. *Geary v Physic* (1826) 5 B & C 234.
41. *Laythoarp v Bryant* (1836) 2 Bing (NC) 735; *The Liverpool Borough Bank v Eccles* (1859) 4 H & N 139; see also Cockburn CJ in *Williams v Lake* (1859) 2 EL & EL 349 at 354.

[9.12] It is important to ensure that the agreement or the memorandum identifies the relevant parties[42] (although it has been held that a beneficiary need not be a party or named as a beneficiary[43]). It is needless to say necessary where a standard form guarantee is to be used to complete the blanks, such as the name of the principal debtor. Additional evidence as to the name of the principal may not be sufficient to rectify such an omission.[44] A manuscript correction as to the name of the principal debtor in the guarantee may be valid notwithstanding the absence of all party consent. In *Lombard Finance Ltd v Brookplain Trading Ltd*,[45] a guarantee was altered, subsequent to its execution, by having the word "company" struck out from the name of the principal debtor. Marks above the alteration purported to show that the parties had initialled the amendment, which they had not in fact done. One of the guarantors contended that the unauthorised alteration made the guarantee void and the purported initialling made it a forgery. The English Court of Appeal held that an unauthorised alteration to a document rendered it void only if it was a material alteration and that an immaterial alteration made in good faith did not amount to a forgery. Effectively, the English courts permit an alteration of a document to correct a misdescription. The justification for this approach is that if the alteration had not been made presumably evidence would have been admissible to show that the principal debtor was simply misdescribed and on that basis the court would order rectification.[46]

Oral Evidence

[9.13] It seems that the courts will allow oral evidence which seeks to explain a term of the guarantee. In *Perrylease Ltd v Imecor AG*[47] the defendant had agreed to guarantee back payments due by its subsidiary. The guarantee referred to leasing agreements without being clear as to which leasing agreements. Scott J considered that the oral evidence sought to explain rather than contradict the guarantee, and was thus admissible to show that it was intended to guarantee payments under all leasing agreements entered into after the date of the guarantee between the plaintiff and the guarantor's subsidiary.

[9.14] However, in *Bank of Ireland v McCabe*[48] the Supreme Court allowed oral evidence to contradict the guarantee which was stated to be "a continuing security" of such obligations as should at any time be owing or remain unpaid to

---

42. *Williams v Lake* (1859) 2 El & El 349; *Evans v Hoare* [1892] 1 QB 593.
43. *Kenney v Employers' Liability Assurance Corporation* [1901] 1 IR 301.
44. See *Imperial Bank of Canada v Nixon* [1926] 4 DLR 1052.
45. [1991] 2 All ER 762.
46. *Ibid* at 765 *per* Dillon LJ.
47. [1987] 2 All ER 373; for comment on this decision see *Fisher* [1987] 2 JIBL 119.
48. Supreme Court, unrep, 19 December 1994; (1995) CLP 99.

the bank. The Supreme Court held that oral evidence was admissible to the effect that the guarantee was given for a specific transaction, since completed. On that basis it decided (without reference to any decided cases)[49] that the guarantee was unenforceable for all obligations owing or unpaid to the bank. In so deciding the Supreme Court overruled the High Court[50] which had held that the oral evidence was "simply an explanation of the circumstances under which the said written guarantee came into existence". The Supreme Court's surprising preference for oral evidence over the written word is a harsh warning to all lenders of the danger of relying upon an all moneys' guarantee. It may thus be appropriate, albeit inconvenient and time consuming,[51] for guarantors to execute an acknowledgement each time a revised or additional facility is being made available to a borrower. Alternatively in the case of corporate guarantors, the board resolution approving the guarantee could specifically provide that the approval covers future advances to the principal debtor.[52]

[9.15] An oral variation of a written guarantee may be upheld by the courts. In *Re a Debtor (No 517 of 1991)*[53] the guarantor claimed that the creditor had agreed orally to allow certain monies to be applied in reduction of the guarantor's liability to the creditor under a written guarantee. Ferris J held that the oral agreement could be relied upon as the Statute of Frauds[54] merely had the effect of making an agreement to which it applied unenforceable.

[9.16] Similarly, oral evidence is admissible to show that the written contract does not reflect the agreement that was entered into, as where the contract was signed and delivered subject to satisfaction of a condition precedent which was never fulfilled.[55]

DISTINGUISHED FROM CONTRACT OF INDEMNITY

"It ... has raised many hair-splitting distinctions of exactly that kind which brings the law into hatred, ridicule and contempt by the public".[56]

[49.] Judgment was delivered by Egan J; Denham J and Blayney J simply concurred.
[50.] Flood J, 25 March 1993.
[51.] Lending to corporate customers will often involve obtaining guarantees from other group members which will require board approval from each company, involving time not only of the directors but of lawyers in drafting or approving the resolutions.
[52.] See further para **[18.56]**.
[53.] [1992] 2 JIBL N-31.
[54.] The Statute of Frauds (Ireland) 1695 s 2 is equivalent to the English Statute of Frauds 1677, s 4.
[55.] *Pattle v Hornibrook* [1897] 1 Ch 25.
[56.] Harman LJ in *Yeoman Credit Ltd v Latter* [1961] 2 All ER 294 at 299.

"An indemnity is a contract by one party to keep the other harmless against a loss, but a contract of guarantee is a contract to answer for the debt, default or miscarriage of another who is to be primarily liable to the promisee."[57]

[9.17] While a guarantee needs to be in writing if it is to be enforceable, an indemnity does not. Needless to say this has given rise to much litigation as to the distinction between a guarantee and an indemnity.[58] It was stated in a 1902 Court of Appeal judgment:[59]

"Of course in one sense all guarantees, whether they come within [s 2] or not, are contracts of indemnity. But the difference between those indemnities which come within the section and those which do not is very shortly thus expressed in the notes to *Forth v Stanton*. These cases establish that the statute applies only to promises made to the person to whom another is already or is to become answerable'".

The manner in which an instrument is described should not be relied upon in ascertaining whether it is a guarantee or an indemnity - "the use of the word 'guarantee' ... is sometimes used to misdescribe what is in law a contract of indemnity and not of guarantee".[60]

[9.18] The nineteenth century decision in *Guild & Co v Conrad*[61] is helpful in clarifying the distinction between a contract of guarantee and a contract of indemnity. At the defendant's request the plaintiff accepted bills of exchange from a firm of merchants on the defendant's promise that he would meet the bills at maturity. Later when the firm got into difficulties, the defendant promised the plaintiff that if he would accept their bills the funds would be provided. It was held that the first promise was a guarantee and the second an indemnity, Lopes LJ stated:[62]

"A promise to be liable for a debt conditionally on the principal debtor making default is a guarantee and is a promise to make good the default of another within the Statute. On the other hand, a promise to become liable for a debt

---

57. Holroyd Pearce LJ in *Yeoman Credit Ltd v Latter* [1961] 2 All ER 294 at 296; cited with approval by Aldous LJ in *British and Commonwealth Holdings plc v Barclays Bank plc* [1996] 1 All ER 381 at 395.
58. For a further outline as to the distinction see *Halsbury's Laws of England* 4th ed, Vol 20, para 109.
59. *Harburg India Rubber Comb Company v Martin* [1902] 1 KB 778 at 784 *per* Vaughan Williams LJ.
60. Lord Diplock in *Moschi v Lep Air Services Ltd* [1972] 2 All ER 393 at 400; see also Lloyd J in *General Produce Co v United Bank Ltd* [1979] 2 LLR 255 at 258 - "The problem of construction is not solved by labelling the document one thing or the other"; see further Lingard, *Bank Security Documents* (3rd ed) para 13.7A.
61. [1894] 2 QB 885.
62. *Ibid* at 895.

whenever the person to whom the promise is made should become liable is not a promise within the Statute of Frauds and need not be in writing."

[9.19] In *Provincial Bank of Ireland v Fisher*[63] the leading judgment in the Irish Court of Appeal[64] approved of perhaps the most clear and helpful words of Vaughan Williams LJ in *Davys v Burnell*:[65]

"... in any case where, in substance and in fact, an obligation has been undertaken by a person to the creditor to pay a debt due from another person, for which that other remains responsible, in the event of his making default, *prima facie* that is a guarantee".

[9.20] In *Commodity Broking Company Ltd v Meehan*[66] the defendant had refused to sign a guarantee but Barron J held nevertheless that he had orally agreed to give an indemnity. In deciding that the defendant had agreed to give an indemnity rather than a guarantee Barron J said:[67]

"There was never any hope that the company could pay its debt. It was not an agreement of the defendant to pay if the principal debtor, the company, did not, which is the essential element of a guarantee; but an agreement to pay in any event, which is an indemnity."

[9.21] In distinguishing between a contract of guarantee and a contract of indemnity, the contract itself must be interpreted as well as the intention of the parties and surrounding circumstances.[68] In *Bryan & Company v Erico Construction Ltd*,[69] the plaintiff, a law firm, agreed to carry out work for the corporate defendant on the individual defendants' oral promise of payment for past and future fees in respect of work for the corporate defendant. The defendants in their defence claimed that the promise was a guarantee and thus unenforceable as it was not reduced to writing. The court considered all the surrounding circumstances had to be taken into account in determining the true intention of the parties. The court held that as the law firm had expressly indicated they would continue to act only if the individual defendants would be responsible for the legal fees, the oral agreement was an indemnity and not a guarantee.

---

63. [1918] 2 IR 521.
64. Sir Ignatius J O'Brien C; the Court of Appeal's decision was affirmed unanimously by the House of Lords [1919] 2 IR 249.
65. [1913] 2 KB 47 at 54.
66. [1985] IR 12.
67. *Ibid* at 18.
68. *Yeoman Credit Ltd v Latter* [1961] 2 All ER 294; *Communities Economic Development Fund v Canadian Pickles Corp* (1992) 85 DLR (4th) 88.
69. [1995] 1 JIBL N-5.

[9.22] As we have seen, a guarantee is a written agreement to answer for the debt of another.[70] Thus if the debt is void, there is nothing to answer for, or if the debt is tainted with illegality, the guarantee will be unenforceable.[71] In *Coutts & Co v Browne-Lecky*[72] Oliver J indicated that where the loan was void, the omission to repay it does not give rise to any obligation as there is no debt, default or miscarriage.

[9.23] Most guarantees now provide by their language that the guarantor indemnifies the creditor as a primary obligation in addition to guaranteeing repayment of the third party debt to the creditor. The purpose of this clause is to enable the creditor to be able to rely on the guarantee as though it were an indemnity, as an indemnity is a primary liability in itself and thus should not be tainted if the loan itself is void. How effective this language will be for the creditor's protection is open to question.[73] Much will depend upon the circumstances of the case. A statement in a guarantee "as a primary obligor and not merely as a surety" has been held to be "merely part of the common form of provision to avoid the consequences of giving time or indulgence to the principal debtor and cannot convert what is in reality a guarantee into an indemnity".[74] If it is clear that the surety is giving a guarantee and an indemnity then the creditor is more likely to be protected in the event that the principal debt is irrecoverable.[75] A weakness in taking a guarantee only, as opposed to a guarantee and an indemnity, is highlighted by the remarks of Lord Denning MR:[76]

> "... if a clause in a guarantee makes the guarantor liable for a larger sum than the mortgagor, that clause is unenforceable. The guarantor is only under a secondary obligation to guarantee the debt of the principal debtor. If the principal debtor's debt is reduced for good reason, equally the guarantor's obligation is reduced. If there is a term in the contract to the contrary, it should be rejected as being repugnant or unreasonable".

---

[70] Para **[9.02]**.
[71] See Chesire, Fifoot & Furmston's *Law of Contract* (13th ed) pp 387-392; *Redmond v Smith* (1844) 7 Man & G 457 (where a contract of insurance to cover an illegal venture was itself illegal).
[72] [1946] 2 All ER 207.
[73] It is likely that an illegality in the underlying transaction which taints a guarantee will taint an indemnity for such transaction.
[74] *Per* Fisher J in *Heald v O'Connor* [1971] 2 All ER 1105 at 1110; see also *State Bank of India v Kaur* [1995] NBC 43 where the Court of Appeal held that a principal debtor clause did not turn a guarantee into an indemnity.
[75] See *General Produce Co v United Bank Ltd* [1979] 2 LLR 255.
[76] *Standard Chartered Bank Ltd v Walker* [1982] 3 All ER 938 at 943; it has been suggested there is nothing objectionable about such an indemnity clause provided it is clear and it has not been mispresented to the guarantor - Lingard, *Bank Security Documents* (3rd ed) para 13.67.

[9.24] A distinction is to be drawn between a loan which is void and therefore unenforceable against both the borrower and the guarantor, and a loan the repayment of which is unenforceable against the borrower, (being *ultra vires* the borrower) but nevertheless enforceable against the guarantor.[77] In *Gerrard v James*[78] money lent to a company for the purchase of its own shares was irrecoverable from the company as it was lent for an illegal purpose and was *ultra vires* the company. The defendants had jointly and severally covenanted with the plaintiff, (1) to guarantee the full and proper performance by the company of the covenants on its part contained in the agreement, and (2) in the event of default being made by the company under its covenants, to accept liability and to guarantee the payments to the plaintiff.

Lawrence J held that:[79]

> "the true meaning of the covenant on the part of the defendants is that, if the company does not perform its obligations under the agreement, the defendants will themselves perform those obligations. The first branch of the covenant is, in my judgment, sufficient to entitle the plaintiff to succeed in this action. But I also think that the second branch applies to the facts of this case. The word 'default' is a word of wide general import, and includes 'failure' and 'omission'. It seems to me immaterial whether the failure or omission by the company to perform its obligations is attributable to its financial inability or to statutory disability, as the liability of the defendants arises, whatever may be the cause of failure. The gist of the bargain entered into by the defendants, in my opinion, was: 'If you, the plaintiff, will advance this £1500 we, the defendants, will pay you, if the company does not pay'."

[9.25] In *Yorkshire Railway Wagon Co v Moclure*[80] three directors who had guaranteed an *ultra vires* borrowing were bound by their guarantee. This decision was followed and applied in *Munster and Leinster Bank Ltd v Barry*.[81] In that case an industrial society obtained a loan from the bank which exceeded

---

77. See *Yorkshire Railway Wagon Co v Moclure* (1881) 19 Ch D 478 and *Gerrard v James* [1925] 1 Ch 616 (although the court in *Heald v O'Connor* [1971] 2 All ER 1105 sought to explain the latter decision on the grounds that the guarantee was construed as an indemnity).

78. [1925] 1 Ch 616; Milnes Holden suggests in *The Law and Practice of Banking* Vol 2 (7th ed) para 19.50, that it would not be surprising if the Court of Appeal over-ruled this decision, although this suggestion is contrary to de Colyar's statement in 1897, in the *Law of Guarantees and of Principal and Surety* (3rd ed) p 210, that "where directors guarantee the performance of a contract of their company which does not bind the latter, as being *ultra vires*, the directors' suretyship liability is enforceable", Lingard in *Bank Security Documents* (3rd ed) para 13.7 regards this proposition as being anomalous and submits that only an indemnifier remains liable once the principal debtor ceases to be liable.

79. *Ibid* at 622.

80. (1881) 19 Ch D 478.

81. [1931] IR 671.

the society's borrowing limit under its rules. The loan was guaranteed by a number of the society's shareholders who were members of the society's managing committee. Johnston J held that having regard to the position of the guarantees in relation to the society and their knowledge of the limitation on the society's borrowing powers, they could not avoid liability on the grounds of *ultra vires*.

[9.26] An exception to the rule that a guarantee will be discharged if the underlying debt discontinues applies in the case of rental payments under a lease which is disclaimed by a liquidator. This turns on the language of s 290(3) of the Companies Act, 1963 which provides that the disclaimer determines the company's liability but does not "affect the rights or liabilities of any other person". In *Re Farm Machinery Distributors Ltd: Tempany v Royal Liver Trustees Ltd*[82] Keane J held that on the liquidator's disclaimer of the lease, the release of the surety was not necessary for releasing the company from liability and thus the disclaimer did not affect the rights and liabilities of the guarantor. In doing so, Keane J indicated he regarded the Court of Appeal's contrary decision in *Stacey v Hill*[83] as being unsatisfactory and declined to follow it. Up until 1996 the decision in *Stacey v Hill*[84] continued to be applied in England by reference to similar statutory provisions as to disclaimer of leases.[85] But, Keane J can feel vindicated by the House of Lords decision in *Hindcastle Ltd v Barbara Attenborough Associates Ltd*[86] which specifically overruled *Stacey v Hill*. The principal judgment was delivered by Lord Nicholls of Birkenhead who explained the English equivalent[87] of s 290(3) of the Companies Act, 1963 as follows:[88]

> "The statute provides that a disclaimer operates to determine the interest of the tenant in the disclaimed property but not so as to affect the rights or liabilities of any other person. Thus when the lease is disclaimed it is determined and the reversion accelerated but the rights and liabilities of others, such as guarantors and original tenants, are to remain as though the lease had continued and not been determined. In this way the determination of the lease is not permitted to affect the rights or liabilities of other persons. Statute has so provided.
>
> .... it is essential to have in mind that the fundamental purpose of an ordinary guarantee of another's debt is that the risk of the principal debtor's insolvency shall fall on the guarantor and not the creditor. If the debtor is unable to pay his

---

82. [1984] ILRM 273; [1984] BCLC 588.
83. [1901] 1 KB 660.
84. *Ibid.*
85. See *Allied Dunbar Assurance plc v Fowle* [1994] BCC 422.
86. [1996] 1 All ER 737.
87. Insolvency Act, 1986, s 178(4).
88. *Ibid* at 748 and 753.

debt when it becomes due, his bankruptcy does not release the guarantor. The discharge of a bankrupt releases him from all his bankruptcy debts, but this does not release a guarantor from the bankrupt; see s 281(1) and (7) of the 1986 Act. The very object of giving and taking a guarantee would be defeated if the position were otherwise. So the guarantor remains liable to the creditor."

[9.27] Where a company is struck off the register of companies, a creditor may apply to the court for its re-instatement on the register.[89] The court may, if it is satisfied that the company was trading when it was struck off or that it is just and equitable that the company be restored to the register, order its restoration. In such event the company will be deemed to have continued in existence as though it had not been struck off. This will have the effect of reviving retroactively a guarantor's liabilities for a dissolved company.[90]

DISTINGUISHED FROM CONTRACT OF INSURANCE

[9.28] A contract of guarantee does not require the creditor to show *uberrima fides*, that is full disclosure of all material facts known to the creditor pertaining to the contract,[91] save where the non-disclosure amounted to a misrepresentation.[92] In the *Royal Bank of Scotland v Greenshields*[93] the Lord President of the Scottish Court of Session indicated:

"The only circumstance in which a duty to disclose would emerge, and a failure to disclose would be fatal to the bank's case, would be where a customer put a question, or made an observation in the hearing of the bank agent, which would inevitably lead anyone to the conclusion that the intending guarantor was labouring under a misapprehension as to the state of the customer's indebtedness".

As *uberrima fides* is required in a contract of insurance, the question may arise as to whether a certain contract is one of guarantee or insurance. The distinction was considered by Romer LJ in *Seaton v Heath*.[94] In the course of his judgment in that case Romer LJ stated:[95]

"... the difference between these two classes of contract does not depend upon any essential difference between the word 'insurance' and the word 'guarantee'. There is no magic in the use of those words. The words, to a great extent, have the same meaning and effect; and many contracts ... may with equal propriety be called contracts of insurance or contracts of guarantee.

89. Companies Act, 1963, s 311(8).
90. *Allied Dunbar Assurance plc v Fowle* [1994] BCC 422.
91. Subject to what is set out in paras **[9.30]-[9.32]** below.
92. *Westpac Securities Ltd v Dickie* [1991] 1 NZLR 657.
93. 3 LDAB 80.
94. [1899] 1 QB 782.
95. *Ibid* at 792.

Whether the contract be one requiring 'uberrima fides' or not must depend upon its substantial character and how it came to be effected ...

... Contracts of insurance are generally matters of speculation, where the person desiring to be insured has means of knowledge as to the risk, and the insurer has not the means or not the same means. The insured generally puts the risk before the insurer as a business transaction, and the insurer on the risk stated fixes a proper price to remunerate him for the risk to be undertaken; and the insurer engages to pay the loss incurred by the insured in the event of certain specified contingencies occurring. On the other hand, in general, contracts of guarantee are between persons who occupy, or ultimately assume, the positions of creditor, debtor, and surety and thereby the surety becomes bound to pay the debt or make good the default of the debtor. In general, the creditor does not himself go to the surety, or represent, or explain to the surety, the risk to be run. The surety often takes the position from motives of friendship to the debtor, and generally not as the result of any direct bargaining between him and the creditor, or in consideration of any remuneration passing to him from the creditor. The risk undertaken is generally known to the surety, and the circumstances generally point to the view that as between the creditor and surety it was contemplated and intended that the surety should take upon himself to ascertain exactly what risk he was taking upon himself."

[9.29] According to a former President of the High Court[96] these tests laid down by Romer LJ "have long been accepted as satisfactory". More recently, they were applied by Blayney J in the High Court in *International Commercial Bank plc v Insurance Corporation of Ireland plc and Meadows Indemnity Company Ltd*.[97] In that case, the plaintiff bank agreed to lend money to Amaxa SA and in consideration of making that loan the first defendant, ICI, undertook by way of "a credit guarantee insurance agreement" to "indemnify" the bank for 100% of the loan. ICI submitted that the credit guarantee insurance agreement was a contract of insurance and not of guarantee and so a contract *uberrima fides*. The court held that:[98]

1. Applying the tests of Romer LJ[99] as to the substantial character of the contract and the manner in which it came to be effected, the contract was not one which required *uberrima fides* on the part of the bank and was in substance a guarantee rather than a contract of insurance, and

2. Having regard to the substantial character of the contract, the manner in which it was expressed and its effect were much closer to a

---

[96.] Davitt P in *Kreglinger and Ferrau Ltd v Irish National Insurance Company Ltd* [1956] IR 116 at 148.

[97.] [1991] ILRM 726.

[98.] The High Court decision was the subject of an unsuccessful appeal to the Supreme Court (31 July 1992) concerning the re-insurance of ICI's risk by Meadows Indemnity Company Ltd.

[99.] In *Seaton v Heath* [1899] 1 QB 782.

guarantee than to a contract of insurance and the agreement contained a number of clauses which are appropriate only to a guarantee (a number of the clauses were found to be essentially the same as the precedent guarantee found in *Butterworths Encyclopaedia of Forms and Precedents*). It was considered significant also that the consideration expressed in the agreement was the granting of the loan which is the standard consideration in contracts of guarantee.

Duty of Disclosure by Bank

[9.30] The statement that a contract of guarantee does not require *uberrima fides* on the part of the bank must be qualified by two decisions. First *Hamilton v Watson*[100] where the House of Lords held that a creditor was not required to disclose to a prospective guarantor anything which might only naturally take place between the creditor and debtor;[101] this decision was explained by Vaughan Williams LJ to the effect that:[102]

> "a creditor must reveal to the surety every fact which under the circumstances the surety would expect not to exist, for the omission to mention that such a fact does exist is an implied representation that it does not. Such a concealment is frequently described as 'undue concealment'."

Secondly, *Levett v Barclays Bank plc*[103] where it was held that "a creditor was under a duty to disclose to the surety contractual arrangements made between the principal debtor and the creditor which made the terms of the principal contract something materially different in a potentially disadvantageous respect from those which the surety might naturally expect". Thus, the distinction as to the duty of disclosure as between contracts of guarantee and of insurance has become blurred and bankers would be well advised not to rely on the non-applicability of *uberrima fides* to contracts of guarantee, but to bear in mind the words of M Burton QC:[104]

> "The principle appears to be that there is imposed upon the creditor a duty to disclose what in general terms can be described as unusual features, unknown to the surety".

[100.] (1845) 12 Cl & Fin 109.
[101.] See also *London General Omnibus Company Ltd v Holloway* [1912] 2 KB 72; *Lloyds Bank Ltd v Harrison* (1925) 4 LDAB 12; *The National Provincial Bank of England (Ltd) v Glanusk* [1939] 3 KB 335; *Westminster Bank Ltd v Cond* (1940) 5 LDAB 263; *Cooper v National Provincial Bank Ltd* [1945] 2 All ER 641.
[102.] In *London General Omnibus Company Ltd v Holloway* [1912] 2 KB 72 at 79 applied in *National Mortgage and Agency Company of New Zealand Ltd v Stalker* [1933] NZLR 1182.
[103.] [1995] 2 All ER 615.
[104.] Sitting as a deputy judge of the High Court in *Levett v Barclays Bank plc* [1995] 2 All ER 615 at 628; see also *Commercial Bank of Australia Ltd v Amadio* (1983) 151 CLR 447.

However, the judge displayed a practical approach to the application of legal principles when indicating that the bank's duty must not be too onerous, by stating:[105]

> "There is not to be a duty on a bank to disclose too much to a guarantor or commercial life becomes impossible. In particular, what is clear is that a bank is under no obligation to disclose to a guarantor facts relating to the impecuniosity or past track record of a debtor, for it would be understood by a surety that the existence of financial problems on the part of the debtor was just the reason why a guarantee was being required."

[9.31] In *National Mortgage and Agency Company of New Zealand Ltd v Stalker*[106] it was held that where a guarantee is given for "all moneys which are now or at any time hereafter may be due or owing" there could be no implied representation or undue concealment, arising from the non-communication by the bank, of the state of the debtor's account, that there was no current indebtedness to which the guarantee could apply - it was for the guarantor to ascertain by enquiring as to the extent of the current indebtedness.

[9.32] A bank must exercise care here as it will be precluded by its duty of confidentiality from making disclosures to the guarantor about the customer whose debt is being guaranteed.[107] In *Lloyds Bank Ltd v Harrison*[108] Sargant LJ was quite categorical on the question:[109]

> "the bank would be wrong in disclosing, without some very special direction by the customer, the whole particulars of the state of the account of that customer to the surety. It may be expected that the customer who is bringing his friend along as a surety has explained the general nature of his position, and has explained it properly".

This prohibition may be waived, either expressly or impliedly, by the customer.[110] Learned authors differ as to whether a customer impliedly consents to disclosure by virtue of introducing the guarantor into the transaction.[111] Where the bank is permitted to make a disclosure it must take extreme care not

---

[105.] *Ibid* at 627.

[106.] [1933] NZLR 1182.

[107.] See para **[3.01]**.

[108.] (1925) 4 LDAB 12.

[109.] *Ibid* at 16.

[110.] See para **[3.01]**.

[111.] See Milnes Holden, *The Law and Practice of Banking* Vol 2 (7th ed) para 19-6 where he highlights the different views of Sir John Paget (consent implied) and Lord Chorley (doubtful that consent is implied), although *Paget's Law of Banking* (11th ed) states (at p 627) that, "where the guarantor does ask for information it is submitted that the bank is best advised to ensure that it has the customer's express authority to override its duties of confidentiality and answer the questions".

to mislead the guarantor through any statement of its bank official or indeed from any omission in such statement.[112]

Where repayment of a consumer loan[113] is guaranteed, statute provides[114] that a copy of the guarantee and of the loan agreement be "(i) handed personally to the guarantor upon the making of the contract, or (ii) sent within 10 days of the making of any contract" to the guarantor. Failure to do so will render the guarantee unenforceable.[115]

BUSINESS OF GIVING GUARANTEES

Prohibition unless Licensed or Exempted

[9.33] Until 1978 it was unlawful (without a licence)[116] and an offence[117] for any person[118] (other than an assurance company) to carry on in Ireland "the business of issuing bonds or contracts of suretyship".[119] In 1978,[120] this prohibition was removed in respect of certain bonds, contracts of suretyship and guarantees issued by the holder of a banking licence[121] ("a licensee") in the course of its banking business or issued by a non-resident bank for the purpose of satisfying a requirement of a licensee.

[9.34] This exception was expanded and simplified in 1989,[122] and extended in 1992,[123] to the effect that the prohibition does not apply to any bond or any contract of suretyship or guarantee:

1. Given (or entered into) by a licensee in the course of its banking business or in the course of their respective businesses ICC Bank plc, Foir Teoranta or ACC Bank plc, or

2. Given (or entered into) by a person, resident outside Ireland, in the course of its banking business:

---

112. See Lord Truro LC in *Owen v Homan* (1851) 3 Mac & G 378 at 396; see further paras **[9.70]**-**[9.74]** below.
113. See further Ch 7.
114. Consumer Credit Act, 1995, s 30(1)(b).
115. *Ibid* s 38; see also para **[9.89]** below.
116. Insurance Act, 1936, s 8(1).
117. Insurance Act, 1936, s 8(2).
118. This includes body corporate - Interpretation Act, 1937, s 11(c).
119. Insurance Act, 1936, s 8 prohibits "assurance business" which is defined in s 3 as including "guarantee insurance business" which itself includes "the business of issuing bonds or contracts of suretyship".
120. Insurance (Amendment) Act, 1978 as amended by the Insurance Act, 1981.
121. Pursuant to the Central Bank Act, 1971.
122. Insurance Act, 1989, s 27.
123. ACC Bank Act, 1992, s 12.

to satisfy, and only for the purposes of, a requirement which is both -

(i) a requirement of a licensee [ICC Bank plc, Foir Teoranta or ACC Bank plc], and

(ii) made solely for the purposes of securing financial facilities to be made available by that licensee [ICC Bank plc, Foir Teoranta or ACC Bank plc].[124]

The point to note is that the prohibition applies (subject to the exceptions indicated above) to the business of issuing bonds and contracts of suretyship, ie guarantees and indemnities. It applies to any person, wherever resident or wherever they carry on business, who issues a bond to a person ordinarily resident in Ireland or accepts a premium for a bond from a person ordinarily resident in Ireland where such issuance or acceptance "was done in the course and as part of the carrying on of a business which is assurance business".[125] In other words, once it gives a guarantee as part of its business, the guarantor (unless it comes within the statutory exception) commits an offence.

[9.35] Since 1 January 1993 a licensee, in the context of guarantee business, now includes any credit institution authorised and supervised by the competent authority of another Member State of the European Union.[126] The guarantee business of that credit institution must be in accordance with that institution's authorisation in its home State.

What Constitutes a Business?

[9.36] A question may often arise in practice as to whether a commercial entity, in giving a once-off guarantee as part of a business transaction, and probably receiving monetary compensation for so doing, is carrying on an assurance business. In *The Minister for Industry and Commerce v Suicre Éireann cpt*[127] Lynch J, in relying upon D'Arcy J's judgment in *Cripps Warburg Ltd v Cologne Investment Company Ltd, Aran Friendly Society*[128] and *Halsbury's Laws of England*,[129] held that the ordinary meaning of the expression to carry on business "presupposes some sort of continuation of activity as contrasted with one or two isolated transactions."[130] But neither D'Arcy J, nor Lynch J made any reference

---

124. Insurance (Amendment) Act, 1978, s 2(1) as amended by the ACC Bank Act, 1992, s 12.

125. Insurance Act, 1936, s 10(2); there is no reference to contract of suretyship in this section - this is perceived as being an oversight rather than a deliberate omission, although the position has not been judicially interpreted.

126. European Communities (Licensing and Supervision of Credit Institutions) Regulations, 1992, SI 395/1992, Reg 20(1) and the Schedule, para 6; these regulations implemented in Ireland the Second Banking Directive (Council Directive No 89/546) EEC of 15 December 1989.

127. [1992] 2 IR 215.

128. [1980] IR 321; see further para **[7.05]**.

129. 4th ed Vol 7(1) para 22.

130. [1992] 2 IR 215 at 231.

to the 1918 House of Lords' decision in *Cornelius v Phillips*[131] which held otherwise.

[9.37] There is less doubt that a business may be deemed to be carried on, even though only one transaction is effected, if it is intended to effect further transactions.[132]

[9.38] A guarantee given in Ireland by a non-resident guarantor will not escape the prohibition of assurance business,[133] except where such assurance is by way of "re-insurance".[134]

EFFECT OF GUARANTEE CONTRARY TO INSURANCE ACTS

[9.39] A question may arise as to the effect of a guarantee given in contravention of the Insurance Acts. Also of relevance will be how such a guarantee will affect the indemnity given to the guarantor. First, the relevant provisions of the Insurance Act, 1936 need to be considered. Secondly, guidance may be obtained from the English courts as to the approach to be adopted when guarantees have been provided contrary to statute.

Statutory Provisions

[9.40] The applicable provisions of the Insurance Act, 1936 are as follows:

8(1) It shall not be lawful for any assurance company or other person to carry on in Saorstát Éireann any assurance business save under and in accordance with a licence ... granted by the Minister ....

(2) Every person (other than an assurance company) who carries on any assurance business in contravention of this section shall be guilty of an offence under this section and shall be liable on summary conviction thereof to a fine not exceeding one hundred pounds together with, in the case of a continuing offence, a further fine not exceeding five pounds for every day during which the offence continues.

9(1) It shall not be lawful for any person (otherwise than in the course of re-insurance) to effect or to endeavour to effect any contract of assurance with an assurance company or any other person which or who is not the holder of an assurance licence entitling such company or person to effect contracts of assurance of the kind so effected or endeavoured to be effected by such person.

(2) Every person who effects or endeavours to effect any contract of assurance in contravention of this section shall be guilty of an offence

---

131. [1918] AC 199.
132. *In re Griffin* (1890) 60 LJQB 235; see para **[7.07]**.
133. See the *London Finance and Discount Co Ltd v Butler and Butler* [1929] IR 90.
134. Insurance Act, 1936, s 10(2).

under this section and shall be liable on summary conviction thereof to a fine not exceeding fifty pounds.

The Act defines[135] "assurance company" as meaning a company (whether registered in Ireland under the Companies Acts or incorporated outside Ireland) which "carries on any assurance business," "assurance business" includes "guarantee insurance business" which means *inter alia* "the business of issuing bonds or contracts of suretyship". The language of s 9 is clear in rendering it unlawful for any person to effect a contract of guarantee with a person who is not authorised to issue guarantees. Accordingly, it would seem to follow that indemnities given in respect of such guarantees are unlawful and unenforceable.[136] Payment under such an indemnity would involve making a payment pursuant to a contract which is contrary to Irish law - the courts will not assist any person seeking to enforce a payment in such circumstances.[137]

Common law

[9.41] In *Bedford Insurance Co Ltd v Instituto de Resseguros do Brasil*,[138] neither the plaintiff nor its broker were authorised to carry on marine insurance business which came within the definition of the relevant statute as "the business of effecting and carrying out" contracts of marine insurance. Parker J held that as the insurance contracts contravened the statutory prohibition of effecting and carrying out insurance contracts without authorisation, they were illegal and void *ab initio* and thus the defendants were not obliged to honour their indemnity in respect of such contracts.

[9.42] However, a contrary conclusion was reached by the court in *Stewart v Oriental Fire and Marine Insurance Co Ltd*.[139] Legatt J held that the relevant statute did not invalidate an unauthorised contract; the statutory prohibition was limited to the carrying on of unauthorised business and it did not follow that because an insurer committed an offence in conducting unauthorised insurance business, contracts of insurance were necessarily unenforceable.

[9.43] The contrary conclusions of these decisions were resolved, albeit by way of *obiter*, by the English Court of Appeal's decision in *Phoenix General Insurance Co of Greece SA v Administratia Asigurarilor de Stat*.[140] In giving the

---

[135.] Section 3.

[136.] The exclusion of re-insurance contracts would not negate the unenforceability of the indemnity where the indemnity is given to support a contract of guarantee which itself is unlawful and unenforceable.

[137.] See *Namlooze Venootschap de Faam v The Dorset Manufacturing Co Ltd* [1949] IR 203 and the Supreme Court's decision in *Fibretex (Societe Personnes Responsobilitie) Ltd v Belier Ltd* (1954) 89 ILTR 141.

[138.] [1984] 3 All ER 766.

[139.] [1984] 3 All ER 777.

[140.] [1987] 2 All ER 152.

judgment of the Court, Kerr LJ pointed out[141] it is settled law that any contract prohibited by statute is illegal and void (on the authority of *Cope v Rowlands*[142]). However, he indicated also that because it is an offence for a party to enter into a certain type of contract it does not necessarily mean that the contract is void,[143] as the statutory prohibition and offence may be designed to protect the public and "good public policy and common sense therefore require that contracts of insurance, even if made by unauthorised insurers, should not be invalidated."[144] In applying the relevant decisions, Kerr LJ stated:[145]

> "The problem is therefore to determine whether or not the 1974 Act prohibits contracts of insurance by necessary implication, since it undoubtedly does not do so expressly. In that context it seems to me that the position can be summarised as follows:
>
> (i) Where a statute prohibits both parties from concluding or performing a contract when both or either of them have no authority to do so, the contract is impliedly prohibited ...
>
> (ii) But where a statute merely prohibits one party from entering into a contract without authority and/or imposes a penalty on him if he does so (ie a unilateral prohibition) it does not follow that the contract itself is impliedly prohibited so as to render it illegal and void ...
>
> (iii) The Insurance Companies Act 1974 only imposes a unilateral prohibition on unauthorised insurers. If this were merely to prohibit them from carrying on "the business of effecting contracts of insurance" of a class for which they have no authority, then it would clearly be open to the court to hold that considerations of public policy preclude the implication that such contracts are prohibited and void .... the unilateral prohibition is not limited to the business of "effecting contracts of insurance" but extends to the business of carrying out contracts of insurance. This is a form of statutory prohibition, albeit only unilateral, which is not covered by any authority ... I can see no convincing escape from the conclusion that this extension of the prohibition has the unfortunate effect that contracts made without authorisation are prohibited by necessary implication and therefore void. Since the statute prohibits the insurer from carrying out the contract (of which the most obvious example is paying claims), how can the insured require the insurer to do an act which is expressly forbidden by statute ...
>
> (iv) It follows that, however reluctantly, I feel bound to agree with the analysis of Parker J in the Bedford case and his conclusion that

---

141. *Ibid* at 171.
142. (1836) 2 M & W 149.
143. Adopting Devlin LJ in *Archbolds (Freightage) Ltd v S Spaglett Ltd (Randall, third party)* [1961] 1 All ER 417 at 425.
144. [1987] 2 All ER 152 at 175.
145. *Ibid* at 176.

contracts of insurance made by unauthorised insurers are prohibited by the 1974 Act in the sense that they are illegal and void, and therefore unenforceable. In particular, I agree with the following passages which led him to this conclusion [1984] 3 All ER 766 at 772 ...

> 'The express prohibition is on the carrying on of insurance business of a relevant class, but, as I have already mentioned, the definition in the case of each class begins, "the effecting and carrying out of contracts of insurance". What therefore is prohibited is the carrying on of the business of effecting and performing contracts of insurance of various descriptions in the absence of an authorisation. It is thus both the contracts themselves and the performance of them at which the statute is directed.'"

Guarantees by Non-Exempted Entity

[9.44] To circumvent the unlawfulness under the Insurance Acts, parties sometimes consider putting together a transaction whereby a non-resident guarantor (without a banking or insurance licence in Ireland) may enter into a guarantee of indebtedness arising out of a transaction whereby the documentation is governed by a foreign law and executed abroad. While such a transaction might be enforced in a foreign court, assuming it to be legal in the jurisdiction of such court, a problem could arise if such foreign judgment is then sought to be enforced in Ireland against, say, the "indemnifier" of the guarantor. An exception to the recognition of foreign judgments under both the Brussels Convention[146] and the Lugano Convention[147] is where the judgment is contrary to the public policy of the jurisdiction of the person against whom the judgment is to be enforced.[148] Thus, it may be unwise to structure a transaction offshore, if ultimately it needs to be enforced against one party in Ireland. Indeed, a foreign court may refuse to enforce the transaction if it is brought to its attention that had the transaction been brought before the Irish courts it would have been unenforceable as being contrary to statute in Ireland.

[9.45] This can be seen from the House of Lords' decision in *Regazzoni v KC Sethia (1944) Ltd.*[149] In that case, the Indian Government had prohibited the export, whether directly or indirectly, of goods to South Africa. The parties

---

[146.] The Convention on Jurisdiction and the Enforcement of Judgments in Civil and Commercial Matters, (signed at Brussels) 1968 incorporated into Irish law by the Jurisdiction of Courts and Enforcement of Judgments (European Communities) Act, 1988, s 3; see also para **[7.69]**.

[147.] The Convention on Jurisdiction and the Enforcement of Judgments in Civil and Commercial Matters, (signed at Lugano) 1988 incorporated into Irish law by the Jurisdiction of Courts and Enforcement of Judgments Act, 1993; see also para **[7.69]**.

[148.] Article 27.

[149.] [1957] 3 All ER 286.

agreed under English law that jute would be delivered to Italy and ultimately sold onto South Africa. An action was taken for damages arising from failure to deliver the jute in Italy. The House of Lords held that the agreement would not be enforced in England as a matter of public policy as its performance would have involved carrying out an act in a friendly country which would have violated the law of that country.

[9.46] The appropriate method for a non-EU credit institution to issue a guarantee is to arrange for the guarantee to be issued by an EU credit institution and to stipulate that a condition of the issuing of such guarantee is the provision by the non-EU credit institution of an indemnity to secure the guarantee. While this obviously entails the introduction of a third party to the transaction at some cost, it enables the transaction to proceed. This is done so on the basis that the guarantee is given by the EU credit institution in the course of its banking business and that the indemnity of the non-EU credit institution is given in the course of its banking business solely for the purpose of satisfying a requirement of the EU credit institution for securing financial facilities to be made available by the EU credit institution.[150]

GUARANTOR'S RIGHT TO HAVE DEBT PAID

[9.47] Whether advising a guarantor, or indeed a person receiving a guarantee, familiarity with the guarantor's rights is essential so that a guarantor will not incur a liability needlessly or the recipient will not prejudice his rights of recovery from the guarantor.

As we have seen, the basic principle of a guarantee is that it is an agreement by the guarantor to discharge a debt due or to become due by the debtor to the creditor.[151] As the guarantor will have a reasonable expectation that the debtor will discharge the debt, and thus exonerate the guarantor from any liability, the guarantor may have the right to require the debtor to pay the debt. An example can be seen from the decision of *Thomas v Notts Incorporated Football Club Ltd.*[152] In that case under the terms of the guarantee the guarantor had the right to discontinue the guarantee on notice to the bank. The guarantor gave notice of discontinuance of the guarantee whereupon the bank closed the account. The guarantor claimed that he had an equitable right to require the football club, being the debtor, to exonerate him from liability under the guarantee by paying it off. The court held that once an account had been closed and there was an

---

[150] So as to comply with s 27 of the Insurance Act, 1989, see para **[9.34]** above, as applied by the European Communities (Licensing and Supervision of Credit Institutions) Regulations, 1992 SI 395/1992, see para **[9.35]** above.

[151] See para **[9.02]**.

[152] [1972] 1 All ER 1176.

accrued fixed liability, a surety was entitled to be discharged from all liability under his guarantee by calling on the debtor to pay off the amount due and it was immaterial that the creditor was bound to make a demand on the guarantor before he could proceed against him and that no demand had been made.

This principle can be seen also from the Lord Chancellor's judgment in *Nisbet v Smith*[153] where he said:[154]

> "It is clear and never has been disputed that a surety, generally speaking, may come into this Court, and apply for the purpose of compelling the principal debtor for whom he is surety to pay in the money, and deliver him from the obligation."

The guarantor has the right also to discharge the principal debt, take over any security held by the creditor for the debt and proceed against the principal debtor to recover the amount paid.[155]

[9.48] The guarantor may not wish to be seen to pursue the principal debtor. According to the Lord Chancellor in *Wright v Simpson*,[156] the guarantor may lodge the guaranteed amount with the creditor and at the guarantor's expense compel the creditor to prove against the principal debtor ultimately for the debtor's bankruptcy or liquidation. Although the creditor has his money such a suit may give him unfavourable publicity which could affect his future business.

[9.49] Before proceeding against the guarantor, the bank is not required to realise security which it has from the principal debtor or co-surety.

> "The true principle is that mere omission to sue does not discharge the surety, because the surety can himself set the law in operation against the debtor."[157]

This principle can be seen clearly from the Supreme Court's decision in *AG v Sun Alliance and London Insurances Ltd*.[158] In that case the defendants gave the Minister for Finance a bond to secure the payment of excise duties which would become due by JJ Murphy and Company Ltd. When the bond was called, the defendant claimed that the Revenue Commissioners should in the first instance take all steps available to it to recover the amount including the exercise of a statutory lien over spirits and imported beer. McWilliam J held in the High

---

[153.] (1789) 2 Bro CC 579.

[154.] *Ibid* at 582.

[155.] See Rose LJ in *Re Bank of Credit and Commerce International SA (No 8)* [1996] 2 BCLC 254 at 270.

[156.] (1802) 6 Ves Jun 714 at 734.

[157.] Lindley LJ in *Carter v White* (1880) 25 Ch D 666 at 672.

[158.] [1985] ILRM 522; for comment on the implications of this decision see Doyle, 'No Guarantors Equity - *Attorney General v Sun Alliance and London Insurances Ltd*' (1986) 4 ILT 138.

Court[159] that under the terms of the bond the defendant became liable immediately upon the default of JJ Murphy and Co and the fact that the Revenue Commissioners may have had another remedy did not affect the defendant's liability. The Supreme Court dismissed the defendant's appeal. McCarthy J, giving the sole judgment of the court, stated:[160]

> "It is well settled that it is not necessary for the creditor, before proceeding against the surety, to request the principal debtor to pay, or to sue him, though solvent, unless this be expressly stipulated in the surety document. There is authority for the proposition that the creditor does not have to resort to securities received by the creditor from the principal debtor".

[9.50] The case of *Lombard and Ulster Banking Ltd v Murray and Murray*[161] is a warning, particularly to directors of companies who give personal guarantees that in reality their guarantees may be the first security to be realised. In that case, the defendants were directors of Verona Investments ("Verona"). The bank advanced monies to Verona and an associate company, Aegis Investments Ltd, on the strength of a mortgage over lands of Verona and personal guarantees from the defendants. Costello J rejected the defendants' submission that the bank could only enforce the mortgages given by the directors in support of their guarantees after the bank had asserted its rights against the two companies, stating unequivocally that,[162] "there is no doubt that a creditor is not bound to sue the principal debtor before suing a surety." As to the suggestion that the doctrine of marshalling[163] would require the bank to enforce Verona's mortgage first, Costello J indicated,[164] "the doctrine cannot be relied on as a defence to proceedings instituted by a creditor against one of several co-sureties".

[9.51] To recover the debt due to it, the bank should first make a demand on the principal debtor[165] (unless the terms of the guarantee specifically state otherwise[166]) and secondly, not take any action to prejudice the value or enforceability of the security held by it from the principal debtor or co-surety.

[159.] [1985] ILRM 576 (14 May 1984).

[160.] [1985] ILRM 522 at 526 (28 February 1985).

[161.] [1987] ILRM 522.

[162.] *Ibid* at 524.

[163.] See Wylie, *Irish Land Law* (3rd ed) paras 13.075-13.080.

[164.] [1987] ILRM 522 at 525.

[165.] See *Dow Banking Corporation v Bank Mellatt* (1983) referred to in Chorley & Smart, *Leading Cases in the Law of Banking* (6th ed) p 318; *Paget's Law of Banking* (11th ed) p 639 states "it is usual and prudent practice" to make a demand first on the principal debtor prior to making a demand on the guarantor.

[166.] See *DFC Financial Services Ltd v Coffey* [1991] BCC 218.

[9.52] When the principal debt has become due, the guarantor has a right to discharge the debt and seek to recover the debt from the principal debtor.[167] However, the right of reimbursement will not be granted to a person who has guaranteed repayment of a debt without being so requested by the principal debtor.[168]

[9.53] While in practice, it seldom happens that a guarantor will pay the debt prior to being called upon to do so, there may be circumstances where a delay by the bank in calling for repayment of the principal debt could prejudice the guarantor as the principal debtor, at the time of maturity of its indebtedness to the bank may be in a financially stronger position and better able to discharge the debt than at a later date. This was explained by Cockburn CJ in *Swire v Redman and Holt*:[169]

> "The relation of principal and surety gives to the surety certain rights. Amongst others the surety has a right at any time to apply to the creditor and pay him off, and then (on giving proper indemnity for costs) to sue the principal in the creditor's name. We are not aware of any instance in which a surety ever in practice exercised this right; certainly the cases in which a surety uses it must be very rare. Still the surety has this right. And if the creditor binds himself not to sue the principal debtor, for however short a time, he does interfere with the surety's theoretical right to sue in his name during such period. It has been settled by decisions that there is an equity to say that such an interference with the rights of the surety, - in the immense majority of cases not damaging him to the extent of even a shilling, - must operate to deprive the creditor of his right of recourse against the surety, though it may be for thousands of pounds. But though this seems ... consistent neither with justice nor common sense, it has been long so firmly established that it can only be altered by the legislature".

[9.54] A guarantor may wish to discharge the principal's debt which has become due where a bank is slow to enforce either the principal security or the guarantee. A guarantor may be well advised to take such action where the assets the subject of the principal security are declining in value and further delay may result in a diminished amount to be realised from its ultimate enforcement. The case of *China and South Sea Bank Ltd v Tan*[170] is a clear illustration of the desirability for a guarantor not to await the inevitable demand and loss. In that case the bank's advance was secured by a mortgage of shares and a guarantee.

---

[167] "There is no doubt that a surety paying a debt is entitled to recover against the principal, as for money paid to his use" - *per* Slesser LJ *Re A Debtor* [1937] 1 Ch 156 at 160; see also Pollock CB in *Brittain v Lloyd* (1845) 14 M & W 762 at 773; *Carter v White* (1880) 25 Ch D 666; *Re Salisbury-Jones, Hammond v Salisbury-Jones* [1938] 3 All ER 459.

[168] *Owen v Tate* [1975] 2 All ER 129.

[169] (1876) 1 QBD 536 at 541.

[170] [1989] 3 All ER 839.

At the time of the debtor's default the value of the shares covered the outstanding loan but the shares ultimately became worthless. The guarantor resisted payment on the ground that the bank had failed to exercise a duty of care. The guarantee in its terms provided that the guarantor's liability would not be affected by any securities held by the bank or any time or indulgence granted by the bank. The Privy Council advised that the tort of negligence did not contradict contractual promises. In an admirably succinct judgment, Templeman LJ highlighted the promise and how the guarantor should mitigate his losses in a declining market for the secured assets:[171]

> "The surety contracts to pay if the debtor does not pay and the surety is bound by his contract. If the surety, perhaps less indolent or less well protected by the creditor, is worried that the mortgaged securities may decline in value then the surety may request the creditor to sell and if the creditor remains idle then the surety may bustle about, pay off the debt, take over the benefit of the securities and sell them."

[9.55] Of course, if the guarantor pays the amount of the debt to the bank he can take an assignment of the bank's right of repayment from the principal debtor and take proceedings against the debtor in his own name.[172] In *Ex p Crisp*[173] the Lord Chancellor stated:[174]

> "Where there is a principal and surety, and surety pays off the debt, he is entitled to have an assignment of the security, in order to enable him to obtain satisfaction for what he has paid over and above his share."

However, until the security is actually transferred to the guarantor, the guarantor does not have an estate or interest in the assets the subject of the security which would be affected by registration of judgment (under the Judgment Mortgage Act 1850) against him.[175]

[9.56] According to the English Court of Appeal,[176] it is possible for a guarantor to discharge his liability by transferring to the bank moneys which he had previously improperly taken from the principal debtor. The majority decision, upholding the earlier decision of Millett J, found that the principal debtor had not suffered loss as the monies were used to reduce the debtor's obligation to the bank - the guarantor simply lost his right of subrogation. Accordingly, the liquidator could not recover the misappropriated funds from the guarantor. Dillon LJ thought otherwise. It must be doubtful whether this extraordinary

---

[171.] *Ibid* at 842.
[172.] Pursuant to the Supreme Court of Judicature Act (Ireland) 1877, see para **[14.03]**.
[173.] (1744) 1 Atk 133.
[174.] *Ibid* at 135; see also the *Privy Council in China and South Sea Bank Ltd v Tan* [1989] 3 All ER 839 at 842.
[175.] *Kennedy v Campbell and Campbell* [1899] 1 IR 59.
[176.] *Derek Randall Enterprises Ltd v Randall* [1991] BCLC 379.

decision would be applied in Ireland. It would seem more equitable that the misappropriated funds be returned to their rightful owner,[177] that the guarantor be called upon to honour his guarantee with his own funds and in the event of his so doing he would have a right of subrogation in respect of the amount paid from his own resources.

GUARANTOR'S RIGHT OF SUBROGATION

"In the course of the legal argument on this aspect [subrogation] I have been referred to a number of textbooks and other authorities and I must confess that at the end of it all I feel ill-equipped to offer any wide-ranging view as to the law of subrogation."[178]

[9.57] A right of subrogation may be defined as being the right of a person who has paid money, on behalf of a debtor to a creditor to step into the shoes of the creditor in respect of the amount paid, thereby giving the payor whatever rights the creditor had, at the time of payment, against the debtor in respect of the debt discharged by the payor. This right of subrogation arises though only where the payor does not otherwise have a right of recovery, such as an indemnity or counter-indemnity from the debtor.[179] The principle of subrogation was given statutory effect by s 5 of the Mercantile Law Amendment Act 1856. As we have already seen, however, this Act was repealed in Ireland on 16 May 1983.[180] Notwithstanding the repeal, it appears that the principle is sufficiently established by case law to mean that the guarantor is subrogated to the creditor's rights upon payment by him to the creditor of the amount of the guaranteed debt.[181] Although decided subsequent to the introduction of the Mercantile Law Amendment Act, 1856 the Vice Chancellor's judgment in *Goddard v Whyte*,[182] where no mention was made of the Act, sets out the courts' approach. Sir John Stuart stated:[183]

"By the law of this Court a surety who satisfies the debt for which he is liable is entitled to have from the creditor whose debt he pays the securities which such creditor has obtained from the debtor; and if such securities are not voluntarily given up it is the right of the surety to come to this Court to have such security delivered up".

[177.] The principal debtor or on its insolvency, its creditors (or shareholders).

[178.] *Per* M Wheeler QC (sitting as a Deputy Judge) in *Re Peake's Abattoirs Ltd* [1986] BCLC 73 at 79; see also Breslin (1996) CLP 248 - "it is difficult for the average lawyer to understand such [subrogation] clauses".

[179.] See *Barclays Bank Ltd v TOSG Trust Fund Ltd* [1984] BCLC 1.

[180.] By the Statute Law Revision Act, 1983, see para **[9.05]**.

[181.] For an application of the principle subsequent to the repeal see in *Re PMPA (Longmile) Ltd (in liq) v Private Motorists Provident Society (in liq)* [1993] 1 IR 190; see para **[9.62]** below.

[182.] (1860) 2 Griff 449.

[183.] *Ibid* at 452; see also Cockburn CJ in *Wulff and Billing v Jay* LR 7 QB 756 at 762.

In *Kennedy v Campbell and Campbell*[184] Kenny J stated:[185]

> "The Mercantile Law Amendment Act gives a surety a statutable right, which, without the Act, a Court of equity would have worked out for him in a properly constituted suit".

[9.58] Perhaps the most lucid explanation in the Irish courts of the guarantor's rights of subrogation is that of Lynch J in *Re 19th Ltd*[186] when he said:[187]

> "The right of subrogation arises from equitable doctrines seeking to do justice between the parties. Where the guarantee is of the whole of the debt and is without limitation the law is quite clear. The surety cannot resort to the creditor's remedies until such time as the creditor has been paid his debt in full whereupon the surety's right to resort to the creditor's remedies arises by subrogation.
>
> If the guarantee is of part only of the debt and the surety has paid that part in full the surety can share in securities held by the creditor as against the principal debtor. This has the effect of encouraging the creditor to manage the debt carefully and if necessary to get in the debt promptly. The creditor should try not to allow the debt to grow with interest to such proportions that there is no hope of the principal debtor being able to pay the debt in full because in that event the surety will have to be called upon to pay the part which he guaranteed. In such circumstances the creditor will have to share the loss with the surety who has paid his share in full by allowing the surety to share *pro tanto* in the benefit of other securities held by the creditor as against the principal debtor. Where the guarantee is of the whole debt but nevertheless limited as to the amount which the surety can be compelled to pay, the surety cannot resort to the creditor's remedies until the creditor has been paid in full."

It is critically important for a bank and its adviser to understand this helpful explanation from Lynch J. The reason for this is that if a bank is lending say £500,000 to a company and the company's directors agree to give a guarantee for £200,000 of the company's indebtedness, unless agreed to the contrary, the bank will be obliged to share with the directors the security which it has from the company upon the directors paying the bank £200,000 (on foot of their guarantee). In such event the bank will hold the primary security from the company as trustee for itself and the guarantors as tenants in common.[188] If, however, the guarantee is stated to be a guarantee of all the company's debts and liabilities to the bank but that the liability of the guarantee is limited to £200,000, the directors will not be entitled to any benefit of the bank's security from the company until the company's indebtedness to the bank has been

---

[184.] [1899] 1 IR 59.
[185.] *Ibid* at 63.
[186.] [1989] ILRM 652.
[187.] *Ibid* at 656.
[188.] *Re Butlers Wharf Ltd* [1995] 2 BCLC 43.

discharged in full.[189] Accordingly, for a bank to ensure that the guarantor does not obtain rights to the debtor's primary security until the debt has been cleared, the guarantee should be drafted in a manner where the entire debt is guaranteed, but subject to a limit (where the guarantor desires only to guarantee a certain amount of the debt).[190]

[9.59] Even where the entire debt is guaranteed but subject to a limit, it remains important for a bank to provide in the guarantee, and thus to be agreed by the guarantor, that the guarantor will not be entitled to prove in competition with the bank in the insolvency of the principal debt until all monies due or to become due to the bank have been discharged in full.[191] This will avoid the bank being caught by an exception to the rule as happened in *Barclays Bank Ltd v TOSG Trust Fund Ltd*.[192] In his judgment Oliver LJ clarified the exception and indicated how it could be counter-acted in the guarantee:[193]

> "Where the guarantee is of the whole of a fluctuating balance (eg as in the case of a guarantee of the debtor's current account with a bank) with a limit on the liability of the surety, such a guarantee is to be construed as a guarantee of part only of the debt and the surety paying up to the limit of his liability will be entitled to that extent to stand in the creditor's shoes and prove in priority to him. The right of the surety in these circumstances to prove in priority to the principal creditor can, however (as it normally is in bank guarantees) be excluded by the express terms of the contract of guarantee. A provision that the guarantee is to be in addition and without prejudice to any other securities held from or on account of the debtor and that it is to be a continuing security notwithstanding any settlement of account is probably sufficient for this purpose but at least there must be some express clause in the contract which can fairly be construed as a waiver by the surety of his rights in favour of the principal creditor."

There is a fine line between this judgment and the decision in *Ulster Bank Ltd v Lambe*[194] where a continuing guarantee of all the defendant's liabilities, existing or to be incurred, subject to a limit was held to be a guarantee of the entire debt (subject to the specified limit).

[9.60] Although such clauses waiving subrogation rights (until the debt due to the bank has been fully discharged) are common, they may be contrary to the European Communities (Unfair Terms in Consumer Contracts) Regulations,

---

[189.] *Ex p Turquand* (1876) 3 Ch D 445; *Re Whitehouse* (1887) 37 Ch D 683; *Re Sass, ex p National Provincial Bank of Ireland Ltd* [1896] 2 QB 12.

[190.] See also *Ellis v Emmanuel* [1874-80] All ER Rep 1081.

[191.] See *The Encyclopaedia of Forms and Precedents* (5th ed) Vol 17(2) Butterworths.

[192.] [1984] BCLC 1.

[193.] *Ibid* at 41.

[194.] [1966] NI 161.

1995,[195] and thus unenforceable as against a guarantor who is a consumer. Even
in the nineteenth century such a clause brought displeasure to the Irish courts. In
Re Gillespie, a bankrupt[196] Miller J felt that the guarantor was unlikely to have
fully understood such a clause and although he was bound by authority to give
judgment against the guarantor he declined to award any costs against him. In
that case the guarantor's liability was limited to £800 although available for any
ultimate balance. Miller J[197] considered the waiver of subrogation rights clause
in the guarantee to be "in contravention of the true spirit" of the £800 limitation
clause and its effect was not to limit the guarantor's obligations to £800 but "it
went much further, and confiscated all rights and privileges conferred upon him,
as a guarantor, by statute, in the event of the person whose debt he had
guaranteed becoming a bankrupt."[198]

Miller J obviously felt the need to send out a warning to all:[199]

> "the public, and the commercial public especially, should know that such form
> of guarantee was intended, although apparently so restricted in its terms, to
> deprive John Gillespie of rights and privileges, possibly never in the
> contemplation of the guarantor, in a manner which may not be very apparent".

In the face of commercial reality this judicial displeasure has largely been
ignored to date.

[9.61] The guarantor's right of subrogation is a right granted in equity, in other
words, subject to the courts being satisfied it is fair to do so.[200] Thus, a guarantor
who discharges his obligation with the principal debtor's monies will not be
subrogated to the bank's right against the principal debtor for such monies.[201] In
ascertaining the court's approach it is helpful to consider the words of Barr J in
Re Chipboard Products Ltd (in liq):[202]

> "The Minister as guarantor having paid the bank a debt which was owing to it
> by the company, has, *prima facie*, a right to stand in the shoes of the bank by
> way of subrogation and to obtain the benefit of whatever securities the bank
> had in respect of the debt. However, this right is an equitable one and the
> granting of it is at the discretion of the court which will allow it only when
> satisfied that to do so is likely to achieve justice between the debtor and its
> guarantor. However, in equity there is an important limitation on the advantage

[195.] SI 27/1995 see para **[18.01]**; see also Breslin, 'Guarantees Under Attack' (1996) CLP 243.
[196.] (1887) 19 LR Ir 198.
[197.] *Ibid* at 201 and 202.
[198.] Pursuant to s 253 of the Irish Bankrupt and Insolvent Act, 1857.
[199.] (1887) 19 LR Ir 198 at 201.
[200.] For further reading see Doyle, 'Reason and Justice in the Law of Subrogation' (1994) ILT 10.
[201.] See *Derek Randall Enterprises Ltd v Randall* [1991] BCLC 379.
[202.] [1994] 3 IR 164 at 174.

which the guarantor may obtain on the exercise of his right to subrogation. He may secure no more than an indemnification of loss.

The essence of the law as to subrogation by a surety is succinctly stated in the following passage in *Halsbury's Laws of England* (4th ed), Vol 16 at para 890:

> "When a surety has paid a debt to a creditor, he is entitled in equity to be subrogated to all the rights possessed by the creditor, and is entitled to have transferred to him any securities which the creditor has taken from the debtor, so as to help him recoup himself".

In simple terms, this means that the guarantor may by subrogation avail of all the rights which the satisfied creditor has against the debtor to recoup from the latter whatever financial loss the guarantor has suffered on foot of his guarantee of liability of the debtor to the creditor".

In that case, the fact that the guarantor, the Minister for Finance, had taken other security in support of his guarantee did not affect his right of subrogation, which was limited to the amount of his loss "ie he is entitled to recoup by subrogation the whole of the principal sum paid by him to the bank and appropriate interest."[203]

[9.62] In the case of joint and several guarantees (which in the case of a group of companies arise typically where one or more are borrowing and all are guaranteeing the indebtedness of the borrowers), such of the guarantors as discharge the liability under the guarantee are entitled to be subrogated to the rights of the others. The liability of the guarantors should be discharged by each of them making an equal payment, in addition to any amount due by it as a primary debtor. This was decided by Murphy J in *Re PMPA (Longmile) Ltd (in liq) v Private Motorists Provident Society (in liq)*,[204] following consideration of the Court of Appeal's decision in *Re Parker, Morgan v Hill*[205] - a decision on the interpretation of s 5 of the Mercantile Law Amendment Act 1856. Although the Act had been repealed in Ireland some time prior to Murphy J's decision,[206] its repeal at least in regard to s 5 (the subrogation right) may not have changed the law applying in Ireland as the section essentially codified the subrogation principles applicable in 1856 under common law and which should still be applicable under Irish common law today. This principle can be seen from Lord Blackburn's decision in *Duncan, Fox & Co v North and South Wales Bank*[207] where he stated:[208]

---

203. *Ibid* at 175; curiously the judge held also that the security held by the Minister did not affect his statutory right of subrogation pursuant to s 5 of the Mercantile Law Amendment Act 1856 notwithstanding the earlier repeal of that Act.
204. [1993] 1 IR 190.
205. [1894] 3 Ch 400.
206. See paras **[9.05]** and **[9.57]**.
207. (1880) 6 App Cas 1.
208. *Ibid* at 19.

"I think it is established by the case of *Derring v Lord Winchelsea* (1787) 2 B
& P 270 and the observations on that case by Lord Eldon in *Craythorne v
Swinburne* (1807) 14 Ves 165, and Lord Redesdale in *Stirling v Forrester*
(1821) 3 Bli 575, that where a creditor has a right to come upon more than one
person or fund for the payment of a debt, there is an equity between the persons
interested in the different funds that each shall bear no more than its due
proportion".

[9.63] The exercise of the subrogation rights does not entail a consideration of
the state of accounts as between co-guarantors. In *Brown v Cork*[209] the English
Court of Appeal held that monies which have been realised from the
enforcement of joint and several guarantees and the proceeds placed in a
suspense account, pending the discharge of the debt, should be distributed
amongst the guarantors, pursuant to their subrogation rights in a just proportion
to which they contributed.[210] The Court held that these monies should be
distributed regardless of any right of set-off which the co-guarantors may have
amongst themselves.

[9.64] If a guarantor is to seek a right of subrogation in respect of any payment
made by him, it is important that the guarantor indicates clearly when making
the payment that he is making the payment pursuant to his guarantee. This
would avoid the consequences of the decision in *Re Peake's Abattoirs Ltd.*[211] In
that case, the proceeds of sale of a mortgaged premises owned by the guarantor
were used by the bank to clear the borrower's indebtedness and the surplus used
to discharge the borrower's creditors. The court held that the proceeds were lent
to the borrower by the guarantor and there was no basis on which the guarantor
could be subrogated to the bank's security.

[9.65] The decision in *Re Peake's Abattoirs Ltd*[212] is a reminder that a right of
subrogation accrues to a person who makes a payment pursuant to its liability
under a guarantee and will not arise where the person has an interest in the
transaction which is distinct from that of a guarantor. In considering whether the
plaintiff was entitled to a right of subrogation in *Huggard v The Representative
Church Body*,[213] O'Connor MR stated:[214]

"the test of a contract of suretyship is not to be found in its result in discharging
the liability of another, but in its main object being to secure another's debt, in

---

[209.] [1985] BCLC 363.
[210.] Although the court applied the Mercantile Law Amendment Act 1856, s 5 it seems clear that
these principles apply at common law in Ireland.
[211.] [1986] BCLC 73.
[212.] *Ibid.*
[213.] [1916] 1 IR 1.
[214.] *Ibid* at 13.

the payment of which the promisor has no interest, and for which he has no liability except such as attaches by reason of the promise to pay. If the promisor has himself an interest in the transaction, he is more than a guarantor - he is a principal debtor".

[9.66] The development of private banking in Ireland over the 1990s has sprung from an increasing number of individuals commanding remuneration levels commensurate with their contribution to the significant growth and development of the Irish economy. The time demands on such individuals and the diminishing influence of the Roman Catholic Church in Irish life, have, amongst other reasons, resulted in a sudden rise in the number of individuals living separately from their spouses. The significance of this phenomenon for guarantees is the increased likelihood of a question arising as to whether the discharge by one spouse pursuant to a guarantee of a debt by the other spouse is to be treated as an advancement by the guarantor for the benefit of his spouse or as a subrogation right entitling the guarantor to take whatever steps the bank could have taken against the spouse. While it may be argued such a question should not arise between spouses who are legally separated, it may be foreseen that such a question could arise in one of the many cases where spouses lead separate lives without being lawfully separated.

[9.67] This question was considered some time ago in the English courts in the case of *Anson v Anson*.[215] In that case a bank account was opened in the wife's name for housekeeping expenses, the husband giving the wife cheques for this account. Some of these payments were lodged by the wife to her personal account; the wife requested the husband to guarantee the housekeeping account which he did. When the parties divorced, the bank demanded payment from the wife who refused and then from the husband who paid under the guarantee. When the husband sought recovery from the wife she claimed the transaction was in the nature of an advancement. Pearson J explained how advancement would operate in the case of a bank guarantee:[216]

> "it must be understood as meaning that there was an intention that the husband should not have the right of reimbursement. For advancement to be presumed in such a transaction it would have to be interpreted as a transaction of a very special character, in that, although the husband gives a guarantee of his wife's account, there is a special arrangement, expressed or implied, between him and his wife whereby he is expected to bear the liability and is not expected, or entitled, if he is called upon to pay and does pay, afterwards to claim reimbursement".

The court held that on the facts the guarantee was given not to relieve the wife of

---

[215.] [1953] 1 QB 636.
[216.] *Ibid* at 641.

her obligations to the bank, but to resolve an immediate emergency, with the intention that the transaction would have the ordinary incidents of a guarantee and thus the wife was liable to reimburse the husband.

The rationale for the concept of reimbursement by the debtor to the guarantor was explained by Pearson J in the following manner:[217]

> "The essence of the matter ... is that the debt is the debt of the principal debtor and so remains, and therefore when the surety is called upon to pay the position has to be put right between the parties so that the liability comes once more to be the liability of the principal debtor."

CO-GUARANTOR'S CONTRIBUTION

[9.68] It was settled over 200 years ago[218] that where there are a number of guarantors for a certain amount, each covenanting by a separate instrument, there is a right of contribution between them.[219] This is to be distinguished from the position where guarantors are bound by different instruments for equal portions of a debt due from the same principal; here each guarantor's covenant is a separate and distinct transaction and there is no right of contribution between them.[220] The right of one co-guarantor to sue the other for contribution arises only when he has paid more than his share in which event he will have the right to be reimbursed whatever he has paid beyond his share.[221] This principle was applied in *Ex p Snowdown; in Re Snowdown*[222] where one of two co-guarantors paid half the debt and sought a contribution. The Court of Appeal held that until a guarantor paid more than his proportion of the debt due by the debtor, he is not entitled to call on his co-guarantor for contribution even where the co-guarantor has not been called upon by the creditor to pay anything.

In *Wolmershausen v Gullick*[223] it was held that a guarantor against whom judgment was obtained by the creditor for the full amount of the guarantee, but who paid nothing, could maintain an action against a co-guarantor to compel him to contribute towards the common liability.

---

217. *Ibid* at 643.
218. *Dering v Lord Winchelsea* (1787) 1 Cox 318.
219. See also *Scholefield Goodman & Sons Ltd v Zyngier* [1985] 3 All ER 105; the Australian courts have extended this principle to letters of comfort, see *Capital Financial Group Ltd v Rothwells Ltd* [1994] 5 JIBL N-96.
220. *Coope v Twynam* (1823) Turn & R 426.
221. *Davies v Humphreys* (1840) 6 M & W 153, following Lord Eldon's decision in *Ex p Giffort* (1802) 6 Ves 805.
222. (1881) 17 Ch D 44.
223. (1893) 2 Ch 514.

It seems a guarantor who brings an action against a co-guarantor for contribution must join the principal debtor in the action (unless the principal debtor is insolvent).[224]

DISCHARGE OF GUARANTOR

> "It is a truism of banking that guarantees are the easiest form of security to take and the most difficult to realise, as there are various ways in which a guarantor may avoid liability."[225]

Non-Existence of Subject Matter

[9.69] There is an implied condition precedent to a guarantee that the subject matter of the guarantee exists.[226] This condition precedent will be implied even where the guarantor "unconditionally" guarantees payment of a debt.[227] Thus it is important to realise that a replacement of the principal debt by another whether through release or novation will discharge the guarantor.[228] In recent years finance leases have become a common source by which corporate bodies raise money.[229] The capital allowances which the bank can avail of make it an attractive form of finance both for the bank and the user of the leased asset. Accordingly, a corporate entity may be able to acquire its equipment through a finance lease at a cheaper rate than through a purchase with borrowed money. The banker may wish to have the lease payments guaranteed. The banker may not see the leased asset as it is chosen by the user, the lessee. A guarantee in respect of lease payments will be unenforceable if there is in fact no asset leased.[230] Nor can the guarantor be bound in such a case by a standard clause in the guarantee to the effect that the guarantor is liable as a primary obligor as such a clause purports to apply where the principal debtor has a defence to recovery.[231] Accordingly, it is essential for bankers to actually ensure that what they are financing does in fact exist and is the subject matter of the lease with the end user.

---

224. *Hay v Carter* [1935] 1 Ch 397.

225. *Legal Decisions Affecting Bankers* Vol 11 p 111.

226. De Colyar's *Law of Guarantees and of Principal and Surety* (3rd ed) p 210.

227. As in *Associated Japanese Bank (International) Ltd v Credit du Nord SA* [1988] 3 All ER 902; for a suggested redrafting of guarantees in the light of that decision see *Credit & Finance Law* Vol 4 (1992) 59.

228. *Commercial Bank of Tasmania v Jones* [1893] AC 313 where there was a novation of the principal debt - the guarantor was discharged although he had agreed that his guarantee would remain in place until he executed a new one.

229. See Explanatory Memorandum to the Borrowing Powers of Certain Bodies Bill, 1996.

230. *Associated Japanese Bank (International) Ltd v Credit du Nord SA* [1988] 3 All ER 902.

231. *Ibid per* Styn J at 914.

Mispresentation

> "The language employed in banking transactions may sometimes be unenlightening as to the legal consequences which flow from them."[232]

Misrepresentation as to Debtor's Account

[9.70] A banker should take care to avoid any misrepresentation on its part being made to a guarantor concerning the account of the principal debtor prior to execution of the guarantee. In *Westminster Bank Ltd v Cond*[233] it was held that the bank manager was under no duty to disclose to a potential guarantor the existence of a subsisting overdraft of the principal debtor:[234] "Mere non-disclosure of a material fact is not sufficient to give relief".[235] However, Tucker J considered:[236]

> "it is also clear that it is the duty of a bank manager, when he is asked a specific question, to give a true, honest, and accurate answer to any question which is directed to him which can be in any way material to the giving of the guarantee."

Paget makes the valid point though that a banker can simply decline to answer a question put to him by the guarantor.[237]

Misrepresentation as to Nature of Guarantee

[9.71] Bankers should note that where they do explain the nature and effect of a guarantee to a guarantor, the banker should be careful to avoid misstating the effect of the guarantee. The consequences of a misstatement can be seen from the English Court of Appeal's decision in *Cornish v Midland Bank plc*.[238] In that case, a customer had executed a mortgage following an explanation from the bank that the mortgage was like a building society mortgage (by being limited to the initial advance). The mortgage in fact secured further advances. The court declined to set aside the mortgage on the ground of undue influence as there was no evidence that the bank had taken advantage of the mortgagor. However, the court also held that in explaining the mortgage to the mortgagor the bank owed her a duty of care and as a result of its negligence in discharging that duty would be liable to pay damages to the mortgagor in respect of her losses.[239]

[232.] Costello J in *O'Keeffe v O'Flynn Exhams and Partners and Allied Irish Banks* High Court, unrep, 31 July 1992 at p 21.
[233.] (1940) 5 LDAB 263.
[234.] See also *Lloyds Bank Ltd v Harrison* (1925) 4 LDAB 12.
[235.] (1940) 5 LDAB 263 at 270 *per* Tucker J.
[236.] *Ibid*
[237.] *Paget's Law of Banking* (11th ed) p 628.
[238.] [1985] 3 All ER 513.
[239.] On the duty of banks to offer advice see Business Law Review June 1986 p 178.

[9.72] A similar position arose in *MacKenzie v Royal Bank of Canada*[240] where a woman hypothecated shares to a bank in support of her guarantee to secure the indebtedness of her husband's company. She received no independent advice and claimed she had been subject to undue influence by her husband. The Privy Council did not consider that there was any onus on the bank to procure independent advice and that her will was not overborne by that of her husband. However, as the bank had incorrectly informed her, the shares were effectively already hypothecated, the bank had misrepresented the position - a misrepresentation of fact. Accordingly, the transaction was set aside - "A contract of guarantee, like any other contract, is liable to be avoided if induced by material misrepresentation of an existing fact, even if made innocently."[241]

[9.73] There is authority for the proposition that a bank should disclose any unusual features of a transaction or of the account being guaranteed as non-disclosure may amount to a misrepresentation sufficient to have the guarantee set aside.[242]

[9.74] The danger in allowing the debtor explain the nature of the guarantee to a guarantor can be seen from the Court of Appeal's decision in *Carlisle and Cumberland Banking Co v Bragg*.[243] In that case, the bank was unable to enforce the guarantee as a result of the debtor informing the guarantor that the guarantee agreement related to an insurance proposal. This decision has since been overruled in England (in *Saunders v Anglia Building Society*[244]) on the grounds that:

> "if ... a person signs a document because he negligently failed to read it, ... he is precluded from relying on his own negligent act for the purpose of escaping from the ordinary consequences of his signature ... this is an ... illustration of the principle that no man may take advantage of his own wrong."[245]

While this statement seems eminently sensible, it is questionable whether an Irish court would have held the covenantor liable bearing in mind that she was a 78 year old widow who could not read the document as she had broken her spectacles and was misled into believing the document purported to have an effect different to what it was.

---

[240]. [1934] AC 468.

[241]. *Ibid* at 475.

[242]. Gibbs CJ in *The Commercial Bank of Australia Ltd v Amadio* (1983) 151 CLR 447.

[243]. [1911] 1 KB 489.

[244]. [1970] 3 All ER 961.

[245]. [1969] 1 All ER 1062 at 1081 *per* Salmon LJ (Court of Appeal) - approved by Lord Pearson (House of Lords) [1970] 3 All ER 961 at 982.

Non-Execution by all Joint and Several Guarantors

[9.75] Unless otherwise agreed, a guarantee given by more than one party on a joint and several basis will be unenforceable unless all guarantors execute and deliver the guarantee.[246] Although at first sight this may seem odd in the sense that any person signing a joint and several guarantee should be aware that he could be liable for the whole debt, the rationale for the rule is that a person signing such a guarantee is doing so on the basis that the other named guarantors will also be signing and it is a material alteration of the contract to change that arrangement without the guarantor's consent. A good illustration of this rule is the case of *Fitzgerald v McCowan*.[247] In that case six of the seven joint and several guarantors signed the guarantee. Some payments were made under the guarantee and it then transpired that one of the guarantors, who had been out of the country, had not signed. It transpired also that this person was insolvent and would not have been able to make any payments under the guarantee if requested. Nevertheless, the court held that the guarantors could revoke the guarantee as they had signed it on the basis that all seven were going to sign. Johnson J said:[248]

> "it has been long well settled that a deed sealed and delivered, even by the party himself, on such a condition is not operative as a deed, or binding on the person who has so sealed and delivered it until the condition is performed. It is not essential that this should be so expressed in words.
>
> ... Parties of the same part usually execute the instrument when it is tendered to them or when it is convenient, on the faith that it will be duly executed by all the necessary parties and not necessarily in the order in which the draughtsman happens to have arranged their names".

[9.76] Essentially, it came down to a misrepresentation by the person taking the guarantee which entitled the guarantors who had signed the contract to revoke it.[249] Accordingly, a banker on taking delivery of an executed guarantee should be mindful of the words of the Master of the Rolls:[250]

> "Where a surety had executed a document in the belief derived from the form of the document that it would be executed by all the sureties named as such in the document as persons who were to sign, he would be relieved from his obligation if all the others did not sign".

[246.] See *Evans v Bremridge* (1856) 8 De GM & G 100; *Hansard v Lethbridge* [1892] 8 TLR 346; *The National Provincial Bank of England v Brackenburg* (1906) 22 TLR 797; *James Graham & Co (Timber) Ltd v Southgage Sands* [1985] 2 All ER 344.

[247.] [1898] 2 IR 1.

[248.] *Ibid* at 8.

[249.] See also *Marston v Griffith and Co Pty Ltd* [1985] 3 NSWLR 294.

[250.] Lord Esher in *Hansard v Lethbridge* (1892) 8 TLR 346 at 347.

This rule applies even where the only non-signing guarantor is taken ill and dies before signing.[251] However, in practice guarantees will usually counteract the effect of this decision by specifically providing in its terms that the guarantors are bound notwithstanding the failure of one or more guarantors to sign the guarantee. The bank or other recipient is not obliged to sign although as a matter of practice it generally does sign.

[9.77] The desirability for a banker to know his guarantors and to be present (or to have a reliable witness to be present) at the time they sign was highlighted in *James Graham & Co (Timber) Ltd v Southgate Sands*.[252] In that case, unknown to the creditor, the signature of one of the joint and several guarantors was forged. The English Court of Appeal held that since there was no contract of guarantee unless all the anticipated guarantors signed, the liability of the joint guarantor under the guarantee was discharged.[253]

[9.78] An example of a simple alteration which rendered the guarantee worthless can be seen from the case of *Ellesmere Brewery Company v Cooper*.[254] In that case, four persons agreed to give a joint and several guarantee for £150, but each guarantor's liability was to be limited to a specified amount - £25 each in the case of two guarantors and £50 each in the case of the other two. The final signatory to the guarantee changed his limit from £50 to £25 and then delivered the guarantee. The court held that the alteration was a material one and the other guarantors were thus discharged; furthermore as a result of their discharge the fourth guarantor was discharged as well.

[9.79] Similarly, the release of one of a number of joint and several guarantors will have the effect of releasing all the guarantors.[255] However, the release of one of a number of several guarantors will not discharge the guarantee of the others, unless the others can show they should have had a right of contribution from the released guarantor which they have lost by the release.[256]

Non-Execution by all Several Guarantors

[9.80] The rule highlighted in *Fitzgerald v McCowan*[257] is to be distinguished from the situation where there is more than one guarantor but each guarantor is

---

[251.] As happened in *The National Provincial Bank of England v Brackenburg* (1906) 22 TLR 797.

[252.] [1985] 2 All ER 344.

[253.] The forgery of a correction in the name of the principal debtor in the guarantee has been held not to discharge the guarantor on the ground that the error as to misdescription was immaterial - *Lombard Finance Ltd v Brookplain Trading Ltd* [1991] 2 All ER 762 see para **[9.12]**.

[254.] [1896] 1 QB 75; applied by Costello J in *Lombard and Ulster Banking Ltd v The Governor and Company of the Bank of Ireland and Brookhouse School* High Court, unrep, 2 June 1987.

[255.] *Mercantile Bank of Sydney v Taylor* [1893] AC 317.

[256.] *Ward v The National Bank of New Zealand Ltd* (1883) 8 App Cas 755.

[257.] [1898] 2 IR 1 - see para **[9.75]** above.

to be severally, but not jointly and severally, liable for up to a specific amount.[258] In *Byblos Bank SAL v Al-Khudhairy*,[259] the bank issued a facility letter offering a company a credit facility of £3 million secured by, *inter alia*, a personal guarantee from the defendant for up to £1.6 million and a personal guarantee from Mr Al Bunnia for £1.1 million. The defendant executed his guarantee but Mr Bunnia did not execute his. Following the appointment of a receiver to the company, the defendant sought leave to defend on the grounds that the transaction envisaged the other guarantee would be given and since this was not obtained he should be released from his guarantee. The English Court of Appeal held that, notwithstanding the terms of the facility letter (as between the bank and the company), there was no express or implied term as between the bank and the defendant that the defendant's liability under the guarantee was dependant on Mr Bunnia executing his guarantee. The Court held that it would be necessary to find such a term before the defendant could be discharged from his guarantee.[260]

[9.81] Lawyers advising a guarantor in such circumstances should take note from the foregoing decision that it should be specifically agreed as between the guarantor and the bank that as a condition for giving the guarantee the other security envisaged will be taken by the bank. Guarantors and their advisers should heed the words of Purchas LJ in the English Court of Appeal's decision in *TCB Ltd v Gray*[261] where he said:[262]

> "... where a guarantor wishes to make his guarantee dependent on the giving of some other valid collateral security by a third party he must establish that this formed part of the contract under which the guarantee was given ... In the absence of it being established by the guarantor that the taking of a valid collateral security is a term of the contract between him and the lender, the guarantor cannot rely on the failure of the lender to provide himself with a valid collateral security, although he may have indicated he was going to do so. Moreover, for such a term of the contract of guarantee to be established not only must it be intended subjectively by the guarantor but it must also be brought home to and accepted by the lender."

[258.] This type of guarantee arrangement is less frequent than joint and several guarantees.

[259.] [1987] BCLC 232.

[260.] The court did consider that the circumstances did not rule out "the prospect, shadowy though it is" that some other material fact might emerge and thus the defendant was given leave to defend.

[261.] [1988] 1 All ER 108.

[262.] *Ibid* at 113.

Partnerships

[9.82] As a partnership is not a separate legal entity, a guarantee of a partnership debt shall, in the absence of agreement to the contrary, be revoked as to future transactions by any change in the constitution of the partnership, that is, the partners.[263] The same applies where the recipient of the guarantee is a partnership.[264] The Partnership Act 1890 in fact codifies the common law on this point namely, that unless otherwise agreed a guarantee is revoked, if the constitution of the principal debtor or beneficiary changes, for example if the principal debtor or the beneficiary amalgamates with another company.[265]

However, it appears that although partners are jointly and severally liable for the debts of the firm (to which they are a partner),[266] the Partnership Act 1890 is silent as to the consequences of a change in the constitution of a partnership which is a guarantor. The prudent course is to provide as a term of the guarantee that a change in the constitution of the principal debtor or beneficiary or guarantor, will not affect the guarantor's liability under the guarantee.

Breach of Covenant

[9.83] By having a guarantee executed under seal, the possibility is not excluded that the guarantee may nonetheless be unenforceable by the bank for breach of covenant. A costly example of this for the bank can be seen from the decision in *Hoon v Bank of Nova Scotia*.[267] In that case the judge of first instance held that the guarantee was enforceable.[268] This decision was upheld by a majority of the British Columbia Court of Appeal[269] before being overruled by a majority of the Supreme Court of Canada.[270] In that case, Hoon had guaranteed debts "in consideration of the bank agreeing to deal with the principal debtors in the way of its business as a bank". The bank then sought further security and a settlement was entered into whereby the bank agreed to postpone payment for a year on receipt of an additional guarantee and tangible security. Following the expiration of the one year period, the bank sought to enforce its security against the guarantor. In rejecting the bank's claim, the Canadian Supreme Court followed the dissenting judgment of Bull JA in the British Columbia Court of Appeal. Bull JA considered that it was the bank's intention from the beginning to call in the debt and the temporary postponement negotiated only on receipt of

---

[263] Partnership Act, 1890, s 18.
[264] *Ibid.*
[265] See *Wright v Russell* (1774) 3 Wils KB 530; *Myers v Edge* (1797) 7 TR 254.
[266] Partnership Act 1890, s 9.
[267] (1966) 56 DLR (2d) 598.
[268] 41 DLR (2d) 558.
[269] (1965) 53 DLR (2d) 239.
[270] (1966) 56 DLR (2d) 598.

further security could not be said to constitute a dealing with its customer "in the way of its business as a bank"; the guarantee could not be enforced as the guarantor's agreement was conditional on the bank performing its covenant under the guarantee which it had failed to do. The particular concern for banks to note here is that the guarantee was executed under seal - thus it was not the absence or insufficiency of consideration, but the breach of covenant by the bank which discharged the guarantor.

Debtor Given Time

"Where a man is surety at law for the debt of another, payable at a given day, if the obligee defeats the condition of the bond, he discharges the security."[271]

[9.84] An agreement by a bank to give time to the principal debtor to discharge the debt beyond the term originally agreed will release the guarantor[272] (unless the guarantor has agreed otherwise[273]). This release will apply even where it is shown that the extension of time was granted only due to the principal debtor's inability to pay his debt on time and the guarantor has not suffered by the extension of time.[274] The rationale for this principle was explained by Eldon LC:[275]

"The rule is this - that, if a creditor, without the consent of the surety, gives time to the principal debtor, by so doing he discharges the surety; that is, if time is given by virtue of positive contract between the creditor and the principal - not where the creditor is merely inactive. And, in the case put, the surety is held to be discharged, for this reason, because the creditor, by so giving time to the principal, has put it out of the power of the surety to consider whether he will have recourse to his remedy against the principal, or not, and because he, in fact, cannot have the same remedy against the principal as he would have had under the original contract".

With regard to the suggestion that the extension of time benefits the surety, Lord Eldon stated:[276]

---

271. The Lord Chancellor in *Rees v Berrington* (1795) 2 Ves Jun 540 at 542.
272. *Provincial Bank of Ireland v Fisher* [1918] 2 IR 521 and [1919] 2 IR 249; *Nisbet v Smith* (1789) 2 Bro CC 579; *Bolton v Buckenham* (1891) 1 QB 278; *Rouse v The Bradford Banking Company Ltd* (1894) AC 586; see also Cotton LJ in *Holme v Brunskill* (1877) 3 QBD 495 at 505.
273. The guarantee itself will, or should, provide that time may be given to the principal debtor without discharging the guarantor - see *The Encyclopaedia of Forms and Precedents* (5th ed) Vol 17(2) Butterworths.
274. *Samuel v Howarth* (1817) 3 Mer 272.
275. *Ibid* at 278.
276. *Ibid* at 279.

"but the law has said that the surety shall be the judge of that, and that he alone has the right to determine whether it is, or is not, for his benefit. The creditor has no right - it is against the faith of his contract - to give time to the principal, even though manifestly for the benefit of the surety, without the consent of the surety."

[9.85] Where the bank grants time to the principal debtor, in the absence of a clause in the guarantee permitting the bank to do so, the onus will be on the bank to prove that the guarantor had consented. Obviously, this can be a fruitful source of argument for lawyers as in *Provincial Bank of Ireland v Fisher*[277] where a majority of the Irish Court of Appeal overruled the High Court's decision in favour of the bank.[278] In considering the nature of the evidence to support the bank's contention that consent was given, Moloney LJ stated:[279]

"knowledge of time having been given is not, *per se*, enough. There must be either direct evidence of consent or evidence from which a jury might reasonably infer it."

[9.86] The granting of time must be distinguished from mere forbearance to sue which in itself does not discharge the guarantor. In *Eyre v Everett*[280] the beneficiary of a bond allowed five years to elapse from the time the bond became payable to the time action for recovery was instigated. During that time the principal debtor became insolvent and left the jurisdiction. In rejecting the plaintiff's contention that the delay was a sufficient reason as to why the bond should not be enforced, Lord Eldon stated:[281]

"The case, therefore, presents nothing more than the passive act of the obligees not suing. But the surety has no right to say that he is discharged from the debt which he has engaged to pay, together with the principal, if all that he rests upon is the passive conduct of the creditor in not suing. He must himself use diligence, and take such effectual means as will enable him to call on the creditor either to sue, or to give him, the surety, the means of suing".

Thus, it is not open to a guarantor to be discharged from its guarantee simply because the bank is dilatory in pressing the principal debtor for payment of the guaranteed debt.[282] However, a guarantor may be able to obtain a court order compelling performance of the guaranteed contract where delay is putting the guarantor's position in jeopardy.[283]

[277.] [1918] 2 IR 521.

[278.] The bank appealed to the House of Lords which unanimously upheld the majority decision of the Irish Court of Appeal [1919] 2 IR 249.

[279.] [1918] 2 IR 521 at 559.

[280.] (1826) 2 Russ 381.

[281.] *Ibid* at 384.

[282.] *Clarke v Birley* (1889) 41 Ch D 422.

[283.] *Hibernian Fire Insurance Co v Dargan* [1941] IR 514.

Guarantor Not Informed of Debtor's Default

[9.87] In *O'Connor v Sorahan*[284] it was decided by the President of the High Court and unanimously by the Supreme Court that a delay on the part of a creditor in informing the guarantor of the debtor's default will not affect the guarantor's agreement to honour his guarantee. While the case involved a landlord and tenant, the Supreme Court judgments indicated clearly the same principles would apply to bankers' advances. In that case the tenant was eight months in arrears on his monthly payments before the guarantor was informed of the tenant's default. The guarantor's claim that only one month's rent should be payable by him was dismissed. Kennedy CJ stated:[285]

> "In the absence of express stipulation for notice, there is not, in my opinion, any equity which confers upon the guarantor an unqualified right to notice of each default in payment of the debts guaranteed".

Fitzgibbon J, in his judgment, alluded to what the guarantor should do to protect himself:[286]

> "There is no room for the application of the equitable doctrine of laches to such a liability. It is in the power of the guarantor to protect himself against an accumulation of indebtedness by making inquiries of his principal from time to time, and by calling upon him to make good any default which has occurred."

[9.88] A bank should beware that if the guarantee, following negotiation of its terms, stipulates that notice of the principal debtor's default is to be given to the guarantor within a stipulated time, the failure to give such notice should a default arise will render the guarantee worthless. In *Eshelby v Federated European Bank Ltd*,[287] it was held by the English Court of Appeal in such circumstances the guarantor's actual liability became operative on the serving of such notice and the failure to do so within the stipulated time meant that the guarantor's liability never became operative.

Non-Compliance with Statutory Procedure

[9.89] It is essential for advisers, when advising on guarantees, to ensure that the statutory procedure under which a guarantee may be issued or enforced must be complied with. Failure to follow any such procedure correctly may result in the guarantor being discharged with unhappy consequences for the recipient of the guarantee and/or its adviser.[288] This is of particular relevance with regard to

---

[284.] [1933] IR 591.
[285.] *Ibid* at 603.
[286.] *Ibid* at 605.
[287.] [1932] 1 KB 423.
[288.] See *Mahon v Irish National Insurance Co Ltd* (1958) XXIV Ir Jur R 41; but see also the Supreme Court in *Wicklow County Council v Hibernian Fire and General Insurance Co* [1932] IR 581.

consumer loans, where statute specifically stipulates that failure to comply with certain requirements renders the guarantee unenforceable.[289]

Material Variation in Contract

[9.90] A material variation in the contract between the bank and the debtor (in respect of which the debtor's obligation is guaranteed by the guarantor) will, without the guarantor's consent, discharge the guarantor.[290] The rationale for this is that a variation in the contract between the bank and the debtor is effectively a change in the contract between the bank and the guarantor.[291] It seems that, to discharge the guarantor, the variation should be a material one.[292] This of course can give rise to dispute as to whether a variation is or is not material;[293] thus uncertainty can arise for persons involved in guarantees or advising on them. In *Holme v Brunskill*[294] the plaintiff agreed to let a farm and 700 sheep upon the defendant's guarantee that the flock would be re-delivered in good order and condition. Subsequently, a field forming part of the farm was taken out of the tenancy, without the guarantor's consent. Upon the termination of the tenancy the flock had reduced in number and condition. The Court of Appeal decided, by a majority, that the guarantor should have been requested to assent to the variation and not having been so requested his guarantee was discharged. Whether the alteration was material was a matter for the surety. Cotton LJ explained the position as follows:[295]

> "The true rule in my opinion is, that if there is any agreement between the principals with reference to the contract guaranteed, the surety ought to be consulted, and that if he has not consented to the alteration, although in cases where it is without inquiry evident that the alteration is unsubstantial, or that it cannot be otherwise than beneficial to the surety, the surety may not be discharged; yet, that if it is not self-evident that the alteration is unsubstantial, or one which cannot be prejudicial to the surety, the Court, will not, in an action against the surety, go into an inquiry as to the effect of the alteration, or allow the question, whether the surety is discharged or not, to be determined by

---

[289.] Consumer Credit Act, 1995 s 38.

[290.] See Murphy J in *The UDT Bank Ltd v Startbrite Ltd* High Court, unrep, 20 April 1993 p 4.

[291.] See Gavan Duffy J in *Jackson v Hayes* (1939) Ir Jur R 59 at 62.

[292.] "A material variation means any variation which cannot be seen without inquiry to be insubstantial, or one which cannot be otherwise than beneficial to the surety" *per* Esson JA in *Alberta Opportunity Co v Zen* (1984) 6 DLR (4th) 620 at 640; in *Jackson v Hayes* (1939) Ir Jur R 59 the High Court held that an agreement which was varied did not discharge the guarantor as it was manifest without inquiry that the variation did not injure the guarantor.

[293.] See the split decisions in *Holme v Brunskill* (1877) 3 QBD 495; *Burnes v Trade Credits Ltd* [1981] 2 All ER 122 and *Alberta Opportunity Co v Zen* (1984) 6 DLR (4th) 620.

[294.] (1877) 3 QBD 495.

[295.] *Ibid* at 505; followed by Gavan Duffy J in *Jackson v Hayes* (1939) Ir Jur R 59 at 62; see also Chitty J in *Bolton v Salmon* [1891] 2 Ch 48 at 54.

the finding of a jury as to the materiality of the alteration or on the question whether it is to the prejudice of the surety, but will hold that in such a case the surety himself must be the sole judge whether or not he will consent to remain liable notwithstanding the alteration, and that if he has not so consented he will be discharged."

Brett LJ, dissenting, felt the difference to be neither material nor substantial concluding,[296] "The doctrine of the release of suretyship is carried far enough, and to the verge of sense". More recently the English Court of Appeal held that a guarantor will be discharged only where the variation was 'not unsubstantial'.[297] The clear warning is for banks to ensure that under the terms of a guarantee, a variation can be made without the specific consent of the guarantor; or if this is precluded, no variation is made at all to avoid the cost of litigation and the uncertainty of a decision of the courts, as to whether the variation was "not unsubstantial".

[9.91] A guarantor's consent will be needed where the duration of a bank facility is extended with a new rate of interest. In *Burnes v Trade Credits Ltd*,[298] the guarantee provided that (1) "any further advances" were to be covered by the guarantee and (2) the creditor was entitled to grant the debtor time or "any other indulgence or consideration" without obtaining the guarantors' consent. At the end of the term the creditor and debtor agreed to extend the term for a year and increased the rate of interest from 9 per cent to 16 per cent. The New South Wales Court of Appeal held that the guarantors were liable on the grounds that the increased interest was a further advance. The Privy Council thought otherwise and held that the term "advance" normally meant the furnishing of money for some specified purpose and the reference to "further advances" meant the lending of an additional principal sum. The claim against the guarantors was not permitted as the effect of the change was to impose an additional liability without their consent.

[9.92] As a matter of practice a bank will ensure that the guarantor's consent is given by virtue of the terms of the guarantee itself.[299] An example of a successful exclusion clause can be seen from the case of *Perry v National Provincial Bank of England*[300] where the security stipulated that the bank could without affecting its rights vary, exchange or release other securities held and "compound with,

---

[296.] *Ibid* at 509.

[297.] *National Westminster Bank plc v Riley* [1986] BCLC 268 (in this case the bank breached the underlying contract with the company but the breach was of a non-repudiatory nature).

[298.] [1981] 2 All ER 122.

[299.] For precedent guarantees see *The Encyclopaedia of Forms and Precedents* (5th ed) Vol 17(2) Butterworths.

[300.] [1910] 1 Ch 464.

give time for payment of, and accept compositions from, and make any arrangement with the debtors or any of them." When the bank discharged the principal debtor in exchange for debentures of a lower amount than what was due to the bank, the guarantor contended that as the debt was discharged so was his secondary liability as guarantor. The Court of Appeal held that the guarantor was still liable for the balance, Cozens Hardy MR stated:[301]

> "it is perfectly possible for a surety to contract with a creditor in the suretyship instrument that notwithstanding any composition, release or arrangement, the surety shall remain liable although the principal does not".

[9.93] The decision of *Holme v Brunskill*[302] was accepted by the Supreme Court in *MacEnroe v Allied Irish Banks Ltd*[303] to the effect that neither a principal debtor nor a bank could make any alteration in the terms of a guaranteed contract unfavourable to the interests of a guarantor without his consent. In that case the guarantor guaranteed debts and liabilities of the company on current account or otherwise. Hamilton J held that the guarantee was discharged by the opening of a third account with the bank. The Supreme Court unanimously allowed the bank's appeal as the guarantee was expressed to be "for any ultimate balance that shall remain unpaid by the Company to you". The court held that as the guarantee did not relate to specific accounts the opening of the third account was not a material variation of the guaranteed contract.[304]

Introduction of the Euro

[9.94] The introduction of the Euro, apart from envisaging a change in the currency of the sum being guaranteed, may result in a change in the base rate of interest from, for example, DIBOR to EURIBOR. However, the impact of the Euro, notwithstanding the consequential variations in the guarantee will not have the effect of "discharging or excusing performance" under the guarantee.[305]

Discharge of Contract

[9.95] The acceptance by the bank of a repudiation of a contract by the principal debtor will not in itself discharge the guarantor's obligation in respect of that contract. The House of Lords set out the courts' approach on this principle in *Moschi v Lep Air Services Ltd*[306] where it held that, unless otherwise agreed, the

---

[301.] *Ibid* at 473.

[302.] (1877) 3 QBD 495.

[303.] [1980] ILRM 171.

[304.] The Court distinguished this from the Privy Council's decision in *National Bank of Nigeria Ltd v Oba MS Awolesi* [1964] 1 WLR 1311 where a guarantee which related to one account was discharged by the opening of a second account.

[305.] Council Regulation (EC) No 1103/97 of 17 June 1997 on certain provisions relating to the introduction of the Euro.

[306.] [1972] 2 All ER 393.

guarantor's obligation was to see to it that the principal debtor performed its obligations, a breach of which entitled the creditor to damages.

Failure to Maintain Primary Security

[9.96] At the time a person agrees to give a guarantee, the guarantor will often give the guarantee in the knowledge and expectation that the bank is obtaining, or has obtained, a charge or other form of security over part or all of the principal debtor's property and assets. This raises the question as to what happens, in the absence of any specific agreement on the point, if the bank fails to obtain or maintain the primary security. This question was considered in the case of *The Northern Banking Company Ltd v Newman and Calton*.[307] Hanna J having reviewed the case law,[308] stated:[309]

> "these authorities establish the following propositions of law:
>
> 1. If it is an express or implied condition of, or collateral to, the arrangement for the guarantee, that an existing security, whether inchoate or complete, should be made or kept effective by the creditor for the benefit of the parties as a counter-security, failure to observe that condition discharges the surety absolutely, inasmuch as he has not got the contract he bargained for.
>
> 2. The mere circumstance that at the time that the surety becomes bound there exists to the knowledge of the surety in the possession of the creditor another security, which is available to the creditor, does not make it an implied term of the contract to maintain the same as effective, breach of which entitles the surety to absolute discharge. It must be found by the Court to be an express or implied term of the contract agreed to and understood to be so by both parties.
>
> 3. If it falls short of being a term of, or collateral to, the contract but there is, in fact, in the possession of the creditor, either at the time of the contract or later, such a counter-security as referred to, it is the duty of the creditor, whether its existence is known to the surety or not, to exercise reasonable care in maintaining it for the benefit of the surety, so as to be available, unimpaired by reason of any negligence, on the discharge of the debt. If he fails in this duty, the surety is entitled to credit against his liability for the damages suffered by such breach of duty by the creditor."

Accordingly, Hanna J held that as the bank had failed to make the primary security effective, the guarantors were discharged from liability. Banks usually circumvent the impact of this decision by providing in the guarantee that the

---

[307.] [1927] IR 520.
[308.] *Carter v White* (1880) 25 Ch D 666; *Polak v Everett* (1876) 1 QBD 669; *Pearl v Deacon* (1857) 24 Beav 186; *Taylor v Bank of New South Wales* (1886) 11 App Cas 596.
[309.] [1927] IR 520 at 538.

guarantor's liability shall not be discharged by the primary security becoming invalid or being released by the bank.[310]

[9.97] Although it appears from case law that mere negligence, inactivity or delay by the bank will not absolve the guarantor from liability,[311] where a bank has been grossly negligent a guarantor may be discharged.[312] For a practitioner this is unsatisfactory due to the absence of any clear distinction in civil proceedings between negligence and gross negligence.[313] The safest course is obviously to preclude such a dispute arising by appropriate language in the guarantee.[314]

[9.98] The case of *The UDT Bank Ltd v Startbrite Ltd*[315] is a clear illustration of how appropriate language in a guarantee will exempt a bank from its failure to perfect the primary security. The case highlights the need for guarantors and their advisers to ensure that the primary security is effected for their own benefit.[316] The facts of the case were that the bank made advances to Clare Textiles Ltd a wholly owned subsidiary of the guarantor. The facility letter indicated that a second charge on the borrower's property would be taken. The charge was not taken to the knowledge of the guarantor, but the guarantor contended that the agreement to give security in the facility letter should have been registered pursuant to s 99 of the Companies Act, 1963[317] so as to preserve the guarantor's rights of subrogation.[318] The guarantee provided that the bank was permitted, without discharging the guarantor's liability:

> "To accept, vary, exchange, renew, abstain from perfecting or release any
> security or securities now held or to be held by the Bank for or on account of

---

[310.] See Lingard, *Bank Security Documents* (3rd ed) Document 4 CL 3.02.

[311.] See the Lord Chancellor in *County Council of the County of Donegal v Life and Health Assurance Association* [1909] 2 IR 700 at 716; O'Byrne J in *Fraher v County Council of Waterford* [1926] IR 505 at 513.

[312.] *Fraher v County Council of Waterford* [1926] IR 505.

[313.] "The words "gross negligence" should never be used in connection with any matter to which the common law relates because negligence is a breach of duty, and, if there is a duty and there has been a breach of it which causes loss, it matter not whether it is a venial breach or a serious breach" *per* Lord Godddard in *Pentecost v London District Auditor* [1951] 2 All ER 330 at 333.

[314.] As in *China and South Sea Bank Ltd v Tan* [1989] 3 All ER 839 see para **[9.54]** and *The UDT Bank Ltd v Startbrite Ltd* High Court, unrep, 20 April 1993, Murphy J see para **[9.98]** below; *Credit Lyonnais Australia Ltd v Darling* (1992) JIBFL 130 where the guarantee provided that the guarantee would not be affected by the bank's omission to complete the primary security or where the primary security is void.

[315.] High Court, unrep, 20 April 1993, Murphy J.

[316.] See also *Credit Lyonnais Australia Ltd v Darling* (1992) JIBFL 130 where the primary security was void due to its registration outside the statutory period. Had the security been properly registered the guarantors would not have been called upon.

[317.] See Ch 17.

[318.] See para **[9.57]-[9.67]**.

any monies payable under the loan agreement or other obligations of the borrower."

Murphy J interpreted this language as follows:[319]

"The words 'abstain from perfecting ... any security' would seem to come close to defeating the defendants argument. However, counsel on the defendants behalf contends that the word 'abstain' means a conscious decision not to perform an act and not mere negligence or inactivity. In the absence of any authority I would be reluctant to decide this case on such a fine distinction although I do accept that the word 'abstain' does have the connotation of deliberate and, usually, self-sacrificing, restraint. However, where the word appears in the context which empowers the creditor to make far reaching changes in the securities to which he is or may be entitled, I believe it would be unrealistic to construe it in this restrictive fashion. The creditor is free under Clause 3(3) aforesaid to 'release' a security without reference to the guarantor. He need not 'renew' a mortgage which is renewable and in that case it matters not whether the failure to renew is due to incompetence or a positive decision in that behalf. In those circumstances, it seems to me, that the word 'abstain' would properly be understood as including 'failing to do' a particular act for whatever reason or for no reason."

There was a further additional provision in the guarantee to the effect that the bank had an absolute discretion without or without the guarantor's assent or knowledge:

"To fail to assert or delay in asserting any right or remedy against the borrower or to fail or delay in pursuing any rights or remedies against the borrower".

Murphy J indicated that:[320]

"Whilst it would seem to me that the sub-paragraph dealing expressly with securities might be more appropriate, sub-paragraph 2 in its express terms does of itself give to the creditor the power not to pursue any rights or remedies available to him and those "rights and remedies" would appear to me to include the right to call for the completion of the second legal charge in accordance with the terms of the facility letter or to perfect his right to his equitable charge."

The fact that the guarantor was aware that the second charge was not created and that the duty, although not the practice, of registering a charge pursuant to s 99 of the Companies Act, 1963 rests with the company rather than the bank[321] supported the court's decision in favour of the bank upholding the guarantor's liability.

[319.] Page 6.

[320.] Page 7.

[321.] Companies Act, 1963, s 100.

The concluding words of Murphy J's judgment should be sufficient to impress upon all banks and their advisers as to the need for an appropriate exclusion clause in a guarantee:[322]

"the terms of the guarantee exclude the operation of the established legal principles which would otherwise require the creditor to perfect and maintain a security which was available for their benefit and through them for the guarantors."

Absence of Continuing Security

[9.99] In preparing a guarantee a bank or its adviser should ensure that the rule in *Clayton's Case*[323] will not operate to extinguish or diminish the indebtedness which may be claimed under the guarantee. There are two aspects which need to be covered here namely, first the necessity to provide that the guarantee is "a continuing security" and, secondly that if the guarantee is terminated by notice from the guarantor or his personal representatives or determined by the bank making a demand it should be provided that the guarantor's liability shall remain notwithstanding any subsequent payment into or out of the account made by the principal debtor.

[9.100] The absence of the first provision will mean that any payment made by the principal debtor will reduce the amount of the debt covered by the guarantee and any subsequent advances made by the bank will not be covered by the guarantee (which covers only the actual indebtedness at the time of the guarantee). As explained by Rigby LJ[324] "the effect of that word ["continuing"] is to extend a guarantee beyond the first sum advanced to sums subsequently advanced, so long as the guarantee is continued". This provision, however, will not extend the guarantee to cover a liability not provided for in the covenant clause.[325] Furthermore, it may be overridden by oral evidence to the effect that the guarantee was given for a particular transaction only.[326]

[9.101] The absence of the second provision will necessitate the bank ruling off the principal debtor's account at the time of the termination or determination of the guarantee in order to preserve the guarantor's liability for such amount.

The leading case on the latter point is that of *Westminster Bank Ltd v Cond.*[327] In that case the guarantee contained the following provision:

---

[322] Page 9.
[323] See para **[4.34]** above.
[324] In *Parr's Banking Company Ltd v Yates* [1898] 2 QB 460 at 466.
[325] See *In re Quest Cae Ltd* [1985] BCLC 266.
[326] *Bank of Ireland v McCabe* (1994) Supreme Court, unrep, 19 December see para **[9.14]** above.
[327] (1940) 5 LDAB 263.

"In the event of this guarantee being determined either by notice by me or my legal personal representatives, or by demand in writing by the bank, it shall be lawful for the bank to continue the account with the principal, notwithstanding such determination, and the liability of myself or my estate for the amount due from the principal at the date when the guarantee is so determined shall remain, notwithstanding any subsequent payment into or out of the account by or on behalf of the principal".

Tucker J stated:[328]

"those words are apt to prevent the application of the rule in *Clayton's Case*. I cannot help thinking that they were designed expressly so to do, and I think they have achieved that object."

Were it not for this clause the bank could have found that, having not ruled off the account, the subsequent payments would have discharged the guaranteed debt and the guarantor's obligations would have been thereby discharged.

Irregular Conduct

[9.102] According to the English Court of Appeal there is no general principle that "irregular" conduct on the part of the bank will discharge the guarantor, even if such conduct is prejudicial to the guarantor. The court held in *Bank of India v Trans Continental Commodity Merchants Ltd and Nashbai Nagjibhai Patel*[329] that a guarantee of foreign exchange facilities was not revocable despite the foreign exchange contracts being conducted in an irregular manner. In the High Court Bingham J[330] considered that a guarantor could be discharged:

1. If the bank acts in bad faith,
2. If the bank is guilty of concealment amounting to misrepresentation,
3. If the bank causes or connives at the default by the principal debtor in respect of which the guarantee is given, or
4. If the bank varies the terms of the contract between it and the principal debtor in a way which could prejudice the guarantor's interests.

Alteration of Guarantee

[9.103] It is self-evident that where a guarantee is altered by a bank, subsequent to its execution and delivery by the guarantor, it will be unenforceable against the guarantor as it is no longer evidence of terms agreed by the guarantor. However in *Co-operative Bank plc v Tipper*[331] an alteration made in pencil was

---

[328.] *Ibid* at 273.
[329.] [1982] 1 LLR 506 and [1983] 2 LLR 298.
[330.] [1982] 1 LLR 506 at 515 approved by the Court of Appeal [1983] 2 LLR 298 at 301.
[331.] [1996] 4 All ER 366.

held not to be an alteration.[332] The court decided it did not stop the bank from seeking rectification for the original error.[333]

COURT PROTECTION

[9.104] A person's liability under a guarantee may be diminished where the debtor (whose liabilities to the bank are guaranteed) comes under the protection of the court.[334] Following the appointment of an examiner to a company, during the protection period,[335] a bank is precluded from commencing any proceedings[336] against a guarantor in respect of that company's indebtedness.[337] This provision should be borne in mind by any banker who is proposing to provide banking facilities to a corporate customer solely or primarily on the financial strength of the guarantor.

[9.105] Where a company is given the protection of the court, an examiner will be appointed to the company.[338] An examiner is required to formulate proposals for a compromise or scheme of arrangement where he is of the opinion:[339]

(a) the whole or any part of the undertaking of the company would be capable of survival as a going concern, and

(b) an attempt to continue the whole or any part of the undertaking of the company would be likely to be more advantageous to the members as a whole, and to the creditors as a whole, than a winding-up of the company, and

(c) the formulation, acceptance and confirmation of proposals for a compromise or scheme of arrangement would facilitate such survival.

The proposals, which have to be confirmed by the court who can modify them,[340] invariably involve a write down of the debt due to each creditor, including creditors with the benefit of guarantees.

The court is not permitted to confirm any proposals unless it is satisfied that:[341]

[332.] "It may be an annotation, it may be a suggestion, but it does not actually alter the substance of the document" *per* Judge Cooke at 372.

[333.] The directors who gave the guarantee were described as both the guarantors and the customer.

[334.] Pursuant to the Companies (Amendment) Act, 1990, s 2(1); for further reading see Courtney, *The Law of Private Companies* (1994) Butterworths, Ch 17; Lynch, Marshall and O'Ferrall, *Corporate Insolvency and Rescue* (1996) Butterworths Ch 10.

[335.] The Companies (Amendment) Act, 1990, s 5(1) provides for a period of three months which may be extended to a fourth month or even longer pursuant to ss 18(3) and 18(4) respectively.

[336.] But not from making a demand.

[337.] Companies (Amendment) Act, 1990, s 5(2)(f).

[338.] Pursuant to the Companies (Amendment) Act, 1990, s 2(1).

[339.] Companies (Amendment) Act, 1990, s 18(1).

[340.] Companies (Amendment) Act, 1990, s 24; for a consideration of the procedure involved see the judgment of Hamilton P in *Re Goodman International and Related Companies* (28 January 1991).

[341.] Companies (Amendment) Act, 1990, s 24(4).

    (i)   the proposals are fair and equitable in relation to any class of members or creditors that had not accepted the proposals and whose interests or claims would be impaired by implementation, and

    (ii) the proposals are not unfairly prejudicial to the interests of any interested party.

[9.106] The guarantor's position was considered in two early unreported decisions. In *Re Presswell Ltd*[342] a group of companies came under the protection of the court. In his proposals for a scheme of arrangement the examiner proposed that Ulster Bank would obtain 25 pence in the pound notwithstanding that the debt due to them was personally guaranteed by two guarantors - indeed the bank suggested that the loans had continued on the basis of the guarantees. The scheme envisaged the discharge of these guarantees. The guarantors filed affidavits showing the extent of their assets which consisted primarily of family homes, holiday residences and certain motor vehicles. Murphy J considered that in the event of the guarantees being called upon, the guarantors would have been adjudicated bankrupt and other creditors would have shown an interest in such proceedings. Accordingly, on the basis of the assets available, Murphy J held that the prospects of recovering a substantial payment from the guarantors was "not great" and therefore the proposals were not in the circumstances unfairly prejudicial to the interests of the bank.

[9.107] A few weeks later Costello J took a somewhat different view in *Re Selukwe Ltd.*[343] In that case Allied Irish Banks was being offered 10 pence in the pound in the proposed scheme of arrangement. Two directors had given joint and several guarantees supported by security and the examiner's proposal envisaged the release of the guarantees. Costello J had this to say:[344]

> "The principal but not the sole objection taken by the Bank is its claim that there is no justification for releasing the personal guarantees of the two directors. I agree with the submissions made on the Bank's behalf in this connection. I can find no reason for depriving the Bank of this security. The reason advanced for this proposal, namely, that the new investors did not wish the directors to face the problem of perhaps having to face bankruptcy proceedings does not justify the examiner's proposal. As long as the proposals contain this provision I think that they are not fair and equitable in so far as the Bank is concerned."

Accordingly, Costello J modified the examiner's proposals by providing that the guarantees remain in place.

[342.] High Court, unrep, 4 November 1991, Murphy J.
[343.] High Court, unrep, 20 December 1991, Costello J.
[344.] *Ibid* at p 2.

[9.108] As already seen, guarantors who honour their guarantees have subrogation rights against the person on whose behalf the debt was guaranteed.[345] The subrogation rights would obviously hamper a company coming out of a scheme of arrangement by burdening it with an immediate debt effectively from its past.[346] Costello J dealt with this by providing that the directors would not be entitled to subrogation rights except where they pay more than 90 per cent of the debts to the bank in which case their subrogation rights would be limited to the sums paid in excess of 90 per cent of the debt (the company's liability to the bank being limited to 10 per cent under the proposed scheme of arrangement).

ASSIGNMENT OF GUARANTEE

[9.109] It seems clear that, unless otherwise agreed, a change in the principal debtor or the holder of the guarantee, whether by way of assignment, transfer or amalgamation will release the guarantee.[347] In practice, any change in the principal debtor will result in a re-negotiation of the facilities and the security. A bank, or other person holding a guarantee, may however wish to assign or transfer the guarantee to another entity, possibly within its own corporate group. Defining the bank (or other holder of the guarantee) in the guarantee itself as including its successors and assigns and any company with which it may amalgamate[348] will avoid the guarantee being released where the bank assigns its interest or changes its constitution.

ASCERTAINMENT OF AMOUNT OWING

[9.110] It is sometimes suggested in practice to use a short form guarantee. A person preparing such a guarantee may be pressurised into omitting what may seem over lawyerly clauses. One such clause is to the effect that a certificate signed by an officer of the obligee shall, save in the case of manifest error, be conclusive evidence against the guarantor as to the amount owing. This clause may be perceived as being somewhat arbitrary and in the case of consumer contracts may well be contrary to the provisions of the European Communities (Unfair Terms in Consumer Contracts) Regulations, 1995.[349] In commercial

---

[345.] See para **[9.57]-[9.67]** above.

[346.] Or as Costello J said at p 3 - "it might well upset the whole balance of the proposals and defeat their object."; the Company Law Review Group's First Report recommended at para 2.33 that a guarantor should not have a right of subrogation where a company is coming out of an examinership pursuant to a scheme of arrangement.

[347.] See Stephenson LJ in *First National Finance Corporation Ltd v Goodman* [1983] BCLC 203 at 209; Partnership Act 1890, s 18.

[348.] As in *First National Finance Corporation Ltd v Goodman* [1983] BCLC 203.

[349.] SI 27/1995 see para **[18.01]** below.

transactions, unless a guarantor can show that a bank acted in bad faith, such clauses are likely to be upheld.[350] The absence of such a clause will necessitate the obligee proving as against the guarantor the amount due by the guarantor notwithstanding that the obligee has already obtained judgment against the principal debtor for the amount demanded. This was decided by the Court of Appeal in *Ex p Young; In re Kitchen*[351] The rationale for this rule and the manner in which it may be avoided were explained by James LJ as follows:[352]

> "It is perfectly clear that in an action against a surety the amount of the damage cannot be proved by any admissions of the principal. No act of the principal can enlarge the guarantee, and no admission or acknowledgement by him can fix the surety with an amount other than that which was really due and which alone the surety was liable to pay. If a surety chooses to make himself liable to pay what any person may say is the loss which the creditor has sustained, of course he can do so, and if he has entered into such a contract he must abide by it".

[9.111] Guarantees usually provide that the guarantor shall pay the bank "on demand". These words are used so that the Statute of Limitations does not run from the date of the execution of the guarantee, as happened in *Parr's Banking Company Ltd v Yates.*[353] In enforcing a guarantee, a bank can avoid having to prove that a demand was made by stipulating in the guarantee itself that a demand is deemed to have been made by service of a demand notice at the guarantor's address (or 48 hours after it having been posted to the guarantor's address). The limitation period from the date upon which the cause of action accrues is six years for a guarantee executed under hand, and twelve years for a guarantee executed under seal.[354] Accordingly, a guarantee executed under hand is more likely to fall foul of the limitation period than one executed under seal.[355]

---

[350] *Dobbs v The National Bank of Australasia Ltd* [1935] 53 CLR 643 where the High Court of Australia held that such a clause was not contrary to public policy as ousting the jurisdiction of the Courts; this decision was applied by the English Court of Appeal in *Bache & Co (London) Ltd v Banque Vernes et Commerciale de Paris SA* [1973] 2 LLR 437 where Lord Denning MR went so far as to state:

> "this commercial practice (of inserting conclusive evidence clauses) is only acceptable because the bankers or brokers who insert them are known to be honest and reliable men of business who are most unlikely to make a mistake. Their standing is so high that their word is to be trusted. So much so that a notice of default given by a bank or a broker must be honoured".

[351] (1881) 17 Ch D 668.

[352] *Ibid* at 671.

[353] [1898] 2 QB 460; see also *Bank of Baroda v Patel* [1996] 1 LLR 391.

[354] Statute of Limitations, 1957.

[355] As happened in *Bank of Baroda v Patel* [1996] 1 LLR 391.

TERMINATION OF GUARANTEE

Right of Termination by Guarantor

[9.112] A guarantee sometimes provides that it may be terminated by the guarantor giving notice of termination, such notice being usually of a month or three months. If such a provision is to be included in a guarantee, a bank should ensure that not only does the guarantee stipulate that the guarantee shall remain in force in respect of any moneys due by the guarantor prior to the expiration of the termination notice but also that the bank may crystallise the principal debt, upon receiving notice of termination, and thereby make a demand on the guarantor prior to the expiration of the termination notice.

[9.113] It should be noted, particularly where, as in most transactions involving guarantees, a guarantee is given as a condition precedent to an advance being made to a borrower, that a guarantee may be withdrawn by the guarantor before any advance is made.[356]

[9.114] It seems that, unless a guarantee stipulates to the contrary, a guarantee may be withdrawn at any time by the guarantor as to future advances which may be made by the holder of the guarantee to the guaranteed debtor.[357] But where the guarantee is in respect of a facility which has already been advanced on the strength of the guarantee, the guarantee may not be withdrawn.[358]

[9.115] In the case of joint and several guarantees the decision in *Egbert v Northern Crown Bank*[359] highlights the need for advisers to consider carefully the language of a guarantee. In that case the guarantee was stated to cover all liabilities "until the undersigned, or the executors or administrators of the undersigned, shall have given the bank notice in writing to make no further advances." One of the guarantors died and his executors notified the bank of his revocation. Fresh advances were made by the bank. The Privy Council held that the language of the guarantee meant that the guarantee was to remain in force until notice was given by all the guarantors (or their executors or administrators). Lord Dunedin stated:[360]

---

[356] *Offord v Davies* (1862) 12 CB (NS) 748.

[357] See Bowen J in *Coulthart v Clementson* (1879) 5 QBD 42 at 46; Lord Coleridge CJ in *Beckett v Addyman* (1882) 9 QBD 783 at 791; Joyce J in *Re Grace, Balfour v Grace* [1902] 1 Ch 733 at 737.

[358] For the distinction between the two types of guarantee see Lush LJ in *Lloyd's v Harper* (1880) 16 Ch D 290 at 319.

[359] [1918] AC 903.

[360] *Ibid* at 907.

"if it had been sought to allow any one to bring the guarantee to an end, either for himself or for all, nothing would have been easier than to express such an intention by such words as 'all or any of the undersigned'."

Death of Guarantor

[9.116] The guarantor's death does not terminate the guarantee. This is based on the principle that a guarantee is a contract and not a bank authority or mandate.[361] However, notice of the guarantor's death whether formal or informal will, in most circumstances, terminate the guarantee.[362] In *Re Whelan decd; Dodd v Whelan*,[363] notice of the guarantor's death was not given to the bank. Subsequently, the bank manager heard in conversation of the guarantor's death. The court held that knowledge of the guarantor's death was sufficient to put the bank on inquiry whether there was any authority to continue the previous course of dealing, and that the guarantee was determined on the date when the bank first had knowledge of the guarantor's death.

[9.117] Instances where a guarantee will not be terminated on notice of death are (1) where it is specifically provided that the guarantee will continue to bind the guarantor's estate following the guarantor's death,[364] and (2) where the holder of the guarantee has given consideration for the guarantee and in respect of an individual obligation on his part.[365]

[9.118] Guarantees often provide a notice period of termination, permitting the guarantor to terminate the guarantee by giving a period of notice.[366] The question may arise as to what happens when the guarantor dies - does his notice of death terminate the guarantee or must the notice period run its full course? This was answered in the case of *Coulthart v Clemenston*.[367] In that case the guarantee provided that it would continue until the expiration of three months' notice being given to the bank manager. Bowen J decided that the notice of termination specified in the guarantee could only be given by the guarantor himself and accordingly upon receiving notice of the guarantor's death, the bank had constructive notice that the guarantee was withdrawn. Bowen J indicated[368] that if the bank wished to provide for a special notice upon the guarantor's death

---

[361.] *Bradbury v Morgan* (1862) 1 H & C 249; *Coulthart v Clementson* (1879) 5 QBD 42; see remarks of the Vice-Chancellor in *Re Whelan decd, Dodd v Whelan* [1897] 1 IR 575 at 577.

[362.] *Coulthart v Clemenston* (1879) 5 QBD 42.

[363.] [1897] 1 IR 575.

[364.] See the remarks of Bowen J in *Coulthart v Clemenston* (1879) 5 QBD 42 at 46-48.

[365.] *Lloyd's v Harper* (1880) 16 Ch D 290.

[366.] See para **[9.112]** above.

[367.] (1879) 5 QBD 42.

[368.] *Ibid* at 48.

to determine the guarantee they could have provided for this in the guarantee itself.

[9.119] Where there is more than one guarantor and the guarantor's obligations are joint and several, the death of one guarantor will not discharge the other guarantor(s). This was decided in *Beckett v Addyman*.[369] The rationale for this point of law was explained by Field J thus:[370]

> "in the present case the death of one of the co-sureties was a possible event which must have been in contemplation of all the parties at the time of the execution of the guarantee.
>
> It is in no sense the act of the creditor; it does not happen from anything done or omitted to be done by him, nor is it an event in any way under his control ...
>
> Moreover it is an event the consequences of which the surety has a control, for as soon as the defendant had notice of Wright's death it was competent to him at once to have revoked his guarantee and thus determined his further liability: *Offord v Davies* 12 CBNS 748.
>
> But ... he has omitted to take the means in his power of determining his further liability, he must ... be taken by thus standing by ... to have induced the plaintiffs to act in making further advances in the belief that he was willing that his several further liabilities should continue".

[9.120] The Civil Liability Act, 1961 provides:[371]

> On the death of a person ... all causes of action (other than exceptional causes of action) subsisting against him shall survive against his estate.

Thus, the guarantor's liability under a guarantee does not terminate upon his death. However, the Civil Liability Act, 1961 provides a limitation period within which the bank must act if it is to institute proceedings on foot of the guarantee. It provides:[372]

(1) In this section "the relevant period" means the period of limitation prescribed by the Statute of Limitations or any other limitation enactment.

(2) No proceedings shall be maintainable in respect of any cause of action whatsoever which has survived against the estate of a deceased person unless either -

    (a) proceedings against him in respect of that cause of action were commenced within the relevant period and were pending at the date of his death, or

---

[369] (1882) 9 QBD 783.
[370] *Ibid* at 789-790; his decision was unanimously upheld by the Court of Appeal.
[371] Section 8(1).
[372] Section 9.

(b) proceedings are commenced in respect of that cause of action
     within the relevant period or within the period of two years
     after his death, whichever period first expires.

[9.121] An interesting application of this statutory provision arose in Barron J's
decision in *The Governor and Company of the Bank of Ireland v O'Keeffe*.[373] In
February 1982 the guarantor died; in May 1982 the bank demanded payment
under the guarantee. Proceedings for such payment were instituted, over two
years later, in February 1985. The defendant contended that the proceedings
were statute barred pursuant to s 9(2)(b) of the Civil Liability Act, 1961. The
court held that the bank's cause of action did not arise until after the demand
was made and since the demand had not been made until after the guarantor's
death, there was no cause of action subsisting against him at the time of his
death and accordingly s 9(2)(b) was inapplicable.

Guarantor's Insanity

[9.122] As with death, the insanity of the guarantor does not terminate the
guarantee but rather notice of the guarantor's insanity does. In *Bradford Old
Bank Ltd v Sutcliffe*[374] it was held by Lawrence J, and confirmed by the Court of
Appeal, that lunacy did not relieve the guarantor from liability of the amount
due on the loan when he became insane, but the guarantee did not cover
advances made after notice of the insanity. He said:[375]

   "The bank, when it had received notice of the lunacy, could no longer make
   advances upon the faith of the guarantee, just as death operates upon a
   continuing guarantee which contains no provision requiring a notice to
   terminate it. The creditor then knows that the guarantor has no longer a
   contracting mind, and consequently cannot be fixed with a contractual liability
   by any act done by the creditor alone".

LETTERS OF COMFORT

   "The parties may, by using clear words, show that their intention is to make the
   transaction binding in honour only, and not in law; and the courts will give
   effect to the expressed intention".[376]

[9.123] There may be circumstances where a party providing credit or an
advance will accept a letter of comfort from the borrower's parent corporation in
lieu of a guarantee. This may arise also in some countries where a State owned
corporation is availing of finance - the State in question may provide a letter of
comfort rather than a guarantee. A letter of comfort will typically indicate that

[373] [1987] IR 47.
[374] (1918) 119 LT 727.
[375] *Ibid* at 728.
[376] Megaw J in *Edwards v Skyways Ltd* [1964] 1 All ER 494; see also *Jones v Vernon's Pools Ltd*
[1938] 2 All ER 626 and *Appleson v H Littlewood Ltd* [1939] 1 All ER 464.

the person giving the letter is aware of the financing transaction and undertakes to maintain its shareholding in the borrower and/or ensure that the borrower is in a position to meet its financial obligations.[377]

[9.124] Letters of comfort are now given less frequently than in the 1980s as a creditor will obtain little comfort from it unless it is legally binding; but the provider of the letter will not wish it to be binding in the sense of a guarantee.[378] The provider of the letter simply wants to give sufficient comfort to the bank (or other creditor) so that the provider's subsidiary will receive the bank's facility yet the provider wishes to incur no legal obligation to the bank should the subsidiary subsequently encounter financial difficulties.[379]

[9.125] Great care is needed both in drafting a letter of comfort and in approving it, as the courts will give effect to it in its strictest terms.[380] A letter of comfort as with any contract, if it is to be enforceable, must contain the three essential elements to a contract namely, (1) offer and acceptance, (2) consideration (unless executed under seal) and (3) intention to create legal relations. It is the third strand which has given rise to much deliberation by the judges when considering whether to enforce a letter of comfort. There is a presumption in commercial contracts that there is an intention by the parties to create legal relations, although this presumption may be rebutted.[381]

[9.126] The current legal position on letters of comfort, as applying in England and Wales,[382] can be seen from the Court of Appeal's decision in *Kleinwort Benson Ltd v Malaysian Mining Corp Bhd*.[383] It held that:

> "A letter of comfort from a parent company to a lender stating that it was the policy of the parent company to ensure that its subsidiary was 'at all times in a position to meet its liabilities' in respect of a loan made by the lender to the subsidiary did not have contractual effect if it was merely a statement of

---

[377.] For further reading see Wood, *The Law and Practice of International Finance* (1980) para 13.5; Butterworths, *Forum Comfort Letters* (1986) September JIBFL 2 (in particular the analysis by Parsons of provisions in Comfort Letters); also less frequently described as letters of responsibility (1978) IBL 288.

[378.] See O'Ceidigh, 'Letters of Comfort and the Liability of the Issuer' (1990) ILT 234.

[379.] Essentially a written "gentleman's agreement" which has been described (by Vaisey J) as, "an agreement which is not an agreement, made between two persons, neither of whom is a gentleman, whereby each expects the other to be strictly bound without himself being bound at all".

[380.] For its impact on audits see Copp, 'Comfort Letters' (1990) Accountancy 81.

[381.] See Chesire, Fifoot & Furmston's *Law of Contract* (13th ed) p 118; Clark, *Contract Law in Ireland* (3rd ed) 1992, p 71.

[382.] The author is not aware of any authority in Ireland on the point.

[383.] [1989] 1 All ER 785; see also Gill, 'Letters of Comfort' - The Need for Continuing Caution' (1989) ILT 235; (1988) JBL 111, (1989) JBL 96 and (1989) JBL 259.

present fact regarding the parent company's intentions and was not a contractual promise as to the parent company's future conduct."

In that case, the defendant was a Malaysian public limited company owned by the Republic of Malaysia. The defendant incorporated a subsidiary and in respect of finance made available to the subsidiary gave a letter to the financier which stated - "It is our policy to ensure that the business of *MMC Metals Ltd* is at all times in a position to meet its liabilities to you under the above arrangements". Hirst J held that as the plaintiff relied on the letter in making finance available, the letter was intended to create legal relations and was enforceable against the defendants. The Court of Appeal unanimously allowed the appeal and held that the letter of comfort was a statement of present fact and not a promise of future conduct; the fact that it was given instead of a guarantee showed that the defendants did not wish to assume a legal liability for repayment but only a moral responsibility.

[9.127] One of the purposes of a comfort letter for the bank is the fact that the parent providing the letter is fully aware of the subsidiary's liabilities and should not dispose of the subsidiary without reverting to the bank. This scenario forms the background to the English Court of Appeal's decision in *Chemco Leasing SpA v Redifussion plc*.[384] In that case the comfort letter stated:

"We assure you that we are not contemplating the disposal of our interest in CMC Italy and undertake to give Chemco prior notification should we dispose of our interest. We undertake to take over the remaining liabilities to Chemco of CMC Italy should the new shareholders be unacceptable to Chemco."

The defendants disposed of their interest in CMC Italy. At the time of the disposal the plaintiffs were not informed by the defendants but became aware of the disposal. They raised the matter with the defendants who undertook to revert, but did not. The Court of Appeal held, somewhat harshly, that as the plaintiffs did not pursue the point with the defendants they had waived their right of objection and could not enforce the terms of the letter.

[9.128] The Australian courts have been less willing to permit the giver of a letter of comfort the liberty to ignore the obligation of such letter.[385] In *Banque Brussels Lambert SA v Australia National Industries Ltd*,[386] the defendant gave the plaintiff a letter of comfort which included the following passages:

---

384. [1987] FTLR 201; see also Gill, 'Letters of Comfort and Intention to Create Legal Relations' (1988) ILT 103; for a detailed comparison on the two Court of Appeal decisions see Brown, 'The Letter of Comfort: Placebo or Promise?' (1990) JBL 281.
385. See *Capital Financial Group Ltd v Rothwells Ltd* [1994] 5 JIBL N-96 where the New South Wales Court of Appeal extended the doctrine of contribution between co-guarantors (see para **[9.68]** above) to persons who had provided letters of comfort.
386. Supreme Court of New South Wales, 12 December 1989 and 5 October 1990.

"We confirm that we are aware of the eurocurrency facility of US$5 million which your bank has granted to Spedley Securities Ltd ...

We take this opportunity to confirm that it is our practice to ensure that our affiliate, Spedley Securities Ltd, will at all times be in a position to meet its financial obligations as they fall due. These financial obligations include repayment of all loans made by your bank under arrangements mentioned in this letter."

The court held that the words of the letter were sufficiently promissory in nature so as to establish the existence of a legally enforceable contractual obligation. It held though that the defendant's failure to ensure that Spedley Securities Ltd was in a position to meet its financial obligations did not trigger an obligation in the nature of a guarantee, but rather an obligation to pay damages to the bank for the loss suffered by it by reason of the defendant's default.

[9.129] A classic example of a letter of comfort can be seen from the letter provided in *Re Atlantic Computers plc (in administration), National Australia Bank Ltd v Soden*.[387] The letter stated:

"Dear Sirs,

Letter of Comfort

We hereby confirm that Altantic Medical Ltd is wholly owned by Atlantic Computers plc. We confirm that we are aware of the facility detailed below and which your bank has granted to Atlantic Medical Ltd."

The facility is then described as a hire-purchase facility expiring on 30 December 1993. The letter continues:

"In consideration of the bank granting such credit, we undertake that without the prior consent of the bank:

(a) that the beneficial ownership of Atlantic Medical Ltd will be maintained by this company during the currency of the facility now to be made available by the bank;

(b) that the moneys owing by Atlantic Medical Ltd to the parent company will not be repaid in priority to any moneys owing or contingently owing by Atlantic Medical Ltd to the bank;

(c) that if Atlantic Medical Ltd is unable to meet its commitment, the parent company will take steps to make arrangements for Atlantic Medical Ltd's present, future or contingent obligations to the bank both for capital and interest to be met.

This document is not intended to be a guarantee and, in the case of para (c) above, it is an expression of present intention by way of comfort only."

Chadwick J, in his judgment reviewed the relevant authorities and stated:[388]

[387.] [1995] BCC 696.
[388.] *Ibid* at 698.

"the question for the court in each case is whether as a matter of construction, in the light of whatever surrounding circumstances may be relevant and admissible, the parties intended to make a contractual promise for the future or to give only a warranty as to present intention."

The court held that paragraph (c) of the letter, read independently of the letter's final paragraph, was phrased in terms which were sufficiently certain as to give rise to an enforceable obligation. However the final paragraph of the letter showed that the parent was giving no more than a warranty as to present intention by way of comfort only and the letter did not impose a contractual obligation. The clear lesson from this decision is that a letter of comfort, once clear in its terms, will be given effect to in accordance with such terms. This highlights the importance of precision in the drafting of such letters.

[9.130] One common law jurisdiction seems to have gone so far as to imply a term in a letter of comfort that the beneficiary be informed of a material change in the circumstances of the provider such that a statement in the letter of comfort should no longer be relied upon, because of its incorrectness; breach of this term giving rise to an action for damages against the corporate officers of the comfort provider.[389] An officer of a corporation should not express any personal commitment in a letter of comfort unless such officer is prepared to incur a personal liability.[390] The decision in *Motemtronic Ltd v Autocar Equipment Ltd*[391] is a reminder of the danger in giving any oral comfort in the course of negotiations. Ultimately, the Court of Appeal found that although an oral statement taken in isolation amounted to a collateral warranty, it needed to be considered against the background of the circumstances of the meeting and was thus a non-binding comfort only. Although the chairman escaped any legal liability, the fact that he needed to go as far as the Court of Appeal to do so must have made him regret giving any oral comfort - a lesson for corporate officers and lawyers.

[389.] *Toronto-Domincan Bank v Leigh Instruments Ltd* (1993) JIBFL 92.
[390.] See *Paulger v Butland Industries Ltd* (1991) JBL 281 where the New Zealand Court of Appeal held the managing director personally liable for debts of the company over which it managed.
[391.] Court of Appeal, unrep, 20 June 1996; see commentary by Vollans (1996) BLR 232.

Chapter 10

Mortgages and Charges of Land

"No one, I am sure, by the light of nature ever understood an English mortgage of real estate."[1]

[10.01] There are principally five methods by which land may be given as security for liabilities incurred or to be incurred by the security provider to the security holder.[2] The first method is where the debtor transfers his title in the land to the creditor on the condition that as soon as the debt is discharged the title will be re-transferred back to the debtor. The second method is where the debtor demises his title in the land to the creditor for a period slightly shorter than the unexpired term held by the debtor on condition that the term granted to the creditor ceases upon discharge of the debt or other liabilities secured by the demise. These first two methods are known as legal mortgages while the third method is known as an equitable mortgage. This involves the debtor depositing, or effectively pledging, his title documents to the lands with the creditor on condition that the documents (or deeds) are returned upon the discharge of the debt or other liability secured by the deposit. The fourth method is for the debtor to charge his land (by way of fixed or specific charge) in favour of the creditor again on condition that the charge will be discharged upon the repayment of the debt or extinguishment of all other liabilities secured by the charge. The fifth method is for the debtor to create a floating charge over his land in favour of the creditor to secure the debts or other obligations of the debtor.[3]

MORTGAGE BY CONVEYANCE OR ASSIGNMENT

[10.02] The typical language used in a security document where title to the debtor's lands are transferred by way of mortgage is as follows:[4]

[1.] Lord Macnaghten in *Samuel v Jarrah Timber and Wood Paving Corporation Ltd* [1904] AC 323 at 326.

[2.] For a brief history of mortgages of land see Fisher and Lightwood's *Law of Mortgages* (10th ed) p 6-7; see also Wylie, *Irish Land Law* (3rd ed) para 12.02.

[3.] For the creation of floating charges see Ch 13.

[4.] "No particular words or form of conveyance are necessary to constitute a mortgage" - *Halsbury's Laws of England* (1st ed) (1912) Vol 21 para 124; for the minimum requirements see the short form of mortgage set out in the Fourth Schedule in the Conveyancing Act 1881; for further reading see Wylie, *Irish Land Law* (3rd 1997) paras 12.24-12.47; for a fuller and helpful discourse on the preparation of mortgages see Black, *The Drafting of Mortgages and their Enforcement*, SYS Lecture 135.

"As security for the mortgagor's covenant[5] to pay all sums due and owing or to become due and owing by the mortgagor to the mortgagee the mortgagor as Beneficial Owner[6]:

   (a) hereby grants and conveys unto the mortgagee ALL THAT AND THOSE so much of the lands, hereditaments and premises described in the Schedule hereto as is of freehold tenure together with all buildings,[7] fixtures (including trade fixtures) and fixed plant and machinery[8] from time to time thereon TO HOLD the same unto the mortgagee in fee simple subject to the proviso for redemption hereinafter contained, and

   (b) hereby transfers and assigns unto the mortgagee ALL THAT AND THOSE so much of the lands and premises described in the Schedule hereto as is of leasehold tenure together with all buildings, fixtures (including trade fixtures) and fixed plant and machinery from time to time thereon TO HOLD the same unto the mortgagee for the residue or residues of the term or respective terms of years for which the mortgagor now holds the same subject to the proviso for redemption hereinafter contained

PROVIDED ALWAYS that if the mortgagor shall on the ninetieth day after the date hereof [9] pay to the mortgagee the principal amount due and payable to the mortgagee together with the interest thereon at the agreed rate then and in such event this mortgage and the lands, hereditaments and premises described in the Schedule hereto shall at the cost and expense of the mortgagor be released by a reconveyance or surrender or as the mortgagor shall direct."[10]

[10.03] The benefit of such a mortgage is that the mortgagee acquires the entire estate and interest of the mortgagor in the lands and premises and the mortgagor has only his equity of redemption.[11] The drawback and indeed danger for the

---

5. A mortgage should contain a covenant by the mortgagor to pay to the mortgagee principal and interest/all sums due and owing or to become due and owing and/or to discharge all liabilities due and to become due by the mortgagor to the mortgagee.
6. The words "as Beneficial Owner" mean that under s 7(1)(c) of the Conveyancing Act 1881, certain covenants are implied by the mortgagor including power to mortgage, lawful for the mortgagee to enter upon default of payment, indemnified against all other incumbrances, covenant for further assurance.
7. It is usual to insert a reference to buildings but not essential as pursuant to s 6(1) of the Conveyancing Act 1881 a mortgage of land is deemed to include and by virtue of the Conveyancing Act 1881 operates to mortgage with the land "all buildings, erections, fixtures" appertaining to the land; see also s 6(2).
8. For mortgages of plant and machinery see Ch 11.
9. This is known as the legal date of redemption referred to in para **[10.06]** below.
10. A mortgagor may require the mortgagee to convey the property to a third party - Conveyancing Act 1881, s 15.
11. Equity of redemption has been defined as the right of the mortgagor to have his property returned to him upon payment of his debt (see para **[10.06]** below).

mortgagee is that all the liabilities running with the land are also transferred. Thus, in the case of a leasehold interest this includes rent and other obligations of the mortgagor under which he holds the lands and premises. The principal obligations apart from paying rent would be the payment of rates, the duty to repair and maintain the property and the duty to insure it against the usual risks. Accordingly, this method is to be avoided at least with regard to leasehold interests and the second method should be adopted.

MORTGAGE BY DEMISE

[10.04] Lands the title to which are not registered in the Land Registry should be mortgaged by way of (conveyance, assignment or) demise to enable the mortgagee to acquire sufficient title to be able to dispose of the title in the event that the power of sale arises.[12] Suitable language to mortgage lands by demise is the following:

> "As security for the mortgagor's covenant to pay all sums due and owing or to become due and owing by the mortgagor to the mortgagee the mortgagor as Beneficial Owner hereby demises unto the mortgagee ALL THAT AND THOSE the lands, hereditaments and premises described in the Schedule hereto together with all buildings, fixtures (including trade fixtures) and fixed plant and machinery from time to time thereon TO HOLD such of the same as are of freehold tenure unto the mortgagee for the term of 1000 years from the date hereof and TO HOLD such of the same as are of leasehold tenure unto the mortgagee for the residue or residues of the term or respective terms of years for which the mortgagor now holds the same less the last three days of such term or respective terms subject as to all such lands, hereditaments and premises to the proviso for redemption hereinafter contained.
>
> PROVIDED ALWAYS THAT if the mortgagor shall on the ninetieth day after the date hereof pay to the mortgagee the principal amount due and payable to the mortgagee together with interest thereon at the agreed rate then and in such event this mortgage and the lands, hereditaments and premises described in the Schedule hereto shall at the cost and expense of the mortgagor be released by a surrender or as the mortgagor may direct."

[10.05] Because the entire interest or estate of the mortgagor has not been mortgaged to the mortgagee the mortgage must provide for the reversionary interest to be held in trust for the mortgagee - otherwise the mortgagee would not be in a position to sell the entire interest or estate in the event of the power of sale arising. The following language is appropriate to fulfil this requirement:

[12.] Conveyancing Act, 1881, s 19; see also *Halsbury's Laws of England* (1st ed) (1912) Vol 21 para 205.

"The mortgagor hereby declares that the mortgagee shall henceforth stand possessed of all the mortgagor's estate and interest of the lands, hereditaments and premises of freehold tenure herein demised in reversion expectant upon the determination of the term of years hereby created and of the lands and premises of leasehold tenure herein demised for the last three days or respective last three days of the term or terms of years for which the same is held by the mortgagor and for any further or other interest which the mortgagor now has or may hereafter acquire or become entitled to in the same or any part thereof in trust for the mortgagee and to be conveyed, assigned or otherwise dealt with whether to the mortgagee or its nominee or otherwise as the mortgagee shall direct but subject to the same equity of redemption as may for the time being be subsisting in the lands, hereditaments and premises herein demised AND the mortgagor hereby authorises the mortgagee to appoint a new trustee or new trustees of any such reversion and in particular at any time to appoint such new trustee or new trustees in the place of the mortgagor or any trustee or trustees appointed herein as if the mortgagor or any such trustee or trustees were incapable of acting the trustee thereof hereby declared AND the mortgagor hereby irrevocably appoints the mortgagee the Attorney of the mortgagor in his name and on his behalf at any time to assign any of the same reversions or any further or other interest the mortgagor has or may hereafter have during the continuance of this security in the lands, hereditaments and premises herein demised to the mortgagee or as the mortgagee shall think fit, including (but without prejudice to the generality of the foregoing) any receiver appointed by the mortgagee under the powers herein contained, subject to such equity of redemption (if any) as may for the time being be subsisting as aforesaid and to do seal and execute all instruments, acts and things necessary or proper for that purpose".

REDEMPTION OF MORTGAGES

[10.06] It is traditional but now less common to stipulate the legal date for redemption of a mortgage.[13] This is the date upon which the mortgagor may redeem the mortgage by paying back the loan together with interest and any costs. This is the legal contractual date for repayment of the loan and the right of the mortgagor to have the title to his mortgaged land returned to him. He cannot redeem earlier.[14] The legal date for redemption is usually the first interest payment date or six months after the date of the mortgage.[15] However, if the mortgage debt is repayable on demand, the demand when made is the date of redemption.[16] In earlier times the failure of the mortgagor to redeem on the legal

---

[13.] See fn 9 in para **[10.02]** above.

[14.] See *Re Hone's Estate* (1873) IR 8 Eq 65; *Knightsbridge Estates Trust Ltd v Byrne* [1939] Ch 441; and *Multiservice Bookbinding Ltd v Marden* [1978] 2 All ER 489.

[15.] See Fisher and Lightwood's *Law of Mortgage* (10th ed) p 545-6.

[16.] See Cousins, *The Law of Mortgages*, p 291.

date of redemption meant that the mortgagor forfeited his land and was still liable to the mortgagee to repay the loan. However, later the courts of equity permitted the mortgagor to redeem subsequently to the legal date of redemption.[17] This right of redemption is known as the equity of redemption.

In permitting a mortgagor to redeem subsequent to the legal date of redemption, the courts seek to prohibit any term in the mortgage which effectively would prevent the mortgagor obtaining title to his property free of all incumbrances once the mortgage debt has been repaid. Any such term is void as being "a clog on the equity of redemption".

Clog on the Equity of Redemption

> "The rule of Equity is, that no onerous engagement of any description can be entered into by a mortgagor with his mortgagee on the occasion of the mortgage"[18]

[10.07] It is unclear at times as to what may or may not be a clog on the equity of redemption. Obviously, it is of real importance to a solicitor who may be involved in advising a financial institution on a structure, created for tax advantage or more precisely avoidance, involving a myriad of cross securities and possibly options, any one of which if deemed to be a clog would negative the effect of a document; this may be critical not only in protecting a party's interests but also possibly in the completion of the structure necessary for the parties to obtain the anticipated tax advantage. It can therefore be of more than academic interest to understand the nature of a clog on the equity of redemption.

[10.08] An early Irish decision on the nature of a clog on the equity of redemption is neatly illustrated in *Chapple v Mahon*.[19] In that case, the mortgagor covenanted in the mortgage to pay the mortgagee at the time the mortgage debt was cleared a commission of 5 per cent on the sum advanced and interest on the commission from the date of the advance. The court held that the agreement was illegal and void as it was contrary to the nature of a mortgage security.

[10.09] In *Re Edwards' Estate*[20] a mortgage giving the mortgagee power to purchase the equity of redemption in the event of default was not upheld by the Court. Hargreave J explained the difficulty in his judgment when he said:[21]

[17.] This is subject to a limitation period of 12 years once a mortgagee has taken possession - Real Property Limitation Act, 1874, s 7.

[18.] Hargreave J in *Re Edwards' Estate* (1861) 11 Ir Ch R 367 at 369.

[19.] (1870) IR 5 Eq 225.

[20.] (1861) 11 Ir Ch R 367.

[21.] *Ibid* at 369.

"I do not doubt that if this contract had been entered into ... after the completion of the mortgage transaction, and when [the mortgagor] had got the money in his pocket, it would be perfectly valid, but then the mortgagor would be under no kind of pressure, and he would be able to exercise his unbiased judgment as to whether it was a fair contract. But when the contract is part of the arrangement for the loan, and is actually inserted in the mortgage deed, it is presumed to be made under pressure, and is not capable of being enforced."

However, one misconception[22] is that mortgages cannot contain a collateral advantage to the mortgagee,[23] who should simply require re-payment of principal and payment of interest prior to re-conveying or re-demising the mortgaged property. As was so aptly explained by Lord Parker of Waddington in the House of Lords,[24] this misconception has arisen because collateral advantages were not upheld for mortgages to secure borrowed money as such advantages were a breach of the usury laws.[25]

[10.10] In his classic judgment on the history and nature of the equity of redemption Lord Parker concluded by stating:[26]

"There is now no rule in equity which precludes a mortgagee, whether the mortgage be made upon the occasion of a loan or otherwise, from stipulating for any collateral advantage, provided such collateral advantage is not either:

    (1) unfair and unconscionable, or

    (2) in the nature of a penalty clogging the equity of redemption, or

    (3) inconsistent with or repugnant to the contractual and equitable right to redeem."

It may be useful to analyse each of these three headings.

(1) Unfair and Unconscionable

[10.11] A clear example of an unconscionable bargain arose in *Chapple v Mahon*.[27] The interest on a mortgage debt was agreed at 10 per cent, but

---

[22.] See for example the judgment of the Master of the Rolls in *Comyns v Comyns* (1871) IR 5 Eq 583.

[23.] See O'Neill Kiely, *The Principles of Equity* (1936) The Fodhla Printing Company Ltd 265.

[24.] In *G and C Kreglinger v New Patagonia Meat and Cold Storage Company Ltd* [1914] AC 25 at 54.

[25.] However, see the earlier judgment of Kay J in a lower court in *James v Kerr* (1888) 40 Ch D 449 where he said at 460 "the rule that a mortgagee should not be allowed to stipulate for any collateral advantage beyond his principal and interest did not depend on the laws against usury. The rule was entirely independent of the rate of interest actually charged. There seems to be less reason than ever for altering it now that persons may agree upon any rate of interest they please."

[26.] *G and C Kreglinger v New Patagonia Meat and Cold Storage Company Ltd* [1914] AC 25 at 61 (the Earl of Halsbury, Lord Atkinson and Lord Mersey, agreed with the judgments of Lord Parker and Viscount Haldane (who delivered a concurring judgment)).

[27.] (1870) IR 5 Eq 225.

reducible to 8 per cent if paid within 21 days after it fell due. The mortgagees were appointed by the mortgagor as agents and receivers over the mortgaged lands, and as such agents, acted so as to delay the payment of rents, which if punctually paid, would have put funds in their hands to pay the interest within 21 days. The court held that the mortgagees could claim interest only at the lower rate.

Although the courts will not permit an unconscionable bargain to stand, they have shown a willingness to permit the mortgage to remain as security for the principal sum advanced and an appropriate rate of interest.[28]

[10.12] It is important to distinguish between a bargain which is unreasonable and a bargain which is unconscionable.[29] The former is permitted but not the latter. This can be seen from the decision in *Multiservice Bookbinding Ltd v Marden*.[30] The defendant lent the plaintiff £36,000 (Sterling), the borrower's covenant to pay capital and interest being linked to the value of the Swiss franc. The mortgage provided (i) interest to be paid at 2 per cent above the bank rate, quarterly in advance on the total principal sum of £36,000 throughout the period of the loan notwithstanding capital repayments, (ii) arrears of interest to be capitalised after 21 days, (iii) neither the loan nor the mortgage to be called in for ten years and (iv) clause 6 (the Swiss franc uplift clause) provided that any sum paid on account of interest or in repayment of capital could be increased or decreased proportionately if at the close of business on the day preceding the payment date the rate of exchange between the Swiss franc and Sterling would vary by more than 3 per cent from 12.07 5/8 Swiss francs to £1 Sterling. At the time of redemption there were just over 4 Swiss francs to £1 Sterling leading to a capital repayment of £87,588 plus interest of in excess of £45,000. The court considered that the rate of interest was unreasonable (due to the indexing of the amount to Swiss francs) and also considered that the payment of interest on the whole sum throughout the whole term despite the capital repayments was unreasonable. However as each party had been separately advised and there was no great inequality in bargaining power, the transaction was upheld. In applying Lord Parker's judgment,[31] the court held:[32]

> "... the plaintiffs must show that the bargain, or some of its terms, was unfair and unconscionable; it is not enough to show that in the eyes of the court it was unreasonable.

---

28. See *Kevans v Joyce* [1896] 1 IR 442, 473.
29. Although Wylie, *Irish Land Law* (3rd ed) para 13.096 suggests that the courts prohibit additional payments "if they are regarded as unconscionable or unreasonable."
30. [1978] 2 All ER 489.
31. In *G and C Kreglinger v New Patagonia Meat and Cold Storage Co Ltd* [1914] AC 25.
32. *Per* Browne-Wilkinson J at 502.

... a bargain cannot be unfair and unconscionable unless one of the parties to it has imposed the objectionable terms in a morally reprehensible manner, that is to say, in a way which affects his conscience."

Browne-Wilkinson J concluded:[33]

"... the test is not reasonableness. The parties made a bargain which the plaintiffs, who are businessmen, went into with their eyes open, with the benefit of independent advice, without any compelling necessity to accept a loan on these terms and without any sharp practice by the defendant. I cannot see that there was anything unfair or oppressive or morally reprehensible in such a bargain entered into in such circumstances."

In the earlier decision of *Knightsbridge Estates Trust Ltd v Byrne*[34] (where the borrower was not permitted to redeem earlier than the agreed period of 40 years), Greene MR stated in the Court of Appeal:[35]

"Equity does not reform mortgage transactions because they are unreasonable. It is concerned to see two things (i) that the essential requirements of a mortgage transaction are observed and (ii) that oppressive or unconscionable terms are not enforced. Subject to this, it does not, in our opinion, interfere."

[10.13] A contrast to these decisions is that of *Cityland and Property (Holdings) Ltd v Dabrah*.[36] In that case, the premium payable on redemption was so large (57 per cent) as to destroy the mortgagor's equity in the property and accordingly interest was allowed but not the premium.

(2) Penalty Clogging the Equity of Redemption

[10.14] A good example of a clog on the equity of redemption can be seen from the decision already referred to in *Chapple v Mahon*.[37] In *Comyns v Comyns*[38] a stipulation that £100 per annum was to be allowed to the mortgagee for managing the lands was held to be void.

In *Browne v Ryan*,[39] the defendant mortgaged his land to the plaintiff to secure a loan of £200 and interest thereon. As part of the same transaction the defendant agreed by an independent deed to sell his land within twelve months, and to give the sale thereof to the plaintiff, who was an auctioneer, and that if the lands were sold otherwise than through the plaintiff he would pay the plaintiff five per cent of the purchase money. The Court of Appeal held that the collateral advantage

---

33. *Ibid* at 503.
34. [1939] Ch 441.
35. *Ibid* at 457.
36. [1967] 2 All ER 639.
37. (1870) IR 5 Eq 225; see para **[10.08]** *infra*.
38. (1871) IR 5 Eq 583.
39. [1901] 2 IR 653.

stipulated for by the mortgagee in the independent deed placed such a fetter on the equity of redemption that it vitiated the agreement. Walker LJ stated the law to be thus:[40]

> "... it has been long settled, and is still the law, that, when once the redemption price has been fixed and arrived at, the mortgagee cannot charge against the mortgagor on account as a charge against the estate to be redeemed any extra payments for commission for himself or otherwise ... and this, though the bargain for the extra payments may have been deliberately made; such a charge by its mere statement clogs the equity of redemption, and involves an assertion that there shall be no redemption till the extra demands are paid."

[10.15] The decision in *Browne v Ryan*[41] may be contrasted with that of *Maxwell v Tipping*.[42] The plaintiff also was already indebted to the defendant for £1500 secured by a mortgage on land with interest at 5 per cent in consideration of a further advance of £300 executed a collateral agreement under which the defendant was appointed agent over the mortgaged lands subject to agency fees. He agreed to pay 6 per cent interest on the total £1800 although the additional one per cent was not charged on the lands. The court held that the collateral agreement, being a new contract for fresh consideration, had not the effect of imposing a fetter on the equity of redemption by reason of increasing the rate of interest payable, or by reason of making the mortgagee the agent of the mortgagor to receive the rents, and empowering him to charge agency fees.

Thus, it is perfectly possible to have collateral contracts to the mortgage which are for the benefit of the mortgagee yet which do not prevent or restrict redemption of the mortgage. Such collateral contracts are permitted.[43] However, collateral contracts which effectively impose a covenant running with the land even after redemption of the mortgage debt will not be upheld.[44]

(3) Contractual and Equitable Right to Redeem

[10.16] A mortgage may not by its terms provide that the mortgagee purchase or have an option to purchase any part or interest in the mortgaged property.[45] The distinction between the contractual and equitable right to redeem is set out succinctly by Lord Parker:[46]

[40.] *Ibid* at 676.
[41.] [1901] 2 IR 653.
[42.] [1903] 1 IR 498.
[43.] See *Biggs v Hoddinott* [1898] 2 Ch 307.
[44.] See *Rice v Noakes & Co* [1900] 1 Ch 213; 2 Ch 445.
[45.] See Lord Parker in *G and C Kreglinger v New Patogonia Meat and Cold Storage Co Ltd* [1914] AC 25 at 50; see also *Re Edwards' Estate* (1861) 11 Ir Ch R 367.
[46.] *Ibid*.

"A condition to the effect that if the contractual right is not exercised by the time specified the mortgagee shall have an option of purchasing the mortgaged property may properly be regarded as a penal clause. It is repugnant only to the equity and not to the contractual right. But a condition that the mortgagee is to have such an option for a period which begins before the time for the exercise of the equitable right has arrived, or which reserves to the mortgagee any interest in the property after the exercise of the contractual right, is inconsistent not only with the equity but with the contractual right itself."

[10.17] The rule that a mortgagee may not, at the time of making the loan and taking security, stipulate that it may purchase the property has been criticised in cases where business persons, properly advised, negotiating at arms length have come to a commercial decision to make such a bargain.[47] In *Samuel v Jarrah Timber and Wood Paving Corporation Ltd*[48] a company gave security over their debenture stock in respect of a loan but also granted the lender an option to purchase. The House of Lords held the option to be void. But the Earl of Halsbury said:[49]

"If a day had intervened between the two parties of the arrangement, the part of the bargain which the appellant claims to be performed would have been perfectly good and capable of being enforced."

However, if the arrangement had been set up to allow a break of a day, such option would still have been void, unless it was clear that the borrower had no commitment at the time of creating the mortgage to give subsequently an option to purchase the mortgaged asset.[50] The courts will look at the substance of the transaction as a whole, rather than the form; accordingly, even if time intervenes between the original mortgage and the later option, the option may be unenforceable.[51]

The underlying principle to be borne in mind by practitioners in devising any structure involving the equity of redemption can be seen from Lord Lindley's judgment in *Samuel v Jarrah Timber and Wood Paving Corporation Ltd*[52] when he said:[53]

"The doctrine 'once a mortgage always a mortgage' means that no contract between a mortgagor and a mortgagee made at the time of the mortgage and as part of the mortgage transaction, or, in other words, as one of the terms of the

---

47. See Lord Macnaghten in *Samuel v Jarrah Timber and Wood Paving Corporation Ltd* [1904] AC 323 at 327.
48. [1904] AC 323.
49. *Ibid* at 325.
50. See for example *Reeve v Lisle* [1902] AC 461; see further O'Neill Kiely, *The Principles of Equity* (1936) p 266.
51. See for example *Lewis v Frank Love Ltd* [1961] 1 WLR 261.
52. [1904] AC 323.
53. *Ibid* at 329.

loan, can be valid if it prevents the mortgagor from getting back his property on paying off what is due on his security. Any bargain which has that effect is invalid, and is inconsistent with the transaction being a mortgage."

MORTGAGE BY DEPOSIT OF TITLE DEEDS

"An equitable mortgage as understood in a Court of Equity may arise in many ways. It arises where without any writing there is a deposit of title deeds by a debtor with his creditor, for the law then presumes that there was an intention to create a security. It will exist where there is a written memorandum accompanying a deposit evidencing the purport of it or the terms upon which the deposit is made and many banks have printed forms to meet such a case; or it may be created by a written memorandum of deposit although no deposit of deeds has been actually made, or it will be created by any agreement in writing to create a charge either immediately, or when the deed to which it refers has been executed ... It may be contained in a mere letter, though the party be not in possession of the property and be waiting for the conveyance to be executed."[54]

[10.18] A popular informal method of taking security over land is for a borrower to deposit his title deeds with a bank or other lender as security for finance made available or to be made available by the lender. Indeed as far back as 1791 it was stated:[55] "It is now fully settled, that a deposit of title-deeds, as security for a debt, does amount to an equitable mortgage."

More recently Kenny J explained the concept of an equitable mortgage with his usual clarity:[56]

"The deposit, as security, of documents of title to land which is not registered gives the person with whom it is made an equitable estate in the lands until the money secured by it is repaid: the remedy for securing payment is to apply to the court for a declaration that the deposit has given a charge on the lands. The right created by the deposit is not limited to keeping the deeds until the money has been paid but gives an equitable estate in the lands."

The title deeds, when deposited in the appropriate manner, will create an equitable mortgage over the lands to which they relate and the fixtures attached thereto.[57]

In the case of lands, the title to which is unregistered the deposit should be of all material title documents;[58] in the case of lands the title of which is registered in the Land Registry, the original land certificate should be deposited.[59] Failure to

---

[54.] Walker LJ in *Re Stevenson's Estate* [1902] 1 IR 23 at 46 (dissenting judgment upheld by the House of Lords in *Fullerton v Provincial Bank of Ireland* [1903] 1 IR 483).

[55.] By Eyre CB in *Plumb v Fluitt* (1791) 2 Anst 432 at 438; see also *Birch v Ellames* (1794) 2 Anst 427.

[56.] *Allied Irish Banks Ltd v Glynn* [1973] IR 188 at 191.

[57.] See *Ex p Price* (1842) 2 Mont D & D 518; *Ex p Tagart* (1847) De Gex 531; *Ex p Dowell* (1848) 12 Jur 411.

[58.] See *Re Lambert's Estate* 13 LR Ir 234; also O'Neill Kiely, *The Principles of Equity* (1936) 309.

deposit the material title document to a property may not be fatal to an equitable mortgage by deposit of title deeds - this will then depend upon the surrounding circumstances.[60] For example in *Simmons v Montague*[61] a deposit of a map of a hotel and the title deeds to a portion of the premises was held to be an equitable mortgage of the entire hotel as the mortgagor had agreed to charge all his interest in the hotel premises. The receipt of a land certificate will not protect a mortgagee where he is deemed to be on notice of facts which shows that the depositor is not lawfully entitled to the land certificate at the time of making the deposit.[62] But where a mortgagee is not on notice[63] of rights of a person not on title or of facts which support such rights, its mortgage will take priority over such rights.[64]

[10.19] Although the mortgagee is bound on redemption of the mortgage to deliver up the title deeds, there is case law to the effect that he is not liable to account to the mortgagor for any damage to the title deeds prior to redemption of the mortgage. In *Gilligan and Nugent v The National Bank Ltd*[65] the mortgagee was not liable for damage to title deeds caused by flooding in its premises as the mortgagor had not repaid the advances made to him. The reasoning behind this approach can be seen from Madden J's judgment where he said:[66]

> "The true key for the solution of the questions raised in this case ... is to be found in the recognition of the principle of law by which title deeds are regarded as part of the realty, and in avoiding the misleading analogies of pledge or bailment of chattels. This principle is the foundation upon which the security of an equitable mortgage by deposit has been built up by a series of decisions...The equitable mortgagee becomes the actual owner of the title deeds by an accomplished fact, and he cannot be deprived of this ownership unless by redemption; he is thus outside the Statute of Frauds. He has acquired this ownership otherwise than by a 'conveyance'; he is, therefore, outside the provisions of the Registry Acts which postpone unregistered "conveyances". The deeds are his property until redemption. Why should a covenant on his part be implied to take reasonable care of what is his own?"

Whether this general statement applies today must be questionable although there could be still circumstances where the mortgagee is not liable for damage

---

59. See Registration of Title Act, 1964, s 105(5).
60. See McMahon J in *Bank of Ireland Finance Ltd v DJ Daly Ltd* [1978] IR 79 at 82.
61. [1909] 1 IR 87.
62. See *Tench v Molyneux* (1914) 48 ILTR 48.
63. For the meaning of notice see paras **[10.46]-[10.51]**.
64. See *Allied Irish Banks Ltd v Glynn* [1973] IR 188.
65. [1901] 2 IR 513.
66. *Ibid* at 532-3.

to the title deeds while under his control provided he had taken reasonable precautions to safeguard them.

[10.20] The advantages in this method of taking a mortgage is its informality and, (in particular for a mortgagor who is an individual) the absence of any registration in the Registry of Deeds or (as the case may be) the Land Registry. Although such mortgages by corporate borrowers will not result in registration in such registries, particulars of the security are required to be registered in the Companies Registration Office.[67] Because of the absence of registration in the Registry of Deeds or the Land Registry there will be a cost saving.[68] A further saving will be the absence of stamp duty as there is no instrument creating the security and therefore no document which requires to be stamped.[69] This method of security is used typically for short term facilities or for employees of the financial institution taking the security in respect of home loan and other finance. In practice, because of its informality, the normal requisitions are often dispensed with. This practice may lead to difficulties should the mortgagee wish to enforce its security, for instance in *The National Bank Ltd v Keegan*[70] the occupant of two rooms in a house subject to a mortgage was entitled to his estate in priority to the mortgagee.

[10.21] The principal disadvantage of this method is the necessity to obtain a court order should the mortgagee wish to enforce its security.[71] Other disadvantages include the absence of covenants to repair and insure the property in favour of the mortgagee and the absence of any restriction on the mortgagor granting leases of the property.

A further disadvantage is that this method is not flexible enough to permit second or subsequent mortgages with regard to property the title to which is registered in the Land Registry as the release of the land certificate to enable registration of the second mortgage will effectively be a release of the first equitable mortgage.

[10.22] The importance for bankers in having a loan properly documented and the consequences for failing to do so can be seen from the case of *O'Keeffe v O'Flynn Exhams and Partners and Allied Irish Banks*.[72] In that case the bank

---

67. See *Re Alton Corporation* [1985] BCLC 27.
68. The current Registry of Deeds fee is £26 (Registry of Deeds (Fees) Order, 1991 SI 360/1991) and the maximum Land Registry fee is £250 (Land Registration (Fees) Order, 1991 SI 363/1991).
69. Stamp duty is payable at the rate of one-tenth of one per cent of the amount secured subject to a limit of £500.
70. [1931] IR 344.
71. See Wylie, *Irish Land Law* (3rd ed) para 13.044.
72. High Court, unrep, 31 July 1992, Costello J; for a discussion of this decision see Coughlan, 'Land Law - Equitable Mortgages and Charges' [1992] 14 DULJ 171.

was requested to provide a joint loan to enable a husband and wife to purchase a house in their joint names. The loan however was granted only to the husband. The property was purchased in the joint names of husband and wife and the title deeds deposited with the bank as security for the loan. The court held that the bank obtained an equitable mortgage over the husband's interest in the property, but obtained no equitable interest over the wife's interest.

For a written record to be obtained of the mortgage and yet to avoid having in existence a stampable document it is the practice for an officer of the mortgagee to take a written note of the transaction and to read the note to the mortgagor at the time the title documents are being deposited.[73] This will avoid any inference that the title documents were deposited simply for safe keeping.[74] It is particularly important for the mortgagee to have sufficient written evidence of the transaction where the title documents were, prior to the mortgage, held by the bank for safe keeping or for some other purpose.[75]

[10.23] An indication as to how strictly courts may construe a transaction against a mortgagee can be seen from the decision in *Re Alton Corporation*.[76] In that case a company borrowed money to purchase a property. The loan agreement provided that (save as disclosed), the company would not create a mortgage or other encumbrance on its property and the loan would rank at least *pari passu* with all other indebtedness; on completion of the purchase, the company's solicitors would undertake to the bank to hold the title deeds to the bank's order, the solicitors would register a notice of the deposit of the land certificate in favour of the bank and that the Land Registry would be instructed to return the land certificate direct to the bank. The court held that, notwithstanding the foregoing, as there was nothing in the loan agreement to indicate that the deposit of the land certificate was to be made as security for the loan, an equitable mortgage had not been created. In addition the court regarded the *pari passu* language as being inconsistent with creating a security interest. Thus, bankers and their advisers when drafting facility letters or loan agreements would do well to heed the words of Sir Robert Megarry VC where he said in his judgment:[77]

> "The court may readily infer an agreement to create an equitable mortgage when money is lent and the borrower deposits title deeds with the lender without a single word passing, but where hundreds of words pass in a

---

[73.] See para **[10.24]** below.
[74.] Although see McMahon J in *Bank of Ireland Finance Ltd v DJ Daly Ltd* [1978] IR 79 at 82 - "The deposit of title deeds by a debtor is prima facie evidence of an agreement for a mortgage of the estate."
[75.] See *The National Bank Ltd v McGovern* [1931] IR 368.
[76.] [1985] BCLC 27.
[77.] *Ibid* at 32.

typewritten document evidently drafted by someone with legal knowledge, and the reference to the deposit of the title deeds wholly abstains from any indication of an intention that the deposit is to secure the loan, would it be right for the court to infer what the parties have abstained from stating or indicating?"

Procedure in taking a Mortgage by Deposit of Title Deeds

[10.24] The title documents should be deposited by all persons who have a legal or beneficial interest in the property, including occupiers who have contributed towards the purchase of the property.[78] Where appropriate, persons with a legal interest in the property should receive independent advice.[79] The form of written record would read along the following lines:

"Memorandum of Deposit

On this day of [date]

[Name of depositor] of [Address of depositor]

[On behalf of - name of corporate mortgagor if appropriate]

deposited with me as duly authorised officer of [name of mortgagee] documents of title relating to [address/description of property] and informed me that he was depositing the same by way of equitable mortgage to secure the payment of all sums now due or to become due to [name of mortgagee] by [name of mortgagor] either alone or jointly with any other person on any account or in respect of any liability whatsoever whether actual or contingent or whether in the character of principal debtor, guarantor or surety or otherwise together with in all cases interest (at such rate as may be agreed from time to time) and all other banking charges.

Signed by a duly

authorised officer on

behalf of [name of   "[Signature]"

mortgagee] in the presence

of:

In the case of a corporate mortgagor the officer of the mortgagor should produce to the mortgagee a certified copy of a board resolution of the mortgagor approving of the creation of the mortgage and authorising the officer to make the deposit.[80]

---

78. See para **[10.36]** below.
79. See *The Northern Banking Company Ltd v Carpenter* [1931] IR 268; *The National Bank Ltd v McGovern* [1931] IR 368; see further Ch 8.
80. See para **[18.56]** below.

[10.25] Previous correspondence such as a letter from the mortgagee, accepted by the mortgagor, offering financial facilities on certain conditions including the condition to grant a mortgage by deposit of title deeds could be deemed to be a registrable document. This would defeat the purpose of taking a mortgage by deposit of title deeds and accordingly a notice of withdrawal of correspondence should be signed by the mortgagor. This notice is designed to have the effect of cancelling all previous correspondence and would be along the following lines:

> "WHEREAS [name of mortgagor] has applied to [name of mortgagee] for certain accommodation on the security of an equitable mortgage by way of deposit of title deeds as a continuing and collateral security NOW IT IS HEREBY AGREED AND DECLARED that all or any written communication from [name of mortgagor] or on its behalf to such proposed deposit prior to this date are hereby withdrawn and cancelled and shall have no operation whatever and the terms and conditions of such equitable mortgage shall be solely determined by oral arrangement to be made between [name of mortgagor] and an officer or representative of [name of mortgagee]
>
> Dated this day of   19
>
> Signed by a duly
>
> authorised officer of
>
> [name of mortgagor]
>
> in the presence of:
>
> Signed by a duly
>
> authorised officer of
>
> [name of mortgagee]
>
> in the presence of:"

Although it is the practice in some financial institutions to have a notice of withdrawal of correspondence signed by its customer prior to the making of the deposit of title deeds, it is not certain that such notice will be effective. If there is no registrable document a subsequent registered mortgage will not take priority. An early decision to this effect occurred in *Re Burke*[81] where Burke deposited title deeds by way of equitable mortgage. There was no letter, memorandum or other instrument in writing accompanying the deposit. Subsequently, Burke executed a marriage settlement which was duly registered. It was held that the equitable mortgage had a prior claim. More recently this approach was applied by Costello P in *National Irish Bank Ltd v O'Connor & Arnold*.[82]

---

[81] 9 LR 124.
[82] High Court, unrep, 9 October 1996.

A facility letter which stipulates that a deposit of title deeds will be made to secure finance being made available may nonetheless be held to be registrable (in the Registry of Deeds or the Land Registry) and indeed stampable. The absence of registration (of a registrable mortgage) means that a subsequent mortgage (including judgment mortgage) taken without notice of the prior equitable mortgage (ie the agreement in the facility letter to create an equitable mortgage) and which is registered will take priority over the prior equitable mortgage.[83] To avoid this problem, it is safer for the facility letter to provide that "such security shall be given as the bank may from time to time designate." This though, creates an uncertainty for the customer who may be asked to give additional security and accordingly it is a risk the customer will have to consider carefully.

[10.26] The practice of having a withdrawal of correspondence signed by the mortgagor arose from the House of Lords' decision in *Fullerton v Provincial Bank of Ireland*[84] which restored the decision of Meredith J after it had been reversed by a majority of the Court of Appeal.[85] In that case, Stevenson wrote a number of letters to his bank manager stating that as soon as he obtained a conveyance to lands in County Westmeath he would deposit it with the bank as security for his overdraft. The deeds were deposited with the bank without any written memorandum of deposit. Subsequently, Stevenson executed a mortgage of the lands in favour of a second mortgagee and this mortgage was duly registered. Meredith J held that the documents of the correspondence:

> "constitute a conveyance within the true construction of the 5th Section of the Irish Registry Act ... and therefore the bank is not entitled to claim priority as in the case of an equitable mortgage by parol deposit of title deeds."

As the documents had not been registered the prior equitable mortgage lost its priority to the subsequent legal mortgage which was registered.

[10.27] The 5th Section of the Irish Registry Act provides:

> "that every deed or conveyance not registered, of any lands comprised in a deed or conveyance a memorial whereof shall be registered in pursuance of the Act, shall be deemed and adjudged fraudulent and void not only as against such a deed or conveyance so registered as aforesaid but likewise against all and every creditor and creditors by judgment etc. contained or expressed in such memorial registered as aforesaid."

---

83. See Wylie, *Irish Land Law* (3rd ed) para 13.146.
84. [1903] 1 IR 483; (1903) 37 ILTR 188.
85. In *Re Stevenson's Estate* [1902] 1 IR 23; (1902) 36 ILTR 49.

In 1832 the word "instrument" was substituted for "conveyance".[86] Accordingly, it is this section which the notice of withdrawal of correspondence seeks to avoid. Thus, the notice of withdrawal of correspondence will not be required where the title to the lands mortgaged is registered in the Land Registry.

It might be noted also, that even if the notice of withdrawal of correspondence is effective, where the mortgagor creates another mortgage, which is registered between the date of the facility letter (which incorporates an agreement to mortgage and is therefore registrable) and the time of the notice of withdrawal of correspondence, the subsequent equitable mortgage by deposit of title deeds will lose priority. A search in the appropriate registry at the time of completion of the equitable mortgage may fail to disclose the existence of the prior mortgage which may be in the course of being stamped prior to registration. In practice, this is unlikely to happen as the intervening mortgagee will or should have the title documents thereby preventing the customer from making the deposit and misleading bank (or the financial institution) making funds available on the security of the deposit. This risk may be minimised by the bank issuing initially a draft of the form of the facility letter prior to issuing the actual facility letter simultaneously with the deposit of title documents.

At the time of taking the deposit, an officer of the mortgagee should not refer to the facility letter as this could have the effect of bringing the facility letter into being a registrable document. If the notice of withdrawal of correspondence is fully effective it may negative replies to requisitions on title given by the customer or his solicitor and indeed the other terms of the facility letter. This poses an additional complicating factor as obviously the bank wishes to rely upon the replies to requisitions and indeed the terms of the facility letter itself.

[10.28] Where a family home is being mortgaged, if the title of such home is in the name of only one spouse, the other spouse should sign his or her consent prior to the mortgage.[87]

A typical form of consent would read:

> "I, [name of spouse], being the lawful spouse of [name of mortgagor] hereby consent for the purpose of compliance with the provisions of the Family Home Protection Act, 1976 to the equitable mortgage of [description of property] as security for [amount of loan/all present and future sums due or to become due by the mortgagor to the mortgagee]. I confirm having given this consent prior to the granting of the equitable mortgage by my lawful spouse.
>
> I confirm also that the implications of the equitable mortgage have been explained to me and I have been recommended by [the mortgagee] to obtain independent legal advice prior to completing this consent form.

---

86. Registry of Deeds (Ir) 1832.
87. See Family Home Protection Act, 1976, s 3; see paras **[10.59]**-**[10.62]** below.

Dated the day of [   ]

Signed by the said

[   ]

in the presence of:"

[10.29] Particulars of a mortgage by deposit of title deeds to land created by a company (formed or registered under the Companies Acts) must be filed in the Companies Registration Office.[88] The Form 47 to be filed with the Registrar of Companies within 21 days of the creation of the mortgage should contain the following information:

(1) "Equitable Mortgage by deposit of title deeds dated the day of [date]."

(2) Amount secured by the mortgage, or if appropriate, "All sums due and owing or to become due and owing by the Company to [name of mortgagee]".

(3) Name, address and occupation of the mortgagee.

(4) Description of the land mortgaged.

The form should be executed and verified in the prescribed manner.[89]

EQUITABLE MORTGAGES

[10.30] Apart from a mortgage by way of deposit of title deeds, an equitable mortgage will be created either where there is an agreement to create a mortgage or where an instrument is executed which shows an intention to create a mortgage. A mortgage of an equitable interest, such as the equity of redemption, is itself also an equitable mortgage.

Agreement to Mortgage

[10.31] An agreement to give a mortgage is itself an equitable mortgage. In *Re Hurley's Estate*[90] it was held that an agreement by a person to execute "a mortgage on all my houses and lands", created a valid equitable mortgage on the person's lands at the time of the agreement. Monroe J stated:[91]

"If a person mortgages or agrees to mortgage all his lands a charge is created in law or in equity on all the lands of which he is then the owner; and in registering an agreement, mortgage or conveyance, the memorial is only required to follow the description contained in the instrument."

---

88. Companies Act, 1963, s 99(2)(d); see para **[17.09]**.
89. See para **[17.54]** below.
90. [1894] 1 IR 488.
91. *Ibid* at 498.

More recently, Costello J stated:[92]

> "It is well established that an agreement in writing to deposit title deeds as a security for a loan creates an equitable charge on the land to which the deeds relate."

In the case of a corporate mortgagor, it should be noted also that a covenant given in a debenture (incorporating a floating charge) to deposit title documents of land, which the mortgagor subsequently acquires, may be registrable in the Registry of Deeds. The absence of such registration will result in the mortgagee losing priority to any subsequently registered security over the same land. Particulars of such covenant should be specified in the Form 47 being filed in the Companies Registration Office in respect of the floating charge. Failure to do so will mean that the mortgagee will be unable to enforce the covenant against the liquidator of the mortgagor or obtain priority in respect of such land against creditors of the mortgagor.[93]

Intention to Mortgage

[10.32]

> "It is now settled, after some conflict of opinion, that any instrument in writing for value, from which an intention can be collected to create a security for a debt on any property of the grantor, whether existing or future, and whether localised by the instrument or not, will create a charge by way of equitable mortgage on such property, and if it be future property when it accrues."[94]

CHARGES OF LAND

Unregistered Land

[10.33] A charge of land, unlike a mortgage, confers no legal estate in the land upon the chargee.[95] Accordingly, the chargee has no power to enter and sell the lands upon default. Section 21 of the Conveyancing Act 1881 enables a mortgagee to exercise the power of sale and "to convey the property sold for such estate and interest therein as is the subject of the mortgage."[96] It should be noted that as a charge does not create any estate or interest in the property, the chargee has no title to convey. The dangers in simply charging land[97] can be seen from the judgment of Johnston J (upheld by the Supreme Court) in *Bank of*

[92.] *O'Keeffe v O'Flynn Exhams and Partners and Allied Irish Banks* High Court, unrep, 31 July 1992 at p 29.
[93.] Companies Act, 1963, s 99(1); see Ch 17.
[94.] Walker LJ in *Coonan v O'Connor* [1903] 1 IR 449 at 471.
[95.] See *Northern Banking Co Ltd v Devlin* [1924] 1 IR 90.
[96.] Mortgage includes charge - see Conveyancing Act 1881, s 2(vi).
[97.] Other than land the title of which is registered in the Land Registry, see para **[10.34]** below.

Ireland v Freeney.[98] In that case, a person charged all his estate and interest in certain lands; the deed provided that the chargee would have the power of sale conferred on mortgagees by the Conveyancing Act, 1881 without the restrictions imposed by s 20 of that Act, with a further declaration by the chargor that he would stand possessed of the estate and interest in trust for the chargee as well as an irrevocable power of attorney in favour of the chargee empowering the chargee to convey the estate as he should think fit. It was held that none of the ancillary powers changed the character of the security from that of an equitable charge and accordingly the chargee was not entitled to possession. As Johnston J pointed out, [99]

> "The deed is primarily a deed of charge, and it does not of itself purport to convey any estate or interest to the bank".

Accordingly, a practitioner should be particularly careful when preparing security not simply to adopt an English form of security from a book of English precedents, which does not create a mortgage by conveyance or demise, as the mortgagee will receive insufficient title to enforce its security.[100]

Registered Land[101]

[10.34] Land, the title to which is registered in the Land Registry, may be charged by the owner.[102] The charge must be in the prescribed form,[103] namely Forms 67 or 68 or otherwise as set out in the Land Registration Rules, 1972.[104] The Registrar of Titles may refuse registration of a charge which is improper in form or which does not indicate with sufficient precision the particular interest or land to be charged.[105] The chargee will not acquire any interest in the land charged until the charge is registered in the Land Registry.[106] A typical form of charge (which incorporates the language required by the Land Registration Rules, 1972) would in its charging clause read as follows:

> "The chargor as Beneficial Owner and as registered owner, or as the person entitled to become registered owner[107] hereby charges ALL THAT AND THOSE the lands, hereditaments and premises described in the Schedule

---

98. [1930] IR 457.
99. *Ibid* at 461.
100. Although see Coughlan, 'Land Law - Equitable Mortgages and Charges' (1992) 14 DULJ 171 where it is suggested that an Irish court will make an order for sale in favour of an equitable chargee.
101. For further reading see Wylie, *Irish Land Law* (3rd ed) paras 12.24-12.29.
102. Registration of Title Act, 1964, s 62(1).
103. *Ibid* s 62(2); Land Registration Rules, 1972 (SI 230/1972), r 52.
104. SI 230/1972, r 113.
105. Land Registration Rules, 1972 (SI 230/1972), r 53.
106. Registration of Title Act, 1964, s 62(2); see para **[10.99]** below.

hereto together with all buildings,[108] fixtures (including trade fixtures) and fixed plant and machinery from time to time thereon with the payment or discharge of all moneys and liabilities hereby covenanted to be paid or discharged by the chargor and the chargor assents to the registration of the charge as a burden on the said property."[109]

The other clauses in the charge should be along the same lines as that of a mortgage including covenants (to keep in repair and insure), powers of sale and appointment of receiver, the grant of a power of attorney and a further assurance clause.

[10.35] The chargee of registered land is entitled to a certificate of charge from the Land Registry.[110] However, it should be noted that except where an equitable mortgage is created by deposit of the land certificate, a registered chargee is neither entitled to the land certificate[111] nor permitted to stipulate that the land certificate be given to the chargee.[112] Nonetheless, in practice a chargee will generally hold the original land certificate. Indeed on receiving a requisition for a land certificate signed by the registered owner of the land authorising delivery to a chargee, the Registrar of Titles is at liberty to deliver the land certificate to the chargee without further enquiring from the registered owner as to whether he is aware of his rights under s 67.[113]

EQUITIES AFFECTING MORTGAGES AND CHARGES

Direct and Indirect Financial Contributions

[10.36] A number of decisions in the 1970s developed the concept of a wife obtaining a beneficial interest in a property owned by her husband to the extent of her financial contributions to the property either direct or indirect.[114] As a result of the Family Home Protection Act, 1976 where a spouse's prior consent is required for the disposal of a family home and the more usual procedure now of having family homes legally owned by spouses as joint tenants, such

---

[107.] A person entitled to become registered owner may charge the land prior to his registration as owner - Registration of Title Act, 1964, s 90.

[108.] It is probably not essential to insert a reference to buildings as pursuant to s 3(1)(c) of the Registration of Title Act, 1964 land includes "houses or other buildings or structures whatsoever and parts of any such houses, buildings or structures whether divided vertically, horizontally or otherwise".

[109.] Registration of Title Act, 1964, s 69(2).

[110.] *Ibid* s 62(5); Land Registration Rules, 1972 (SI 230/1972), rr 156 and 157.

[111.] *Ibid* s 67(1); Land Registration Rules, 1972 (SI 230/1972) r 106.

[112.] *Ibid* s 67(2).

[113.] See *Re Associated Banks* [1944] Ir Jur R 29.

[114.] *C v C* [1976] IR 254; *Heavey v Heavey* (1977) 111 ILTR 1; *McGill v LS* [1979] IR 238; for a discussion of these and other cases see Cooney, 'Wives, Mistresses and Beneficial Ownership' (1979) Ir Jur 1; *Curran v Curran and AC Barlett (Ireland) Ltd v Curran and Curran* High Court, unrep, 10 March 1981, McWilliam J.

decisions are becoming of less relevance for properties involving disputes between spouses. However, increasingly two persons may live together in a property without being lawfully married.[115] Accordingly, such decisions are relevant to a prospective mortgagee and its solicitor when investigating title prior to the taking of security.

The legal effect of the early decisions (which are obviously still relevant for homes held in the name of one spouse) was summarised by Finlay P in *W v W*[116] where he stated:[117]

Direct Financial Contribution

"Where a wife contributed by money to the purchase of a property by her husband in his sole name in the absence of evidence of some inconsistent agreement or arrangement the court will decide that the wife is entitled to an equitable interest in that property approximately proportionate to the extent of her contribution as against the total value of the property at the time the contribution was made."

Indirect Financial Contribution

"Where a wife contributes either directly towards the repayment of mortgage instalments or contributes to a general family fund thus releasing her husband from an obligation which he otherwise would have discharged liabilities out of that fund and permitting him to repay mortgage instalments she will in the absence of proof of an inconsistent agreement or arrangement be entitled to an equitable share in the property which had been mortgaged and in respect of which the mortgage was redeemed approximately proportionate to her contribution to the mortgage repayments: to the value of the mortgage thus redeemed and to the value of the property at the relevant time."

[10.37] The dual approach of the direct and indirect financial contribution[118] was confirmed more recently by the Supreme Court in *N v N and C*[119] where it was held that the redemption of any form of charge or mortgage on a property consists of the acquisition by the owner or mortgagor of the estate in the property the subject matter of the mortgage. Therefore there is no distinction in principle between contributions made by a wife directly or indirectly towards the repayment of a mortgage and a contribution to the acquisition of an interest in property by an original purchaser. There may be instances, however, where a

---

115. As in the case of *McGill v LS* [1979] IR 238; paradoxically the constitutional ban on divorce, recently repealed, resulted in an increasing number of persons living together who were unable to become husband and wife.

116. [1981] ILRM 202.

117. *Ibid* at 204.

118. A useful example of a spouse obtaining a beneficial interest in a house from contributing to a family fund can be seen in *FG v PG* [1982] ILRM 155.

119. [1992] ILRM 127.

spouse simply obtains an interest in the furniture and not in the house itself, as where the purchase price and mortgage repayments are effectively provided by the other spouse's employer.[120]

No deemed Contribution

"Where a wife expends monies or carries out work in the improvement of a property which has been originally acquired by and the legal ownership in which is solely vested in the husband she will have no claim in respect of such contribution unless she established by evidence that from the circumstances surrounding the making of it she was lead to believe (or of course that it was specifically agreed) that she would be recompensed for it. Even where such a right to recompense is established either by an expressed agreement or by circumstance in which the wife making the contribution was lead to such belief it is a right to recompense in monies only and cannot and does not constitute a right to claim equitable share in the estate of the property concerned."

[10.38] The use of the trust concept was developed by the courts as the legal basis on which the title is held for the contributor.[121] In *C v C*[122] Kenny J stated:[123]

"When the matrimonial home is purchased in the name of a husband, either before or after a marriage, the wife does not become entitled, as wife, to any share in its ownership either because she occupies the status of wife or because she carries out household duties. In many cases, however, the wife contributes to the purchase price or mortgage instalments. Her contributions may be either by payment to the husband of monies which she has inherited or earned, or by paying the expenses of the household so that he has the money which makes it possible for him to pay the mortgage instalments ... the correct and most useful approach to these difficult cases is to apply the concept of a trust to the legal relationship which arises when a wife makes payments towards the purchase of a house, or the repayment of the mortgage instalments, when the house is in the sole name of the husband. When this is done, he becomes a trustee for her of a share in the house and the size of the share depends upon the amount of the contributions which she has made towards the purchase or the repayment of the mortgage."

[120.] See *McC v McC* [1986] ILRM 1.

[121.] On the application of the trust concept see Mee, 'Joint Ownership of the Family Home' [1992] 86 ILSI Gazette 59; for a detailed criticism of the judicial approach to the trust concept see Mee, 'Trusts of the Family Home' [1992] 14 DULJ 19; for a full treatment of the application of resulting trusts see Keane, *Equity and the Law of Trusts in the Republic of Ireland* (1988) Butterworths paras 12.12-12.16.

[122.] [1976] IR 254.

[123.] *Ibid* at 257 and 258; see also McWilliam J in *Power v Conroy* [1980] ILRM 31 at 32.

The use of the trust concept was set out in Northern Ireland by Lord MacDermott LCJ in *McFarlane v McFarlane*.[124] Lord MacDermott however considered, that where the contribution was indirect, a beneficial interest would only pass where there was an arrangement or agreement to that effect. His judgment was applied by Keane J in *MG v RD*[125] where he held that an air hostess who contributed to family finances did not obtain a beneficial interest in the family home. He concluded by stating:[126]

> "If the law in this country were that substantial contributions by a wife to household expenses which were the responsibility of the husband and which left him with more money to repay the mortgage instalments automatically entitled the wife to a beneficial interest in the relevant property, the plaintiff in the present case would succeed. For the reasons I have given, I am satisfied that this proposition does not correctly state the law; and I must accordingly dismiss the plaintiff's claim."

[10.39] More recently, in *Midland Bank plc v Dobson and Dobson*[127] the English Court of Appeal held that, although it had been the common intention of the husband and wife that she should have a beneficial interest in the house, the wife was unable to establish any such interest to prevent enforcement of the mortgage. The Court held that no resulting, implied or constructive trust arose, since it had not been agreed that she should act to her detriment in reliance on the common intention[128] - her household expenditure had not been made on that understanding, she had made no direct contribution to the purchase price or to any of the mortgage repayments, and her performance of household duties was perfectly consistent with her husband's sole ownership of the house.

[10.40] The current position on the trust concept may be considered to be correctly set out by Henchy J in the Supreme Court when he stated:[129]

> "Where the matrimonial home has been purchased in the name of the husband, and the wife has, either directly or indirectly, made contributions towards the purchase price or towards the discharge of mortgage instalments, the husband will be held to be a trustee for the wife of a share in the house roughly corresponding with the proportion of the purchased money represented by the wife's total contribution. Such a trust will be inferred when the wife's contribution is of such a source and kind as will justify a conclusion that the acquisition of the house was achieved by the joint efforts of the spouses.

[124.] [1972] NI 59; see also its application in *Allied Irish Banks Ltd v McWilliams* [1982] NI 156.

[125.] High Court, unrep, 28 April 1981.

[126.] *Ibid* p 18.

[127.] [1985] FLR 314.

[128.] On the requirement for a beneficiary to alter her position to her detriment for a trust to be created see Patten, 'Acquiring an Interest in the Home' (Conference Paper 1981).

[129.] In *McC v McC* [1986] ILRM 1 at 2; referred to by Egan J in *L v L* [1992] ILRM 115 at 125.

When the wife's contribution has been indirect (such as by contributing, by means of her earnings, to a general family fund) the courts will, in the absence of any express or implied agreement to the contrary, infer a trust in favour of the wife, on the ground that she has to that extent relieved the husband of the financial burden he incurred in purchasing the house."

A person who contributes to the discharge of mortgage payments on a property will not lose his beneficial interest emanating from such contribution even where he declines to take a transfer of the legal title. Thus the next of kin of such a contributor may acquire rights to the property in respect of which such contributions were made.[130]

[10.41] Even where title to a house is put into the name of one party to avoid the other from being disbarred from claiming social security, the courts will give effect to an acknowledgement of joint beneficial ownership. In *Tinsley v Milligan*[131] the English Court of Appeal by a majority upheld such an arrangement, Nicholls LJ stating:[132]

"the common law has drawn a distinction, not always clear or convincing, between (a) enforcing an illegal contract and (b) enforcing proprietary rights even though they are derived under an illegal contract. In general the court will assist in case (b)."

Their decision was upheld by a 3-2 majority in the House of Lords[133] which was held that where property interests are acquired as a result of an illegal transaction a party to the illegality can recover by virtue of a legal or equitable property interest if, but only if, he can establish his title without relying on his own illegality even if it emerged that the title on which he relied was acquired in the course of carrying through an illegal transaction. Clearly therefore, while an arrangement deriving from an illegal contract may be upheld, there is by no means judicial agreement on the matter.

[10.42] Efforts to have a wife's role in the home, as recognised by Article 41 of the Constitution of Ireland, acknowledged as entitling her to a beneficial interest failed in the decision of *L v L*.[134] The Supreme Court held unanimously that to allow the courts to extend the circumstances in which a wife may claim a beneficial interest in the family home to a situation where she has made no direct or indirect financial contribution to the acquisition of the property or to a family fund, but who has performed the constitutionally preferred role of wife and mother in the home would not be to develop any principle known to the

---

130. *Murray v Murray* [1996] 3 IR 251.
131. [1992] 2 All ER 391.
132. *Ibid* at 402.
133. [1993] 3 All ER 65.
134. [1992] ILRM 115.

common law but rather to create an entirely new right; such a course of action would constitute legislation and would be a usurpation by the courts of the function of the legislature.[135]

[10.43] In the case of two persons, who are unmarried to each other, living together in a premises the courts may need to consider more clearly the underlying implied agreement between the parties.[136] In *Lloyds Bank plc v Rosset*[137] the House of Lords held that in resolving a dispute between two persons who had shared a home in circumstances where one party was entitled to the legal estate and the other party claimed to be entitled to a beneficial interest, the fundamental question which had to be resolved was whether, on the basis of evidence of express discussions between the parties and independently of any inference to be drawn from their conduct in the course of sharing the property and managing their joint affairs, there had been at any time prior to the acquisition of the property, or exceptionally at some later date, any agreement, arrangement or understanding reached between them that the property was to be shared beneficially coupled with detrimental action or alteration of position on the part of the person claiming the beneficial interest, or failing that, whether there had been direct contributions to the purchase price by the person claiming the beneficial interest from which a constructive trust could be inferred.

[10.44] In *Bristol and West Building Society v Henning*[138] the English Court of Appeal held that where a property is subject to a beneficial interest or other property right, such as a licence to occupy, and both the legal owner and the person claiming the beneficial interest agree to raise a mortgage on the property, such agreement will be construed as being a common intention that the legal owner as trustee should have power to grant a mortgage to a third party, to the extent of granting to the third party a mortgage which has priority over any beneficial interests in the property. Although this decision will have little application to spouses in Ireland, due to the Family Home Protection Act, its logic[139] is nonetheless difficult to counter and could be applied to persons sharing a property which is legally owned by one party.

---

135. For a critical comment of this decision see Jackson, 'Family Law - The Constitution and Beneficial Ownership of the Family Home' [1992] 14 DULJ 153.
136. See *Hammond v Mitchell* [1992] 2 All ER 109.
137. [1990] 1 All ER 1111.
138. [1985] 2 All ER 606.
139. *Ibid*, see the judgment of Browne-Wilkinson LJ with which the other members of the Court agreed.

Family Law Act, 1981[140]

[10.45] Where two or more persons have agreed to marry one another, wedding gifts of property to either or both of them are presumed to be given to them as joint owners.[141] Where an agreement to marry is terminated, the rules of law concerning the rights of spouses to beneficial interests in property apply also to the rights of the parties to the terminated agreement.[142] What these rules of law are however is open to some doubt.[143] Despite this, mortgagees should be aware of the potential for beneficial interests arising - Requisition 25[144] specifies the appropriate queries to be raised. A statutory declaration should be required to verify the position and the application of the Family Law Act is usually incorporated in the statutory declaration verifying the position under the Family Home Protection Act, 1976.[145]

DOCTRINE OF NOTICE[146]

"the recognised text-books ... are unanimous that a purchaser or mortgagee who omits to make such inquiries and inspections as a prudent and reasonable purchaser, or mortgagee, acting on skilled advice would have made will be fixed with notice of what he would have discovered if he had made the inquiries and inspections which ought reasonably to have been made by him."[147]

[10.46] The basis for the foregoing quotation arises from s 3(1)(i) of the Conveyancing Act 1882. As McWilliam J said,[148] if this sub-section is put in a positive form it appears to correctly state the position as to notice namely:

A mortgagee[149] shall be affected by notice of any instrument, fact or thing if it is within his own knowledge, or would have come to his knowledge if such

---

[140.] Enacted on 23 June 1981.
[141.] Family Law Act, 1981, s 3.
[142.] *Ibid*, s 5.
[143.] See O'Donnell, 'Conveyancing and the Family Home' SYS Lecture 146 at p 30 - "... the points which I have made ... tend to show that the whole section is a nonsense".
[144.] 1996 Edition of the *Law Society of Ireland Objections and Requisitions on Title*.
[145.] See para **[10.72]** below.
[146.] See generally, Fisher and Lightwood's *Law of Mortgages* (10th ed) pp 461-470; Wylie, *Irish Land Law* (3rd ed) paras 3.069-3.093; Keane, *Equity and the Law of Trusts in the Republic of Ireland* (1988) para 5.07-5.14; Kenny J in *Bank of Ireland Finance Ltd v Rockfield Ltd* [1979] IR 21 at 37; Costello J in *Re Fuller and Company Ltd, O'Connor v McCarthy Walsh and Field* [1982] IR 161.
[147.] Kenny J in *Northern Bank Ltd v Henry, Henry and First National Building Society* [1981] IR 1 at 16; see also the Lord Justice of Appeal in *Carroll v Keayes* (1873) IR 8 Eq 97 at 132; see also O'Byrne J in *Heneghan v Davitt, Davitt and Rowley* [1933] IR 375 at 379.
[148.] *Ibid* at 6.
[149.] The Act uses the word purchaser which by s 1(4)(ii) is deemed to include mortgagee.

inquiries and inspections had been made as ought reasonably to have been made by him.

A person may be on notice in any of three circumstances namely, (a) actual notice - facts coming within a person's own knowledge, (b) constructive notice - facts which would have come within a person's own knowledge if appropriate inquiries/inspections had been made and (c) imputed notice - where a person's agent has actual or constructive notice.[150] The first two types of notice (actual and constructive) are covered in s 3(1)(i) of the Conveyancing Act 1882; the third type (imputed) is covered in s 3(1)(ii) of that Act.

[10.47] An illustration of constructive notice can be seen from the decision of *Somers v Weir*.[151] In that case, the plaintiff agreed to purchase a family home from the defendant's husband. When the plaintiff's solicitor sought a family home consent from the defendant, the defendant's husband made a statutory declaration to the effect that the defendant was uncontactable but was in any event not relying on the house as a family home and by virtue of a separation agreement had no interest in the family home. On a subsequent sale of the property the defendant's consent was sought and refused. The Supreme Court held, overruling Doyle J, that at the date of the purported assignment by the defendant's husband, the plaintiff was affected by constructive notice of the rights of the defendant because the continued existence of her statutory right to have her consent sought and of her other claims would have come to the knowledge of the plaintiff's solicitor if such inquiries had been made as ought reasonably to have been made by him and that, by reason of the failure to make such inquiries, the plaintiff had failed to discharge the onus of establishing that she had acquired "in good faith" the lessee's interest in the property and that, accordingly, the purported assignment by the defendant's husband to the plaintiff was void. Henchy J said pointedly:[152]

> "The inescapable conclusion is that the true facts ... would have come to the plaintiff's knowledge if (to use the words of the Act of 1882) 'such inquiries and inspections had been made as ought reasonably to have been made.' Therefore, the plaintiff must be held to have purchased with notice of those facts, so that the property she acquired (or purported to acquire) was not acquired in good faith."

[10.48] An even more striking example of this doctrine and the need for appropriate enquiries to be made and followed through when taking security is the decision in *Northern Bank Ltd v Henry, Henry and First National Building*

---

[150] *The Governor and Company of the Bank of Ireland v Smyth and Smyth* [1995] 2 IR 459 at para **[10.64]** below; see further, Sheridan, 'Notice and Registration' (1950) 9 NILQ 33.
[151] [1979] IR 94; 113 ILTR 81.
[152] *Ibid* at 110; and 89 respectively.

Society.[153] In that case, the plaintiff took a second charge on the first and second defendants' house, the first charge having previously been taken by the third defendant. The plaintiff took up the title deeds and had a search done but did not investigate title further, no doubt relying "in the interests of business expediency"[154] on the investigation previously undertaken by the first mortgagee. By failing to raise requisitions on title, the plaintiff was unaware that the wife of the owner had an equitable interest in the property and that there was litigation pending concerning the property. The Supreme Court held, affirming the decision of McWilliam J, that the wife's claim to be entitled to an equitable estate in the house would have come to the knowledge of the plaintiff if such inquiries and inspections had been made as ought reasonably to have been made by them in accordance with the standard described in s 3(1) of the Conveyancing Act 1882 and, accordingly at the date of the mortgage the plaintiff was deemed to have had constructive notice of the wife's claim. All three Supreme Court judges considered in their separate written judgments that the test to be applied is an objective one and is one which a reasonable mortgagee should apply and not what might be applied in the particular circumstances.[155] Thus, a person taking a mortgage of land without investigating the title to the land will be fixed with constructive notice of all that he would have discovered upon the usual investigation of title.[156]

[10.49] Although both Courts indicated that inspection of the property was not necessary,[157] a more recent English decision fixed the mortgagee with notice of what it considered it should have discovered through its surveyor's inspection. In *Kingsnorth Trust Ltd v Tizard*[158] the wife, who had contributed to the purchase money, occupied the spare room in the family home which was unregistered property. The husband when applying for the loan indicated he was single but informed the surveyor he was married but separated. The Court held that the fact that the husband was married at the time the surveyor made his valuation report was a fact material to the transaction between the husband and the plaintiff. Accordingly, when the surveyor discovered that the husband was married but separated from the wife, he was under a duty to look for signs of occupation by anyone other than the husband and the children and to communicate the information to his principals, ie the plaintiff; his knowledge that the husband had a wife was deemed to be the plaintiff's knowledge. In any event, the reference in the report to the husband's "son and daughter" should itself have put the plaintiff

---

153. [1981] IR 1.
154. *Ibid* at 8 per Henchy J.
155. *Ibid* per Henchy J at 9, Kenny J at 19 and Parke J at 20.
156. See *Gainsborough v Whitcombe Terra Cotton Clay Co Ltd* (1885) 53 LT 116.
157. *Ibid per* McWilliam J at 6 and Kenny J at 19.
158. [1986] 2 All ER 54.

on further inquiry which would have led them to discover the wife's beneficial interest in the matrimonial home, with the result that, by virtue of the English equivalent of s 3(1)(i) of the Conveyancing Act 1882,[159] the plaintiff had knowledge of such equitable rights as the wife had and the mortgage took effect subject to those rights.

[10.50] Accordingly, it should be noted that any prior equitable interest of a spouse (or other person) will rank in priority to a mortgagee's subsequent mortgage/charge unless the mortgagee can show that it acquired its interest *bona fide* for value without actual or constructive notice of the spouse's equitable interest.[160] A spouse, with a prior equitable interest, who remains silent in the presence of a representative of a proposed mortgagee may not be able to set up the prior equitable interest when the mortgagee seeks subsequently to enforce its security - this was the result of *Ulster Bank Ltd v Shanks*.[161] However, in view of the decision in *The Governor and Company of the Bank of Ireland v Smyth and Smyth*,[162] a silent spouse is less likely to have his or her prior equitable interest defeated.

[10.51] Increasingly, solicitors when retained by bankers to complete a transaction involving a mortgage or charge are requested to do the minimum possible on the grounds of time and cost. Bankers themselves are under increasing competition from other bankers and therefore do not wish to be seen by their customers as taking an uncommercial approach to what is essentially a business transaction - the lending of money and the taking of security. Although the *Northern Bank v Henry* case involved taking security to support a guarantee, the principles are the same and the decision is a reminder to bankers and more particularly their legal advisers as to the necessity to raise appropriate requisitions on title even where the title has been investigated previously by another mortgagee.

Occupiers' Rights[163]

> A purchaser must pay heed to anyone in occupation if he is to be sure of getting a good title ... a wise purchaser or lender will take no risks. Indeed, however

---

[159] The Law of Property Act 1925, s 199(1)(ii) (a).

[160] See *Allied Irish Banks Ltd v McWilliams* [1982] NI 156.

[161] [1982] NI 143.

[162] [1995] 2 IR 459; see para **[10.64]** below.

[163] For useful articles (i) on the judicial application of such rights see Sweeney, 'Occupiers' Rights: A New Hazard for Irish Conveyancers?' (1981) 75 ILSI Gazette 103; (ii) on the earlier judicial approach see Taylor, 'Land Registration - Occupiers' Rights' (1971) NLJ 784 and 821; (iii) on the nature of enquiries to be made - Pearce, 'Joint Occupation and the Doctrine of Notice' (1980) Ir Jur 211; and (iv) on suggested precautions for mortgages see Conlon, 'Beneficial Interests, Conveyancers and the Occupational Hazard' (1985) ILSI Gazette 59.

wise he may be he may have no ready opportunity of finding out; but, nevertheless, the law will protect the occupier.[164]

[10.52] Section 72(1) of the Registration of Title Act, 1964 provides that all registered land is subject to specified burdens. One of those burdens includes:[165]

> the rights of every person in actual occupation of the land or in receipt of the rents and profits thereof, save where, upon enquiry made of such person, the rights are not discharged.

The date when the interest is protected by actual occupation is the date of the transfer and not the date when the transfer is registered in the Land Registry.[166] The (English) Law Commission's Report on The Implications of *Williams & Glyn's Bank Ltd v Boland*[167] indicates an interpretative difficulty with the section.[168] Paragraph 12 of the Report includes the following:

> "The meaning of 'actual occupation' in this context is by no means clear. It has often been said to be a matter of fact, not law; and the words were described in Boland as ordinary words of plain English which should be interpreted as such, connoting physical presence rather than some legal entitlement. Yet as a fact actual occupation is not always easy either to discern or to establish: a person's occupation may be vicarious (for example, through a deserted wife or a caretaker) and must apparently have some degree of permanence. Moreover, as a concept, actual occupation can be exceedingly elusive: for example, in the particular context of rating law personal residence is not a necessary adjunct of actual occupation, and actual occupation is not necessarily terminated by lengthy absences. The breadth of interpretation given to the term in this context affords no confidence that its interpretation in the conveyancing context is liable to be any more precise."

In *Kingsnorth Trust Ltd v Tizard*,[169] it was held that for physical presence in a house to amount to actual occupation of the house it did not have to be either exclusive or continuous and uninterrupted. It seems also that a person who is not physically in occupation may claim protection if his employee or representative occupies on his behalf.[170]

[10.53] It was not until the House of Lords' decision of *Williams & Glyn's Bank Ltd v Boland*,[171] involving the application of the English equivalent of

---

[164.] Russell LJ in *Hodgson v Marks* [1971] 1 Ch. 892 at 932; see also the Lord Justice of Appeal in *Carroll v Keayes* (1873) IR 8 Eq 97 at 134.

[165.] Paragraph (j).

[166.] See *Abbey National Building Society v Cann* [1990] 1 All ER 1085.

[167.] Cmnd 8636.

[168.] The English equivalent to s 72(1)(j) is s 70(1)(g) of the Land Registration Act 1925.

[169.] [1986] 2 All ER 54.

[170.] See Oliver LJ in *Abbey National Building Society v Cann* [1990] 1 All ER 1085 at 1101.

[171.] [1980] 2 All ER 408; on the implications of the decision for lenders see also *Paget's Law of Banking* (11th ed) pp 602-605.

s 72(1)(j)[172] that conveyancers really took note of the hazards facing purchasers and mortgagees of land.[173] In this case, title to the property was registered in the name of the husband although both husband and wife contributed to the purchase price. Without the wife's knowledge the husband granted a mortgage of the property to secure a guarantee of his business debts - the bank failing to inquire at the time whether the wife had any interest in the property. Both the Court of Appeal and the House of Lords held that the wife was a person in actual occupation of the land within the meaning of the Act (since she was physically living in the property) and accordingly the wife's interest was protected as against the bank.

It should be noted that the mere fact of occupation by a spouse or other person is not as such protected by s 72(1)(j).[174] What is protected are the rights of such person in occupation.[175] Accordingly, where such person has an equitable interest in the property that equitable interest will be protected. Protected interests will include the estate of the mortgagor's tenants.[176] Although it appears that inspection of the property may not be necessary for a mortgagee or chargee,[177] where an inspection is carried out the mortgagee will be fixed with notice of what the surveyor discovered or ought to have discovered from his inspection.[178]

[10.54] As a result of the *Williams & Glyn's* decision the Law Society introduced the following additional requisitions on title in their standard requisitions:[179]

> 13.9 Has any person other than the Vendor made any direct or indirect
>   financial contribution or been the beneficiary of any agreement or

---

[172.] Section 70(1)(g) of the Land Registration Act 1925.

[173.] See also Robert Reid QC, The Legal Implications of *Williams & Glyn's Bank Ltd v Boland* (Conference Paper 1981) - "The decision in *Williams and Glyn's* created a stir, not so much because of any novelty in what was decided, but because the House of Lords at last made the legal profession take its head out of the sand and seriously consider what had been the law, for at any rate eight years, since the decision of the Court of Appeal in *Hodgson and Marks* in 1971."

[174.] *Guckian and Guckian v Brennan and Sheridan* [1981] IR 478; see also *City of London Building Society v Flegg* [1987] 2 WLR 1266 and Oliver LJ in *Abbey National Building Society v Cann* [1990] 1 All ER 1085 at 1096.

[175.] See the dissenting judgment of Russell LJ in the English Court of Appeal in *National Provincial Bank Ltd v Ainsworth* [1964] 1 All ER 688 at 701 approved unanimously by the House of Lords [1965] 2 All ER 472.

[176.] See *Woolwich Equitable Building Society v Marshall* [1952] Ch 1.

[177.] *Northern Bank Ltd v Henry, Henry and First National Building Society* [1981] IR 1 *per* McWilliam J at 6 and Kenny J at 19.

[178.] *Kingsnorth Trust Ltd v Tizard* [1986] 2 All ER 54.

[179.] Requisition 14.5 of the 1996 edition of the Law Society's *Objections and Requisitions on Title*; for further practical suggestions see Russell, '*Williams and Glyn's Bank Ltd v Boland and Brown*: *The Practical Implications*' [1981] NILQ 3.

arrangement whereby that person has acquired an interest in the property or any part of it?

13.10 If so, furnish details now of the interest acquired or claimed.

[10.55] Another requisition on title, and indeed a normal completion requirement for registered titles, is a declaration by the chargor declaring that none of the burdens specified in s 72 of the Registration of Title Act, 1964 affect the property, known as a Section 72 Declaration. However, reliance should not be placed on this declaration concerning any rights of an occupier because enquiry should be made to such occupier. Although the words in the section "upon enquiry made of such person" may be construed as enquiries made concerning such person, it has been judicially held that such reference means enquiry to such person.[180] However, the possibility of a mortgagee claiming damages for misrepresentation cannot be excluded and obviously solicitors should take full and complete instructions prior to replying to requisitions or queries on title to avoid any claim for damages for their negligent reply or for failing to advise the mortgagor of the necessary legal requirements.

A claim for damages against a mortgagor for misrepresentation may be of little value if the mortgagor is unable in the first instance to repay the debt or liabilities owing by it to the mortgagee. Accordingly, a mortgagee may have little real remedy for being unable to enforce its mortgage where it finds an undisclosed occupier has rights over the mortgaged property. The lack of sympathy for mortgagees in this predicament is epitomised by the Law Commission's Report on The Implications of *Williams & Glyn's Bank Ltd v Boland*[181] where it states:[182]

> "So far as lenders are concerned, it may perhaps be argued that they are well capable of taking care of themselves; they can insure, or increase their charges, to cover the occasional 'Boland' loss so that such losses are borne by the general body of borrowers, without perceptible hardship to the individual."

[10.56] The beneficial rights of occupiers, illustrated by the *Williams & Glyn* decision, apply also to corporate bodies. For example, a premises owned by a company may be occupied by other companies in the same group. Potential difficulties may arise where a company in the group has a significant unconnected minority shareholder who may claim that such shareholder has made a financial contribution to the property and should receive a return or more

---

[180.] See Blayney J in *Doherty v Doherty and Friends Provident Life Office* [1991] 2 IR 458 at 462; [1992] ILRM 372 at 375; Vaughan Williams LJ in *Hunt v Luck* [1902] 1 Ch 428 at 433; see also para 18 of The Law Commission's *Report on the Implications of Williams & Glyn's Bank Ltd v Boland* (Cmnd 8636).

[181.] Cmnd 8636.

[182.] *Ibid* para 64.

likely should have its occupation protected against a mortgagee who seeks to enforce its mortgage against the legal owner.

Although the *Williams & Glyn* decision dealt with titles which are registered, it is equally important in the context of carrying out a proper investigation of title for unregistered land in accordance with the notice requirements of s 3 of the Conveyancing Act 1882.[183]

[10.57] The decision in *Williams & Glyn* involved the owner mortgaging his property some time following its purchase. Most financing transactions for personal borrowers involve the creation of a mortgage/charge at the time of the purchase of the property to secure the finance raised for the purchase. The House of Lords' decision in *Abbey National Building Society v Cann*[184] indicates that a mortgagee/chargee need not be concerned with this section where the mortgage/charge is completed simultaneously with the purchase pursuant to a prior agreement to create such an encumbrance.[185] The two judgments (with which the three other Lords agreed) were delivered by Lord Oliver and Lord Jauncey. Lord Oliver stated:[186]

> "The reality is that, in the vast majority of cases, the acquisition of the legal estate and the charge are not only precisely simultaneous but indissolubly bound together. The acquisition of the legal estate is entirely dependent on the provision of funds which will have been provided only against an agreement that the estate will be charged to secure them ... The reality is that the purchaser of land who relies on a building society or bank loan for the completion of his purchase never in fact acquires anything but an equity of redemption, for the land is, from the very inception, charged with the amount of the loan without which it could never have been transferred at all and it was never intended that it should be otherwise."

Lord Jauncey stated:[187]

> "It is of course correct as a matter of strict legal analysis that a purchaser of property cannot grant a mortgage over it until the legal estate has vested in him. The question however is whether having borrowed money in order to complete the purchase against an undertaking to grant security for the loan over the property the purchaser is, for a moment of time, in a position to deal with the legal estate as though the mortgagee had no interest therein ...
>
> ... In my view a purchaser who can only complete the transaction by borrowing money for the security of which he is contractually bound to grant a mortgage to the lender co instanti with the execution of the conveyance in his favour

---

[183.] See Murray J in *Ulster Bank Ltd v Shanks* [1982] NI 143 at 146.
[184.] [1990] 1 All ER 1085.
[185.] For further discussion see Cranston, *Banks - Liability and Risk* pp 88-94.
[186.] [1990] 1 All ER 1085 at 1100.
[187.] *Ibid* at 1107.

cannot in reality ever be said to have acquired even for a scintilla temporis the unencumbered fee simple or leasehold interest in land whereby he could grant interests having priority over the mortgage or the estoppel in favour of prior grantees could be fed with similar results. Since no one can grant what he does not have, it follows that such a purchaser could never grant an interest which was not subject to the limitations on his own interest."

However, the mortgagee/chargee will be concerned to see that its customer, the purchaser, obtains vacant possession of the property it is financing. Accordingly, its solicitor will need to consider the possibility of occupiers' rights when reviewing the replies given by the vendor's solicitor to the requisitions on title raised by the purchaser's solicitor.

[10.58] The benefits of a mortgagee insisting that a person with beneficial interests in a property about to be mortgaged should be independently advised by a solicitor can be seen from the outcome of *Doherty v Doherty and Friends Provident Life Office*.[188] In that case, the wife financed the construction of a family home the title of which was registered solely in the name of the husband. Friends Provident Life Office advanced a loan to the husband on the security of a mortgage on the family home. Requisitions on title were furnished to and obtained from the husband who made a s 72 declaration. The wife signed a consent to the mortgage for the purposes of the Family Home Protection Act, 1976. Although Blayney J held that as the wife had made financial contributions towards the construction of the house she had acquired a beneficial interest which was an unregistered burden within the meaning of s 72, there was no obligation on Friends Provident Life Office to explain the consequences of the mortgage to the wife as she was independently advised; furthermore as the wife's conduct amounted to a representation that she had no beneficial interest in the property there was no duty to enquire of her as to whether or not she had such an interest; accordingly she was estopped from asserting her interest in priority to the mortgage. In coming to his conclusion Blayney J relied on an earlier High Court decision with similar results.[189]

It may be imprudent however for practitioners to rely entirely on a family home consent as waiving the consenter's beneficial interests. This applies particularly where a spouse consents to the other spouse mortgaging his (or her as the case may be) interest in the property (as required by the Family Home Protection Act, 1976). In this case however Mrs Doherty consented "to the within mortgage of our family home." It is therefore a safer course to provide that all interests of occupiers are mortgaged or charged.[190] Otherwise to obtain vacant possession

---

188. [1991] 2 IR 458; [1992] ILRM 372; see further Ch 8.
189. *Harrison v Harrison* High Court, unrep, 20 June 1989, Barrington J.

the mortgagee may be required to prove that the mortgage was taken without (either actual or constructive) notice.

SPOUSE'S CONSENT

Family Home Protection Act, 1976[191]

[10.59] The Family Home Protection Act, 1976 came into force on 12 July 1976. Section 3(1) of that Act states:

> Where a spouse, without the prior consent in writing of the other spouse, purports to convey any interest in the family home to any person except the other spouse, then, the purported conveyance shall be void.

[10.60] A number of words call for further clarification namely, convey and conveyance, interest and family home. Conveyance includes a mortgage and an enforceable agreement to grant a mortgage (convey also includes mortgage).[192] Mortgage is defined as including "an equitable mortgage, a charge on registered land and a chattel mortgage."[193] Interest is defined as meaning "any estate, right, title or other interest, legal or equitable".[194] The expression family home means "primarily, a dwelling in which a married couple ordinarily reside ... in addition, a dwelling in which a spouse whose protection is in issue ordinarily resides or, if that spouse has left the other spouse, ordinarily resided before so leaving."[195] It was held in *The Governor and Company of the Bank of Ireland v Slevin*[196] that the limitation of the definition of "family home" to a "dwelling" was quite clearly for the purpose of separating a dwelling house from any other enterprise and a mortgage or charge created without the spouse's prior consent was void only insofar as it related to the dwelling but not otherwise.[197]

The section does not apply where an enforceable contract for sale is entered into prior to 12 July 1976 but the sale is not completed until on or after that date.[198]

[190.] See para **[10.67]** below; for a form of acknowledgement of no claim by an occupier see Russell, '*Williams v Glyn's Bank Ltd v Boland and Brown*: The Practical Implications' [1981] NILQ 3.

[191.] See generally Wylie, *Irish Conveyancing Law* (2nd ed, 1996) para 16.61-16.73; Carroll, 'The Family Home Protection Act' SYS Lecture 124.

[192.] Family Home Protection Act, 1976, s 1(1).

[193.] *Ibid.*

[194.] *Ibid*; see also *The Governor and Company of the Bank of Ireland v Purcell* [1989] IR 327; [1988] ILRM 480 and [1990] ILRM 106; see further para **[10.70]** below.

[195.] Family Home Protection Act, 1976, s 2(1); for a consideration of this sub-section see Finlay CJ in *National Irish Bank Ltd v Graham, Graham* [1994] 2 ILRM 109.

[196.] [1995] 2 IR 454.

[197.] See also *Allied Irish Banks plc v O'Neill and Kidd* [1995] 2 IR 473.

[198.] *Hamilton v Hamilton and Dunne* [1982] IR 466.

353

The section does not apply also where both spouses convey an interest in the family home,[199] as the section "is directed against unilateral alienation by one spouse".[200]

[10.61] There are three exceptions to the requirement of consent[201] namely:

1. The court may in certain circumstances dispense with the spouse's consent.[202] This basically arises only if the court considers the spouse is being unreasonable in withholding consent,[203] the spouse whose consent is required has deserted [204] or the spouse whose consent is required is incapable of consenting.[205]

2. In respect of a conveyance made by a spouse in pursuance of an enforceable agreement made before the marriage of the spouses.[206]

3. (a) if the conveyance is made to a purchaser for full value,

    (b) if the conveyance is made, by a person other than the spouse making the purported conveyance, to a purchaser for value, or

    (c) if the conveyance's validity depends on the validity of a conveyance in respect of which any of the conditions in (a) or (b) or (2) above is satisfied.[207]

Purchaser is defined as including a mortgagee or other person who in good faith acquires an estate or interest in property.[208] "Full value" is stated to mean "such value as amounts or approximates to the value of that for which it is given."[209]

[10.62] To come within this exception it is accordingly essential to act in "good faith" and to do so the onus is on the person seeking to uphold the transaction.[210] Henchy J set out the requirements as follows:[211]

> "The question whether a purchaser has acted in good faith necessarily depends on the extent of his knowledge of the relevant circumstances. In earlier times the tendency was to judge a purchaser solely by the facts that had actually came

---

[199.] *Nestor v Murphy and Murphy* High Court, unrep, 23 October 1979, Henchy J.

[200.] *Ibid*, Henchy J at page 3.

[201.] See also Family Home Protection Act, 1976, s 3(8)(b) (as introduced by the Family Law Act, 1995).

[202.] Family Home Protection Act, 1976, s 4(1).

[203.] *Ibid*, s 4(2).

[204.] *Ibid*, s 4(3).

[205.] *Ibid*, s 4(4).

[206.] *Ibid*, s 3(2).

[207.] *Ibid*, s 3(3).

[208.] *Ibid*, s 3(6).

[209.] *Ibid*, s 3(5).

[210.] *Ibid*, s 3(4).

[211.] *Somers v Weir* [1979] IR 94 at 108; (1979) 113 ILTR 81 at 88.

to his knowledge. In the course of time it came to be held in the Court of Chancery that it would be unconscionable for the purchaser to take his stand on the facts that had come to his notice to the exclusion of those which ordinary prudence or circumspection or skill should have called to his attention when the facts at his command beckoned him to look and inquire further, and he refrained from doing so, equity fixed him with constructive notice of what he would have ascertained if he had pursued the further investigation which a person of reasonable care and skill would have felt proper to make in the circumstances. He would not be allowed to say "I acted in good faith, in ignorance of those facts, of which I learned only after I took the conveyance" if those facts were such as a reasonable man in the circumstances would have brought within his knowledge."

An indication of the difficulty in coming with the "good faith" requirement can be seen from the Supreme Court's decision in *Somers v Weir*.[212] In that case, the defendant left the family home with the children and the husband contracted to sell the home to the plaintiff. When the plaintiff's solicitor required the defendant's written consent to the sale, he was informed by the husband's solicitor that the defendant had left the house some years ago and was no longer relying on it as her family home, that the husband was abroad and that the defendant's address was unknown. On returning to Dublin the husband made a statutory declaration in which he stated that the defendant had not relied on the home as her family home since he and the defendant had separated and that by virtue of a separation agreement (which was not exhibited) she had no interest in the home. The sale was completed. The following year when re-selling the house the purchaser insisted on the defendant's written consent to the previous sale and so the plaintiff sought the defendant's consent. The High Court held that the plaintiff had done all that was reasonably necessary to acquaint herself with the title of the defendant's husband and granted a consent pursuant to s 4 of the Act. However the Supreme Court unanimously allowed the appeal and over-turned the consent.

The Supreme Court held that at the date of the purported assignment by the defendant's husband, the plaintiff was affected by constructive notice of the rights of the defendant because the continued existence of her statutory right to have her consent sought and of her other claims would have come to the knowledge of the plaintiff's solicitor if such inquiries had been made as ought reasonably to have been made by him and that by reason of the failure to make such inquiries, the plaintiff had failed to discharge the onus of establishing that she had acquired "in good faith" the lessee's interest in the property and that, accordingly, the purported assignment by the defendant's husband to the plaintiff was void.

[212.] [1979] IR 94; (1979) 113 ILTR 81.

More recently the Supreme Court held, in *Allied Irish Banks plc v Finnegan and Finnegan*,[213] that where the bank relied upon exemption (3)(a)[214] it had to show that it did not have any actual or constructive notice of the possible invalidity of the consent.[215]

Procedure in Practice

[10.63] When acting for a mortgagee it is essential, not only to have the mortgagor's spouse give his/her prior written consent[216] but also, to ascertain that in respect of unregistered land the vendor's spouse has given his/her written consent to all conveyances and assignments of the lands since 12 July 1976.

The principal initial issue here is for the mortgagee to establish whether or not the mortgagor (and previous vendors) has a spouse and to obtain verification. The reported court decisions concern principally situations where a married couple who ordinarily resided in the property in question have separated and one spouse either refuses to consent or is or appears to be uncontactable.

In ascertaining the situation the mortgagee's solicitor should raise the following queries:[217]

1.   Is the property or any part thereof the vendor's "family home" as defined in the Act.

2.   If the answer to 1. is in the affirmative, furnish the prior written consent of the vendor's spouse and verify the marriage by statutory declaration exhibiting therein copy civil marriage certificate...

3.   If the answer to 1. is in the negative, state the grounds relied upon, and furnish now draft statutory declaration for approval verifying these grounds.

4.   In respect of all "conveyances" (as defined in the 1976 Act) of unregistered property made on or after the 12 July 1976 furnish spouses' prior written consents where appropriate together with verification of marriage by statutory declaration exhibiting therein copy civil marriage certificate or where consent is not necessary please furnish evidence verifying same by way of statutory declaration.

5.   (a)   Did/does the property or any part thereof comprise the "family home" of any person other than the vendor or previous owner.

---

213. [1996] 1 ILRM 401.

214. See para **[10.61]** above.

215. [1996] 1 ILRM 401 at 405 *per* Blayney J (Hamilton CJ and O'Flaherty J concurring).

216. For a form of consent see para **[10.28]** above and para **[10.67]** below.

217. As set out in requisition 24 of the 1996 Edition of the Law Society's *Objections and Requisitions on Title*.

(b) If so, give the name of such person and give the nature of the "interests" as defined in the 1976 Act (if any) in the property.

(c) In relation to any such person having an "interest" furnish the prior written consent of that person's spouse to any "conveyance" (as defined as aforesaid) of that person's interest in the property or any part thereof since 12 July 1976 and verify such spouse's marriage by statutory declaration exhibiting therein copy civil marriage certificate.

(d) If such person did not have an "interest" as above in the property or any part of it state the grounds relied upon and furnish now draft statutory declaration for approval verifying those grounds.

Independent Advice for Consenting Spouse

[10.64] Practitioners have become increasingly aware of the desirability of arranging for a spouse prior to giving his/her consent to obtain independent advice.[218] The necessity for such independent advice was confirmed by the Supreme Court's decision in *The Governor and Company of the Bank of Ireland v Smyth and Smyth*.[219] In this case, the bank failed to obtain possession of a family home where the wife of the owner successfully pleaded that her consent (pursuant to s 3 of the Family Home Protection Act, 1976) was not a true consent in that she was not advised to obtain independent legal advice and that she did not have a proper understanding of what she was signing. In holding that the charge was thus void Geoghegan J in the High Court[220] applied the equitable principles referred to by the English Court of Appeal in *Barclays Bank plc v O'Brien*.[221] Geoghegan J considered that the views expressed by Scott LJ in the English Court of Appeal "represent Irish law". Geoghegan J quoted at length from the head-note in the All England Reports[222] as indicating the current position in Ireland. As it is now essential for lenders in Ireland and their advisers to take heed of these words, it is appropriate that the head-note as adopted by Geoghegan J be remembered:[223]

> "as a matter of policy married women who provided security for their husband's debts and others in an analogous position such as elderly parents on whom pressure might be brought to bear by adult children, were to be treated as

---

[218.] See further Ch 8.

[219.] [1995] 2 IR 459.

[220.] High Court, unrep, 26 March 1993.

[221.] [1992] 4 All ER 983; this decision was subsequently upheld by the House of Lords see further para **[8.08]**.

[222.] [1992] 4 All ER 983 at 984.

[223.] High Court, unrep, 26th March 1993 Geoghegan J at pp 7 and 8.

a specially protected class of sureties so that where the relationship between the surety and the debtor was one in which influence by the debtor over the surety and reliance by the surety on the debtor were natural and probable features of the relationship, the security given by the surety would in certain circumstances be unenforceable notwithstanding that the creditor might have no knowledge of and not have been responsible for the vitiating feature of the transaction. The circumstances in which equity would hold that the security given by a surety in that protected class was unenforceable were:

(i)   if the relationship between the debtor and the surety and the consequent likelihood of influence and reliance was known to the creditor,

(ii) if the surety's consent to the transaction was procured by undue influence or material misrepresentation on the part of the debtor or the surety lacked an adequate understanding of the nature and effect of the transaction,

(iii) if the creditor, whether by leaving it to the debtor to deal with the surety or otherwise, failed to take reasonable steps to try and ensure that the surety entered into the transaction with an adequate understanding of its nature and effect and that the surety's consent to the transaction was a true and informed consent. Accordingly, although each case within the protected class depended on its own facts, as a general rule a creditor who took security from a married woman for her husband's debts ought to take reasonable steps, such as advising her to take independent advice or, if she declined to do so, offering a fair explanation of the security document before she signed it, to see that she understood the transaction she was entering into ...".

The bank appealed to the Supreme Court which unanimously held that a "consent" for the purposes of s 3 of the Family Home Protection Act, 1976 must be a fully informed consent, with the spouse understanding what he or she was consenting to; as the wife believed the charge affecting the land would not affect the family home, the consent was held to be invalid. Blayney J held that [224] first, the validity of the spouse's consent depended solely on whether the spouse had full knowledge of what she was doing; secondly, the fact that the bank was not aware of her lack of knowledge was immaterial as it had constructive notice of her lack of knowledge, since if the bank's solicitor had enquired as to the state of the spouse's knowledge in regard to what was covered by the charge, the bank would have discovered she believed the charge did not apply to the family home. Accordingly, the bank was treated as having constructive knowledge of what the enquiries would have revealed.[225]

The court further held that the bank did not owe any duty to the consenting spouse, but rather the bank's agent ought to have made enquiries to protect the

[224.] [1995] 2 IR 459 at 469 (Hamilton CJ and Egan J agreeing with his judgment).
[225.] See Conveyancing Act 1882, s 3, see para **[10.48]** above.

bank's own interests, since if the spouse had consented to the charge after it had been fully explained to her and after she had received independent advice it was unlikely that her consent could have been challenged.[226]

[10.65] In the subsequent case of *The Bank of Nova Scotia v Hogan and Hogan*,[227] the Supreme Court highlighted the consequences which flowed from the requirement to obtain the consent of a non-owing spouse to a mortgage of a family home.[228] Murphy J stated:[229]

"... two consequences flow, first, that a grantee or purchaser must, in his own interest, ensure that the necessary statutory consent is forthcoming and, secondly, that the consent, if given, is a true consent, that is to say, constitutes a decision which represents a fully free exercise of the independent will of the spouse concerned."

Verification Not a Family Home

[10.66] Requisition 24.3 requests the submission of a statutory declaration. The extent of corroboration required for the statutory declaration to be acceptable was set out by Costello J in *Reynolds and Reynolds v Waters*.[230] In that case the vendor's solicitor replied to the equivalent of Requisition 24.3 as follows:[231]

"the vendor will on completion furnish statutory declaration verifying that he has been separated from his wife who deserted him prior to his taking up residence in the premises in sale and that his wife from whom he is now divorced has never resided in the premises."

The purchaser's solicitor sought the wife's consent or a joint declaration that the premises were not a family home. The vendor's solicitor maintained that the declaration of the vendor was adequate evidence under the Family Home Protection Act that the property was not a family home within the meaning of the Act. In deciding that the purchaser's solicitor's requirements were unreasonable, Costello J stated:[232]

"if (a) the purchaser's solicitor has made all proper enquiries (by, for example, utilising Requisition 52 of the Law Society's Requisitions [now Requisition 24.3]); and (b) has been informed of facts which, if true, establish that the dwelling is not a family home and that these facts will be verified by statutory

---

226. For further commentary on this decision see Wylie, *Irish Conveyancing Law* (2nd ed, 1996) para 16.69.
227. [1996] 3 IR 239.
228. Pursuant to the Family Home Protection Act, 1976, s 3.
229. [1996] 3 IR 239 at 246 (O'Flaherty J and Blayney J agreed with his judgment).
230. High Court, unrep, 1 March 1982.
231. *Ibid* page 3.
232. *Ibid* page 7; for a criticism of Costello J's approach see O'Donnell, 'Conveyancing and the Family Home' - SYS Lecture 146.

declaration; and (c) neither the purchaser nor his solicitor has any reason to doubt the accuracy or the veracity of the statements in the proposed statutory declaration; then it is not reasonable for the purchaser's solicitor to insist on corroboration of the vendor's declaration and in its absence to call on the vendor to obtain a declaration from the Court. By accepting the draft declaration in such circumstances he will have done all that he can reasonably be required to do so. Should it subsequently transpire that due to carelessness or fraud he had been misinformed and that the premises were in fact a family home, then the purchaser would have acquired the property in good faith and if full value was paid for it the conveyance will be protected by s 3(3)(a) of the Act."

Costello J rejected the submission of the purchaser that he was not bound to accept the vendor's statutory declaration because the vendor's financial interest in the transaction raised the question of his trustworthiness and justified a request for corroboration.

Form of Consent

[10.67] The standard form of consent on a conveyance or assignment would read as follows:

> I, [   ] being the spouse of the within named vendor hereby consent for the purposes of s 3 of the Family Home Protection Act, 1976 to the sale by the Vendor of the within premises for the sum of £ ___ .

On a mortgage it would read as follows:

> I, [   ] being the lawful spouse of the within named Mortgagor in consideration of the Bank granting or continuing banking facilities or other accommodation for as long as the Bank may think fit to the Mortgagor or to third parties guaranteed by the Mortgagor or guaranteeing banking facilities or other accommodation at the Mortgagor's request at any other bank on the Mortgagor's account or on that of third parties hereby:
>
> (a) CONSENT to the granting of the within demise for the purposes of compliance with the provisions of the Family Home Protection Act, 1976 and I confirm having subscribed my name hereunder prior to the execution of the within Mortgage by the Mortgagor; and
>
> (b) DEMISE unto the Bank all my estate, right, title and interest (if any) in the Mortgaged Property with the payment to the Bank of all moneys covenanted to be paid by my said spouse, the Mortgagor and subject to all the within terms, covenants and conditions in so far as the same may be applicable thereto TO HOLD such of the same as are of freehold tenure unto the Bank for the term of 1,000 years from the date hereof and TO HOLD such of the same as are of leasehold tenure unto the Bank for the residue of the respective terms of years for which the same is held less the last three days of each of such terms subject as to all the Mortgaged Property to the proviso for redemption

hereinbefore contained and henceforth I shall stand possessed of the reversion hereby reserved in such estate, right, title and interest (if any) in trust for the Bank subject to such equity of redemption (if any) as may for the time being be subsisting therein by virtue of these presents to dispose thereof as the Bank may direct and I hereby authorise the Bank to appoint a new trustee or trustees of the said reversion or reversions at any time or times in my place or of any trustee appointed under this power as if he or they were incapable of acting in the trusts hereof and I hereby irrevocably appoint the Secretary for the time being of the Bank my attorney to assign in my name and on my behalf at any time the said reversion or reversions to the Bank as the Bank shall think fit and subject to such equity of redemption (if any) as may for the time being be subsisting as aforesaid and to execute and do all instruments and acts necessary or proper for that purpose.

SIGNED SEALED and DELIVERED

by the said [   ]

in the presence of [   ]:

It is recommended that the memorial (to be filed in the Registry of Deeds) would end with the following words (immediately prior to the reference of witnesses to the deed of assurance):

and it was further witnessed that for the consideration therein the Mortgagor's spouse did thereby endorse her prior consent to the said Mortgage and did thereby demise unto the Bank all her estate, right, title and interest (if any) in the property set out in the First Schedule of the said Mortgage and in the Schedule hereto.

The purpose of paragraph (b) is to ensure that whatever beneficial interest in the premises the spouse has should be subject to the mortgage. This will be subject to the spouse receiving appropriate independent advice[233] and not being subject to any other vitiating elements.

[10.68] It is not essential that the spouse's consent be endorsed on the contract or indeed on the deed of assurance. In *Kyke v Tiernan and Tiernan*[234] the vendor's wife signed a letter (drafted by the vendor) consenting to the sale but refused to sign her consent to the deed. McWilliam J held that:[235]

"As the statute provides that the consent must be in writing, the consent contained in the letter ... is sufficient to comply with the section."

He explained his decision as follows:[236]

---

[233] See para **[10.64]** above.
[234] High Court, unrep, 15 July 1980 McWilliam J.
[235] *Ibid* page 9.

"... I suppose it could be said, on a strict interpretation of section 3 of the Act, that there must be a consent in writing to each conveyance, that is to say, both to the contract and to the final conveyance to the purchaser, but I cannot imagine that it could have been the intention of the legislature to require two consents for the completion of one transaction, namely, the sale of one house, and thus leave a purchaser in the position of conducting all the work and incurring all the expense necessary for the completion of a purchase only to find that a spouse had changed his or her mind about giving consent and require the whole transaction to be abandoned."

However, a spouse who signs his/her consent to a loan application for a loan to be made to the other spouse on the stated security of the family home is not deemed by such signature to have consented for the purposes of the Family Home Protection Act, 1976.[237]

Prior Consent

[10.69] The statutory requirement is "prior consent in writing of the other spouse";[238] thus subsequent, simultaneous or retrospective consent is not permissible. The courts, however, are not slow to be creative to administer justice fairly where there might otherwise be a technical escape for a mortgagor. In *Bank of Ireland v Hanrahan*,[239] the defendant deposited his land certificate with the bank to secure a loan. The bank manager pointed out to the defendant that his wife's consent was needed. The defendant having handed over the land certificate went to get his wife who gave her consent later in the day. The court held prior consent had been given. O'Hanlon J stated:[240]

"If the attempt by the Defendant to effect a mortgage by equitable deposit of his land certificate was already complete before his wife called in to execute the consent, then it was not a "prior consent in writing" as required by the Act, and the transaction should be regarded as void.

However, my ultimate conclusion ... is that the Bank and the Defendant impliedly agreed to the retention by the Bank of the land certificate as mere custodians thereof until such time as the Defendant's wife came in to sign the necessary consent, and that a tacit agreement should be implied as between the Bank and the Defendant that as and from the time when Mrs Hanrahan signed the consent, the character in which the land certificate was held by the Bank should change and that from that time forward they should be entitled to retain it in the capacity of equitable mortgagee."

236. *Ibid.*
237. See *Standard Life Assurance Co Ltd v Satchwell* High Court, unrep, 12 December 1990, Egan J (as reported in *The Irish Times* on 13 December 1990).
238. Family Home Protection Act, 1976, s 3(1).
239. High Court, unrep, 10 February 1987 O'Hanlon J.
240. *Ibid.* p 3.

Further Advances

[10.70] Prior to November 1987 it had been generally assumed that once a spouse had consented to the family home being mortgaged to secure present and future advances no further consent would be required, if the lender made further monies available on the security of the mortgage. The decision though of Barron J in *Bank of Ireland v Purcell*[241] changed such assumption. In that case, a family home was mortgaged by way of deposit of title deeds in 1975 to secure present and future advances. When further advances were made no consent was obtained from the non-owning spouse. Barron J held that as the Act required consent for the mortgage of "any interest in the family home" the security could not cover these further advances. He acknowledged that although the estate had been conveyed by the initial mortgage the interest of the mortgagor depends at any one time on the amount borrowed and the value of the equity of redemption (and thus the mortgagor's interest in the lands) is altered on each occasion a further advance is made. Barron J pointed out that a person who has a mortgage for present and future advances may continue to rely on the security for further advances until he receives notice of a second mortgage whereupon his rights in respect of further advances thereafter are subordinated to the mortgagee.[242] As the bank had notice that the premises were a family home their rights in respect of the further advances were subordinated to the rights of the spouse. His decision (and his reasons) was unanimously upheld by the full Supreme Court.[243]

Premises owned by a corporate body

[10.71] Following the enactment of the Family Home Protection Act, 1976 there was considerable difference of opinion among practitioners as to the appropriateness of seeking a statutory declaration where a property was owned by a company, as of course it could not be a company's "family home".[244] In *Walpoles (Ireland) Ltd v Jay*[245] McWilliam J held that a company does not require consent under the Family Home Protection Act for any conveyance it makes as it can have no spouse. However, the judge recognised that[246] even where a company has the title to the property being transferred, another person

---

[241] [1989] IR 327; [1988] ILRM 480; see also O'Connor, 'Equitable Mortgages and a Spouse's Consent' (1988) ILT 227.
[242] See Naish C in *Re O'Byrne's Estate* (1885) 15 LR Ir 373; Wylie, *A Casebook on Irish Land Law* p 469.
[243] [1989] IR 327; [1990] ILRM 106.
[244] See O'Donnell, 'Conveyancing and the Family Home', SYS Lecture 146.
[245] High Court, unrep, 20 November 1980.
[246] *Ibid* p 6.

may have, or have had, a legal or equitable interest in such property and if an individual his or her spouse's consent may be required.[247]

Statutory Declarations

[10.72] The form of statutory declaration required to be given varies depending upon the category of person mortgaging or charging the property. Standard forms for a number of categories have been prepared by the Conveyancing Committee of the Law Society of Ireland; these include:[248]

[**Husband & Wife - Family Home**]

IN THE MATTER OF THE FAMILY HOME PROTECTION ACT 1976/

THE FAMILY LAW ACT 1981/ JUDICIAL SEPARATION AND

FAMILY LAW REFORM ACT 1989/FAMILY LAW ACT, 1995/FAMILY LAW (DIVORCE) ACT, 1996

We, [ ] both of [ ] both aged 18 years and upwards, SOLEMNLY AND SINCERELY DECLARE as follows:

1. This declaration relates to the property known as [ ] in the County of [   ] (being the property comprised in folio [   ] County [ ]) (hereinafter called "the property").

2. The property is our family home within the meaning of that term in the Family Home Protection Act, 1976, as amended by the Family Law Act, 1995.

3. We have been married once and once only, namely to each other, on the day of   19 . We are each the lawful spouses of the other. We refer to a photocopy of our civil marriage certificate upon which we have endorsed our names prior to making this declaration.

4. None of the provisions of the Family Law Act, 1981 (hereinafter called "the Act of 1981") apply to the property because neither of us has been party to an agreement to marry which has terminated within the past three years, and no proceedings of any kind have been threatened or instituted in relation to the property under any of the provisions of the Act of 1981.

5. No proceedings of any kind have been instituted or threatened, and no application or order of any kind has been made, in relation to the property, under any of the provisions of the Judicial Separation and Family Law Reform Act, 1989, of the Family Law Act, 1995 ("the 1995 Act") or of the Family Law (Divorce) Act, 1996 ("the 1996 Act"), and the assurance of the property to the party or parties mentioned in paragraph 8 hereof is not a disposal for the purposes of

---

[247.] For a discussion of this decision see Lyall, 'Conveyancing - The Family Home Protection Act 1976 and Conveyances other than by Spouses' [1984] 6 DULJ 158.

[248.] January 1998.

defeating a claim for relief (as defined in section 35 of the 1995 Act and section 37 of the 1996 Act).

6. The property is not subject to any trust, licence, tenancy or proprietary interest in favour of any person or body corporate arising by virtue of any arrangement, agreement or contract entered into by either of us, or by virtue of any direct or indirect financial or other contribution to the purchase thereof, or by operation of law, or otherwise, and the property is held free from encumbrances.

7. We understand the effect and import of this declaration which have been fully explained to us by our solicitor.

8. We make this solemn declaration conscientiously believing it to be true for the satisfaction of [name of mortgagee/chargee] and pursuant to the provisions of the Statutory Declarations Act, 1938.

DECLARED at [   ] in the County of [   ]

by the said [   ] and

this day of [   ] 19

before me, a Commissioner for Oaths/

Practising Solicitor and I know the

Declarants.

_____

Commissioner for Oaths/Practising Solicitor

[single person]

IN THE MATTER OF THE FAMILY HOME PROTECTION ACT 1976/

THE FAMILY LAW ACT 1981/JUDICIAL SEPARATION AND

FAMILY LAW REFORM ACT 1989/FAMILY LAW ACT, 1995/FAMILY LAW (DIVORCE) ACT 1996

I, [   ] aged 18 years and upwards SOLEMNLY AND SINCERELY DECLARE as follows:

1. This declaration relates to the property known as [   ] in the County of [   ] (being the property comprised in folio [   ] County [   ]) (hereinafter called "the property").

2. The property is not a family home within the meaning of that term in the Family Home Protection Act, 1976 as amended by the Family Law Act, 1995. No married couple has ordinarily resided therein since I acquired an interest therein.

3. I am not and never have been married to any person under the law of this or any other civil or religious jurisdiction, and no proceedings have been instituted or threatened by any person alleging the contrary.

4. None of the provisions of the Family Law Act, 1981 (hereinafter called "the Act of 1981") apply to the property because I have not been party to an agreement to marry which has been terminated within the past three years and no proceedings of any kind have been threatened or instituted in relation to the property under any of the provisions of the Act of 1981.

5. The property is not subject to any trust, licence, tenancy or proprietary interest in favour of any person or body corporate arising by virtue of any arrangement, agreement or contract entered into by me or by virtue of any direct or indirect financial or other contribution to the purchase thereof, or by operation of law, or otherwise, and the property is held free from encumbrances.

6. I understand the effect and import of this declaration which have been fully explained to me by my solicitor.

7. I make this solemn declaration conscientiously believing it to be true for the satisfaction of [name of mortgagee/chargee] pursuant to the provisions of the Statutory Declarations Act, 1938.

DECLARED at [   ] in the County of [   ]

by the said [   ]

this day of 19__

before me a Commissioner for Oaths/Practising Solicitor

and I know the Declarant.

Commissioner for Oaths/Practising Solicitor

[Company]

IN THE MATTER OF THE FAMILY HOME PROTECTION ACT 1976/

THE FAMILY LAW ACT 1981/JUDICIAL SEPARATION AND

FAMILY LAW REFORM ACT 1989/FAMILY LAW ACT, 1995/FAMILY LAW (DIVORCE) ACT, 1996

I, [   ] of [   ] aged 18 years and upwards SOLEMNLY AND SINCERELY DECLARE as follows:

1. This declaration relates to the property known as [ ] in the County of [ ] (being the property comprised in folio [   ] County [   ]) (hereinafter called "the property").

    The property is owned by [   ] (hereinafter called "the company") of which I am a director.

2. The property is not a family home within the meaning of that term in the Family Home Protection Act, 1976 as amended by the Family Law Act, 1995. No married couple has ordinarily resided therein since the company acquired an interest in the property. No lease, letting

agreement, tenancy agreement, licence or similar agreement has been made by the company which would entitle any person to reside in the property. No officer, director, member, tenant, invitee or licensee of the company has ever resided therein.

3.   None of the provisions of the Family Law Act 1981 (hereinafter called "the Act of 1981") to the property and no proceedings of any kind have been threatened or instituted in relation to the property under any of the provisions of the Act of 1981.

4.   No proceedings of any kind have been instituted or threatened, and no application or order of any kind has been made, in relation to the property, under any of the provisions of the Judicial Separation and Family Law Reform Act, 1989, of the Family Law Act 1995 ("the 1995 Act") or the Family Law (Divorce) Act, 1996 ("the 1996 Act"), and the assurance of the property to the party or parties mentioned in paragraph 7 hereof is not a disposal for the purposes of defeating a claim for relief (as defined in s 35 of the 1995 Act and section 37 of the 1996 Act).

5.   The property is not subject to any trust, licence, tenancy or proprietary interest in favour of any person or body corporate arising by virtue of any arrangement, agreement or contract entered into by the company, or by virtue of any direct or indirect financial or other contribution to the purchase thereof, or by operation of law, or otherwise, and the property is held free from encumbrances.

6.   I understand the effect and import of this declaration which has been fully explained to me by the company's solicitor, and I am authorised by the company to make this declaration.

7.   I make this solemn declaration conscientiously believing it to be true for the satisfaction of [name of mortgagee/chargee] and pursuant to the provisions of the Statutory Declarations Act, 1938.

DECLARED at

in the County of [   ]

by the said [   ]

this day of 19__

before me, a Commissioner for Oaths/

Practising Solicitor, and I know the

Declarant,_____

Commissioner for Oaths/Practising Solicitor

LAND COMMISSION'S CONSENT

[10.73] For primarily historical reasons,[249] a person (who is not otherwise exempted) is required to obtain the written consent of the Land Commission[250]

[249.] For the historical background see Wylie, *Irish Conveyancing Law* (2nd ed, 1996) paras 16.37-16.43.

in order to take an interest, including a mortgage or charge, whether legal or equitable, in any land which is not situated in "a county borough, borough, urban district or town".[251] Among those exempted from this requirement are Irish citizens and banks named in the Third Schedule to the Central Bank Act, 1942.[252] Where an interest in non-urban land is being acquired, the mortgage or charge must contain a certificate by the mortgagee or chargee that it is either exempted from such consent (by reference to the specific exemption),[253] or has obtained the appropriate consent and any conditions attached to such consent have been complied with.[254] The issue of such a certificate necessitates the execution of the mortgage or charge by the mortgagee or chargee.[255] The Land Commission's consent may be given retrospectively.[256] In practice there is little, if any, difficulty in obtaining such consent (including retrospective) for mortgages and charges.[257] Recently, the requirement to obtain such consent was abolished where the mortgagee or chargee is an individual whose principal place of residence is in a Member State of the European Communities or other European State which is a contracting party to the European Economic Area Agreement or a body corporate incorporated in such a State and having its registered office, central administration or principal place of business within such a State.[258]

HOUSING LOANS

[10.74] The provisions of Part IX of the Consumer Credit Act, 1995[259] must be complied with in respect of a loan agreement or facility letter made by a mortgage lender where the loan is secured by a mortgage or charge over a freehold or leasehold estate or interest in a "house" where:[260]

---

250. Land Act, 1965, s 45(2)(a).
251. *Ibid* s 45(1).
252. *Ibid* s 45(1).
253. Section 45(1) of the Land Act, 1965 lists ten categories of "qualified persons".
254. Section 45(3)(a); for the suggested form of such certificate see the guide issued by the Incorporated Law Society of Ireland in September 1965 on certain provisions of the Land Act 1965.
255. Execution of a charge is also required for Land Registry purposes to comply with the requirement to certify an address of the chargee in the State, see para **[10.34]** above.
256. Land Act, 1965, s 45(9)(a).
257. A guide issued in September 1965 by the Incorporated Law Society of Ireland on certain provisions of the Land Act 1965 did indicate that, "The power to give retrospective consent will be used exceptionally".
258. Land Act 1965 (Additional Category of Qualified Persons) Regulations 1995 (SI 56/1995), reg 2.
259. Implemented on 13 May 1996 (SI 121/1996); for further reading see Elliot, 'Housing loans under Consumer credit Act 1995 (1996) CLP 195.
260. Consumer Credit Act, 1995, s 115(1); see definition of housing loan in s 2(1).

(a) the loan is made for the purpose of enabling the borrower [being a consumer[261]] to provide or improve the house or to purchase the said estate or interest, or

(b) the loan is made for the purpose of refinancing a loan within the meaning of paragraph (a), or

(c) the house is to be used or to continue to be used as the principal residence of the borrower or his dependants".

The definition of "house" is all embracing as it "includes any building or part of a building used or suitable for use as a dwelling and any out-office, yard, garden or other land appurtenant thereto or usually enjoyed therewith".[262]

A "mortgage lender" means:[263]

(1) a credit institution,[264] or

(2) any other person of a class prescribed, or

(3) a person whose business includes the making of housing loans, provided that at least 50 per cent by number of all business loans outstanding to him, in whole or in part, at any time comprises loans secured by mortgage of residential property, or

(4) a local authority.[265]

Valuation Report

[10.75] When considering whether or not to grant a housing loan, a mortgage lender will seek a report on the valuation of the asset being provided as security for the loan namely, the house. Following the furnishing of the report to the mortgage lender, the consumer will be informed whether or not his application for a housing loan is successful. At the time of informing the consumer, the mortgage lender is required to provide the consumer with a copy of the valuation report.[266] The mortgage lender is required to attach to (or include in) the report "a note stating clearly the nature and purpose of the report".[267] The mortgage lender is precluded from charging the consumer for the cost of the report if the loan application for a loan is refused.[268]

[261.] See definition of borrower in s 2(1).

[262.] Consumer Credit Act, 1995, s 2(1).

[263.] *Ibid* as amended by SI 127/1996.

[264.] As defined in s 2(1) as amended by SI 127/1996 and as further amended by SI 369/1996.

[265.] For its application see further SI 186/1997.

[266.] Consumer Credit Act, 1995, s 123(1).

[267.] *Ibid* s 123(2).

[268.] *Ibid* s 123(3).

Insurance of House

[10.76] A mortgage lender will require insurance to be taken out on the house against the risk of fire and other hazards. The consumer may choose any insurer[269] and any intermediary for the purpose of taking out the insurance.[270] The mortgage lender is required to give written notification to the consumer of his right of choice and also the nature and extent of the required insurance.[271]

Costs of Investigating Title

[10.77] Section 125 of the Consumer Credit Act, 1995 stipulates that a mortgage lender shall pay the costs of any investigation of title to any property offered as security by a consumer acting as borrower and such costs shall not be recoverable from the consumer. Although the section refers to "any property" it is considered that this prohibition relates only to housing loans at least with regard to loans being made by credit institutions by virtue of the statutory definition of mortgage lender.[272]

Mortgage Protection Insurance

[10.78] The Consumer Credit Act, 1995[273] imposes an obligation on a mortgage lender to arrange a life assurance policy which provides a capital sum to discharge the housing loan in the event of the borrower's death (on the basis that payments in the meantime will have been made). There are certain limited exceptions to this requirement.[274]

Information, Documents and Warnings

[10.79] To alert a mortgagor to the possible consequences of taking up a housing loan and entering into a mortgage, a mortgage lender is required to ensure that,[275] (a) an information document, (b) an application form for a housing loan, or (c) any document approving a housing loan, shall include the following notice:

"WARNING

YOUR HOME IS AT RISK IF YOU DO NOT KEEP UP PAYMENTS ON A MORTGAGE OR ANY OTHER LOAN SECURED ON IT"

---

[269] Provided it is an insurer within the meaning of the Insurance Act, 1989 (see Consumer Credit Act, 1995, s 115(2)).
[270] Consumer Credit Act, 1995, s 124(1).
[271] *Ibid* s 124(2).
[272] Meaning "a credit institution making housing loans" (Consumer Credit Act, 1995, s 2(1)).
[273] Section 126(1).
[274] See s126(2).
[275] Consumer Credit Act, 1995, s 128(1).

and in the case of a housing loan carrying a variable rate of interest,[276] the notice shall include:

"THE PAYMENT RATES ON THIS HOUSING LOAN MAY BE
ADJUSTED BY THE LENDER FROM TIME TO TIME".

The legislation fails to ensure that a warning will be seen by a borrower as these notices must be stipulated on any of the documents rather than all of them.[277] Thus, the benefit of the warning to the consumer will be completely lost if the mortgage lender, in satisfying the statutory requirements, simply puts the warning on an information document[278] which the consumer might never see. A further warning is required on all of the three categories in the case of an endowment loan.[279]

[10.80] A mortgage lender is required to ensure that a housing loan agreement shall contain on the front page a notice in the following form,[280]

IMPORTANT INFORMATION as at [date]

1. Amount of credit advanced £
2. Period of Agreement
3. Number of Repayment Instalments
4. Amount of Each Instalment £
5. Total Amount Repayable £
6. Cost of this credit (5 minus 1) £
7. APR*
8. Amount of endowment premium £
   (if applicable)
9. Amount of mortgage protection premium (if applicable) £
10. Effect on amount of instalment of 1% increase in
    first year in interest rate** £

* Annual Percentage Rate of Charge

** This is the amount by which the instalment repayment will increase in the event of a 1% increase at the start of the first year in the interest rate on which the above calculations are based.

[10.81] A mortgage lender is required to issue a copy of the mortgage to a borrower (in respect of a housing loan) at the time the loan is made (or as soon as practicable thereafter).[281] The mortgage lender is also required to issue an

---

[276.] *Ibid* s 128(2).
[277.] By virtue of the word "or" instead of "and" as applies in ss 121(5), 132 and 133.
[278.] As defined by the Consumer Credit Act, 1995, s 115(2).
[279.] Consumer Credit Act, 1995, s 133.
[280.] Consumer Credit Act, 1995, s 129(1) as applied by the Consumer Credit Act, 1995 (section 129) Regulations, 1995 SI 132/1996.
[281.] Consumer Credit Act, 1995, s 130(a).

annual statement to the borrower, indicating the total amount of the loan outstanding.[282]

[10.82] A mortgage lender is required to ensure that in respect of[283] (a) the making, accepting or administering of an application for a loan, (b) the valuation of the security for the loan, (c) legal services in connection with the loan, (d) services provided by a mortgage agent in relation to the loan, or (e) non-acceptance of an offer or approval of a loan, "a statement of reasonable prominence" that such a fee is payable, specifying the amount of it or how it is determined, must be included in or attached to (i) any information document, (ii) any application form, and (iii) any approval of a loan.

Interest Arrears and Redemption

[10.83] Where it is the policy of a mortgage lender to charge interest in arrears on housing loans, any communication in relation to arrears of payments must state the amount of the increase in interest rates and other charges; such information is required also to be specified in "any information document relating to application form for, or document approving, such a loan."[284] A communication which refers to the possibility of taking possession under a mortgage must contain an estimate of the cost to the borrower of taking possession.[285]

[10.84] A borrower is allowed to repay the housing loan prior to the agreed date of redemption without incurring a fee for such pre-payment.[286] This is subject to certain exceptions such as where the rate of interest is fixed,[287] in which case a statement must be set out showing how the amount is to be calculated (such statement being on an information document, an application form, loan approval and a communication varying the terms of a housing loan).[288]

SOLICITORS' UNDERTAKINGS

"Practising solicitors are not to be regarded as potential fraudsters or accomplices to fraud. ... *Prima facie* they are to be taken to be men and women of good character whose word is their bond and whose statements do not require that degree of confirmation and cross-checking which might well be appropriate in the case of statements by others who are not members of so respected a profession."[289]

---

282. *Ibid* s 130(b).
283. *Ibid* s 132.
284. *Ibid* s 134(1).
285. *Ibid* s 134(2).
286. *Ibid* s 121(1).
287. *Ibid* s 121(2).
288. *Ibid* s 121(5).
289. Lord Donaldson of Lymington MR in *United Bank of Kuwait Ltd v Hammoud* [1988] 3 All ER 418 at 429; see also *A Guide to Professional Conduct of Solicitors in Ireland* - para 7.1 - "The word of a solicitor should be his bond".

[10.85] A person who wishes to purchase a property will retain a solicitor for the purpose of investigating the title to the property and to carry out appropriate searches so that the purchaser will obtain an unencumbered good marketable title to what in many cases will be the most significant investment the purchaser has ever made. To purchase a property, a person will almost invariably require financial assistance from a bank, a building society or other financial institution. Until fairly recent times, the lender would retain its own solicitor to investigate title and carry out searches on its behalf. Although the interests of the purchaser and the lender are not the same and conflicts of interest may arise,[290] to minimise costs it is now normal, in the case of residential purchases, for one solicitor to act on behalf of both parties.The lender will advance funds to a solicitor (chosen by the customer) on the solicitor's undertaking to use the proceeds for the purchase of the property and to hold the title documents in trust for the lender pending their stamping and registration and thereafter furnish them to the lender.

Similarly, where property is to be sold, to prepare the conditions of sale for an auction or draft contract for a private treaty sale, the vendor's solicitor will take up the title documents from the lender on his undertaking to hold them in trust for the lender and to return them on demand.

Thus, solicitors' undertakings form an integral part of the purchase and sale of residential property. The Law Society have laid down general principles applicable to solicitors' undertakings namely:[291]

> "An undertaking of a solicitor is binding in law and, furthermore, the failure by a solicitor to honour an undertaking is unprofessional conduct. A solicitor is responsible for carrying out an undertaking given by any member of his staff whether or not that member of staff is admitted to practise as a solicitor. A principal or a partner should sign each undertaking given by any member of his staff whether or not that member of staff is admitted to practise as a solicitor. A principal or a partner should sign each undertaking where an undertaking is given in writing by a firm of solicitors.
>
> A solicitor should be guided by the following principles in giving an undertaking:
>
> (a) an undertaking should not be given lightly and should only be given when it is clearly necessary to do so in the interests of the client;
>
> (b) if an undertaking is given it will be deemed to be the personal undertaking of the solicitor giving it, unless the contrary be proved. The onus of proving the contrary lies on the solicitor asserting that the undertaking was not given personally;

[290.] See ILSI Gazette 77 (1983) 277 where a practice note indicated that a bank's solicitor who agreed to act for the customer "would be foolish".

[291.] *A Guide to Professional Conduct of Solicitors in Ireland* - para 7.3; for further obligations imposed on persons giving an undertaking see the Conveyancing Act 1881, s 9.

(c) a solicitor, who gives an undertaking on behalf of a client for which he
does not intend to accept personal responsibility, should express this
intention clearly in the undertaking by appropriate words."

Despite Lord Donaldson's remarks set out above, as Lord Donaldson himself
also remarked there do exist dishonest solicitors.[292] Where a lender is presented
by its customer with the name of a solicitor whom the customer wishes to retain
and thereby the lender is requested to rely on such solicitor's undertaking, if the
solicitor is not familiar to the lender, the lender may consider it prudent to
ascertain from the Law Society that the solicitor has not been struck off the
register of solicitors or otherwise censured.

[10.86] A standard form of solicitor's undertaking has been agreed between the
Conveyancing Committee of the Law Society and the legal advisers of the
principal financial institutions[293] providing finance for the purchase of houses.
The Law Society's Conveyancing Committee has recommended to solicitors
that the agreed form of undertaking[294] be used for all residential mortgage loans
approved after 1 February 1997 and that no alternative documentation should be
used.[295]

[10.87] As the agreed form of undertaking contains specific authority from the
customer for his solicitor to act and give the undertaking on his behalf, the
lender will not be required to ascertain and verify the authority.[296] However,
obviously this does not cater for the fraudulent customer. An example of how a
solicitor or firm of solicitors may be caught where an undertaking is not as
tightly drafted as it might be can be seen from *United Bank of Kuwait Ltd v
Hammoud*.[297] This decision involved two cases both involving the same solicitor
by the name of Emmanuel. In the first case Emmanuel, a salaried partner in a
firm of solicitors, gave an undertaking on behalf of the firm without the
knowledge of the other partners to the bank that funds of the customer would be

---

[292.] *United Bank of Kuwait Ltd v Hammoud* [1988] 3 All ER 418 at 429.

[293.] ACC Bank, AIB Bank, AIB Finance, Bank of Ireland, EBS, First National Building Society,
ICC Bank, ICS Building Society, Irish Life Home Loans, Irish Nationwide Building Society,
Irish Permanent plc, National Irish Bank, Norwich Irish Building Society, TSB Bank and
Ulster Bank Ltd.

[294.] Which should be signed only by a partner or principal of the firm and should set out any
intended qualification to a certificate of title.

[295.] When issuing the recommendation the Law Society stated: "This recommendation is endorsed
by the Solicitors Mutual Defence Fund Ltd and Solicitors are advised that failure to utilise the
agreed documents may engender difficulty with their Professional Indemnity Insurance
Cover."

[296.] For the treatment of ostensible authority by the Courts see *Kett v Shannon and English* [1987]
ILRM 364 (Supreme Court) and *Thomas Williamson Ltd (In Receivership) v Bailieborough
Co-operative Agricultural Society Ltd* High Court, unrep, 31 July 1986, Costello J.

[297.] [1988] 3 All ER 418.

transferred to the bank. In the second case Emmanuel was employed as an assistant solicitor but in charge of a branch office. A similar undertaking was given.

The English Court of Appeal held that where a solicitor who had actual authority to represent himself as being a practising solicitor with an established firm gave an undertaking which the receiver of the undertaking was entitled to assume was given in the context of an underlying transaction which was part of the usual business of a solicitor, the undertaking would be enforced against the firm as having been given with ostensible authority and therefore binding on the firm. It further held that, on the facts as presented to the banks, a reasonably careful and competent bank would have concluded that the undertaking was given in the context of an underlying transaction which was part of the usual business of a solicitor. In each case, therefore, the lender had discharged the burden of proving that Emmanuel had had ostensible authority to bind the firm of solicitors which employed him.

A number of points from this decision should be noted by both bankers and solicitors:[298]

1. For the court to enforce a solicitor's undertaking as such, it is an essential requirement that there be a promise made in his capacity as a solicitor.

2. The promise of one partner binds the other members of the firm if it was an act for carrying on in the usual way business of the kind carried on by the firm.[299]

3. A contract made by a servant or other agent binds the principal if it was made with the ostensible authority of the principal.

4. A third party is concerned only as to whether a transaction appears to be of a kind that is within the ordinary authority that the agent is held out as having, not whether it is in fact a transaction of that kind.

5. The opening by the bank of a loan account for the customer was consideration supporting the giving of the undertaking.

6. The giving of the undertaking was an act for carrying on in the usual way the business of solicitors - solicitors regularly give undertakings in the ordinary course of their business and this is often regarded as a key feature of the service they provide.

7. On the information given to the bank by the solicitor, a reasonably careful and competent bank would most probably have concluded

---

[298.] [1988] 3 All ER 418 the first four points are taken from the judgment of Staughton LJ at 427; the rest from the judgment of Glidewell LJ at 420.
[299.] Partnership Act 1890, s 5.

that there was an underlying transaction of a kind forming part of a solicitor's business, and thus that the undertaking was an act for the carrying on of such business.

[10.88] The English Court of Appeal's approach and outline of the principles involved is consistent with the approach of the Irish courts. The *United Bank of Kuwait* case is a stark reminder to all solicitors in a partnership that their partner or indeed employee may bind the firm, and accordingly each partner in that firm, to a financial commitment to be met ultimately out of the personal assets of each partner. Where there are insufficient assets to cover the lender's loss, as a result of the fraudulent dishonour of a solicitor's undertaking, the lender may be able to recover his loss from the Law Society's Compensation Fund. Section 21(4) of the Solicitors (Amendment) Act, 1960 states:

> Where it is proved to the satisfaction of the Society that any person has sustained loss in consequence of dishonesty on the part of any solicitor or any clerk or servant of a solicitor in connection with that solicitor's practice as a solicitor or in connection with any trust of which that solicitor is a trustee, then, subject to the provisions of this section, the Society shall make a grant to that person out of the Fund and the amount of the grant shall be such as represents in the opinion of the Society full indemnity for that loss.

[10.89] The operation of this section in favour of a bank can be seen from the High Court's decision, and its unanimous approval by the Supreme Court in *The Trustee Savings Bank v The Incorporated Law Society*.[300] In that case Herbert Mulligan a partner in Francis X. Mulligan & Son, solicitors, sought a loan to purchase a property. The bank agreed to advance the loan on the undertaking of the firm provided it was signed by another partner. Mulligan supplied the undertaking with a forged signature of his partner. Mulligan failed to repay the loan, was struck off the roll of solicitors and the firm also failed to honour the undertaking. The bank sought to recover its loss from the Law Society's Compensation Fund.

In upholding the High Court's decision that the bank was entitled to recompense, the Supreme Court held that the test was whether Herbert Mulligan had acted dishonestly in connection with his practice as a solicitor. If so, the Society is obliged to compensate persons who sustained loss as a consequence thereof. In the circumstances, the issue of a letter on the notepaper of his practice amounted to dishonesty in connection therewith, and the bank was entitled to compensation. Finlay CJ in giving the judgment of the Court specifically approved of Johnson J's conclusion in the High Court:[301]

---

[300] [1988] ILRM 541 and [1989] ILRM 665 (see also [1987] IR 430 for High Court judgment).
[301] *Ibid* at 545 and 669 respectively.

"... when the bank requested an undertaking from FX Mulligan & Son, at that time Mr Mulligan acted dishonestly by

(1) writing an undertaking on behalf of FX Mulligan & Son, the contents of which he knew to be false;

(2) forging the signature of his partner, John F. Carroll, which he also knew to be dishonest.

This he did on behalf of FX Mulligan & Son of which he was a practising partner and ... in perpetrating the falsehoods and dishonesties in this event ... Mr Mulligan was acting and purported to act and held himself out as acting as FX Mulligan & Son and what was done was done in the name of his practice."

CERTIFICATES OF TITLE

Form of Certificate

[10.90] As with solicitors' undertakings,[302] the principal financial institutions and the Law Society have agreed a form of certificate of title to be given by borrowers' solicitors to the lending financial institution at the time of the drawdown of residential property mortgage loans. The solicitor certifying the title is required to carry out a proper investigation of title to the property to be mortgaged, attend at the signing[303] and arrange for stamping and registration.[304] The certificate of title should certify that, subject to qualifications previously agreed with the lender, the borrower has "good marketable title" to the property. This means "a title of a quality commensurate with prudent standards of current conveyancing practice in Ireland".[305] The solicitor is also required to certify that he or his firm holds professional indemnity insurance cover with a qualified insurer[306] for a sum which is in excess of the amount being advanced to the borrower.

Duty of a Solicitor

[10.91] The duty of a solicitor, who will usually be acting for the borrower in the purchase of the property, in giving the certificate of title to the lender is onerous. He is essentially required to act also for the lender, other than in the actual preparation of the mortgage itself.[307] Specific guidelines have been issued which should be followed by certifying solicitors. These include:

[302.] See para **[10.85]** above.

[303.] All security documents should be signed in the presence of and witnessed by a solicitor.

[304.] Before passing over the loan cheque the solicitor should ensure he has sufficient funds to pay for the stamping and registration.

[305.] As stated on the agreed form of certificate.

[306.] As defined under SI 312/1995.

[307.] The agreed form of certificate of title specifically excludes any certification concerning the terms of the mortgage or any other document prepared by the lender.

1. The solicitor should ensure that there should be compliance with any requirements specified in the special conditions in the lender's letter of offer.

2. The title must be freehold or leasehold, with an unexpired term of at least 70 years, unless the solicitor is satisfied that the lessee has a statutory right to purchase the fee simple under the ground rents legislation. If land registry title, it must be either absolute or good leasehold.

3. The property must be free from encumbrances to ensure that the lender shall have a first legal mortgage/charge.

4. The consideration expressed in the purchase deed/building agreement must be as stated in the loan approval/offer. If there is any discrepancy, this must be brought to the attention of the lender prior to drawing down the cheque. The amount of the loan may be reduced in the event of such a discrepancy.

5. There must be no restrictions on mortgaging the property. Any necessary consent from a housing authority, for example, must be obtained and compliance with any condition procured.

6. The borrower(s) signature(s) on the mortgage (including any non-owning spouse or other person who may be required to join the mortgage) must be made in the presence of and witnessed by a solicitor.

7. For properties not forming part of a housing estate, there must be with the title a declaration of identity declaring that the property and its essential services are entirely within the boundaries of the lands the subject matter of the lender's security.

8. If title to the property vests in the sole name of one spouse, and if the Family Home Protection Act, 1976 applies, a prior consent to the mortgage must be completed, signed and dated by the mortgagor's spouse (even if the property will not become a family home (vesting in sole name) until immediately after completion it is, nonetheless, recommended that the prior consent is signed by the relevant spouse as possession may have been taken informally or partially beforehand).

9. (a) There must be no person other than the borrower with any estate or interest, beneficial or otherwise, in the property and this must be confirmed by a statutory declaration of the borrower.

    (b) If there is any such person with any such estate or interest by reason of making a contribution to the purchase price or otherwise howsoever, that person should, after the mortgagor signs the mortgage, execute a deed of confirmation so as to supplementally mortgage any such estate or interest to the lender. Where appropriate the beneficiary's spouse should sign his/her prior consent to the deed of confirmation.

(c) If there is a right of residence the person entitled thereto must sign a deed of confirmation except in the event of such right being an exclusive right in which event the right of residence must be released prior to the execution of the mortgage.

(d) It should be noted that a sole mortgagor's spouse already signing the prior Family Home Protection Act, "Consent to Mortgage" may be a beneficiary nonetheless because of, eg direct or indirect financial contribution. If there is any doubt in this respect, the beneficiary should, after the mortgagor signs the mortgage, execute a deed of confirmation so as to supplementally mortgage any such estate or interest to the lender.

10. If the lender requires that the non-owning spouse joins in the mortgage deed there should be compliance with this requirement.

11. Any spouse signing the Family Home Protection Act consent or any non-owning spouse joining in the mortgage or any person signing the deed of confirmation or consent thereto must receive independent legal advice (or, after receiving legal advice from the borrower's solicitor of the serious implication of not taking such advice, must sign an explicit waiver of the right to be so advised which waiver must be placed with the title deeds).

12. Searches must include those against the borrower and, when a purchase is completed in advance of the mortgage, searches must be updated to the date of the mortgage.

Liability of a Solicitor

[10.92] Obviously, a solicitor who gives incorrect information to a lender, on the strength of which the lender advances funds, leaves himself open to an action for damages due to his negligence. The damages though may not correlate to the loss suffered by the lender, as can be seen from the instructive decision of the English Court of Appeal in *Bristol and West Building Society v Mothew (t/a Stapley & Co)*[308] In that case, the customer's solicitor inadvertently failed to inform the society, in breach of the society's instructions to the solicitor, that the

---

[308.] [1996] 4 All ER 698.

customer was taking out a second mortgage to rank behind the society's first mortgage. Following the customer's default and the sale of the house, the society brought an action against the solicitor for its loss alleging breach of contract and negligence in failing to inform the society of the arrangements (which was admitted) and breach of trust (which was denied). The Court held that, where a lender sued his solicitor for having negligently given him incorrect advice or information it was sufficient for him to prove that he relied on the advice or information and he did not have to prove that he would not have acted as he did if he had been given the proper advice or the correct information. Accordingly, it was sufficient for the society to prove that it relied on the representations in the report and it did not have to prove that it would not have made the mortgage advance if it had known the true facts.

But in giving the principal judgment of the Court, Millett LJ pointed out the distinction between a duty to advise someone as to what course of action he should take with a duty to provide information for the purpose of enabling someone else to decide upon the course of action, he stated:[309]

> "In the former case, the defendant is liable for all the foreseeable consequences of the action being taken. In the latter case, however, he is responsible only for the consequences of the information being wrong. The measure of damages is not necessarily the full amount of the loss which the plaintiff has suffered by having entered into the transaction but only that part, if any, of such loss as is properly attributable to the inaccuracy of the information.
>
> ... the society will not have to prove that it would not have made the mortgage advance if it had known the true facts; but it will be required to establish what it has lost as a result of the existence of the second charge and the purchasers' indebtedness to the bank."

As for the allegation of breach of trust, the Court held that since the solicitor's conduct in providing incorrect information to the society was due to an oversight, it constituted a breach of duty of which he was unaware and, therefore such conduct and his subsequent application of the mortgage money in accordance with his instructions did not constitute a breach of trust. Furthermore, the defendant was not guilty of breach of fiduciary duty since his failure to report the true state of affairs was due to an inadvertent failure and was not due to disloyalty or infidelity.

[10.93] The court's approach in holding a solicitor accountable for the consequences of his negligence but no more can be seen also from the subsequent case of *Bristol and West Building Society v Fancy & Jackson (a firm)*.[310] In that case, the borrower's solicitor in giving a report to the building

---

[309.] *Ibid* at 706.
[310.] [1997] 4 All ER 582.

society was alleged to have failed (i) to report circumstances which suggested that the true purchase price was lower than that stated in the offer letter, (ii) to report circumstances which suggested that on completion the borrower would be in breach of a special condition in the offer letter, and (iii) to obtain proper security. The court held *inter alia* that:

1. Where a solicitor returned an unqualified report he thereby warranted to the society that he knew of no reason why he could not give a confirmation that the mortgage transaction in respect of which he was seeking authority to proceed would be completed in accordance with the terms in the society's special conditions. Furthermore, the solicitor was under an obligation to inform the society if he subsequently became aware that the confirmation could no longer be relied upon and would therefore be in breach of duty if he failed to do so.

2. Where a solicitor who was under a duty to take reasonable care to provide information on which someone else would decide upon a course of action was negligent in the provision of that information, he was not responsible for all the consequences of that course of action, he was only responsible for the consequences of that information being wrong.

Although the courts ensured, in these cases, that the careless or negligent solicitor was not required to indemnify the society for all its losses in the transaction, the cases themselves highlight the possibility of negligence actions arising due to any oversight on the part of a solicitor in issuing a certificate of title.

[10.94] Solicitors may draw comfort from the recent English Court of Appeal decision in *National Home Loans Corp plc v Giffen Couch & Archer*,[311] where it was held that where a solicitor, in the course of acting for both borrower and lender in a remortgage transaction, discovered information casting doubt on the borrower's ability to repay the loan, he was not under a duty to report that information to the lender unless his instructions required him to do so. However, in *Mortgage Express Ltd v Bowerman & Partners*,[312] the English Court of Appeal held a solicitor, acting for both sides, negligent when she failed to inform the lender of information which came to her knowledge which cast doubt on the valuation of the property the subject of the security.

[311.] [1997] 3 All ER 808.
[312.] [1996] 2 All ER 836.

REGISTRATION IN THE REGISTRY OF DEEDS[313]

Mortgages of Unregistered Land

[10.95] To maintain priority against subsequent mortgages or judgment mortgages, a mortgage of unregistered land should be registered in the Registry of Deeds at the earliest opportunity following its execution.[314] For this purpose a memorial namely, a short precis of the mortgage should be prepared and executed under seal. The memorial should be typed on "vellum or parchment".[315] The form of the memorial should be the form for memorials of mortgages as published by the Law Society's Conveyancing Committee and circulated with the Law Society's Gazette of December 1990.[316] This reads as follows:

> "A MEMORIAL of Indenture of Mortgage dated the day of 199 and made between [   ] of, [   ] (therein and hereinafter called "[   ] "), of the one part and [   ] of [   ] (therein and hereinafter called "[   ] ") of the other part.
>
> WHEREBY after reciting as therein IT WAS WITNESSED that for the consideration therein the [   ] as beneficial owner did thereby convey/demise unto [   ] ALL THAT AND THOSE the Property described in the Schedule hereto and thereto TO HOLD the same unto as therein set forth subject to the proviso for redemption therein contained.
>
> WHICH said Indenture as to the due execution thereof by [   ] was witnessed by: [name, address and description]
>
> WHICH said Indenture as to the due execution thereof by [   ] was Witnessed by: [name, address and description]
>
> SCHEDULE
>
> [description of property by reference to[317] "the county and barony, or the town or county of a city, and parish, or the town and parish"]
>
> Signed and Sealed
>
> by the said
>
> in the presence of:
>
> 1st Witness
>
> 2nd Witness

[313.] See generally Wylie, *Irish Land Law* (3rd ed) Ch 22; Madden, *Registration of Deeds* (1868, McGee).

[314.] Registration of Deeds Act (Ireland), 1707 ss 4 and 5.

[315.] *Ibid s* 6.

[316.] This publication sets out also a list of queries which arise most frequently from the Registry of Deeds (reproduced in the Dublin Solicitors Bar Association Newsletter of 1/92).

[317.] Registry of Deeds (Ireland) Act, 1832, s 29.

The above named [   ] Maketh Oath and Saith that he is a Subscribing Witness to the Deed, of which the above writing is a Memorial, and also to said Memorial; and that he saw Deed and Memorial duly executed by the said [   ] and the name subscribed as Witness to said Deed and Memorial, respectively, is this Deponent's proper name and handwriting.

Sworn before me this day of 19

at

in the County of

and I know the Deponent.

_____

Commissioner for Oaths/Practising Solicitor

[10.96] The memorial is required to be executed under seal by either the mortgagor or the mortgagee.[318] The execution must be "attested by two witnesses" one of which must have been a witness to the execution of the mortgage.[319] It should be noted that the witnesses to the sealing of a document by a corporate body as prescribed by the corporate body's articles of association or other constitutional document are not witnesses for the purposes of the Act. Although registration may be accepted by the Registrar it is extremely doubtful that the requirements of the Act have been complied with unless two additional independent witnesses attest to the execution.[320]

[10.97] It is the duty of the Registrar to check that the memorial conforms with the requirements of the statute and to compare it with the mortgage.[321] It should be noted that the Registrar's acceptance of the memorial for registration is not conclusive proof of its conformity either with the deed or with the statutory requirements.[322] Practitioners would be well advised to heed the words of *Madden* in his practical treatise on the registration of deeds where he states:[323]

> "The fact that the Registry Office is in the habit of receiving and entering memorials of a certain class, does not conclusively prove their legal admissibility, or the validity of the act of registration. The Registrar receives, and puts on the files in his book, whatever is brought him, at the peril of the party bringing it."

_____

[318.] Registration of Deeds Act (Ireland), 1707, s 6.

[319.] *Ibid.*

[320.] See Meredith, 'Witnessing and Attestation' (1983) 77 ILSI Gazette 83.

[321.] As to the statutory requirements see Registration of Deeds Act (Ireland) 1707, s 7; Wylie, *Irish Land Law* (3rd ed) para 22.07; Madden, *Registration of Deeds* (1868, McGee) p 43.

[322.] See Madden, *Registration of Deeds* (1868, McGee) p 79.

[323.] *Ibid* at p 49.

On approving a mortgage for registration the Registrar "endorses upon it a certificate mentioning the certain day and time when the memorial is registered, and also the book, page and number in which it is entered."[324] This is important to note because the priority as between registrable mortgages[325] is "according to the priority of time of registering such memorial".[326]

[10.98] Following completion of a mortgage, the mortgage and the memorial should be stamped.[327] The memorial cannot be registered unless it and the mortgage to which it refers have been properly stamped.[328]

REGISTRATION IN THE LAND REGISTRY

[10.99] Where a charge is taken on the land the title of which is registered in the Land Registry it is imperative to file the charge, duly stamped,[329] in the Land Registry together with appropriate ancillary documentation.[330] The charge will rank in priority for registration in the order in which it is received by the Land Registry[331] (provided the charge is not withdrawn for alteration[332]). When registration is completed it will take effect as of the date of the application.[333] Upon and only upon registration, the chargee will acquire the same rights as though it had obtained a mortgage by deed including the power to sell the estate or interest which is subject to the charge.[334] Indeed the legislation[335] provides that the Registrar of Titles need not be concerned with any mortgage, charge or debenture created by a company unless such incumbrance is registered as a burden or protected by caution or inhibition.

It should be noted that the register of ownership of lands is "conclusive evidence" of the owner's title and of any charge on the register.[336] The land certificate issued by the Land Registry showing the owner's title to the land is

---

[324.] Registration of Deeds Act (Ireland) 1707, s 7.

[325.] An equitable mortgage by deposit of title deeds without any writing is not a registrable mortgage (*Re Driscoll* 1 Ir Eq 285); see also *Re Burke* 9 LR Ir 24.

[326.] Registration of Deeds Act (Ireland) 1707, s 4; on priorities see further Wylie, *Irish Land Law* (3rd ed), paras 13.141-13.162.

[327.] The mortgage (unless it is a collateral or additional security) at the rate of one tenth of one per cent of the amount secured subject to a maximum duty of £500; the memorial at £26 (Registry of Deeds (Fees) Order, 1991 SI 360/1991).

[328.] See an Act to amend the Laws relating to Inland Revenue (1861) 24 & 25 Vic c 91 s 34].

[329.] With the same duty as for a mortgage - see fn 327 above.

[330.] Registration of Title Act, 1964, s 69.

[331.] Land Registration Rules, 1972 SI 230/1972 rule 61(1).

[332.] *Ibid* r 65.

[333.] *Ibid* r 63.

[334.] Registration of Title Act, 1964, s 62(6).

[335.] *Ibid* s 80.

[336.] *Ibid* s 31(1); see further Fitzgerald, 'The Conclusiveness of the Register of Titles in Ireland' SYS Lecture 127.

"*prima facie* evidence" of his title.[337]Accordingly, any person wishing to ascertain the rights of ownership to registered lands should make a search of the relevant folio on the register and not rely on the land certificate. Furthermore rule 159 of the Land Registration Rules, 1972[338] specifically states that a land certificate or indeed certificate of charge is not deemed to certify the ownership of a charge which appears thereon.[339]

To submit the charge for registration,[340] the chargee's solicitor will prepare an application in the form as set out in Form 17 of the Land Registration Rules, 1972[341] namely,[342] the name of the chargee, the charge to be registered as a burden on the folio mentioned in the heading, the amount of Land Registry fees[343] submitted, the name of the person to whom the land certificate and other documents are to be re-issued. The documents submitted (which are to be listed on the form) should include the original land certificate[344] (if issued), the original stamped[345] charge and a certified copy[346] together with the certificate of registration of charge where the chargor is a company registered under the Companies Acts.

There is provision for an application to be submitted without the certificate of registration of charge.[347] In practice, the Registrar used to accept only those applications submitted with the certificates of charge. However, as a result of the delays running up to 12 months from the time registration is applied for in the Companies Registration Office until the issue of the certificate of registration of charge, registration may be proceeded without the certificate.[348] In the meantime, the chargee may use a caution or inhibition to obtain protection.[349]

---

[337] *Ibid* s 105(4).

[338] SI 230/1972.

[339] See also Griffith, 'Land Registry Practice' (1977) 71 ILSI Gazette 99 at 103.

[340] A list of common errors made in submissions was published by the Law Society's Conveyancing Committee and distributed with the December, 1990 Gazette (reproduced in The Dublin Solicitors' Bar Association Newsletter of 1/92).

[341] SI 230/1972.

[342] *Ibid* r 57.

[343] Land Registration Rules, 1972 (SI 230/1972), rules 59(2) and 60; the fees are fixed from time to time by the Minister for Justice (Registration of Title Act, 1964 s14(1)); the current maximum are £250 (Land Registration (Fees) Order, 1991 (SI 363/1991).

[344] *Ibid*, r 59(3) and r 162; Registration of Title Act, 1964, s 105.

[345] *Ibid*, r 59(2).

[346] *Ibid*, r 181.

[347] *Ibid*, r 114.

[348] See further Ch 17.

[349] See paras **[10.100]-[10.101]** below.

Apart from checking that the charge is in proper form and its execution has been witnessed,[350] the Registrar of Titles is also under "the duty" to ascertain that the appropriate stamp duty has been paid on the instrument.[351]

CAUTIONS

[10.100] When taking a charge over registered land, prior to submitting the charge for registration in the Land Registry, the chargee must first execute the charge, stamp the charge, and where the chargor is a company, obtain the Certificate of Registration of Charge from the Registrar of Companies.[352]Any delay in applying for registration leaves the register open for other burdens to be entered.[353] To protect the chargee's interest a caution may be lodged with the Registrar of Titles to the effect that no dealing should be done with the land until notice has been served on the cautioner.[354] The form of caution is as set out in Form 81 of the forms provided by the Land Registration Rules, 1972.[355] An affidavit as set out in Form 82 is required to be made by the cautioner stating the basis on which the caution is made.[356] The Registrar of Titles will then send a notice to the registered owner in Form 83 of the entry of the caution.[357] Following lodgment of the caution, the Registrar of Titles may not without the consent of the cautioner register any dealing in the land.[358] However, the cautioner has only seven days to respond to the Registrar, following the service of a notice by the Registrar in Form 84 or 85, after which the caution will lapse.[359] If the cautioner objects to the proposed dealing he may be required to give sufficient security to indemnify every person against damage by the delay in registration.[360]

Another, but less used, protective mechanism is an inhibition. This is generally used with regard to unregistered rights. Any person interested in registered land or a charge thereon may apply to the Registrar of Titles for an entry to be made on the relevant folio inhibiting for a time or until the occurrence of a certain event any dealing with the registered land or charge.[361]

[350.] See para **[10.34]** above.

[351.] Registration of Title Act, 1964, s 104.

[352.] See Ch 17.

[353.] Priority is given in the order in which documents are received by the Land Registry (r 61 of the Land Registration Rules, 1972 SI 230/1972).

[354.] Registration of Title Act, 1964, s 97(1).

[355.] SI 230/1972; rule 131(1).

[356.] *Ibid* r 131(2); a person who lodges a caution "without reasonable cause" will be liable to compensate any person damaged thereby (Registration of Title Act, 1964, s 97(5)).

[357.] *Ibid* r 131(4).

[358.] Registration of Title Act, 1964, s 97(2).

[359.] *Ibid* s 97(3) and rules 132 and 136 of the Land Registration Rules, 1972 SI 230/1972.

[360.] *Ibid* s 97(4).

[361.] *Ibid* s 98; for the procedure involved see rr 137-145 inclusive of the Land Registration Rules, 1972 (SI 230/1972).

PRIORITY SEARCH

[10.101] A further temporary protective mechanism for a chargee of registered land is a priority search. A person who has agreed to lend money on the security of a charge may apply to the Registrar of Titles to make an official search.[362] This application is to be made in duplicate in the format of Form 104 or 105 of the Forms specified in the Land Registration Rules, 1972.[363] The Registrar shall issue a certificate[364] in a prescribed form[365] and shall at the request of the applicant make an entry in the register in the form of an inhibition.[366] However, for the applicant to retain priority, the instrument must be submitted for registration within 14 days after the date of the issue of the Registrar's Certificate.[367]

JUDGMENT MORTGAGES

[10.102] A creditor who obtains a judgment for a sum of money against a debtor may, by filing a copy of an affidavit (the original of which is filed in the High Court Central Office) in the Registry of Deeds or the Land Registry[368] (as the case may be) effectively convert his judgment into a mortgage of the debtor's land (as specified in the affidavit). The judgment mortgage which results from such filing will have priority over mortgages subsequently registered in the Registry of Deeds[369] and in the Land Registry.[370] The affidavit should contain appropriate details of the judgment and of the debtor's lands to be subjected to the judgment mortgage.[371]

The effect of this filing can be seen from s 7 of the Judgment Mortgage (Ireland) Act, 1850 which states:

> And be it enacted, that the registration as aforesaid of such affidavit shall operate to transfer to and vest in the creditor registering such affidavit all the lands, tenements, and hereditaments mentioned therein, for all the estate and interest of which the debtor mentioned in such affidavit shall at the time of such

---

[362] *Ibid* s 107 and Land Registration Rules, 1972 (SI 230/1972) r 191.

[363] SI 230/1972.

[364] Registration of Title Act, 1964, s 107.

[365] Form 104A or 105A of the Land Registration Rules, 1972 (SI 230/1972).

[366] Registration of Title Act, 1964, s 108(1); Form 106 of the Land Registration Rules, 1972 (SI 230/1972) - see r 193.

[367] *Ibid* s 108(2); Land Registration Rules, 1972 (SI 230/1972) rule 192; see also Wylie, *Irish Conveyancing Law* (2nd ed, 1996) para 15.41.

[368] *Ibid* s 69(1)(i) and 71; Land Registration Rules, 1972 (SI 230/1972) r 118(1).

[369] For a basic outline see Keane, *Equity and the Law of Trusts in the Republic of Ireland* (1988) Butterworths para 5.15.

[370] Registration of Title Act, 1964, s 74.

[371] As to the requirements of the affidavit see Wylie, *Irish Land Law* (3rd ed) paras 13.168-13.178; see Madden, *Registration of Deeds* (1868, McGee) Part II Ch. II.

registration be seised or possessed at law or in equity ... but subject to redemption on payment of the money owing on the judgment ... and such creditor ... shall, in respect of such lands, tenements and hereditaments, or such estate or interest therein as aforesaid, have all such rights, powers, and remedies whatsoever as if an effectual conveyance, assignment, appointment, or other assurance to such creditor of all such estate or interest, but subject to redemption as aforesaid, had been made, executed, and registered at the time of registering such affidavit.

[10.103] A point to bear in mind for this section is that as the judgment mortgagee obtains the debtor's title, so too does he obtain the debtor's obligations in respect of such title. Thus, the judgment mortgagee incurs the obligations running with a leasehold title as he has effectively taken an assignment of the title and not a security by way of sub-demise. Thus a creditor should endeavour to register his judgment only against freehold land, particularly as the very fact that he has an unsatisfied judgment would indicate that the debtor is unlikely to be able to discharge its payments promptly under any leasehold interests it holds.

Identification of Lands

[10.104] The Judgment Mortgage (Ireland) Act, 1850 provides at s 6 that:

such affidavit shall specify the county and barony, or the town or county of a city, and parish, or the town and parish, in which the lands to which the affidavit relates are situate, and where such lands lie in two or more counties or baronies, or parishes or streets, or partly in one barony, parish, or street and partly in another, the same shall be distinctly stated in such affidavit.

[10.105] These and the other requirements under s 6 make it incumbent upon a practitioner registering a judgment mortgage to pay particularly close attention to inserting the relevant and appropriate details in an affidavit.[372] Its stringent requirements afford an opportunity for a subsequent incumbrancer and its adviser to examine closely the details of the affidavit to ascertain whether it has fully complied with the statutory requirements.[373] In 1901 Lord Ashbourne stated:[374]

"There are few Acts of Parliament which have changed the law so much, or which have given to the legal profession so much occupation, or so much scope for developing their talents. Every line of this 6th section, indeed every word and syllable of it, has been threshed out backwards and forwards."

[372.] For registered land see also the requirements of r 119 of the Land Registration Rules, 1972 (SI 230/1972).

[373.] See also r 121 of the Land Registration Rules, 1972 (SI 230/1972).

[374.] In *Re Kane* [1901] 1 IR 520 at 523.

In *Re Murphy and McCormack*,[375] the Supreme Court held that Wylie J was wrong when he held in the High Court that the omission of the name of the barony from the affidavit did not affect the validity of the registration of the judgment; the Supreme Court held that such omission was fatal to its validity. In *Re George Flannery*[376] the affidavit stated that the debtor's lands were in the parish of New Ross. The debtor's lands were situated in what was popularly known as the parish of New Ross but in fact were in the parish of St. Mary's. Kenny J held that the affidavit was defective and that no judgment mortgage had been created. The harshness of this decision was explained by Kenny J in his judgment:[377]

> "As every judgment-mortgage affidavit registered in the Registry of Deeds has to be entered in the books and indexes kept in that office as if it were a memorial of a deed, and as the parish in which the lands are situate must be shown in the index of lands when the property is in a town or in a county of a city, the omission or serious misdescription of the parish in the affidavit may lead to incorrect entries being made in the indexes.
>
> The provision in section 6 of the Act of 1850 that the parish should be stated is to enable the affidavit to be registered correctly in the Index of Lands and in the abstract book so that those searching will not be misled. But if a parish which does not exist is referred to in the affidavit, it cannot be correctly registered and, in my opinion, is defective."

[10.106] More recently the decision of Costello J[378] and the endorsement of his views by the Supreme Court[379] indicate the courts may in future adopt a less fastidious approach. McCarthy J put it thus:[380]

> "If the property is clearly and adequately identified, so that none could be under any misapprehension, in a manner that would be appropriate to a conveyance of the property, is the legitimate charge to be defeated by the omission of a detail of which few may know and with which even fewer be concerned? I think not."

In *The Irish Bank of Commerce v O'Hara*[381] the defendant contended that the affidavit did not comply with s 6 as it did not specify the parish in which the property was situate. Both Courts held it was not clear that Dun Laoghaire was a town[382] and that therefore the requirement to state the parish was open to doubt;

[375.] [1930] IR 322.

[376.] [1971] IR 10.

[377.] *Ibid* at 13 and 14 respectively.

[378.] *The Irish Bank of Commerce v O'Hara* High Court, unrep, 10 May 1989; see also Doyle, 'A Fresh Look at the Judgment Mortgage (Ireland) Act' 1989 ILT 304.

[379.] Supreme Court, unrep, 7 April 1992; ILSI Gazette April 1993.

[380.] Supreme Court, unrep, 7 April 1992, p 2.

[381.] Supreme Court, unrep, 7 April 1992.

the purpose which the 1850 Act was intended to achieve was achieved by the description as given. The Courts did indicate though that care is needed to ensure that the lands are properly identified.

Costello J explained:[383]

> "... if non-compliance with the section arises from a misdescription then it is very likely that this would be fatal to the judgment mortgage. But if non-compliance arises from a mere omission of a statutory requirement this will not automatically invalidate the judgment mortgage. The purpose of the requirement relating to the location of the lands is to identify with precision the location of the lands affected by the judgment mortgage and to enable persons subsequently dealing with the judgment debtor and his lands to be warned of its existence."

[10.107] A misdescription with regard to an unnecessary detail will not invalidate an affidavit. In *Frayne v O'Dowd*[384] the debtor's acreage was overstated - the Circuit Court held this to be irrelevant as it was not a requirement to state the acreage.

Description of Debtor

[10.108] Section 6[385] provides that the affidavit shall specify the debtor's "title, trade or profession" as well as his "usual or last known place of abode". In *Dardis and Dunns Seeds Ltd v Hickey*[386] the debtor's description as a farmer instead of as a mechanic was fatal to the validity of the affidavit. This decision was taken in reliance on the decision in *Murphy v Lacey*[387] where an affidavit was held to be ineffective because it described the debtor, who had been a farmer but had since become a farm labourer, as a farmer. More recently in *Allied Irish Banks plc v Griffin*,[388] the debtor, who was a farmer, was described as a widow. Denham J held that widow indicated marital status and where a person holds an occupation it is not a title, trade or profession as required by the Act; accordingly the affidavit was invalid. In quoting from Wylie's *Irish Land Law*, Denham J implied that "widow" would be appropriate if the debtor had no trade or profession.[389]

---

382. For a further discussion of the meaning of a town see Kenny J in *Dardis and Dunns Seeds Ltd v Hickey* High Court, unrep, 11 July 1974; Wylie, *A Casebook on Land Law* p 479.
383. High Court, unrep, 10 May 1989.
384. (1951) 85 ILTR 114.
385. Judgment Mortgage (Ireland) Act 1850.
386. High Court, unrep, 11 July 1974 Kenny J; Wylie, *A Casebook on Irish Land Law* p 479.
387. (1896) 31 ILTR 42.
388. [1992] 2 IR 70; [1992] ILRM 590.
389. *Ibid* at pp 74 and 593 respectively.

Judgment Mortgage Registered Subsequent to Contract for Sale[390]

[10.109] A bank proposing to make finance available to a customer who has contracted to purchase land may be faced with a difficulty on closing if the final searches show that a judgment mortgage has been registered against the vendor subsequent to the contract for sale. The decision in *Tempany v Hynes*[391] is instructive as to the rights of the parties concerned.

The respective interests of a vendor and a purchaser in lands following the completion of a contract of sale but prior to the completion of the deed of assurance (and registration in the case of registered land) was set out by Henchy J in the Supreme Court:[392]

"When a binding contract for the sale of land has been made, whether the purchase money has been paid or not, the law ... treats the beneficial ownership as having passed to the purchaser from the time the contract was made ... From then until the time of completion, regardless of whether the purchase money has been paid or not, the vendor, in whom the legal estate is still vested, is treated for certain purposes ... as a trustee for the purchaser. But, coupled with this trusteeship, there is vested in the vendor a substantial interest in the property pending completion. Save where the contract provides otherwise, he is entitled to take and keep for his own use the rents and profits up to the date fixed for completion. It is clear, therefore, that between contract and completion the vendor has a beneficial interest in the property which is capable of being charged by a judgment mortgage ... Since the judgment creditor (by registering his judgment as a judgment mortgage) could not acquire any greater estate or interest in the land than the registered owner had at the time of such registration, all that could pass to the judgment creditor here was the interest in the land which the registered owner had after the making the contract to sell, namely, an interest which would pass out of existence once the sale had been completed, the purchase money paid and the purchaser registered as full owner. It follows, therefore, that if the defendant completes the purchase and becomes registered as full owner, the post-contract judgments will no longer affect the lands and he will be entitled to have them cancelled from the folios".

[390.] See further Keane, *Equity and the Law of Trusts in the Republic of Ireland* (1988) Butterworths para 5.16.

[391.] [1976] IR 101; for a detailed critical analysis of the majority decision see Lyall, 'The Purchaser's Equity: An Irish Controversy' (1989) ILT 270.

[392.] *Ibid* at 109; see also Kennedy CJ in *Re Murphy and McCormack* [1930] IR 322 at 327; for further discussion on this see Wylie, *Irish Conveyancing Law* (2nd ed, 1996) paras 12.02-12.10; Kenny J in his judgment (with which O'Higgins CJ agreed) adopted a somewhat different approach; but as was pointed out by Keane in *Equity and the Law of Trusts in the Republic of Ireland* (1988) para 5.16 that although this "represents, of course, the law, ... it is thought that the decision is somewhat doubtful".

Henchy J pointed out[393] that the purchaser's right to have the judgment mortgage discharged is now given statutory recognition by s 71(4)(c) of the Registration of Title Act, 1964 which provides that the creditor's affidavit charging the debtor's interest in land is subject to: "all unregistered rights subject to which the judgment debtor held that interest at the time of registration of the affidavit."

This sub-section avoids the mischief which arose in *Pim v Coyle*[394] where a purchaser who delayed in registering his transfer found his title subject to judgment mortgages registered subsequent to his agreement to purchase the lands. That decision appeared to turn on the fact that it was a voluntary transfer as it was not followed in similar circumstances where the transfer was given for value.[395]

The respective positions of the parties is the same with regard to unregistered titles:

> "... it is well settled ... that a judgment mortgage, created under the Judgment Mortgage Act, 1850, by the registration of the necessary affidavit in the Registry of Deeds, only affects such property as the judgment debtor, at the time of the registration, lawfully possesses as of his own right, and that the judgment creditor takes subject to all equities by which the judgment debtor is bound."[396]

Spouse's Consent

[10.110] A mortgage over an interest in a family home created by a spouse without the other spouse's prior written consent is void.[397] However, a judgment mortgage is effected by the creditor filing an office copy of an affidavit (containing requisite details) in the Registry of Deeds, but no interest is mortgaged or purported to be mortgaged by any spouse. Accordingly, a spouse's consent is not required for the registration of a judgment mortgage.[398] As Carroll J explained:[399]

> "A judgment mortgage, if registered against a family home, is not a disposition by a spouse purporting to convey an interest in the family home. It is a unilateral act by a judgment creditor and the creation of the judgment mortgage is effected by the registration in the Registry of Deeds (in the case of unregistered land) of the affidavit of judgment which has already been filed in

---

393. *Ibid* at 110.
394. [1907] 1 IR 330.
395. In *Re Murphy and McCormack* [1930] IR 322 and in *Re Mabel Strong* [1940] IR 382.
396. O'Byrne J in *Re Mabel Strong* [1940] IR 382 at 402.
397. Family Home Protection Act, 1976, s 3(1) (subject to certain exceptions).
398. See *Murray v Diamond* [1982] ILRM 113; Wylie, *A Casebook on Irish Land Law* p 476; see also *Containercare (Ireland) Ltd v Wycherley and Wycherley* [1982] IR 143.
399. In *Containercare (Ireland) Ltd v Wycherley and Wycherley* [1982] IR 143 at 150 and 153.

court ... where the estate or interest of a spouse is vested by operation of law in a judgment mortgage, that judgment mortgagee takes free from any obligation to obtain the consent of the other spouse to a disposition by the judgment mortgagee."

A judgment creditor may nonetheless have difficulty in enforcing a judgment mortgage over a family home as the Court may decline to order a partition or a sale in lieu of partition.[400]

Partnerships

[10.111] A judgment against a partnership may be converted to a judgment mortgage on the firm's property.[401]

Procedure in Practice

[10.112] A creditor who has obtained judgment for a sum of money against a landowner may convert his judgment into a judgment mortgage by swearing an affidavit setting out precisely the details as required by s 6 of the Judgment Mortgage (Ireland) Act 1850. Where there are joint creditors in respect of the same debt the swearing of an affidavit by one of the creditors on behalf of all is sufficient.[402]

In certain exceptional circumstances, the affidavit may be sworn by a person other than the creditor.[403] When the Registrar in the Registry of Deeds is presented with an office copy of the affidavit, the Registrar is obliged to register it.[404] Similarly, with regard to land the title of which is registered, once the copy affidavit is presented to the Registrar, the Registrar is obliged to register it on the appropriate folio[405] in the manner as set out in Form 74 of the Land Registration Rules, 1972.[406]

The failure to re-register judgments every five years in accordance with the provisions of the Judgment Mortgage (Ireland) Act, 1850 does not affect the priority of the registered judgment creditors *inter se*, but only as regards subsequent mortgagees, creditors or purchasers.[407]

A judgment obtained in England can be converted into a judgment mortgage in Ireland pursuant to the Judgments Extension Act 1868.[408]

[400.] See *First National Building Society v Ring and Ring* [1992] 1 IR 375.

[401.] *Magner v Johnstone* [1926] IR 472.

[402.] See *Re Kane* [1901] 1 IR 520.

[403.] See *McLoughlin v Strand Housing Ltd* (1952) 86 ILTR 167 - creditor was absent in Malaysia for a year on a merchant vessel; see also r 119(2)(a) of the Land Registration Rules, 1972 (SI 230/1972).

[404.] See Madden J in *Re Robert Phelan* [1912] 1 IR 91 at 94.

[405.] Registration of Title Act, 1964, s 71; *Re Robert Phelan* [1912] 1 IR 91.

[406.] SI 230/1972, rule 118(2).

[407.] *Re Boyse's Estate* [1910] 1 IR 292.

[408.] In *Re Cleland's Estate* [1909] 1 IR 1.

In the case of registered land there is also an enabling provision for the registration of a burden as affecting land any judgment or order of a court[409] or a *lis pendens*.[410] The procedure for registration is set out in the Land Registration Rules, 1972.[411]

RELEASE OF MORTGAGES[412]

[10.113] Upon payment or discharge of the debt for which the mortgage has been granted the mortgagor is entitled to have the mortgage released. Ideally, the discharge of the debt and the release of the mortgage happen simultaneously. In practice for non commercial loans, there is usually a delay in the issue of the release due to the sealing requirements of the mortgagee. While this is unsatisfactory the reality is that solicitors are required to complete a purchase and a mortgage on the basis of an undertaking from another solicitor to furnish a release.

When acting for a person redeeming a mortgage, it is important to ensure that the person receives back the full absolute title to the land mortgaged. An imperfect deed, however, may be sufficient in that the surrender will be implied on the handing over of the mortgage.[413] In practice, the mortgagor's solicitor should prepare a draft deed of release for approval by the mortgagee's solicitor, prior to preparing an engrossment.[414] The appropriate language to be used in a deed releasing property which has been mortgaged by conveyance is as follows:

> "the mortgagee hereby releases and conveys unto the mortgagor ALL THAT AND THOSE [description of property] TO HOLD the same unto the mortgagor in fee simple".

Where property has been mortgaged by demise the following language should be used:

> "the mortgagee hereby releases and surrenders unto the mortgagor ALL THAT AND THOSE [description of property] to the intent that the term of years created by the Mortgage may merge and be extinguished in the reversion expectant upon the determination thereof."

The following additional language should then be inserted whether the property has been mortgaged by conveyance, assignment or demise:

[409.] Registration of Title Act, 1964, s 69(1)(h).

[410.] *Ibid* s 69(1)(i); see also Wylie, *Irish Land Law* (3rd ed) para 13.165.

[411.] SI 230/1972, rr 127 and 128 respectively.

[412.] For further reading see Wylie, *Irish Conveyancing Law* (2nd ed, 1996) paras 19.55-19.56; Fisher and Lightwood's *Law of Mortgage* (10th ed) p 569.

[413.] See *Haigh v Brooks* (1839) 10 Ad & El 309.

[414.] Assuming the mortgagee does not have a standard form of release impressed on its mortgage.

"To the intent that all the property mortgaged by the Mortgage shall henceforth be held by the mortgagor freed and discharged from all and any mortgage created by the Mortgage and from all moneys interest and costs and all claims and demands of the mortgage thereunder."

[10.114] A release of an equitable mortgage by deposit of title deeds may be effected by returning the deeds to the mortgagor. This procedure of course is not possible where a builder deposits his title deeds to a housing estate and sells individual houses. A letter of release from the mortgagee will be sufficient to release the property from the mortgage.[415]

[10.115] Where a charge has been registered on a folio in the Land Registry, the Registrar is obliged to register on the folio the discharge of the charge at the request of the registered owner of the charge or upon the chargee's receipt.[416] A chargor's solicitor should prepare a discharge in the form as set out in Form 71A of the Schedule of Forms to the Land Registration Rules, 1972.[417]

[10.116] At the time of the execution of any release or discharge in favour of a company, a note of such release or discharge should be set out in the Companies Office Form 49. This form is prepared by the mortgagor/chargor and executed under seal; the mortgagor's/chargor's company secretary and a director are required to make a declaration as to its correctness before a Commissioner for Oaths or practising solicitor. On receipt of this form, the Registrar of Companies will notify the mortgagee or chargee who then has 21 days within which to object to its filing.[418] Where a mortgage or charge has been partially released, the appropriate Companies Office form is Form 49A.

---

[415] See Milnes Holden, *The Law and Practice of Banking* Vol 2 (7th ed, 1986) para 6-22; see also Rowley, *Conveyancing and Equitable Charges* (1962) 26 Conv 445.

[416] See Registration of Title Act, 1964, s 65.

[417] SI 230/1972; assuming the charge does not have a standard form of discharge impressed on its charge.

[418] This procedure may be criticised as leaving a mortgagee or chargee open to having its security satisfied on the register where the notification from the Registrar has been inadvertently over-looked.

Chapter 11

Mortgages and Fixed Charges of Chattels

PRIORITY OF SECURED CREDITOR

[11.01] A company[1] may create a security interest over its assets so as to give the holder of that security interest a right, upon certain events, of taking possession of the assets, disposing of them and utilising the proceeds towards the discharge of the debt secured by the security interest. The enforcement of security, however, will usually trigger the receivership or liquidation of a company (in practice a creditor wishing to enforce its security will appoint a receiver over the secured assets). Where a company's assets are sold and the proceeds distributed to its creditors (and shareholders), the law sets out the priority of creditors to be satisfied in the event that the proceeds are insufficient to satisfy all creditors and shareholders.[2]

Priority of Fixed Charges

[11.02] A secured creditor will usually obtain priority over all other creditors of an insolvent company,[3] save where an involvement company comes under the protection of the court.[4] This arises by virtue of s 284 of the Companies Act, 1963 which applies the bankruptcy rules to the winding up of insolvent companies.[5] Section 76 of the Bankruptcy Act, 1988 sets out by reference to the First Schedule of that Act the proof of debts. Under para 24 of the First Schedule to the Bankruptcy Act a "secured creditor" may realise its security and then prove for the balance if its security is insufficient to discharge the debt due to it. A "secured creditor" is defined as meaning "any creditor holding any mortgage, charge or lien on the debtor's estate or any part thereof as security for a debt due to him".[6]

---

1. Within the meaning of the Companies Act, 1963, s 2(1).
2. Companies Act, 1963 s 284.
3. An exception to this is where a secured creditor has a fixed charge on book debts - see para **[14.00]**.
4. Pursuant to the Companies (Amendment) Act, 1990, s 2(1); see in *Re Atlantic Magnetics Limited* [1993] 2 IR 561.
5. See Kenny J in *Re Tailteann Freight Services Ltd (in liq); Freaney v The Governor and Company of the Bank of Ireland* [1975] IR 376 at 381.
6. Bankruptcy Act, 1988 s 3.

[11.03] The meaning of mortgage may be ascertained from Lindley MR's definition in *Santley v Wilde*[7] where he described a mortgage as, "a conveyance of land or an assignment of chattels as a security for the payment of a debt or the discharge of some other obligation for which it is given."[8]

The words of Atkin LJ in *National Provincial and Union Bank of England v Charnley*[9] give a clear meaning as to what is meant by a charge:

> "I think there can be no doubt that where in a transaction for value both parties evince an intention that property, existing or future, shall be made available as security for the payment of a debt, and that the creditor shall have a present right to have it made available, there is a charge, even though the present legal right which is contemplated can only be enforced at some future date."

A lien may be described as a right, either by contract, or by law under which the person holding an asset may retain possession until the debt (in respect of which the asset is held) is discharged.[10]

Priority of Floating Charges

[11.04] Section 285(2) of the Companies Act, 1963[11] sets out certain debts which in a winding up[12] "shall be paid in priority to all other debts". The owners of such debts are known as preferential creditors.[13] Any doubt raised by the wording at the commencement of s 285(2) as to whether preferential creditors rank in priority to secured creditors is removed by sub-s (7)(b) which makes it clear that the debts listed in sub-s (2), "have priority over the claims of holders of debentures under any floating charge created by the company". In other words, if the secured creditor has a mortgage, charge or lien over an asset it will be entitled to the proceeds of that asset in priority to the preferential creditors provided his security is not deemed to be a floating charge,[14] and provided his security does not rank in priority behind an earlier floating charge.[15]

---

7.   [1899] 2 Ch 474 at 474.

8.   This definition is adopted by O'Neill Kiely, *The Principles of Equity as applied in Ireland* (1936), The Fodhla Printing Company Ltd 263.

9.   [1924] 1 KB 431 at 449.

10. See Fisher and Lightwood's *Law of Mortgage* (9th ed) 5; see also Goode, *Legal Problems of Credit and Security* (2nd ed, 1988) 14.

11. As amended - see McCann, *Butterworths Ireland Companies Acts 1963-1990* (1993).

12. Companies Act, 1963' s 98 extends this to a receivership.

13. For a detailed treatment see Lynch, Marshall & O'Ferrall, *Corporate Insolvency and Rescue* (1996) Butterworths, paras 4.34 to 4.53; see also Courtney, *The Law of Private Companies* (1994) Butterworths, paras 19.129-19.131; Keane, *Company Law in the Republic of Ireland* (2nd ed, 1991) Butterworths, paras 38.72-38.75.

14. See *Richards v Overseers of Kidderminster* (1896) 2 Ch 212 and *Re Lewis Merthyr Consolidated Colleries Ltd* [1929] 1 Ch 498.

15. See in *Re Manning Furniture Ltd* [1996] 1 ILRM 13.

Effective Security for Creditors

[11.05] In view of the continuing expansion, and threat of expansion, of creditors entitled to priority over the holders of floating charges,[16] creditors have sought ways of taking security which would have the operational benefit for the chargor as being a floating charge and yet still be regarded as a fixed charge.[17] This has resulted in much judicial interpretation both in Ireland and in other common law jurisdictions as to the characteristics which distinguish a fixed charge from a floating charge.[18] In more recent times, the concept of automatic crystallisation has been introduced whereby a floating charge is created in favour of the creditor but upon certain stipulated events the charge crystallises and becomes fixed. This is the classic case of endeavouring to satisfy the creditor by giving him first priority[19] as well as satisfying the creator of the charge by enabling it to carry on its business in the normal course of events.[20]

THE NATURE OF A FIXED OR SPECIFIC CHARGE

[11.06] If a charge is not to be regarded as being a floating charge, it must be what is known as a fixed or specific charge. The principal judicial decisions arise where a liquidator seeks to establish whether a particular security is a floating charge and therefore ranks subsequent in priority to the preferential creditors. The legal argument accordingly has tended to prove or disprove that the particular security has the characteristics of a floating charge - if it does not, then by a process of elimination it must be a fixed or specific charge.

[11.07] In recent times this process was first considered by the Irish courts in December 1978 in *Re Lakeglen Construction Ltd (in liq).*[21] Costello J initially sought guidance from Farwell J's judgment in *Illingworth v Houldsworth*[22] which indicated that if it was intended the charge was to remain dormant until some future date and the company was to go on dealing with the charged assets

---

16. In 1994 the Company Law Review Group were asked to examine whether specific preference should be given to farmer creditors.
17. See Keane J in *Re Keenan Brothers Ltd* [1985] IR 401 at 415; [1985] ILRM 254 at 264; see also Corporate Briefing Jan 1989 39; Pennington, *Fixed Charges over Future Assets of a Company* (1985) 6 Co Law 9 and *Butterworths Banking & Financial Law Review 1987* p 177-200.
18. See *Re Keenan Brothers Ltd* [1985] IR 401; [1985] ILRM 641; [1986] BCLC 302; *Re Atlantic Computer Systems plc* [1992] 1 All ER 476; *Re Atlantic Medical Ltd* [1993] BCLC 386; *Re CCG International Enterprises Ltd* [1993] BCLC 1428; *Re GE Tunbridge Ltd* [1995] 1 BCLC 34; *Royal Trust Bank v National Westminster Bank* [1995] BCC 128.
19. See *Griffiths v Yorkshire Bank plc* [1994] 1 WLR 1427 - although doubts have been cast on the correctness of this decision - see *The Company Lawyer* 16 [1995] 291.
20. For automatic crystallisation see para **[13.12]**.
21. [1980] IR 347 (also referred to as *Kelly v McMahon Ltd*).
22. [1904] AC 355.

until then, the security would contain the true elements of a floating charge. Costello J considered whether the parties at the time of executing the debenture intended that the book debts (which were subject to the charge, the nature of which was unspecified) would be dealt with by the company as though the debenture had not been created, until the debenture holder became entitled to intervene. In his deliberations Costello J noted that what had to be borne in mind was the following:

1   The company was a trading company,

2   The parties expressly agreed that the company was to be permitted to carry on its business, and

3   In the normal course of affairs it would create difficulties for a trading company if it were required to hand over to the debenture holder its book debts as it received them from time to time.

Costello J concluded that:[23]

> "in the absence of provisions to the contrary ..., when permission to trade is given in a debenture, permission to receive book debts is more readily to be inferred than is an arrangement by which the company is required to hand them over to a debenture holder".

Costello J found that the absence of restrictive provisions preventing the company from dealing with its book debts in the normal course of business supported the inference that it was intended by the parties that the charged assets be dealt with from time to time in the normal course without regard to the charge created by the debenture.

[11.08] The following July in *Welch v Bowmaker (Ireland) Ltd and The Governor and Company of the Bank of Ireland*[24] the Supreme Court considered the language of a debenture which specified that, first all the company's undertaking, property and assets present and future were charged and, secondly the hereditaments and premises specified in the schedule were specifically charged. Although the lands in question were not specified in the schedule Costello J had held in the High Court that such lands were nevertheless the subject of a specific charge as the debenture was stated to have been issued subject to the conditions endorsed thereon, the first of which provided that the charge created over the company's lands and premises for the time being was a specific charge. The majority of the Supreme Court, however, held that the particular provisions of the charging clause overrode the conditions of the

---

[23.] [1980] IR 347 at 353.

[24.] [1980] IR 251.

debenture and accordingly the charge over the lands in question was not specific but floating.

Parke J, who was particularly critical of the draftsman of the debenture,[25] set out guidelines for establishing the true nature of the charge when he said,[26]

> "In construing a document, a court is not entitled to speculate as to what the parties intended to say; the court's task is to ascertain what is the true meaning and intention of the words used by the draftsman. If the words are free from inconsistency or ambiguity, it is not permissible to work outside the document itself or to attempt to ascribe any forced or strained meaning for such words in order to justify a particular construction. If (as in the present case) there is inconsistency between certain provisions of the document, it is necessary to consider the entire document and the facts and circumstances surrounding its execution in order to ascertain which of the conflicting expressions must take precedence in determining the true meaning of the document."

It seems that inconsistent provisions in a debenture which are inapplicable to the subject matter of the charge will be ignored in construing the nature of the charge.[27]

[11.09] It was six years later in 1985 when the Supreme Court again considered the distinction in *Re Keenan Brothers Ltd (in liq)*.[28] In that case the Supreme Court heard an appeal from Keane J's decision in the High Court [29] which held that a debenture which purported to create a fixed charge over book debts was in reality a floating charge.

Although the Supreme Court unanimously took a contrary view to the High Court, the judgments of Keane J and the principal judgments in the Supreme Court of Henchy and McCarthy JJ took much the same route in laying out the decisive factors. Both courts approved and adopted Lord Macnaghten's statement in *Illingworth v Houldsworth*[30] that:

> "A specific charge ... is one that without more fastens on ascertained and definite property or property capable of being ascertained and defined; a floating charge, on the other hand, is ambulatory and shifting in its nature, hovering over and so to speak floating with the property which it is intended to affect until some event occurs or some act is done which causes it to settle and fasten on the subject of the charge within its reach and grasp".

[25.] *Ibid* at 259.
[26.] *Ibid* at 261.
[27.] See *Re Cimex Tissues Ltd* [1994] BCC 626.
[28.] [1985] IR 401; [1985] ILRM 641; [1986] BCLC 242.
[29.] [1985] IR 401; [1985] ILRM 254; [1985] BCLC 302.
[30.] [1904] AC 355 at 385.

[11.10] Also considered and adopted by both courts in that decision, and indeed by Costello J in *Re Lakeglen Construction Ltd (in liq)*[31] was the stated characteristics of a floating charge by Romer LJ in the English Court of Appeal[32] where he indicated that a charge which contained the following three characteristics would be a floating charge:

> "(1) if it is a charge on a class of assets of the company present and future;
>
> (2) if that class is one which in the ordinary course of the business of the company, would be changing from time to time; and
>
> (3) if you find that by the charge it is contemplated that, until some future step is taken by or on behalf of those interested in the charge, the company may carry on its business in the ordinary way as far as concerns the particular class of assets I am dealing with."

Romer LJ pointed out that a charge may still be a floating charge even if it did not possess all three characteristics; this point was made also by Hoffmann J in *Re Brightlife Ltd*.[33] But both the Supreme Court in Ireland[34] and the High Court in Northern Ireland,[35] when considering whether a charge was fixed or floating, acknowledged in their respective decisions the first two characteristics applied to the case in question and then set about establishing whether the third criterion applied before holding in each case that the charge was floating.[36]

The critical part of these characteristics is the third one, namely, the intention that until the debenture holder intervenes the chargor may continue to deal with the charged assets in the normal course of its business.[37] Hence, in endeavouring to establish whether a particular security is or is not a floating charge the courts examine the security to ascertain if the chargor was restricted from dealing with the charged asset in the normal course of business.[38] There may be circumstances though where a rather loose restriction does not render a purported fixed charge a floating one.[39]

---

[31] [1980] IR 347 at 354.

[32] In *Re Yorkshire Woolcombers Association Ltd* [1903] 2 Ch 284 at 295.

[33] [1986] BCLC 418 at 427; see also Pennington, 'Fixed Charges over Future Assets of a Company' (1985) 6 Co Law 9 at 18 and *Butterworths, Banking & Financial Law Review 1987* at 192 - "The absence of one or more of these features will signify an intention to create a fixed charge, but it does not inevitably follow that a fixed charge is created because the legal requirements for a floating charge may not be satisfied".

[34] *Re Holidair Ltd* [1994] 1 IR 416.

[35] *Re Armagh Shoes Ltd* [1984] BCLC 405.

[36] Both cases involved a charge on book debts but the Northern Ireland case concerned also a charge on plant, machinery, fixtures, fittings and ancillary equipment.

[37] See in particular McCarthy J in *Re Keenan Brothers Ltd (in liq)* [1985] IR 401 at 424; [1985] ILRM 641 at 649.

[38] See Blayney J in *Re Holidair Ltd* [1994] 1 IR 416 at 445; although see Millett LJ in *Re Cosslett (Contractors) Ltd* [1997] 4 All ER 115 see para **[11.15]** below.

[39] See *Re Cimex Tissues Ltd* [1994] BCC 626 dealt with in para **[11.14]** below.

Restricted Use of Charged Asset

[11.11] The statement in the security that it is a fixed charge, and thus the declared intention of the parties that it is fixed, is not in itself sufficient.[40] It must be clear that the stated intention brought into effect in reality a fixed charge. There should be a requirement that the use of the assets the subject matter of the fixed charge be restricted or under the control of the fixed charge holder such as in the debenture and charge considered in *Re Keenan Brothers Ltd (in liq)*[41] where the book debts were required to be paid into a designated account and not disposed of or diminished or withdrawn from the designated account without the prior written consent of the debenture holder or chargee. In the Supreme Court, Henchy J[42] was satisfied that:

> "the restricted use permitted to the company of the assets charged was incompatible with the essence of a floating charge ... the charge, far from being floating or dormant or hovering over those assets, had fixed on them to such an extent that they were unusable in the ordinary course of business save at the discretion of the Bank ... such a degree of sequestration of the book debts when collected made those monies incapable of being used in the ordinary course of business and meant that they were put, specifically and expressly, at the disposal of the Bank ... assets thus withdrawn from ordinary trade use, put in the keeping of the debenture holder, and sterilised and made indisposable save at the absolute discretion of the debenture holder, have the distinguishing features of a fixed charge."

[11.12] The following year in the High Court, Barron J stated:[43]

> "since the purpose of a floating charge is to enable the borrower to use its property unrestricted by the existence of the charge so long as the charge remains floating, a test to ascertain the true nature of the charge is to determine whether the instrument of charge does or does not permit such unrestricted use of the property charged."

[11.13] Whether unrestricted use of the property charged is permitted or not depends upon the terms of the charge and not upon the action taken subsequent to the creation of the charge. In *Re Wogan's (Drogheda) Ltd*[44] the deed which provided that a fixed charge over book debts was created contained a covenant requiring the chargor to pay all moneys it received in respect of book debts into

---

[40.] See McCarthy J in *Re Keenan Brothers Ltd (in liq)* [1985] IR 401 at 421; [1985] ILRM 641 at 647; see Blayney J in *Re Holidair Ltd* [1994] 1 IR 416 at 445; see also Barron J in *Re AH Masser Ltd (In Receivership)* [1986] IR 455 at 457; Hutton J *Re Armagh Shoes Ltd* [1984] BCLC 405 at 419.

[41.] [1985] IR 401 at 424; [1985] ILRM 641 at 649.

[42.] *Ibid* at 419; *Ibid* at 645; his judgment was supported by Finlay CJ, Walsh J and Hederman J.

[43.] In *Re AH Masser Ltd (In Receivership)* [1986] IR 455 at 457.

[44.] [1993] 1 IR 157.

banking accounts as may be designated by the lender. As no banking account was subsequently designated, Denham J held that only a floating charge had been created. However, the Supreme Court unanimously held that evidence of the conduct of the parties subsequent to the date of the charge was inadmissible[45] and as the terms of the deed were such as to create a fixed charge, a fixed charge was deemed to have been created. This interpretation is not entirely satisfactory as the effect is for the parties to agree on a set of restrictions in the charge, which will have the effect of granting the chargee priority over the preferential creditors (should the need arise), and to operate in a manner without paying any adherence to such restrictions.[46]

[11.14] In *Re Holidair Ltd*[47] the Supreme Court held that a covenant in a mortgage debenture requiring the chargor to carry on business in a proper and efficient manner, together with the absence of a restriction on withdrawing moneys which had become the proceeds of book debts, negatived the purported creation of a fixed charge over book debts even though the mortgage debenture contained a provision whereby the chargor was required to pay the book debts when realised to such account as the chargee could designate.

Licence to deal with charged asset

[11.15] The three decisions[48] of the Supreme Court in the 1980s and 1990s concerning the distinction between fixed and floating charges have involved a consideration only of book debts. In England the point came up for consideration in respect of machinery in *Re Cimex Tissues Ltd.*[49] In that case a toilet roll manufacturer created a debenture in which it charged by way of fixed charge plant and machinery specified in a valuation annexed to the debenture.

The machinery was used in the manufacturing process and this was not of a type which would be charged on a regular basis. The debenture however contained covenants usually associated with a floating charge in that it provided that the company could not deal with the charged property otherwise than for the purpose of getting in and realising them in the ordinary course of business and not sell the charged property except in the ordinary course of business and for the purpose of carrying on its trading business. The court held that the covenants were inapplicable to the charged property by virtue of their nature and that a

---

[45] Following the decision of *Whitworth Estates Ltd v Miller* [1970] AC 583.
[46] Goode, *Legal Problems of Credit and Security* (2nd ed) p 9 - "A creditor cannot claim a fixed security interest in an asset and at the same time allow the debtor the right to continue to treat the asset as his own."
[47] [1994] 1 IR 416.
[48] *Re Keenan Brothers Ltd* [1985] IR 401; [1985] ILRM 641; *Re Wogan's Drogheda Ltd* [1993] 1 IR 157 and *Re Holidair Ltd* [1994] 1 IR 416.
[49] [1994] BCC 626.

fixed charge had been created as a licence for the chargor to deal to some extent with the charged assets was not necessarily inconsistent with a fixed charge. The court indicated that the extent to which a licence to deal with the charged assets was compatible with a fixed charge would depend on the circumstances of the case and nature of the property charged. The rationale for this approach can be seen from the judgment of Mr Burnton QC where he stated:[50]

"Both a fixed and a floating charge are present securities. In my judgment, the difference between them relates to the nature of the interest of the lender in the charged property immediately created by the debenture before any crystallising event occurred. A fixed charge attaches to the charged property in specie either immediately or as soon as it is acquired by the chargor. The interest of a floating chargee is not specific prior to crystallisation. The floating chargee is, in effect, given a security interest in the fund of assets over which the charge is created.

If the crucial difference between a fixed charge and a floating charge is in the nature of the interest of the chargee prior to any event of crystallisation, it would follow that a licence for the chargor to deal to some extent with the charged assets is not necessarily inconsistent with a fixed charge. If, however, the licence to deal given to the chargor is extensive, the charge will be floating, since in this circumstances there is in effect no attachment of the charge to any specific asset: see Goode, *Legal Problems of Credit and Security*, at p 56. The extent to which the licence to deal is compatible with a fixed charge must depend on all the circumstances of the case, and in particular on the nature of the charged property. Where the charged property is stock, or book debts - i.e. where the assets are naturally fluctuating - the court will readily conclude that a liberty for the chargor to deal with the charged assets is inconsistent with a fixed charge. Where, as in the present case, the assets are specific and do not necessarily fluctuate, some liberty to release the charged assets may not be inconsistent with a fixed charge. Conversely, however, on this basis a floating charge over present goods, not extending to future goods, is not a conceptual impossibility.

If this analysis is correct, one would expect to find cases where there was a fixed charge notwithstanding that, under the instrument creating the charge, the chargor had the right to deal, to some extent, with the charged assets. *Holroyd v Marshall* (1862) 10 HL Cas 191 is such a case."

Control of Asset

[11.16] Conversely, a charge may be a floating charge even where the chargor does not have an unfettered freedom to deal with the charged assets. In *Re*

---

50. *Ibid* at 635.

Cosslett (Contractors) Ltd[51] Millett LJ clarified that it is the element of control which is the distinguishing feature; he said:[52]

> "The judge held that it is of the essence of a floating charge that until the charge crystallises the chargor should retain an unfettered freedom to carry on his business in the ordinary way ... But with respect the converse does not follow. The chargor's unfettered freedom to deal with the assets in the ordinary course of his business free from the charge is obviously inconsistent with the nature of a fixed charge; but it does not follow that his unfettered freedom to deal with the charged assets is essential to the existence of a floating charge. It plainly is not, for any well drawn floating charge prohibits the chargor from creating further charges having priority to the floating charge; and a prohibition against factoring debts is not sufficient to convert what would otherwise be a floating charge on book debts into a fixed charge (see *Re Brightlife Ltd* [1986] 3 All ER 673 at 676, [1987] Ch 200 at 209 per Hoffmann J).
>
> The essence of a floating charge is that it is a charge, not on any particular asset, but on a fluctuating body of assets which remain under the management and control of the chargor, and which the chargor has the right to withdraw from the security despite the existence of the charge. The essence of a fixed charge is that the charge is on a particular asset or class of assets which the chargor cannot deal with free from the charge without the consent of the chargee. The question is not whether the chargor has complete freedom to carry on his business as he chooses, but whether the chargee is in control of the charged assets."

FORM OF SECURITY

[11.17] Thus, if by taking a security interest it is intended that the creator will be permitted to trade with the charged assets in its normal course of business and those charged assets are of a type which would revolve on a regular basis, a number of creditors (known as preferential creditors) are given a statutory priority over the holder of that security interest.[53] A secured creditor may avoid losing priority by obtaining title to the asset with a proviso for the return of title on the payment of the secured debt.[54] Traditionally, lenders took title to lands and buildings by way of sub-demise or conveyance granting a right of redemption on the payment of the secured debt and a floating charge on all other assets. Although it has been suggested that a mortgage of chattels cannot be created by demise,[55] the Court of Appeal has held[56] that where lands were

---

[51.] [1997] 4 All ER 115.
[52.] *Ibid* at 127.
[53.] See para **[11.04]** above.
[54.] See paras **[10.02]-[10.03]**.
[55.] Cousins, *The Law of Mortgages* p 48.
[56.] *National Provincial and Union Bank of England v Charnley* [1924] 1 KB 431.

demised "together with all and singular the fixed and movable plant machinery and fixtures implements and utensils now or hereafter fixed to or placed upon or used in or about" the lands for the residue of the term of the lease less the last 10 days, an equitable charge over the chattels was created ranking in priority to subsequent charges.[57]

In many cases title to plant, machinery and equipment are assigned (not charged) to the lender as security for the repayment of monies owing or which may become due. This demise or assignment is in the true nature of a mortgage[58] rather than a mere charge.[59]

Fixed Security over Future Chattels

[11.18] At common law title to a chattel could not be assigned if at the time of the assignment the chattel did not exist.[60] Writers on the subject are agreed that the decision in *Holroyd v Marshall*[61] had the effect of permitting assignments in equity of future property.[62] The facts may be summarised to the effect that there was an agreement to purchase "machinery, implements and things" specified in a schedule to the deed and fixed in a mill and that all "machinery, implements and things" which should be fixed or placed in the mill should be subject to the agreement. The Lord Chancellor, Lord Westbury held that, "immediately on the new machinery and effects being fixed or placed in the mill, they became subject to the operation of the contract, and passed in equity to the mortgagees."[63] Subsequently in *Tailby v The Official Receiver*[64] the House of Lords held that an assignment of future book debts was not too vague to take effect and operated to pass the beneficial interest in a book debt which came into existence after the date of the assignment. Lord Watson held that the assignee

---

[57.] It was held that a floating charge was created over the chattels referred to in the security.

[58.] Cousins, *The Law of Mortgages* p 48 - "where the chattel is mortgaged ... it is by way of assignment of the legal title with a proviso, express or implied, for reassignment on redemption"; see also Forde, *Commercial Law* (2nd ed, 1997) para 5.061 - "A chattel mortgage is an absolute assignment of ownership to the mortgagee, subject to a proviso for re-assignment when the debt has been paid off".

[59.] For a brief description of the distinction see the Crowther 'Report on Consumer Credit' Cmnd 4596 para 4.17; see also Goode, *Legal Problems of Credit and Security* (2nd ed, 1988) p 14.

[60.] Gough, *Company Charges* (2nd ed 1996) p 39; see also Goode, *Legal Problems of Credit and Security* (2nd ed 1988) p 32.

[61.] (1862) 10 HLC 191.

[62.] Gough, *Company Charges* (2nd ed 1996) p 77; Goode, *Legal Problems of Credit and Security* (2nd ed 1988) p 33; but see the earlier decision in *Langton v Horton* (1842) 1 Hare 549 which held that a deed of assignment by way of mortgage of a ship together with her cargo was a valid assignment in equity of the future cargo to be taken during the particular voyage as well as of the cargo which existed at the time of the assignment.

[63.] (1862) 10 HLC 191 at 211.

[64.] (1888) 13 App Cas 523.

should obtain the benefit of the security, in respect of future acquired assets, provided the asset:

> "on its coming into existence, ... shall answer the description in the assignment, or, in other words, ... shall be capable of being identified as the thing, or as one of the very things assigned. When there is no uncertainty as to its identification, the beneficial interest will immediately vest in the assignee."[65]

[11.19] The importance of careful drafting is illustrated by the decision in *Reeve v Whitmore*[66] where it was held that an assignment of existing chattels by way of mortgage, accompanied by a power to the mortgagee to put a manager in possession, and a licence to the mortgagee to enter and seize after-acquired chattels, does not operate as an equitable assignment of such after-acquired chattels, or create in the mortgagee any present equitable interest in them. The concept of a valid security on future chattels was confirmed by the Lord Chancellor in giving judgment when he said:[67]

> "If there had been, either upon the face of the deed expressly, or there could have been collected from the provisions of the deed by necessary implication, a contract or agreement between the parties that the mortgagee should have a security attaching immediately upon the future chattels to be brought on the premises, the mortgagee would have had a present interest in all those materials, whether manufactured or raw which after the date of the security might have been brought on the brickfield."

Fixed Security over Substituted Chattels

[11.20] The decision in *Holroyd v Marshall*[68] was applied and approved in Ireland with regard to substituted chattels in *The Merchant Banking Company of London (Ltd) v Spotten*.[69] Spotten assigned by way of mortgage or charge to the bank all its linens and other goods at present in the possession or custody of a specified third party. The deed provided that if the bank sanctioned the sale of goods, Spotten would at all times retain goods to the gross value presently held and keep an account of all goods held in substitution. In deciding that the principle of *Holroyd v Marshall* was applicable to the deed, the Lord Chancellor held: "that all parcels of future goods which where so substituted for those removed became liable to and attached by the lien."

A chattel mortgage will not cover substituted assets, for those specifically mortgaged, unless the mortgage states that it is to include substituted goods -

---

65. *Ibid* at 533.
66. (1838) 4 D J & S 51.
67. *Ibid* at 16.
68. (1862) 10 HLC 191.
69. (1877) IR 11 Eq 586.

this applies even if the intention of the parties is clear that the mortgage includes substituted assets.[70]

[11.21] Any suggestion that these decisions were made prior to or around the time of the judicial establishment of a floating security, and therefore refer to the effective creation of only a floating security over future assets is removed by the words of Vaughan Williams LJ in *Re Yorkshire Woolcombers' Association Ltd*:[71]

> "I do not think that for a 'specific security' you need have a security of a subject matter which is then in existence. I mean by 'then' at the time of the execution of the security; but what you do require to make a specific security is that the security whenever it has once come into existence, and been identified or appropriated as a security, shall never thereafter at the will of the mortgagor cease to be a security. If at the will of the mortgagor he can dispose of it and prevent its being any longer a security, although something else may be substituted more or less for it, that is not a 'specific security'.

Assets Changing from Time to Time

[11.22] The principle of creating a valid mortgage or charge over chattels is well established.[72] However, the decision in *National Provincial Bank of England Ltd v United Electric Theatres Ltd*[73] is a reminder that certain requirements have to be satisfied to take the security, even a mortgage, out of the category of a floating security.

The decision, although not generally referred to in other works, is an important one for any practitioner who drafts security documents. The facts of the case were that by a mortgage, for securing the payment of moneys, the defendants conveyed to the plaintiffs hereditaments and premises described in the schedule "together with all and singular the fixed and movable plant machinery and fixtures implements and utensils now or hereafter fixed or placed upon or used in or about the said hereditaments and premises," to hold the same unto the plaintiffs absolutely subject to the proviso for redemption contained therein. The court stated that:[74]

> "it is quite plain that as far as the chattels were concerned this mortgage did not intend to interfere with the ordinary carrying on by the defendants of their theatre business, with all the necessary changes in plant, machinery, utensils, and chattels that such carrying on of the business would from time to time

---

70. See *Re Zegalski and M Zegalski Pharmacy Ltd* (1972) 31 DLR (3d) 766.
71. [1903] 2 Ch 284 at 294.
72. See *Flory v Denny* (1852) 7 Ex 581; *Maughan v Sharpe* (1864) 17 CBNS 443; and observations of Bowen LJ in *Johnson v Diprose* [1893] 1 QB 512 at 517.
73. [1916] 1 Ch 132.
74. *Ibid* at 138 *per* Astbury J.

necessitate; and indeed the mortgage itself specified that the defendants should conduct the business of their various theatres in a regular and proper manner in all respects".

In deciding that the security was a floating rather than a fixed security, the court applied the test of Romer LJ in *Re Yorkshire Woolcombers Association Ltd*[75] of the three characteristics of a floating charge and found that:[76]

> "where a company like the defendants carry on a considerable number of theatres, and charge the whole of their present and future stock in trade, furniture, loose effects, plant, machinery, and so on that may be upon the various premises, and agree to carry on their business in the ordinary course, ... that is a charge upon a class of chattels all of which in the ordinary course of business would or might be changed or removed from time to time."

[11.23] Similarly, in the security created in *Re Armagh Shoes Ltd*[77] it was stated that:

> "the Mortgagor ... charges ... by way of Fixed Charge all ... plant machinery fixtures fittings and ancillary equipment now or at any time hereafter belonging to the Mortgagor".

Hutton J noted the reference in the security to "now or at any time hereafter belonging to the Mortgagor" and hence "the Deed ... contemplates that the Company will from time to time in the future and in the ordinary course of its business change its plant, machinery, fixtures, fittings and ancillary equipment".[78]

Similar words used in the security in *National Provincial Bank of England Ltd v United Electric Theatres Ltd*[79] -"now or hereafter fixed or placed" - had the same effect (in showing the intention of the parties to permit the chargor to carry on business in the normal course with regard to the charged assets).

[11.23] In *Re GE Tunbridge Ltd*[80] the court, in acknowledging that the first and third of Romer LJ's criteria for a floating charge were present considered whether the second characteristic applied namely, if the class of assets charged is one which in the ordinary course of the company's business would be changing from time to time. The facts of the case were that the company, which was in the business of selling and repairing motor cars, charged "(a) by way of Fixed Charge, the Fixed Assets ... (b) by way of Floating Charge, the Floating Assets ...". The Fixed Assets were described as those listed in the First Schedule

---

75. [1903] 2 Ch 284 at 295; see also para **[11.10]** above.
76. [1916] 1 Ch 132 at 140.
77. [1984] BCLC 405.
78. *Ibid* at 408.
79. [1916] 1 Ch 132.
80. [1995] 1 BCLC 34.

which after listing certain assets concluded, "All other assets (not being Floating Assets) now owned or hereafter acquired by the Chargor or in which it now has or in the future acquires an interest" The Floating Assets were defined as motor vehicles and spare parts. The question arose as to whether the fixed charge caught other assets referred to in the First Schedule namely, office furniture, typewriting, electronic equipment, tools and fixed or semi-fixed equipment. The court considered it to be unrealistic that these other assets would not or might not be charged or removed from time to time and accordingly a floating charge had been created as all three of Romer LJ's criteria for a floating charge had been satisfied. In giving judgment Sir Mervyn Davies did however state:[81]

> "The position might have been otherwise had the debenture contained a schedule in which there were itemised the particular chattels that the parties regarded as being susceptible of a fixed charge."

DRAFTING A MORTGAGE OR FIXED CHARGE OVER CHATTELS

Operative Words of Security

[11.24] The operative words of a security which creates a mortgage over chattels or a fixed charge over chattels varies considerably in practice. Many securities simply state that a fixed charge or an assignment is created over certain types of chattels,[82] or in some cases chattels particulars of which are set out in a schedule attached to the security.[83] Both of these routes have largely gone unchallenged,[84] presumably because of the statement of intention[85] to create a fixed security and, where particulars of the asset are scheduled, the certainty of the subject matter. Many of such securities however contain few or no covenants showing a clear intention that the chattel can be dealt with subject only to the direction and

---

[81.] *Ibid* at 39.

[82.] See for example the debenture in *Re Lakeglen Construction Ltd (in liq)* [1980] IR 347 clause 3L(a) of which was unchallenged and which stated: "The company ... hereby assign unto the major creditors all their respective fixed and moveable plant machinery equipment fixtures implements and utensils to hold the same unto the major creditors absolutely." Costello J stated at 352 in passing that this clause created an assignment.

[83.] See Astbury J in *National Provincial Bank of England Ltd v United Electric Theatres Ltd* [1916] 1 Ch 132 at 141.

[84.] It may be simply a matter of "judicial indifference" as remarked by Cousins, *The Law of Mortgages* p 7 where the author points out the distinction in the remedies applicable to a mortgagee and a chargee.

[85.] "It is quite clear that no particular form of words is necessary for the purpose of creating a charge. It is enough that the parties have made it plain by the language they have used that it was their intention to create it." Bankes LJ in *National Provincial and Union Bank of England v Charnley* [1924] 1 KB 431 at 440; although see *Re Armagh Shoes Ltd* [1984] BCLC 405 where the stated intention to create a fixed charge was insufficient because the deed contained "no express provisions restricting the company from dealing with the assets charged".

control of the security holder - a requirement which is considered to be necessary to create a fixed security over book debts.[86]

[11.25] To avoid any doubt that such a security may nevertheless leave the asset as part of the mortgagor's assets subject to the prior rights of preferential creditors,[87] the following language[88] will have the effect of transferring title to the mortgagee:

> "The mortgagor as beneficial owner hereby assigns[89] to the mortgagee all and singular the plant, machinery and equipment particulars of which are set out in the schedule hereto ('the Mortgaged Property') to hold unto the mortgagee absolutely by way of security for the payment of all monies and the discharge of all obligations covenanted herein to be paid and discharged ('the Secured Obligations') provided always that if the Secured Obligations have been paid and discharged then the mortgagee at the request and cost of the mortgagor shall re-assign the Mortgaged Property to the mortgagor or as it may direct."

The schedule to the deed should set out a list of the plant, machinery and equipment by reference to descriptions and distinguishing features such as manufacturer's serial number; it should end with the words:

> "... together with all substitutions, replacements and renewals thereof provided always that any component or other item which is at any time removed from the foregoing shall remain subject to the security created by this deed until such time as a substitution, replacement or renewal shall have been installed in or on the property referred to above in accordance with clause [   ] (d) of this deed [ie the covenant to replace] whereupon the component or item replaced shall be released from the mortgage herein created."

Unlike an assignment by way of security, a charge is not a document "which transfers the property with a condition for re-conveyance, but is a document which only gives a right to payment out of a particular fund or particular property, without transferring that fund or property."[90]

[86.] See *Re Lakeglen Construction Ltd (in liq)* [1980] IR 347; *Re Keenan Brothers Ltd (in liq)* [1985] IR 401; [1985] ILRM 641; *Re Armagh Shoes Ltd* [1984] BCLC 405.

[87.] Pursuant to s 285(2) of the Companies Act, 1963.

[88.] See Sheridan, *Rights in Security* (1974), Collins p 117 - "To create a legal mortgage of a chattel it is necessary to vest the legal title in the mortgagee ... if the title is passed as security, with a contractual right to redeem, the transaction is a legal mortgage"; see also Ramage, 'Chattel Mortgages' (1971) 121 NLJ 291.

[89.] the words "assign ... by way of security" are set out in the form of bill of sale in the Schedule to the Bills of Sale (Ireland) Act (1879) Amendment Act, 1883 which is to be used for specifically charging goods and chattels by individuals see para **[11.38]** below; see also Costello J in *Re Lakeglen Construction Ltd (in liq)* [1980] IR 347 at 352.

[90.] Denham J in *Tancred v Delogoa Bay and East African Railway Co* (1898) 23 QBD 239 at 242; *Palmer v Carey* [1926] AC 703 at 706; *National Provincial & Union Bank of England v Charmley* [1924] 1 KB 431 at 449; *Re Charge Card Services Ltd* [1986] 3 All ER 289 Millett J 309.

[11.26] It has been suggested[91] that a proviso stipulating that a mortgagor retains possession until default operates as a redemise by the mortgagee, or that there is an express or implied licence to the mortgagor to deal with the chattel in the way of trade.[92] However, the suggestion that the mortgagor retains possession of the chattel until default as bailee only[93] is the more attractive one for maintaining both the concept of avoiding the statutory priority given to preferential creditors in respect of the secured chattel and the avoidance of any language associated with the concept of a floating charge.

Assets caught by Security - "fixed plant and machinery"

[11.27] It is fairly usual for a mortgage to provide that a fixed charge is created over designated lands of the chargor "together with all buildings fixtures (including trade fixtures) and fixed plant and machinery from time to time thereon" and a floating charge over the undertaking and other assets. Most bankers would probably contemplate that this language would create a fixed charge over heavy plant and machinery, which even if not bolted to the floor of the premises could not be removed without the help of a fork-lift truck. However, the decision in *Re Hi-Fi Equipment (Cabinets) Ltd*[94] is a warning that this is not so.

In that case, the chargor owned items of machinery which were free standing and attached to the floor of its factory by their own weight. The chargor charged by way of fixed charge its lands fixtures fixed plant and machinery and created a floating charge over its other assets. The question arose as to whether the machinery was fixed plant and machinery and therefore subject to the fixed charge. Harman J held that the word "fixed" governed both plant and machinery and rejected the submission that it should be contrasted with the reference to fixtures - "the phrase 'fixed plant and machinery' has the connotation of plant and machinery in some way firmly attached to the premises despite the apposition of the phrase 'fixtures (including trade fixtures)'".[95] Accordingly, the machinery was caught by the floating charge and its proceeds subject to the prior right of preferential creditors.

The decision and the references made three times by the judge to the "unhappy" drafting is a stark reminder to lawyers and their clients of the importance of detail. It appears the bank did not suffer in the case because the chargor's

---

[91.] Fisher and Lightwood's *Law of Mortgage* (9th ed) p 73.

[92.] It is submitted either of these suggestions would give rise to the danger of a floating charge being deemed to have been created with its concept of granting the chargor a licence to carry on his trade in the normal course without reference to the charge - see para **[13.08]**.

[93.] Ramage, 'Chattel Mortgages' (1971) 121 NLJ 291.

[94.] [1988] BCLC 65.

[95.] *Ibid* at 73.

directors had given guarantees to the bank supported by charges over their private residences. The fact that the security over the machinery was held not to be fixed meant that the bank looked to the directors' assets to cover their loss. Accordingly, the attention to detail in a security document is required also by the guarantor's lawyer in approving the document. The term "fixed plant and machinery" may be contrasted with the term "movable plant". In *National Provincial Bank of England v Charnley*[96] it was held that "all the movable plant used in or about the premises" caught motor vans.[97]

Assets caught by Security - "plant"

[11.28] The meaning of the word "plant" has been considered by the Irish courts when deciding on tax allowances. Both the High Court[98] and the Supreme Court[99] have adopted the definition given by Lindley LJ in *Yarmouth v France*[100] namely:

"... in its ordinary sense, it includes whatever apparatus is used by a businessman for carrying on his business - not his stock-in-trade which he buys or makes for sale; but all goods, chattels, fixed or moveable, live or dead, which he keeps for permanent employment in his business".

In *Inspector of Taxes (O'Culachain) v McMullan Brothers Ltd*[101] a question arose as to whether canopies over the forecourts of petrol filling stations constituted plant. In the Supreme Court, Blayney J stated:[102]

"if the canopies are part of the apparatus used for the carrying on of the business, then they constitute plant. On the other hand, if they are simply the building or part of the building or the setting in which the business is carried on, and serve no other purpose, they are not plant".

The Supreme Court upheld the findings of Judge Martin in the Circuit Court that the canopies performed other functions as well as providing shelter namely:[103]

"the provision of an attractive setting for the sale of the appellant's products, they advertise and promote the appellant's products, they create an overall

96. [1924] 1 KB 431.
97. Note Harman J's remarks in *Re Hi-Fi Equipment (Cabinets) Ltd* [988] BCLC 65 at 73 - "I do not believe a fixed charge is appropriate to motor vehicles."
98. McWilliam J in *Inspector of Taxes v McCann* [1984] ILRM 679 at 681.
99. Blayney J in *Inspector of Taxes v McMullen Brothers Ltd* [1995] 2 IR 217 at 227; [1995] 2 ILRM 498 at 506; see also *Inspector of Taxes v Roscommon Race Course Committee* [1996] 1 IR 163; [1996] 2 ILRM 81.
100. (1887) 19 QBD 647 at 658.
101. [1995] 2 IR 217; [1995] 2 ILRM 498.
102. [1995] 2 ILRM 498 at 506; O'Flaherty J and Denham J agreed with the judgment of Blayney J.
103. *Ibid* at 507.

impression of efficiency and of financial solidarity and most important of all, they attract customers."

Thus the canopies were held to be plant.

The Supreme Court subsequently applied the same principles in *Inspector of Taxes (O'Grady) v Roscommon Race Course Committee.*[104] The question arose as to whether a stand for viewing races was plant. The Inspector of Taxes suggested it was not on the grounds of *Browne v Burnley Football and Athletic Co Ltd*[105] where the court held that a stand was not plant. O'Flaherty J stated:[106]

> "The Burnley stadium stand is in a different category. In fact it provided seating accommodation for patrons. The patrons paid to get in, sit down and watch the matches. At Roscommon Races, in contrast, the patrons in general will spend only a small part of the duration of the races in the stand. There are substantial periods of time between one race and another. I have no doubt that the races constitute a very important social occasion as well as everything else. The spectators will circulate, meet with friends, express opinions on the prospects of the horses, place bets, go to the bars and so forth. When a race is about to start they will tend to congregate in the stand to get a good view. ... The stand is truly not the place of business of the respondents but rather an attractive addition to their actual business which is that of promoting and organising horse races."

Accordingly, the stand was held to be plant.

Assets caught by Security - "machinery"

[11.29] Equipment which requires the application of force by means of agitation will constitute machinery.[107] So also will a process which requires the use of force by mechanical means for the achievement of a specified purpose.[108]

Covenants in Security

[11.30] The following are covenants which might usefully be incorporated into a chattel mortgage:

> "The mortgagor hereby covenants with the mortgagee that at all times during the subsistence of this security the mortgagor shall:
>
> (a) keep as bailee for the mortgagee the Mortgaged Property in its sole and exclusive possession at the address specified in the Schedule hereto;

---

[104] [1996] 1 IR 163; [1996] 2 ILRM 81.

[105] [1980] 3 All ER 244.

[106] [1996] 1 IR 163 at 168; Blayney J and Barrington J agreed with the judgment of O'Flaherty J.

[107] *Denis Coakley & Co Ltd/Arkady Feed Ltd v Commissioner of Valuation* [1996] 2 ILRM 90.

[108] *Beamish & Crawford Ltd v Commissioner of Valuation* [1980] ILRM 149.

(b) pay punctually all rents, rates, taxes and all other outgoings payable in respect of the premises in which the Mortgaged Property shall be situate and shall keep and produce on demand to the mortgagee all receipts for such payments;

(c) ensure that in so far as the Mortgaged Property is affixed to any land or building it shall be capable of being removed without damage to it or to any such land or building and that such steps are taken to ensure that the title to the Mortgaged Property does not pass to the owner of such land or building;

(d) keep the Mortgaged Property in good order and repair and replace any part of the Mortgaged Property as may be destroyed, damaged or worn out with new parts of similar quality, and permit the mortgagee, or any person authorised by the mortgagee, to enter upon the premises at which the Mortgaged Property is located for the purpose of inspecting and examining its condition;

(e) insure and keep insured the Mortgaged Property with insurers previously approved in writing by the mortgagee against loss or damage by accident, fire, theft, lightning, explosion, civil commotion, earthquake, landslide, storm, tempest, burst pipes, malicious damage, aircraft (and articles dropped therefrom), impact and such other risks as the mortgagee shall from time to time request to the full replacement value thereof from time to time free from restriction or excess and stipulating therein that no monies are to be paid to the mortgagor without the prior written consent of the mortgagee and in the event that any such monies are received by the mortgagor without such consent such monies shall be held by the mortgagor as trustee for the mortgagee and the mortgagor shall on demand pay and transfer the same to the mortgagee Provided Always that all monies received in respect of such insurance shall at the option of the mortgagee be applied either in replacing, restoring or reinstating the Mortgaged Property or towards discharging the Secured Obligations;

(f) pay punctually all premiums payable in respect of the insurance referred in (e) above, produce the receipts for such payment to the mortgagee on demand, maintain such insurances in full effect and not do or omit to do anything whereby the said insurance will or may be vitiated and in default of the mortgagor effecting or keeping in place such insurance the mortgagee may insure and keep insured the Mortgaged Property as aforesaid, without being under any obligation to do so and all money expended by the mortgagee under this clause shall be immediately due and payable to the mortgagor together with interest at [specify rate by reference to mortgagee's rate or DIBOR] from the date of payment by the mortgagee;

(g) obtain from the insurer covering the risks referred to in (e) above a written undertaking in favour of the mortgagee to the effect that it shall give the mortgagee ten days written notice prior to permitting the insurance referred to in (e) above becoming ineffective for any reason;

(h) not sell, assign, let, pledge, mortgage, charge, encumber or part with possession of or otherwise deal with the Mortgaged Property or any interest therein or (without the prior written consent of the mortgagee) create or permit to be created any lien on the Mortgaged Property whether for repairs or otherwise;

(i) not without the prior written consent of the mortgagee make any alterations, additions or improvements to the Mortgaged Property (other than pursuant to paragraph (d) above); and

[(j) affix to the Mortgaged Property a plate or notice to the effect that the Mortgaged Property is owned by the mortgagee]."

A point of particular concern to a mortgagee is that ownership carries with it responsibilities. It is essential therefore that insurance is in place at all times. A mortgagee may be faced with the prospect of the insurance cover lapsing, the mortgagor not being in a position to renew the insurance thereby putting the onus on the mortgagee to insure. If the mortgagee renews the policy the costs may not be recoverable from the mortgagor who may be insolvent; if the mortgagee does not renew the policy there may be a concern that any third party incurring injury in using the mortgaged asset may have a remedy against the mortgagee. It is for this reason that some banks do not apply or incorporate the provisions of paragraph (j) into their standard security. The affixing of such a plate however will protect the mortgagee from the mortgagor disposing of the chattel to a purchaser without notice of the mortgagee's interest.

[11.31] It is suggested that the covenant clause should be followed by an indemnity clause along the following lines:

"The mortgagor hereby indemnifies and agrees to hold the mortgagee indemnified against all claims, proceedings or damages made or awarded in respect of any loss, damage or injury whatsoever arising out of or in connection with the Mortgaged Property."

The chattel mortgage should include the power of sale for the mortgagee.

SECURITY CREATED ORALLY

[11.32] It may be noted that while it is preferable to set out clear and precise terms of the security, there appears to be no reason why an effective security over chattels cannot be taken by word of mouth.[109] However, a person wishing

---

[109.] See Crossley Vaines, *Personal Property* (2nd ed) p 321 - "There is no doubt that a mortgage of chattels may be made by word of mouth"; the authorities given for this statement however are *Reeves v Capper* (1838) and *Flory v Denny* (1852) both of which uphold security executed under hand rather than under seal; see also Sheridan, *Rights in Security* (1974), Collins p 114; Bell, *Modern Law of Personal Property in England and Ireland* (1989), Butterworths p 191; Goode, *Legal Problems of Credit Security* (2nd ed, 1988) pp 31-32, *GB Peacock Land Co Ltd v Hamilton Mills Producers Co Ltd* [1963] NZLR 576.

to take a chattel mortgage will want not only to have the terms of the security certain but also written evidence to produce in court proceedings should the need arise. Accordingly, a written instrument to effect the security will be used. It may be noted though that the English Court of Appeal have upheld a security over a chattel without reference to any document.[110]

MORTGAGES OF CHATTELS BY INDIVIDUALS

Bills of Sale Acts

> "One undesirable result of the Acts has been to produce a vast amount of expensive litigation, and of decisions not always easily reconcilable on any consistent ground of principle or with each other".[111]

[11.33] Where individuals, or a group of individuals working together as a partnership, create a mortgage or charge over chattels and moveables as security for any debt or for the payment of money, the bills of sale legislation[112] must be complied with in order to create effective security.[113] The bills of sale legislation applies to assignments and other assurances of personal chattels including powers of attorney[114] as well as licences to take possession of personal chattels as security for any debt.[115] The expression "personal chattels" includes "goods, furniture and other articles capable of complete transfer by delivery" as well as including, when assigned separately from land, fixtures and growing crops.[116] It includes also machinery used in or attached to any factory or workshop other than fixed power machinery or pipes.[117] It does not include a life assurance policy given as collateral security for a loan.[118]

[11.34] Under the Bills of Sale (Ireland) Act, 1879 chattels comprised in a bill of sale (which had been and continued to be duly registered) were not deemed to be in the possession, order or disposition of the person who granted the bill.[119]

---

110. *Newlove v Shrewsbury* (1888) 21 QBD 41.
111. Robbins, *The Law of Mortgages* (1897) Stevens and Sons, Ltd; Sweet & Maxwell, Ltd, Vol 1 p 189.
112. The Bills of Sale (Ireland) Acts, 1879 and 1883.
113. For further reading see Maguire, 'The Bill of Sale: The Forgotten Relation?' (1997) CLP 3.
114. "The inclusion of "powers of attorney" in the definition of a bill of sale is intended to prevent instruments operating really as bills of sale from being framed in the form of powers of attorney, in order to erode the provisions of the Acts and escape the necessity of registration. It is clear that such instruments, if given by way of security for money, will be void as not being according to the statutable form" - Robbins, *The Law of Mortgages* Vol 1 (1897) p 198.
115. Bills of Sale (Ireland) Act, 1879, ss 3 and 4.
116. *Ibid* s 4.
117. *Ibid* s 5.
118. See *Carpenter v Deen* (1889) 23 QBD 566.
119. Bills of Sale (Ireland) Act, 1879, s 20.

However, this was repealed by the Bills of Sale (Ireland) Act (1879) Amendment Act, 1883.[120] The effect of this repeal is that where the grantor of a bill of sale is adjudged a bankrupt prior to a default under the bill of sale,[121] the proceeds of the chattels will be available to the bankrupt's creditors in priority to the grantee of the bill of sale.[122]

[11.35] It should be noted that a bill of sale of stock (as defined in the Agricultural Credit Act, 1978[123]) is void and incapable of being registered under the Bills of Sale Acts.[124] Accordingly, a bill of sale which creates security over chattels should exclude such chattels as are stock within the meaning of the Agricultural Credit Act, 1978 and such stock should be charged in accordance with the provisions of that Act.

Attestation and Registration

[11.36] Every agreement by which a power of distress is given over personal chattels by way of security for any present, future or contingent debt is deemed to be a bill of sale[125] and therefore to be effective must comply with the statutory requirements for bills of sale.[126] To comply with the statutory requirements each bill of sale must be duly attested and registered under the legislation within seven days of its creation.[127] Failure to do so will render the agreement void.[128] The form of attestation and registration is provided for in the legislation[129] (but where the time for registering a bill of sale expires on a day on which the registrar's office is closed, the registration will be valid if made on the next following day on which the registrar's office is open[130]). The first of the two Bills of Sale Acts required the attestation of a bill to be done by a solicitor and for it to be stated that before the execution of the bill of sale its effect had been explained to the grantor by the attesting solicitor.[131] Rather curiously this was repealed by the second Act[132] so that there is no statutory requirement to explain

---

[120.] Section 15.

[121.] This could arise prior to an instalment becoming due.

[122.] See *Re Hayes* [1899] 2 IR 206; *Hollinshead v P and H Egan Ltd* [1913] 2 IR 487; [1913] AC 564.

[123.] Section 23(1) see further para **[11.42]**.

[124.] Agricultural Credit Act, 1978, s 36(1).

[125.] Bills of Sale (Ireland) Act, 1879, s 6.

[126.] Under the Bills of Sale (Ireland) Acts, 1879 and 1883.

[127.] Bills of Sale (Ireland) Act, 1879, s 8 as amended by Bills of Sale (Ireland) Act (1879) Amendment Act, 1883, s 8.

[128.] *Ibid.*

[129.] *Ibid* s 10 and Bills of Sale (Ireland) Act (1879) Amendment Act, 1883, s 10.

[130.] Bills of Sale (Ireland) Act, 1879, s 22.

[131.] *Ibid* s 10(1).

[132.] Bills of Sale (Ireland) Act (1879) Amendment Act, 1883 s 10.

its effect to the grantor. The form of the bill of sale as set out in the Schedule to the 1883 Act requires the grantor to execute the bill under seal in the presence of a witness who is required to state his or her name, address and description. In *Simms v Trollope & Sons*[133] the Court of Appeal held that a bill of sale was void where the witness, who had no occupation, did not indicate his "description". One of the judges[134] stated that the word description as used in the Act "includes a description of the profession, trade or occupation of the witness or, if he has no profession, trade or occupation, his style."

[11.37] It should be noted that registration must be renewed every five years otherwise the registration becomes void.[135] Security over personal chattels by companies does not require to be registered under the Bills of Sale legislation;[136] but where such security is created by an industrial and provident society registration is required.[137] The Rules of the Superior Courts[138] set out the manner in which a memorandum of satisfaction may be recorded.

Any person is entitled, on payment of an appropriate fee, to search the register and make extracts from a bill of sale.[139]

Form of Bill of Sale

[11.38] Each bill of sale given by way of security for the payment of money is void unless it is done in accordance with the form[140] as set out in the schedule to the Bills of Sale (Ireland) Act (1879) Amendment Act, 1883.[141] Accordingly, it is essential to ensure that there is no material divergence from the statutory

---

[133.] [1897] 1 QB 24.

[134.] *Ibid* at 27.

[135.] Bills of Sale (Ireland) Act, 1879, s 11.

[136.] Bills of Sale (Ireland) Act (1879) Amendment Act, 1883, s 17; see also in *Re Royal Marine Hotel Co, Kingstown (Ltd)* [1895] 1 IR 368.

[137.] See in *Re North Wales Produce and Supply Society Ltd ex p Priddle* [1922] 2 Ch 340; *Re The Drogheda and District Co-operative Society Ltd* (1924) 58 ILTR 42.

[138.] SI 15/1986 Order 81.

[139.] Bills of Sale (Ireland) Act (1879) Amendment Act, 1883 s 16; the Rules of the Superior Courts SI 15/1986 Order 81 rule 4; the extracts which may be taken from a search are confined to the date of execution, registration, renewal of registration, and satisfaction, names, addresses and occupations of parties and amount of consideration.

[140.] For precedent forms and commentary see *The Encyclopaedia of Forms and Precedents* (5th ed) Vol 4, Butterworths (1986).

[141.] *Ibid* s 9 - "the section does not avoid bills of sale for not being made in the form in the schedule, but only bills of sale which are not made in accordance with the form ... A bill of sale is surely in accordance with the prescribed form if it is substantially in accordance with it, if it does not depart from the prescribed form in any material respect." - Bowen LJ in *Ex p Stanford* (1886) 17 QBD 259 at 269-270.

form.[142] As to what is a material divergence, the full English Court of Appeal stated:[143]

"A divergence only becomes substantial or material when it is calculated to give the bill of sale a legal consequence or effect, either greater or smaller, than that which would attach to it if drawn in the form which has been sanctioned, or if it departs from the form in a manner calculated to mislead those whom it is the object of the statute to protect".

This was applied in *Kelly & Co v Kellond*[144] where the Court of Appeal held that an assignment by way of security over chattels specifically described in a schedule, "together with all other chattels and things, the property of the mortgagor, now in or about the premises, and also all chattels and things which may, at any time during the continuance of this security, be in or about the same or any other premises of the mortgagor (to which the said chattels or things or any part thereof may have been removed), whether brought there in substitution for, or renewal of, or in addition to the chattels and things hereby assigned," was void, as the assignment by including goods not specifically described in the schedule gave a greater legal effect than if the assignment were confined to the goods specifically described in the schedule.

[11.39] Thus, each bill of sale (which must set forth the consideration for which it is given[145]) must have annexed to it a schedule containing an inventory of the personal chattels comprised in the bill of sale - any chattels not "specifically described" in the schedule will not be caught by the security.[146] Accordingly, a general description will not be sufficient.[147] The rationale for the requirement of a specific rather than a general description was elucidated by Fry LJ in *Carpenter v Deen*[148] where he said:[149]

[142.] See *Myers v Elliott* (1886) 16 QBD 526; *Jackson v Eaton* 39 ILTR 41.

[143.] *Ex p Stanford* (1886) 17 QBD 259 at 270.

[144.] (1888) 20 QBD 569; the decision was upheld in the House of Lords in *Thomas v Kelly and Baker* (1888) 13 App Cas 506.

[145.] See Schedule to the Bills of Sale (Ireland) Amendment Act, 1883; the consideration must be correctly stated, in *Re George O'Kelly* (1895) 29 ILTR 148 a bill of sale was held to be void as it referred to consideration "now paid" when in fact it had been paid some months previously; a bill of sale for less than £30 is void under s 12 of the Bills of Sale (Ireland) Act (1879) Amendment Act, 1883.

[146.] Bills of Sale (Ireland) Act (1879) Amendment Act, 1883 s 4; see the split decision in *Carpenter v Deen* (1889) 23 QBD 566.

[147.] See *Witt v Banner* (1888) 20 QBD 114 where Lord Esher MR stated that "specifically described" "must mean that they are to be as specifically described as is usual in such inventories as are usually made for business purposes with regard to the particular subject-matter".

[148.] (1889) 23 QBD 566.

[149.] *Ibid* at 574; quoted with approval by Lopes LJ in *Davidson v Carlton Bank Ltd* [1893] 1 QB 82 at 86.

"In considering what is the meaning of the words 'specifically described' ... we should look at the scope and object of the section ... they are to facilitate the identification of the articles enumerated in the schedule with those that are to be found in the possession of the grantor: that is to say, to render the identification as easy as possible and to render any dispute as to the intention of the parties as rare as possible, and to shut the door to fraud and controversy, which almost always arise when general descriptions are used".

However, any fixtures, plant or trade machinery which is brought onto land or premises to replace fixtures, plant or trade machinery caught by the security will be subject to the security as though originally specified in the schedule.[150]

Description and Substitution of Chattels

[11.40] An example of the need to comply strictly with the terms of the legislation can be seen from the decision in *Davies v Jenkins*.[151] A farmer having previously borrowed £40, borrowed an additional £50 and as security executed a bill of sale over farm stock described as "Stock, two horses, four cows". The bill was expressed to be in consideration of £90 now due and owing. The bill was held to be void as:

1.   The description of the stock was too vague and contrary to s 4;

2.   The bill had no receipt clause and was thus not in the statutory form; and

3.   The consideration was misstated as the £50 advanced at the time the bill was executed was not now owing.[152]

The judgments in that decision are instructive as to the degree of description of the chattels required in the bill of sale. Darling J stated:[153] "it was usual to describe horses by their colour, a greater degree of particularity was required in the case of horses than in that of cows".

As for substitution of chattels, Channell J stated:[154]

"Upon the question whether the description of particular chattels is sufficient, a distinction is to be drawn between those chattels which are customarily changed from time to time and replaced by the substitution of others, and those which are not. Tables and chairs in a private house are not customarily changed in that fashion, at all events not with any degree of frequency, and a very specific description of them is not required. But live stock on a farm must

---

[150.] Bills of Sale (Ireland) Act (1879) Amendment Act, 1883 s 6(2).

[151.] [1900] 1 QB 133.

[152.] See also in *Re George O'Kelly, a Bankrupt* 29 ILTR 148 where a bill of sale was void because the consideration previously paid was referred to as "now paid".

[153.] *Ibid* at 136.

[154.] *Ibid*.

necessarily, in consequence of death or other causes, be replaced with much greater frequency, and require a more specific description. Merely to specify their number is not enough. So, too, chattels forming the stock-in-trade of a shop, such as the pictures in *Witt v Banner*[155] are in the nature of things intended to be parted with and replaced with others whenever the opportunity arises. Therefore, in their case the description is specifically required to be specific."

Enforcement

[11.41] The legislation, however, imposes certain limitations on enforcement. Personal chattels assigned under a bill of sale can be seized only:[156]

(1) If the grantor shall make default in payment of the sum or sums of money thereby secured at the time therein provided for payment, or in the performance of any covenant or agreement contained in the bill of sale and necessary for maintaining the security;

(2) If the grantor shall become a bankrupt, or suffer the said goods or any of them to be distrained for rent, rates or taxes;

(3) If the grantor shall fraudulently either remove or suffer the said goods, or any of them, to be removed from the premises;

(4) If the grantor shall not, without reasonable excuse, upon demand in writing by the grantee, produce to him his last receipts for rent, rates and taxes;

(5) If execution shall have been levied against the goods of the grantor under any judgment at law.

Even after the grantee takes possession, the grantor may within five days apply to the High Court who may restrain the grantee from retaining possession if it is satisfied that the cause of seizure no longer exists. Chattels cannot be sold within five days of seizure.[157]

MORTGAGES OF AGRICULTURAL STOCK

"The 'Chattel Mortgage' is a common form of security for agricultural loans in the Argentine Republic and some other countries of the New World. It is not likely to achieve the same general success in this country, due to entirely different farming conditions."[158]

[11.42] The requirements of the Agricultural Credit Act, 1978 need to be considered where security is to be created over stock within the meaning of that Act.[159] Stock is defined as including (and therefore not necessarily limited to):[160]

[155.] (1887) 20 QBD 114.

[156.] Bills of Sale (Ireland) Act (1879) Amendment Act, 1883, s 7.

[157.] *Ibid* s 13.

[158.] RC Barton, chairman, Agricultural Credit Corporation Ltd - Appendix No. 19 to the *Report of the Commission of Inquiry into Banking, Currency and Credit* 1938 P No 2628.

[159.] For further reading see Maguire, 'Agricultural Chattel Mortgages' (1997) CLP 170.

[160.] Agricultural Credit Act, 1978, s 23(1).

(a) animals and birds of every kind and the progeny and produce of such animals and birds,

(b) insects and fish of every kind and the progeny and produce of such insects and fish,

(c) agricultural crops (whether growing on or severed from the land),

(d) trees (whether growing on or severed from the land),

(e) any product derived from any of the foregoing,

(f) machinery, implements, vehicles, fixtures, fittings and materials used in or for the production, manufacture, processing, preparation for sale or marketing of any agricultural or fishery produce.

The definition, particularly items (e) to (f), is exceptionally wide in that technically all leather goods such as briefcases, shoes and jackets as well as all goods made of wood such as furniture and wooden shelving are caught. The reference to machinery and vehicles used for the sale or marketing of any agricultural[161] produce is also wide. The width of the definition is obviously unhelpful to lawyers who are required to carry out all necessary registrations so that the lawyer's client's security is properly safeguarded. Taken literally virtually every floating charge over a company's[162] undertaking would require registration under the Act as some of the assets the subject of the undertaking are likely to fall within at least one of the categories.

It should be noted though that in order for "stock" to be subject to the Act it must be "the absolute property" of the mortgagor[163] (save where the loan is made to purchase the stock and at the time the chattel mortgage is created the stock has not yet been acquired[164]). Thus machinery with a valid retention of title affecting it will not be "stock".

Registration and Priority

[11.43] The Agricultural Credit Act, 1978 stipulates that[165] "no chattel mortgage shall have effect until it is registered ... in the register or every register (as the case may be) of chattel mortgages in which it is capable of being registered." The priority of chattel mortgages are governed by the times at which they are registered.[166]

---

161. "Agricultural" is defined in s 3(1) of the Act.
162. Although Costello J held that a debenture created by a company does not require to be registered under the Act - see para **[11.45]** below.
163. Agricultural Credit Act, 1978, s 23(4).
164. *Ibid* s 24; this section was enacted to overcome the difficulty highlighted by RC Barton in Appendix No 19 (para 14-17) to the *Report of the Commission of Inquiry into Banking, Currency and Credit* 1938 P No 2628.
165. *Ibid* s 26(5).
166. *Ibid* s 34(1).

Every "chattel mortgage" is capable of being registered within a month "after its date" in the register of chattel mortgages serving the area in which the mortgagor's land is situated (or where the land is in more than two areas in each register).[167] The register is kept in the Circuit Court Office serving the area.[168] Any party to a chattel mortgage may register it;[169] in practice the mortgagee's solicitors will or should register it.

[11.44] The Act defines a "chattel mortgage" as meaning:[170]

> an instrument under seal made between a recognised borrower of the one part and a recognised lender of the other part which is
>
> (a) a floating chattel mortgage, or
>
> (b) a specific chattel mortgage, or
>
> (c) both a floating chattel mortgage and a specific chattel mortgage.

A "recognised borrower" is "any person"[171] who may receive credit facilities from a "recognised lender" or who gives security to a recognised lender as principal or surety.[172] A "recognised lender" is ACC Bank plc or any "recognised bank".[173]

Any bank may apply to the Minister for Finance to be appointed as a recognised bank.[174] The appointment though is at the discretion of the Minister.[175] Accordingly, if a chattel mortgage is created in favour of a person who is not a recognised lender, registration under the Act is neither required nor permissible as the chattel mortgage is not a chattel mortgage within the meaning of the Agricultural Credit Act.

[11.45] Although a recognised borrower is defined as any person rather than as any individual and therefore may include a body corporate,[176] the High Court has held that a debenture incorporating a charge over agricultural stock created by a company in favour of a recognised lender does not require to be registered under the Agricultural Credit Act. In *Re Castlemahon Poultry Products Ltd (in liq)*[177] the company's liquidator submitted that debentures incorporating charges over agricultural stock which had been created in favour of two recognised

---

[167.] *Ibid* s 26(2).

[168.] *Ibid* s 26(1).

[169.] *Ibid* s 26(3).

[170.] *Ibid* s 23(1).

[171.] This includes a body corporate - see Interpretation Act, 1937, s 11(c).

[172.] Agricultural Credit Act, 1978, s 23(1).

[173.] *Ibid*.

[174.] The names of recognised banks are available from the Department of Finance.

[175.] Section 25(2).

[176.] See Interpretation Act, 1937, s 11(c).

[177.] High Court, unrep, 13 December 1985, Costello J.

lenders were ineffective in relation to the stock as they had not been registered under the Act. However, the court held that such charges were effective on the grounds that the Oireachtas did not intend the debentures to be registered as chattel mortgages on the grounds that (1) the debentures were not chattel mortgages within the meaning of the Act, (2) there already existed a registration system for debentures under the Companies Acts,[178] and (3) the registry of chattel mortgages under the Act is not open to public inspection but is limited to certain bodies and officers.[179]

The liquidator chose not to appeal the decision. It is submitted that it would be imprudent for a solicitor, when taking security for a recognised lender over agricultural stock from a company, to rely on this decision. In any event the registration procedure is inexpensive[180] and straightforward.[181]

The three grounds on which Costello J based his decision are each open criticism:

(1) Simply because the instrument under seal, which complies with all the ingredients of the statutory definition of "chattel mortgage", contains other terms does not of itself result in the chattel mortgage ceasing to be a chattel mortgage. If that were the case there would be endless possibilities for documents to be prepared containing extraneous and irrelevant material sufficient to bring any chattel mortgage outside the requirements of the Act,

(2) The existence of a registration system for companies under the Companies Acts does not exempt companies from registering where appropriate in the Registry of Deeds or the Land Registry; companies are specifically excluded by statute[182] from registering security under the Bills of Sale legislation - there is no such exclusion under the Agricultural Credit Act, 1978; furthermore, if a company creates a specific chattel mortgage over stock and no other security interest is created by the instrument, such security will not fall within one of the heads requiring registration under the Companies Act[183] as had it been executed by an individual[184] it would not have been registered as a bill of sale by virtue of the exclusion under the Agricultural Credit Act.[185]

---

178. Companies Act, 1963, s 99.

179. Agricultural Credit Act, 1978, s 26(6).

180. The registration form requires a stamp of 25p.

181. The stamped one page registration form should be delivered with the stamped original chattel mortgage to the County Registrar (of the County or Counties where the agricultural stock is situated) within a month after its creation.

182. Bills of Sale (Ireland) Act (1879) Amendment Act, 1883, s 17.

183. Companies Act, 1963, s 99(2).

184. *Ibid* paragraph (c).

185. Section 36(1).

If Costello J's decision is sound it means on a strict interpretation of "the legislation" a specific chattel mortgage created by a company need not be registered in any register. The Act itself clearly envisages companies creating chattel mortgages;[186]

(3) Although the registers of chattel mortgages are not open to public inspection they are open to inspection by any recognised lender[187] and therefore the majority of persons likely to grant credit to or take security from a company. There is in any event a duty on every person seeking credit to disclose in writing to the potential creditor whether or not there is subsisting any chattel mortgage and if so its particulars.[188]

Chattel Mortgages by Sureties

[11.46] The Agricultural Credit Act, 1978 has been drafted unsatisfactorily in that while it is clear from the definition of "recognised borrower"[189] that a guarantor as well as a borrower may come within the definition, and therefore the requirements of the Act, the definitions of both a floating chattel mortgage and a specific chattel mortgage apply to charges secured with the payment to the recognised lender "of any money advanced or to be advanced to the recognised borrower".[190] Thus, despite the apparent intention[191] of the Oireachtas to catch third party security, a security given solely in support of a guarantee does not fall within the definition of "chattel mortgage". This apparent oversight is particularly inexcusable in the light of the Report of the Commission of Inquiry into Banking, Currency and Credit 1938.[192] The chairman[193] of the Agricultural Credit Corporation Ltd[194] when commenting upon the definition of chattel mortgage under the Agricultural Credit Act, 1927[195] stated in the Report,[196] "... nor would it be possible to take a chattel mortgage to secure an indirect liability, such as a guarantee."[197] Thus although a recognised borrower can be a guarantor under the Agricultural Credit Act a chattel mortgage created by a guarantor as

---

[186.] Section 31(2); see also the definition of mortgagor in s 23(1).
[187.] Agricultural Credit Act, 1978, s 26(6).
[188.] *Ibid* s 35(1).
[189.] See para **[11.44]** above.
[190.] Agricultural Credit Act, 1978, s 23(1).
[191.] By virtue of the statutory definition of recognised borrower.
[192.] P No 2628.
[193.] Mr RC Barton.
[194.] Now ACC Bank plc.
[195.] No 24 of 1927, repealed by the Agricultural Credit Act, 1978.
[196.] Appendix No 19 para 11.
[197.] In para 13 Mr RC Barton set out a suggested definition which had it been adopted would have avoided the current unsatisfactory position.

guarantor will not fall to be registered as it is not a chattel mortgage within the meaning of the Act.

Chattel Mortgages for advances

[11.47] Both a specific chattel mortgage and a floating chattel mortgage come within the Act whether taken for moneys already advanced or which may be advanced to the recognised borrower.[198]

Specific Chattel Mortgages

[11.48] A specific chattel mortgage catches "specific stock" charged wherever such stock is situated.[199] A specific chattel mortgage can attach to "stock" which is purchased subsequent to the creation of the mortgage where the loan which the chattel mortgage secures has been given to purchase the after-acquired stock.[200] A duly registered specific chattel mortgage operates and has the effect:[201]

    (a) to prohibit the mortgagor from selling or otherwise transferring the ownership or possession of any stock comprised therein without giving to the mortgagee at least 7 days' previous notice in writing of his intention to effect the sale or transfer,

    (b) to prohibit the mortgagor from selling or otherwise transferring ownership or possession for less than a fair and reasonable price,

    (c) to impose on the mortgagor, in the event of any of the stock dying or being stolen or being destroyed by fire or other agency, the obligation to notify the mortgagee of such event within 7 days after it occurs,

    (d) to impose on the mortgagor, in the event of his selling or otherwise transferring the ownership or possession of any of the stock, the obligation to give forthwith to the mortgagee notice in writing of the sale or transfer, with such particulars thereof as the mortgagee may require,

    (e) to impose on the mortgagor, in the event of his selling or otherwise transferring the ownership or possession of any of the stock, the obligation to pay to the mortgagee, within 7 days after the sale or transfer, all sums secured by the chattel mortgage or such lesser sum as the mortgagee may in writing agree to accept or to apply the proceeds of the sale or transfer in such other manner as may have been previously authorised by the mortgagee,

    (f) to imply a covenant on the part of the mortgagor to pay to the mortgagee on demand the principal money and interest secured by the chattel mortgage at the time and in the manner thereby appointed, and

---

[198.] Agricultural Credit Act, 1978, s 23(1).
[199.] *Ibid.*
[200.] *Ibid* s 24.
[201.] *Ibid* s 27(1).

(g) to impose on the mortgagor the obligation to preserve and keep safe the stock therein comprised and (save as may be otherwise authorised by the chattel mortgage or the mortgagee or as may be necessary for any intended lawful sale) not to remove such stock from his land.

The Act provides that upon a default by the mortgagor in complying with any of the foregoing obligations:

"the whole of the principal money secured by the chattel mortgage shall, on demand by the mortgagee for payment thereof, become and be due and be forthwith payable notwithstanding anything contained in the chattel mortgage."[202]

Rather curiously an exception is made for covenant (f). Accordingly, it should be remembered when drafting a chattel mortgage for a specific provision to be inserted specifying that a default in a payment obligation can trigger a demand for payment of all principal moneys secured by the chattel mortgage.

The Act specifies that offences, carrying the sanction of a fine and/or imprisonment[203] for up to 2 years, are committed where the mortgagor sells stock without appropriate notice or fails to transfer the proceeds of the sold stock to the mortgagee.[204] The statutory provisions of the effect of a specific chattel mortgage are required to be endorsed on every specific chattel mortgage (although failure to do so will not invalidate the mortgage).[205]

Floating Chattel Mortgages

[11.49] A floating chattel mortgage applies to a charge of stock "from time to time on the recognised borrower's land".[206] In relation to a recognised borrower, land is defined as meaning,[207] "the buildings or land or buildings and land in or on which the recognised borrower carries on business or which he uses in connection with his business."

A duly registered floating chattel mortgage has the effect:[208]

(a) to create an ambulatory and shifting charge of the principal money and interest secured thereby on all stock the property of the mortgagor from time to time on the land to which the chattel mortgage relates (in this section referred to as the land), and

---

[202.] *Ibid* s 27(2).
[203.] Imprisonment seems to have been provided at the suggestion of RC Barton - see *Report of the Commission of Inquiry into Banking, Currency and Credit* 1938 P No. 2628 Appendix No 19 para 20.
[204.] *Ibid* s 27(3).
[205.] *Ibid* s 27(4).
[206.] *Ibid* s 23(1).
[207.] *Ibid*.
[208.] *Ibid* s 30(1).

    (b) to prohibit the mortgagor from selling any of the stock at any time on the land otherwise than in the ordinary course of business, and

    (c) to impose on the mortgagor the obligation of maintaining the stock from time to time on the land at a level of value equivalent (as near as may be having regard to the ordinary course of business) to the value of the stock on the land at the date of the chattel mortgage,[209] and

    (d) whenever the mortgagor sells any of the stock for the time being on the land and does not within one month replace such stock by new stock sufficient to bring the value of the stock on the land as near as may be to the value of the stock on the land at the date of the chattel mortgage, to impose on him the obligation of paying such (if any) part of the proceeds of such sale as the mortgagee shall require to the mortgagee in reduction or discharge of the principal money secured by the chattel mortgage and any interest and costs due thereon and to confer on the mortgagor the right to pay the whole or any part of such proceeds of sale to the mortgagee in reduction or discharge of such principal money and interest and costs.

There is also an implied covenant that the mortgagor will pay the mortgagee the principal money and interest secured by the chattel mortgage at the times and in the manner specified in the mortgage.[210]

Crystallisation of a Floating Chattel Mortgage

[11.50] The legislation is far reaching in that it specifically enables and indeed encourages a recognised lender to serve a notice of crystallisation of the floating charge, thereby turning the floating chattel mortgage into a specific chattel mortgage.[211] The procedure itself is somewhat cumbersome as the following steps must be taken:

    1. Part of the principal money must be unpaid for 28 days (after the date appointed for payment) or part of the interest must be in arrears and unpaid for 56 days (after it has become due) or there has been a breach of some provision contained in, or implied in, the security by s 30(2),[212]

---

[209] A mortgagor whose business is encountering difficulty is unlikely to comply with this requirement - see RC Barton para 7 of Appendix No 19 to the *Report of the Commission of Inquiry into Banking, Currency and Credit* 1938 P No 2628.

[210] Agricultural Credit Act, 1978, s 30(2).

[211] *Ibid* s 31(1).

[212] *Ibid* s 31(1)(a) (other than a covenant to pay principal or interest); but the covenant implied by s 30(2) is a covenant to pay the principal money and interest at the time and in the manner appointed by the chattel mortgage.

2. The mortgagee must take an inventory of the stock on the mortgagor's land,[213]

3. After having taken the inventory of stock the mortgagee must serve a notice[214] of crystallisation on the mortgagor,[215]

4. The mortgagee must then within seven days of serving the notice send a copy of the notice and the inventory by registered post[216] to the Circuit Court Offices where the floating chattel mortgage is registered.[217]

This procedure, when carried out, has the effect of converting the floating chattel mortgage into a specific chattel mortgage of all stock on the recognised borrower's land at the time of service of the notice.[218]

Monitoring Stock

[11.51] The holder of a specific chattel mortgage or of a floating chattel mortgage may "on any day on which a civil process may be served" enter land "between the hours of sunrise and sunset" and take an inventory of the stock.[219] The mortgagee may arrange for one of its agents or employees to carry out this exercise.[220]

AGRICULTURAL CO-OPERATIVE SOCIETIES

Certification

[11.52] Any society registered under the Industrial and Provident Societies Act, 1893 may apply to the Minister for Agriculture for a certificate certifying that the society is an agricultural co-operative society for the purposes of the Agricultural Co-operative Societies (Debentures) Act, 1934.[221] The requirements for a successful application are set out in the Agricultural Co-Operative Societies (Debentures) Regulations, 1949[222] and include a statement

---

[213.] *Ibid* s 31(1)(c).

[214.] Upon which there should be endorsed a copy of s 27 of the Act - Agricultural Credit Act, 1978, s 31(3).

[215.] *Ibid* s 31(1)(b).

[216.] Section 31(2)(a) provides that a notice may be served by delivery to the mortgagor or by it being left at the mortgagor's usual place of abode or business or in the case of a company at its registered office.

[217.] *Ibid* s 31(1)(d).

[218.] *Ibid* s 31(1)(i).

[219.] Agricultural Credit Act, 1978, s 29(1); this seems to have been enacted following the suggestion of RC Barton in Appendix No 19 para 31 of the *Report of the Commission of Inquiry into Banking, Currency and Credit 1938* P No 2628.

[220.] *Ibid* s 29(3).

[221.] No 39 of 1934; see Agricultural Co-operative Societies (Debentures) Act, 1934, s 3(1).

[222.] SI 141/1949 - see reg 4.

by the society as to the amount which it desires to secure by the issue of debentures. Before issuing the certificate the Minister must be satisfied that the objects of the co-operative society are "wholly or substantially agricultural".[223]

Issue of Debentures

[11.53] The Act provides that an agricultural co-operative society (which is authorised by its rules to borrow money) may at any time issue debentures to any "authorised lender" for the purpose of securing to such lender the repayment, with or without interest, of any money lent (or intended to be lent) by such lender to such society.[224] Thus, a debenture may be given for principal obligations but not as guarantor. The form of the debenture may create fixed and/or floating charges over the society's property and undertaking.[225] The debenture should state - "This debenture is issued under the Agricultural Co-operative Societies (Debentures) Act, 1934 (No 39 of 1934)."[226] An "authorised lender" includes,[227] "any corporate body lawfully carrying on banking business"[228] as well as any other body corporate or person approved by the Minister for Agriculture.[229]

Where the committee of the agricultural co-operative society has the power under its rules to borrow money, and the proposed borrowing is within any limit, the committee should approve of such borrowing and security; where the committee does not have this power a special meeting of the shareholders of the society must be convened for the purpose of considering and, if thought fit, passing a resolution authorising the borrowing and the giving of security.[230]

Registration

[11.54] The authorised lender is required, within twenty-one days after the issue to it of a debenture by an agricultural co-operative society, to apply to the Minister for Agriculture for registration of the security in the Department of Agriculture; failure to apply for such registration within the statutory time period will render the debenture "null and void".[231] The application for registration of a debenture (or a charge on uncalled capital) must contain all the particulars for completing the Register of Charges.[232] The format of the Register

---

[223]. Agricultural Co-operative Societies (Debentures) Act, 1934, s 3(2)(b).

[224]. *Ibid* s 4(1).

[225]. *Ibid* s 4(3).

[226]. Agricultural Co-Operative Societies (Debentures) Regulations, 1949, reg 9(1).

[227]. Agricultural Co-operative Societies (Debentures) Act, 1934, s 2.

[228]. *Ibid* s 2(1)(f).

[229]. *Ibid* s 2(1)(g).

[230]. *Ibid* s 4(2).

[231]. *Ibid* s 4(6).

[232]. Agricultural Co-Operative Societies (Debentures) Regulations, 1949 SI 141/1949, reg 11; the Department of Agriculture require a copy of the debenture to be supplied with the application for registration.

and thus the requirements to complete the registration are set out in the Schedule to the Agricultural Co-Operative Societies (Debentures) Regulations, 1949.[233] The Register is open to inspection by the public.[234]

Registration of a debenture (or charge on uncalled capital) issued by an agricultural co-operative society is deemed to "be notice to all persons having dealings with such society of the existence of such issue of debentures or of such charge, as the case may be".[235]

Ministerial Consent

[**11.55**] It might be noted that the statutory requirement that a debenture be issued by an agricultural co-operative society only with the consent of the Minister for Agriculture[236] has been repealed,[237] but there has been no corresponding repeal to the statutory requirement that an agricultural co-operative society be required to obtain the consent of the Minister for Agriculture when borrowing money on the security of a charge on its uncalled capital.[238]

---

[233] SI 141/1949 - see reg 10(1).

[234] Agricultural Co-operative Societies (Debentures) Act, 1934, s 9(3); Agricultural Co-Operative Societies (Debentures) Regulations, 1949, reg 10(2).

[235] Agricultural Co-operative Societies (Debentures) Act, 1934, s 9(4).

[236] *Ibid* s 5.

[237] Agricultural Credit Act, 1978, s 7.

[238] Agricultural Co-operative Societies (Debentures) Act, 1934, s 6.

Chapter 12

Pledges and Trust Receipts

NATURE OF A PLEDGE

[12.01] One of the simplest ways of taking security is to take possession of the asset given as security for the payment of a debt and to retain that asset until the debt is discharged or, in the event of failure to pay the debt, to sell the asset and retain sufficient of the proceeds to discharge the debt. The form of such a security is known as a pledge.[1] The giving of a pledge (ie the delivery of the asset) has the additional benefit for the pledge or that particulars of the pledge are not required to be filed in the Companies Registration Office[2] nor indeed, in the case of an individual, registered as a bill of sale.[3]

As possession of the asset is required, the circumstances in which the security may be used are somewhat limited. Nevertheless, it has proved to be a particularly useful form of security where the production and sale of an asset are being financed. In Ireland this applies most specifically to the processing and sale of beef, as well as other agricultural products.

However, a bank will not wish to hold the asset on its premises; but provided control is held by the bank a pledge will be effective. In its simplest form, the borrower will deliver certain specified assets to the bank (or other lender) and the borrower will sign a letter of pledge. Unlike a mortgage or charge the letter of pledge will not be effecting the security but simply setting out the terms under which a pledge has been granted or may from time to time be granted.[4] The letter will indicate that the assets have been pledged to the bank as security for the loan to be held until repayment of the loan, whereupon the asset will be returned to the borrower; in the event of failure to repay the loan, the bank is authorised to sell the asset.

---

1. For further reading see Milnes Holden, *The Law and Practice of Banking* Vol 2 (7th ed) Part 6; *Paget's Law of Banking* (11th ed) Ch 33; Lingard, *Bank Security Documents* (3rd ed) Ch 17; Sheridan, *Rights in Security* (1974) Collins pp 144-174.
2. See Ch 17 below.
3. "The policy of the legislation [Bills of Sale Acts] is to preclude a borrower from giving a misleading impression of affluence, by requiring public registration of other persons' interests in things of which the borrower is in possession. If possession is given to the lender, there is no need for registration" - Sheridan, *Rights in Security* (1974) Collins p 145.
4. See further paras **[12.21]**, **[12.27]** and **[12.28]** below.

[12.02] There are many judicial statements as to what constitutes a pledge[5] - the one which is perhaps most pertinent is that of Holmes LJ in the Court of Appeal where he stated:[6]

> "A pledge to secure a debt may be defined to be a delivery of goods and chattels to the creditor as a pawn to secure payment of the sum due. Delivery of the goods pledged is an essential element; but the delivery may be either actual or constructive. The pledgee has only a special property in what is pledged, the general property continuing in the pledgor; but the pledgee is entitled to hold the goods until payment of the debt; and, upon failure of payment, to sell them."

[12.03] The goods pledged or to be pledged must be in existence. As possession is required for a pledge, a pledge cannot be given in respect of goods which do not exist.[7]

[12.04] A pledgee will not be able to rely on a pledge of goods unless the pledgor has absolute title to the goods.[8] Thus, a pledgee should establish that the goods to be pledged are not leased from a third party; otherwise the third party lessor may be able to repossess the pledged goods.[9] It should be established also that the pledgor does not hold the goods subject to any retention of title in favour of a third party. In addition, a search should be made against the file of a potential corporate pledgor in the Companies Registration Office to ascertain that there is no specific charge over the goods or more probably a floating charge. If there is a floating charge over the pledgor's present and future assets a written waiver should be obtained from the chargee excluding the pledged goods from the charge. A negative pledge will almost certainly be included in a security document creating a floating charge.[10] Thus, a waiver should be obtained to avoid a breach of the negative pledge. In the case of securities, enquiries as to title are not sufficiently made "by merely asking the question of the broker, 'Are these your own securities?' to be answered sufficiently by 'Yes' or 'No'; but they might entail the duty of at least a *prima facie* case of ownership being shown".[11] Accordingly, as with other security, a pledgee should satisfy

---

5. Hold CJ in *Coggs v Bernard* (1703) 92 ER 107, Erle Ch J in *Martin v Reid* (1862) 11 CBNS 730, Lord Esher MR and Bowen LJ in *Ex p Hubbard, In re Hardwick* (1866) 17 QBD 690, Cotton LJ in *Ex p Official Receiver, In re Morritt* (1886) 18 QBD 222 at 232; see also Gough, *Company Charges* (2nd, ed 1996) p 21.

6. *Doherty v Kennedy* [1912] 1 IR 349 at 376 (the Court of Appeal's decision was reversed in part by the House of Lords in *Dublin City Distillery (Great Brunswick Street, Dublin) Ltd v Doherty* [1914] AC 823).

7. See Wills J in *Gilbertson and Co v Anderson and Coltman Ltd* (1901) 18 TLR 224.

8. See Mellor J in *Donald v Suckling* (1866) LR 1 QB 585 at 610.

9. *Singer Manufacturing Co v Meredith* (1900) 34 ILTR 108.

10. See para **[13.18]**.

11. The Vice-Chancellor in *Mulville v Munster and Leinster Bank* 27 LR Ir 379 at 393.

himself that the goods are not only in existence but also that the full absolute unencumbered title to them is held by the pledgor.

[12.05] A person who has taken a pledge from a mercantile agent, who is in possession of the goods with the consent of the owner, will be protected if the pledge is taken prior to an advance of any monies and the pledgee acts in good faith without notice of the agent's lack of authority to make the pledge.[12] A *bona fide* pledgee without notice is protected also where he takes a pledge from either a vendor of goods who retains possession following the sale, or a purchaser of goods who has taken possession of the goods prior to the discharge of the vendor's rights.[13]

TAKING A PLEDGE OF GOODS

[12.06] The methods by which a pledge may be taken have been set out by the Privy Council:[14]

> "At the common law a pledge could not be created except by a delivery of possession of the thing pledged, either actual or constructive. It involved a bailment. If the pledgor had the actual goods in his physical possession, he could effect the pledge by actual delivery; in other cases he could give possession by some symbolic act, such as handing over the key of the store in which they were. If, however, the goods were in the custody of a third person, who held for the bailor so that in law his possession was that of the bailor, the pledge could be effected by a change of the possession of the third party, that is by an order to him from the pledgor to hold for the pledgee, the change being perfected by the third party attorning to the pledgee, that is acknowledging that he thereupon held for him; there was thus a change of possession and a constructive delivery: the goods in the hands of the third party became by this process in the possession constructively of the pledgee."

The Privy Council went on to state that the transfer of a bill of lading operated also as a transfer of the possession as well as the property in the goods.

[12.07] Delivery may be effected through any of the following methods:

1. Delivery of the goods themselves,
2. Delivery of the documents of title to the goods,
3. Delivery of the means of control of the goods, or

[12.] The Factors Act, 1889, ss 2 and 4; see also *Lloyds Bank Ltd v Bank of America National Trust and Savings Association* [1938] 2 All ER 63; [1938] 2 KB 147.

[13.] The Factors Act, 1889 ss 8 and 9; the Sale of Goods Act, 1893 s 25.

[14.] Lord Wright in *Official Assignee of Madras v Mercantile Bank of India Ltd* [1935] AC 53 at 58.

4. Delivery of an order or warrant to a third party (under whose control the goods are) and the attornment by the third party.

Documents of Title

[12.08] In banking transactions delivery of the goods themselves to the bank is usually impractical. The first alternative to taking possession of the goods themselves is receiving the documents of title to the pledged goods. Indeed the Privy Council has observed:[15]

> "it is obvious that the ordinary process of financing transactions in goods is much facilitated by ability to pledge the goods by the simple process of pledging the documents of title."

Statutory recognition was given previously by s 3 of the Factors Act, 1889 which provides that, "a pledge of the documents of title to goods shall be deemed to be a pledge of the goods." However, the House of Lords have held that this statutory provision has no application to a pledge of documents of title by any person other than a mercantile agent within the meaning of the Factors Act.[16]

[12.09] The Factors Act, 1889 defines[17] (for the purpose of that Act) document of title as including:

> any bill of lading, dock warrant, warehouse-keeper's certificate, and warrant or order for the delivery of goods, and any other document used in the ordinary course of business as proof of the possession or control of goods, or authorising or purporting to authorise, either by endorsement or by delivery, the possessor of the document to transfer or receive goods thereby represented.

However, notwithstanding the width of this definition, as the Factors Act was enacted in connection with dealings by mercantile agents, it is generally considered that the expression "documents of title" when dealing with pledges refer only to bills of lading and statutory warrants.[18] Indeed, immediately following his statement that goods may be pledged by pledging documents of title, Lord Wright said:[19]

> "It need not be repeated that bills of lading stand apart, nor need it be observed here that some warehousing companies have, by means of private Acts, assimilated their warrants or delivery orders to bills of lading for this purpose."

---

15. *Ibid* at 60.
16. *Inglis v Robertson and Baxter* [1898] AC 616.
17. Section 1.
18. See Paget's *Law of Banking* (11th ed) p 562.
19. *Official Assignee of Madras v Mercantile Bank of India Ltd* [1935] AC 53 at 60.

Thus the transfer of a bill of lading will amount to delivery of possession of the goods to the pledgee without further action on the part of the pledgor:

> "property in the goods passes by such indorsement and delivery of the bill of lading, whenever it is the intention of the parties that the property should pass, just as under similar circumstances the property would pass by an actual delivery of the goods".[20]

A bill of lading remains a document of title, the endorsement and delivery of which will pass title to the goods, until the goods are delivered on shore to the person entitled to them.[21] However, it should be noted that the endorsement of a bill of lading and delivery to the endorsee will not give title to the endorsee to goods which form part of a larger consignment the subject of the bill of lading.[22] A word of caution however, a *bona fide* transferee for value of a bill of lading will not be entitled to the goods, unless the transferor had not merely possession of the bill of lading but a right to transfer it.[23]

The reference to warehousing companies by Lord Wright include the Dublin Port and Docks Board who have been authorised to act as warehousemen[24] and to issue certificates and warrants for goods warehoused.[25] A person named in such a certificate is deemed to be owner of the goods specified in the certificate.[26] Warrants for delivery issued by the Dublin Port and Docks Board are transferred by special endorsement and entitle the person named in the warrant (or the endorsee) to the delivery of the goods specified in the warrant.[27]

Means of Control

[12.10] Constructive delivery arises where the goods are placed at the disposal of and under the control of the pledgee such as in a warehouse.[28] A good illustration of constructive delivery, being sufficient delivery to constitute a pledge, can be seen from the facts of *Hilton v Tucker*.[29] The relevant facts were that Hilton lent moneys to Tucker (the pledgor) on the security of a collection of prints. The collection was stored in a room hired and paid for by the pledgor.

---

20. Bowen LJ in *Sanders Brothers v Maclean & Co* (1883) 11 QBD 327 at 341.
21. *Barclays Bank Ltd v Commissioners of Customs and Excise* [1963] 1 Lloyd's Rep 81.
22. *Burdick v Sewell* (1884) 10 App Cas 74 and *The Aramis* [1989] 1 Lloyd's Rep 213.
23. *Gurney v Behrend* (1854) 3 El & Bl 622.
24. The Dublin Port and Docks Act, 1869 s 106.
25. *Ibid* s 107.
26. *Ibid* s 108.
27. *Ibid* s 109.
28. For a general discourse on the concept of constructive delivery see Stoljar, 'The Delivery of Chattels' (1958) 21 MLR 27.
29. (1888) 39 Ch D 669; the correctness of this decision has been doubted by Sheridan, *Rights in Security* (1974 Collins) 148, but in doing so Sheridan lays out the facts of the case in a manner which does not in all respects conform to the Law Reports.

The key of the room was given to Larking, an employee of the pledgor, who was to make a catalogue of the collection. The pledgor wrote to Hilton stating:

> "the collection was moved in today ... Larking has the key, which I place entirely at your disposal."

Subsequently, the pledgor wrote to Hilton acknowledging the advance and, that the goods pledged were to be held until the loan had been repaid, stating:

> "I hereby request and authorise you to retain possession of my collection of engraved portraits, prints, and other property now deposited by me in a certain room in Oxford Mansions, Oxford Street, the key of which room is at present in your possession or power".

Kekewich J held that the pledge was perfected by delivery of the key to Larking which amounted to constructive delivery of the prints to Hilton. His decision was not affected by the fact that the pledgor's housekeeper held a duplicate key for housekeeping purposes.

Kekewich J though sounded a word of caution on the conclusiveness of the key effecting constructive delivery - "I do not rely on the fact of the key having been handed over". But he went on:[30]

> "There are several cases cited on the interesting question of the effect of delivery of a key. I think, when they are examined, they all really come to this, that the delivery of the key in order to make constructive possession must be under such circumstances that it really does pass the full control of the place to which admission is to be gained by means of the key; as, for instance, where timber is deposited in a warehouse. The delivery of the key is the symbol of possession where the possession itself is practically impossible".

[12.11] Kekewich J's point that the delivery of the key must be such as to pass full control is illustrated by the subsequent decision in *Wrightson v McArthur and Hutchisons (1919) Ltd.*[31] The defendant, as security for monies due to the plaintiff, set aside certain goods in two rooms on its premises. The rooms were locked and the keys handed to the plaintiff. Two letters were written evidencing the arrangement, the second of which stated, "The goods to be locked up, the keys in your possession, and you to have the right to remove same as desired". The court held that notwithstanding that the rooms were on the defendant's premises, the plaintiff acquired possession of the goods upon delivery to him of the keys of the rooms in which the goods were stored; in addition, and of importance to the court, the defendant had given the plaintiff the licence to enter the rooms and remove the goods. Accordingly, the liquidator of the defendant did not have a right to the goods. Rowlatt J considered that if the keys had been

---

30. *Ibid* at 676.
31. [1921] 2 KB 807.

delivered without the licence to remove the goods at any time, possession of the goods would not have passed. He stated further that the delivery of the key should not be a symbolic delivery, but as having the effect as giving actual control.[32]

Attornment

[12.12] The concept of attornment arises out of s 29(3) of the Sale of Goods Act, 1893 which provides that:

> Where the goods at the time of sale are in the possession of a third person, there is no delivery by seller to buyer unless and until such third person acknowledges to the buyer that he holds the goods on his behalf; provided that nothing in this section shall affect the operation of the issue or transfer of any document of title to goods.

Thus, where the goods are under the possession and control of an independent warehouseman, in the absence of transferring documents of title, the warehouseman must attorn to the pledgee. This was not required in *Hilton v Tucker*[33] nor in *Wrightson v McArthur and Hutchisons (1919) Ltd*[34] as in the former case the person holding the key was an employee of the pledgor and in the latter the key was actually handed to the pledgee.

[12.13] A delivery order, which is not a document of title, will be effective to pass possession of the goods where it is delivered to the third party warehouseman and the warehouseman acknowledges that he holds the goods as bailee for the deliveree.[35] The timing of the attornment may prove to be critical in establishing who is to bear the loss for damage to goods held by the warehouseman. The case of *Wardar's (Import & Export) Co Ltd v W Norwood & Sons Ltd*[36] is a reminder of the importance for bankers and all persons involved in the agri-business to have proper control over the movement of agricultural products at all stages.

Because of its particular relevance to the more usual pledging arrangements in Ireland, it is worth considering the facts of the case. The plaintiff purchased 600 cartons of frozen kidneys from the defendant (which was part of a consignment of 1500 cartons imported from Argentina and held in a cold store). The plaintiff examined the kidneys in the cold store and arranged to take delivery at 8 o'clock the following morning. On arriving at the stipulated time, the plaintiff's carrier

---

[32.] For a fuller treatment of the delivery of a key as giving possession, see Bell, *Modern Law of Personal Property in England and Ireland* (1989) Butterworths pp 46-51.

[33.] (1888) 39 Ch D 669.

[34.] [1921] 2 KB 807.

[35.] See Lord Parker of Waddington in *Dublin City Distillery (Great Brunswick Street, Dublin) Ltd v Doherty* [1914] AC 823 at 852 and para **[12.08]**.

[36.] [1968] 2 QB 663.

gave the delivery order (which was the defendant's authorisation to release the goods to the carrier) to the cold store and loading began. The carrier turned on the refrigeration in his van at 10 o'clock at which time he noticed that the cartons still on the pavement were dripping. Loading was completed at noon and the carrier signed a receipt for the kidneys with a qualification that they were received "in soft condition." The refrigeration in the van reached the required temperature at 1 o'clock (five hours after loading commenced). The kidneys were found to be unfit for consumption. The English Court of Appeal unanimously found in favour of the defendant as the moment the cold store received, and acknowledged (by permitting loading to commence), the delivery order was the moment that the property in the kidneys passed to the plaintiff.

[12.14] Although as a general rule the risk in the property does not pass until the property itself passes,[37] there may be circumstances which give rise to a passing of the risk even where the property remains with the vendor or pledgor. This arose in *Sterns Ltd v Vickers Ltd*[38] where the plaintiff purchased from the defendant 120,000 gallons of white spirit which was part of a larger quantity in a certain tank owned by a storage company. On receiving the delivery warrant, the plaintiff agreed with the storage company that the spirit would remain where it was and the plaintiff would pay storage charges to the storage company. The spirit deteriorated. It was held notwithstanding that the property had not passed to the plaintiff (as it had not been separated from the bulk and appropriated to the plaintiff), the risk nevertheless had passed to the plaintiff. As the Court of Appeal pointed out, the defendant had satisfied its bargain and the plaintiff had the right to demand delivery from the storage company.

[12.15] Attornment will not have been created when a warehouseman receives a delivery order and neither objects to it nor acknowledges it.[39] Scrutton LJ set out a guide as to what constitutes an attornment. He said:[40]

> "I think, myself, that a very little will suffice to create an attornment. If the warehouseman writes on the order in the presence of the messenger the word "accepted", so that he sees it; if he makes delivery of part of the goods, as in the case of *Gillett v Hill* where a delivery of five sacks of flour in compliance with an order to deliver "5 sacks ex 20", was held to be an admission of the possession of twenty sacks; if he makes a claim for charges on the person presenting the delivery order; or if he tells him that he has entered his right to the goods in his books. In each of those cases I think it ought to be found that

---

37. Sale of Goods Act, 1893, s 20.
38. [1923] 1 KB 78.
39. *Laurie and Morewood v Dudin and Sons* [1926] 1 KB 223; see also *Farina v Home* (1846) Ex 16 Mee & W 119 and *M'Ewan v Smith* (1849) 2 HLC 309.
40. *Ibid* at 237.

the warehouseman had attorned. But I do not see how it is possible to get an attornment or recognition of the title of the person named in the order out of the mere fact that an order is brought by a messenger and given to a clerk, where nothing is done which is communicated to the other party".

Book Entries

[12.16] Bankers are from time to time put under pressure from their customers to cut any documentation and procedures to the minimum so as not to interfere with the customer's business of earning a return from its undertaking with the minimum of documentation. This pressure in turn leads to pressure being put on lawyers advising bankers on the requirements for effective security. The dangers of setting up a procedure which, while going through the motions of creating a pledge, in reality fall short of the requirements can be seen from the contrasting House of Lords decisions in *Young and Knight v Lambert*[41] and *Dublin City Distillery (Great Brunswick Street, Dublin) Ltd v Doherty*.[42]

[12.17] In *Young and Knight v Lambert*[43] imported goods were stored by their owner in a customs warehouse. The owner pledged the goods to the owner's financiers; a note of the pledge was entered in the book of the customs' chief officer with a request for the goods to be held subject to the orders of the financiers. The Privy Council held that there had been constructive delivery and the financiers were pledgees of the goods.

[12.18] In *Dublin City Distillery (Great Brunswick Street, Dublin) Ltd v Doherty*[44] money was advanced to a distillery company on the security of manufactured whiskey. The whiskey was stored in a warehouse which could be accessed only by the company and the excise officer jointly. Each time an advance was made, the lender's name was entered in a stock-book against particulars of the whiskey; the lender's name was also entered in a separate book called "the register of mortgages." A trade invoice and a document called a warrant containing particulars of the whiskey and stating it to be deliverable to the lender were both delivered to the lender. The excise officer though was not aware of the transaction. The entry of the lender's name in the stock-book was made in pencil - when the particular whiskey was sold, the warrants were returned, the lender's name was removed and the purchaser's name was entered in ink. Further whiskies were "pledged" to replace those sold. The House of Lords held that a pledge had not been created. Lord Atkinson considered that the evidence showed that the warrants were regarded as the security and not as

---

[41.] (1870) LR 3 PC 142.
[42.] [1914] AC 823.
[43.] (1870) LR 3 PC 142.
[44.] [1914] AC 823.

evidence of the pledgee's rights with regard to goods already delivered to the pledgee. Lord Atkinson stated:[45]

> "This evidence ... leaves it quite uncertain whether the company did not, in their dealings with this whisky in the first instance, practically ignore the alleged pledge, and treat the whisky as their own ... the evidence, documentary and oral, such as it is, does not establish that there was a constructive delivery ... of the whisky."

These words should be heeded by any person thinking of taking a short cut to putting security in place.

[12.19] It will be noted that in *Young and Knight v Lambert*[46] the entry in the book was not temporary and the officer in charge was requested to hold the goods to the order of the pledgee. This should be borne in mind when considering the following passage from Lord Parker of Waddington's judgment in *Dublin City Distillery (Great Brunswick Street, Dublin) Ltd v Doherty*[47] which is set out here as it is a useful guideline as to what constitutes sufficient delivery to effect a pledge:

> "It is quite certain that at common law a pledge cannot be created unless possession of the goods the subject of the pledge be delivered to the pledgee. When the goods in question are in the actual possession of the pledger, possession of them is, as a rule, given to the pledgee by actual delivery of the goods themselves. There are, however, cases in which possession may pass to the pledgee without actual delivery, for example, whenever there is some agreement between the parties the effect of which is to change the possession of the pledger from a possession on his own account as owner into a possession as bailee for the pledgee. Such an agreement operates as a delivery of the goods to the pledgee and a redelivery of the goods by the pledgee to the pledger as bailee for the purposes mentioned in the agreement. A mere book entry cannot, however, have this effect. When the goods are not in the actual possession of the pledger, but of a third party as bailee for him, possession is usually given by a direction of the pledger to the third party requiring him to deliver them to, or hold them on account of, the pledgee, followed either by actual delivery to the pledgee or by some acknowledgement on the part of the third party that he holds the goods for the pledgee. The form in which such direction or acknowledgement is given is immaterial. Where the third party is a warehouseman the direction usually takes the form of a delivery order and the acknowledgement of a warrant for delivery of the goods or an entry in the warehouse books of the name of the pledgee as the person for whom the goods are held. The acknowledgement, whatever its form, does not change the nature

---

45. *Ibid* at 849.
46. (1870) LR 3 PC 142.
47. [1914] AC 823 at 852.

of the warehouseman's possession. He still holds as bailee, but for the pledgee instead of the pledger. He has simply attorned to the pledgee."

The arrangement failed to operate as a pledge because as Lord Summer stated:[48]

"no change took place in the character of the company's possession sufficient to complete an agreement to give a pledge by actually putting the pledgee in possession."

The lesson to be learnt by bankers and lawyers is, to avoid the possibility of losing the security and/or being engaged in protracted litigation,[49] the appropriate security requirements should be insisted upon.

Time of Delivery

[12.20] Delivery of the goods to be pledged need not be contemporaneous with the advance which the goods secure. In *Hilton v Tucker*[50] (referred to above[51]), the pledge of the collection of prints was agreed upon at the time of the first advance, but was not put in place until 34 days thereafter when the pledgor wrote to Hilton indicating that the prints were in the room, Larking having the key which was to be at Hilton's disposal. Kekewich J said:[52]

"It seems to me that the transaction may be divided into two parts, and that though fraud may intervene in any case, however careful lawyers or actors may be, still remembering that, in the meantime, there is no property in the lender until he has got the goods, it seems to me a very small opening for fraud to hold that the delivery need not be actually contemporaneous with the pledge. My view of the law certainly is, that if money is advanced, as here, on a contract that goods shall be delivered and that those goods are delivered in pursuance of that contract, the same legal results follow as if the money was handed over with one hand and the goods received with the other".

[12.21] Care should be taken, though, to ensure that a pledge is created and not a charge or bill of sale. Thus an agreement giving the lender the right to take possession, either immediate or otherwise, of the goods as security for a loan will be void unless registered pursuant to the Bills of Sale Acts[53] or (as the case may be) the Companies Act, 1963.[54] However, an agreement which records a

---

48. *Ibid* at 865.
49. The case of *Young and Knight v Lambert* was heard by a judge of the Superior Court of Canada whose decision was overruled by the full Superior Court; their decision was affirmed by the Court of Queen's Bench before it was overruled by the Privy Council; the case of *Dublin City Distillery (Great Brunswick Street, Dublin) Ltd v Doherty* was heard by the High Court in Ireland whose decision was affirmed by a majority of the Court of Appeal before being overruled by the House of Lords.
50. (1888) 39 Ch D 669.
51. In para **[12.10]** above.
52. (1888) 39 Ch D 669 at 677.
53. The Bills of Sale (Ireland) Act, 1879, ss 3, 4 and 8; see *Ex p Parsons; In re Townsend* (1886) 16 QBD 532.
54. Section 99(2)(c); see paras **[17.06]**-**[17.07]**.

pledge and regulates the right of the pledgee to sell goods will not be avoided pursuant to the Bills of Sale Acts.[55] The distinction was explained by Lord Esher MR when he said:[56]

> "... the essence of a pledge is that the grantee says to the grantor, I will lend you money if and when you deposit certain goods with me. It is not, I will lend you money on the security of an authority to take possession of certain goods."

Pledgee Licensing Pledgor to use Goods

[12.22] A pledgee who has possession, whether actual or constructive, may permit the pledgor or another party to have the use of the pledged goods for a specific purpose, without thereby losing the benefit of his pledge. This may be done even where the goods are actually in the possession of the pledgor.

An example of a pledgee permitting a pledgor to retain physical possession is *Reeves v Capper*.[57] The facts of the case were that the captain of a ship pledged his chronometer to the ship's owner in consideration of an advance, the owner allowing the captain the use of the chronometer for his next voyage. The terms of the agreement evidencing the arrangement stated:

> "In consideration of your advancing me £100, on account of this voyage, instead of the usual advance of £50, I make over to you as your property, until the said sum is repaid, my chronometer and all my nautical instruments, now on board the 'Don Giovanni', you allowing me the use of the same for this voyage".

Tindal CJ held that these words gave the captain *"no interest in the chronometer, but only a licence or permission to use it, for a limited time"*, and that the possession of the captain during and after the voyage was the possession of the owner.

[12.23] In *Martin v Reid*[58] the plaintiff pledged his horse and cart to Mr Bowers. Mr Bowers took possession of the horse but, not having enough room, left the cart with the plaintiff on the understanding that Mr Bowers could collect the cart as he pleased. On Mr Bowers' insolvency the plaintiff re-took the horse, but Mr Bowers' assignee seized the horse and cart. The court held that the plaintiff was not entitled to possession as there had been sufficient delivery of the horse and cart to vest the property in Mr Bowers.

[12.24] This principle applies also to bills of lading which are released by the pledgee to enable the pledgor to sell the cargo. In *North Western Bank Ltd v*

---

55. *Ex p, In re Hardwick* (1886) 17 QBD 690; approved by the House of Lords in *Charlesworth v Mills* [1892] AC 231.
56. *Ibid* at 697.
57. (1838) 132 ER 1057.
58. (1862) 11 CBNS 730.

John Poynter, Son, & Macdonalds,[59] it was held that the release of the bill of lading did not affect the pledgee's security and the pledgee was entitled to the proceeds of the cargo.

[12.25] The principle of the pledgee permitting the pledgor to obtain possession of the pledged goods for a particular purpose, without affecting the pledge, has been criticised by Sheridan in *Rights in Security*[60] as being contrary to the Bills of Sale legislation which are designed to protect the public dealing with persons who have apparent title to goods. Sheridan considers that the concept of a licence "is a word-game which does not reflect commercial realities". However, Sheridan acknowledges that *Reeves v Capper*[61] has not been judicially disapproved. Although Sheridan considers the decision in *Martin v Reid*[62] to be "probably no longer of authority", presumably because of the subsequent Bills of Sale Acts, there appears to be no judicial disapproval of the decision. Indeed the principle has given rise to the concept of trust receipts.

TRUST RECEIPTS

[12.26] The decisions which enabled a pledgee to part with possession of the pledged goods without losing the benefit of the pledge have been adapted to the modern day use of a pledge in banking transactions. This has been facilitated by the use of trust receipts or letters of trust. One of the earlier judicial approvals of the use of trust receipts occurred in *Re David Allester Ltd.*[63] In that case the company, which pledged goods to a bank as security for a loan, wished to obtain possession of the bill of lading and supporting documentation to enable it to sell the goods and use the proceeds to discharge the loan. To enable the company to do this, the bank requested the company to sign a letter addressed to the bank in the following terms:

> "We have to acknowledge receipt of invoice, bill of lading, and copy of insurance policy representing ... We receive the above in trust on your account, and we undertake to hold the goods when received, and their proceeds when sold, as your trustees. We further undertake to keep this transaction separate from any other and to remit you direct the entire net proceeds as realized, but not less than [the amount of the loan] within 28 days from this date.
>
> We undertake to cover the goods by insurance against fire and to hold the policy or policies on your behalf."

[59.] [1895] AC 56.
[60.] (1974) Collins pp 149-150.
[61.] (1838) 132 ER 1057.
[62.] (1862) 11 CBNS 730.
[63.] [1922] 2 Ch 211.

The company's liquidator claimed that the trust receipt was invalid as either (1) being an unregistered bill of sale, or (2) an unregistered mortgage or charge on the company's book debts. On the first point, the court held that the document did not fall within the definition of a bill of sale; the bank's rights as pledgee were complete upon delivery of the bills of lading and other documents; the trust receipt was merely an authority by the pledgee authorising the pledgor to sell the goods on the pledgee's behalf; the pledge and the pledgee's rights did not arise under the document but under the original pledge. The court held that the bank as pledgee had the right to realise the goods from time to time, and it was more convenient to allow the realisation to be made by experts - the pledgors - and the pledgee was entitled to do this. The court found on the second point, that the trust receipt was not a mortgage or charge in the true sense as there was no intention that the trust receipt give such a charge - the trust receipt simply enabled the goods to be realised.

[12.27] It should be noted that the pledge of the goods arose under a previous oral arrangement together with the delivery of the bills of lading and other documents. Where a pledge is actually effected by a letter of pledge or, if possession is not transferred, by a letter of hypothecation,[64] the document effecting the pledge will be void for want of registration under the Bills of Sale Acts or the Companies Acts.[65] This point is illustrated by the decision in *Ladenburg & Co v Goodwin, Ferreira & Co Ltd.*[66] In that case, the defendant gave the plaintiff (as security for advances) duplicate bills of lading, copy invoices of goods shipped and a letter "hypothecating the shipments or the proceeds thereof."

The court held that the letter of hypothecation gave a mortgage or charge, not on the goods, but, on the proceeds; thus, being a charge on the company's book debts it was void against the company's liquidator as its particulars were not registered as required by the Companies (Consolidation) Act, 1908.[67]

The court considered that the intention of the letter of hypothecation was that the company should give the bank a mortgage or equitable security on the goods where it could be enforced, otherwise on hypothecation of the proceeds.

---

64. Letter of hypothecation should not be confused with letters of pledge, see further Lingard, *Bank Security Documents* (3rd ed) para 17.71 and Gutteridge & Megrah, *The Law of Bankers' Commercial Credits* (6th ed) pp 186, 187.

65. Registration however is not required if the arrangement falls within an exemption under s 4 of the Bills of Sale (Ireland) Act, 1879, such as being "transfers of goods in the ordinary course of business of any trade or calling" as in *Ex p North Western Bank* (1872) LR 15 Eq 69 (where the advance was made in the ordinary course of trade) or as being "documents used in the ordinary course of business of any trade or calling" as in *Re Hamilton Young & Co* [1905] 2 KB 772.

66. [1912] 3 KB 275.

67. Equivalent to the Companies Act, 1963, s 99(2)(e) see paras **[17.14]**-**[17.20]** below.

[12.28] The decision can be contrasted with the later decision of in *Re David Allester Ltd*[68] in that the pledging arrangement itself arose under the letter of hypothecation, whereas in the later decision the pledge had already taken place and the letter simply stipulated the terms upon which the pledgor was permitted to take possession of the goods.

PRACTICAL OPERATION OF PLEDGES AND TRUST RECEIPTS

[12.29] In the everyday business of banking, the security given to bankers by the proper and effective use of pledges and trust receipts is particularly beneficial where the customer manufactures or produces goods to be sold outside the State;[69] the bank for its part wishes to have recourse to the goods (or their proceeds) prior to any other creditor of the customer,[70] and the customer for its part wishes to avoid the payment of stamp duty which is payable on mortgages or charges.[71]

[12.30] An effective manner of utilising this form of security[72] is as follows:

1. The bank writes a letter (a facility letter) to the company offering to provide bank facilities upon certain conditions including a condition that the goods will be pledged to the bank upon such terms as the bank may stipulate;

2. Following acceptance of the letter[73] the company signs (by one of its officers, under hand) a general letter of pledge[74] agreeing the terms upon which the bank shall have a pledge over all documents

---

[68.] [1922] 2 Ch 211.

[69.] On the advantages and disadvantages of goods as security see Milnes Holden, *The Law and Practice of Banking* Vol 2 (7th ed) p 259.

[70.] A fixed charge over goods is impractical where the goods are rotating as supplemental charges will need to be taken unless the banker wishes to establish that a fixed charge can effectively be taken over future goods.

[71.] Currently at the rate of one-tenth of one per cent of the amount secured subject to a limit of IR£500; it is possible though that a memorandum of pledge could come within the definition of equitable mortgage of the Stamp Act, 1891 s 86(2) and therefore be stampable at the rate of 5 pence per £100 secured.

[72.] For a further exposition of trust receipts in practice see *Phang Sin Kat* (1987) 2 JIBFL 87.

[73.] The commitment by the company in the facility letter to grant a pledge, "even though money be advanced on the faith of it, is not in itself sufficient to pass any special property in the chattel to the pledgee" - Lord Atkinson in *Dublin City Distillery (Great Brunswick Street, Dublin) Ltd v Doherty* [1914] AC 823 at 843.

[74.] For a precedent form see Lingard, *Bank Security Documents* (3rd ed) Document 7 (with a suitable modification in clause 10 for the governing law of Ireland and submission to the jurisdiction of the High Court of Ireland and appointment of persons to accept legal proceedings in Ireland); see also *The Encyclopaedia of Forms and Precedents* (5th ed) Vol 4 document 37.

deposited with the bank from time to time[75] (which will be held as continuing security for the discharge of sums due or to become due by the company to the bank). Alternatively, the company may sign (under hand) a letter of pledge in respect of each transaction with the details of the goods pledged set out in a schedule. It should be noted that the general letter of pledge or, as the case may be, the letter of pledge specific to a transaction, does not bring about the pledge - it simply sets out the terms which will apply as and when documents are pledged;

3. The goods are then pledged by any of the methods already indicated, for example in the case of goods (awaiting shipment) being stored in a warehouse, owned by a third party, the warehousekeeper on receiving the goods attorns to the bank by signing a letter of attornment in the following terms:

> "To [name and address of bank] ('the Bank')
>
> We, the undersigned [name of warehousekeeper], as the owners of the premises specified in the schedule hereto in which the goods specified in the schedule hereto ('the Goods') are warehoused and stored by us for the owners thereof ([name of pledgor]), hereby acknowledge that, by irrevocable agreement with such owners, we hold the Goods in the name of and for the account of the Bank and, in consideration of the Bank permitting the Goods to be stored at our warehouse and for other good and valuable consideration (the receipt of which we hereby acknowledge), we irrevocably undertake with the Bank not to release the Goods to any person save on the instructions of a delivery order from the Bank. We hereby waive in favour of the Bank any lien which we may now, or at any time in the future, have over the Goods for unpaid storage charges or otherwise.
>
> Schedule
>
> Description of the Goods:
>
> Address of premises where the Goods are stored:
>
> [Date] [Signature of Warehousekeeper]"

4. The Attornment together with any supporting documentation in relation to the goods is delivered to the bank. Upon attornment (but not before),[76] the third party warehousekeeper acts as the bank's agent

---

75. Such an agreement is not registrable.
76. "The warehouseman holds the goods as the agent of the owner until he has attorned in some way to [the pledgee], and agreed to hold the goods for him; then, and not till then, does the warehouseman become a bailee for the latter; and then, and not till then, is there a constructive delivery of the goods. The delivery and receipt of the warrant does not *per se* amount to a delivery and receipt of the goods" - Lord Atkinson in *Dublin City Distillery (Great Brunswick Street, Dublin) Ltd v Doherty* [1914] AC 823 at 847.

in holding the goods and is not permitted to release the goods without the bank's express written approval. When the pledgor requires the goods to be transported, the bills of lading will be pledged to the bank who will authorise the release of the goods from the warehouse. If the warehouse is some distance from the ship, the independent carrier of the goods will sign a similar attornment to that of the warehousekeeper.

[12.31] If the warehouse is not owned by an independent third party but by the pledgor (and thus the pledgor has physical control of the location), then following the pledge of the goods to the bank the pledgor should sign a trust receipt[77] indicating clearly that it is holding the goods and their proceeds in trust for the bank. It is important that the trust receipt be signed after a pledge of the goods has been taken. If the circumstances are such that a trust receipt is executed prior to the pledge, then particulars of the trust receipt will need to be registered pursuant to the Bills of Sale Acts, or as the case may be, the Companies Acts.[78]

LOSS OF PLEDGE BY FRAUD

> "The truth is that almost every aspect of commercial dealing is not proof against the possible result of the frauds, that a lawyer, thinking of the possibilities of such things, might suppose to be so easy, but which in business in fact occur so rarely."[79]

[12.32] This statement of the English Court of Appeal in 1938 will no doubt give rise to differing views amongst bankers and lawyers depending upon their relative experience. The fact is though, that a pledge coupled with a release of possession under a trust receipt requires a degree of trust (not usually associated with taking security) between the provider of funds and the corporate borrower. An example of circumstances where a trusting banker suffered loss occurred in *Lloyds Bank Ltd v Bank of America National Trust and Savings Association*.[80] The plaintiffs advanced money to a company on the security of bills of lading taken under a letter of hypothecation. To enable the company to sell the goods

---

77. The form of trust receipt may be as used in *David Allester Ltd* (see para **[12.26]** above) or as in Lingard, *Bank Security Documents* (3rd ed) Document 8 (with suitable modifications for governing law, jurisdiction and process agent); see also *The Encyclopaedia of Forms and Precedents* (5th ed) Vol 4 document 38; or *Encyclopaedia of Banking Law* F (358).
78. The trust receipt in these circumstances is a declaration of trust without transfer and thus falls within the definition of bills of sale in s 4 of the Bills of Sale (Ireland) Act, 1879; for a company as well as being registered pursuant to s 99(2)(c) the trust receipt will in such circumstances also be registrable as being a charge on book debts; see also *Ladenburg & Co v Goodwin, Ferreira & Co Ltd* [1912] 3 KB 275.
79. MacKinnon LJ in *Lloyds Bank Ltd v Bank of America National Trust and Savings Association* [1938] 3 KB 147 at 166; [1938] 2 All ER 63 at 73 (where the quotation is marginally different).
80. *Ibid.*

the subject of the bills of lading, the plaintiffs released the bills of lading to the company who signed a trust receipt acknowledging that the goods and the proceeds of sale were held in trust for the plaintiffs. Subsequently, the company pledged the documents referred to in the trust receipt with the defendants who took the pledge without knowledge of the plaintiffs' interest. The Court of Appeal held that the company and the plaintiffs acting in combination were the owners and that the company's broker had possession of the documents with the consent of the owner; accordingly the defendants were protected under s 2 of the Factors Act 1889 and thus acquired a valid pledge in priority to the previous pledge to the plaintiffs.

LEGALITY OF A PLEDGE

[12.33] Where an agreement to pledge is illegal, a pledgee's right to retain the pledged goods may be upheld by the courts. In *Taylor v Chester*,[81] the plaintiff pledged half of a £50 bank note with the defendant as security for money due for the consumption of food and drink in a brothel and for taking part in a debauchery. The court held that the plaintiff, who had not tendered payment, was not entitled to claim that the contract of pledge was unenforceable due to its illegality. To succeed in his claim he had to show the illegality of the agreement and as such "he was precluded from obtaining 'the assistance of the law' to recover it back".[82]

[12.34] The Pawnbrokers Act, 1964 (as amended by the Consumer Credit Act, 1995[83]) applies to every transaction entered into in respect of a pledge on which a loan or advance not exceeding £5,000 is made by a pawnbroker to a pledgor.[84] A pawnbroker is defined as including any person who carries on the business of taking goods and chattels in pawn.[85] A person is prohibited from carrying on the business of a pawnbroker at any premises unless he holds a licence in respect of such premises.[86] To obtain a licence an application must be made to the Director of Consumer Affairs (accompanied by a fee of £1,000).[87] A separate application must be made in respect of each premises from which the business will be carried out.[88] The Director may refuse the application on certain stipulated grounds[89] such as unsatisfactory evidence of "good character" or "financial

[81.] (1869) 4 LR QB 309.
[82.] *Ibid* at 315.
[83.] Sections 153 and 154; Eighth Schedule.
[84.] Pawnbrokers Act, 1964, s 3 (as amended).
[85.] *Ibid* s 2.
[86.] *Ibid* s 7 (as amended).
[87.] *Ibid* s 8 (as amended).
[88.] *Ibid* s 8(1) (as amended).
[89.] *Ibid* s 8(3) (as amended).

stability" but also if the applicant holds a bookmaker's licence, an intoxicating liquor licence, a gaming licence, a moneylender's licence or an auctioneer's licence. The licence needs to be re-applied for annually.[90] A pawnbroker is required to display in a conspicuous place in his premises a notice ("printed in large and legible characters") setting out certain prescribed information such as rate of interest on loans, details of redemption, surplus on sale of pledged goods and damage to pledged goods.[91] In addition a pawnbroker is required[92] to "keep displayed in large and legible characters over the outer door of the premises in which he carries on the business of a pawnbroker his name and the word 'Pawnbroker'". The Pawnbrokers Act, 1964 sets out detailed stipulations as to the procedures which the pawnbroker must follow in conducting his business. Prior to the amendment of the Pawnbrokers Act (on 13 May 1986), the £5,000 limit was £50 and thus the legislation has become increasingly obsolete as persons in need of finance (for £50) tended to rely more on credit unions and moneylenders to satisfy their requirements. It is uncertain whether this relative obsolescence can now be revived.

PLEDGEE'S RIGHT OF SALE

[12.35] A pledgee has an implied power of sale over goods which have been pledged to him as security for a loan.[93] One of the earlier judgments concerning pledges was that of Holt CJ in *Coggs v Bernard*[94] where he outlined six types of bailment. A pledge or pawn he considered conferred on the pledgee or pawnee a "special property" in the thing pledged or pawned. This "special property" has been referred to on a number of occasions in subsequent decisions.[95] In *Ex p Hubbard; in re Hardwick*,[96] Bowen LJ explained that the special property passed to the pledgee so that the goods could be dealt with by the pledgee if necessary to enforce his rights and that the general property in the goods remained with the pledgor. Bowen LJ's explanation was quoted with approval by Kekewich J in *Hilton v Tucker*.[97] Lord Mersey though considered that the

---

[90.] *Ibid* s 8(4) (as amended).

[91.] *Ibid* s 13(1)(b), second schedule.

[92.] *Ibid* s 13(1)(a).

[93.] *Pigot v Cubley* (1864) 15 CBNS 701.

[94.] (1703) 92 ER 107.

[95.] Blackburn J in *Donald v Suckling* (1866) LR 1 QB 585 at 613, Blackburn J in *Harper v Godsell* (1870) LR 5 QB 422, Bramwell LJ in *Babcock v Lawson* (1880) 5 QBD 284, Field J in *Burdick v Sewell* (1883) 10 QBD 363 at 366, Cotton LJ in *Ex p Official Receiver; In re Morritt* (1886) 18 QBD 222 at 232, Lord Macnaghten in *Bank of New South Wales v O'Connor* (1889) 14 App Cas 273 at 282, Cozens-Hardy J in *Harold v Plenty* [1901] 2 Ch 314 at 316, Cherry LJ in *Doherty v Kennedy* [1912] 1 IR 349 at 384, Rowlatt J in *Wrightson v McArthur and Hutchisons (1919) Ltd* [1921] 2 KB 807 at 815.

[96.] (1886) 17 QBD 690.

[97.] (1888) 39 Ch D 669 at 673.

expression "special property" created no property at all - he preferred the term "special interest".[98]

[12.36] The "special property" or "special interest" in the pledged goods enables the pledgee to sell the goods upon the pledgor's failure to satisfy the debt due to the pledgee. This principle can be seen from the judgment of Cotton LJ in the Court of Appeal's decision in *Ex p Official Receiver; In re Morritt*,[99] where he said:[100]

> "A contract of pledge carries with it the implication that the security may be made available to satisfy the obligation, and enables the pledgee in possession (though he has not the general property in the thing pledged, but a special property only) to sell on default in payment and after notice to the pledgor, although the pledgor may redeem at any moment up to sale."

Thus, once payment of the secured debt is tendered to the pledgee, the special property in the goods is terminated and possession of the goods must be returned to the pledgor. In *Burdick v Sewell*,[101] Field J stated that:[102]

> "the legal effect [of the pledge] is that only a special property passes from the borrower to the lender, although coupled with the power of selling the pledge and transferring the whole property in it on default in payment at the stipulated time, if there be any, or at a reasonable time after demand and non-payment, if no time for repayment be agreed upon. Moreover until such default, although the lender may assign the pledge to another to the limited extent of his own interest in it, ie, as a security for the amount due, he cannot pass the whole and entire property in the goods to another, for by the contract the general property remains in the pawnor; who by virtue of that general property may determine the special property by tender of the secured amount, and may immediately recover the pledge on refusal in a possessory action."

[12.37] The pledgee's right to sell the pledged goods may be exercised only following the pledgor's failure to satisfy the secured debt on the appointed day or, if there is no appointed day, following a demand for payment and the failure of the pledgor to meet that demand.[103] Where no time has been stipulated for satisfaction of the secured debt, the pledgor may satisfy the debt at any time during his life.[104] Where no redemption date has been stipulated the pledgee may exercise his power of sale on the death of the pledgor.[105] The death of the

---

98. *The Odessa* [1916] AC 145 at 158, 159.
99. (1886) 18 QBD 222.
100. *Ibid* at 232.
101. (1883) 10 QBD 363.
102. *Ibid* at 367.
103. *Pigot v Cubley* (1864) 15 CBNS 701 and *France v Clark* (1883) 22 Ch D 830.
104. *Kemp v Westbrook* (1749) 27 ER 1030.
105. *Ratcliff v Davis* (1610) 80 ER 733.

pledgee does not affect redemption of the pledge.[106] A pledgee who exercises his power of sale on[107] or prior to the appointed day for payment will be liable to an action for conversion. The pledgor's damages will be the actual damage incurred by it as a result of the conversion. Thus the pledgor will be entitled only to nominal damages if the pledgee can show that the pledgor had no intention to redeem the pledge on the appointed day.[108]

[12.38] In exercising his power of sale, which may be done without the court's assistance,[109] the pledgee must exercise due care. The Privy Council has stated[110] that a pledgor:

"... must appropriate the proceeds of the sale to the payment of the pledgor's debt, for the money resulting from the sale is the pledgor's money to be so applied. The pledgee must account to the pledgor for any surplus after paying the debt. He must take care that the sale is a provident sale, and if the goods are in bulk he must not sell more than is reasonably sufficient to pay off the debt, for he only holds possession for the purpose of securing himself the advance which he has made."

[12.39] A contract of sale for pledged goods by the pledgee will not carry with it any implied warranty of title. However, a purchaser may be able to recover his money if he can show that it was understood by both parties that the purchaser would acquire full title to the goods.[111]

[12.40] It should be noted that a pledgee's right of sale is not equivalent to a mortgagee's right to foreclose. The distinction was explained by Jessel MR in *Carter v Wake*[112] where he stated that under a legal mortgage, conveyance of the legal ownership was transferred to the mortgagee the benefit of which could not be exercised until the mortgagor defaulted - the same principle applied to an equitable mortgage by deposit of title deeds because effectively that was an agreement to execute a legal mortgage (carrying the rights of a legal mortgagee). However, a pledgee never has the absolute ownership and cannot foreclose. That the distinction is not just an academic point can be seen from the facts of *Carter v Wake*.[113] The defendant deposited certain Canadian bonds with the plaintiff as security for a debt. The bonds were redeemable at par in 1890 but at

---

106. *Ibid.*
107. *Johnson v Stear* (1863) 15 CBNS 330 where it was held that the pledgor has the whole of the appointed day to redeem the pledge.
108. *Ibid.*
109. Lord Mersey in *The Odessa* [1916] AC 145 at 159.
110. *Ibid.*
111. *Morley v Attenborough* (1849) 154 ER 943.
112. (1877) 4 Ch D 605.
113. *Ibid.*

the time of the action were redeemable at a considerable discount. On the defendant's default the plaintiff, rather than selling the bonds at a discount, wished to foreclose the equity of redemption so that he could redeem the bonds in 1890. The court granted the plaintiff an order for sale but not the right to foreclose on the equity of redemption.[114] Thus a pledgee may obtain a sale but not a foreclosure.[115]

[12.41] During the continuation of the pledge, at all times prior to its determination, the pledgee owes a duty to the pledgor to exercise care in safeguarding the pledged goods. Where the goods are destroyed by fire, there is a *prima facie* presumption that the pledgee was negligent. If the pledgee fails to discharge the onus of disproving negligence, the pledgor may recover the difference in the value of the goods and the amount of the advance received and not repaid to the pledgee (and be discharged from repaying the advance).[116]

[114] The Court's decision in *Carter v Wake* (1877) 4 Ch D 605 was applied and followed in *Fraser v Byas* [1895] 11 TLR 481.
[115] Cozens-Hardy J in *Harold v Plenty* [1901] 2 Ch 314 at 316.
[116] *Foley v O'Hara* (1920) 54 ILTR 167.

Chapter 13

Floating Charges

"The floating charge was invented by Victorian lawyers to enable manufacturing and trading companies to raise loan capital over debentures. It could offer the security of a charge over the whole of the company's undertaking without inhibiting its ability to trade."[1]

PURPOSE OF FLOATING CHARGES

[13.01] The purpose of creating a floating charge is, as far as the chargor is concerned, to give security for its debts - a security which would usually cover all the assets and indeed undertaking of the chargor, yet at the same time enable the chargor to carry on its business in the ordinary course without interference from the chargee; effectively the principle is that the chargor can carry on its business as though the floating charge did not exist.[2] For a person who wishes to make funds available to companies to finance their business, the funds can be made available in the knowledge that their repayment with interest are secured on the assets and undertaking of the borrower or guarantor. As a matter of practice floating charges are not given by individuals[3] (save in the case of floating chattel mortgages over agricultural stock[4]).

However, the effectiveness of a floating charge[5] has diminished over time. The chargor's debts due to preferential creditors will be paid in priority to moneys due to the holder of a floating charge in the event that a liquidator is appointed to the chargor,[6] or indeed where the chargee exercises its rights under the security and appoints a receiver.[7] However, a creditor can, by a close monitoring of the

---

[1.] Hoffmann J in *Re Brightlife Ltd* [1986] BCLC 418 at 427.

[2.] See Lindley LJ in *Biggerstaff v Rowatt's Wharf Ltd* [1896] 2 Ch 93 at 101.

[3.] "In principle ... there seems to be no reason why a floating charge should not be created by partners or an individual running a business. The difficulty is one of machinery: registers of bills of sale, land and other property must record the precise property charged: there is no suitable register for floating charges" - Sheridan, *Rights in Security* (1974) Collins 127.

[4.] See para **[11.49]**.

[5.] See Robbie and Gill, 'Fixed and Floating Charges: A New Look at the Bank's Position' (1981) JBL 95; Cork Committee, *Insolvency Law and Practice* paras 104-106 and 1526-1527.

[6.] Companies Act, 1963, s 285(2) sets out a list of categories of debts which in a winding up of a company "shall be paid in priority to all other debts"; this category and the extent of such priority enjoyed by such persons has been extended - see McCann, *Butterworths Ireland Companies Act 1963-1990* (1993).

[7.] Companies Act, 1963, s 98.

debtor's financial position, in theory keep abreast of developments in the debtor's financial position. The reality unfortunately is often otherwise - it is not uncommon for very experienced bankers to be misled by information provided in management accounts.[8] Usually by the time bankers receive a company's annual audited accounts the information is of historical value only.

Apart from ranking in priority to unsecured creditors of the chargor, the holder of a floating charge has the benefit of being able, on the happening of pre-agreed stipulated events, to appoint a receiver and manager over the assets and undertaking of the chargor. The appointment of a receiver and manager enables the holder of a floating charge to manage the chargor's business and dispose of its assets until the debt due to the floating chargee has been discharged.

NATURE OF FLOATING CHARGES

[13.02] The nature and characteristics of a floating charge are discussed in many learned publications on banking and company law.[9] Perhaps the best Irish elucidation of the nature of a floating charge is contained in the judgment of Keane J in *Re Keenan Bros Ltd (in liq)*[10] where he said:

"There is no definition of the expression 'floating charge' in the Companies Acts 1963 to 1983, but the essential characteristics of such a security have been the subject of discussion in a number of cases. I think that one has to bear in mind at the outset that this form of charge made its first appearance in England by a by-product of the joint stock companies ... In order to borrow money, such companies offered as security not merely their fixed assets, but also assets which were regularly turned over in the course of business such as the companies' stock in trade. It was obviously cumbersome and impractical to charge such assets specifically with the repayment of advances, since it would mean the constant execution and release of securities as the assets were disposed of and replaced. Hence the concept developed of a charge which did not attach to any specific assets of the company, remained dormant until the mortgagee intervened and in the interim did not prevent the mortgagor from using the assets in question in the ordinary course of his business".

---

8. The reader though will find little evidence of this fact in the law reports. The chargor simply collapses and the chargee is left to take whatever is left. If fraud is involved there are legal remedies available but the practicalities are such that rarely can such remedies be successfully pursued.
9. *Encyclopedia of Banking Law* paras 1051-1080; Lingard, *Bank Security Documents* (3rd ed, 1993) pp 155-172; Gough, *Company Charges* (2nd ed, 1996) Part Two; Picarda, *The Law Relating to Receivers, Managers and Administrators* (2nd ed 1990) pp 16-40; Goode, *Legal Problems of Credit and Security* (2nd ed 1988) pp 46-77; Sheridan, *Rights in Security* (1974 Collins) pp 126-137; Cork Committee, *Insolvency Law and Practice* paras 101-103 and 1523-1525; see also Courtney, *The Law of Private Companies* (1994), paras 14.040-14.065; *Pennington's Company Law* (6th ed) pp 446-466.
10. [1985] IR 401 (Keane J's decision was reversed in the Supreme Court on other grounds).

[13.03] Keane J went on to cite Romer LJ's description of a floating charge which arguably is the best known of all, namely:[11]

> "I certainly do not intend to attempt to give an exact definition of the term 'floating charge', nor am I prepared to say that there will not be a floating charge within the meaning of the Act which does not contain all the three characteristics that I am about to mention, but I certainly think that if a charge has the three characteristics that I am about to mention it is a floating charge:
>
> 1. If it is a charge on a class of assets of the company present and future;
> 2. If that class is one which in the ordinary course of the business of the company, would be changing from time to time; and
> 3. If you find that by the charge it is contemplated that, until some future step is taken by or on behalf of those interested in the charge, the company may carry on its business in the ordinary way as far as concerns the particular class of assets I am dealing with".

[13.04] Lord Macnaghten's description in the same case is also well known - this description is helpful in ascertaining the nature and meaning of a floating charge. Lord Macnaghten said:[12]

> "A floating charge ... is ambulatory and shifting in its nature, hovering over and so to speak floating with the property which it is intended to affect until some event occurs or some act is done which causes it to settle and fasten on the subject of the charge within its reach and grasp."

These tests, particularly that of Romer LJ, have been applied continually by the courts to debentures to ascertain whether a security is a floating charge.[13]

[13.05] The Agricultural Credit Act, 1978 specifically provides for a floating security to be created over "stock" within the meaning of the Act. The Act states such a floating security shall have effect:[14]

1. To create an ambulatory and shifting charge on the property,
2. To prohibit the mortgagor from selling the charged property otherwise than in the ordinary course of business, and

---

[11.] *Re Yorkshire Woolcombers Association Ltd* [1903] 2 Ch 284 at 295.

[12.] *Illingworth v Houldsworth* [1904] AC 355 at 358; See also Farrar 'Floating Charges and Priorities' (1974) 8 Conv 315 "it is now settled that a floating charge is a present equitable mortgage which is not specific but shifting until crystallisation when it settles and becomes a fixed equitable charge."

[13.] See *National Provincial Bank of England Ltd v United Electric Theatres Ltd* [1916] 1 Ch 132; *Re Lakeglen Construction Ltd* [1980] IR 347 at 354; *Re Armagh Shoes Ltd* [1984] BCLC 405; *Re Keenan Bros Ltd* [1985] IR 401; *Re Holidair Ltd* [1994] 1 IR 416; *Re Cimex Tissues Ltd* [1994] BCC 626; *Supercool Refrigeration and Air Conditioning v Hoverd Industries Ltd* [1994] 3 NZLR 300 at 316; *Re GE Tunbridge Ltd* [1995] 1 BCLC 34 at 37; *Re Cosslett (Contractors) Ltd* [1997] 4 All ER 115.

[14.] Section 30(1).

3. To impose on the mortgagor the obligations of maintaining the charged assets at a level of value equivalent to the value at the date of the charge.

[13.06] To put it simply, a company which creates a floating charge remains free to carry on business and utilise its charged assets in the ordinary course of its business as though the charge did not exist;[15] but nevertheless immediately upon the occurrence of certain stipulated events the charge will attach to the assets. The moment the charge attaches to the assets, the charge is said to have crystallised. A debenture containing a floating charge may contain restrictions on the charged assets, such as a covenant by the chargor not to create any further charges over its assets (known as a negative pledge)[16] or a prohibition on factoring debts.[17]

The typical wording used to create a floating charge is:

> "As security for moneys due or to become due to the chargee the company hereby charges in favour of the chargee by way of first floating charge all its undertaking, property and assets whatsoever and wheresoever both present and future".

A common alternative is to begin with the words "As security for moneys hereby covenanted to be paid"; it may be stating the obvious that a covenant be provided in the debenture under which the chargor covenants to pay all sums of money etc to the chargee.[18] The word "undertaking" means the whole business entity of the company.[19] In what is generally regarded as being the first reported decision concerning a floating charge,[20] Gilford LJ stated:[21]

> "the word 'undertaking' had reference to all the property of the company, not only which existed at the date of the debenture, but which might afterwards become the property of the company. And I take the object and meaning of the debenture to be this, that the word 'undertaking' necessarily infers that the company will go on, and that the debenture holder could not interfere until either the interest which was due was unpaid, or until the period had arrived for the payment of the principal, and the principal was unpaid ... I hold that under

---

15. Or a licence is given to the company to carry on its business - see Romer J in *Robson v Smith* [1895] 2 Ch 118 at 124.
16. See para **[13.18]** below.
17. See Millett LJ in *Re Cosslett (Contractors) Ltd* [1997] 4 All ER 115 at 127, see para **[11.15]**.
18. As a minimum this will avoid embarrassing remarks as made by Hoffmann J in *Re Shoe Lace Ltd* [1992] BCC 367 at 368 - "It is a curiosity of this document that it contains no covenant to pay anything".
19. *Commercial Union Assurance Company Ltd v TG Tickler Ltd* High Court, unrep, 4 March 1959.
20. *Re Panama, New Zealand and Australian Royal Mail Co* (1870) LR 5 Ch App 318.
21. *Ibid* at 322.

these debentures they [the debenture holders] have a charge upon all property of the company past and future, by the term 'undertaking'."

Ordinary Course of Business

[13.07] The whole concept of the floating charge arose out of the requirement of the creditor on the one hand to have security for the repayment of its facilities and for the debtor to be able to continue to carry on and manage its business as it sees fit without the hindrance of a charge attached to its assets. In the earliest reported floating charge decision, subsequent to the foundation of the State, Lavery J stated:[22]

"The nature of a floating security ... is that it leaves the Company free to dispose of its property by sale or otherwise in the ordinary course of its business. The Company may mortgage or sell part or even the whole of its property - if not *ultra vires* - and may issue debentures, government stock and other securities. A debenture constituting a floating security over the undertaking and assets of a company does not specifically affect any particular assets until some event occurs or some act on the part of the mortgagee is done which causes the security to crystallise into a fixed security".

In *Re Holidair Ltd*[23] the fact that the chargor had covenanted in the security "to carry on business in a proper and efficient manner" was held to be inconsistent with a fixed charge and the Supreme Court held unanimously that such a covenant meant that the chargor was meant to deal with the charged assets unhindered by the chargee and thus the security had the characteristics of a floating charge.

A purchaser of property, which is the subject of a floating charge, is entitled to reasonable evidence that the charge has not crystallised.[24] Accordingly, it is a customary and prudent precaution for such a purchaser to require the vendor of the property to produce a current letter from the floating chargee confirming that the charge has not crystallised.

[13.08] The judgments in *Re Old Bushmills Distillery Co; ex p Brett*[25] highlight the 19th century decisions on the nature of a floating charge and the progressiveness of the judiciary in moulding this form of security to facilitate trade. Lord Ashbourne stated that:[26]

[22.] In *Halpin v Cremin* [1954] IR 19 at 24.
[23.] [1994] 1 IR 416.
[24.] See in *Re Horne and Hellard* (1885) 29 Ch D 736.
[25.] [1897] I IR 488.
[26.] *Ibid* at 495.

"Courts are now anxious to uphold all reasonable *bona fide* transactions that are entered into for the purpose of keeping up the business of a Company and saving it from collapse or paralysis from want of the sinews of war".

The concept of "a licence to trade" being permitted by the holder of a floating charge[27] was adverted to by Lord Ashbourne in his judgment:[28]

"Debentures constitute what is called a 'floating' security, that is to say, they allow the Company to deal with its assets in the ordinary course of business until the Company is wound up or stops business, or a receiver is appointed at the instance of the debenture-holders, or, as it has been said (see *In re Standard Manufacturing Company*),[29] they constitute a charge, but give a licence to the Company to carry on its business".[30]

In the same case Walker LJ after saying that a floating security does not become a fixed charge, "till the event happens on which they are made payable", continues:[31]

"I think the result may be stated as follows: It is involved in such a charge that the Company shall continue a going concern and the debenture-holder has no power to interfere till his charge becomes payable. He can claim no account of mesne profits or challenge any authorised dealing by the Company with its property or business. The directors, as masters, carry on meantime the business for which the Company was incorporated according to its constitution, and remain clothed with the power of doing all things necessary for carrying on that business, including the meeting of special emergencies. Assets may be withdrawn by sale, and the proceeds then take their place, or other assets may be substituted or additional assets added by trading; but the floating security follows the concern, reduced or added to, through every form of its trading existence, which existence continues as if the debentures were not there till the floating charge becomes a fixed one".

[13.09] To understand the meaning of a floating charge and the concept of carrying on business in the ordinary course, the reader need look no further than

---

[27.] It can apply also to a fixed charge see *Re Cimex Tissues Ltd* [1994] BCC 626.

[28.] In *Re Old Bushmills Distillery Co; ex p Brett* [1897] 1 IR 488 at 500.

[29.] [1891] 1 Ch 641.

[30.] This was quoted from Romer J's judgment in *Robson v Smith* [1895] 2 Ch 118; on the licence to trade concept note Buckley LJ's decision in *Evans v Rival Granite Quarries Ltd* [1910] 2 KB 979 where the learned judge stated, "A floating security is not a specific mortgage of the assets, plus a licence to the mortgagor to dispose of them in the course of his business, but is a floating mortgage applying to every item comprised in the security, but not specifically affecting any item until some event occurs or some act on the part of the mortgagee is done which causes it to crystallise into a fixed security ... the real bargain between the parties ... is that the mortgagee gives authority to the company to use all its property until the licence to carry on business comes to an end."

[31.] [1897] 1 IR 488 at 507.

the short but pertinent judgment of Henchy J in *Re Keenan Bros Ltd (in liq)*[32] in which he said:[33]

> "A floating charge, so long as it remains floating, avoids the restricting (and in some cases, paralysing) effect on the use of the assets of the company resulting from a fixed charge. While a charge remains a floating one, the company may, unless there is agreement to the contrary, deal with its assets in the ordinary course of business just as if there were no floating charge."

The terms of virtually every debenture which incorporates a floating charge contain covenants by the chargor (i) to carry on and conduct its business in a proper and efficient manner, and (ii) not without the chargee's consent, to sell, transfer or dispose of any part of its undertaking or assets other than in the usual course of trading and for the purpose of carrying on its business.[34]

CRYSTALLISATION OF FLOATING CHARGES

[13.10] As already indicated,[35] at the moment a charge crystallises it attaches and fastens onto the assets (the subject of the charge). Once a floating charge crystallises, the assets the subject of the charge are effectively held by the chargeholder in priority to all other interests. This is because the effect of crystallisation is that "there is an equitable assignment to the debenture holder of all the property which is subject to the floating charge".[36] This can be seen also from the more recent decision in *Re Tullow Engineering (Holdings) Ltd, Grace v Tullow Investments Ltd.*[37] In that case, the company granted a floating charge over shares it held in Tullow Oil plc. It subsequently granted an option to purchase those shares in favour of Tullow Investments Ltd. Following the appointment of a receiver by the chargeholder and thus the crystallisation of the floating charge, the option holder sought to exercise its option to purchase the shares. Blayney J indicated that had the option been exercised prior to the appointment of a receiver it would have constituted a contract of sale and purchase but, "the effect of the crystallisation of the floating charge which occurred was that there was an immediate equitable assignment of the shares to the debentureholders so that, in equity, they became the owners of the shares."[38]

[32.] [1985] IR 401; "The judgments of Henchy and McCarthy JJ describe more clearly than any recent English judgment the distinction between a fixed and a floating charge" - Berg, 'Charges Over Book Debts: A Reply' [1995] JBL 433 at 440.

[33.] *Ibid* at 418.

[34.] For an interesting case as to how agreements were structured so as to come within the exception of sales in the ordinary course of business see *AE Coveney v HS Persse Ltd and Gardiner* [1910] 1 IR 194.

[35.] Paras **[13.03]** and **[13.06]**.

[36.] *Tempany v Hynes* [1976] IR 101 *per* Kenny J at 116.

[37.] [1990] 1 IR 452.

[38.] *Ibid* at 458.

It should be noted though that this "equitable assignment" does not affect assets which the company possesses but does not own, such as goods the subject of a hire purchase agreement or subject to retention of title.[39]

The assets which are subject to the crystallised charge include not only the assets held by the company at the time the charge crystallises but also assets which the company subsequently acquires (provided of course such assets come within the description of the charged property).[40]

The question then arises as to when does a floating charge crystallise?[41] At the end of the 19th century Lord Macnaghten, in describing the nature of a floating charge, stated:[42]

> "It is of the essence of such a charge that it remains dormant until the undertaking charged ceases to be a going concern, or, until the person in whose favour the charge is created intervenes".

[13.11] The authorities are generally consistent in concluding that a floating charge will crystallise on the appointment of a liquidator or receiver to the chargor and also where the chargor otherwise ceases business.[43] In regard to the latter: "the material event is a cessation of business and not, if that is something different, ceasing to be a going concern".[44]

Thus, the sale of the chargor's business will cause a floating charge over its assets to crystallise as the sale will amount to a cessation of its business.[45]

Other authorities, however, adopt a narrower viewpoint, particularly in Ireland.[46] In *Halpin v Cremin*[47] Lavery J held that a floating charge had not crystallised notwithstanding that the chargor had closed down its operations - the learned judge held that "The charge becomes specific on the appointment of a receiver or on a winding-up". This view, it is suggested, is based on an innate

---

[39.] See Kenny J in *Re Interview Ltd* [1975] IR 382 at 395.

[40.] *Lynch v Ardmore Studios (Ireland) Ltd and Hayes* [1966] IR 133.

[41.] For an inclusive treatment as to when a floating charge crystallises see Courtney, *The Law of Private Companies* (1994) Butterworths, paras 14.053-14.059.

[42.] *The Governments Stock and Other Securities Investment Co Ltd v The Manila Railway Co Ltd* [1897] AC 81 at 86.

[43.] *Encyclopedia of Banking Law* paras 1071-1080; Lingard, *Bank Security Documents* (3rd ed, 1993) para 9.19; Gough, *Company Charges* (2nd ed, 1996) pp 135-136; Picarda, *The Law Relating to Receivers, Managers and Administrators* (2nd ed, 1990) 29-31; Goode, *Legal Problems of Credit and Security* (2nd ed, 1988) pp 60-62; Sheridan, *Rights in Security* (1974) Collins, p 134.

[44.] Nourse J in *Re Woodroofes (Musical Instruments) Ltd* [1985] WLR 543; see also Romer J in *Robson v Smith* [1895] 2 Ch. 118 and Joyce J in *Edward Nelson & Co Ltd v Faber & Co* [1903] 2 KB 367; to be distinguished from Lord Macnaghten in *Governments Stock and Other Securities Investment Co Ltd v Manila Rly Co* [1897] AC 81 at 86.

[45.] See *Re The Real Meat Co Ltd* [1996] BCC 254.

[46.] Keane, *Company Law in the Republic of Ireland* (2nd ed, 1991), Butterworths, para 22.28.

[47.] [1954] IR 19.

conservatism and cautiousness. This unchallenged authority is a reflection that in recent times the matter has not come before the Irish courts for consideration.[48] It may be anticipated that this restrictive view will not prevail when the concept of crystallisation is considered again by the Irish courts.[49]

Automatic Crystallisation by Agreement

[13.12] A number of English decisions[50] have indicated that at the time the floating charge is created the parties may agree upon certain events, the happening of which will cause the floating charge to crystallise.[51] This approach is epitomised by the judgment of Nourse J in *Re Woodroffes (Musical Instruments) Ltd*[52] where he stated:[53]

"Although the general body of informed opinion is of the view that automatic crystallisation is undesirable ... I have not been referred to any case in which the assumption in favour of automatic crystallisation on cessation of business has been questioned. On that state of the authorities it would be very difficult for me to question it, even if I could see a ground for doing so. On the contrary, it seems to me that it is in accordance with the essential nature of a floating charge. The thinking behind the creation of such charges has always been a recognition that a fixed charge on the whole undertaking and assets of the company would paralyse it and prevent it from carrying on its business. On the other hand it is a mistake to think that the chargee has no remedy while the charge is still floating. He can always intervene and obtain an injunction to prevent the company from dealing with its assets otherwise than in the ordinary course of its business."

---

[48] For an interesting discussion on the concept of automatic crystallisation on the chargor ceasing to carry on business see Gill, 'Ceasing to carry on Business and the Concept of Automatic Crystallisation of Floating Charges' (1986) 4 ILT 160.

[49] See Courtney, *The Law of Private Companies* (1994) Butterworths, para 14.061.

[50] *Re Woodroffes (Musical Instruments) Ltd* [1985] BCLC 227 and *Re Brightlife Ltd* [1986] BCLC 418; *Re Permanent Houses (Holdings) Ltd* [1988] BCLC 563; see also Buckley LJ's judgment in *Evans v Rival Granite Quarries Ltd* [1910] 2 KB 979 where he stated that a floating security "is a mortgage presently affecting all the items expressed to be included in it, but not specifically affecting any item till the happening of the event which causes the security to crystallise as regards all the items. This crystallisation may be brought about in various ways. A receiver may be appointed, or the company may go into liquidation and a liquidator be appointed, or any event may happen which is defined as bringing to an end the licence to the company to carry on business."

[51] This view is supported by *Pennington's Company Law* (6th ed) p 447 where the author points out the distinction between crystallisation on the happening of a stipulated event and crystallisation on enforcement of the security subsequent to the happening of a stipulated event. Lingard submits that "there is no objection in principle to an automatic cyrstallisation clause" - Lingard, *Bank Security Documents* (3rd ed, 1993) para 9.26.

[52] [1985] BCLC 227.

[53] *Ibid* at 233.

The effect of such crystallisation prior to the appointment of a receiver or liquidator will, according to the English decisions, give the debentureholder priority over the preferential creditors of the chargor - a priority it would not otherwise have had. It was decided in *Re Brightlife Ltd*[54] that a debt secured by a floating charge, which had automatically crystallised by agreement, ranked in priority to the preferential debts. In the course of his judgment Hoffmann J stated that:[55]

> "In *Re Griffin Hotel Co Ltd*,[56] [Bennett J] decided in that case that the priority given by the statute to preferential debts applied only if there was a charge still floating at the moment of the winding up ... It follows that if the debenture-holder can manage to crystallise his floating charge before the moment of winding up, s 614(2)(b) gives the preferential creditors no priority".

Hoffmann J acknowledged that in the usual case of crystallisation before winding up, namely by appointment of a receiver, preferential creditors would still be entitled to priority under the Companies Act,[57] and that the relevant sections[58] were presumably "intended to ensure that in all cases preferential debts had priority over the holder of a charge originally created as a floating charge". But the judge pointed out that the decision in *Re Griffin Hotel Co Ltd*[59] "revealed a defect in the drafting" of the legislation. He went on:

> "it meant, for example, that if the floating charge crystallised before winding up, but otherwise than by the appointment of a receiver, the preferential debts would have no priority under either section. For example, if crystallisation occurred simply because the company ceased to carry on business before it was wound up, as in *Re Woodroffes (Musical Instruments) Ltd*,[60] the preferential debts would have no priority".[61]

In so deciding, Hoffmann J specifically rejected the arguments by the Commissioners of Customs and Excise that public policy required restrictions on crystallising events, as a winding up or appointment of a receiver is required to be noted on the chargor's file in the Companies Registry whereas a notice of crystallisation need not be registered. The result it was contended might be prejudicial to third parties who gave credit to the chargor.[62]

---

54. [1986] BCLC 418.
55. *Ibid* at 424.
56. [1941] Ch 129.
57. Section 196 (broadly equivalent to s 98 of the Companies Act, 1963).
58. Sections 614(2)(b) and 196 of the Companies Act 1985 (broadly equivalent to s 85(2) and s 98 respectively of the Companies Act, 1963) which according to Hoffmann J originated in the Preferential Payments in Bankruptcy Amendment Act 1897.
59. [1941] Ch 129.
60. [1985] BCLC 227.
61. The English Parliament has since passed amending legislation closing this loop-hole.
62. The concept of crystallisation without enforcement was rejected on the grounds of public policy by the British Columbia Supreme Court in the *Queen v Consolidated Churchill Copper Corp Ltd* [1979] 90 DLR (3rd) 357.

[13.13] This latter argument is an attractive one.[63] However to avoid any suggestion that the public could be prejudiced, it is suggested that notice of the automatic crystallisation be inserted on the Form 47 so that the public would at least be on notice of the possibility of an automatic crystallisation.

An example of how an automatic crystallisation clause can work in favour of a group of companies borrowing can be seen from the decision in *Re Permanent Houses (Holdings) Ltd*.[64] The company executed a debenture which incorporated a floating charge. The terms of the debenture provided that the floating charge would crystallise automatically upon an event of default under the debenture. The bank demanded payment of moneys due thereby precipitating an event of default and crystallisation of the floating charge. The bank demanded payment also from the guarantor of the company's debts. The guarantor discharged the debt and took the benefit of the bank's security. The court held that s 196 of the Companies Act 1985[65] gave the preferential creditors priority over the holders of a charge only if that charge was a floating charge at the time of the receiver's appointment and, as the charge had crystallised prior to the receiver's appointment, the floating charge was no longer a floating charge at the time of such appointment. Accordingly, the holder of the floating charge, namely the guarantor, was entitled to the proceeds in priority to the preferential creditors.

[13.14] If the recent English decisions are correct,[66] it is clearly desirable to incorporate crystallisation clauses into floating charge debentures. The debentureholder in priority so that the proceeds of the assets, the subject of the crystallised charge, pass to the ever-increasing preferential creditors (although not to the extent of crystallising without anyone knowing about it). It will usually be preferable to exclude book debts from the crystallisation clause.[67] Debentures should obviously be drafted with sufficient care to enable the crystallisation to take effect both at the instance of the debentureholder upon certain agreed events and prior to the time a receiver would be appointed.[68]

---

[63] See Farrar, 'The Crystallisation of a Floating Charge' (1976) 40 Conv 397 - "At present the law seems to be moving too far in the direction of the debenture holder and the effect of the law at present might be to give rise to a fixed equitable charge descending on the assets of the company unknown to any of the parties, for example where a complex borrowing limit provision has been exceeded and the document provides that such an event gives rise to crystallisation".

[64] [1988] BCLC 563.

[65] Equivalent to s 98 of the Companies Act, 1963.

[66] See also *Re Manurewa Transport Ltd* [1971] NZLR 909.

[67] To avoid the problems caused to the security holder by the Taxes Consolidation Act, 1997, s 1001, see para **[14.36]**.

[68] Boyle, 'The Validity of Automatic Crystallisation Clauses' (1979) JBL 231; Farrar, 'World Economic Stagnation puts the floating Charge on Trial (1980) 1 Co Law 83; Campbell, 'Determining the Exact Time of Crystallisation' (1983) 4 Co Law 36; Boyle, 'A Case of Crystallisation and Priorities' (1985) 6 Co Law 277; Jones, 'Crystallisation of Floating Charges' (1989) 1 JIBL 34.

One can only speculate as to how the Irish courts would treat such a clause. It is doubtful that the courts would refuse to allow their operation simply on the grounds of public policy (as in *The Queen v Consolidated Churchill Copper Corp Ltd*[69]), as the Supreme Court has shown a willingness to allow the intention of the parties to prevail.[70] Although as against that, the Supreme Court has not been shy about finding a way to circumvent an agreement in a debenture between the chargor and chargee.[71]

[13.15] A somewhat curious decision is the Australian decision of *Stein v Saywell*[72] where it was held that preferential creditors lost priority to the debenture holder under a floating charge which became specific after the presentation by a creditor of a winding-up petition but prior to the making of a winding-up order.[73] This decision is all the more difficult to justify in view of the fact as Barwick CJ correctly pointed out in his dissenting judgment that, "once the order is made the winding up is deemed to have commenced with the lodgement of the petition."

[13.16] The argument to be made in support of crystallisation at the instance of the debenture holder has statutory authority by virtue of the Agricultural Credit Act, 1978, s 30 of which provides that where moneys secured by a floating chattel mortgage remain unpaid or there has been a breach of covenant by the mortgagor, the mortgagee may serve on the mortgagor "a notice in writing declaring that the floating chattel mortgage has become fixed".[74] The effect of such a notice is that:[75]

> the floating chattel mortgage with effect on and from the date of the service of the notice shall ... become and be fixed, and shall have effect as a specific chattel mortgage of all stock which is on the said land at the time of the service of the said notice.

[69.] (1979) 90 DLR (3rd) 357.

[70.] *Re Keenan Bros Ltd* [1985] IR 401.

[71.] *Re Holidair Ltd* [1994] 1 IR 416.

[72.] (1969) 121 CLR 529.

[73.] Gregory, 'Some Problems of Automatic Crystallisation' (1986) Insolvency Law & Practice p 31, writes that the weakness of the Australian decision is that it ignores the definition or scope of the charge as described by Romer J or by Lord Macnaghten in *Re Yorkshire Woolcombers Association Ltd* and that a receiver appointed after crystallisation is still appointed under the floating charge as crystallisation is part and parcel of the content of the floating charge.

[74.] There are certain specific requirements to be met under s 31(1) of the Agricultural Credit Act, 1978 before such a notice can be served including a requirement that the mortgagee must before service of the notice take an inventory of the stock on the land to which the floating chattel mortgage relates; see para **[11.50]**.

[75.] Section 31(1)(i).

The outcome of an Irish decision is awaited with interest. While each argument has its attractions,[76] it would be reasonable to assume that should the Irish courts decide that the triggering of an automatic crystallisation clause is effective,[77] and thus priority is given to the debenture holder ahead of the preferential creditors, amending legislation[78] will be implemented to reverse that effect. This would follow what was done in Australia subsequent to the *Stein v Saywell* decision[79] and what was so surreptitiously done in Ireland subsequent to the Supreme Court's decision in *Re Keenan Brothers Ltd*.[80]

Decrystallisation

[13.17] The Supreme Court has shown that the crystallisation of a floating charge will not impede the role of an examiner who is appointed to a company with assets over which a floating charge has crystallised. In *Re Holidair Limited*,[81] the Supreme Court held that a floating charge which had crystallised on the appointment of a receiver to the company de-crystallised on the subsequent appointment of an examiner to the company. It seems unclear why the court felt it necessary to consider this point as the holder of a charge, whether fixed or floating, is not permitted to utilise the charged assets during such time as an examiner is appointed to the company.[82]

[76.] For further discussion on the contrasting views see Milman, 'Guidance on bank debentures' (1987) 8 Co Law 30; Wilkinson, 'Automatic Crystallisation of Floating Charges' (1987) 8 Co Law 75; Wilkinson, 'Automatic Crystallisation of Floating Charges' (1986) Insolvency Law & Practice 162; 'A Review of *Re Woodroffes (Musical Instruments)* and *Re Brightlife Ltd*'; Gill, 'Crystallisation of Floating Charges and Preferential Creditors' (1986) 4 ILT 231.

[77.] As argued by Courtney, *The Law of Private Companies* (1994) Butterworths para 14.064.

[78.] For a summary of earlier efforts by the legislature to protect the rights of unsecured creditors from floating charges see Hoffmann J's judgment in *Re Brightlife Ltd* [1986] BCLC 418.

[79.] The position in England has also been amended by the legislature - the Insolvency Act 1986 Schedule 13, enables the preferential creditors to obtain priority over the holder of a floating charge which has crystallised prior to the appointment of a receiver, thereby to that extent negativing the effect of the decisions in *Re Woodroffes (Musical Instruments) Ltd* and in *Re Brightlife Ltd*.

[80.] The provisions of s 115 of the Finance Act, 1986 (now s 1001 of the Taxes Consolidation Act, 1997) were introduced into Dáil Éireann 13 days prior the enactment of the Bill. No indication of such draconian legislation was given by the Minister for Finance in his budget speech nor did it appear when the Bill was presented to Dáil Éireann. The provisions first appeared in the Bill as passed by Dáil Éireann on 13 May 1986 without any public announcement and took effect on 26 May 1986.

[81.] [1994] 1 IR 416.

[82.] Save with the consent of the examiner - Companies (Amendment) Act 1990, s 5(2)(d); in *Re Atlantic Magnetics Limited* [1993] 2 IR 561 the examiner was permitted to utilise the proceeds of a fixed charge on book debts; see also Courtney, *The Law of Private Companies* (1994) Butterworths para 17.049.

NEGATIVE PLEDGE

[13.18] As we have seen, it is essential, if the floating charge is to have any value, that a subsequent chargee will not somehow obtain priority over the chargor's assets. This could be obtained if the chargor creates a fixed charge over part or all of its assets in favour of a third party.[83]

To avoid losing priority,[84] the debenture containing the floating charge should be drafted in a manner so as to include a clause restraining the chargor from creating subsequent charges ranking in priority to or *pari passu* with the floating charge. This clause is what is known as a negative pledge clause.[85] The wording of a typical negative pledge clause is:[86]

> "The chargor hereby covenants that it shall not, [and shall procure[87] that none of its subsidiaries shall,] without the prior written consent of the chargee, create or attempt to create or permit to subsist any mortgage, charge, pledge, debenture, lien (other than a lien arising in the ordinary course of business by operation of law) or other encumbrance on the undertaking, property, assets and rights charged herein or on any part thereof".

It can be seen that the principal purpose of the foregoing negative pledge covenant is to ensure that the anticipated proceeds from the pool of assets being charged by the floating charge will not be diluted through subsequent charges.[88] In a sense the company creating the charge with the negative pledge is agreeing with the chargee, typically its banker, that it will not go elsewhere for its secured finance without agreement from the bank.

[13.19] The concept of a negative pledge gives rise to public policy issues. Whether a negative pledge could be unenforceable as being contrary to Articles 85 and/or 86 of the Treaty of Rome[89] was considered in *Oakdale (Richmond) Ltd v National Westminster Bank plc*.[90] The court held that such restriction was

---

[83.] On winding up or receivership of the chargor, the holder of a fixed charge will, with some exceptions, rank in priority to all other creditors in respect of the proceeds of the assets the subject of the fixed charge - see para **[11.02]**.

[84.] As in *Wheatley v Silkstone and Haigh Moor Coal Co* (1885) 29 Ch D 715.

[85.] See also paras **[7.32]-[7.34]**; for a concise treatment see Goode, *Legal Problems of Credit and Security* (2nd ed, 1988) pp 17-23; for a more detailed discussion see Gabriel, *Legal Aspects of Syndicated Loans* (1986) Butterworths pp 82-97.

[86.] On the drafting and usefulness of such clauses (albeit for Euro-bond issues) see Boardman and Crosthwait, 'Wither the Negative Pledge' [1986] 3 JIBL 162; and see also Hobbs, 'The Negative Pledge: A Brief Guide' [1993] JIBL 269; for additional material see Buckheit, 'Negative Pledge Clauses: The Games People Play' IFLR (July 1990); 'How to Negotiate the Negative Pledge Clause' (December 1992); 'How to Negotiate Permissible Liens' (January 1993).

[87.] "Procure" is preferable to "not permit" - see Boardman and Crosthwait, 'Wither the Negative Pledge' [1983] 3 JIBL 162 at 163.

[88.] For a useful and more detailed treatment of the negative pledge, see Kalderen and Siddiqi, *Sovereign Borrowers* (1984) Butterworths.

not anti-competitive (or an abuse of a dominant position) as the chargor could always discharge the indebtedness to the bank and have the charge released (thereby releasing itself from the negative pledge).

The Supreme Court has set its face against such clauses where its effect has been to prevent the company from obtaining alternative sources of finance. In *Re Holidair Ltd*[91] a group of companies charged their assets under a mortgage debenture. The companies agreed under the debenture that for as long as any moneys remained owing to the debenture holder the companies would not borrow moneys without the debenture holder's consent. An examiner who was appointed to the group sought directions as to whether he could borrow from another source. Costello J held in the High Court that the examiner could not break the company's contracts and must take the company as he found it. The Supreme Court found however that the negative pledge was a constraint likely to be detrimental to the company and that the examiner was entitled[92] to take the necessary steps to rectify, halt and prevent the negative pledge and, subject to the court's sanction,[93] borrow moneys elsewhere.

[13.20] The negative pledge covenant itself is unlikely to give sufficient protection to the chargee. Although a breach of the negative pledge clause by the chargor will give rise to a right of action on the part of the chargee, the exercise of such a right of action would in most circumstances be meaningless as the chargor's assets available to pay any damages awarded are in any event already charged (albeit under a floating security) in favour of the chargee.[94] The breach of covenant though, in most properly drafted debentures, trigger an event of default and a right of automatic crystallisation of the floating charge.

If the cause of the breach of the negative pledge covenant is the creation of a fixed charge in priority to the floating charge, the negative pledge covenant may be of little use. This can be seen from the Supreme Court's decision in *Welch v Bowmaker (Ireland) Ltd and The Governor and the Company of the Bank of Ireland*.[95] In that case, the company created a floating charge over lands not specifically described in the debenture a condition of which stated that the company was not at liberty to create other security in priority to or *pari passu*

89. See Rosovsky, 'Negative Pledge Clauses and Articles 85 and 86 of the Treaty of Rome' (1989) 4 BJIBFL 416; for a contrary view see Hobbs, 'The Negative Pledge; A Brief Guide' [1993] 7 JIBL 269.
90. [1997] 1 BCLC 63; see para **[7.33]**.
91. [1994] 1 IR 416.
92. Pursuant to the Companies (Amendment) Act, 1990, s 7(5).
93. Companies (Amendment) Act, 1990, s 9.
94. On the possibility of a right of action by the chargeholder against a subsequent chargee see Stone, 'Negative Pledges and the Tort of Interference with Contractual Relations' [1991] 8 JIBL 310.
95. [1980] IR 251.

with the debenture. The second defendant subsequently took a mortgage by deposit of title deeds over lands the subject of the floating charge. The Supreme Court held that at the time of the deposit of the title deeds, although the second defendant was aware of the debenture it was not aware of its terms and thus its subsequent mortgage took priority. Henchy J stated that: "it is settled law that there is no duty on the bank in a situation such as this to seek out the precise terms of the debenture."[96]

In supporting Henchy J, Parke J posed the question:[97]

> "is it to be said that, although the Companies Act, 1963, makes provision for the registration of certain particulars regarding charges created by a company, it is obligatory upon a third party dealing with that company to go beyond the particulars which have been recorded in the register in the Companies Office in accordance with the section in order to ascertain whether he may deal safely with the company in the ordinary course of a business transaction between them?"

From this passage it may be deduced that a note of the negative pledge was not made on the Form 47.

[13.21] A form of protection can be obtained by filing a note of the negative pledge in the chargor's file in the Companies Registration Office.[98] The chargee's solicitor will, or should, ensure that the Form 47 giving particulars of the charge contains full details of the negative pledge clause. The filing in the Companies Registration Office of the details of the covenant, on the same Form 47 which is being filed containing short particulars of the floating charge, should put third parties, namely other potential lenders, on notice. Being on notice will preclude them from obtaining priority as even if a fixed charge is taken, priority will be obtained only if the charge has been obtained by a creditor *bona fide* without notice.[99] While actual notice will suffice, the question arises as to whether a person is bound by constructive notice. The Supreme Court has indicated that "actual or constructive notice of the prohibition must be shown before the subsequent mortgagee can be said to be deprived of priority".[100] However, although there is support for this view,[101] it seems more likely that the

---

96. *Ibid* at 256, quoting as authority *Re Standard Rotary Machine Co* (1906) LT 829; *Wilson v Kelland* [1910] 2 Ch 306 and *G & T Earle Ltd v Hemsworth RDC* (1928) 44 TLR 605.

97. *Ibid* at 262.

98. See also paras **[17.81]-[17.90]** inclusive.

99. Farrar, 'Floating Charges and Priorities' (1974) 38 Conv 315 - "it is now clearly established that knowledge of the existence of such a clause operates in equity to prevent a subsequent mortgagee obtaining priority".

100. Henchy J in *Welch v Bowmaker (Ireland) Ltd and The Governor and Company of the Bank of Ireland* [1980] IR 251 at 256.

101. Hobbs, 'The Negative Pledge: A Brief Guide' [1993] 7 JIBL 269.

Supreme Court would now follow the principles of its decision in *Roche and Roche v Peilow & Peilow*[102] in requiring a subsequent chargee to follow the prudent course (and the common practice) of examining the company file in the Companies Registration Office to ascertain whether a negative pledge clause was stated on the Form 47 filed by the first chargee, and (assuming the restriction is filed) thereby fix it with constructive notice.[103]

[13.22] Where a negative pledge is being given in an unsecured transaction,[104] for example, where a company is raising funds from investors and agrees not to give security to the investors or to other investors or bankers, it is not unusual to add at the end of the negative pledge covenant:

> "unless the benefit of such security is at the same time or prior thereto, extended equally and rateably to secure monies due or to become due hereunder".

In practice the use of this clause has declined as there is a view, which is not unsound, that for this clause to be effective and enforceable particulars should be registered in the Companies Registration Office[105] as an agreement to create a charge is itself a charge (albeit equitable) and therefore registrable.[106] There is also a view that such clauses cannot in equity give such a security interest.[107] Thus there remains uncertainty as to their legal effect.[108]

INVALIDITY OF FLOATING CHARGES

[13.23] To discourage creditors from obtaining floating charges prior to the imminent collapse of the chargor, and thereby obtain priority over the unsecured creditors, the legislature have provided that in certain circumstances the holder of a floating charge will not obtain any advantage.

Section 286 of the Companies Act, 1963 provides that the creation of any mortgage or charge within six months prior to the chargor's winding-up shall in certain circumstances be deemed to be a mortgagor's fraudulent preference and be invalid.[109] The potential invalidity period is two years where the security is created in favour of "a connected person".[110]

[13.24] Section 288(1) of the Companies Act, 1963 provides that:[111]

[102.] [1985] IR 232.

[103.] "Lack of enquiry may amount to lack of good faith" - Lynch, Marshall, O'Ferrall, *Corporate Insolvency and Rescue* (1996) Butterworths, para 4.69.

[104.] For reading on the negotiation of such clauses see *Buckheit* (1990) IFLR 10; (1992) IFLR 28; (1993) IFLR 31; for a useful treatment on the functions, variations and weaknesses of negative pledge covenants see Wood*, Law and Practice of International Finance* (Sweet & Maxwell 1980) para 6.2.

[105.] Pursuant to the Companies Act, 1963 s 99.

[106.] Penn, Shea & Arora, *The Law and Practice of International Banking* Vol 2 (1987) para 6.43.

[107.] See Maxton, 'Negative Pledges and Equitable Principles' [1993] JBL 458.

[108.] For further reading see Stone, 'The 'Affirmative' Negative Pledge' [1991] 9 JIBL 364.

where a company is being wound up, a floating charge on the undertaking or property of the company created within 12 months before the commencement of the winding up shall, unless it is proved that the company immediately after the creation of the charge was solvent, be invalid, except as to money actually advanced or paid, or the actual price or value of goods or services sold or supplied, to the company at the time of or subsequently to the creation of, and in consideration for, the charge, together with interest on that amount at the rate of 5 per cent per annum.

Thus every floating charge created within 12 months of the winding up of the chargor is at risk.[112]

Section 288(3) of the same Act provides that:

Where a floating charge on the undertaking or property of a company is created in favour of a connected person, subsection (1) shall apply to such a charge as if the period of 12 months mentioned in that subsection were a period of 2 years.

The term "connected person" encompasses a wide spectrum and includes[113] a director, a shadow director, a person connected with a director, a related company, trustee of or a surety or guarantor of a director, shadow director, connected person or related company.

[13.25] Section 288(3) was introduced by the Companies Act, 1990.[114] The background to this provision can be traced to the 1958 Report of the Company Law Reform Committee (known as the Arthur Cox Report).[115]

At the time of the Arthur Cox Report the risk period for all floating charges was three months.[116] The Report considered the three month period to be too short and recommended a change to 12 months for directors and connected persons and six months otherwise.[117] The Report, in pointing out how directors could circumvent the section, stated:[118]

---

[109] For further reading see Courtney, *The Law of Private Companies* (1994) Butterworths, para 19.048-19.066; Lynch, Marshall, O'Ferrall, *Corporate Insolvency and Rescue* (1996) Butterworths, paras 7.69-7.77; Keane, *Company Law in the Republic of Ireland* (2nd ed, 1991) Butterworths, paras 38.80-38.83.

[110] Companies Act, 1963, s 286(3).

[111] As amended by the Companies Act, 1990, s 136.

[112] See also Courtney, *op cit*, paras 19.070-19.079; for a learned and useful discussion of the English equivalent (the Insolvency Act 1986, s 245) see Lingard, *Bank Security Documents* (3rd ed, 1993) paras 6.2-6.5.

[113] Section 288(4).

[114] Section 136.

[115] Pr 4523.

[116] Companies (Consolidation) Act, 1908, s 212.

[117] Para 158.

[118] Para 159.

"A method of evading s 212 of the Act of 1908 has been used on a number of occasions. A director who has advanced money to a company without getting a debenture secured by a floating charge arranges with the company, when a winding up is imminent, that the company will repay the advance to him, that he will make a new advance of the same amount to the company and that the new advance will be secured by a floating charge. Such a floating charge would not seem to be invalid as money is paid to the company at the time of the creation of the floating charge. We recommend that such a charge should be declared to be invalid."

[13.26] In assessing whether a floating charge is invalidated, the section needs to be carefully scrutinised. The first point to note is that the section opens with the words, "where a company is being wound up". Thus if prior to the winding up the floating charge crystallises and the chargee realises funds through a sale of the charged assets and such funds are used to reduce or discharge indebtedness secured by the floating charge, the section cannot be used subsequently by a liquidator to recover the funds realised from the security.[119]

[13.27] In any proceedings arising under this section between competing creditors it is not necessary for the company to be joined as a party to the proceedings.[120]

"except as to money actually advanced or paid"

[13.28] However, if a person makes funds available to the chargor in consideration for and at the time of, or subsequent to, the creation of the charge, to the extent of such funds made available plus 5 per cent the charge will not be invalidated by s 288. The rate of 5 per cent per annum has remained unchanged since 1908.[121]

The replacement of an unsecured debt with moneys secured on a floating charge will not satisfy the exception relating to moneys advanced. The expression "money actually advanced or paid" means the net amount and not the gross. In *Revere Trust Ltd v Wellington Handkerchief Works Ltd*[122] £400 was advanced at the time of the security being given and £310 was paid by the chargor to the security holder to discharge an earlier debt. The Northern Ireland Court of Appeal held that the security was valid for £90 plus five per cent thereon. Andrews LJ indicated:[123]

"It is our duty in my opinion to look, not at the mere form, but at the reality of the transaction. The object of the section was to prevent companies which were

---

[119.] *Mace Builders (Glasgow) Ltd v Lunn* [1985] BCLC 154 and [1987] BCLC 55.

[120.] *Smurfit Paribas Bank Ltd v AAB Export Finance Ltd (No 2)* [1991] 2 IR 19.

[121.] Companies (Consolidation) Act, 1908, s 212.

[122.] [1931] NILR 55.

[123.] *Ibid* at 61.

in extremis giving charges on their property for past debts to the prejudice of other creditors. If the device adopted in this case were countenanced by the court, it seems to me that the section would become valueless, as it could be evaded in every case by the mere intercharge of cheques".

[13.29] This principle was extended where the security holder was a separate entity from the earlier creditor but within the same group. In *Re GT Whyte & Co Ltd*[124] the company owed Lloyds Associated Banking Co Ltd, a wholly owned subsidiary of Lloyds Bank Ltd, £12.75 million. The creditor demanded payment, Lloyds Bank advanced the money to the company to discharge the debt and as security for the new advance the company granted Lloyds Bank a floating charge. The company went into liquidation eleven months later. The court held that the floating charge was effectively a substitution of a better security for the company's indebtedness to Lloyds and the exception as to moneys advanced could not be relied upon. When considering the expression "money actually advanced or paid", Nourse J stated:[125] "the primary question in each case is whether the transaction is in substance for the benefit of the company and not merely the substitution of a security for an unsecured debt".

"at the time of"

[13.30] The guiding principle of this expression from an early Irish case was that expressed by Powell J:[126]

"As a general rule, a payment made on account of the consideration for the charge and in anticipation of its execution, and in reliance on a promise to execute it, although made some days before its execution, is made at the time of its creation, within the meaning of the section."

In elaborating on this statement, Powell J quoted from Neville J whose judgment was upheld by the Court of Appeal in *Re Columbian Fireproofing Co Ltd*:[127]

"The question is, what is the meaning in this section of the words `at the time of' the creation of the charge? I think, whether any particular payment comes within these words, it must always be a question of fact depending on the circumstances of a particular case. The word 'time' in this connexion must always be, to some extent, indefinite, for the creation of the security and the payment of the money cannot be simultaneous; and I think that a payment made on account of the consideration for the security in anticipation of its creation and in reliance on a promise to execute it, although made some days before its execution, is made at the time of its creation within the meaning of the section."

---

124. [1983] BCLC 311.
125. *Ibid* at 317.
126. In *Re Olderfleet Shipbuilding and Engineering Co Ltd* [1922] 1 IR 26 at 39.
127. [1910] 1 Ch 758 at 765.

It was held in *Re Daniel Murphy Ltd*[128] that moneys advanced after an agreement to give a charge, but before the execution of the charge, are advanced at the time of the charge within the meaning of the Act,[129] provided that any delay in having the charge completed and registered was not intended to deceive creditors and was not unreasonable or culpable. The rationale for this approach was given by Kenny J in his judgment, namely:[130]

> "... it is desirable that lenders should be encouraged to advance money when a promise to create a charge has been given, for that is usually the time when the money is urgently needed."

In *Re F and E Stanton Ltd*[131] it was held that payments made some time before the creation of a floating charge were made "at the time of" its creation provided the payments were made in anticipation of the charge and in reliance of it and the chargee had not procured or acquiesced in any delay in obtaining the charge (even though ultimately the charge was taken four days prior to a petition being presented to wind up the chargor). Maugham J did indicate in the course of his judgment that a delay of greater than four or five days does require an explanation.

The approach adopted by the Court of Appeal in *Re Columbian Fireproofing Co*[132] was effectively applied by Maugham J, by the two Irish decisions (referred to above) and by Barron J in *Smurfit Paribas Bank Ltd v AAB Export Finance Ltd (No 2)*[133] where, after reviewing the authorities, he stated:[134]

> "In order to treat payments made to the company before the execution of the charge as payments made at the time of the charge, the necessary elements to be established are: - an honest transaction; advances made before the execution of the charge and reasonable expenditure in and about the preparation and execution of the charge."

[13.31] A difficulty with this line of authority is that the Court of Appeal's approach to the words "at the time of" was specifically rejected by the English Court of Appeal in *Re Shoe Lace Ltd*.[135] In giving the leading judgment in the Court of Appeal Sir Christopher Slade stated:[136]

---

128. [1964] IR 1.
129. The Companies (Consolidation) Act, 1908, s 212, the relevant part of which is identical to the Companies Act 1963, s 288.
130. [1964] IR 1 at 6.
131. [1929] 1 Ch 180, applying the Court of Appeal's decision in *Re Columbian Fireproofing Co* [1910] 2 Ch 120.
132. [1910] 2 Ch 120.
133. [1991] 2 IR 19.
134. *Ibid* at 30.
135. [1993] BCC 609.
136. *Ibid* at 619.

"The words 'at the time of or subsequently to the creation of ... the charge' ...
were clearly included by the legislature for the purpose of excluding from the
exemption the amount of moneys paid to the company before the creation of
the charge, even though they were paid in consideration for the charge."

In *Re Shoe Lace Ltd*[137] the directors of a company resolved to create a debenture
on 20 March 1990. Moneys were advanced to the company on 3 April, and
again in May, June and 16 July before the debenture was executed on 21 July.
The company was compulsorily wound up in November 1990. The Court of
Appeal upheld Hoffmann J's decision[138] that the payments were not made at the
time of creation of the charge.[139] Sir Christopher Slade set out the position
succinctly:[140]

"In a case where no presently existing charge has been created by any
agreement or company resolution preceding the execution of the formal
debenture, then, in my judgment, no moneys paid before the execution of the
debenture will qualify for the exception under the subsection, unless the
interval between payment and execution can be regarded as contemporaneous
... it is always open to the lender not to lend until the charge has actually been
executed; this must be the prudent course".

Although the courts' decisions in *Re Shoe Lace Ltd*[141] contrast with the earlier
Irish decisions,[142] the rationale of the English Court of Appeal's decision carries
more conviction and should be the line to be adopted henceforth.

"in consideration for"

[13.32] It was held in *Re Daniel Murphy Ltd*[143] that the word "consideration"
bears a different meaning in the section from the meaning it bears in the law of
contract in that the section makes past consideration - the giving of a charge -
effective consideration for cash subsequently advanced in reliance upon it. The
court decided that cash advanced after the promise to grant the charge was given
was money advanced in consideration of the charge within the meaning of the
section.

---

137. [1993] BCC 609.
138. [1992] BCLC 636.
139. The wording of s 245 of the English Insolvency Act 1986 is somewhat different to the Irish
legislation which uses language previously used in English legislation. The Court of Appeal
regarded the distinction as being immaterial.
140. [1993] BCC 609 at 620.
141. [1993] BCC 609.
142. And with the decision in *Re Fairway Magazines Ltd* [1993] BCLC 643.
143. [1964] IR 1.

[13.33] In *Re Yeovil Glove Co Ltd*,[144] the English Court of Appeal held that the words "in consideration for" (in the equivalent English legislation[145]) meant "by reason of" or "having regard to the existence of". In so deciding the Court upheld the decision of Plowman J;[146] Willmer LJ stated:[147]

> "I agree with the learned judge that the expression 'in consideration for the charge' means in this context 'in consideration of the fact that the charge exists', and that the relevant question of fact is whether the payments subsequently made would have been made if the charge had not been given. If that is right, the learned judge's finding of fact that unless the charge had been given the bank would not have allowed the company to go on operating its accounts would seem to be conclusive against the liquidator".

The court approved and applied the decision of Romer J in *Re Thomas Mortimer Ltd*.[148] In that case, an insolvent company owing £58,180 to its bank created a floating charge in favour of its bank as security for £50,000. Thereafter the company made payments to the bank of £41,311 and drew out from its account £51,248. Romer J held that the payments in went towards discharging the pre-charge debt and the subsequent drawings was cash paid to the company subsequently to the creation of and in consideration for the charge.

"unless ... the company ... was solvent"

[13.34] The critical test in this section are the words, "unless it is proved that the company immediately after the creation of the charge was solvent". The debentureholder seeking to uphold the charge thus has to prove the solvency of the chargor at the time the chargor created the security.

This section was considered by the High Court in 1978 and the decision of McWilliam J was unanimously affirmed by the Supreme Court in 1980. It was held in *Re Creation Printing Co Ltd, Crowley v Northern Bank Finance Corporation Ltd and GP Kelso Ltd*[149] that:

1. Immediately after the creation of the floating charge, the chargor had been unable to pay its debts as they became due and accordingly, had not been solvent within the meaning of s 288;[150]

---

[144] [1964] 2 All ER 849.
[145] Companies Act, 1948, s 322.
[146] [1962] 3 All ER 400.
[147] [1964] 2 All ER 849 at 861.
[148] (1925) 4 LDAB 3.
[149] [1981] IR 353; Milman, 'Test of Commercial Solvency Rejected' (1983) 4 Co Law 231.
[150] See also the Companies Act, 1963, s 214 which provides that: "A company shall be deemed to be unable to pay its debts (c) if it is proved to the satisfaction of the court that the company is unable to pay its debts, and in determining whether a company is unable to pay its debts, the court shall take into account the contingent and prospective liabilities of the company."

2. Where a company intended to continue to conduct its business after it had created a floating charge, the value of its fixed and moveable assets at that time must be ignored in determining whether it had been solvent within the meaning of s 288;

3. For the purpose of establishing that a company was solvent within the meaning of s 288, the onus of proof lies on the person who asserts the validity of the floating charge.

[13.35] This decision was applied in *Smurfit Paribas Bank Ltd v AAB Export Finance Ltd (No 2)*[151] where Barron J stated:[152]

"The test of insolvency, that the company should be unable to pay its debts as they fell due, is one laid down in *Crowley v Northern Bank Finance*.[153] It is taken in distinction to the test of balance sheet assets. The company must be able to pay its debts in the way in which it proposes to pay them, ie by continuing in business. So it cannot take into account the value of any assets needed to continue the business save insofar as such assets might be available as security for a loan."

[13.36] A floating charge created by a company, within 12 months prior to the commencement of its winding up, in favour of an officer[154] of the company to secure indebtedness to such officer, and such indebtedness was wholly or partly discharged, will be invalid to the extent of the repayment of the indebtedness unless it is proved that the company immediately after the creation of the charge was solvent.[155]

[151.] [1991] 2 IR 19.

[152.] *Ibid* at 27.

[153.] [1981] IR 353.

[154.] Companies Act, 1963, s 289(3) defines "officer" for the purpose of that section as including, "the spouse, child or nominee of an officer." This may include a shadow director - see MacCann, *Butterworth Ireland Companies Acts*, (1993) fn 4d to s 289.

[155.] Companies Act, 1963, s 289(1).

Chapter 14

Security over Debts

ASSIGNMENT OF DEBTS BY WAY OF SECURITY[1]

[14.01] The assignment of debts appears to have begun around the time of the English conquest of Ireland in the twelfth century when the Jews assigned debts to the Crown towards the discharge of their tax liabilities.[2] However, following the expulsion of the Jews from England at the end of the thirteenth century,[3] common law did not recognise the assignment of a debt. This was due first to the impossibility of delivery of possession, secondly to the perception that it constituted maintenance, thirdly that the debt was a personal matter between the debtor and creditor and fourthly that a debt was too uncertain to be assigned.[4]

Assignment under the Judicature Act

[14.02] Statutory recognition was given to the assignment of a debt by the Supreme Court of Judicature Act (Ireland), 1877, s 28(6) of which reads:

> Any absolute assignment, by writing under the hand of the assignor (not purporting to be by way of charge only), of any debt or other legal chose in action, of which express notice in writing shall have been given to the debtor, trustee, or other person from whom the assignor would have been entitled to receive or claim such debt or chose in action, shall be and be deemed to have been effectual in law (subject to all equities which would have been entitled to priority over the right of the assignee if this Act had not passed) to pass and transfer the legal right to such debt or chose in action from the date of such notice, and all legal and other remedies for the same, and the power to give a good discharge for the same, without the concurrence of the assignor ...

[14.03] Where a debt is assigned by way of security, for the assignee to sue the debtor without joining the assignor:

(i)   the assignment must be absolute (subject to a proviso for redemption),

(ii)   it must be of the entire debt, and

(iii)   notice of it must be given to the debtor.

---

[1] For further treatment of this subject see *Chitty on Contracts* (26th ed) Vol 1 Ch 19.
[2] *Bailey* 47 (1931) LQR 516, 48 (1932) LQR 248 and 547.
[3] *Ibid.*
[4] Biscoe, *Credit Factoring* (Butterworths, 1975) p 96.

The principal benefit of being able to take an assignment of a debt in compliance with the Judicature Act, as security for moneys due by the assignor to the assignee, is that the assignor drops out of the arrangement and the assignee has direct recourse to the debtor. Title to the debt is effectively passed to the assignee so that, in the event of the assignor's liquidation, the assignee will have priority to that debt in preference to the assignor's other creditors.[5] If the debtor is a Department of the State or a semi-State agency the benefits of having the debt assigned are obviously greater in that the solvency of the debtor should not be a concern, which it might otherwise be. It should be noted though that such a debtor may well preclude, in its agreement with the creditor, the creditor assigning the benefit of the debt. In *Helston Securities Ltd v Hertfordshire County Council*,[6] a contractor agreed to carry out road works for the County Council. The contract provided that the contractor could not assign the contract or any part of it without the County Council's consent. The contractor assigned the amount owing to him to the plaintiff. The court held the assignment to be invalid and that the County Council was entitled to refuse payment to the plaintiff. The decision is a warning to legal advisers when preparing an assignment to ensure that the subject matter is capable of assignment. The question then arises as to what are the requirements to come within the provisions of the Judicature Act so as to obtain the benefits of that Act.

[14.04] Although the assignment must be absolute and "(not purporting to be by way of charge only)", an assignment may nonetheless be taken by way of security and still comply with the Judicature Act. This principle was established in *Burlinson v Hall*[7] and followed in *Tancred v Delagoa Day and East Africa Railway Co*[8] where in each case an assignment to secure moneys due or to become due was taken with a proviso for redemption or re-assignment. In the former case Day J, in explaining the distinction between an absolute assignment by way of security and a charge, stated that the deed although not absolute as a sale was "absolute as contradistinguished from conditional", and that the assignee can deal as he thinks fit. He pointed out that:[9]

> "a charge differs altogether from a mortgage. By a charge the title is not transferred, but the person creating the charge merely says that out of a particular fund he will discharge a particular debt. But a charge differs from an assignment. A charge on a debt confers rights on the person to whom the charge is given to have it enforced by assignment - not by action against the

---

5. *Rutter v Everett* (1895) 2 Ch 872.
6. [1978] 3 All ER 262.
7. (1884) 12 QBD 347.
8. (1889) 23 QBD 239.
9. (1884) 12 QBD 347 at 350.

debtor, but by proceedings against the person who created the charge to assign the debt."

The latter decision was supported by the Court of Appeal in *Hughes v Pump House Hotel Co Ltd*[10] where Cozens-Hardy LJ stated:

"The principle of the decision [*in Tancred v Delagoa Bay and East Africa Railway Co*] ought not to be confined to the case where there is an express provision for reassignment. Where there is an absolute assignment of the debt, but by way of security, equity would imply a right to a reassignment or redemption, and the sub-section would apply to the case of such an absolute assignment ... A mortgage is not mentioned in the enactment; but, where there is an absolute assignment of the debt, the limiting words as to a charge only are not sufficient to exclude a mortgage".

[14.05] The reference to "any debt" means the entire debt. In *Conlan v Carlow County Council*[11] it was held that an assignment of part of a debt is not within s 28(6) of the Supreme Court of Judicature Act (Ireland),1877. However, the court held that the assignee of part of a debt may maintain a common law action in respect of such part, where all persons interested in the debt are parties to the action.

Notice of Assignment

[14.06] The statute prescribes that "express notice in writing" be given to the debtor. Any delay in giving notice does not affect the legality of the assignment itself but until notice is given the assignee leaves himself open to the assignor entering into a further assignment with a third party and notice of that second assignment being given to the debtor prior to notice of the first assignment. In such event, the first assignee will lose priority as against the debtor to the second assignee.[12] The delay in giving notice however will not affect the assignee's rights against the assignor and upon subsequent notice being given the assignee acquires the right to sue in his own name without joining the assignor. Until the notice is given the assignment remains valid in equity.[13]

There is no stipulation as to who should give the notice. In view of the fact that the assignor will have a relationship with the debtor and that the assignee might not have, it is common practice for the assignor to give notice to the debtor in a form and manner agreed with the assignee. Despite the "postal rule" under the law of contract,[14] notice is considered to have been given when it has been

---

[10.] [1902] 2 KB 190.
[11.] [1912] 2 IR 535; 46 ILTR 183.
[12.] Rule in *Dearle v Hall* (1823-28) 3 Russ 1.
[13.] *Grundy v Broadbent* [1918] 1 IR 433.
[14.] See Chesire Fifoot & Furmston's *Law of Contract* (13th ed) Butterworths, p 53.

received by or on behalf of the debtor. This was established by the decision in *Holt v Heatherfield Trust Ltd*[15] where Atkinson J held:[16]

"The date of 'such notice' is the date of a notice which has been given to the debtor, and refers back to the express notice in writing mentioned earlier in the section. It is express notice in writing given to the debtor, and, in my judgment, the date of such notice is the date on which it is received by or on behalf of the debtor. If the notice arrives at his place of business, and he happens to be away and does not see it personally for another day or two, I think that would be immaterial; it would be received on his behalf. I think it is the date of the receipt by him or on his behalf. It cannot be the date of the notice, because a notice might be written and dated a week before it was posted, and it would be absurd to suppose that that would be effective."

Accordingly, the notice of assignment should contain a form of acknowledgement for completion by the debtor who on receipt of the notice of assignment should be asked to acknowledge receipt in the form of the attached acknowledgement. The form of acknowledgement will not only acknowledge receipt of the notice of assignment but will also acknowledge:

1. That the amount of the debt specified is due and payable,

2. That the debtor has no set-off or counterclaim in respect of the debt, and

3. The debtor has not received any prior notice of an assignment.[17]

[14.07] Care must be taken in the notice of assignment either to enter the date of assignment correctly or not at all. In *WF Harrison & Co Ltd v Burke*[18] the English Court of Appeal followed an earlier decision[19] by holding that a notice which referred to an assignment of 6 December 1954, rather than the correct date of 7 December 1954, did not comply with the requirements of the Judicature Act. As Lord Denning explained in a subsequent decision,[20] "the short ground of those decisions was that the notice with a wrong date was a notice of a non-existing document". The notice of assignment, however, does not need to take any particular form to comply with the requirements of the Judicature Act. Widgery LJ pointed out in the English Court of Appeal,[21] "that the only formality required by the section is that express notice in writing be given to the debtor". In the same case Lord Denning said:[22]

[15.] [1942] 2 KB 1.

[16.] *Ibid* at 6.

[17.] See also Milnes Holden, *The Law and Practice of Banking* Vol 2 (7th ed, 1986) Ch 29.

[18.] [1956] 1 WLR 419.

[19.] *Stanley v English Fibres Industries Ltd* (1899) 68 LJ QB 839.

[20.] *Van Lynn Developments Ltd v Pelias Construction Co Ltd* [1969] 1 QB 607.

[21.] *Ibid* at 615.

[22.] *Ibid* at 613.

"It seems to me to be unnecessary that it [the notice] should give the date of the assignment so long as it makes it plain that there has in fact been an assignment so that the debtor knows to whom he has to pay the debt in the future."

[14.08] The historical and indeed current practice of indicating the date of the assignment on the notice of assignment arises from the wish of the assignor to avoid any misunderstanding as to what debt has been assigned. As Widgery LJ has pointed out[23] there is no particular form required other than that it be in writing. A suggested simple form of assignment is:

Notice of Assignment

To: [Name and address of debtor]

Take notice that we have assigned the debt of £[amount of debt] due by you to us in favour of [name of assignee]. Kindly acknowledge receipt by signing the attached notice of acknowledgement and send it to [name of assignee]

Dated the [ ] day of [ ]

Signed for and on behalf of assignor

Notice of Acknowledgement

To: [Name and address of assignee]

We hereby acknowledge receipt of a notice of assignment dated [ ] day of [ ] in respect of a debt of £[ ] due by us to [name of assignor]. We hereby confirm that the said debt is due and payable without set-off or counterclaim and we have not received any prior notice of assignment in respect of the said debt.

Signed for and on behalf of debtor.

Obviously, the actual form of notice and acknowledgement will vary depending upon the complexity of the arrangements. The date in the notice of assignment is simply a way of recording when the notice was sent. As already indicated[24] the notice may be given by the assignee but in practice, on the assignor's execution of the assignment, the assignor should execute the notice and hand it to the assignee who will deliver it to the debtor.

Equitable Assignment

[14.09] For a debt to be assignable under the Judicature Act, it must be a definite and ascertained amount[25] and although authorities differ, it must be a present debt (future debts are not assignable at law).[26] Where an assignment does not

---

[23.] *Ibid* at 615.

[24.] Para **[14.06]**.

[25.] *Jones v Humphrey* [1902] 1 KB 10.

[26.] *Re Clarke* (1887) 26 Ch D 348; *Holt v Heatherfield Trust Ltd* [1942] 2 KB 1; but see Lord Alverstone CJ in *Jones v Humphrey* [1902] 1 KB 10.

comply with the requirements of the Judicature Act, the courts of equity may nonetheless give effect to the assignment provided consideration has been given for the assignment.[27] Lord Watson in his judgment in *Tailby v The Official Receiver*[28] sets out the position clearly:

> "The rule of equity which applies to the assignment of future choses in action is, as I understand it, a very simple one. Choses in action do not come within the scope of the Bills of Sale Acts, and though not yet existing, may nevertheless be the subject of present assignment. As soon as they come into existence, assignees who have given valuable consideration will, if the new chose in action is in the disposal of their assignor, take precisely the same right and interest as if it had actually belonged to him, or had been within his disposition and control at the time when the assignment was made. There is but one condition which must be fulfilled in order to make the assignee's right attach to a future chose in action, which is, that, on its coming into existence, it shall answer the description in the assignment, or, in other words, that it shall be capable of being identified as the thing, or as one of the very things assigned. When there is no uncertainty as to its identification, the beneficial interest will immediately vest in the assignee".

A drawback however is that the assignor will not have dropped out of the contract and will need to be joined in any action by the assignee for the recovery of the debt.[29] However, the assignor may by power of attorney or by agreeing to the appointment of a receiver over its debts, on the occurrence of stipulated events, effectively have given authority to the assignee or its agent to take steps to recover the debt in the name of the assignor.

Notwithstanding that the creditor is required to have the assignor join in any proceedings for recovery of the debt where the debt has been assigned by way of equitable assignment, it is still prudent, unless there are compelling commercial reasons otherwise, to give notice of the assignment to the debtor. This is to maintain priority over subsequent equitable assignments[30] and to indicate to the debtor that he pays the assignor at his peril rather than paying the creditor who is now the owner of the debt.[31]

The ultimate effect of the foregoing is that if a creditor wishes to take debts as security for moneys owed to it by a person, it may take an assignment of present debts by having the person execute an absolute assignment subject only to a proviso for redemption on satisfaction of the moneys due and arrange for notice

---

[27.] *Holroyd v Marshall* 10 HLC 191; *Re Clarke* (1887) 26 Ch D 348; *Tailby v The Official Receiver* (1888) 13 App Cas 523; *Holt v Heatherfield Trust Ltd* [1942] 2 KB I.

[28.] (1888) 13 App Cas 523 at 533.

[29.] See the judgment of Viscount Cave LC in *Performing Right Society Ltd v London Theatre of Varieties* [1924] AC 1.

[30.] *Marchant v Norton, Power & Co* [1901] 2 KB 829.

[31.] *Brice v Bannister* (1878) 3 QBD 569.

of such assignment with attendant paying instructions to be given to the debtor. If the creditor wishes to take future debts as security for moneys owing to it, or if it does not wish to give notice to the debtor, the courts will give effect to such assignments, provided all other matters as to capacity and execution are complied with.

Registration of Assignments

[14.10] Particulars of an assignment of a book debt,[32] whether absolute or otherwise, which is given by a company to secure the payment of a debt or obligation, should be filed in the Companies Registration Office within 21 days of the creation of the assignment.[33] Otherwise the assignment will be void as against the liquidator and any creditor of the Company.[34]

[14.11] A good illustration of this point is the English decision in *Re Kent & Sussex Sawmills Ltd*.[35] In that case a bank provided financing facilities for a company in connection with its contract with the Ministry of Fuel and Power. A condition of the bank's facility was the completion by the company of a letter of authorisation to the Ministry which stated:

> "With reference to the above-mentioned contract, we hereby authorise you to remit all moneys due thereunder direct to this company's account at Westminster Bank Ltd, Crowborough, whose receipt shall be your sufficient discharge. These instructions are to be regarded as irrevocable unless the said bank should consent to their cancellation in writing ..."

When the company went into liquidation, the bank contended that the letter amounted to a sale to the bank by the company of its debt to it under the contract.

In his judgment Wynn-Parry J noted that in *Bell v The London and North Western Railway Co*[36] a railway contractor gave his bankers a letter directing the railway company to pass the cheques which might become due to him "to his account with the bank", and it was held that that was not an equitable assignment, but that it would have been if it had directed the cheques to be passed to the bank. Wynn-Parry J held that this decision would have been followed if the company's letter had stopped at the end of the first sentence, but the additional words to be considered were:

> "these instructions are to be regarded as irrevocable unless the said bank should consent to their cancellation in writing ...".

---

32. For its meaning, see para **[14.15]** below.
33. Companies Act, 1963, s 99(2)(e), paras **[17.14]**-**[17.18]**.
34. Companies Act, 1963, s 99(1).
35. [1947] 1 Ch 177; see also para **[17.28]**.
36. (1852) 15 Beav 548.

Wynn-Parry J continued:[37]

> "Effect must be given to those words and, in my judgment, the proper way of construing this letter, looking at it as a whole, is never to lose sight of the circumstances that the relationship of the two parties in question, the company and the bank, was that of borrower and lender, and that this letter was brought into existence in connection with a proposed transaction of borrowing by the company and lending by the bank. So regarded, I think the opening words of the second sentence fall naturally into the picture and that they must be regarded as having been introduced for the protection of the bank. Once that is admitted, it throws light on the whole of the letter and serves to underline what is obviously equally the intention of the first sentence, namely to provide protection for the bank. It, therefore, appears to me that the result of that is to take this case out of *Bell v London & North Western Railway Company* and to lead to the conclusion that I must treat this letter as amounting to an equitable assignment."

This then posed the question as to whether the assignment was one by way of sale or by way of security. Wynn-Parry J stated that *prima facie* in looking at any documentation in the context of a borrower and a lender one could expect to discover that the document was intended to be given as security for the repayment of indebtedness. Counsel for the bank however put forward the view that the ultimate test must be whether there is an equity of redemption and that the letter disclosed no equity of redemption. Wynn-Parry J, held however, that by implication an equity of redemption is to be discovered in the language of the second sentence, as there was no commercial business reason for those words except on the basis that the parties deliberately contemplated that circumstances might arise for the bank's cancellation of the instructions. The court thus decided that the letter constituted an equitable assignment by way of security, thus constituting a charge on book debts, and was void as against the liquidator because particulars were not registered within the statutory period.

The decision in *Re Kent & Sussex Sawmills Ltd*[38] is of relevance to the practitioner in Ireland as there are many financings where debts due to companies (whether due by Departments of State, local authorities or otherwise) are assigned to banks as security for bonds issued by banks on behalf of their customers. Such assignments may require registration, depending on the wording of the assignments.[39]

[14.12] Another decision of note for bankers and their lawyers when financing construction contracts is that of *Contemporary Cottages (NZ) Ltd v Margin*

[37.] [1947] 1 Ch 177 at 180.

[38.] [1947] 1 Ch 177.

[39.] See further paras **[17.14]-[17.18]**.

Traders Ltd.[40] In that case the plaintiff, which carried on the business of erecting and selling cottages, assigned the benefit of each contract to build a cottage to the defendant as security for loans made in respect of each contract. Notice of the assignments was given to each owner but particulars of the assignments were not registered.

In deciding that the assignments were properly classified as charges and not as absolute assignments, the High Court of Auckland noted that the Court of Appeal when previously considering such question[41] had applied Cave J's decision in *Beckett v Tower Assets Co*,[42] where Cave J stated that the real question to be decided is the intention of the parties. To ascertain that intention what must be considered, according to Cave J, is:

1. The form of the transaction,

2. The substance of the transaction,

3. The position of the parties, and

4. The circumstances under which the transaction came about.[43]

The Auckland High Court considered those factors from which the parties' intentions should be inferred and found each of the factors pointed to an intention to create security, namely:

1. The form of the transactions was more appropriate to a loan and charge rather than sale and assignment - loan memoranda, covenants for reassignment on repayment of the loans, recitals in the assignments specifying, (a) request for a loan, (b) agreement to make an advance, (c) execution of memorandum pursuant to the Moneylenders Act, and (d) agreement to grant security for a loan,

2. The substance of the transactions was that of loans,

3. The position of the parties was clearly that of finance company and building company. These factors led him to the decision that the assignments were properly classified as charges and not as absolute assignments, and

4. The circumstances under which the loans came about could be described as the common situation of a construction company receiving working capital by loans against its construction work.

[40.] [1981] 2 NZLR 114.

[41.] *Automatic Association (Canterbury) Inc v Australasian Secured Deposits Ltd* [1973] NZLR 417.

[42.] [1891] 1 QB 1.

[43.] See also *Saunderson and Co (in liq) v Clark* (1913) 29 TLR 579.

[14.13] A useful and comprehensive guide as to ascertaining whether an assignment is one by way of sale (not requiring registration) or one by way of mortgage or charge (requiring registration) is set out in Romer LJ's decision in the English Court of Appeal in *Re George Inglefield Ltd*.[44] Because of its clarity in highlighting the differences and its help in focusing the mind of a practitioner in deciding whether or not an assignment requires registration it may be useful to set out the relevant passage:

> "... the essential differences that exist between a transaction of sale and a transaction of mortgage and charge. In a transaction of sale the vendor is not entitled to get back the subject-matter of the sale by returning to the purchaser the money that has passed between them. In the case of a mortgage or charge, the mortgagor is entitled, until he has been foreclosed, to get back the subject-matter of the mortgage or charge by returning to the mortgagee the money that has passed between them. The second essential difference is that if the mortgagee realises the subject-matter of the mortgage for a sum more than sufficient to repay him, with interest and the costs, the money that has passed between him and the mortgagor he has to account to the mortgagor for the surplus. If the purchaser sells the subject-matter of the purchase, and realises a profit, of course he has not got to account to the vendor for the profit. Thirdly, if the mortgagee realises the mortgage property for a sum that is insufficient to repay him the money that he has paid to the mortgagor, together with interest and costs, then the mortgagee is entitled to recover from the mortgagor the balance of the money, either because there is a covenant by the mortgagor to repay the money advanced by the mortgagee, or because of the existence of the simple contract debt which is created by the mere fact of the advance having been made. If the purchaser were to resell the purchased property at a price which was insufficient to recoup him the money that he paid to the vendor, of course he would not be entitled to recover the balance from the vendor."

Greene LJ's judgment in the English Court of Appeal in *Ashby, Warner & Co Ltd v Simmons*[45] is also helpful. The Court held in that case that registration was not required.

[14.14] Although it may be considered by some that whether or not an assignment is registrable is simply a matter of academic debate and when in doubt register, it should be borne in mind that in practice it is more usual for the practitioner to be asked by the assignee not to register if at all possible to accommodate the wishes of the assignor, particularly where the assignor has given a negative pledge to other creditors. The burden of deciding whether or not to register falls squarely on the assignee's legal adviser (although it is the assignor's duty to register where appropriate[46]).

---

44. [1933] 1 Ch 1 at 27.
45. [1936] 2 All ER 679; see para **[17.28]**.
46. Companies Act, 1963, s 100(1).

The points for the practitioner to note from the decisions in *Re Kent & Sussex Sawmills Ltd*[47] and *Contemporary Cottages (NZ) Ltd v Margin Traders Ltd*[48] are:

1. A company's letter of authorisation to its debtor to discharge the debt by payment to its account in a bank (rather than direct to a bank) does not of itself constitute an equitable assignment requiring registration.

2. A letter as in (1) with an additional indication that the instructions are irrevocable except with the consent of the bank is an equitable assignment by way of security particulars of which are required to be registered in the Companies Registration Office.

3. An assignment of debt with a proviso for re-assignment or discharge of moneys due or with a provision, whether expressly stated or which can be implied from the surrounding circumstances, that the assignment is security for finance being made available will require registration under s 99 of the Companies Act, 1963.

In each case however, the debt the subject of the assignment must be a "book debt" otherwise particulars of the assignment are not registrable[49] (unless the assignment secures the issue of debentures or is deemed to be a floating security[50]).

FIXED CHARGES OVER BOOK DEBTS AND OTHER DEBTS[51]

Meaning of Book Debt

[14.15] The need may arise when examining the nature and operation of fixed charges over book debts to understand the meaning of book debts. This is due to the fact that particulars of charges on book debts of a company are required to be registered in the Companies Registration Office[52] but not particulars of a charge on debts[53] that are not book debts (other than where the charge secures the issue of debentures or it is a floating charge). The question as to whether a debt is a book debt is equally relevant to an assignment of debts by way of security.[54]

---

47. [1947] 1 Ch 177.
48. [1981] 2 NZLR 114.
49. The Companies Act, 1963, s 99(2)(e) requires registration of particulars of charges, mortgages or assignments by way of security of "book debts of the company"; see further para **[17.14]**.
50. Paragraphs (a) and (f) of the Companies Act, 1963, s 99(2).
51. This section proved the basis of a paper delivered by the author to the Center for International Legal Studies - Salzburg 1996.
52. Companies Act, 1963, s 99(2)(e).
53. For a discourse on the notion of debt see MacCormack, 'Debt' (1977) Ir Jur 187.
54. See paras **[14.10]-[14.14]** above.

A book debt may be described as a debt which arises in the ordinary course of trade and which is, or should in the normal course of business be, entered in the books of a trading company.[55] If a debt is not a book debt, it will nonetheless be caught by any security which charges "book debts and other debts" of the company.[56]

Development of Book Debt Security

[14.16] As banks increasingly sought to take full advantage of the benefits of a fixed charge to counteract the preferential status of the Revenue Commissioners,[57] inevitably a series of court decisions was required to clarify the question as to whether it is possible to take a fixed charge over future book debts.[58] The current process began in 1978 with *Siebe Gorman & Co Ltd v Barclays Bank Ltd*[59] and the law continued to develop[60] with the decisions in *Re Lakeglen Construction Ltd,*[61] *Re Armagh Shoes Ltd,*[62] *Re Keenan Brothers Ltd,*[63] *Re AH Masser Ltd,*[64] *Re Wogan's (Drogheda) Ltd,*[65] *Re Holidair Ltd,*[66] and *Re New Bullas Trading Ltd.*[67]

[14.17] In *Siebe Gorman & Co Ltd v Barclays Bank Ltd*[68] Slade J held in the English High Court that:[69]

> "It is perfectly possible in law for a mortgagor, by way of continuing security for future advances, to grant to a mortgagee a charge on future book debts in a form which creates in equity a specific charge on the proceeds of such debts as soon as they are received and consequently prevents the mortgagor from

---

55. For the meaning of book debt see also Gough, *Company Charges* (2nd ed, 1996) Butterworths 677-681, and *Pennington's Company Law* (6th ed) Butterworths 499.
56. To ascertain Whether or not a debt comes within the meaning of book debt see paras **[17.14]**-**[17.38]**.
57. See Companies Act, 1963, ss 98 and 285; Johnston, 'Charges over Moveables - Fixed or Floating?', The Irish Centre for Commercial Law Studies, 18 January 1996.
58. For a further review of the issues see Courtney, *The Law of Private Companies* (Butterworths, 1994) para 14.032 to 14.039.
59. [1979] 2 LLR 142.
60. For a review of the legal development of fixed charges over book debts see Berg, 'Charges Over Book Debts: A Reply' (1995) JBL 433; Marks, 'Taking Charges Over Book Debts' The Irish Centre for Commercial Law Studies, 18 January 1996.
61. [1980] IR 347.
62. [1984] BCLC 405.
63. [1985] IR 401.
64. [1986] IR 455.
65. [1993] 1 IR 157.
66. [1994] 1 IR 416.
67. [1993] BCLC 1389 and [1994] 1 BCLC 485.
68. [1979] 2 LLR 142.
69. *Ibid* at 159.

disposing of an unencumbered title to the subject matter of such charge without the mortgagee's consent, even before the mortgagee has taken steps to enforce its security".

In that case, clause 3 of the debenture provided that:

"The Company as beneficial owner hereby charges with payment or discharge of all monies and liabilities hereby covenanted to be paid or discharged by the Company:

... (d) by way of first fixed charge all book debts and other debts now and from time to time due or owing to the Company".

Slade J went on to say:

"I see no reason why the Court should not give effect to the intention of the parties, as stated in clause 3(d), that the charge should be a first fixed charge on book debts".

Clause 5 of the debenture stated:

During the continuance of this security the Company ...

(c) shall pay into the Company's account with the bank all monies which it may receive in respect of the book debts and other debts hereby charged and shall not without the prior consent of the bank in writing purport to charge or assign the same in favour of any other person and shall if called upon to do so by the bank execute a legal assignment of such book debts and other debts to the bank".

Although in the circumstances the bank's charge was held not to be effective as a fixed one (due to the absence of notice of the restrictive provisions), the decision is nevertheless of real importance as it proved to be the benchmark for the widespread taking of fixed charges over future book debts in Ireland and the Supreme Court's ultimate approval of such charges.[70]

[14.18] In December 1978 in *Re Lakeglen Construction Ltd*[71] Costello J was called on to consider whether a fixed charge was created by a debenture which provided that as security for the payment of moneys agreed to be paid:

"the company and the holding company as beneficial owners hereby charge in favour of the major creditors all their respective book debts and all rights and powers of recovery in respect thereof to hold the same unto the major creditors absolutely."

The debenture showed a clear intention to create fixed charges over other assets and a floating charge over the undertaking. While it could be inferred from the order in which the assets were set out in the debenture (first an assignment of

---

[70.] *Re Keenan Brothers Ltd* [1985] IR 401.
[71.] [1980] IR 347.

plant, machinery, equipment, printing implements and utensils, secondly a charge on book debts, thirdly a fixed charge on goodwill and uncalled capital, fourthly a fixed charge on shares and fifthly a floating charge on "all other their respective undertakings and assets") that a fixed charge was intended, taking into account the absence of the reference to a fixed charge and the absence of any other restrictive provisions, Costello J held the charge to be a floating one.

[14.19] While at the time some considered this judgment to be the answer to the decision in *Siebe Gorman*, it was clear from a reading of the judgment that Costello J's judgment was not inconsistent or contrary to that of Slade J. Indeed in his concluding remarks in his judgment Costello J stated:

> "In reaching the conclusions which I have just stated, I have not ignored the recent judgment of Slade J in *Siebe Gorman v Barclays Bank*. It seems to me, however, that the provisions of the document which Slade J was considering were considerably different to those in the present case and that no great assistance is to be found from the conclusions he reached on the facts before him".

In reaching his conclusion, Costello J asked the question whether at the time of execution did the parties intend that the company would remain free to receive the book debts as though the debenture had not been created. In answering the question the judge considered that the points to bear in mind were the fact that:

1. The company was a trading company,

2. The parties agreed that the company was permitted to carry on its business, and

3. In the normal course it would create difficulties for the company if it was required to hand over its book debts to the debenture holder as and when it received them. The judge held that the absence of a direction to hand over the book debts supported the inference that it was intended the company was permitted to deal with its book debts in the ordinary course of its business.

Costello J concluded his analysis of the debenture by reference to the tests laid down in the decisions of *Houldsworth v Yorkshire Woolcombers Association Ltd*[72] and *Illingworth v Houldsworth*[73] by stating:

> "I am satisfied that the parties intended that the company should carry on its business in the ordinary way and that for this purpose it was licensed (until some future contingency arose which would justify the intervention by the

---

72. [1903] 2 Ch 284.
73. [1904] AC 355.

debenture holders) to receive payment for its debtors from time to time without regard to the charge created by the debenture over the book debts".

[14.20] It was a further three years before a decision of substance arose on this topic - this time it was in the Northern Ireland High Court where Hutton J held in *Re Armagh Shoes Ltd*[74] that a fixed charge over future book debts had not been created. Although this judgment did not uphold a charge which was stated to be a fixed charge, the validity of such charges continued to be undecided as in that case it appeared the validity of the charge might have been upheld had there been appropriate restrictions on the company dealing with its book debts - restrictions which had by then been brought into operation in the drafting of many of such charges.

The deed provided that the mortgagor:

"as beneficial owner hereby charges in the favour of the Bank by way of Fixed Charge all receivables debtors plant machinery fixtures fittings and ancillary equipment now or at any time hereafter belonging to the Mortgagor".

In endeavouring to ascertain whether the charge was in reality fixed or floating, Hutton J like others before him, cited Romer LJ's test of a floating charge.[75] Hutton J considered that the words, "now or at any time hereafter belonging to the Mortgagor" indicated that the company would from time to time in the future and in the ordinary course of its business change its plant and ancillary equipment. He considered that if the adjective "Fixed" was omitted from the term "Fixed Charge", the Deed contemplated that until some future step is taken by the chargee, the company could carry on its business in the ordinary way. He went on:[76]

"Therefore the question arises whether the description of the charge as a "fixed charge" constitutes the charge a fixed charge and prevents it from being a floating charge. In my judgment it does not, and I consider that the authorities establish that where the remainder of the wording of a deed reveals the three characteristics described by Romer LJ, the fact that the deed by its express words purports to create a fixed or specific charge does not operate to prevent the charge from being a floating one".

Hutton J considered that his judgment was distinguishable from that of Slade J in *Siebe Gorman & Co Ltd v Barclays Bank Ltd*[77] as there was no clause similar to clause 5(c) of the *Siebe Gorman* debenture. Hutton J held that it was "a necessary implication from the deed that the company was to have the right or licence to deal with the assets, comprised within the ambit of the charge, in the

---

[74] [1984] BCLC 405.
[75] See para **[13.03]**.
[76] [1984] BCLC 405.
[77] [1979] 2 LLR 142.

ordinary course of its business until the Bank decided to enforce the charge" and accordingly the charge was a floating charge.

[14.21] A further three years elapsed before the High Court in Ireland held in *Re Keenan Brothers Ltd*[78] that a debenture, which specified that a charge was fixed and furthermore provided for the proceeds to be paid into a special account, did not in fact create a fixed charge over future book debts. By this stage it had become common practice for banks to take fixed charges over future book debts with in many cases the additional protection of a procedure for the payment of proceeds into a special account.[79] Keane J's decision was welcomed by those who considered such charges could not effectively be created, but the judgment drew much criticism.[80] Despite signalling the apparent death of fixed charges over future book debts,[81] banks continued to include them in their debentures and on 22 November 1985 the concept was given the ultimate seal of approval by an unanimous decision of the Supreme Court.

The facts of the case were that the company created a charge in favour of Allied Irish Banks Ltd and a debenture in favour of Allied Irish Investment Bank Ltd.[82] Clause 2 of the charge read:

> "The company as beneficial owner and by way of continuing security HEREBY CHARGES with the payment of the principal moneys, interest and other lawful charges as aforesaid all the book debts and other debts present and future of the company which said charge shall be a first fixed charge".

The charge also contained the following:

> "The company shall pay into an account with the bank designated for that purpose all monies which it may receive in respect of the book debts and other debts hereby charged and shall not without the prior consent of the bank in writing make any withdrawals or direct any payment from the said account.
> The company shall if called upon to do so by the bank:

> (a) execute a legal assignment of its book debts and other debts to the bank;

> (b) deliver an account to the bank of the particulars of and the amounts due in respect of its book debts and other debts at that date.

> The company shall not without the prior consent in writing of the bank purport to charge, waive, assign or otherwise deal with its book debts or other debts in favour of any other person."

---

78. [1985] IR 401.
79. Johnston, 'Fixed Charges over Book Debts' (1985) BLR 104.
80. McCormack, 'Fixed Charges on Future Book Debts' (1987) Co Law 3; Pearce, 'Fixed Charges on Book Debts' (1987) JBL 18.
81. Byrne and Tomkin, 'Charges on Book Debts - *Siebe Gorman* in Ireland' (1985) NLJ 443.
82. [1985] IR 401 at 404.

Subsequently, the company and the bank entered into an agreement which provided that the bank would open an account designated, "Book Debts Receivable Account" in the joint names of the bank and the company, and that all book debts and other debts received by the company should be lodged to the credit of that account and no withdrawals should be made except by a cheque or other instrument signed by the company and countersigned by the bank. The agreement provided also that at the company's request the bank might at its discretion permit the company from time to time to withdraw or transfer from that account moneys required by the company for carrying on its business.

Although the agreement was signed only three months prior to the appointment of a provisional liquidator to the company it was nonetheless implemented and any question of fraudulent preference was not raised.

The debenture contained similar but not identical provisions. As well as specifying the charge to be, "by way of first fixed legal charge its present and future book debts and all rights and powers in respect thereof" and containing a negative pledge, the debenture provided that:

7. The company at all times during the continuance of this security:

    7.1 Shall pay all moneys received by it from time to time in respect of book debts into an account with Allied Irish Banks Ltd at 36 Tullow Street, Carlow, designated for that purpose and shall not without the prior consent of the bank in writing make any withdrawal from the said account nor direct any payment to be made from the said account.

    7.2 Shall from time to time furnish to the bank such financial statements and information respecting its assets and liabilities as the bank may reasonably require and in particular an itemised list of full particulars of all book debts outstanding at any given date.

    7.3 Shall not without the consent in writing of the bank carry on its business other than in the ordinary and normal course.

    7.4 Shall not without the consent in writing of the bank assign, discount, remit, waive or otherwise diminish or dispose of its book debts other than by collecting the same and lodging the proceeds in accordance with the provisions of clause 7.1 hereof.

For the purposes of the Court's decision, both the charge and supplemental agreement and the debenture were considered together. In line with Costello J's judgment in *Re Lakeglen Construction Ltd*,[83] Keane J began his judgment in the High Court by considering the meaning of a floating charge.[84] Keane J then

---

[83.] [1980] IR 347.
[84.] See para **[13.02]**.

497

examined in detail the language of the charge and debenture and highlighted the inconsistencies which he perceived between the language of the instruments and the explicit statement of the charges being fixed.

Keane J held that:[85]

> "The intention was to enable the company to collect the book debts, lodge them to its bank account and use them in the business in the ordinary way. The banks for their part could at any time freeze the account if they considered the financial position so demanded. If the charge subsequently crystallised, as by the appointment of a receiver, the bank would have been able to ensure that its security was not dissipated. If that was indeed the intention, then it is difficult to imagine why the charge should be described other than as a floating charge; one which remained dormant until the happening of certain events and which in the interval did not preclude the company from making use of the assets in the course of its business ... where the intention of the parties, inferred from the instrument read as a whole, is to create a floating rather than a fixed security, this intention should not be treated as displaced by the fact that the partners have, for whatever reason, chosen to give the charge thus created an inapposite description."

[14.22] In holding that the charge and debenture both created floating charges over the company's book debts, Keane J chose to disagree with Slade J in *Siebe Gorman & Co Ltd v Barclays Bank Ltd*[86] and agreed with the approach of Hutton J in *Re Armagh Shoes Ltd*,[87] although in the author's view the judgments of Slade J and Hutton J are not inconsistent. Keane J stated that after concluding on the matter he noted the Report of the Review Committee on Insolvency Law under the chairmanship of Sir Kenneth Cork recommended a reversal of the *Siebe Gorman* decision.[88] It might be noted though that the Review Committee did so in the context of other amending legislation which would *inter alia* reduce the impact of preferential creditors and thereby restore the holder of a floating charge to a position it once enjoyed. The Review Committee also regarded, incorrectly in the author's view, the judgments of Slade J and Hutton J as being inconsistent.[89]

Keane J's final reasoning of his decision betrayed perhaps his willingness to make new law along the lines of the Review Committee which in referring to Slade J's decision stated:[90]

---

[85]. [1985] IR 401 at 410.
[86]. [1979] 2 LLR 142.
[87]. [1984] BCLC 405.
[88]. Cmnd 8558.
[89]. Para 1586 Cmnd 8558.
[90]. Para 1585 Cmnd 8558.

"this effectively reproduces all the advantages of the floating charge (from the point of view of the creditor) with none of its disadvantages. Moreover ... it would be all to easy to create a hybrid security with the best of both worlds if the law were left unchanged".

In concluding, Keane J stated:[91]

"What the banks have sought to do in the present instance is to create a hybrid form of charge which incorporates all the advantages of a floating charge with none of the statutory limitations on its operation. The borrower continues to use the asset in the course of its business to his own benefit, and to the benefit of the lender who continues to earn interest on his loan, in the knowledge that he can at any time realise his security if his prospects of ultimate repayment appear in peril. At the same time, he is protected from the consequences that would normally ensue for a lender who offers money on the security of the floating charge within twelve months of a winding-up or in circumstances where the preferential creditors are owed substantial sums".

[14.23] Despite the criticism of Keane J's judgment, his line of argument was such that notwithstanding his failure to distinguish between the judgments of Slade J and Hutton J the outcome of the appeal was far from certain. The Supreme Court though finally established that fixed charges on future book debts is not only possible but had effectively been created by the charge and the debenture.

In a particularly succinct and clear judgment Henchy J began:[92]

"One of the essential differences between a fixed charge and a floating charge given by a company is that a fixed charge takes effect, upon its creation, on the assets that are expressed to be subject to it, so that those assets, as they then exist, or, when the charge applies to future assets, as soon as they come into existence, will stand encumbered by the charge, and the company will be able to deal with those assets only to the extent permitted by the terms of the charge".

Henchy J considered that since the present and future book debts were stated to be subject to a fixed charge and since they were:

"to be segregated in a special account and there to be virtually frozen and rendered unusable by the company save with the prior consent in writing of the Bank, I consider that the charge, far from being floating or dormant or hovering over those assets, had fixed on them to such an extent that they were unusable in the ordinary course of business save at the discretion of the Bank. The charge therefore was, as it was expressed to be, a fixed charge".

---

91. [1985] IR 401 at 415.
92. *Ibid* at 418.

McCarthy J considered at some length Keane J's judgment in the High Court and its inconsistencies with the common law decisions on the topic. In answer to Keane J's assertion that the charge was hybrid and effectively the bank was having it both ways,[93] McCarthy J had this to say:[94]

> "Whilst acknowledging that the charge is somewhat hybrid in form because of the concession in respect of the collection of debts and lodgment to a special account, I do not recognise in it the ordinary characteristics of a floating charge ie that it may crystallise on the happening of some future event. If the borrower, the company, is driven to such financial straits that it is prepared to effect an immediate charge upon its book debts, the existence of which charge is, in effect, published to the commercial and financial world, I do not accept that an elaborate system set up to enable the company to benefit by the collection of such debts detracts from its qualifying as a specific or fixed charge".

McCarthy J found support in *Tailby v The Official Receiver*[95] and *Evans, Coleman & Evans Ltd v RA Nelson Construction Ltd*[96] for the concept of a fixed charge on future book debts and held that the charge and debenture effected what they were intended to namely, a fixed charge on the company's present and future book debts.

[14.24] The other members of the Supreme Court namely, Finlay CJ, Walsh J and Hederman J all agreed with the judgments of Henchy J and McCarthy J.[97] Walsh J though made the interesting point that the proceeds of the book debts lodged to the Book Debts Receivable Account were not subject to the fixed charge:

> "As the relationship between the banker and customer is one of debtor and creditor all sums from time to time standing to credit in that account were owed by the Bank to the company and were not book debts due to the company or debts in the contemplation of the deed of charge or the debenture, even though the account was opened to receive the collected book and other debts due to the company, which of course ceased to be debts from the moment they were collected".

This suggestion has received the subsequent support of the English High Court[98] where it was held that a bank balance does not fall within the term "book debts and other debts".

---

93. See para **[14.22]** above.
94. [1985] IR 401 at 424.
95. (1883) 13 App Cas 523.
96. 16 DLR 123.
97. One English commentator has indicated: "The judgments of Henchy and McCarthy JJ describe more clearly than any recent English judgment the distinction between a fixed and a floating charge" - Berg, 'Charges Over Book Debts: A Reply' (1995) JBL 433 at 440.
98. In *Re Brightlife Ltd* [1986] BCLC 418.

This raises the point that to be fully secured the banks should take a charge on the book debts receivable account.[99]

[14.25] A year later Barron J delivered a judgment in the High Court which clarified, to the extent that it was needed, the distinction between a fixed and floating charge. In *Re AH Masser Ltd*[100] the wording of the debenture, which was virtually identical to the wording of the security in *Siebe Gorman & Co Ltd v Barclays Bank Ltd*,[101] was along the lines much used by banks in Ireland at the time.

The charging clause provided that the company "charges by way of first fixed charge all book debts and other debts now and from time to time due or owing to such company ..."

The restrictive clause provided that:

"during the continuance of this security each company shall pay into an account or accounts of such company with the banks or any of them all monies which it may receive in respect of the book debts and other debts hereby charged and shall not without the prior consent in writing of the trustee, purport to charge, assign or otherwise dispose of the same in favour of any other person ..."

Barron J considered the two tests in ascertaining the true nature of the charge were first whether the instrument of charge permits unrestricted use of the property charged and secondly whether or not an immediate assignment in equity has been created by the charge. Barron J found that these questions were both answered by the restrictive clause as:[102]

"This clause clearly restricts the manner in which the company can deal with the proceeds of its book debts. It also restricts the company from purporting to charge, assign or otherwise dispose of its book debts and other debts. This is a recognition that the company would not be entitled to do so. If so, then it is a recognition that the book debts and other debts are assigned in equity at the date of execution of the deed or at the date of the creation of such debt if this occurs subsequently".

Although as Barron J pointed out,[103] the restrictions were not as extensive as in *Re Keenan Brothers Ltd*[104] he considered the essential restriction was that which prevented the company from charging, assigning or otherwise disposing of its book debts. The importance of the restrictive clause was underlined by Barron J

[99.] As in *Re New Bullas Trading Ltd* [1993] BCLC 1389 and [1994] 1 BCLC 485; see paras **[14.30]** and **[14.31]** below.
[100.] [1986] IR 455.
[101.] [1979] 2 LLR 142.
[102.] [1986] IR 455 at 457.
[103.] [1986] IR 455 at 459.
[104.] [1985] IR 401.

in holding that notwithstanding the charging clause as seeking to create a fixed charge, if the provisions of the charging instrument contradict such expressed intention, the contrary provisions shall prevail.[105] This was also the approach adopted in England in *Re Brightlife Ltd*[106] where the debenture was expressed to create a fixed charge over book debts but the restrictive provisions simply stated that the chargor could not without the chargee's prior written consent "except in the ordinary course of business ... deal with its book or other debts". These provisions are more appropriate to a floating charge and accordingly Hoffmann J held the charge to be floating.

[14.26] The criteria for the drafting of a fixed charge over book debts appeared to be well established by the decision in *Re Keenan Brothers Ltd*[107] and *Re AH Masser Ltd*.[108] These decisions gave certainty to lawyers and bankers alike for six years until the courts' decisions in *Re Wogan's (Drogheda) Ltd*.[109] In that case, the company charged by way of first fixed charge its book debts and other debts and receivables present and future. The charge contained a covenant requiring the company to:

> "pay into such banking account or accounts as may be designated for such purpose by the lender ... all monies which it may receive in respect of book debts and other debts or securities and not without the prior consent of the lender in writing to withdraw or deal with such monies."

Denham J held:

1. The statement in the charge that it was fixed was not conclusive;

2. All the criteria laid down by the Supreme Court in *Re Keenan Brothers Ltd*[110] must be met before the charge could be regarded as a fixed charge;

3. One of the criteria was the establishment of a special bank account to be designated and controlled by the lender into which the company was to lodge the proceeds of all book debts;

4. The restrictive provisions contained in the charge did not, without the designation of a specific bank account, suffice to bring the charge within the ambit of the decision in *Re Keenan Brothers Ltd*; and

---

105. [1986] IR 455 at 457.
106. [1986] BCLC 418.
107. [1985] IR 401.
108. [1986] IR 455.
109. [1993] 1 IR 157.
110. [1985] IR 401.

5.   Since no specific bank account had been designated by the chargee after the debenture was given, the charge was a floating and not a fixed charge.

In the context of the requirement that a charge over a moveable or fluctuating asset must incorporate restrictions on the chargor as to its freedom to utilise in order to take it out of the category as being a floating charge,[111] Denham J's short judgment encapsulated the salient points, including the application of the Supreme Court's only decision at that stage on fixed charges over book debts.[112]

[14.27] The Supreme Court, however, reversed Denham J's judgment by latching on to the point that evidence as to whether or not a designated account was opened was inadmissible. They decided that the effect of the terms of the charge was such as to confer the precise characteristics of a fixed charge set out by them in *Re Keenan Brothers Ltd.*[113] The fact that a designated account was opened and operated in *Re Keenan Brothers Ltd* and not in *Re Wogan's (Drogheda) Ltd* was seen by the Supreme Court as being immaterial in creating a fixed charge. The effect of this decision was thus to relax the controls otherwise seen as necessary to bring the charge into the category of being fixed.[114] This led to some uncertainty which is never helpful to lenders and their advisers in taking such security.[115] Indeed the decision, which is difficult to reconcile with both earlier and subsequent decisions, may have led to a false sense of comfort for some bankers and lawyers.

[14.28] Two years later the opportunity arose again for the Supreme Court to give guidance. In *Re Holidair Ltd*[116] a group of companies charged by way of first fixed charge all book debts and other debts present and future. The debenture provided that the companies would pay into such bank account as the chargee may from time to time select all moneys which it received in respect of such debts and would not without the prior written consent of the chargee dispose of such moneys in favour of any other person. Consistent with the Supreme Court's test of what constitutes a fixed charge as laid down in *Re Wogan's (Drogheda) Ltd,*[117] the chargee did not designate a bank account for the book debts proceeds and such proceeds were used by the companies in the

---

[111.] See para **[11.15]**.

[112.] *Re Keenan Brothers Ltd* [1985] IR 401.

[113.] [1985] IR 401.

[114.] For a strong criticism of the logic of the Supreme Court's decision see Fealy, 'Fixed Charges over Book Debts: A Loosening of the Reins?' (1993) ILT 133.

[115.] See (1993) 11 Palmer's in Company 1; Johnston, 'Bank Finance - Searching for Suitable Security' (1994) 1 CLP 3.

[116.] [1994] 1 IR 416.

[117.] [1993] 1 IR 157, see para **[14.26]** above.

normal course of their business. In holding that the charge was fixed, Costello J applied what had been decided previously in the Irish courts. He stated:[118]

> "It is well established that in construing a charge contained in a debenture the court is not bound by the parties' description of the charge and must, in order to ascertain their intention, consider all its provisions. But if, as here, the parties describe the charge as a 'fixed charge' and support their description by provisions which restrict the use permitted by the borrower of the assets charged in a manner incompatible with the essence of a floating charge, this is persuasive evidence that the charge should be treated as a fixed charge (see: *Re Keenan Brothers Ltd* [1985] IR 401, *Re AH Masser Ltd* [1986] IR 455 and *Re Wogan's (Drogheda) Ltd* [1993] 1 IR 157). I think that in this case the proper construction of the debenture is that the parties intended that the charge would be a fixed one. They referred to it as a fixed and provided (a) that the book debts would be paid into an account designated by the trustee and (b) that the assignment or disposal of the book debts could only take place with the consent of the trustee.
>
> The trustee did not in fact designate a special account under para 3.08 until the appointment of the examiner and allowed the companies to use the book debts in the ordinary course of business. But the Supreme Court has made clear in *Re Wogan's (Drogheda) Ltd* [1993] 1 IR 157 that such concession does not justify the court construing the charge as a floating charge. The Chief Justice pointed out that the court was prohibited from construing a deed in accordance with the conduct of the parties subsequent to its date ..."

[14.29] The Supreme Court managed to find a way of reversing Costello J's decision and distinguishing it from its own judgment in *Re Wogan's (Drogheda) Ltd.*[119] The Supreme Court decided:

1. The sole issue is whether the provisions in the debenture permitted the companies to carry on their business in the ordinary way in so far as concerned their book debts;

2. The restriction in the debenture on the disposal of book debts was not applicable to cash received in respect of book debts;

3. If the charge had required the book debts to be paid into a designated account, such requirement would be contrary to the covenant in the debenture by the companies to carry on and conduct their businesses "in a proper and efficient manner".

4. As there was no restriction in the debenture preventing the companies from using the proceeds of the book debts in the normal way for the purpose of carrying on their businesses, the charge had the third

---

118. [1994] 1 IR 416 at 427.
119. [1993] 1 IR 157.

characteristic referred by Romer LJ in *Re Yorkshire Woolcombers'*
Association Ltd[120] and was accordingly a floating and not a fixed
charge.

Distinction between charges over book debts and their proceeds

[14.30] Just prior to the *Holidair* decisions the English Court of Appeal upheld
the intended effect of a charge which created a fixed charge on book debts
which provided that the company should pay the proceeds of its book debts into
a bank account but thereafter in the absence of directions as to its use by the
chargee, the proceeds be released from the fixed charge and be subject to a
floating charge.

The ingenious drafting of the debenture in *Re New Bullas Trading Ltd*[121] had the
effect of giving the chargee the required priority over the Inland Revenue in
respect of the company's book debts which had not been collected at the time of
appointment of an administrative receiver but yet enabled the company to
effectively treat the charge as floating by allowing the company unrestricted use
of the proceeds. The only fetter on the company's freedom was a prohibition on
selling, assigning, factoring or discounting the book debts - a prohibition which
might not be out of place in a floating charge.

A review of the terms of the debenture brings to mind the words of Keane J in
Re Keenan Brothers Ltd:[122]

> "What the banks have sought to do in the present instance is to create a hybrid
> form of charge which incorporates all the advantages of a floating charge with
> none of the statutory limitations on its operation. The borrower continues to use
> the assets in the course of his business to his own benefit, and to the benefit of
> the lender who continues to earn interest on his loan, in the knowledge that he
> can at any time realise his security if his prospects of ultimate repayment
> appear in peril."

The debenture in *Re New Bullas Trading Ltd*[123] provided that the company
created in favour of 3i a fixed charge over "the book debts and other debts due
or owing to the Company both present and future". It further stated that:

> "During the continuance of this security the Company shall:
>
> (A) (i) pay into a current account or a separate designated account (as
>   3i may require) of the Company with the Bank all moneys
>   which it may receive in respect of the book debts and other
>   debts hereby charged and ... pay or otherwise deal with such

---

120. [1903] 2 Ch 284; see para **[13.03]**.
121. [1993] BCLC 1389 and [1994] 1 BCLC 485.
122. [1985] IR 401 at 415.
123. [1993] BCLC 1389 and [1994] 1 BCLC 485.

moneys standing in such account in accordance with any
directions from time to time given in writing by 3i; ...

(ii) in the absence of any directions from 3i any moneys received
by the Company and paid into such account in respect of the
book debts and other debts hereby charged shall upon such
payment in stand released from the fixed charge on such debts
hereinbefore by this Debenture created and shall stand subject
to the floating charge hereinbefore by this Debenture created
over the other property and assets of the Company;

(iii) any such release shall in no respects derogate from the
subsistence and continuance of the said fixed charge on all
other book and other debts of the Company for the time being
outstanding.

(B) if called upon to do so by 3i execute a legal assignment of such book
debts and other debts to 3i in such terms as 3i may require ...

(C) deal with such book debts and other debts in accordance with any
directions from time to time given in writing by 3i ... and in default of
and subject to any such directions deal with the same only in the
ordinary course of getting in and realising the same (but not sell assign
factor or discount the same in any way)."

In a very full and well researched judgment, Knox J held[124] that the charge had
failed the test of fulfilling the criteria to be a fixed charge as established by the
decisions in *Siebe Gorman & Co Ltd v Barclays Bank Ltd*,[125] *Re Keenan
Brothers Ltd*[126] and *Re Brightlife Ltd*.[127]

[14.31] In its appeal, the debenture holder relied primarily on an alternative
submission to that made before Knox J,[128] in that the security provided for a
fixed charge over uncollected book debts and a floating charge over their
proceeds. This approach broke new ground as previous judgments in Ireland,
Northern Ireland[129] and England[130] had not distinguished between book debts
and their proceeds, with one notable exception. The exception was the judgment
of Walsh J in *Re Keenan Brothers Ltd*,[131] which at the time was overshadowed

---

[124.] [1993] BCLC 1389.
[125.] [1979] 2 LLR 142.
[126.] [1985] IR 401.
[127.] [1986] BCLC 418.
[128.] See Nourse LJ at [1994] 1 BCLC 485 at 491.
[129.] See in particular *Northern Bank Ltd v Ross* [1991] BCLC 504 where the Northern Ireland
Court of Appeal held that moneys lodged to an account for the payment of cheques and credit
cards were subject to the chargor's charge on book debts and other debts.
[130.] Although Hoffman J held in *Re Brightlife Ltd* [1984] BCLC 418 that moneys in a bank account
were not caught by a charge on "book debts and other debts" as the prohibition in the security
on the company dealing with its book or other debts "otherwise than in the ordinary course of
getting in and realising the same" could not apply to moneys in a bank account.
[131.] [1985] IR 401.

by the establishment in that case of the legal possibility of taking a fixed charge over present and future book debts. Walsh J stated:[132]

> "Book debts and other debts cease to be such the moment they are discharged by the debtors, irrespective of whether the payment is made directly to the creditor or, on his order, to some other party on his account.
>
> As the relationship between the banker and customer is one of debtor and creditor all sums from time to time standing to credit in that account were owed by the Bank to the company and were not book debts due to the company or debts in the contemplation of the deed of charge or the debenture, even though the account was opened to receive the collected book and other debts due to the company, which of course ceased to be debts from the moment they were collected.
>
> I do not find it necessary to identify what particular monies were or are the subject of the fixed charge beyond repeating my opinion that none of the monies in the receivable account were ever so subject after they were lodged to that account."

The English Court of Appeal[133] accepted the distinction that book debts cease to exist as such once they are paid into the company's account[134] (or paid by the company to the bank). Accordingly, the court held that a fixed charge had been created over uncollected book debts but a floating charge over their proceeds.

The significance of the Court of Appeal's decision in *Re New Bullas Trading Ltd*[135] can be gauged from the deluge of commentary on it, virtually all supporting and welcoming the decision.[136] The decision's principal impact should be the consideration by all potential chargeholders and their legal advisers of the form of fixed charge over book debts so as not to diminish the prospect of ranking ahead of preferential creditors upon the chargor's insolvency.

Restrictions not anti-competitive

[14.32] The restrictive provisions of paying book debt proceeds into a specific account under a fixed charge over book debts have been challenged on the

---

132. *Ibid* at 417.

133. Judgment of Nourse LJ [1994] 1 BCLC 485 at 487.

134. See also Chadwick J in *Oakdale (Richmond) Ltd v National Westminster Bank plc* [1997] 1 BCLC 63 at 75; for a judgment failing to make that distinction see Tompkins J in *Supercool Refrigeration and Air Conditioning (in Receivership and Liquidation) v Hoverd Industries Ltd* [1994] 3 NZLR 300 where the High Court, Auckland held that a fixed charge which required the chargor to pay into its bank account all monies received in respect of its book debts was not fixed as there was no restriction on withdrawals.

135. [1994] 1 BCLC 485.

136. See Petkovic [1994] 5 JIBL 183; Berg (1994) JIBFL 93; Naccarato and Street (1994) JIBFL 109; Gregorian (1994) 15 Co Law 181; Ward [1994] 2 JIBL N-38; Breslin (1995) 2 CLP 32; Berg (1995) JBL 433.

grounds that they are in conflict with Articles 85 and 86 of the Treaty of Rome. In *Oakdale (Richmond) Ltd v National Westminster Bank plc*[137] the company sought a declaration that the requirement, under the debenture it had given to the defendant bank, to pay its book debt proceeds into its bank account and be restricted from its use thereof were prohibited and void under Articles 85 and 86. Chadwick J said the test was whether the restrictions imposed in the bank's standard mortgage debenture were necessary for rendering the transaction which was to be effected by that debenture properly operable, or whether they went further.[138] He found that such restrictions were necessary for a specific charge over book debts to be effective and that if banks were not willing to lend on the security of book debts the ability of small trading companies to obtain finance would be curtailed. The judge concluded,[139] "Far from being anti-competitive, the clause promotes competition because it enables a company to obtain additional finance from its banks under an all-moneys debenture". Therefore the challenge under Article 85 was not sustainable. With regard to Article 86 the judge found that National Westminster Bank did not enjoy a dominant position within the market for lending to small trading companies; nor did the lending terms, which reflected what any sensible bank lender would regard as necessary to protect itself against the credit risk, amount to an abuse of any dominant position which it might enjoy.

DRAFTING A FIXED CHARGE OVER BOOK DEBTS

[14.33] It is a daunting prospect for any lawyer in preparing a fixed charge over book debts to prepare a document which meets first the bank's requirement of giving it priority over the customer's preferential creditors and secondly, the customer's requirement not to execute a charge which will restrict the manner in which it conducts its ongoing business. Indeed, book debts have been described as being "a challenging asset over which to take a fixed charge".[140] In preparing such a security the four principal court decisions[141] need to be considered.[142] The fact that all four decisions reversed the judgments given in the courts below is not reassuring for the draftsman when required by his client to prepare security which will give effect to its wishes.[143]

[137.] [1997] 1 BCLC 63.

[138.] *Ibid* at 75.

[139.] *Ibid* at 76.

[140.] Gregorian (1994) 15 Co Law 181.

[141.] *Re Keenan Brothers Ltd* [1985] IR 401 see paras **[14.21]-[14.24]**; *Re Wogan's (Drogheda) Ltd* [1993] 1 IR 157 see paras **[14.26]-[14.27]**; *Re Holidair Ltd* [1994] 1 IR 416, see paras **[14.28]-[14.29]**; *Re New Bullas Trading Ltd* [1993] BCLC 1389 and [1994] 1 BCLC 485, see paras **[14.30]-[14.31]**.

[142.] For an analysis of the latter three decisions see Dobbyn and Reid, 'The Effectiveness of Fixed Charge on Book Debts: The Irish Experience' [1994] 8 JIBL 321.

[143.] The judges, whose decisions in all three Irish cases were reversed, have each subsequently been promoted - Keane J and Denham J to the Supreme Court and Costello J to President of the High Court.

[14.34] A fixed charge over present and future book debts is usually incorporated in a debenture which provides for charges, whether fixed or floating, over other assets of the chargor. However such a fixed charge can be taken in a document of its own. The first clause of such a charge would typically provide that the chargor will pay on demand all moneys now or at any time hereafter due or owing to the chargee in respect of any liability whether actual or contingent and whether in the character of principal debtor or guarantor or surety or otherwise. The second clause would be the charging clause. There is no specific formula - a simple provision charging by way of fixed charge all present and future book debts of the chargor would be sufficient for most purposes. A comprehensive clause would read along the following lines:

> "The chargor as beneficial owner hereby charges by way of continuing security with the payment to the chargee of the principal money interest and other monies hereby agreed to be paid or intended to be hereby secured by way of first fixed charge (i) all book debts and other debts now and from time to time hereafter due owing or incurred to the chargor together with the benefit of all rights, securities and guarantees of any nature whatsoever now or at any time enjoyed or held by it in relation thereto, (ii) all its rights title and interest in and to all other debts in and to which the chargor has any right title or interest (all the debts and benefits referred to in (i) and (ii) being hereinafter collectively called 'the debts'), and (iii) all monies from time to time in the account of the chargor with the chargee used for the receipt of the debts."

The third clause would be the covenant which should effectively copperfasten the nature of the security by imposing strict limits on the extent to which the chargor can deal with the debts.[144] While the following covenants are the most desirable for the chargee's viewpoint, there may be good commercial reasons why the third, fourth and fifth may not be practical or acceptable. It is probably essential, if the security is to be construed as fixed (over both debts and their proceeds) rather than floating, that the first two covenants be given without amendment.[145] For the first covenant to be given the chargor should have access

---

[144.] Apart from the decisions already cited, the absence of restrictions was held to be the fatal flaw in a "specific charge" over book debts *in Re Pearl Maintenance Services Ltd, Re Pearl Building Contracts Ltd* [1995] BCC 657.

[145.] Apart from *Re Keenan Brothers Ltd* [1985] IR 401 and *Re Holidair Ltd* [1994] 1 IR 416; see also Chadwick J in *Oakdale (Richmond) Ltd v National Westminster Bank plc* [1997] 1 BCLC 63 at 75:

> "In order that the specific charge over book debts shall be effective it is necessary to provide for the bank to have control over the proceeds of collection of those debts... A bank which takes a charge over book debts will not be fully protected unless it can insist that the proceeds of collection of the book debts are paid into a specified account: that is to say, an account under its control or, at least, an account in credit at another bank to which it can give notice of its charge".

to other cash, from its banker or otherwise, to enable it to carry on its business. The following is a suggested covenant clause:

"The chargor hereby covenants with the chargee that during the continuance of the security hereby created:

(i) it shall procure that the chargor's present and future debtors shall pay to the chargee (in or towards the reduction or discharge of the chargor's indebtedness to the chargee) all moneys due owing or incurred in respect of the debts and to the extent that any such moneys come into the hands of the chargor they shall be immediately remitted to the chargee and any moneys not so remitted shall be held by the chargor as trustee for the chargee;

(ii) it shall not without the prior written consent of the chargee purport to charge, sell, assign, factor, discount or otherwise dispose of, or permit to subsist any charge or lien over, the debts in favour of any other person and shall if called upon to do so by the chargee execute a legal assignment of the debts to the chargee;

(iii) it shall not without the prior written consent of the chargee permit or agree to any variation of the rights attaching to the debts or any of them;

(iv) it shall not without the prior written consent of the chargee release, exchange, compound, set-off, grant time or indulgence in respect of or in any other manner deal with all or any of the debts save as herein expressly provided;

(v) it shall at its own expense institute continue or defend all such proceedings in connection with the debts as the chargee may require; and

(vi) it shall not carry on its business in relation to the book debts and other debts herein charged otherwise than as set out in this clause;

and in case of default by the chargor in the performance of any of the foregoing covenants it shall be lawful for but not obligatory upon the chargee to do whatever may be necessary to make good such default and all sums expended by the chargee in that behalf shall be added to the monies hereby secured and bear interest accordingly".

It should be mentioned that there is no particular rule as to the language of the foregoing provided it is clear from whatever language is used that a fixed charge is created. Indeed, it is probably more common that the chargor covenants to pay moneys into a designated account with the chargee and agrees not to withdraw moneys from that account without the chargee's consent. The suggested clause (i) above removes any doubt that the moneys may somehow belong to the chargor. The alternative and more common covenant to pay moneys into a designated account of the company will be necessary where the chargee is not the bank in receipt of the book debt proceeds. This will apply where the chargee is not a clearing bank. In such cases, the chargee's consent to withdraw will be required and depending upon the circumstances the clearing bank's consent may also be needed.[146]

The subsequent clauses of the security will set out the standard provisions of a charge including the right to enforce the security by appointing a receiver or otherwise, the powers of a receiver, the application of proceeds, the appointment of any person nominated by the chargee and any receiver as attorney for the chargor. The other aspects of taking a security interest will need to be considered including the capacity of the chargor,[147] the title to the debts,[148] the approval for giving the charge[149] and registration of particulars of the charge.[150]

[14.35] Where the customer wishes to use its book debts proceeds in the normal course of its business (which will happen more often than not), then the approach adopted by the draftsmen in *Re New Bullas Trading Ltd*[151] should be adopted. Although this approach has not been considered by the Irish courts, in view of Walsh J's judgment in *Re Keenan Brothers Ltd*[152] there seems no reason why the English Court of Appeal's decision in *Re New Bullas Trading Ltd*[153] should not be followed. Accordingly the charging clause could remain the same as in para **[14.34]** but, assuming the chargor has charged its undertaking, property and assets (not otherwise specifically charged) by way of floating charge, the covenant clause could state:

"The chargor hereby covenants with the chargee that during the continuance of the security hereby created:

(i)   it shall pay into such account as may be designated from time to time by the chargee all moneys which it may receive in respect of its book debts and other debts and any moneys not remitted shall be held by the chargor as trustee for the chargee;

(ii) it shall pay or otherwise deal with such moneys (specified in (i) above) in accordance with such directions as may from time to time be given by the chargee and in the absence of any such directions such moneys shall on receipt by the chargor be released from the fixed charge granted herein but shall be subject to the floating charge granted herein provided always that such release shall not affect the subsistence and continuance of the fixed charge granted herein on all book debts and other debts of the chargor present and future".

[146.] See *William Gaskell Ltd v Highley Nos 1,2,3* [1994] 1 BCLC 197; see para **[14.45]** below.

[147.] See para **[18.30]**.

[148.] This may seem self evident but in *Re Marwalt Ltd* [1992] BCC 32 a charge on book debts "did not bite" as beneficial ownership was held by a third party.

[149.] See para **[18.56]**.

[150.] See paras **[14.10]**-**[14.14]**; see also Ch 17.

[151.] [1993] BCLC 1389 and [1994] 1 BCLC 485.

[152.] [1985] IR 401 at 416.

[153.] [1994] 1 BCLC 485.

The covenants set out in (ii) to (iv) inclusive in para **[14.34]** should then be repeated as covenants (iii) to (v) here.

SECTION 1001, TAXES CONSOLIDATION ACT 1997

"If banks are not willing to lend against book debts - because adequate security over those debts cannot be taken - the ability of small trading companies to obtain finance will be curtailed."[154]

[14.36] The success of the bank in the Supreme Court in *Re Keenan Brothers Ltd*[155] proved to be a pyrrhic victory for the banking community and indeed industry at large. In the following Spring when the Finance Bill was introduced into Dáil Éireann, there was no indication of any amending legislation, nor indeed on the second printing of the Finance Bill as amended in Committee. However on 13 May 1986 a new s 115 appeared and became law on 27 May before there was time for consideration of its consequences, not only for banks but more particularly industry dependant upon secured banking finance for its operations. This section stated:

Where a person holds a fixed charge (being a fixed charge which is created on or after the passing of this Act) on the book debts of a company (within the meaning of the Companies Act, 1963) and the company fails to pay any relevant amount for which it is liable, then the said person shall, on being notified accordingly in writing by the Revenue Commissioners, become liable to pay such relevant amount on due demand, and on neglect or refusal of payment may be proceeded against in like manner as any other defaulter:

Provided that:

(i)   the amount or aggregate amount which the person shall be liable to pay in relation to a company in accordance with this section shall not exceed the amount or aggregate amount which that person has, while the fixed charge on book debts in relation to the said company is in existence, received, directly or indirectly, from that company in payment or in part payment of any debts due by the company to that person, and

(ii) this section shall not apply to any amounts received by the holder of the fixed charge from the company before the date on which he is notified in writing by the Revenue Commissioners that he is liable by reason of this section for payment of a relevant amount due by the company.

[154.] Chadwick J in *Oakdale (Richmond) Ltd v National Westminster Bank plc* [1997] 1 BCLC 63 at 76.
[155.] [1985] IR 401.

"Relevant amount" is defined in the second sub-section as being amounts which a company is liable to remit to the Revenue Commissioners in respect of PAYE and VAT.

[14.37] As a result of this enactment many banks ceased to take fixed charges over book debts as a general rule and simply relied upon a floating charge, notwithstanding its inferior status on a receivership or liquidation of the chargor. Other banks though, continued to take this form of security while keeping a close watch on the customer's financial viability.

As s 115 effectively reduced the level of security which a business could offer its bankers, inevitably the level of finance available to industry diminished. The Task Force on Small Business,[156] in recommending the repeal of the legislation, stated in its Report:[157]

> "For many trading companies, their book debts are a major, if not the main source of collateral that they can offer to banks in negotiating a loan. As a result of s 115, the value of book debts as a security has been considerably diminished.
>
> We discussed the effects of this provision with representatives of the associated banks. All indicated that it had had an adverse effect on their willingness to lend to small businesses and on the terms on which they did so".

[14.38] The Minister of Finance's budget speech of 1995 indicated that s 115 would be amended "to limit this difficulty ... for small companies seeking bank finance". The amendment however (brought about by s 174 of the Finance Act, 1995[158]) was somewhat disingenuous in that it purported to restrict the effect of s 115 provided the Revenue Commissioners were notified of the charge within 21 days of its creation. The form of notification required by the section is the receipt by the Revenue Commissioners of a copy of the Form 47 filed in the Companies Registration Office (thereby saving the Revenue Commissioners the trouble of searching themselves and at the same time requiring the corporate taxpayer or its banker to arrange for an additional copy of the relevant Form 47 to be sent to it). In many instances, following the implementation of the Act, the Revenue Commissioners sought further details such as VAT numbers from the persons who filed the Forms 47 in compliance with the Act. Section 174 has been described as "a slick way of providing the Revenue with more information and illustrative of their ever-increasing powers to intrude into people's affairs".[159] The reform, which was essentially cosmetic, did not lead to a change

---

[156.] March 1994, chaired by Seamus Brennan TD, Minister for Commerce and Technology.

[157.] *Ibid* at para 3.8.

[158.] For an analysis of s 174 and background to the amendment of s 115 see Courtney, *Company Law Review 1995* (Round Hall Sweet & Maxwell).

[159.] Editorial, Commercial Law Practitioner, (1995) 2 CLP 242.

in banking practice, thereby leading to criticism from both the Revenue Commissioners and the Small and Medium Enterprises Association.[160]

[14.39] The current position of the legislation, since re-enacted as s 1001 of the Taxes Consolidation Act, 1997 is that any holder of a fixed charge on book debts, (created on or after 27 May 1986) becomes liable to pay the arrears of the chargor's VAT or PAYE ("the relevant amount") on demand to the Revenue Commissioners provided that:

(a)   (i) it applies only to payments of the relevant amount which the company subsequently fails to pay, after notification

(ii) it does not apply to amounts received by the chargee before the date of notification, and

(iii) if within 21 days of the creation of the charge or the passing of the Act (whichever is the later) the copy of the Form 47 (relating to the charge) is filed with the Revenue Commissioners, the chargee is liable only for the arrears accrued after the date of notification.

(b) the amount payable is not to exceed the amount received by the chargee in payment of debts while the charge subsists.

[14.40] The Act applies only to holders of fixed charges over book debts[161] created (on or after 27 May 1986) by companies which are "formed and registered" under the Companies Act, 1963 (or where such company existed on 23 December 1963). Accordingly, the legislation does not apply to foreign companies carrying on business in Ireland through branches or otherwise (unless it was incorporated on or prior to 23 December 1963). Although foreign companies carrying on business in Ireland must register under the Companies Act, 1963,[162] they are not formed under that Act.

The real impact of the enactment is that the proviso does not limit the amount which the chargee is required to pay to the amount which the chargee receives pursuant to its fixed charge over book debts, as one would have thought, but the limit is to all amounts received by the chargee. The effect of this is that if a bank has a fixed charge on its customer's lands and book debts and the Revenue Commissioners serve a notice on the bank that the customer is in arrears on its PAYE and/or VAT payments due to it, then the moneys received by the bank from the book debt proceeds and also the proceeds of the sale of the lands must be handed over to the Revenue Commissioners until the customer's arrears have been discharged. Hence the importance for bankers and their advisers to understand that if a fixed charge over book debts is to be taken, the financial

---

[160.] See *The Irish Times*, 2 December 1995, p 17.
[161.] Thus not debts which are not book debts, see para **[17.14]-[17.26]**.
[162.] Companies Act, 1963, s 352.

position will require very close monitoring to avoid the potential of a serious drain on the value of the bank's other security. An additional point to note is that the PAYE and VAT arrears are not limited to a year, which they are under their statutory preferential status.[163]

Another danger is that although the legislation refers to a fixed charge on the book debts, an assignment of debts by way of security would be caught if particulars of such assignment are registered in the Companies Registration Office pursuant to s 99(2)(e) of the Companies Act, 1963.[164] Failure to register particulars of such an assignment of course is likely to render the security void against the liquidator and creditors.[165]

A further point to bear in mind, not so much in taking the security, but when the chargor encounters trading difficulties is where a bank having taken a floating charge serves, or is deemed to have served, a notice of automatic crystallisation.[166] The effect of such notice would be to trigger the potential operation of s 1001. However, as the particulars of the security would have been registered as a floating charge, the Revenue Commissioners would not be aware of the automatic crystallisation and the prospect of a s 1001 notice might be somewhat remote.

[14.41] One method of mitigating the effects of the legislation is for the bank to release the security as soon as it receives a notice from the Revenue Commissioners. However, if the notice is served when the company is in financial difficulties, or indeed while in receivership or liquidation, although a release of the security will avoid the bank remitting proceeds from the sale of other secured assets, the benefit of the fixed charge on book debts will have been lost.

A further precaution which may be taken is for banks and their advisers when preparing fixed charges over book debts to provide either in the facility letter or loan agreement that the company will be liable to gross up any payments so that if the bank is required to comply with a s 1001 notice, the company will be liable to remit such further sums to the bank as will be sufficient so that the bank will receive for its account the amount owing to it. In practice, where such an event arises the company is likely to be insolvent and the bank will suffer loss due to the deficiency.

In practice this section causes particular concern in leasing transactions where part of the security may be an assignment of rentals under the lease.[167] It is not

---

[163.] Companies Act, 1963, s 285 for PAYE and Value Added Tax; see further Taxes Consolidation Act 1997, ss1000 and 995.
[164.] See paras **[14.10]-[14.14]** and Ch 17.
[165.] Companies Act, 1963, s 99(1); see *Orion Finance Ltd v Crown Financial Management Ltd* [1994] 2 BCLC 607, see para **[17.33]**.
[166.] See para **[13.12]-[13.16]**.
[167.] See paras **[14.43]-[14.44]** below.

unusual for the amounts involved in such transactions, in particular aviation, to be significant. Accordingly this statutory provision must be constantly borne in mind each time security over debts, whether by way of assignment or charge, is being contemplated. In such instances it is worthwhile to consider avoidance mechanisms.

[14.42] Despite the very real concerns of banks and other financial institutions it appears that the Revenue Commissioners have not utilised this legislation to any significant extent. It is not difficult to see why - the effect of its use where the company continues to trade would be an immediate siphoning off of effectively the company's working capital (which might otherwise be re-advanced) by the bank, causing the imminent collapse of the company (with the resultant loss of further taxation to the Revenue Commissioners).

However, the legislation has been beneficial to the Revenue Commissioners in that it has resulted in many banks which would otherwise have taken fixed charges over book debts resorting simply to floating charges. The book debt proceeds on the company's receivership or liquidation are paid in the first instance to the preferential creditors,[168] of which the Revenue Commissioners are invariably the most prominent. Accordingly, notwithstanding the decisions of the judiciary, the Revenue Commissioners have effectively restored their supremacy.

EQUIPMENT LEASES

[14.43] Leasing and other finance companies will often create security over their lease and hire agreements to support finance made available to them by their bankers. Usually the security is drafted in a manner incorporating the rental stream. The question arises as to whether such security is a fixed or a floating charge on book debts. This is relevant first, as to what priority the bankers will have upon the leasing company's insolvency and secondly whether the provisions of s 1001 of the Taxes Consolidation Act, 1997 apply.[169] Typically the security creates an assignment and/or charge over the leasing company's right, title and interest in the agreements under which it hires out the equipment to the user.

In *Re Atlantic Computer Systems plc*[170] the English Court of Appeal[171] had no doubt that security over designated hiring agreements did not come within Romer LJ's test of a floating charge[172] nor was it ambulatory within the meaning

---

[168.] Companies Act, 1963, s 98 and s 285.

[169.] See paras **[14.36]-[14.42]** above.

[170.] [1992] 1 All ER 476.

[171.] For a criticism of the rationale of the Court's decision see Marks, 'Taking Charges over Book Debts' The Irish Centre for Commercial Law Studies, 18 January 1996.

[172.] In *Re Yorkshire Woolcombers' Association* [1903] 2 Ch 284; see para **[13.03]**.

as enunciated by Lord Macnaghten.[173] In giving the judgment of the court Nicholls LJ stated:[174]

> "The notable feature of the present case is that the charges were not ambulatory. The property assigned by the company was confined to rights to which the company was entitled under specific, existing contracts. The assignments consisted of the company's rights 'under or by virtue of' subleases each of which was already in existence at the time of the assignments and each of which was specifically identified in the relevant deeds of assignment. In each case the payments due to the company under a specific sublease were charged as security for the payments due by the company under the headlease relating to the same equipment. The company's right to receive future instalments from end-users in due course pursuant to the terms of these subleases was as much a present asset of the company, within Romer LJ's reference to 'present and future' assets of a company, as a right to receive payment of a sum which was immediately due. Romer LJ's reference to future assets was a reference to assets of which, when the charge was created, the company was not the owner. That was the position in that case. That is not the position in this case."

As for the suggestion that it was a floating security because the company could carry on its business unhindered by the intervention of the security holder, Nicholls LJ stated:[175]

> "The company was to be at liberty to receive and use the instalments until AIB chose to intervene. We are unpersuaded that this results in these charges, on existing and defined property, becoming floating charges. A mortgage of land does not become a floating charge by reason of the mortgagor being permitted to remain in possession and enjoy the fruits of the property charged for the time being. This is so even if the land is leasehold and the term is very short, and as such the asset charged is of a wasting character. So here: the mere fact that for the time being the company could continue to receive and use the instalments does not suffice to negative the fixed character of the charge."

That decision was followed and applied in *Re Atlantic Medical Ltd.*[176]

[14.44] In *Royal Trust Bank v National Westminster Bank*[177] Jonathan Parker J sought to extend this principle to the rentals of future hire agreements which were not specified in the assignment. This decision was criticised[178] on the

---

[173.] In *Illingsworth v Houldsworth* [1904] AC 355; see para **[13.04]**.

[174.] [1992] 1 All ER 476 at 494.

[175.] *Ibid.*

[176.] [1993] BCLC 386; see also at para **[17.33]** *Orion Finance Ltd v Crown Financial Management Ltd* [1994] 2 BCLC 607.

[177.] [1995] BCC 128.

[178.] Whiteson, (1995) 11 Insolvency Law & Practice 55.

grounds that the security met the three criteria of Romer LJ in his statement as to what form of security could amount to a floating charge.[179] The Court of Appeal unanimously allowed the appeal and held the security to be a floating security.[180] In that case as security for its obligations to its financier, RTB, a leasing company assigned:

"all the rights benefits and interests of the company present and future in the agreements including ... the right to receive all rentals and other payments whatsoever due or to become due under or by virtue of the agreements."

"the agreements" were defined as meaning:

"All hire lease or hire purchase agreements from time to time entered into between the company and its customer in connection with the equipment hire business carried on by the company and deposited with and assigned to the bank under or pursuant to this deed and any and every continuation thereof or substitution therefor".

In the Court of Appeal Millett LJ confirmed that restrictions which were optional were not restrictions at all; he held:[181]

"The company is bound to pay all moneys collected from customers in respect of deposited agreements into a special account at the bank from which it has no right to make withdrawals without the prior written consent of the bank - but only if required to do so by the bank. The inference is plain. Unless and until the bank imposes such a requirement, the company is under no such obligation. It is not obliged to pay the money to the bank, even though the money represents the proceeds of assets which have been charged to the bank. It is free to pay the money into a bank account of its own - as indeed it did, for the No 2 account was an historic account which had been in existence before the arrangements with the bank were entered into, and it was not a trust account or one designated by the bank to receive the money, nor was it an account over which the bank had any control.

The company's right to withhold agreements and deal with them free from any security interest of the bank so long as they are not needed to maintain the required level of cover, even if they have been financed by the proceeds of deposited agreements (as it was clearly envisaged that they would be), is in my opinion inconsistent with the construction which the judge placed upon the charge.

... the proper characterisation of a security as 'fixed' or 'floating' depends on the freedom of the chargor to deal with the proceeds of the charged assets in the ordinary course of business free from the security. A contractual right in the chargor to collect the proceeds and pay them in to its own bank account for use

179. See para **[13.03]**.
180. [1996] 2 BCLC 682; [1996] BCC 613.
181. *Ibid* at 705, 706; *Ibid* at 619.

in the ordinary course of its business is a badge of a floating charge and is inconsistent with the existence of a fixed charge."

ASSIGNMENT

[14.45] Any doubt which may have existed as to whether an assignment of a fixed charge over book debts could somehow result in the fixed charge becoming a floating one was removed by the decision in *William Gaskell Group Ltd v Highley Nos 1, 2, 3*.[182] In that case, the debentures provided for a fixed charge over all the companies' book debts in favour of Midland Bank with the proceeds of the book debts to be paid into a special account of the bank with a prohibition on withdrawal from such special account without the bank's prior consent. The bank assigned the charge to Waldis Investments. Morritt J held:[183]

"The effect of the assignment has been to divide the identity of the person whose consent is required, in the sense that Midland Bank, or such other bank as holds the account, would have to make the decision as banker whether or not to pay the cheque when the account was in debit, but the consent of the debenture holder continues to be required after the assignment. He has to decide whether or not to permit the special account to be drawn on at all and, if so, for what purpose. After the assignment, that person is Waldis Investments. Far from the restrictions falling away because they are, as alleged, commercially inoperable, it seems to me that they remain exactly the same as they were before but require the consent of Waldis Investments."

Thus the assignment of the fixed charge did not transform them into floating charges.

---

[182] [1994] 1 BCLC 197.
[183] *Ibid* at 205.

Chapter 15

Security over Deposits

[15.01] A number of publications indicate that cash is the best security available.[1] However, the Companies (Amendment) Act, 1990 and the application by the Supreme Court of that Act in *Re Atlantic Magnetics Ltd*[2] make it a far from satisfactory security in Ireland.

[15.02] The manner in which this security may be taken is for the deposit holder to execute a security document over its deposit in favour of the security holder.[3] The form of security itself may simply be a charge, either on its own or as part of a debenture under which other assets are charged. Alternatively, it may be an assignment by way of security over moneys held in the account (subject to a right of redemption) - this form of security should be taken only when the security holder is not holding the deposit.

[15.03] Most securities over deposits have been in favour of the bank holding the deposit - sometimes referred to as "cash-backed security". The bank advances moneys or perhaps grants a guarantee facility under which it gives a performance bond/letter of credit/VAT bond to a third party at the request of its customer who deposits an equivalent amount of moneys with the bank and charges it in favour of the bank.

SECURITY BY WAY OF CHARGE

Historical Conceptual Impossibility

[15.04] In 1984 Murphy J stated in the course of his judgment in *Re Euro Travel Ltd; Dempsey v The Governor and Company of the Bank of Ireland*:[4]

> "I find it difficult to accept the proposition that the company was purporting to charge monies in the hands of the bank itself with monies due by the company to the bank".

[1.] Milnes Holden, *The Law and Practice of Banking* (7th ed) Vol 2 para 30-1; Lingard, *Bank Security Documents* (3rd ed) para 18.1; Mather, *Securities Acceptable to the Lending Banker* (4th ed) p 257.

[2.] [1993] 2 IR 561; see para **[15.26]** below.

[3.] For an excellent article on security over cash see Hutchinson, 'Charge-backs, Set-off and Flawed Assets; Taking Security over Self-Held Cash Deposits' (1996) CLP 55.

[4.] High Court, unrep, 28 May 1984 at p 7.

His decision rested on other points which were in any event overruled by the Supreme Court. No one seemed to notice that Murphy J was doubting the technical ability of a company to charge its deposit in favour of the bank holding the deposit. The form of security seemed to be too well established.[5]

[15.05] Two years later Murphy J's statement was vindicated by the English High Court in *Re Charge Card Services Ltd.*[6] In deciding that it was not possible for a charge to be created in favour of a debtor over his own indebtedness to a creditor, Millett J stated:[7]

> "a charge in favour of a debtor of his own indebtedness to the chargor is conceptually impossible.
>
> A debt is a chose in action; it is the right to sue the debtor.[8] This can be assigned or made available to a third party, but not to the debtor, who cannot sue himself. Once any assignment or appropriation to the debtor becomes unconditional, the debt is wholly or partially released. The debtor cannot, and does not need to, resort to the creditor's claim against him in order to obtain the benefit of the security; his own liability to the creditor is automatically discharged or reduced.
>
> In *Halesowen Presswork & Assemblies Ltd v Westminster Bank Ltd,*[9] Buckley LJ stated, in a passage subsequently approved in the House of Lords by Viscount Dilhorne, Lord Simon and Lord Cross,[10] that he could not understand how it could be said with any kind of accuracy that the bank had a lien on its own indebtedness to its customer."

[15.06] This decision gave rise to much criticism.[11] The Final Report of the Legal Risk Review Committee in England[12] stated:

[5.] Although in *Broad v Commissioner of Stamp Duties* [1980] 2 NSWLR 40 Lee J held that a mortgage or charge over a credit balance in favour of the bank holding the credit was impossible as "there can be no mortgage or charge in favour of oneself of one's own indebtedness to another".
[6.] [1987] BCLC 17.
[7.] *Ibid* at 39 at 41.
[8.] "This view that a debt is just a right to sue must be at least 200 years out of date" - Wood, *'Charge Card* Revisited' (1988) Feb IFLR 26 at 27; see also *Evans* (1996) 17 Co Law 102 at 106.
[9.] [1970] 3 All ER 473 and 487.
[10.] [1972] 1 All ER 641 at 646, 651, 653; Lord Hoffmann indicated in his judgment in *Re Bank of Credit and Commerce International SA (No 8)* [1997] 4 All ER 568 at 576 "that these observations were directed to the use of the word "lien" which is a right to retain possession, rather than to the question of whether the bank could have any kind of proprietary interest".
[11.] See Dillon LJ in *Welsh Development Agency v Export Finance Company Ltd* [1992] BCLC 148 at 166; see McCracken, *The Banker's Remedy of Set-Off* (Butterworths, 1993) Ch 8; Parsons [1987] 3 JIBL 165; Wood (1987) Co Law 262; (1988) Feb IFLR 26, (1988) July IFLR 4; (1988) Oct IFLR 4; Mayo [1992] 7 JIBL 257; Calnan (1996) JIBFL 111; for a contrary view see Goode, *Legal Problems of Credit and Security* (2nd ed) pp 110 and 124-129; Bamford (1988) May IFLR 8; (1988) Aug IFLR 4; Pollard [1988] JBL 127 and 219.
[12.] October, 1992.

"the *dictum* in the decision appears to be contrary to previous decided appeal cases which were binding on the Charge Card court".

While it was suggested that some writers in condemning the decision "have been driven to near hysteria",[13] the Legal Risk Review Committee's Report made uncomfortable reading for bankers and their lawyers, in stating,[14]

"It is probable that there are a large number of existing transactions where the parties believe, wrongly if the *Charge Card* decision is followed, that security is in place. The distinction which that case makes between debts by reference to the parties between whom they are owed bears little relation to commercial practice. Legal decisions of this kind tend to bring the law into disrepute and create real risks for business".

Nonetheless, the Registrar of Companies in England and Wales took note by announcing that he would no longer register charges over deposits in favour of the bank holding the deposit.[15] It seems, prudent lawyers ignored the Registrar's announcement and continued to present particulars for registration for fear that the Registrar could be wrong and the security unenforceable for lack of registration.[16] In any event, the decision in *Re Charge Card Services Ltd*[17] ran contrary to the decision of a more senior court in *Ex p Caldicott, In re Hart*,[18] where the Court of Appeal held that a charge by a depositor over his deposit in favour of the depositee was valid security which could be enforced outside the depositor's bankruptcy.[19] Accordingly, many bankers continued to take charges over deposits.[20] The decision, however, caused enough uncertainty as to give rise to a practice recommendation from the Financial Law Panel in London.[21] Indeed some common law jurisdictions enacted legislation to counteract its effect.[22]

[13.] Bamford, '*Charge Card* - the Case for the Defence' (1988) May IFLR 8.

[14.] At para 6.5 in Appendix 2.

[15.] Lingard, *Bank Security Documents* (3rd ed) para 18.2.

[16.] Parsons, 'Re-Drafting Bank Security Documents Following *Charge Card Services*' [1987] 3 JIBL 165 at 169.

[17.] [1987] BCLC 17.

[18.] (1884) 25 Ch D 716.

[19.] The deed provided that £8,750 placed on deposit should be a security for, and stand charged with, the payment to the bank of the balance for the time being owing from the firm to the bank on their current account.

[20.] See Rowbotham, 'Can Banks Secure their own Deposits' (1987) IFLR 18.

[21.] Security over Cash Deposits - a Practice Recommendation - July 1994.

[22.] Hong Kong - Law Amendment and Reform (Consolidation) Ordinance S15A, applied in *Tam Wing Chuen v Bank of Credit and Commerce Hong Kong Ltd (in liq)* [1996] 2 BCLC 69; Bermuda, 'Charge and Security (Special Provisions) Act 1990; Cayman Islands - the Property (Miscellaneous Provisions) Law 1994'.

[15.07] In December 1995, the English Court of Appeal sought to explain and clarify the decision in *Re Bank of Credit and Commerce International SA (No 8)*.[23] The clarification given by the Court of Appeal (which included Millett LJ) was seen as an effort to justify the 1986 decision of Millett J (as he then was).[24] Rose LJ stated:[25]

> "... we would affirm his decision that a charge-back does not create and vest in the chargee a proprietary interest in the debt which he owes to the chargor; and that it is not, therefore, a charge properly so called within the meaning of s 395 of the Companies Act 1985.[26]
>
> Charge-backs are a commonplace. Charges over bank deposits in favour of the bank ... are everyday examples. It is important that such routine financing arrangements should not be put at risk. If the reasoning in *Re Charge Card Services Ltd* led to the conclusion that chargebacks were invalid or ineffective to give security in the event of the chargor's insolvency, then that reasoning would be suspect."

This explanation was highly unsatisfactory as Millett J clearly indicated a charge-back was impossible.[27] In acknowledging that a charge-back did not achieve its intention but nonetheless gave a security interest, Rose LJ stated:[28]

> "Since a charge-back is incapable of vesting a proprietary interest in the chargee, its effect is purely contractual. It takes effect according to its tenor. The terms of the letters of charge/lien in the present case[29] expressly prohibit the depositor from dealing with the deposit or from withdrawing it while the principal debt is unpaid and gives the bank power to set off the amount of the deposit against the principal debt. We should expect these consequences to follow from the use of the word 'charge' itself, even if they were not expressly spelled out in the document creating the charge-back.
>
> These provisions fetter the depositor's use of the deposit while the principal debt remains unpaid. In his hands the deposit - his chose in action - is a flawed asset. If he becomes insolvent, the asset forms part of the insolvent estate, but it

---

23. [1996] 2 BCLC 254; also known as *Morris v Agrichemicals Ltd* [1996] BCC 204.
24. Segal, 'Conceptual Implausibility in the Court of Appeal' [1996] 6 JIBL 397 - "is an appeal of a first instance decision based on an appellate judgment written by the judge of first instance a conceptual impossibility? The point is, of course, that Millett LJ, the judge who gave the Charge Card decision, was a member of the panel in the Court of Appeal and clearly had a significant hand in writing the judgment. The result is, not surprisingly, something of an apologia and piece of self-justification".
25. [1996] 2 BCLC 254 at 267.
26. Equivalent to the Companies Act, 1963, s 99.
27. See para **[15.05]** above.
28. [1996] 2 BCLC 254 at 268.
29. In this case a bank loan was secured by a purported charge from a third party over the third party's deposit with the bank but without any covenant (in the nature of a guarantee or otherwise) from the third party - a strict collateral security.

remains a flawed asset subject to the same contractual restrictions as before. If the charge-back secures a pre-existing obligation of the depositor, as in *Re Charge Card Services Ltd*, the bank is entitled, and may be bound to set off the amount of the deposit against it under r 4.90. The same result will follow if the charge-back is supported by a personal covenant or guarantee of the depositor.

If the charge-back is a non-recourse collateral security which secures the debt of a third party, the bank will be unable to set off the amount of the deposit against the debt owing to it from the third party. But this will be of little if any practical significance. The bank has the money; the depositor's trustee or liquidator cannot obtain payment while the debt of the third party is outstanding. But it will be his duty to get in the deposit as one of the assets of the estate. It will almost invariably be in the interests of the general body of creditors for him to permit the bank to recoup itself out of the deposit, take delivery of any other securities which the bank holds for the principal debt, and seek to recover from the principal debtor".

This form of security known as a "flawed asset security" is, the author believes, unsatisfactory for a banker as it cannot set off the two liabilities but must await what may be a long process of liquidation. A bank will wish to close its account and utilise its resources for other business.

[15.08] The thinking behind the courts' decisions in *Re Charge Card Services Ltd*[30] and in *Re Bank of Credit and Commerce International SA (No 8)*[31] was understandable in the context of a mortgage or security by way of assignment but not in the context of a charge.[32] As already seen,[33] a mortgage is the transfer of an asset to be held absolutely by the mortgagee subject to the right of the mortgagor to have the asset transferred back to it upon the discharge of the obligations or liabilities for which the mortgage is taken. A security by way of assignment is effectively the same as a mortgage.[34] If the debt due by the bank to its customer (ie the customer's deposit with the bank) is transferred by the customer back to the bank, the debt is extinguished.

Feasibility of Charge-Back

[15.09] However, a charge, in contrast to a mortgage, is the setting aside by the chargor of its property (the subject of the charge) out of which the chargee may

---

30. [1987] BCLC 17.
31. [1996] 2 BCLC 254.
32. Support for this can be found in McCracken, *The Banker's Remedy of Set-Off* (Butterworths 1993) p 180; although Goode, *Legal Problems of Credit and Security* (2nd ed) pp 125-129 suggests that the *Charge Card Services* decision is correct with regard to charges.
33. See para **[10.02]-[10.03]**.
34. *Ibid*; see para **[11.25]**.

help itself in discharge of the chargor's obligations or liabilities to the chargee.[35]
In *Re Charge Card Services Ltd* [36] Millett J stated:[37]

> "The essence of an equitable charge is that, without any conveyance or
> assignment to the chargee, specific property of the chargor is expressly or
> constructively appropriated to or made answerable for payment of a debt, and
> the chargee is given the right to resort to the property for the purpose of having
> it realised and applied in or towards payment of the debt."

In other words, a charge is an encumbrance in favour of the chargee but it does
not transfer title to the asset - title passes only if and when the chargee exercises
its power of enforcement under the terms of the charge. Accordingly, when the
customer charges its deposit in favour of the bank holding the deposit, it is
simply saying to the bank that this debt which you owe to me may be held by
you as security for my obligations or indebtedness to you. If I fail to discharge
these, then you may have the debt back or as much of it as will discharge my
obligations or indebtedness; in the meantime no one else will have a prior right
to that debt either before or after my bankruptcy/liquidation.

[15.10] This distinction between a mortgage (or security by way of assignment)
and a charge was clarified and confirmed by the House of Lords in its judgment
in upholding the Court of Appeal's decision in *Re Bank of Credit and
Commerce International SA (No 8)*,[38] albeit on different grounds. Lord
Hoffmann in giving the decision of the House of Lords explained how a charge
(but not a mortgage) could be taken by the holder of a deposit, over the
deposit:[39]

> "A charge is a security interest created without any transfer of title or
> possession to the beneficiary ... The depositor's right to claim payment of his
> deposit is a chose in action which the law has always recognised as property.
> There is no dispute that a charge over such a chose in action can validly be
> granted to a third party. In which respects would the fact that the beneficiary of
> the charge was the debtor himself be inconsistent with the transaction having
> some or all of the various features which I have enumerated? The method by
> which the property would be realised would differ slightly: instead of the
> beneficiary of the charge having to claim payment from the debtor, the
> realisation would take the form of a book entry. In no other respect, as it seems
> to me, would the transaction have any consequences different from those which
> would attach to a charge given to a third party. It would be a proprietary

---

35. See para **[11.25]**.
36. [1987] BCLC 17.
37. *Ibid* at 40; see also *Swiss Bank Corporation v Lloyds Bank Ltd* [1980] 2 All ER 419 and [1981]
    2 All ER 449.
38. [1997] 4 All ER 568 (also referred to as *Morris v Rayners Enterprises Inc*).
39. *Ibid* at 576.

interest in the sense that, subject to questions of registration and purchaser for value without notice, it would be binding upon assignees and a liquidator or trustee in bankruptcy. The depositor would retain an equity of redemption and all the rights which that implies. There would be no merger of interests because the depositor would retain title to the deposit subject only to the bank's charge. The creation of the charge would be consensual and not require any formal assignment or vesting of title in the bank. If all these features can exist despite the fact that the beneficiary of the charge is the debtor, I cannot see why it cannot properly be said that the debtor has a proprietary interest by way of charge over the debt."

Accordingly, it is now permissible in England and, in view of what must be seen as the correct approach adopted by Lord Hoffmann,[40] in other common law jurisdictions including Ireland that an effective first fixed charge can be created by a depositor over its deposit with a bank to secure its indebtedness to the bank. Lord Hoffmann was not shy about delivering some retribution to Millett J for the mayhem he caused in *Re Charge Card Services Ltd*[41] by indicating, "I think that the courts should be very slow to declare a practice of the commercial community to be conceptually impossible. Rules of law must obviously be consistent and not self-contradictory". Nevertheless, the difficulty in giving security to the holder of the deposit remains where such security is given by way of mortgage or security assignment.

SECURITY BY WAY OF FLAWED ASSET

[15.11] The approach of a flawed asset arrangement is advocated by a number of commentators in England.[42] Under this arrangement a person deposits funds with a bank on the terms that it is not repayable until certain conditions are fulfilled. The principal condition is that no moneys are due or owing by the depositor to the bank. Thus the bank simply has the right to retain the deposit until the depositor's indebtedness is cleared. This approach remains to be tested in the courts.[43] Although it appears not to create a charge, it may offend public policy under the *pari passu* principle.[44] Furthermore, it is not clear how a liquidator of a depositor is expected to discharge the bank debt if he has no recourse to funds and cannot utilise the deposit.[45]

[40.] Although his decision on this point was *obiter* it is likely to be followed.

[41.] [1987] BCLC 17.

[42.] Shea [1986] 3 JIBL 192; Rowbotham (1987) Jan IFLR 19; Parsons [1987] 3 JIBL 165; Pollard (1988) JBL 219.

[43.] Calnan states in 'Security over Deposits after re BCCI (No 8)' (1996) JIBFL 11 at 116:
"Although it is theoretically possible to establish the deposit as a flawed asset, it will be very difficult to achieve in practice and is fraught with uncertainties in the bankruptcy or liquidation of the customer".

[44.] Companies Act, 1963, s 275, see para **[15.18]** below.

[45.] Hutchinson (1996) CLP 55 at 66 suggests that a liquidator would be duty bound to allow the bank set the deposit against the principal debt so that he can recover the balance of the deposit, but he queries whether a liquidator should permit the bank to do so where there will be no balance coming back to the liquidator.

SECURITY BY WAY OF ASSIGNMENT

Form of Security

[15.12] Some banks, where they are part of a group of companies, particularly if more than one entity in the group is licensed to take deposits,[46] can request their customer to place their deposit in another entity in the group. This approach was a useful method of providing effective security while avoiding the problems caused by Millett J's decision in *Re Charge Card Services Ltd.*[47] (the bank holding the security being a separate entity from the bank holding the deposit). Now that these problems have been resolved, at least with regard to charges,[48] the security by way of assignment is likely to be confined principally to structural financing transactions.

An assignment over a deposit held with another institution in favour of the lender will be the cleanest form of security. The language creating the security might read as follows:

> "the company as beneficial owner hereby assigns to the lender all the company's right, title and interest in and to all sums from time to time standing to the credit of the company's account with the bank and all rights, benefits and proceeds thereof provided that if at any time the company is under no obligation present or future, actual or contingent to the bank under [the facility letter (as defined)], the lender will at the request and cost of the company reassign the property hereby assigned to the company or as it may direct".

Notice of Assignment

[15.13] Notice of the security should be given to the bank holding the deposit and an acknowledgement sought. This will bring the security within the requirements of a legal assignment pursuant to the Supreme Court of Judicature Act (Ireland) 1877.[49] The notice and its acknowledgement might read as follows:

Notice of Assignment

To: [name of bank holding account]

[address]

("Account Holder") [Date]

---

46. Pursuant to the Central Bank Act, 1971, s 9.
47. [1987] BCLC 17; it is pointed out by Lingard, *Bank Security Documents* (3rd ed) para 18.29 that this procedure destroys any possibility of set off or of netting-off for prudential purposes.
48. By the House of Lords in *Re Bank of Credit and Commerce International SA (No 8)* [1997] 4 All ER 568 see para **[15.10]** above; although this part of the decision was obiter and thus not binding it is likely to be adopted in subsequent court decisions.
49. Section 28(6); see further para **[14.02]**.

The undersigned refer to the accounts opened by [name of company] ("the Company") with the Account Holder and such other accounts from time to time held by the Company with your bank (the "Charged Accounts").

NOW WE HEREBY GIVE YOU NOTICE that:

1. By a deed of assignment dated [date], made between the Company and [name of security holder] ("the Lender") the Company assigned by way of security all sums from time to time standing to the credit of the Charged Accounts in favour of the Lender.

2. Dealings on the Charged Accounts by the Company are permitted unless and until the Lender shall notify you that no further dealings are permitted, in which event you are hereby irrevocably authorised and instructed to pay any moneys comprised within the Charged Accounts to the Lender or its order at such place as the Lender may from time to time direct.

The authority and instructions herein contained may only be revoked or varied in writing jointly executed by the undersigned.

For and on behalf of

[name of company]

_____

For and on behalf of

[name of security holder]

_____

Acknowledgement of Notice

of Assignment

To: [Name of company]

[Name of security holder]

[date]

We acknowledge receipt of a notice of assignment dated [date] from [name of company] ("the Company") and [name of security holder] ("the Lender") (the "Notice") in respect of the Charged Accounts (as defined in the Notice) and for good and valuable consideration (the receipt and sufficiency whereof is hereby acknowledged) we agree that:

1. We consent to the creation of the security granted by the Company in favour of the Lender pursuant to the assignment dated, [date];

2. We have received no notice of any prior charge, assignment or encumbrance of the property thereby stated to be assigned;

3. We will not without your joint prior written consent, vary, rescind or otherwise alter or terminate the agreement between the Company and ourselves regulating the Charged Accounts and the terms upon which the moneys comprised within the Charged Accounts held by us or in any way prejudice the rights, title and interests assigned in favour of the Lender.

4. We will not claim to set-off[50] to the prejudice of the Lender any of the moneys comprised within the Charged Accounts against any claim we may have against the Company howsoever arising.

For and on behalf of

_____

Duly authorised officer

[name of bank holding account]

[15.14] Particulars of the assignment, when given by a company, should probably be registered in the Companies Registration Office within 21 days of the creation of the assignment.[51] This is on the grounds that it is a charge on a "book debt" that is, a debt owing by the bank holding the deposit to the chargor. If it is not deemed to be a book debt[52] - and in accounting terms for a company's balance sheet it will be treated as "cash at bank" rather than "debtors"[53] - then registration is not required. In the most recent judgment touching on the issue, Lord Hoffman stated:[54]

> "In my view, this is a matter on which banks are entitled to make up their own minds and take their own advice on whether the deposit charged is a `book debt' or not. I express no view on the point, but the judgment of my noble and learned friend Lord Hutton in *Northern Bank Ltd v Ross* [1990] BCC 883 suggest that, in the case of deposits with banks, an obligation to register is unlikely to arise".

However, it is advisable, and indeed the practice, to register as a matter of precaution.[55]

---

50. In the absence of this acknowledgement the bank holding the account will be entitled to set off monies due to it by the customer at the time of receipt of notice (but not monies owing subsequent to the receipt of notice) against the account even after receipt of notice of assignment - *Business Computers Ltd v Anglo-African Leasing Ltd* [1977] 2 All ER 741; see also Kay LJ in *Biggerstaff v Rowatt's Whart Ltd* [1896] 2 Ch 93 at 105.

51. Pursuant to the Companies Act, 1963, s 99; see paras **[17.21]-[17.26]** below.

52. "In principle I doubt that monies due by a banker to its customer and whether or not recorded in books or other documents would properly be described as book debts in that sense" - per Murphy J in *Re Euro Travel Ltd, Dempsey v The Governor and Company of the Bank of Ireland* High Court, unrep 28 May 1984 at p 8.

53. Lingard, *Bank Security Documents* (3rd ed) para 18.23 submits the accounting convention is immaterial as it simply differentiates debts owed by banks from those owed by other debtors.

54. In *Re Bank of Credit and Commerce International SA (No 8)* [1997] 4 All ER 568 at 577.

55. This is dealt with more fully at paras **[17.21]-[17.26]**.

SECURITY BY WAY OF LETTER OF SET-OFF[56]

[15.15] A lender who does not wish to use a third party bank as a depositee may take effective security by way of a letter of set-off over the customer's account with it.[57] Apparently the practice of set-off arose following the Supreme Court's decision in *The Governor and Company of the Bank of Ireland v Martin and Martin*.[58] In that case, the bank was prohibited from setting off moneys in a customer's deposit account against the customer's liability to the bank under a guarantee as the customer had not specifically consented to the set-off.[59] A letter of set-off, provided it has been carefully drafted to avoid creating an encumbrance, can be effective without registering particulars against the corporate customer's file in the Companies Registration Office.[60] It is inappropriate for a letter of set-off to provide for a lien on the amounts in the account as such amounts are not a tangible asset[61] - the security does not relate to specific coins or notes but simply money. A letter of set-off, by not creating an encumbrance, will have the benefit also of avoiding a breach by the customer of most types of negative pledge covenants.[62] This is particularly useful in the case of large corporate bodies who may engage in non-recourse leasing transactions to diminish their tax liability. The structure of such transactions often involves the placing of a deposit as security for an obligation of the depositor under the transaction. It should be noted that such a deposit placed in a

---

[56.] For an excellent treatment see McCracken, *The Banker's Remedy of Set-Off* (Butterworths 1993) Ch 8.

[57.] See also The Financial Law Panel, *Security over Cash Deposits - A Practice Recommendation*, July 1994; for further reading see Shannon, *Contractual Set-Off as a form of Bank Security from an Irish incorporated company* (Irish Centre for Commercial Law Studies 1992); see also Earley, 'Set-off Rights Available to Banks in Ireland' [1997] 4 JIBL 153; it is however subject to public policy considerations pursuant to the Companies Act, 1963 s 275 (see para **[15.16]** below.

[58.] [1937] IR 189; see Murphy J in *Re Euro Travel Ltd, Dempsey v Bank of Ireland* unrep 28 May 1984 p 9.

[59.] See para **[4.24]** above.

[60.] See Goode, *Legal Problems of Credit and Security* (2nd ed) p 173; see also Lingard, *Bank Security Documents* (3rd ed) para 18.7; although a contrary view is taken by Pollard in *Credit Balances as Security - II* (1988) JIBL 219 at 220; see also McCracken, *The Banker's Remedy of Set-Off* (Butterworths, 1993) p 183; it should be noted though in England a contractual set-off is more likely to be registrable, as a charge under the Companies Act 1985 (as amended by the Companies Act 1989, s 93) includes a security interest - a position not prevailing in Ireland; but see Shannon, *Contractual Set-Off as a Form of Bank Security from an Irish incorporated company (Irish Centre for Commercial Law Studies 1992)* pp 29 and 33 where he considers a contractual right of set-off does create a charge but is not registrable on the grounds that a bank balance is not a book debt.

[61.] See O'Connor MR in *Re Morris: Coneys v Morris* [1922] 1 IR 136 at 138.

[62.] See further McCracken, *The Banker's Remedy of Set-Off* (Butterworths, 1993) pp 165-6; see also *Paget's Law of Banking* (11th ed) Butterworths p 547.

transaction where recourse against the depositor is limited to the deposit, may be used to pay the bank's general creditors in the event of the bank's insolvency rather than being used for the purpose of the transaction.[63] Accordingly, the creditworthiness of the bank should not be overlooked when structuring such a transaction.

[15.16] A simple letter of set-off might read along the following lines:

LETTER OF SET-OFF

To: [Name and address of Bank]

In consideration of your making available or continuing to make available to us or on our behalf banking accommodation and/or other financial facilities for so long as you may think fit:

1. We hereby irrevocably authorise and empower you pending payment of any bills, notes, overdrafts, loans, guarantees or other contingencies in respect of which we may be or become liable to you whether as principal, surety or otherwise on any account or in any other manner whatsoever ("Such Liabilities"), and notwithstanding that Such Liabilities may be contingent to hold and retain all monies which now or hereafter may stand to our credit on any current account with you until such time as all Such Liabilities are discharged in full.

2. Where Such Liabilities become due and payable, to the extent that Such Liabilities become due and payable, sums standing to our credit on any fixed term deposit account or other such account which would otherwise become payable to us at a future date shall without further notice or demand become immediately due and payable and subject to the right of set-off herein contained and, for the avoidance of doubt, we hereby consent to the early expiration of the term for which those sums were deposited.

3. Where sums standing to our credit on any deposit account (whether fixed term or otherwise) may become due and payable before Such Liabilities become due and payable we hereby irrevocably agree and consent to the date on which those sums are to become due and payable being postponed until Such Liabilities become due and payable.

4. We hereby covenant not to withdraw, pledge, charge, hold in trust, encumber or otherwise deal with all such monies, until Such Liabilities are discharged in full. If notice of a meeting of members or creditors is given to consider a resolution to wind us up or a notice is given that a petition to appoint an examiner or to wind us up is to be presented to the courts or we act in breach of the covenant herein contained, all Such Liabilities shall become immediately due and payable and such notice or breach shall constitute sufficient and proper authority for you to set-off, transfer or apply any credit in any

---

[63.] See *Tam Wing Chuen v Bank of Credit and Commerce Hong Kong Ltd* [1996] BCC 388.

of our accounts with you (including those accounts referred to at clauses 2 and 3 hereof) (together the "Accounts") towards the repayment or discharge of Such Liabilities,

5. You are hereby irrevocably and unconditionally authorised and empowered to set-off, transfer and apply such monies in the Accounts or any part thereof from time to time in or towards satisfaction of Such Liabilities entirely at your own discretion without further notice or demand and such set-off, transfer and application will be a good and valid discharge of such monies so applied without further endorsement or authorisation whatsoever.[64]

6. For the avoidance of doubt, it is understood that where the provisions of this Letter conflict with the instructions contained in any mandate given to you by us or on our behalf the provisions of this Letter shall prevail.

7. This letter shall be governed by the laws of Ireland.

Dated this day of

SIGNED by

for and on behalf of

[name of depositor]

in the presence of:

The language should be sufficient to precipitate amounts on deposit becoming immediately due and payable as required to come within the set-off requirement of mutuality.[65] It should also have the effect of giving the necessary contractual authority to a banker to set-off funds lodged with it against amounts owed to it. In *The Governor and Company of the Bank of Ireland v Martin and Martin*[66] the Supreme Court held that, except where a depositor has consented, a bank is not entitled to set off a deposit of a guarantor to discharge a debt due by the principal debtor to the bank.

Infringement of Negative Pledge

[15.17] The balance of authority suggests that a charge over a bank balance would not require registration[67] as it is a charge on a debt and not on a book debt.[68] While the author believes that a contractual letter of set-off which does

---

[64.] Turing [1996] JIBL 170 at 174 points out that security by set-off rather than by mortgage or charge has the added benefit that the secured party should not have to first demand the secured indebtedness to give the security provider the opportunity to redeem.

[65.] See Pollard, 'Credit Balances as Security - II' (1988) JBL 219 at 227; thereby getting around the impediment of being unable to combine accounts of different categories (*Bradford Old Bank, Ltd v Sutcliffe* [1918] 2 KB 833) see further para **[4.21]**.

[66.] [1937] IR 189 at 203.

[67.] Pursuant to the Companies Act, 1963, s 99(2)(e).

[68.] See paras **[17.21]-[17.26]** (notwithstanding the practice to register such charges).

not create an encumbrance should not infringe a covenant given by the customer to a third party not to create any mortgage, charge, pledge, lien or encumbrance over its assets, it must be pointed out that English authority indicates otherwise. In *Swiss Bank Corporation v Lloyds Bank Ltd*[69] Buckley LJ in the Court of Appeal[70] stated:[71]

> "... whether a particular transaction gives rise to an equitable charge ... must depend on the intention of the parties ascertained from what they have done in the then existing circumstances. The intention may be expressed or it may be inferred. If the debtor undertakes to segregate a particular fund or asset and to pay the debt out of that fund or asset, the inference may be drawn, in the absence of any contra indication, that the parties' intention is that the creditor should have such a proprietary interest in the segregated fund or asset as will enable him to realise out of it the amount owed to him by the debtor".

The court applied the test of Atkin LJ in *National Provincial and Union Bank of England v Charnley*,[72] namely:

> "... there can be no doubt that where in a transaction for value both parties evince an intention that property, existing or future, shall be made available as security for the payment of a debt, and that the creditor shall have a present right to have it made available, there is a charge, even though the present legal right which is contemplated can only be enforced at some future date."

Letters of Set-off and Public Policy

[15.18] There may be a possibility that a contractual arrangement to bring about mutuality, which would not otherwise exist, could be contrary to what may be regarded as the public policy provisions of s 275 of the Companies Act, 1963.[73] This stipulates that, subject to the Act's provisions as to preferential payments[74] and to agreements as to subordination:[75] "the property of a company on its winding up shall be applied in satisfaction of its liabilities *pari passu*."

[15.19] The application of this principle can be seen from the English case of *British Eagle International Airlines Ltd v Compagnie Nationale Air France*.[76] In that case, the plaintiff and defendant were international airlines and were parties

---

[69.] [1980] 2 All ER 419.
[70.] The Court's decision was upheld by the House of Lords - [1981] 2 All ER 449.
[71.] [1980] 2 All ER 419, at 426.
[72.] [1924] 1 KB 431, at 449.
[73.] See Rose LJ in *Re Bank of Credit and Commerce International SA (No 8)* [1996] 2 BCLC 254 at 262; Lord Hoffmann in *Re Bank of Credit and Commerce International SA (No 8)* [1997] 4 All ER 568 at 573; see also Shea [1986] 3 JIBL 192 at 196; Parsons [1987] 3 JIBL 165 at 168.
[74.] Principally arising pursuant to the Companies Act, 1963, s 285.
[75.] Companies Act, 1963, s 275(2).
[76.] [1975] 2 All ER 390.

to the IATA clearing house agreement. This provided for regular settling of debts by way of set-off with the balance to be paid by the person in deficit. The liquidator of the plaintiff sought to disclaim the clearing house agreement. Both the High Court and the Court of Appeal held that the clearing house agreement was binding on the liquidator. However, the House of Lords by a three to two majority decided otherwise. They held that insofar as the parties to the clearing house arrangements had, by agreeing that simple contract debts were to be settled in a particular way, contracted out of the English equivalent to s 275 which provided for the payment of unsecured debts *pari passu*. Accordingly, the arrangements were contrary to public policy and the general rules of liquidation prevailed. Thus on its liquidation, the plaintiff became entitled to recover payment of debts due to it by other airlines and the airlines which had rendered services to it could only prove in the plaintiff's liquidation for the sums due to it. In giving the principal judgment of the majority Lord Cross quoted[77] a passage from the decision of James LJ in *Ex p Mackay*:[78]

"a man is not allowed by stipulation with a creditor, to provide for a different distribution of his effects in the event of bankruptcy from that which the law provides."

Lord Cross continued:

"The documents were not drawn so as to create charges but simply so as to set up by simple contract a method of settling each other's mutual indebtedness at monthly intervals ... The 'clearing house' creditors are clearly not secured creditors. They are claiming nevertheless that they ought not to be treated in the liquidation as ordinary unsecured creditors but that they have achieved by the medium of the 'clearing house' agreement a position analogous to that of secured creditors without the need for the creation and registration of charges on the book debts in question".

He concluded by indicating that the suggestion by Air France that they had contracted out of the *pari passu* principle of the English equivalent to s 275 was contrary to public policy.

A useful explanation of that decision was given subsequently by Gibson J in *Carreras Rothmans Ltd v Freeman Mathews Treasure Ltd*[79] where he said:[80]

"the principle that I would extract from that case is that where the effect of a contract is that an asset which is actually owned by a company at the commencement of its liquidation would be dealt with in a way other than in accordance with [the English equivalent to s275], then to that extent the

---

77. [1975] 2 All ER 390, at 410.
78. (1873) 8 Ch App 643, at 647.
79. [1984] BCLC 420.
80. *Ibid* at 436.

contract as a matter of public policy is avoided, whether or not the contract was entered into for consideration and for bona fide commercial reasons and whether or not the contractual provisions affecting that asset is expressed to take effect only on insolvency."

[15.20] This explanation and analysis was approved by Costello J in *Glow Heating Ltd v The Eastern Health Board, Rooney and Building and Engineering Ltd (in liq).*[81] Costello J indicated that s 275 does not mean that every contract by which a party obtains superior rights to ordinary creditors is void. This would conflict with retention of title clauses and retention clauses in building contracts. In referring to the decision in *British Eagle International Airlines Ltd v Compagnie Nationale Air France,*[82] Costello J said:[83]

"The House of Lords decision in no way conflicts with the well established principle of insolvency law that a liquidator takes the company's property subject to the liabilities which affected it in the company's hands."

[15.21] The authorities, such as they are, still leave open the question as to whether a contractual letter of set-off could be found to be contrary to public policy. It is the absence of a charge in a letter of set-off[84] which leaves the bank's security in the hands of the judiciary, for:

"the statutory duty of the liquidator in each case[85] is to collect the assets of the company and to apply them in discharge of its liabilities. For this purpose unsecured creditors, unless preferred or deferred, rank equally and share *pari passu* [(see s 275 of the Companies Act, 1963)]. The assets which the liquidator is able to collect and distribute are however necessarily those which are free from a charge."[86]

The application of Costello J's decision to a letter of set-off would indicate that the exercise of the set-off prior to the commencement of the company's liquidation will be effective (unless the letter itself is executed within a fraudulent preference period and such preference is proved[87]). If it is not so exercised, then the bank will have to prove its claim as a creditor in the liquidation and show that the deposit and the indebtedness (to it) are "mutual credits or debts".[88]

[81.] [1988] IR 110, at 119.

[82.] [1975] 2 All ER 390.

[83.] [1988] IR 110, at 120.

[84.] Thereby avoiding the problems created by registration, negative pledges and the *Charge Card Services* decision.

[85.] Whether the winding up is compulsory or voluntary.

[86.] Lord Brightman in *Roberts Petroleum Ltd v Bernard Kenny Ltd (in liq)* [1983] 1 All ER 564 at 572.

[87.] Companies Act, 1963, s 286.

[88.] Within the meaning of para 17(1) of the First Schedule to the Bankruptcy Act, 1988.

[15.22] In *Re Euro Travel Ltd; Dempsey v The Governor and Company of the Bank of Ireland*,[89] Eurotravel Ltd arranged for Bank of Ireland to issue a guarantee in respect of its travel agent business. Eurotravel Ltd gave the bank an indemnity, in respect of its liability under the guarantee, under which the bank was authorised to honour its guarantee and to debit such moneys held by the bank from Eurotravel Ltd. The bank received a demand under the guarantee and paid on foot of it. The bank did not debit any amount from the company's account with it but purported to do so after a liquidator was appointed to the company. The High Court held[90] that the bank was not entitled to debit moneys but the Supreme Court allowed the bank's appeal. In allowing the bank's appeal Henchy J, in delivering the Supreme Court's principal judgment, distinguished the case from *Re Fenton*,[91] where the bank's right of set-off was disallowed, as on the relevant date the bankrupt had not been called upon to pay and so on that date there was no debt owed that could be set off.[92] In *Re Euro Travel; Dempsey v The Governor and Company of the Bank of Ireland*[93] the bank was not proving in the winding up but relying on its contractual right to deduct which had arisen once demand had been made on it under the guarantee. Henchy J held:[94]

> "To say that when the liquidator takes over, the assets of the company vest in him is a less than complete statement of the legal position. The general rule is that he acquires only such title to the assets as the company had - no more, no less. He cannot take any better title to any part of the assets than the company had. This means that he takes the assets subject to any pre-existing enforceable right of a third party in or over them.
>
> When, on the passing of the winding up resolution ..., the moneys standing to the credit of Eurotravel in its current and deposit accounts in the Bank on that date became vested in the liquidator, they became so vested subject to the right over those accounts that had been created in favour of the Bank by the [indemnity]. That right was originally a contingent one and it was to the effect that if the Bank was called on ... by the trustees to pay £75,000, while it would be bound to do so, it could reimburse itself by debiting Eurotravel's accounts with that sum. But when the trustees called on the Bank to pay them £75,000 ... and the Bank became forthwith bound to make that payment, Eurotravel's accounts in the Bank became actually rather than contingently subject to the Bank's right to debit. It was that state of contractual liability that those accounts

---

89. Supreme Court, unrep, 6 December 1985.
90. High Court, unrep, 28 May 1984 Murphy J.
91. [1931] 1 Ch 85.
92. See also *Re a Debtor (No 66 of 1955) ex p The Debtor v The Trustee of the Property of Waite* [1956] 3 All ER 225 where the guarantor had not paid anything on the relevant date and therefore could not set-off anything on that date.
93. Supreme Court, unrep, 6 December 1985.
94. Page 8 and following.

passed to the liquidator. Immediately before the liquidator took over .... the Bank was entitled to say that it was bound to pay the £75,000 and entitled to recover it forthwith by debiting it against Eurotravel's accounts.

The fact that the Bank did not pay the £75,000 or exercise its right to debit until after the winding up had commenced seems to me to be irrelevant for present purposes. What matters is that Eurotravel's bank accounts passed to the liquidator subject to the Bank's enforceable right to pay the £75,000 and to debit that sum against those accounts. The intervention of the winding up did not override or pre-empt the Bank's ability to give effect to that right, any more than it would affect an enforceable lien or charge on those accounts existing on the relevant date. If follows that the Bank's accrued right to debit took precedence over the liquidator's title to the accounts".

Letters of Set-Off by Guarantors

[15.23] Letters of set-off have been upheld even where given by a third party guarantor over the guarantor's deposit with the bank. In *MS Fashions Ltd v Bank of Credit and Commerce International SA (No 2)*[95] the directors of a number of companies agreed to guarantee their company's debts to BCCI. They declared that as a separate and independent obligation the company's liabilities could be recovered from them "as principal debtor and/or by way of indemnity" and shall be repaid on demand whether or not demand was made on the company. In support of this, they deposited moneys with the bank and agreed that the bank could at any time, without further notice, appropriate by way of set-off or otherwise the deposited moneys in or towards satisfaction of the directors' indebtedness to the bank.

In the English Court of Appeal, Dillon LJ held:[96]

"There is a debt presently due from each of the companies to BCCI and equally due from Mr Amir or Mr Ahmed as the case may be as a principal debtor to BCCI and there is the liability from BCCI to Mr Amir and Mr Ahmed for the deposits. That satisfies, entirely, in my judgment, the requirements for statutory set-off ... and consequently r 4.90[97] has automatic effect."

The critical feature here was that although the nature of the directors' obligations was by way of guarantee and thus a contingent debt, the language of the security made them primarily liable for the debt and thus the directors were liable notwithstanding that no demand had been made under the guarantee.

[95.] [1993] BCLC 1200; [1993] 3 All ER 769 the case involved three actions and it is referred to also as *High Street Services Ltd v Bank of Credit and Commerce International SA* [1993] BCC 70 and 360.

[96.] [1993] BCLC 1200 at 1217; [1993] 3 All ER 769 at 785; [1993] BCC 360 at 364.

[97.] The English equivalent to paragraph 17(1) of the First Schedule to the Bankruptcy Act, 1988 - it should be noted though in England under r 4.90 mutual credits or debts as between a bankrupt and a creditor shall be set-off, whereas in Ireland such credits or debts may be set off.

Accordingly, the set-off requirement of mutual debits and mutual credits was applicable.[98]

Rule against Double Proof

[15.24] Cash-backed security is given often to secure a bank's liability which may arise from providing, at the customer's request, a bond, letter of credit or other form of surety obligation. The rule against double proof may prevent a bank from exercising its rights under a contractual letter of set-off.[99] This may arise where an insolvent customer defaults and the beneficiary of the bank's surety obligation proves his debt against the customer and then calls on the bank as guarantor to meet the debt. In such circumstances, while the bank could enforce an assignment of a deposit to meet its obligations under the guarantee it cannot exercise a right of set-off. The bank's exercise of its set-off means a second claim in respect of the same debt is being made against the customer. In these circumstances, the bank as guarantor will need to pursue the principal debtor through its right of subrogation to the right of the principal creditor.[100]

On a point of procedure, to avoid being caught on a double proof prohibition, a bank which has given a bond or guarantee on behalf of its customer, such as for VAT or Customs & Excise, should on being presented with a demand honour the bond first and then utilise its contractual set-off and indemnity from the customer to recompense itself. As Lord Evershed MR indicated:[101]

> "The reasoning of the judgments [in *Re Fenton* [1931] 1 Ch 85] is clear authority for the proposition ... that, if at the relevant date a guarantor has not paid the principal creditor ... there is no 'debt due' to the guarantor from the principal debtor capable of forming the subject of a set-off, under s 31 of the Bankruptcy Act 1914, against a debt due from the guarantor to the principal debtor".

POOLING ARRANGEMENTS

[15.25] In more recent times, as businesses in Ireland have grown and the principal commercial entities incorporate a number of subsidiaries for trading in different divisions, banks servicing such customers have been requested to operate a pooling arrangement whereby one company's overdraft may be covered by another company's surplus both for interest purposes and exposure.

---

98. See the judgment of Hoffmann LJ [1993] BCLC 1200 at 1210; [1993] 3 All ER 769 at 779; [1993] BCC 70 at 75-6 see also the remarks of the same judge (Lord Hoffman) in *Bank of Credit and Commerce International SA (No 8)* [1997] 4 All ER 568 at 573.
99. Final Report of the Legal Risk Review Committee (October 1992).
100. See para **[9.57]**.
101. In *Re A Debtor (No. 66 of 1955), ex p The Debtor v The Trustee of the Property of Waite* [1956] 3 All ER 225 at 229.

Typically, such an arrangement will be secured by each company guaranteeing the indebtedness to the bank of each other company in the group and letters of set-off executed. While such an arrangement should be effective, circumstances may apply where a liquidator seeks the directions of the court on the grounds that the transfer of moneys from one company to another were a fraudulent preference.[102] Alternatively, a member, creditor, liquidator, receiver[103] or examiner[104] may apply to the court to have the transfer of such moneys returned to the transferor on the grounds of the initial transfer being "a fraud on the company, its creditors or members."[105]

However, it is always open to a liquidator or creditor to apply to have the debts of one company in a group discharged by another on the grounds that the group companies were effectively trading as one company.[106] As a minimum, the bank should ensure that the companies in the group have the capacity to have their surplus used to discharge indebtedness of other companies in the group.[107]

Court Protection

[15.26] It should be noted that if an examiner is appointed to a company,[108] or a company otherwise comes under the protection of the court,[109] not only is a bank precluded from enforcing security against the company[110] or a guarantee in respect of the company's obligations[111] but set-off between bank accounts cannot be implemented. The Companies (Amendment) Act, 1990 s 5(2)(h)[112] provides:

> no set-off between separate bank accounts of the company shall be effected, except with the consent of the examiner, and in this paragraph 'bank account' includes an account with any person exempt by virtue of s 7(4) of the Central Bank Act, 1971 from the requirement of holding a licence under s 9 of that Act.

[102.] Companies Act, 1963, s 286 (as amended by the Companies Act, 1990, s 135), see Courtney, *The Law of Private Companies* (Butterworths, 1994), paras 19.048-19.066; see also Keane, *Company Law in the Republic of Ireland* (2nd ed) paras 38.80 to 38.83.

[103.] Companies Act, 1990, s 178.

[104.] Companies Act, 1990, s 180(2).

[105.] Companies Act, 1990, s 139; see Courtney, *The Law of Private Companies* (Butterworths, 1994) paras 19.067-19.069; see also Keane, *Company Law in the Republic of Ireland* (2nd ed) para 38.84.

[106.] Companies Act, 1990 ss 140 and 141.

[107.] See *Re Frederick Inns Ltd* [1994] 1 ILRM 387, see also commercial benefit paras **[18.59]-[18.62]** below.

[108.] Pursuant to the Companies (Amendment) Act, 1990 s 2(1).

[109.] *Ibid* s 3(7).

[110.] *Ibid* s 5(2)(d).

[111.] *Ibid* s 5(2)(f).

[112.] As inserted by the Companies Act, 1990, s 181(1)(c).

The Company Law Review Group[113] recommended the repeal of the section in its First Report.[114] It pointed out that, first the section treated bank creditors differently to other types of creditors[115] and, secondly the Central Bank had indicated that the restriction created difficulties in implementing internationally accepted practices of allowing offsets for capital adequacy purposes.

This restriction has effectively meant that cash is no longer the security it was once thought. An examiner who is appointed to a company with cash either charged to a bank or subject to a letter of set-off will be able to utilise, with the court's approval, such cash for his own expenses.[116] Furthermore an examiner, with the court's approval, may borrow money for working capital purposes and such borrowings may be secured on the cash deposits in priority to the person already holding a first fixed security over the cash deposit.[117] In practice this has led to banks, anxious to provide facilities for their customers, setting up offshore structures to minimise the risk of their security being endangered.[118]

Set-off in Financial Contracts

[15.27] The prohibition on set-off between bank accounts for a company under the protection of the court discouraged banks and other finance houses from using Ireland as a base for their activities. When it became clear that this provision could hinder the development of the International Financial Services Centre,[119] the legislature enacted the Netting of Financial Contracts Act, 1995.[120] Essentially this Act provides that netting or the set-off of money provided by way of security as contained within a netting agreement will be enforceable, notwithstanding anything contained in any rule of law relating to bankruptcy, insolvency or receivership, or in the Companies Acts or the Bankruptcy Act, 1988.[121]

[15.28] However, the benefit of the Act is somewhat more limited than appears at first in that a netting agreement is an agreement which is made between two

---

[113.] Established in March 1994 by the Minister for Enterprise and Employment, Mr Ruairi Quinn.

[114.] December 1994, para 2.34.

[115.] "There is no ground for believing that the right of set-off possessed by a banker differs in principle from that enjoyed by any other person who occupies at the same time the position of debtor and creditor to the same individual or corporation" - Fitzgibbon J in *The Governor and Company of the Bank of Ireland v Martin and Martin* [1937] IR 189 at 204.

[116.] See Finlay CJ in *Re Atlantic Magnetics Ltd* [1993] 2 IR 561 at 577.

[117.] See *Re Atlantic Magnetics Ltd* [1993] 2 IR 561.

[118.] See Johnston, 'Bank Finance - Searching for Suitable Security' (1994) CLP 3 at 5.

[119.] Located on disused docklands in Dublin.

[120.] No 25 of 1995, enacted on 1 August, 1995; for commentary see Foy, 'The Netting of Financial Contracts Act 1995 - a delectable piece of legislative dynamite' (1996) JIBFL 234.

[121.] Section 4(1); this is subject to the possible application of certain provisions of these Acts, such as fraudulent preference.

parties only, in relation to financial contracts,[122] which provide for the termination of those contracts for the time being in existence, the determination of the termination values of those contracts and the set-off of the termination values so determined so as to arrive at a net amount due.[123] The set-off must be provided to secure solely an obligation under a financial contract[124] - accordingly a general letter of set-off or security incorporating a set-off will not obtain the benefit of the Act. The set-off or security must be dedicated to the chargor's obligations under the netting agreement. This can result in a proliferation of security documents if there are a significant number of companies in a group wishing to avail of swaps and similar contracts. This is then multiplied by the number of banks in a syndicate or club who may be making such facilities available.

ATTACHMENT BY THE REVENUE COMMISSIONERS

[15.29] A further weakness of security over a deposit is the risk, obviously greater for a company encountering financial difficulties, that the Revenue Commissioners will serve an attachment notice on the bank. Section 1002(2)(a) of the Taxes Consolidation Act, 1997[125] stipulates that the Revenue Commissioners may serve a notice on any person (whom the Revenue Commissioners believe owe money to the relevant taxpayer) that the relevant taxpayer is in arrears[126] on the discharge of any tax, interest or unpaid tax, or penalty to the Revenue Commissioners.[127] The notice from the Revenue Commissioners will direct the recipient, such as a bank holding a deposit from a customer and thus owing a debt to the customer:[128]

> (I) to deliver to the Revenue Commissioners, within the period of 10 days from the time at which the notice of attachment is received by him, a return in writing specifying whether or not any debt is due by him to the taxpayer at the time the notice is received by him, and if any debt is so due, specifying the amount of the debt:
>
> Provided that where the amount of the debt due by the relevant person to the taxpayer is equal to or greater than the specified amount in relation to the taxpayer, the amount of the debt specified in the return shall be an amount equal to the specified amount,[129] and

---

122. As defined in s 1.
123. *Ibid.*
124. *Ibid.*
125. Originally enacted as s 73 of the Finance Act 1988 and subsequently amended by s 241 of the Finance Act 1992.
126. The taxpayer must be at least one month in arrears - Taxes Consolidation Act, 1997, s 1002(3).
127. The explanatory memoranda to the Finance Bill 1988 (s 69) and the Finance Bill 1992 (s 220) are particularly helpful in setting out the procedure.
128. Taxes Consolidation Act, 1997, s 1002(2)(a)(iii).
129. Special provision is made where the depositor is a joint depositor - Taxes Consolidation Act, 1997, s 1002(2)(a)(iii).

(II) if the amount of any debt is so specified to pay to the Revenue Commissioners within the period aforesaid a sum equal to the amount of the debt so specified.

[15.30] A person on whom a notice may be served is "a person in respect of whom the Revenue Commissioners have reason to believe that he may have, at the time a notice of attachment is received by him in respect of a taxpayer, a debt due to the taxpayer".[130]

In respect of a financial institution a "debt" is defined as a "deposit" held:

(I) to the credit of the taxpayer for his sole benefit; or

(II) to the credit of the taxpayer and any other person or persons for their joint benefit.

Finally, a "deposit" is defined as meaning:[131]

a sum of money paid to a financial institution on terms under which it will be repaid with or without interest and either on demand or at a time or in circumstances agreed by or on behalf of the person making the payment and the person to whom it is made.

Where a banker makes a payment to the Revenue Commissioners, following receipt of such a notice, the banker must "forthwith give the taxpayer concerned a notice in writing specifying the payment, its amount and the reason for which it was made".[132] The payment made by the banker to the Revenue Commissioners will be deemed to have reduced the banker's indebtedness to the customer by the amount of such payment.[133]

[15.31] Where the amount owed by the bank is less than the tax arrears, the bank will be obliged to remit further moneys to the Revenue Commissioners to the extent that it receives further deposits or otherwise owes money to the taxpayer until the tax arrears are cleared,[134] or until the taxpayer is declared bankrupt or wound up.[135] Any moneys paid by a banker to its customer following receipt of such an attachment notice which has the effect of reducing the banker's indebtedness to the customer below the level of tax arrears stated in the notice will not reduce the banker's indebtedness to the customer.[136] Thus, the banker will have simply paid money gratuitously to its customer. In view of the wording of the statute it is unlikely that the banker could subsequently maintain

---

[130.] From the definition of "relevant person", Taxes Consolidation Act, 1997, s 1002(1)(b).

[131.] Taxes Consolidation Act, 1997, s 1002(1)(b).

[132.] *Ibid* s 1002(3)(a).

[133.] *Ibid*, s 1002(13).

[134.] *Ibid*, s 1002(4)(a).

[135.] *Ibid*, s 1002(1) - see definition of "relevant period".

[136.] *Ibid*, s 1002(6).

an action against the customer for the return of the moneys on a quasi-contractual basis or otherwise.[137]

Clearly a company's principal bankers will be at greatest risk as the Revenue Commissioners will be aware, from the payment by cheque of previous taxes, of the identity of the company's clearing banker. A company's annual audited accounts will typically name a company's principal bankers.

[15.32] Whether a notice of attachment pursuant to s 1002 can upset security over deposits is open to some debate - the result is likely to depend on the manner in which security is taken.[138] Any moneys held by the bank as security will come within the definition of "deposit", except arguably moneys held pursuant to a flawed asset arrangement. Moneys held on deposit but subject to a mortgage, charge or assignment by way of security may not come within the definition of "debt", as although it is a deposit held to the credit of the taxpayer, it is not held "for his sole benefit"; arguably it is not held for the "joint benefit" of the taxpayer and the security holder as their interests are different. Thus any deposit the subject of a charge (or other encumbrance) or held on terms that it may be utilised to discharge a certain liability or obligation should not be subject to the provisions of an attachment notice. However, moneys held until a certain contingency occurs or moneys held subject to a contractual right of set-off (where such set-off has not been exercised at the time of receipt of the notice) will be subject to the consequences of an attachment notice. It is arguable though that if the terms upon which the money is held on deposit include a covenant not to withdraw such moneys (without actually containing a lien) as specified in clause 4 of the letter of set-off set out in para **[15.16]** above, such moneys are not therefore held for the sole benefit of the account holder and thus cannot be attached by these provisions.[139]

[15.33] A mitigating factor to the width of the legislation is that an attachment notice may not be given where the taxpayer (or the recipient of the notice) is an undischarged bankrupt or a company being wound up.[140] However, this does not preclude a notice being given when the taxpayer is in receivership. It seems such a notice could not be given when the taxpayer is under the protection of the court.[141]

[137.] *Ibid*, s 1002(6)(b).

[138.] For further reading see Breslin, 'Revenue Power to attach debts under section 73 Finance Act, 1988; Implications for Credit Institutions' (1995) CLP 167 - see in particular his suggestion at footnote 39 that a floating charge over an account which crystallises on the issue of an attachment notice will take priority because it will have crystallised prior to receipt of the notice.

[139.] Unless it could be contended that the moneys were held for "the credit of the taxpayer" and the bank or for the "joint benefit" of the taxpayer and the bank.

[140.] Taxes Consolidation Act, 1997, s 1002(16).

[141.] Companies (Amendment) Act, 1990 s 5(2)(c).

[15.34] In 1994 a solicitor sought a declaration that s 73 (as it then was) was invalid under Articles 34, 40 and 43 of the Constitution. In refusing the application Geoghegan J concluded:[147]

> "[The Attachment Notice] is undoubtedly a very unsatisfactory feature of the legislation and a suitable amendment might be considered. I should add that even in a meritorious case I would not envisage that in any circumstances the section itself or any subsection would be declared unconstitutional but conceivably there might be cases where the actual service of the notice under the section amounted to an unconstitutional exercise of the Revenue Commissioners' powers."

[142.] *Orange v The Revenue Commissioners* [1995] 1 IR 517, at 524.

Chapter 16

Security over Shares

[16.01] The Bills of Sale Acts and s 99 of the Companies Act, 1963 are designed to inform creditors or potential creditors of a person that such person has created security over his/its assets. In practice one of the principal attractions of a security over shares, other than a floating security or a security securing the issue of debentures, is the absence of any public registration requirement.[1] This is an important consideration for many companies who wish to keep "a clean sheet" concerning security registered against them in the Companies Registration Office.[2]

NATURE OF SECURITY

[16.02] There are two principal methods by which fixed security over shares is taken - a legal mortgage and an equitable mortgage (or charge) by way of deposit of the share certificate evidencing title to the shares being mortgaged. A share certificate is *"prima facie* evidence of the title" of the registered holder to the shares.[3] It is a "representation" by the company "that at the date of the certificate the person named therein was owner of the shares".[4] A practitioner in Ireland is requested sometimes, particularly by lawyers from the United States of America, to take a pledge of shares. There has been some discussion as to whether the deposit of share certificates as security is a pledge or an equitable mortgage.[5] The judgment at the turn of the century of Cozens-Hardy J in *Harold v Plenty*[6] is sometimes quoted as effectively settling the point.[7] In that case a

---

[1.] Security over shares is not registrable under the Bills of Sale Acts 1879-1883 - see *Lee & Co (Dublin) Ltd v Egan Wholesale Ltd* High Court, unrep, 27 April 1978/23 May 1978/18 October 1979/18 December 1979 Kenny J; the Companies (No 2) Bill 1987 proposed to amend s 99 by requiring registration of mortgages of shares but the proposal was dropped prior to the implementation of the Bill as the Companies Act, 1990.

[2.] Such a security though would contravene any negative pledge given by the chargor.

[3.] As executed under the common seal of the company - Companies Act, 1963, s 87(1); the share certificates of a public company may be executed under its official seal for securities pursuant to s 3 of the Companies (Amendment) Act, 1977.

[4.] *Per* Romer LJ in *Rainford v James Keith & Blackman Company Ltd* [1905] 2 Ch 147 at 154.

[5.] See Sheridan, *Rights in Security* (Collins, 1974) pp 249-251.

[6.] [1901] 2 Ch 314.

[7.] Lingard, *Bank Security Documents* (3rd ed) Butterworths at para 15.3; Courtney, *The Law of Private Companies* (1994) Butterworths at para 10.025; Forde, *Company Law* (1992) The Mercier Press at para 9.67

certificate of shares was deposited as security for a debt; Cozens-Hardy J stated:[8]

> "I do not think that this is properly a case of pledge. A share is a chose in action. The certificate is merely evidence of title ... The deposit of the certificate by way of security for the debt ... seems to me to amount to an equitable mortgage, or, in the other words, to an agreement to execute a transfer of the shares by way of mortgage."

However, even prior to that decision, in his *Treatise on the Law of Mortgages*, Robbins wrote:[9]

> "... it has been repeatedly held that where there is a deposit of certificates of shares by way of security, accompanied by the execution by the borrower of a complete legal transfer of the shares or of a transfer in blank which the lender can complete by filling in the name of the transferee, the transaction is to be regarded as a mortgage entitling the depositee of the certificates on default to foreclose the shares or to an order for sale in lieu of foreclosure."

It should be said that in most cases where a banker or other lender makes finance available to its customer, the value of a security over shares is minimal particularly where the shares charged are those of a private company (which they are in most instances). Nevertheless, bankers are often happy to take this form of security as it gives them an element of control over the shares should its customer (usually the parent company) default in its obligation to the banker. Thus, while this form of security is not usually taken, it is not uncommon to do so.

Implied Power of Sale

[16.03] Where shares are transferred by way of security and the transferee's name registered, in the absence of any mortgage document, there is an implied power of sale upon default of payment. If there is a time fixed for payment, the power of sale may be exercised upon default; if there is no time stipulated reasonable notice must be given before the power of sale is exercised.[10]

Guidelines as to what is reasonable notice can be obtained from the majority judgments in *Deverges v Sandeman, Clark & Co*[11] where Stirling J stated:[12]

> "The notice must give a reasonable opportunity to the mortgagor to pay what is due under the mortgage; and I think it is at least desirable that it should fix a

---

8. [1901] 2 Ch 314 at 316.
9. Robbins, *A Treatise of the Law of Mortgages Pledges and Hypothecations* Vol 1 Stevens & Sons Ltd; Sweet & Maxwell Ltd (1897) at p 280.
10. *Deverges v Sandeman, Clark & Co* [1902] 1 Ch 579.
11. *Ibid.*
12. *Ibid* at 593.

day for that purpose, and also convey to the mind of the mortgagor that, if he fails to avail himself of the opportunity given to redeem, the mortgagee will be in a position to put in force his rights."

Cozens-Hardy J stated:[13]

"Assuming the true relation between the parties to be that of mortgagor and mortgagees of shares, I think it is settled law ... that the mortgagees have a power of sale, provided that a reasonable time has elapsed after notice requiring payment. The notice need not state that the mortgagees will sell; it is sufficient that the notice requires payment of the mortgage money."

He concluded:[14]

"Having regard to the nature of the property, a fortnight, or at the outside a month, would in the present case be a reasonable time."

The same principle applies where share certificates together with a blank transfer are deposited by way of security. In *Stubbs v Slater*[15] the Court of Appeal held that the fact that the mortgagee in giving notice requiring payment made a mistake as to the amount due on the security and demanded too much was not a ground for invalidating the exercise of his implied power of sale.

[16.04] The enforcement of security over shares will not be precluded even if recovery of the debt, for which the shares are given as security, is barred under the Statute of Limitations.[16] The rationale for this is that the deposit of the share certificates was an equitable assignment of the shares to the bank to the extent of the debt; the bank had thus acquired property rights in the shares.

LEGAL MORTGAGE OF SHARES

[16.05] The form of a mortgage over shares is along similar lines to a mortgage of any other asset.[17] Thus, it will embody as a minimum a covenant to pay, the mortgage clause, the power of sale, the power of appointing a receiver, a power of attorney and a continuing security clause. The mortgage clause will create the security over the shares for which certificates are from time to time deposited with the mortgagee. This will facilitate the taking of additional security without the need to execute a supplemental security form. It is more common now for it to be stated that the security attaches also to all rights deriving from the shares including option rights, bonus issues, rights issues, dividends, interest and all

---

[13.] *Ibid* at 596.
[14.] *Ibid* at 597.
[15.] [1910] 1 Ch 632.
[16.] *The London and Midland Bank Ltd v Mitchell* [1899] 2 Ch 161.
[17.] For an appropriate form see *The Encyclopedia of Forms and Precedents* (5th ed) Vol 4 Form 29 (Butterworths, 1986); see also Lingard, *op cit*, Document 6.

other distributions. This latter aspect triggers the possible need to register the security when created by a company as being a security over book debts.[18]

[16.06] Following the execution of the mortgage, the mortgage together with the original share certificates to which they relate (showing the mortgagor as registered owner of the shares) and an executed share transfer form[19] are delivered to the mortgagee, or its agent. Where the mortgagor is an individual, the share transfer can be executed under hand. The form of transfer set out in the First Schedule to the Stock Transfer (Forms) Regulations, 1996[20] provides that bodies corporate "should execute under their common seal".[21] The mortgagee, or its agent, should ascertain from the share certificates that the shares are fully paid up. The mortgagee will stamp the share transfer, which can be stamped nominally by reference to it being "a transfer by way of security for a loan".[22] The mortgage itself is subject to stamp duty at the rate of one-tenth of one per cent of the amount secured (subject to a limit of £500)[23] unless it is collateral to other security similarly stamped, in which event it is stampable at £10.[24]

[16.07] Following stamping, the mortgagee should present the share certificate together with the stamped transfer for registration to the secretary of the company whose shares have been mortgaged. The secretary should then present the transfer to the board for registration within two months.[25] Upon approval by the board, the secretary will enter the transferee's name in the share register in place of the transferor and issue a new share certificate in the transferee's name (with the transferor's certificate being cancelled).[26] Section 81 of the Companies Act, 1963 provides that "it shall not be lawful for the company to register a transfer of shares ... unless a proper instrument of transfer has been delivered to the company". *Keane*[27] indicates that this section ensures that stamp duty is not avoided.[28] But in *Powell v London and Provincial Bank*[29] the English Court of

---

18. Companies Act, 1963, s 99(2)(e).
19. Regulation 23 of Part I of Table A stipulates that the transfer is to be "in any usual or common form or any other form which the directors may approve;"
20. SI 263/1996.
21. Courtney, *The Law of Private Companies* (1994) Butterworths at para 10.006 suggests that as a share is a chose in action, its transfer by a company can be executed under hand.
22. See paragraph (c) on reverse of share transfer form.
23. Stamp Act 1891 as amended.
24. *Ibid.*
25. Companies Act, 1963, s 86; see also para **[16.30]** below.
26. Companies Act, 1963, Table A, Part I, reg. 8 (as amended by the Companies (Amendment) Act, 1977, s 5(2)).
27. *Company Law in the Republic of Ireland* (2nd ed, 1991) Butterworths, para 20.08.
28. See also s 86 of the Companies Act, 1963 under which a transfer means "a transfer duly stamped".
29. [1893] 2 Ch 555.

Appeal indicated that the registration of an unstamped transfer should not invalidate the transfer and thus the registration. This is re-enforced by the more recent English Court of Appeal's decision in *Nisbet v Shepherd*.[30] In that case, the stock transfer form omitted to state the consideration and was unstamped. Nevertheless, the court held that the registration pursuant to that unstamped transfer was effective. The court decided that "the document sufficiently recorded the transaction; the defects in the form were mere irregulatories".[31] Leggatt LJ stated:[32]

> "... the phrase [proper instrument of transfer] does not mean the instrument complying in all respects with statutory requirements. In this context, 'proper' means no more than 'appropriate' or 'situate'. What it had to be suitable for was stamping".

[16.08] Upon registration, the mortgagee (or its nominee) then becomes the legal owner of the shares and should receive a share certificate to that effect. Unless there is a default by the mortgagor, the mortgagor will typically retain the right to vote at meetings and to receive dividends (although some mortgages provide that the dividends may at the discretion of the mortgagee be utilised towards discharging the mortgagor's obligations to the mortgagee).

[16.09] Since 1 April 1996, a new system known as CREST has come into operation under which title to shares (in a company which has so resolved by directors' resolution) may be transferred without a written instrument in accordance with a computer-based system and procedures laid down by the Companies Act, 1990 (Uncertificated Securities) Regulations, 1996.[33] However, security over shares is more usually taken in respect of the shares of private companies which still use the share certificate and share transfer form for transferring title rather than CREST.

Equity of Redemption

[16.10] The mortgage itself should provide also for the return of the mortgaged shares to the mortgagor upon the discharge of all the mortgagor's obligations secured by the mortgage.[34] When the debt or obligation, for which the mortgage is held, has been discharged, the mortgagee holds the shares and all rights emanating therefrom as "a bare trustee for the mortgagor".[35] A mortgagee who

---

[30.] [1994] BCC 91.

[31.] *Per* Leggatt LJ (with whom the other members of the Court agreed) at 95.

[32.] *Ibid* at 94.

[33.] SI 68/1996; for a helpful article on the operation of CREST see McHugh, 'CREST in Ireland: the Uncertificated Securities Regulations, 1996' (1996) CLP 219.

[34.] The equity of redemption see para **[10.06]**.

[35.] *Per* Kelly LJ in *McGrattan v McGrattan* [1985] NI 28 at 31 applying *Brotherston v Hatt* (1706) 2 Vern 574.

seeks recovery of the debt due to it will not be in a position to obtain judgment if he cannot return the mortgaged shares to the mortgagor.[36] The mortgage should provide that upon redemption, the mortgagor will accept delivery of the same class of shares as those mortgaged, to obviate the possible need of the mortgagee to return the identical shares mortgaged.[37] However, failure to do so may not be critical for the mortgagee as the loss to the mortgagor is the value of the shares which the mortgagor will receive in any event upon the return of shares of the same class.[38]

Regulatory Issues

[16.11] Where the legal mortgagee is a person licensed by the Central Bank of Ireland to carry on banking business in Ireland,[39] the approval of the Central Bank is required where that person wishes to acquire not less than ten per cent of the total shares or of the total voting rights in another entity.[40] However, the Central Bank is permitted, subject to such conditions as it sees fit, to exempt a class of transactions from the approval requirements where the Central Bank is satisfied that "the interest in shares is not being beneficially acquired by a holder of a licence or is being acquired only in the course of its normal business to secure the issue of a loan made by the holder to the undertaking or business concerned".[41] The Central Bank has issued letters to certain banks exempting such banks from having to obtain approval where the transaction falls within one of the criteria specified above.

[16.12] Consideration may need to be given also to the Mergers, Take-Overs and Monopolies (Control) Act, 1978. This Act provides that where two or more enterprises come under common control, title to the shares being transferred will not pass unless the Minister for Enterprise, Trade and Employment so designates, or fails to designate upon the expiration of three months from the notification being made to the Department of Enterprise, Trade and Employment.[42] Common control is triggered if one entity holds more than 25 per cent of another.[43] However, the Act applies only where two or more of the enterprises involved each have gross assets of not less than £10 million or a

---

[36.] See *Trustee of Ellis and Company v Dixon-Johnson* [1925] AC 489.

[37.] This would not be relevant for an equitable mortgage where the shares are not transferred to the name of the mortgagee or its nominee.

[38.] See *Crerar v Bank of Scotland* 2 LDAB 248.

[39.] Pursuant to s 9 of the Central Bank Act, 1971 (as amended by s 32 of the Central Bank Act, 1989).

[40.] Central Bank Act, 1989 s 76.

[41.] *Ibid* s 75(2)(b).

[42.] Mergers, Take-Overs and Monopolies (Control) Act, 1978 s 3.

[43.] *Ibid* s 1(3) as amended by s 15(2) of the Competition Act, 1991.

turnover of not less than £20 million in the most recent financial year.[44] Although there is an exclusion for licensed banks, such a bank will need to bear in mind that the Act may be applicable to a potential purchaser of the shares from the bank should the bank need to enforce the security. The application of the Competition Act, 1991 should not be completely discounted.

[16.13] Part III of the Companies Act, 1990 requires a person who has any interest in 5 per cent of the nominal value of the share capital in a public limited company to notify the company of such interest.[45] However, "an exempt security interest" can be disregarded.[46] An interest in shares is an exempt security interest where it is held by the holder of a banking license issued by the Central Bank, an insurance company, a trustee savings bank, post office savings bank, ACC Bank plc, ICC Bank plc or a member of a recognised stock exchange carrying on business as a stockholder[47] and "it is held by way of security only for the purposes of a transaction entered into by the person or body concerned in the ordinary course of business of such person or body."[48]

EQUITABLE MORTGAGE OF SHARES

[16.14] What is perhaps currently more common in practice is an equitable mortgage. Under this form of security, the share certificate together with an executed but undated share transfer with the name of the transferee unspecified, are delivered to the mortgagee and a form of mortgage or memorandum of deposit executed and delivered.[49] The wording of this form will be virtually the same as the form of legal mortgage. In time this form of security may decline, at least for shares in public companies, as a result of the transfer and registration of transferees under a computer based system.[50] The equitable security document will be subject to stamp duty as for the legal mortgage.

[44.] *Ibid* s 2(1) as amended by the Mergers, Take-Overs and Monopolies (Control) Act, 1978 (section 2) Order, 1993 SI 135/1993.

[45.] Companies Act, 1990 ss 67-71.

[46.] *Ibid* s 78(1).

[47.] *Ibid* s 78(4)(a).

[48.] *Ibid* s 78(4)(b).

[49.] It has been suggested that a deposit of a share certificate without a transfer form will operate like a deposit of title deeds to land and be deemed to give the depositee the remedies of a mortgagee - see Robbins, *A Treatise on the Law of Mortgages, Pledges and Hypothecations* Vol 1 Stevens & Sons Ltd; Sweet & Maxwell Ltd (1897) p 282.

[50.] Pursuant to the Companies Act, 1990 (Uncertificated Securities) Regulations, 1996 SI 68/1996; see para **[16.28]** below; for further reading on the impact of these regulations for security over shares see Evans, 'Crest: Payment, Security and other Related Issues for Banks' (1996) 6 JIBFL 259 and 7 JIBFL 314.

DOCUMENTATION ISSUES

Power of Attorney

[16.15] The power of attorney is particularly important where the security is taken by way of equitable mortgage. This is to enable the mortgagee to complete the transferee's name in the share transfer, date it and deliver it. Its importance can be seen from the English Court of Appeal's decision in *Powell v London and Provincial Bank.*[51] In that case a stock certificate, an undertaking to complete an assignment when required and an executed blank transfer were deposited with the bank as security for an advance. The bank completed the stock transfer form and had its name registered as holder of the stock. The court held that the transfer was not a deed (which was required) and therefore did not pass legal title to the stock.

[16.16] Accordingly, the power of attorney in a mortgage should irrevocably appoint the mortgagee to be the mortgagor's attorney and in the mortgagor's name on his behalf and as the act and deed of the mortgagor to sign, seal, execute and deliver all deeds, instruments, mortgages and things as the mortgagee may consider necessary for completing all assurances of the mortgagor and for exercising the power of sale or other disposal by executing instruments of transfer, including the completion of partially completed instruments executed by the mortgagor, or exercising any voting rights conferred under the terms of the security.

Voting

[16.17] Typically, the security will provide that so long as the mortgagor is not in default on its agreement with the mortgagee, the mortgagor will have the right to attend at general meetings of the company and to vote. As far as the company is concerned the person who has the right to vote is the person whose name is on the register.[52] The mortgagee (whose name is not on the share register) may nonetheless be in a position to direct to the mortgagor the manner in which it should vote. In *Puddephatt v Leith*[53] an advance was secured by a mortgage of shares with the mortgagee's name being entered on the share register. The mortgagee gave an undertaking to the mortgagor to the effect that he would vote as directed by the mortgagor. Upon his failure to do so the court granted the

---

51. [1893] 2 Ch 555.
52. See Companies Act, 1963 s 116 (register of members), s 31 (definition of member) and Table A Part I Reg 63 (votes of members); *Wise v Lansdell* [1921] 1 Ch 425; *Kinsella v Alliance and Dublin Consumers Gas Company* High Court, unrep, 5 October 1982 Barron J; *Siemens Bros & Co Ltd v Burns* [1918] 2 Ch 324.
53. [1916] 1 Ch 200.

mortgagor a mandatory injunction compelling the mortgagee to vote in the manner directed by the mortgagor.

Dividends

[16.18] Likewise, generally the mortgage will stipulate that unless the mortgagor is in default under his agreement with the mortgagee, the mortgagor will have the right to receive dividends. Dividends can be subject to a stop notice.[54]

Stop Notice

[16.19] To maintain effective priority over a subsequent lien by the company on the shares,[55] to inhibit transfers by the mortgagor and to minimise the more remote possibility of the mortgagor either procuring duplicate share certificates from the unsuspecting secretary of the company or selling the shares to a third party without notice of the mortgage,[56] and indeed to formally put the company on notice of the mortgagee's interest,[57] it is prudent for the mortgagee, or its agent, to serve a stop notice on the company secretary. This notice which is provided for in the Rules of the Superior Courts,[58] will take the following form:[59]

NOTICE AS TO STOCK

The High Court

In the matter of [name of company whose shares are mortgaged]

And in the matter of the Chancery (Ireland) Act, 1867.

To:[Name of company whose shares are mortgaged]

Take notice that the following shares in the capital of your company namely [ ] ordinary shares in the name of [name of mortgagor] have been mortgaged in favour of [name of mortgagee] and accordingly, this notice is to stop the transfer of the said shares but not the payment of dividends thereon (or the transfer of the said shares and the payment of dividends thereon) pursuant to Order 46, rules 5 to 13, of the Rules of the Superior Courts.

Dated:

Signed:

[54.] See para **[16.19]** below.
[55.] See Robbins, *op cit* p 277.
[56.] See *Rainford v James Keith & Blackman Company Ltd* [1905] 2 Ch 147.
[57.] See *Rearden v Provincial Bank of Ireland* [1896] 1 IR 532 and *Re Morrissey and Morrissey* [1961] IR 442 at paras **[16.21]** and **[16.20]** respectively.
[58.] SI 15/1986, Order 46.
[59.] *Ibid* Form No 28, Appendix C.

[name of mortgagee's solicitor]

Solicitor for [name of mortgagee]

An affidavit must be sworn by the mortgagee's solicitor and filed in the High Court Central Office. The form of affidavit will state:[60]

AFFIDAVIT AS TO STOCK

The High Court

In the matter of [name of company whose shares are mortgaged]

And in the matter of the Chancery (Ireland) Act, 1867

I,	[name of mortgagee's solicitor] of [address of mortgagee's solicitor] make oath and say as follows:

1.	[name of mortgagee] of [mortgagee's address] is according to the best of my knowledge, information and belief, beneficially interested in part of the ordinary share capital in [name of company whose shares are being mortgaged] incorporated in Dublin on the [ ] day of [ ] registration number [ ].

2.	To the best of my knowledge, information and belief, the said property in which the said [name of mortgagee] is beneficially interested as aforesaid consists of [ ] ordinary shares in [name of company whose shares are being mortgaged] issued, allotted to, and registered in the name of [name and address of mortgagor].

Sworn this [ ] day of [ ]

in the City of [ ]

before me a Commissioner

for Oaths/Practising Solicitor and I know the

Deponent.

_____

Commissioner for Oaths/Practising Solicitor

This affidavit is filed on behalf of [name of mortgagee]. Notice for it are to be sent to [ ].

The procedure is to file the affidavit and the notice in the High Court Central Office an attested copy of the affidavit together with a duplicate of the notice authenticated by the seal of the High Court should be then served on the company whose shares have been mortgaged.[61] The notice may be withdrawn by a written request by the person by whom or on whose behalf the notice was served.[62] Following service of the notice, until withdrawn, it is not lawful for the

_____

60.	*Ibid* Form No 27 Appendix C.
61.	*Ibid* Order 46 rule 6.
62.	*Ibid* Order 46 rule 11.

company to permit a transfer of its shares or where applicable pay dividends to the registered shareholder.[63] If the company subsequently receives a request from the registered shareholder (or a person acting on his behalf) to transfer the shares or pay dividends the company cannot accede to such request for eight days unless the court orders otherwise.[64]

[16.20] The effect of a stop notice is to put the keeper of the company's share register upon enquiry should a dealing be presented to him, other than by the mortgagee, in respect of these shares. Although a company is not permitted to enter a notice of any trust on its share register,[65] the usefulness of a stop notice can be seen from the decision in *Re Morrissey and Morrissey.*[66] In that case the company had a provision in its articles of association, similar to regulation 7 of Part I of Table A of the Companies Act, 1963, to the effect that the company is entitled to treat the person whose name appears on the register in respect of a share as the absolute owner of the share and it is not under an obligation to recognise any trust, equity, equitable claim or partial interest in a share whether or not it has express notice. Shareholders deposited their certificates in respect of shares in the company, with a bank as security for advances. No transfer was registered but the bank gave notice of their interest in the shares to the company. The High Court held that (1) while the articles of association prevented the company from being bound by a notice of trust from its shareholders, the articles did not preclude the bank from giving notice, (2) by giving such notice the bank had taken the necessary steps to perfect its title and had indicated to the company in the only way available to it that it did not consent to the shareholders' requested ownership, and (3) accordingly the bank's interest prevailed. In giving judgment Budd J followed the decisions in *Bradford Banking Co v Briggs*[67] and *Rearden v Provincial Bank of Ireland.*[68] In the latter case, the Master of the Rolls stated in his judgment:[69]

> "It could never have been the object of the legislature to enable the Company ... to ignore for their own purposes and interests the rights of other persons of which they have actual knowledge."

[16.21] It was held in *Rearden v Provincial Bank of Ireland*[70] that a company cannot seek to exercise a lien on its shares pursuant to its articles of association[71]

[63.] *Ibid* Order 46, rule 10.
[64.] *Ibid* Order 46, rule 12.
[65.] Companies Act, 1963 s 123; see also Table A, Part I, reg 7.
[66.] [1961] IR 442.
[67.] (1886) 12 App Cas 29.
[68.] [1896] 1 IR 532.
[69.] *Ibid* at 567.
[70.] [1896] IR 532.
[71.] See reg 11 of Part I of Table A to the Companies Act, 1963.

after it has received notice that the shares are beneficially held by a person whose name is not on the share register. In the Court of Appeal Palles CB stated:[72]

> "The mere fact of notice does not convert the Company into trustees for the persons of whose beneficial interest they have notice; but if, having that notice, they advance money to the trustee, on the security of the trust property, their conduct is not protected by the section and they participate in a breach of trust. So, too, they seek to commit a breach of trust by claiming, under colour of a lien created after such notice, to appropriate to the payment of their own debt property which to their knowledge is trust property."

[16.22] The effect of the failure of a mortgagee to give either a stop notice or to have the shares transferred into its name can be seen from the decision of Budd J in *Re Donal McClement, a bankrupt*.[73] In that case, upon the shareholder's bankruptcy, his shares which he had mortgaged by way of deposit of the share certificates were deemed to be in his order and disposition.[74]

Notice

[16.23] The serving of a stop notice will not give the mortgagee any improvement in its rights over persons (other than the mortgagor) having a prior equitable interest in the mortgaged shares.[75] An instructive case as to how an equitable mortgagee who takes the usual precautions can be prejudiced is that of *Coleman v London County and Westminster Bank Ltd*.[76] Annie Coleman settled debentures on trust, and executed a deed of transfer in favour of the trustee Edward Coleman. The transfer was not registered. One of the beneficiaries assigned his interest to his wife for value. Subsequently Annie Coleman obtained an advance from a bank on the security of the debentures. The bank inspected the register and found Annie Coleman to be the registered owner. Subsequently the bank discovered the settlement; it then arranged for the debentures to be transferred into its name and had its name entered on the register. The assignee brought an action against the bank claiming entitlement to the beneficial interest of the shares which had been assigned to her. The Court held that the assignee had priority as her equitable interest was prior in time to the equitable mortgage in favour of the bank and the bank could not improve its position (by having itself registered as legal owner) following its discovery of the settlement.

---

72. [1896] 1 IR 532 at 578.
73. [1960] IR 141.
74. See also *Re Butler, a bankrupt* [1900] 2 IR 153.
75. *Re AD Holmes* (1885) 29 Ch D 786.
76. [1916] 2 Ch 353.

[16.24] Accordingly, any notice served by a mortgagee of its equitable mortgage will not give it priority over any prior equitable interest in the mortgaged shares. Furthermore a mortgagee will not be able to obtain full legal rights over shares by way of legal mortgage where it is on notice of any prior rights.

[16.25] The decisions in *Moore v The North Western Bank*[77] and on similar facts, in *Ireland v Hart*,[78] are an even grimmer warning to lenders on the security of shares. In the latter case a man who held shares as trustee for his wife gave the defendant an executed blank transfer for the shares as security for a loan. The defendant, who had no notice of the wife's title, completed the transfer and presented it for registration. In holding that the wife's equitable interest prevailed, Joyce J stated:[79] "a legal title is not acquired as against an equitable owner before registration".

If the defendant had no notice of the prior equitable interest he might have acquired title had he been able to register the transfer prior to the action brought by the wife.[80]

[16.26] The serving of a stop notice will also avoid the possibility of a shareholder obtaining a duplicate certificate from the company secretary on the grounds that the original (held by the bank as security) was lost. A subsequent security taken by another bank over the duplicate share certificate will result in difficulties for all parties concerned. The company secretary should prevent such a scenario if he has been presented previously with a stop notice.

Transferring Title

"A transfer is not legally complete until the transferee has been registered in the books of the Company."[81]

[16.27] The rationale for a person taking security is to utilise the benefit of the security should the mortgagor default on its obligations to the mortgagee. The utilisation of security will take the form of disposing of the asset and using the proceeds towards the discharge of the mortgagor's obligations to the mortgagee. If there is a surplus after such discharge, the surplus is returned to the mortgagor.

[77.] (1891) LJ Ch 627.
[78.] [1902] 1 Ch 522.
[79.] *Ibid* at 529.
[80.] See Keane, *Equity and the Law of Trusts in the Republic of Ireland* (1988) Butterworths, para 5.06.
[81.] Johnston J in *Tangney v The Clarence Hotels Company Ltd* [1933] IR 51 at 61.

Directors' Discretion

[16.28] The articles of association of a company, which is a binding contract as between the members *inter se* and as between the members and the company,[82] regulate the manner in which title to shares in the company may be transferred.[83] This is subject to the company not having passed a resolution by its directors that title to any class of its shares may be transferred by means of "a relevant system" (under regulation 8(2) of the Companies Act, 1990 (Uncertificated Securities) Regulations, 1996[84]).

[16.29] In taking security over shares, therefore, it is essential for the mortgagee to become familiar with the company's articles of association.[85] Private companies are required, in their articles of association, to restrict the right of transfer of their shares.[86] Most private companies adopt Part II of Table A of the Companies Act, 1963 as their articles of association, subject to some minor modifications. Regulation 3 of Part II states:

> "The directors may, in their absolute discretion, and without assigning any reason therefor, decline to register any transfer of any share, whether or not it is a fully paid share".

Although the directors are required to pass a formal resolution[87] to this effect within two months[88] if they wish to refuse registration,[89] they are not obliged to give any reason for such refusal,[90] and indeed in most circumstances would be well advised not to give a reason.[91] Although this regulation enables the directors to refuse registration without giving any reason, their refusal must be

---

82. *Powell Duffryn plc v Petereit* The Times European Law Report 15 April 1992; see also Ross J in *Clark v Workman* [1920] IR 107; for a review of the decided cases see Ussher, *Company Law in Ireland* 1986, Sweet & Maxwell pp 163-169.
83. Companies Act, 1963 s 79.
84. SI 68/1996; see para **[16.06]** above.
85. "They constitute a contract between every shareholder and all the others, and between the company itself and all the shareholders. It is a contract of the most sacred character, and it is on the faith of it that each shareholder advances his money" *per* Ross J *in Clark v Workman* [1920] 1 IR 107 at 112.
86. Companies Act, 1963 s 33.
87. See *Tett v Phoenix Property and Investment Co Ltd* [1984] BCLC 599.
88. See para **[16.30]** below.
89. For further detail on the directors' powers to refuse registration see Courtney, *The Law of Private Companies* (1994) Butterworths paras 10.027 to 10.047.
90. See *Re Dublin North City Milling Company* [1909] 1 IR 179; although see *Shaw & Co Ltd Hughes' Case* (1896) 21 VLR 599.
91. See *Re Hafner; Olhausen v Powderley* [1943] IR 426 and *Tett v Phoenix Property and Investment Co Ltd* [1984] BCLC 599; *Muir Mills Co Ltd of Cawnpore v Condon* (1900) 1 LR 22 All 410; see also Hannigan, 'Share Transfer Problems in the Private Company' (1990) 11 Company Lawyer 170.

exercised *bona fide* in what they consider to be in the interest of the company.[92] In the absence of evidence to the contrary the directors will be taken as having acted *bona fide* [93] If a court is to order directors to register where their refusal is due to an improper motive, it seems "the court must not only find that the directors had an invalid motive, but it must also find that they had no valid motive that might be itself sufficient".[94] But it was held in *Re Hafner; Olhausen v Powderley*[95] that the exercise of the directors' discretion through an improper motive enabled the court to infer from the directors' lack of explanation that their refusal was not a *bona fide* exercise of their discretion. In the High Court Black J explained:[96]

> "Once a reason which was invalid was proved to the satisfaction of the Court, the rule [that directors who do not state any reason for refusing a transfer must be presumed to have had valid reasons and that no unfavourable inference can be drawn from their silence] ceased to hold good, and the Court felt itself free to examine the possibility of other reasons that would not be invalid and even to comment upon and draw inferences from the directors' failure to state their reasons".

[16.30] To refuse registration, the company through its board must exercise the right to refuse registration of a transfer within two months of the transfer being lodged with it, and notice of such refusal must be given to the transferee.[97] If the directors fail to exercise their right of refusal within two months of the transfer being presented for registration, their right of refusal will lapse and the transferee is entitled to be registered:[98]

> "If there is unnecessary delay in placing the transfers before the board, the power of veto must, I think, be regarded as lost, so that the right of transfer becomes unrestricted."[99]

Where the board is evenly split as to whether or not a share transfer should be registered and there is no casting vote, the board will have failed to exercise their right to refuse registration and accordingly the transferee is entitled to be registered.[100]

[92.] See Ross J in *Clark v Workman* [1920] 1 IR 107 and Lord Greene MR *Re Smith and Fawcett Ltd* [1942] 1 All ER 542; see also *Popely v Planarrive Ltd* [1997] 1 BCLC 8.

[93.] *Berry v Tottenham Hotspur Football & Athletic Co Ltd* [1936] 3 All ER 554; see also *Popely v Planarrive Ltd* [1997] 1 BCLC 8 which held that the onus was on the transferee to prove that the directors had not acted *bona fide*.

[94.] *Per* Black J in *Re Hafner; Olhausen v Powderley* [1943] IR 426 at 441.

[95.] [1943] IR 426.

[96.] *Ibid* at 441; this part of his decision was unanimously upheld by the Supreme Court.

[97.] Companies Act, 1963 s 84(1); Table A, Part I, reg 26.

[98.] *Moodie v W & J Shepherd (Bookbinders) Ltd* [1949] 2 All ER 1044.

[99.] *Per* Pennycuick J in *Re Swaledale Cleaners Ltd* [1968] 1 All ER 1132 at 1136.

[100.] *Re Hackney Pavilion Ltd* [1924] 1 Ch 276; *Shepherd's Trustee v Shepherd* 1950 SC (HL) 60.

[16.31] Where the directors exercise their right of refusal but fail to inform the transferee of their refusal, such failure will not entitle the transferee to be registered. This was decided in *Popely v Planarrive Ltd*[101] which held that such a failure may well expose the directors to civil or criminal liability, but could not relate back and turn the proper exercise of the directors' powers into a nullity.

[16.32] While the transferor may submit the executed and stamped transfer to the company for registration,[102] in practice it is the transferee who will submit the share transfer to the company for registration,[103] as indeed it is the transferee whose duty it is to stamp the transfer.[104] Furthermore, the transferee is "the proper person" to take proceedings against the company to compel registration.[105] The transferor is not obliged to procure registration - his only duty following delivery of the executed transfer together with the share certificate is not to do anything which may prevent registration.[106] In *Hooper v Hertz*[107] a shareholder executed a blank transfer and handed it over together with a share certificate for the purpose of securing a loan. Following a payment default by the shareholder, the bank completed the transfer and sent it to the company for registration with a share certificate. The shareholder disputed the validity of the transfer. The Court of Appeal held that the shareholder was liable in damages for failing in his obligation to do nothing to prevent or delay registration of the transferee.

[16.33] Accordingly, it is prudent for a chargee to require that where such a provision exists that the articles of association be amended by the addition of a new article to read:

> "Notwithstanding anything contained in these Articles, the directors shall not decline to register any transfer of shares, nor may they suspend registration thereof, where such a transfer is executed or delivered for registration by any person to whom such shares have been mortgaged or charged by way of security, or by any nominee of such person, pursuant to the power of sale under such security and a certificate by any officer of such person that the shares were

---

[101.] [1997] 1 BCLC 8.

[102.] Companies Act, 1963, s 83.

[103.] "When the transfer has been executed and handed over to the transferee, it is then for the latter to pay the consideration money and to get the transfer registered" *per* Brett MR in *Skinner v City of London Marine Insurance Corporation* (1884-85) 14 QBD 882 (approved in *Tangney v The Clarence Hotels Company Ltd* [1933] IR 51).

[104.] Stamp Act 1891, s 122.

[105.] See Johnston J in *Tangney v The Clarence Hotels Company Ltd* [1933] IR 51 at 59.

[106.] *The London Founders Association Ltd and Palmer v Clarke* (1888) 57 LJ QB 290; *Hickens Harrison Woolston & Co v Jackson & Sons* [1943] 1 All ER 128.

[107.] (1906) 75 LJCH 253.

so charged and the transfer was so executed or delivered shall, save in the case of manifest error, be conclusive evidence of that fact."

The mortgagee should ensure that a special resolution is passed amending the articles of association to this effect.[108] Of course, unless it has security over more than 25 per cent of the voting shares it will not be in a position to block a reversal of such change unless it can successfully contend that such change would be oppressive to it as a minority shareholder.[109] It should also be borne in mind that where an equitable mortgage is taken, the mortgagor's name will remain on the share register and therefore will retain the right to vote in respect of such shares.[110] It is inappropriate for the directors to covenant not to block a share transfer as such a covenant would be unenforceable against future directors; it could also be seen as fettering the future discretion of the directors and thus causing them a difficulty in complying with their fiduciary duties to the company. A restriction in the articles of association preventing alteration will be invalid, although members may agree outside the articles of association on restrictions as to the alteration of the articles.[111]

[16.34] It might be noted that the articles of association of most companies will provide that the company has a lien over all partly paid shares and the dividends in respect of such shares.[112] This lien will rank in priority to a subsequent mortgage or charge of shares.[113] Furthermore, the directors are usually empowered to sell such shares.[114] It is always unwise for a person to take a legal mortgage of partly paid shares as upon registration he will be liable for further calls on the shares.[115]

[16.35] The Companies Act, 1990 (Uncertificated Securities) Regulations, 1996[116] provides that,[117] "title to securities may be evidenced and transferred without a written instrument provided that such title is evidenced and transferred in accordance with these regulations." These regulations envisage an approved

---

[108.] Companies Act, 1963 s 15(1).

[109.] Companies Act, 1963, s 205.

[110.] See para **[16.17]** above.

[111.] See *Russell v Northern Bank Development Corporation Ltd* [1992] BCLC 1016; [1992] BCC 578; Lingard suggests otherwise - see Lingard, *op cit,* para 15.27.

[112.] Companies Act, 1963 Table A Part I reg 11 (although the directors may not exercise the lien after receipt of notice of the mortgage see para **[16.20]** above).

[113.] *Close Corporation (Australia) Pty Ltd v North Sydney Brick and Tile Co Ltd* [1995] 10 JIBL N-199 (Supreme Court of New South Wales).

[114.] Companies Act, 1963 Table A Part I reg 12.

[115.] *Ibid* reg 15; calls on members means calls on persons whose names are on the share register - Companies Act, 1963 s 31(2).

[116.] SI 68/1996.

[117.] *Ibid* reg 4(1).

operator entering into an agreement with the Revenue Commissioners as to the payment of stamp duty on transfers of title to securities through a computer based system.[118] The company must have passed a board resolution (with notice thereof to its members[119]) to the effect that title to its shares or any class of shares may be transferred by means of a relevant system[120] (provided the members have not previously passed a resolution precluding the directors from passing such a board resolution[121]). This resolution will have the effect of overriding any contrary provision concerning the transfer of such shares in the company's articles of association.[122]

Pre-emption rights

[16.36] It is likely also in a private company that there is a pre-emption right on the transfer of shares between current members, whereby a member wishing to transfer his shares must offer them to other members prior to offering them to any third party.[123] This pre-emption right would be circumvented by a mortgagee if the company adopted an article, as in paragraph **[16.33]** above, precluding the directors from having the option of refusing to register a transfer. In addition, a procedure should be provided in the pre-emption article to the effect that, notwithstanding any other term of that article, where a person pursuant to a power of sale under any security wishes to transfer such shares the foregoing pre-emption provisions will not apply. It is more doubtful whether in practice such a provision will be agreed to as the members will effectively be foregoing their right to exclude non-members, whereas an amendment to regulation 3 of Part II of Table A[124] is more likely to be readily agreed to as usually the circumstances in creating security over shares are that of parent/subsidiary rather than in the nature of a joint venture or partnership where the pre-emption right occurs. There appears to be a diversity of opinion as to whether beneficial title to the shares passes on the transfer of shares in contravention of a pre-emption provision in the company's articles of association.[125] Clearly the legal title does not pass until the transferee is registered.[126] However, it has been held that where a security holder purports to

---

[118] *Ibid*, reg 4(3).
[119] *Ibid*, reg 8(4).
[120] *Ibid*, reg 8(2).
[121] *Ibid*, reg 8(6).
[122] *Ibid*, reg 8(3).
[123] For a more detailed commentary on pre-emption rights on the transfer of shares see Courtney, *op cit*, paras 10.048-10.062.
[124] As set out in para **[16.33]** above.
[125] See Courtney, *op cit*, paras 10.057-10.059.
[126] See fn 81 above.

sell shares in contravention of the pre-emption right not only will it fail to pass the legal title but also the equitable title.[127]

In the case of some private companies there may be no pre-emption right in the articles of association. Such right may, particularly in the case of joint ventures, be contained in a separate shareholders agreement. Accordingly, the person taking security should obtain a warranty from the proposed mortgagor that all agreements relating to the mortgagor's shares, being offered as security, are disclosed to the mortgagee.

Public companies

[16.37] A public company may have some restriction on the transfer of its shares. Where Part I of Table A of the Companies Act, 1963 is adopted as the articles of association of the company, the directors may decline to register a transfer of shares "to a person of whom they do not approve" or where the registration "in their opinion, may imperil or prejudicially affect the status of the company in the State".[128] Shares which are the subject of a listing on the Stock Exchange are not subject to any transfer restriction. Where the directors do not have power to refuse to register a transfer:

> "they are entitled to have a reasonable time after the transfer is made in order to make inquiries for the purpose of finding out if the transfer is in order; but, after being satisfied on this point, they are bound at the next meeting to register the transfer".[129]

In *Kinsella v Alliance and Dublin Consumers Gas Company*[130] a number of share transfers had not been registered in time for a shareholders' meeting. Nevertheless the Court held that "all reasonable efforts" had been taken by the company to register the transfers in time for the meeting and accordingly the decisions taken at the meeting were not invalid.[131]

Liability of Mortgagee for False Transfer

[16.38] When taking a transfer of shares a lender should be satisfied as to the integrity of the shareholder. An example as to how a lender may find itself indemnifying a company for loss it has suffered can be seen from the case of *Sheffield Corporation v Barclay*.[132] In that case, the bank sent to the corporation

---

[127.] See *Hunter v Hunter* [1936] AC 222 - "A mortgagee of shares cannot split up the interest of the mortgagor and sell the mortgagor's beneficial interest while retaining for himself the legal title" *per* Viscount Hailsham LC at 248.
[128.] Regulation 24 which also stipulates other reasons.
[129.] Per Joyce J in *Ireland v Hart* [1902] 1 Ch 522 at 528.
[130.] High Court, unrep, 5 October 1982, Barron J.
[131.] This did not prevent shareholders from convening a further meeting.
[132.] [1905] AC 392.

stock transfers which were purported to be executed by the registered holders of stock as security for a loan. The corporation acted on the stock transfer and issued a fresh certificate; the bank subsequently sold the stock to a third party. It was discovered later that the signature on the initial stock transfer had been forged and the corporation was obliged to indemnify the stockholder. The House of Lords held that the bank was obliged to indemnify the corporation for its loss. This was on the basis that there was an implied contract between the bank and the corporation under which not only was the title of the person presenting the transfer warranted, but that there was an agreement to keep the person acting on the request for registration indemnified against loss resulting from such registration.[133]

[16.39] Although the bank was not found to be negligent, the judgment of the Lord Chancellor, the Earl of Halsbury, is a clear reminder to banks, and their lawyers, of the responsibility which they undertake when taking security for a loan. The Lord Chancellor said:[134]

> "I do not suggest that there was any negligence - perhaps business could not go on if people were suspecting forgery in every transaction - but their position was obviously very different from that of the corporation ... They cannot refuse to register ... and they cannot inquire into the transaction out of which the transfer arises. The bank, on the other hand, is at liberty to lend their money or not. They can make any amount of inquiries they like. If they find that an intended borrower has a co-trustee, they may ask him or the co-trustee himself whether the co-trustee is a party to the loan, and a simple question to the co-trustee would have prevented the fraud. They take the risk of the transaction and lend the money. The security given happens to be in a form that requires registration to make it available, and the bank 'demand' ... that the stock shall be registered in their name or that of their nominees ... This was done, and the corporation by acting on this 'demand' have incurred a considerable loss."

ALTERNATIVE FORMS OF SECURITY

[16.40] There may be occasions where it is not appropriate to use a standard or traditional form of mortgage or charge. This may arise from the commercial circumstances of the transaction, such as where the security provider wishes to utilise its shares by purchasing and selling but always maintaining a certain pool to which the creditor will have first recourse. On such occasions the security may be structured as an irrevocable authorisation from the shareholder to the creditor. Ideally, the shares should be registered in the name of the creditor.

[133.] This decision applied the general principle of law established in *Dugdale v Lovering* LR 10 CP 196.
[134.] [1905] AC 392 at 396.

Alternatively, the creditor may hold the share certificates and blank transfers executed by the shareholder with an irrevocable authority to complete the transfers. This arrangement may be appropriate where the shares are listed on an exchange and are easily and freely transferable. This flexibility is not suitable for shares in a private company due to the share transfer restrictions and the restriction on offering such shares to the public.[135] The success of this form of security depends upon the speed with which the creditor can utilise the security. These structures involve a full consideration of the legal issues which may arise particularly upon insolvency and bankruptcy and persons lending on such structures should be aware of the pitfalls.

[16.41] Other circumstances may dictate that a mortgage cannot be taken but a lien with a power of sale - this may be appropriate in the case of co-operative societies. Another example of taking a lien rather than a mortgage arises in the case of companies having shares with unlimited liability. It is obviously undesirable to take a mortgage of shares from an unlimited company. Another point to watch regarding a legal mortgage, is obtaining title to all the shares in a company thereby reducing the number of member below the legal minimum to maintain limited liability.[136] The legal minimum[137] can be maintained by transferring one share (in the case of a private company) to a nominee company to hold in trust for the mortgagee.[138]

Where a public company issues bearer securities, title passes by delivery and accordingly these may be pledged.[139]

APPLICABLE LAW

[16.42] Many transactions have become increasingly international. This is particularly so with regard to the ownership and charging of shares. Questions as to the applicable law may arise where for example, no choice of law is expressed in the security document and a US corporation creates security over its shares in its Irish incorporated subsidiary in favour of an English bank. In the example given, while the parties are free to contract under English or New York law, applicable law may become relevant, particularly in the context of enforcement of the security. The principal decision on the point is that of the English Court of Appeal in *Macmillan Inc v Bishopsgate Investment Trust plc (No 3)*.[140] In that case the plaintiff, a Delaware corporation controlled by the late Robert Maxwell,

---

[135.] Companies Act, 1963, s 33(1) and Table A, Part II, reg 2.

[136.] Companies Act, 1963, s 36.

[137.] Two for private company (unless it is a single member company) and seven for a public company (Companies Act, 1963, s 36).

[138.] See Hoffmann J in *Nisbet v Shepherd* [1994] BCC 91 at 95.

[139.] See Ch 12.

[140.] [1996] 1 All ER 585.

had a majority shareholding in B Inc, a company incorporated in New York where the shares were registered. The shares were transferred to the first defendant, an investment trust controlled by Robert Maxwell - those shares were to be held as nominee for the plaintiff pursuant to a written agreement. In breach of trust and without the plaintiff's knowledge, Robert Maxwell agreed to give the shares to three banks as security for loans to companies owned by him. Following his death, the shares were transferred to the banks in New York. The plaintiff claimed recovery of the shares which had been given as security in breach of trust; the banks claimed priority as they had acquired the shares in good faith and for value. The preliminary question to be decided was the applicable law. The Court held that consistently with the general rule relating to movables and land, the appropriate law to decide questions of title to shares in a company was the law of the place where the shares were situated (the *lex situs*) which was in the ordinary way the law of the place where the company was incorporated.[141] The rationale for the approach is probably best put in the judgment of Aldous LJ where he stated:[142]

> "As a matter of principle I believe the appropriate law to decide questions of title to property, such as shares, is the *lex situs*, which is the same as the law of incorporation. No doubt contractual rights and obligations relating to such property fall to be determined by the proper law of the contract. However, it is not possible to decide whether a person is entitled to be included upon the register of the company as a shareholder without recourse to the company's documents of incorporation, as interpreted according to the law of the place of incorporation. If that be right, then it is appropriate for the same law to govern issues as to title, including issues as to priority; thus avoiding recourse to different systems of law to answer essentially a single question. Further, it is to the courts of that place which a person is likely to have to turn to enforce his rights."

A closer reading of the decision elicits the fact that Aldous LJ was in a minority in holding that the applicable law was the place of incorporation. Auld LJ[143] held the applicable law to be that of the place where the share register is kept, while Staughton LJ[144] wavered on the point. In the case in question the place of

---

[141.] Applied *in re Harvard Securities Ltd (in liq), Holland v Newbury* [1997] 2 BCLC 369.
[142.] [1996] 1 All ER 585 at 620.
[143.] *Ibid* at 608 - "In my view, there is authority and much to be said for treating issues of priority of ownership of shares in a corporation according to the *lex situs* of those shares. That will normally be the country where the register is kept, usually but not always the country of incorporation."
[144.] *Ibid* at 602 - "I conclude that an issue as to who has title to shares in a company should be decided by the law of the place where the shares are situated (*lex situs*). In the ordinary way ... that is the law of the place where the company is incorporated. There may be cases where it is arguably the law of the place where the share register is kept."

incorporation and location of the share register were the same so the difference was of academic interest only. Aldous LJ found support from decisions of the Exchequer Court of Canada[145] and the United States Supreme Court[146] for his proposition that the applicable law is that of the country of incorporation.[147] The distinction should be unimportant in Ireland as a company incorporated in Ireland is not permitted to keep its share register outside the State.[148]

[16.43] The same principles do not apply however where, in the absence of a choice of law clause, the shares are freely transferable or negotiable. *In re Harvard Securities Ltd (in liq), Holland v Newbury*,[149] Harvard, a dealer of securities, purchased shares in Australian and United States companies. Shares in the Australian companies were in the same format as those typically held in Ireland where the owner is registered. The US shares were registered in the name of the English Association of American Bond and Shareholders Ltd. The share certificates in respect of these shares stated that the shares were transferable only on the books of the company upon surrender of the certificate. However, the back of the certificate contained a blank transfer signed on behalf of the registered owner and stamped with the words that the owner "hereby guarantees that all necessary papers have been filed with the Registrar and/or transfer agents to ensure transfer". These certificates were kept by the owner in London. The Court held that the applicable law in establishing beneficial ownership in respect of (i) the Australian shares was Australian law being the place of the location of the Australian companies, and (ii) the US shares was English law, as the shares were freely negotiable and thus the applicable law was the place where the certificates were held.

[145.] *Braun v Custodian* (1944) 3 DLR 412 where the applicable law to the shares of a Canadian company registered in New York was held to be subject to the place of incorporation.

[146.] *Jellenick v Huron Copper Mining Co* (1900) 177 US 1 where Harlan J in giving the court's judgment stated - "As the habitation or domicile of the Company is and must be in the State that created it, the property represented by its certificates and stock may be deemed to be held by the Company within the State whose creature it is, whenever it is sought by suit to determine who is the real owner. This principle is not affected by the fact that the defendant is authorised by the laws of Michigan to have an office in another State, at which a book showing the transfers of stock may be kept."

[147.] See also Neuberger J *in re Harvard Securities Ltd (in liq), Holland v Newbury* [1997] 2 BCLC 369 at 374, 5.

[148.] Companies Act, 1963, s 116(6).

[149.] [1997] 2 BCLC 369.

Chapter 17

Registration of Mortgages and Charges

[17.01] Certain mortgages and charges created by companies are required to have their prescribed particulars delivered[1] to the Registrar of Companies within 21 days after their creation.[2] Not all mortgages or charges created by a company require registration. To ascertain whether particulars of a mortgage or charge should be registered, consideration needs to be given as to whether the security falls within one of the categories listed in s 99(2) of the Companies Act, 1963.

CATEGORIES OF CHARGES[3] REQUIRING REGISTRATION

A charge for the purpose of securing any issue of debentures[4]

[17.02] In practice, a charge for the purpose of securing any issue of debentures arises infrequently as companies do not as a general rule raise funds by the issue of debentures, or at any rate debentures which are secured by a charge on the company's assets.[5] The definition of "debenture" in the Companies Act, 1963 is not particularly helpful as it is defined as including "debenture stock, bonds and any other securities of a company whether constituting a charge on the assets of the company or not".[6] Buckley states, "No one seems to know exactly what 'debenture' means."[7]

Chitty J has described a debenture as meaning "a document which either creates a debt or acknowledges it, and any document which fulfils either of these conditions is a 'debenture'".[8]

[17.03] The Court of Appeal in Wellington, New Zealand[9] has held that the word "issue", "must be construed as referring in a collective sense to the aggregate of a number of individual debentures issued by a company."[10]

---

1. As to the duty of delivering particulars see para **[17.71]**.
2. Companies Act, 1963, s 99; for further reading see McCormack, 'Registration of Company Charges' (1984) 2 ILT 67; Courtney, *The Law of Private Companies* (1994) Butterworths, Ch 15.
3. Charge includes mortgage - s 99(10).
4. Companies Act, 1963, s 99(2)(a).
5. Strictly speaking, the raising of funds by companies through the issue of commercial paper is the raising of funds by the issue of debentures, see paras **[7.72]**-**[7.82]**.
6. Companies Act, 1963, s 2(1).
7. *Buckley on the Companies Acts* (1981) 14th ed, p 250.
8. In *Levy v Abercorris Slate and Slab Company* (1887) 37 Ch D 260 at 264.
9. In *Automobile Association (Canterbury) Inc v Australasian Secured Deposits Ltd (in liq)* [1973] 1 NZLR 417.
10. *Ibid per* Richmond J at 425.

[17.04] A point for practitioners to bear in mind is that, when reviewing s 99(2) of the Companies Act, 1963 to ascertain whether a charge over a particular asset is registrable, where the charge does not attach to an asset referred in s 99(2) or is not a floating charge it may nonetheless be registrable if the charge is given as security for the issue of debentures. An example where such a charge may arise is where a company issues debentures to investors who may be investing in the company. The payment of such debentures may be guaranteed by a bank who may obtain an indemnity from the company supported by a charge on assets not otherwise registrable, such as a fixed charge over shares.

A charge on uncalled share capital of the company[11]

[17.05] A charge on uncalled share capital of the company generally arises where uncalled share capital is referred to as part of a company's assets being charged under a mortgage debenture which incorporates a fixed and floating charge over the entire assets and undertaking of the company creating the security.

A charge created or evidenced by an instrument which, if executed by an individual, would require registration as a bill of sale[12]

[17.06] The Bills of Sale (Ireland) Acts, 1879 and 1883 provide that charges created over certain specified assets as security for a debt or for the payment of money must be registered as a bill of sale. These specified assets include "articles capable of complete transfer by delivery".[13] These Acts do not apply to debentures issued by incorporated companies secured on chattels or goods of such companies.[14] Accordingly, a mortgage or charge of any of the specified assets referred to in the Bills of Sale Acts where created by a company must be registered under the Companies Acts but not under the Bills of Sale Acts.[15] This head of registration most commonly arises where a company creates a mortgage or charge over machinery or equipment.[16]

[17.07] Goods held under a contractual lien as security for monies due will not be subject to registration under this head,[17] as "the word 'charge' does not in its

---

11. Companies Act, 1963, s 99(2)(b).
12. *Ibid* s 99(2)(c).
13. Bills of Sale (Ireland) Act, 1879, ss 3 and 4.
14. Bills of Sale (Ireland) Act (1879) Amendment Act, 1883, s 17; applied in *Re Royal Marine Hotel Company, Kingstown (Ltd)* [1895] 1 IR 368; see also in *Re Standard Manufacturing Co* [1891] 1 Ch 627.
15. For a discourse on the 19th century legislation giving rise to this distinction see the Court of Appeal's judgment in *Re Standard Manufacturing Co* [1891] 1 Ch 627.
16. See Ch 11.
17. *Waitomo Wools (NZ) Ltd v Nelsons (NZ) Ltd* [1974] 1 NZLR 484.

ordinary and accepted legal sense embrace a legal possessory lien even ... if the contract gives a right of sale."[18]

A charge on land, wherever situate, or any interest therein, but not including a charge for any rent or other periodical sum issuing out of land[19]

[17.08] Clearly where a company executes a mortgage or charge over land, the prescribed particulars of such security must be filed for registration with the Registrar of Companies.[20] Such particulars are required also where an equitable mortgage has been created by the deposit of title deeds, even where such deposit is not accompanied by a written memorandum confirming the reason for the deposit.[21]

Deposit of Title Deeds

[17.09] A difficulty may arise where title documents are deposited with a bank and there is nothing to indicate the reason for the deposit. In the absence of registration, a liquidator of the company making the deposit will seek to show that the deposit was by way of equitable mortgage which is void for want of registration.[22] A bank which has taken title documents as security for monies due will not be able to rely on any lien over the documents in the absence of registration.[23] In the matter of *Farm Fresh Frozen Foods Ltd (in liq)*[24] the company agreed with its bank to deposit title deeds with the bank as security for a loan. As a prior charge had to be cleared the deeds were not in fact delivered until the day a petition to wind up the company was presented to the High Court. Keane J stated:[25]

> "There is authority for the proposition that where an equitable mortgage is created by deposit of title deeds there is an implied contract that the mortgagee may retain the deeds until he is paid ... But it is also clear that when such a mortgage is avoided for non-registration, this contractual right of retention is avoided also."

[17.10] Keane J rejected also the proposition that the bank could rely on a general lien on the grounds that the title deeds came into the bank's possession by virtue of an express contract for the advancing of money on the security of an equitable mortgage by deposit of title deeds.

[18.] *Ibid per* Richmond J at 491.
[19.] Companies Act, 1963, s 99(2)(d).
[20.] *Ibid*.
[21.] See *Re Wallis & Simmonds (Builders) Ltd* [1974] 1 All ER 561.
[22.] Companies Act, 1963, s 99(1).
[23.] See in *Re Molton Finance Ltd* [1968] 1 Ch 325.
[24.] [1980] ILRM 131.
[25.] *Ibid* at 134.

[17.11] It is in the interest of any lender to have a written memorandum taken at the time of the deposit (to rebut any claim that they were deposited for safe keeping).[26] This may also be in the interest of the company's directors if they are giving personal guarantees as additional security. Even where a loan is granted simultaneously with a deposit of title deeds to land, the lender may still be unable to discharge the onus on him and satisfy the court that a charge was intended to be created.[27]

Solicitor's Undertaking

[17.12] A further difficulty may arise where there is a letter or series of letters from a company's solicitor indicating that a charge will be created over land upon its purchase by the company. An indication of this difficulty arose in *Fullerton v Provincial Bank of Ireland*,[28] where the House of Lords restored the High Court decision (which had been reversed by a majority of the Court of Appeal[29]) which held that the letters did amount to an agreement to create a charge and therefore required registration to preserve priority. In that case, several letters were written by a customer to the bank in some of which he stated that as soon as he had the deed of conveyance of the estate he would deposit it with the bank. As Walker LJ said in his dissenting judgment in the Court of Appeal, which the House of Lords upheld:[30]

> "An equitable mortgage as understood in a Court of Equity may arise in many ways ... It may be contained in a mere letter, though the party be not in possession of the property and be waiting for the conveyance to be executed."

Vendor's Lien

[17.13] A vendor's lien which arises in the course of the sale of land is not a charge for the purpose of registration and particulars of such a lien do not require registration. Any doubt on this point was clarified in the High Court in *Bank of Ireland Finance Ltd v DJ Daly Ltd*.[31] McMahon J considered and followed the decision of Brightman J in *London Cheshire Co v Laplagrene Co*[32] where he held:[33]

> "that an unpaid vendor's lien was the creature of the law; that it did not depend on contract but on the fact that the vendor had a right to a specific performance

---

26. For the form of memorandum see para **[10.24]** above.
27. See *Re Alton Corporation* [1985] BCLC 27.
28. [1903] 1 IR 483.
29. In *Re Stevenson's Estate* [1902] 1 IR 23.
30. *Ibid* at 46.
31. [1978] IR 79.
32. [1971] Ch 499.
33. [1978] IR 79 at 84.

of his contract and that, accordingly, it was not registrable ... If registration were necessary, every vendor selling to a company would be put to the inconvenience of having to register the unpaid vendor's lien as a matter of course on the off chance that circumstances might arise which would render it necessary for the vendor to rely on the unpaid vendor's lien."

A Charge on Book Debts of the Company[34]

[17.14] The principal question which arises under this heading is the meaning of book debt. If certain proceeds are not a book debt and do not fall under another head of charge, the absence of registration of a charge over such proceeds will not be fatal for the charge holder in the event of the appointment of a liquidator to the chargor.[35] The meaning of book debt appeared to be first discussed in *Shipley v Marshall*[36] where the Court considered the meaning of book debts as used in the Bankruptcy Act 1861. Erle CJ said:[37]

"By 'book debts' the legislature doubtless intended to describe debts in some way connected with the trade of the bankrupt ... it is enough to say that this was a debt connected with and growing out of the plaintiff's trade".

Williams J said,[38] "the meaning of the statute is ... all debts due to the bankrupt in respect of which entries could be made in the ordinary course of his business".

Byles J said:[39] "they must be such debts as are commonly entered in books".

[17.15] This latter definition was the one most preferred by Pennycuick J in *Paul & Frank Ltd v Discount Bank (Overseas) Ltd.*[40] Buckley J's interpretation in *Independent Automatic Sales Ltd v Knowles & Foster*[41] of what *Shipley v Marshall*[42] decided arguably offers the best summary of the judicial position on the meaning of book debt:[43]

"*Shipley v Marshall*, I think establishes that, if it can be said of a debt arising in the course of a business and due or growing due to the proprietor of that business that such a debt would or could in the ordinary course of such a business be entered in well kept books relating to that business, that debt can

---

34. Companies Act, 1963, s 99(2)(e).
35. As in *Re Kum Tong Restaurant (Dublin) Ltd (in Liq); Byrne v Allied Irish Banks Ltd* [1978] IR 446.
36. (1863) 14 CBNS 566.
37. *Ibid* at 570.
38. *Ibid* at 571.
39. *Ibid* at 573.
40. [1966] 2 All ER 922 at 926.
41. [1962] 3 All ER 27.
42. (1863) 14 CBNS 566.
43. [1962] 3 All ER 27 at 34, and see also *Contemporary Cottages (NZ) Ltd v Margin Traders Ltd* [1981] 2 NZLR 114.

properly be called a book debt whether it is in fact entered in the books of the business or not".

[17.16] In *Independent Automatic Sales Ltd v Knowles & Foster*,[44] the plaintiff signed a letter of hypothecation in favour of the defendants whereby it was agreed that the plaintiff's bills of exchange and other hire-purchase agreements deposited with the defendants and the proceeds thereof would be pledged to the defendants as security for the payment of moneys. The letter of hypothecation and deposit were held to be void as against the plaintiff's liquidator for lack of registration. Buckley J held that:[45]

> "... the charge constituted by the deposit of one of these agreements was a charge on each and all of the benefits of the plaintiff company under that agreement. If those benefits included any rights which can properly be described as 'book debts' the charge was, in part at least, a charge on book debts and therefore registrable under the section."

Thus, the security over the hire-purchase agreement was a charge on a debt existing at that time, although not then due, and such a debt was a book debt, since the debt could in the ordinary course of business properly be entered in well-kept books relating to the company's business.

[17.17] The subsequent English decision in *Paul & Frank Ltd v Discount Bank (Overseas) Ltd*[46] mitigated the extent to which s 99 applies, particularly where evidence can be shown that the debt would not in the normal course of business be entered in the company's books. The plaintiff signed a letter authorising the Board of Trade Export Credits Guarantee Department to pay the first named defendant any moneys which might become payable under the export credit insurance policy being prepared to cover the liabilities of the plaintiff's foreign customers. At the hearing of the action evidence of accountancy practice was given on which:

1.   It was common ground that the export credit policy would not be entered as a book debt in the company's accounts at the date of the letter of authorisation;

2.   The court found that the policy would not in practice be entered as a book debt before the admission of liability and ascertainment of amount; and

3.   That the policy would not, in practice, be entered as a book debt even after the admission of liability and ascertainment of amount.

---

44.   [1962] 3 All ER 27.
45.   *Ibid* at 34.
46.   [1966] 2 All ER 922.

Pennycuick J held that, on the evidence of accountancy practice, the plaintiff's claim that the letter of authorisation was void for lack of registration failed - the plaintiff failed to establish that the letter of authorisation was a letter in respect of a book debt. In establishing whether or not a particular chose in action is a book debt within the meaning of (the equivalent to) s 99 Pennycuick J stated:[47]

> "In order to ascertain whether any particular charge is a charge on book debts within the meaning of the section, one must look at the items of property which form the subject-matter of the charge at the date of its creation and consider whether any of those items is a book debt. In the case of an existing item of property, this question can only be answered by reference to its character at the date of creation. Where the item of property is the benefit of a contract and at the date of the charge the benefit of the contract does not comprehend any book debt, I do not see how that contract can be brought within the section as being a book debt merely by reason that the contract may ultimately result in a book debt. Here the ECG policy admittedly did not comprehend any book debt at the date of the letter of authority, and that seems to me to be an end of the matter".

[17.18] That judgment was approved and applied by Lynch J in *Farrell v Equity Bank Ltd*.[48] In that case, the defendant advanced funds to a company on condition that the company authorised its insurance brokers to remit to the defendant any premiums which might be refunded. The company's liquidator submitted that the policies were the company's property which had been converted to refunds and that the defendant not having a charge on the policies could not have a charge on the refunds of such policies. Alternatively the liquidator submitted that if there was a charge it was a charge on book debts and was void for lack of registration. Lynch J held that a charge had been created over the refunds which were not book debts, and therefore the letter of authorisation was not void for lack of registration. He applied the English decision of *Paul & Frank Ltd v Discount Bank (Overseas) Ltd*[49] and held that:[50]

> "The mere possibility that future refunds of premiums might become payable in amounts that were wholly unascertained and might never arise at the date of the creation of the charge does not make that transaction a book debt which must be registered pursuant to s 99 of the Act of 1963."

When considering the meaning of book debt, Lynch J stated:[51]

---

47. [1966] 2 All ER 922 at 927.
48. [1990] 2 IR 549.
49. [1966] 2 All ER 922.
50. [1990] 2 IR 549 at 554.
51. *Ibid* at 553.

"There is no definition of the term 'book debt' in the Act of 1963 or so far as I could find in any other Act either.[52] The term is however defined for bankruptcy purposes in Halsbury's *Laws of England*, (4th edition), Vol 3 at para 525 footnote 4, as follows:

> "Book debts' mean all such debts accruing in the ordinary course of a man's trade as are usually entered in trade books but to constitute a book debt it is not necessary that the debt should be entered in a book."

[17.19] The same approach was adopted in the subsequent case of *Jackson and Allied Irish Bank Capital Markets plc v Lombard and Ulster Banking Ltd.*[53] The company obtained loans from the defendant to pay insurance policy premiums and as security for the loans it assigned to the defendant moneys which might have become payable under the policies and all premiums which might be refunded. The second plaintiff had a fixed charge over all "book debts and other debts" owed to the company. Costello J held that the moneys owed to the company in respect of premium refunds were not "book debts" of the company, but were "other debts" of the company (and thus were caught by the charge).

[17.20] Although there appears to be no Irish authority which either defines a "book debt" or refers to any statutory definition, s 2 of the Book Debts Act 1896 of Victoria, Australia defines a book debt as meaning:

> any debt due or to become due at some future time to any person on account of or in connection with any profession, trade or business carried on by such person whether entered in any book or not.

The distinction between a charge on future book debts which is registrable and a charge on contingent book debts which is not registrable can be a fine one and thus not a satisfactory one for a practitioner.[54] The safer course for the practitioner is to register when in doubt. However, a practitioner is often put under pressure by banks not to register so that the banker's customer does not have a note of the charge appear in *Stubbs Gazette*.[55] In such circumstances a careful study of the judgments in *Farrell v Equity Bank Ltd*,[56] *Jackson and Allied Irish Bank Capital Markets Plc v Lombard and Ulster Banking Ltd*[57] as

---

[52.] See, however, the Instruments Act 1958 of Victoria, s 83 of which states the phrase book debts means, "any debt due or to become due at some future time to any person on account of or in connection with any profession trade or business carried on by such person whether entered in any book or not and includes future debts of the same nature although not incurred or owing at the time of the assignment."
[53.] [1992] 1 IR 94.
[54.] See a discussion on this unsatisfactory position in Penn, Shea and Arora, *The Law Relating to Domestic Banking* (1987) Sweet & Maxwell para 21. 16.
[55.] Published by Dun & Bradstreet Limited.
[56.] [1990] 2 IR 549.
[57.] [1992] 1 IR 94.

well as those in *Independent Automatic Sales Ltd v Knowles & Foster*[58] and *Paul & Frank Ltd v Discount Bank (Overseas) Ltd*[59] and their application to the particular circumstances should be carried out.

Charge over Bank Account

[17.21] In taking an assignment or charge over moneys in a bank account, or which may from time to time be in a bank account, the practitioner is required to consider whether particulars of the security should be registered in the Companies Registration Office against the provider of the security pursuant to s 99 of the Companies Act, 1963. While the safe view is obviously to register particulars of a charge over a bank account,[60] the company may prefer to avoid registration and the bank is likely to wish to facilitate its customer thereby requiring the lawyer to decide whether registration can be safely dispensed with.

Moneys standing to the credit of a company in its bank account are clearly moneys owing to the company by its banker and thus a debt due by the banker to the company. Such a debt would in the ordinary course of business be entered in the books of a company and therefore *prima facie* would be a book debt.[61] As such, a charge over it should be registered.[62] In practice it usually is so registered.

Case law suggests that moneys in a bank account may not be a book debt.[63] The entry in the books may not be in the trading books of the company and accounting treatment is generally different - a balance sheet will show trading debts appearing under "Debtors" and monies in a bank account appearing under "Cash at Bank".[64] Allen JA in the Alberta Supreme Court stated[65] that "... the monies on deposit in the bank account would not, in business, be considered to be 'book debts'."

[17.22] In *Re Keenan Bros Ltd*[66] Walsh J stated in the Supreme Court:[67]

"As the relationship between banker and customer is one of debtor and creditor all sums from time to time standing to credit in that account were owed by the

---

[58.] [1962] 3 All ER 27.

[59.] [1966] 2 All ER 922.

[60.] See Lingard, *Bank Security Documents* (3rd ed) Butterworths para 3.19.

[61.] See para **[17.15]** above.

[62.] Pursuant to s 99(2)(e) of the Companies Act, 1963.

[63.] Although see *Re Rick Cobby Haulage Pty Ltd (in liq); Jackson v Esanda Finance Corporation Ltd* [1992] 11 JIBL N-195 where the Supreme Court of South Australia held that security over moneys lodged in an account was void as against the company's liquidator due to the absence of registration as being a charge on a book debt.

[64.] As required by the Companies (Amendment) Act, 1986 s 4(1) Sch Part I format of balance sheets.

[65.] *Bank of Nova Scotia et al v Royal Bank of Canada* (1975) 59 DLR (3d) 107 at 120.

[66.] [1985] IR 401.

[67.] *Ibid* at 417.

Bank to the company and were not book debts due to the company or debts in the contemplation of the deed of charge or the debenture, even though the account was opened to receive the collected book and other debts due to the company, which of course ceased to be debts from the moment they were collected."

[17.23] These remarks were made in the context of the collection and realisation of book debts which had been transformed into cash at bank. The point did not need to be decided in *Re Keenan Bros Ltd*[68] but it did come up for decision in *Re Brightlife Ltd*.[69] Hoffmann J held that moneys standing to the company's credit in the bank account were not caught by its specific charge over its book debts and other debts. He stated:[70]

"I do not think that the bank balance falls within the term 'book debts or other debts' as it is used in the debenture. It is true that the relationship between banker and customer is one of debtor and creditor. It would not therefore be legally inaccurate to describe a credit balance with a banker as a debt. But this would not be a natural usage for a businessman or accountant. He would ordinarily describe it as 'cash at bank' ...

If [the charging clause] stood alone, I might have been left in some doubt over whether 'debts' was being used in a commercial or strictly legal sense. But in my judgment the ambiguity is resolved by the use of the same words in cl 5(ii), which prohibits Brightlife from dealing with its 'book or other debts' without the prior consent in writing of Norandex 'otherwise than in the ordinary course of getting in and realising the same'. A credit balance at the bank cannot sensibly be 'got in' or 'realised' and the proviso cannot therefore apply to it. If 'book debts or other debts' includes the bank balance, the consequence is that Brightlife could not have dealt with its bank account without the written consent of Norandex. It would have had to obtain such consent every time it issued a cheque. The extreme commercial improbability of such an arrangement satisfies me that the parties used 'book debts and other debts' in a sense which excludes the credit balance at the bank".

[17.24] The same judge was presented with similar facts two years later in *Re Permanent Houses (Holdings) Ltd*,[71] where he decided that moneys in the chargor's bank account were not caught by the chargor's fixed charge over book debts. Hoffmann J made it clear that his decision in both cases rested on the construction of the debentures. He stated:[72]

[68.] *Ibid.*
[69.] [1986] BCLC 418.
[70.] *Ibid* at 421.
[71.] [1988] BCLC 563.
[72.] *Ibid* at 566.

"I should perhaps take the opportunity to say, if it was not sufficiently clear, that *Re Brightlife Ltd* did not decide that a credit balance at a bank could not in any context be a 'book debt' or 'other debt'. In particular, I did not and do not express any opinion on whether a credit balance is a 'book debt' for the purposes of [the English equivalent of s 99(2)(e) of the 1963 Act]."

These words should be heeded by any lawyer who thinks that registration of a charge over a bank account can be safely dispensed with.[73]

[17.25] The courts of Northern Ireland considered the issue in *Northern Bank Ltd v Ross*.[74] In that case the company created a fixed charge over its book and other debts and opened a special account. Cash received and held in this special account from the sale of stock was held by Nicholson J to be caught by the charge. The judge indicated that if the monies had been lodged to a general trading account he would have regarded such monies as being "cash at bank". However, on appeal Hutton LCJ held that such monies were not caught by the charge. He stated:[75]

"I consider that 'cash at bank' includes all monies in a bank account whether or not the account is used as a trading account and that the term 'book debts and other debts' does not include 'cash at bank'."

This decision was specifically referred to with approval by Lord Hoffmann in *Re Bank of Credit and Commerce International SA (No 8).*[76]

[17.26] The prudent course, of registering particulars of charges over bank accounts, is adopted in practice as there appears to be no definitive decision that a charge over monies standing to the credit of the chargor in its bank account is not a book debt.[77]

Assignment of Book Debts by way of Sale or by way of Security

[17.27] It should be noted that the document to be registrable, must create or evidence a charge.[78] In *Stoneleigh Finance Ltd v Phillips*[79] invoice financing documents were held not to be registrable as no charge was created. Russell LJ stated:[80]

---

73. MacCann's statement in Butterworths, *Companies Acts 1963-1990* (1993) that: "A bank balance is not a book debt" when dealing with s 99 of the 1963 Act should be treated with caution.
74. [1991] BCLC 504.
75. *Ibid* at 511.
76. [1997] 4 All ER 568 at 577; see also para **[15.10]**.
77. The Final Report of the Legal Risk Review Committee (October 1992) states at para 11.1: "whether a bank deposit is a book debt within the registration requirements have been discussed in the cases and in the legal literature but never satisfactorily resolved."
78. See *Stoneleigh Finance Ltd v Phillips* [1965] 1 All ER 513 and Turner J in *Paintin and Nottingham Ltd v Miller Gale and Winter* [1971] NZ LR 164 at 179.
79. [1965] 1 All ER 513.
80. *Ibid* at 525.

"It is clear that this section has no application to a transaction unless it is one which operates to charge property as security for the payment of money ... It is not sufficient under sub-s 2(c) to find an instrument which if executed by an individual would require registration as a bill of sale: it is necessary also to find a charge."

Russell LJ went on however to sound a note of warning, which is particularly applicable today to practitioners who may be under pressure from bankers (who themselves may be under pressure from their customers) to arrange financing in a manner designed to avoid registration and the consequential publicity. He said:[81]

"It is, however, also true to say that the section cannot be evaded by making what is in fact a charge in form an absolute assignment, or by otherwise adopting a form which does not accord with the real transaction between the parties."[82]

[17.28] In endeavouring to ascertain whether a document is a sale of a book debt not requiring registration or a charge of a book debt which does require registration, it is necessary to discover whether or not the document explicitly or otherwise incorporates an equity of redemption.[83] In *Re Kent & Sussex Sawmills Ltd*[84] a company gave irrevocable instructions to the Ministry of Fuel and Power to remit moneys due to it under a contract with the Ministry direct to its bankers. In his judgment Wynn-Parry J said:[85]

"In my judgment, by implication an equity of redemption is to be discovered in the language of the second sentence. I can see no commercial business reason for the introduction of those words: 'These instructions are to be regarded as irrevocable unless the said bank should consent to their cancellation' except on the basis that the parties deliberately contemplated that circumstances might arise in which it would become desirable that a cancellation of the instructions should be given by the bank. The existence of the previous sentence appears to be to operate strongly to lead to the conclusion that there was nothing in the nature of a sale."

Accordingly, the court held that the letter of authority amounted to an equitable assignment by way of security and constituted a charge on the book debts of the

---

81. *Ibid.*
82. See also *Saunderson and Co (in liq) v Clark* (1913) 29 TLR 579 where a purported absolute assignment of a book debt was void for lack of registration as a security assignment - Lusk J stated: "He had to look at the substance and not to the form of the transaction in order to ascertain whether it was affected by the section. It was impossible for the parties to a transaction by way of mortgage or charge to alter the effect of the enactment by adopting a form which did not accord with the real transaction between them."
83. See paras **[10.06]-[10.17]**.
84. [1946] 2 All ER 638.
85. *Ibid* at 641.

company. As this charge had not been registered it was void against the company's liquidator. In contrast to this in *Ashby, Warner & Co Ltd v Simmons*[86] a letter of authority and direction given to a debtor to pay a certain sum out of a contract to a third party was held not to be a charge as the document did not contain any suggestion that it was a hypothecation but was intended to be an absolute assignment of a specified amount in satisfaction of that part of a debt.

Factoring or Block Discounting of Debts[87]

"It is now well-established that factoring or block discounting amounts to a sale of book debts, rather than a charge on book debts, even though under the relevant agreement the purchaser of the debt is given recourse against the vendor in the event of default in payment of the debt by the debtor."[88]

[17.29] Finance by way of block discounting involves a financier and its customer entering into an agreement whereby the financier purchases specified debts of the customer at a discount and the financier then collects those debts. Where the debts are purchased outright no charge is involved and therefore there is no registration requirement. However, where the debts are assigned as security for advances by the financier, such assignment requires registration as a charge on book debts. In *Lloyds & Scottish Finance Ltd v Cyril Lord Carpets Sales Ltd*,[89] the House of Lords dismissed an appeal from Northern Ireland and held that assignments of debts under a block discounting agreement were not registrable although if the assignments were considered on their own, independent of the master trading agreement, they might be considered as assignments by way of security. Overall, the master trading agreement, from which the specific assignments emanated, showed that the real intention was to operate under the trading agreement which provided for the sale and purchase of debts.

[17.30] In *Re Curtain Dream plc*[90] the nature of the transaction was established by examining the real intention of the parties. The financier extended by facility

---

86. [1936] 2 All ER 697.
87. "... raising money on the strength of receivables is known by different names in different industries. In the instalment credit industry, for example, sale of receivables is known as block discounting, though a refinement of it is rather confusingly called agency block discounting. In other cases the arrangement is referred to as factoring and where the facility does not include credit control, ledger administration and debt collection, practitioners call it invoice discounting" - Oditah, *Legal Aspects of Receivables Financing* (1991) para 2.9. For a standard factoring agreement see *The Encyclopaedia of Forms and Precedents* (5th ed) Butterworths, Vol 4, p 178, Form 45.
88. Dillon LJ in *Welsh Development Agency v Export Finance Co Ltd* [1992] BCLC 148 at 154.
89. (1979) 129 NLJ 366; [1992] BCLC 609; for a commentary on this decision see Giddins, 'Block Discounting - Sale or Charge?' (1980) 130 NLJ 207.
90. [1990] BCLC 925.

letter a line of credit to the company which entered into a trading agreement with the financier whereby the company would invoice the financier for the merchandise provided in the trading agreement and the financier would re-invoice the merchandise to the company with a provision that the merchandise would remain the financier's property until the company paid for it. The court held that the relationship of the parties was that of borrower and lender and the transaction taken as a whole was one of mortgage or charge with moneys being lent by the financier and the security being created by the company to secure the advance. Accordingly, the transaction was unenforceable against the company's bankers who had appointed a receiver due to the absence of registration.

[17.31] The difficulty in distinguishing between a sale and a security can be seen from *Welsh Development Agency v Export Finance Co Ltd*[91] where the English Court of Appeal allowed an appeal from the financier. Dillon LJ adverted to the difficulty in distinguishing the nature of the transaction when he said in the course of his judgment:[92]

> "... there is no one clear touchstone by which it can necessarily and inevitably be said that a document which is not a sham and which is expressed as an agreement for sale must necessarily, as a matter of law, amount to no more than the creation of a mortgage or charge on the property expressed to be sold. It is necessary therefore to look at the provisions in the master agreement as a whole to decide whether in substance it amounts to an agreement for the sale of goods or only to a mortgage or charge on goods and their proceeds."

In that case, the company contracted to sell goods to overseas buyers. The financier made a standing offer to purchase all goods from the company and the company would in turn sell the goods to the overseas buyers as the financier's agent, the financier being an undisclosed principal. Payment by the buyers was to be made to a bank account of the company but under the control of the financier. The plaintiff had a charge over the company's book debts and in the company's receivership claimed that the moneys owed by the overseas buyers were subject to the fixed charge. The Court of Appeal held that these moneys belonged to the financier and not the company as payment for the goods which the financier had purchased and which had been sold on its behalf by the company.

It might be noted that the structure of the financing avoided the company selling debts to the financier as such sale could have contravened its charge in favour of the Welsh Development Agency. The sale of the goods to the financier avoided any negative pledge or any covenant not to factor, discount or assign, the company's debts.

[91.] [1992] BCLC 148.
[92.] *Ibid* at 161.

[17.32] For a practitioner it is critical to be able to distinguish between a transaction of sale and a transaction of mortgage and charge as failure to register particulars of the latter could render the practitioner liable to a negligence suit if a financier loses its security by the failure to register. The practitioner may not have the option of registering, when in doubt, if his customer wishes to avoid the publicity associated with registration. This can leave the practitioner in an unsatisfactory position.[93] The essential differences between the two types of transactions were set out by Romer LJ in *Re George Inglefield Ltd*:[94]

> "In a transaction of sale the vendor is not entitled to get back the subject matter of the sale by returning to the purchaser the money that has passed between them. In the case of a mortgage or charge, the mortgagor is entitled, until he has been foreclosed, to get back the subject matter of the mortgage or charge by returning to the mortgagee the money that has passed between them ... if the mortgagee realises the subject matter of the mortgage for a sum more than sufficient to repay him, with interest and the costs, the money that has passed between him and the mortgagor he has to account to the mortgagor for the surplus. If the purchaser sells the subject matter of the purchase, and realizes a profit, of course he has not got to account to the vendor for the profit ... if the mortgagee realizes the mortgaged property for a sum that is insufficient to repay him the money that he has paid to the mortgagor, together with interest and costs, then the mortgagee is entitled to recover from the mortgagor the balance of the money ... If the purchaser were to resell the purchased property at a price which was insufficient to recoup him the money that he had paid to the vendor, of course he would not be entitled to recover the balance from the vendor."

This test was criticised by Dillon LJ in *Welsh Development Agency v Export Finance Co Ltd*[95] as being somewhat limited in that:

> "... there may be a sale of book debts, and not a charge, even though the purchaser has recourse against the vendor to recover the shortfall if the debtor fails to pay the debt in full and that there may be a sale of book debts, even though the purchaser may have to make adjustments and payments to the vendor after the full amounts of the debts have been got in from the debtors."

While the framework set out by Romer LJ may not encompass all transactions, and although subject to criticism,[96] it does provide useful ground rules. Support for the line taken by Romer LJ was given in a more recent English Court of

---

[93] "It is ... fair to say that as regards registration, the law has chosen to draw a difficult, and in some sense, arbitrary distinction between a mortgage of receivables which is registrable, and a sale or discounting of receivables which is exempt" - Oditah, *Legal Aspects of Receivables Financing* (1991) para 2.12.
[94] [1933] Ch 1 at 27.
[95] [1992] BCLC 148 at 161.
[96] See Oditah, 'Financing Trade Credit: *Welsh Development Agency v Exfinco*' [1992] JBL 541.

Appeal decision. In outlining the courts' approach to the difficulty in distinguishing between a sale and a security, Millett LJ stated:[97]

> "Once the documents are accepted as genuinely representing the transaction into which the parties have entered, its proper legal categorisation is a matter of construction of the documents. This does not mean that the terms which the parties have adopted are necessarily determinative. The substance of the parties' agreement must be found in the language they have used; but the categorisation of a document is determined by the legal effect which it is intended to have, and if when properly construed the effect of the document as a whole is inconsistent with the terminology which the parties have used, then their ill-chosen language must yield to the substance.
>
> Unhappily there is no single objective criterion by which it is possible to determine whether a transaction is one of sale and repurchase or security. In a well-known passage in *Re George Inglefield Ltd* [1933] Ch 1 at 27, [1932] All ER 244 at 256-257 Romer LJ explained the essential differences between a transaction of sale and a transaction of mortgage or charge. They are threefold. (1) In a transaction of sale the vendor is not entitled to recover the property sold; in the case of a mortgage or charge the mortgagor is entitled to redeem the mortgage and recover the mortgaged property. (2) If a purchaser sells the property he has purchased, he may keep any profit he had made on the transaction; if a mortgagee does so, he must account for the profit to the mortgagor. (3) If a purchaser sells the property he has purchased and makes a loss on the transaction, he cannot recover his loss from the vendor; if a mortgagee realises the mortgaged property for less than he is owed, he may recover the balance from the mortgagor.
>
> The difficulty is that no single one of these features may be determinative. The absence of any right in the transferor to recover the property transferred is inconsistent with the transaction being by way of security; but its existence may be inferred, and its presence is not conclusive. The transaction may take the form of a sale with an option to repurchase, and this is not to be equated with a right of redemption merely because the repurchase price is calculated by reference to the original sale price together with interest since the date of the sale. On the other hand, the presence of a right of recourse by the transferee against the transferor to recover a shortfall may be inconsistent with a sale; but it is not necessarily so, and its absence is not conclusive. A security may be without recourse. Moreover, the nature of the property may be such that it is impossible or at least very unlikely that it will be realised at either a profit or loss. Many financing arrangements possess this feature. The fact that the transferee may have to make adjustments and payments to the transferor after the debts have been got in from the debtors does not prevent the transaction from being by way of sale."

---

97. In *Orion Finance Ltd v Crown Financial Management Ltd* [1996] 2 BCLC 78 at 84.

Finance Leases

[17.33] A more recent and tax efficient way in which money may be raised and secured is through a finance lease.[98] A finance lease has been described as:[99]

> "a lease of equipment by a lessor (normally a bank or finance company) under which equipment is leased for the full term of its expected useful life at a rent which will recoup to the lessor the full cost of the equipment with interest and with a return on the lessor's investment."

The case of *Orion Finance Ltd v Crown Financial Management Ltd*[100] affords a useful illustration of finance leases and the need to be vigilant in registration. Orion Finance purchased a computer and sold it to Atlantic Computer Systems plc ("Atlantic") under a hire purchase agreement; Atlantic then leased the computer under a seven year finance lease to Crown Financial Management Ltd ("Crown"), the user of the computer. The rent due to Atlantic under the finance lease was assigned to Orion Finance and Crown were notified of the assignment. Particulars of the assignment were not registered pursuant to the English equivalent of s 99 of the Companies Act, 1963.[101] The assignment was made because the hire purchase agreement specified that Atlantic would assign to Orion Finance all moneys due to it under the lease "as security for its obligations" under the hire purchase agreement. Orion Finance acknowledged that the assignment of the rents was to be in satisfaction of moneys due under the hire purchase agreement. Vinelott J held that the assignment was clearly an assignment of future book debts; it was an assignment by way of security and void for non-registration. Furthermore, even though Crown had been notified of the assignment, as the registration requirements had not been complied with, the assignment was unenforceable against Crown. Vinelott J's decision was upheld by the Court of Appeal.

Proceeds of Sale

[17.34] A charge over proceeds of sale is not registrable. This was decided in *Re Kum Tong Restaurant (Dublin) Ltd; Byrne v Allied Irish Banks Ltd*.[102] Many purchases of residential houses are completed by what is known as "bridging finance". This arises where a financial institution makes funds available to a purchaser to enable the purchaser to complete a purchase (before he sells his own property) with a view to satisfying the pre-conditions of the loan sanction shortly afterwards. The rate of interest applying to the "bridging finance" is

[98.] See explanatory memorandum to the Borrowing Powers of Certain Bodies Bill, 1996.
[99.] By Vinelott J in *Orion Finance Ltd v Crown Financial Management Ltd* [1994] 2 BCLC 607 at 609.
[100.] [1994] 2 BCLC 607 and [1996] 2 BCLC 78.
[101.] Companies Act, 1985, s 395.
[102.] [1978] IR 446.

generally higher than that applying to the loan. Nonetheless, it enables a person to proceed with the purchase notwithstanding that his own equity has not been contributed to the purchase (as it is still tied into the present house being sold). To obtain "bridging finance" a purchaser will need to have its solicitor give an irrevocable written undertaking to the financial institution to hold the title documents of the property being sold in trust for the bank and, on completion of the sale, to remit the sale proceeds to the bank (less the costs of disposal) to discharge the bridging finance.

In *Re Kum Tong Restaurant (Dublin) Ltd: Byrne v Allied Irish Banks Ltd*,[103] a company which was in financial difficulty obtained "bridging finance" from a bank to continue in business until completing the sale of land. The company's solicitors gave a letter of undertaking to the bank under which they undertook, "to hold such documents of title to the said premises as we may have in trust for the Bank and to hand over sufficient monies out of the proceeds of the sale to redeem this bridging finance as soon as the sale is closed." Before completion of the sale an order winding up the company was made and the liquidator sought to obtain the sale proceeds. McWilliam J held that the clear intention of the letter was to charge the proceeds of sale, that the letter was effective to do this and that the purchase price was not a book debt within the meaning of s 99. Accordingly the charge created was not void for lack of registration.

Lien on Sub-Freights

[17.35] As already indicated, a vendor's lien arising from the sale of land does not require registration pursuant to s 99 of the Companies Act, 1963.[104] However, a lien on sub-freights under a time charter is registrable as a charge on book debts. That was decided in *Re Welsh Irish Ferries Ltd*[105] in which Nourse J clearly distinguished such a lien from a vendor's lien for unpaid purchase money and held that the lien on sub-freights created an equitable charge on amounts due from the shipper to the charterer and therefore required registration.

Letters of Hypothecation

[17.36] Care needs to be taken where letters of hypothecation are used.[106] These generally arise with regard to shipping or other trade documents. In *Ladenburg & Co v Goodwin, Ferreira and Co Ltd (in liq) and Garnett*,[107] the company gave

---

[103.] *Ibid*.

[104.] Para **[17.13]** above.

[105.] [1985] BCLC 327; for the decision's impact on commercial practice see Milman, *The Company Lawyer* (1985) Vol 6 No. 5.

[106.] See *Mercantile Bank of India Ltd v Chartered Bank of India, Australia and China and Strauss & Co Ltd* [1937] 1 All ER 231 where letters of hypothecation were held to be floating charges but their enforcement prior to the company's liquidation was upheld, see para **[17.58]** below.

[107.] [1912] 3 KB 275.

the plaintiffs duplicate bills of lading, copies of invoices of goods shipped by them and a letter "hypothecating the shipments or the proceeds". Goods were sold to the company's customers and shipped on bills of lading made out to the customers' orders. Upon the company's liquidation, the plaintiffs claimed to be entitled under the letter of hypothecation to the proceeds of a shipment of goods. It was held that the letter of hypothecation gave a mortgage or charge on the proceeds of the goods and that such charge was a charge on the company's book debts and therefore void against the liquidator for lack of registration.

[17.37] This case can be contrasted with *Re David Allester Ltd*[108] where a company as security for advances had pledged goods to its banker by delivering bills of lading, invoices, insurance policies. On release of such documents the company signed a letter acknowledging receipt of the documents and stating:

> "we receive the above in trust on your account, and we undertake to hold the goods when received, and the proceeds when sold, as your trustees."

It was held that this was not a charge on book debts as the bank already had its security by the pledge and that the letter was not intended to give a charge, but to enable the goods to be realised on the bank's behalf.

[17.38] An exception to the requirement to register particulars of a charge on book debts arises under s 99(6) which stipulates that:

> Where a negotiable instrument has been given to secure the payment of any book debts of a company, the deposit of the instrument for the purpose of securing an advance to the company shall not, for the purposes of this section, be treated as a charge on those book debts.

To avail of this exception it is essential that the negotiable instrument actually be delivered. An agreement to deliver without actual delivery is not sufficient.[109]

A floating charge on the undertaking or property of the company[110]

[17.39] The nature of a floating charge has already been discussed.[111] The significant point concerning the application of this head is that if security is created over certain specified assets which are not otherwise referred to in s 99(2) of the Companies Act, 1963, particulars of such security should be registered unless there is no doubt that the security is a fixed one. For example, the creation by a company of a charge over shares held by it will require

---

[108.] [1922] 2 Ch 211.

[109.] See *Chase Manhattan Asia Ltd v Official Receiver and Liquidator of First Bangkok City Finance Ltd* [1990] BCC 514 (s 80(5) of the Hong Kong Companies Ordinance is identical to s 99(6) of the Companies Act, 1963).

[110.] Companies Act, 1963 s 99(2)(f).

[111.] See para **[13.02]**.

registration unless it is clear that a fixed charge over the shares has been created.[112]

A charge on calls made but not paid[113]

[17.40] As with the second head of charge this head will arise typically in the context of a comprehensive mortgage debenture under which a company charges all its assets in favour of the chargee. It was enacted following a recommendation by the Company Law Reform Committee 1958.[114]

A charge on a ship or aircraft or any share in a ship or aircraft[115]

[17.41] Section 99(2)(h) was extended by s 122 of the Companies Act, 1990 to include aircraft which prior to the implementation of that section on 1 August 1991[116] applied only to ships or shares therein.[117] However, even prior to that extension, charges on aircraft were as a matter of practice registered and indeed did require to be registered as an assignment of a personal chattel pursuant to the Bills of Sale Acts by virtue of s 99(2)(c) as being a charge which if created by an individual would require registration as a bill of sale. Accordingly, it is not clear as to why this amendment was made.

[17.42] If a company creates a charge over a vessel (or a share therein) which is not a ship, registration of the charge is not required. The distinction was considered by the Supreme Court in *Re South Coast Boatyard Ltd, Barber v Burke*.[118] That case involved a charge which had been created over a number of yachts. The liquidator of the chargor sought to set aside the charge for lack of registration. The Supreme Court upheld McWilliam J's decision that yachts were not ships, but were vessels and therefore the charge did not require to be registered pursuant to either s 99(2)(c) or (h).

Kenny J considered the meaning of "ship" at the time of the enactment of the Companies Act, 1963, saying:[119]

> "The court is, in my opinion, entitled to have regard to the way in which English was spoken and used in 1963. If, in that year, any Irishman or, indeed Englishman went to Dun Laoghaire during the sailing season and saw the many

---

[112.] For examples where a floating charge was deemed to be created rather than a fixed charge see *Re Lakeglen Construction Ltd* [1980] IR 347 para **[11.09]** and *Welch v Bowmaker (Ireland) Ltd* [1980] IR 251 para **[11.08]**.
[113.] Companies Act, 1963, s 99(2)(g).
[114.] Under the chairmanship of Arthur Cox.
[115.] Companies Act, 1963, s 99(2)(h) (as amended by the Companies Act, 1990 s 122).
[116.] SI 117/1991.
[117.] Its application to ships or shares therein was introduced in the Companies Act, 1963 following the recommendation of the Report of the Company Law Reform Committee 1958.
[118.] [1980] ILRM 186.
[119.] *Ibid* at 190.

yachts in the harbour, he would say that the British Rail vessel was a ship, that the yachts were yachts and the rowing boats, boats. If he were pressed on what he called yachts, he would say that they were vessels. He would never dream of calling any of the yachts there, irrespective of their size, ships."

Walsh J stated:[120]

"The term 'vessel' does not include everything that floats. For example, it would not include a raft but it would certainly include everything which would be called a boat or a ship".

These passages may be helpful for a practitioner who has to consider whether a charge over an object which floats, such as a boat, requires registration. To summarise, a charge on a ship or a share therein requires registration pursuant to s 99(2)(h). A charge on any other object that floats requires registration pursuant to s 99(2)(c) as a charge on a personal chattel unless such object is a vessel.

A charge on goodwill, on a patent or a licence under a patent, on a trade mark or on a copyright or a licence under a copyright[121]

[17.43] These items[122] will be incorporated in a comprehensive mortgage debenture given as security for advances. In certain instances such charges require registration also in other registries.

REGISTRATION NOT REQUIRED

[17.44] The purpose of registration,[123] apart from complying with the legal requirement to do so,[124] is to put the public on notice that a charge has been created in favour of the particular chargee.[125] Many companies, to maintain their credit standing amongst financial institutions, seek to avoid having charges registered against them. In addition, a company may have given negative pledge covenants to its bankers and would obviously not wish to default on such a covenant (although creating an unregistrable charge would in most circumstances be a default under a negative pledge covenant). A financial institution making funds available to a company, which endeavouring to facilitate its customer's requirements and at the same time obtain effective

---

[120.] *Ibid* at 187.

[121.] Companies Act, 1963, s 99(2)(i).

[122.] Introduced by the Companies Act, 1963 following the recommendation of the Report of the Company Law Reform Committee 1958.

[123.] For further reading see Gough, *Company Charges* (2nd ed,1996) Part Three.

[124.] Pursuant to s 99 of the Companies Act, 1963.

[125.] Notice of the registration is published in Stubbs Gazette - "The object of that legislation is that those that are minded to deal with limited companies shall be able, by searching a certain register, to find whether the company has incumbered its property or not" *per* Buckley J in *Re Jackson & Bassford Ltd* [1906] 2 Ch 467 at 476.

security, will in such circumstances request its solicitor to confirm that a charge given over a certain asset will be effective as against a liquidator notwithstanding the absence of registration. Such a solicitor, apart from satisfying himself as to the legal position, will be required to have a creative mind in many instances to facilitate what may at face value be two incompatible requirements.

[17.45] Since 1963 the only serious attempt to extend the category of registrable securities by legislation arose at the time of the publication of the Companies Bill 1987, re-published as the Companies (No 2) Bill 1987 following the change of government in the early part of that year. Section 94 of the Bill proposed two significant extensions, both of which had been recommended (although not implemented) in England in 1982 by the *Report of the Review Committee on Insolvency Law and Practice*.[126] The Bill proposed to extend the book debts registration requirement to "a charge on any debts or other liabilities owing or incurred to the company"; it also proposed registration for, "a charge on the company's interest in any stocks, shares or marketable securities". The latter had been suggested previously as necessary to cut off anti-avoidance mechanisms.[127] The proposed extension to include charges over any debts or other liabilities would, if implemented, have had the dubious effect of requiring assignments by way of security of contingent liabilities and contingency under insurance policies registrable. Ultimately these proposed extensions were not proceeded with and the only extension related to a charge on an aircraft or a share in an aircraft.[128]

[17.46] The Companies Bill 1987 also proposed, following the suggestion of the Cork Report in England,[129] that the particulars of charges delivered to the Registrar of Companies should "include a monetary limit of a fixed and definite sum on the amount secured by the charge"; the proposal provided that any variation in the amount which would be verified by submitting further particulars to the Registrar of Companies would be void if delivered within 3 months prior to the company's winding up and that any excess over the limit would be void as against a liquidator.[130] This proposal, which was designed to

---

126. Cmnd 8558 under the chairmanship of Sir Kenneth Cork.
127. FitzGerald, Ir Jur 1968; the 1962 English *Report of the Company Law Committee* Cmnd 1749 under the chairmanship of Lord Jenkins stated at para 301: "we do not think all charges should be registered ... but we think section 95(2) should be extended to cover charges created by a company over any shares held by it in a subsidiary."
128. Companies Act, 1990, s 122(a); this may have followed a similar extension in England under the Companies Act, 1985, s 396 of which requires the registration of a charge on an aircraft (the English legislation does not refer to any share in an aircraft presumably because typically shares are taken in ships but not aircraft - a point missed perhaps by the Irish draftsman, who may ultimately prove to be more thorough in the age of securitisation of assets).
129. Cmnd 8558 para 1567.
130. Section 94 introducing new s 99(2) to (4) to the Companies Act, 1963.

inform creditors of the level of indebtedness,[131] would have given rise to a number of practical difficulties and a possible avoidance mechanism.[132] Accordingly, the proposals were not enacted.

[17.47] However, the draftsman reserved his position by inserting new provisions whereby the category of registrable charges may now be amended by Ministerial regulation rather than by parliamentary legislation. The Minister for Enterprise, Trade and Employment may by regulation add to or remove any description of a charge requiring registration.[133] Any regulation made by the Minister must be laid before each House of the Oireachtas "as soon as may be" and if either House annuls the regulation within 21 days of sitting after the regulation is laid before it, the regulation shall be annulled (without prejudice to the validity of previous acts).[134]

PROCEDURE FOR REGISTRATION

The prescribed particulars of the charge

[17.48] The prescribed particulars of a charge by a company[135] which are required to be filed with the Registrar of Companies are set out in Form No 47.[136] In the first column of the form the date and description of the instrument are required to be set out. If the charge is created otherwise than by instrument, such as deposit of title deeds as security, a description of the transaction should be set out. For example, equitable mortgage by deposit of title deeds.

[17.49] In the second column the amount secured by the charge needs to be set out. This is rarely now a monetary amount; it is usually stated to be all moneys due or to become due by the company to [name of chargee] whether as principal, surety or otherwise together with interest, commission and other charges.
The Form 47 as printed by the Companies Registration Office provides in the third column for the names, addresses and occupations of the persons entitled to the charge.[137]

[17.50] Column (3) of the Forms Order and the fourth column of the printed Form 47 indicate that "Short particulars of the property charged should be

---

[131.] A company is obliged to provide this information on its annual return which is made up 14 days after a company's annual general meeting and subsequently filed for public inspection with the Registrar of Companies.

[132.] See Glackin and Johnston, *The Incorporated Law Society of Ireland Seminar on the Companies (No 2) Bill 1987* - 10 May 1988.

[133.] Companies Act, 1963, s 99(2A) and s 99(2B), introduced by s 122(b) of the Companies Act, 1990.

[134.] Companies Act, 1963, s 99(2C), introduced by s 122(b) of the Companies Act, 1990.

[135.] Within the meaning of the Companies Act, 1963, s 2.

[136.] Companies (Forms) Order, 1964, SI 45/1964.

[137.] Column (4) of the Companies (Forms) Order, 1964 SI 45/1964.

given". The following is a specimen of the short particulars to be given from a comprehensive mortgage debenture.

1. Mortgage over all that and those the lands known as [description of lands] together with all buildings, fixtures (including trade fixtures) and fixed plant and machinery from time to time thereon.

2. Specific charge over all that the property described in folio [number of folio] of the register of [freeholders] [leaseholders] county [name of county] together with all buildings, fixtures (including trade fixtures) and fixed plant and machinery from time to time thereon.

3. First specific equitable charge over all estates or interests in any freehold or leasehold properties (except those referred) to in 1 and 2 above) now or at any time hereafter belonging to or charged to the company and the proceeds of sale thereof together with all buildings, fixtures (including trade fixtures) and fixed plant and machinery from time to time thereon.

4. First specific charge over all book debts and other debts whether actual or contingent now or at any time due or owing to the company and the benefit of all securities and guarantees now or at any held by the company in relation thereto.

5. First fixed charge over all monies standing to the credit of the company in the company's account held with the security holder used for the receipt of the proceeds of its book debts and other debts.

6. First fixed charge over all stocks, shares, securities or other interests (together with all rights in respect thereof or incidental thereto) in any of the company's subsidiaries now or at any time belonging to the company.

7. First fixed charge over all the goodwill, trademarks, copyrights, registered designs and other intellectual property and uncalled capital of the company both present and future.

8. First fixed charge over the benefit of all or any licences presently or hereafter acquired by the company.

9. First floating charge over the undertaking and all property, assets and rights of the company whatsoever and wheresoever both present and future.

[17.51] In addition to short particulars of the property charged, it has become standard practice to indicate any restrictions which the chargor is obliged under the charge to comply with when dealing with the charged assets. The first of the two following paragraphs is a standard restriction of which notice is given in the

Form No 47 where a floating charge has been created. The second is notice of the right of the charge holder to convert the charge into a fixed charge.

(a) The security provides that the company shall not without the prior written consent of the security holder either sell or otherwise dispose of any of the assets of the company the subject of the security contrary to the provisions of the security or create or permit to exist any mortgage, debenture, charge, pledge, lien or other interest on or affecting any part of such floating charge ranking in priority to or pari passu with the same.

(b) The security provides that the security holder may at any time in accordance with the terms of the security by notice to the company convert the floating charge into a specific charge as regards any assets specified in the notice.

[17.52] The following are standard restrictive provisions indicated where a fixed charge has been created over future book debts:

(i) The security provides that the company shall collect and realise all book debts and other debts thereby charged and shall until payment thereof to the designated account as therein hold all the proceeds of such collection as realised upon trust for the security holder.

(ii) The security provides that the company shall pay into a designated account with the security holder all monies it receives in respect of the book debts and other debts thereby charged and shall not without the security holder's prior written consent withdraw any monies or direct any payment to be made from such designated account.

(iii) The security provides that the company shall not without the prior written consent of the security holder purport to charge, assign or otherwise dispose or permit to subsist any charge or lien over the book debts and other debts and uncalled capital thereby charged in favour of any other person and shall if called upon to do so by the security holder execute a legal assignment of the same to the security holder.

(iv) The security provides that the company shall not without the prior written consent of the security holder permit or agree to any variation of the rights attaching to the book and other debts thereby charged or any of them, release, exchange, compound, set-off, grant time or indulgence in respect of or in any other manner deal with all or any other book debts and other debts thereby charged save as expressly provided in the security.

[17.53] Column (5), which arises rarely in practice, refers to the amount and rate per cent of the commission, allowance or discount paid directly or indirectly by the company in consideration for the subscription of debentures.

Verified in the prescribed manner

[17.54] Although the Form No 47 specifically states the manner in which the prescribed particulars should be verified, perhaps the greatest number of rejections of filed Forms 47 result from the inaccurate completion of the verification.[138] The usual procedure is that although it is the statutory duty of the company creating the charge to submit the prescribed particulars,[139] the security holder will arrange for the filing of the particulars (as such filing is essentially for the benefit of the security holder). The chargee's solicitor will typically prepare the Form 47 simultaneously with the engrossment of the charge. At the time the charge is executed, a person duly authorised on behalf of the company, usually a director or the secretary, will sign the form, indicate his position in relation to the company and date the form. The chargee's solicitor will then verify the particulars by signing where indicated for verification and shall state the nature of his interest for example, solicitor for the chargee. The date should then be inserted. On occasions, perhaps due to time pressure, the chargee's solicitor will simply sign as applicant, indicating that application is being made as solicitor for the chargee and date the form. In this instance a certified copy of the instrument must be submitted together with the completed form to the Registrar of Companies.[140] Where the chargor completes the form with verification from the chargee, a copy of the instrument is not required to be filed.

Within 21 days after the date of its creation

"Where there is in fact an instrument creating or evidencing a mortgage or charge ... on the true meaning of that section the date of the creation of the mortgage or charge is the date when that instrument was executed and is not the date when any money is subsequently advanced, so as to make an effective charge for the amount of that money".[141]

[17.55] Where an instrument is dated, the date on the instrument is *prima facie* evidence that that was the date of its execution or creation.[142] The safest

---

[138.] See Power, *Practice and Procedure in the Companies Registration Office* (The Irish Centre for Commercial Law Studies) 11 December 1997.
[139.] Companies Act, 1963, s 100.
[140.] The instrument is not put on the company file but returned to the chargee's solicitor simultaneously with the issue of the certificate of registration of charge; the alternative method of verification under the seal of the company is rarely used.
[141.] Sargant J in *Esberger & Son Ltd v Capital and Counties Bank* [1913] 2 Ch 366 at 373.
[142.] See Bosanquet J in *Anderson v Weston and Badcock* (1840) CP 6; Bing NC 292 at 300.

procedure for any solicitor to follow is to regard the date of creation of a charge as being the date of its execution[143] or where this cannot be ascertained, the date the chargor's board resolved to execute the security.[144] In this context, the wording of the resolution is important. For example, where a board approves the terms of a debenture and resolves that it be created and that a director or directors be authorised to execute the debenture or a sealing committee be authorised to seal the debenture, the date of execution, even if subsequent, may be regarded as the date of creation.[145] The concept of execution and holding in escrow, which has been followed by some lending institutions, and which is a practice the author believes is likely to give rise to muddle and inadvertence if not strictly adhered to, was given judicial recognition in *Re CL Nye Ltd.*[146] In that case a charge was sealed and handed undated to the bank's solicitor. The following month the solicitor reported to the bank that the title was valid and the security good whereupon the bank advanced money to the company. Although the case was decided on other issues,[147] Harman LJ found that the date of creation of the security was the date the charge became effective namely, the date when the solicitor reported that the security was good.[148]

Where a deed of charge is not dated and there are no escrow arrangements, the date of creation of the charge is the date the deed of charge is delivered, following its execution, to the chargee or its solicitor.[149]

CONSEQUENCES OF NON-REGISTRATION

[17.56] Section 99(1) of the Companies Act, 1963 provides that every charge to which sub-s (2) applies shall, so far as security is conferred under the charge on the company's property or undertaking:[150]

    (i)   be void against the liquidator and any creditor of the company,

---

[143.] See in *Re Columbian Fireproofing Company Ltd* [1910] 2 Ch 120; see also Buckley J in *Re The Harrogate Estates Ltd* [1903] 1 Ch 498 at 502, "The twenty-one days ... run from the date, not of the resolution which authorised the charge, but from the date at which the charge was created in favour of a person entitled to the benefit of the charge."

[144.] See *Re Olderfleet Shipbuilding and Engineering Company Ltd* [1922] I IR 26.

[145.] In *Re Olderfleet Shipbuilding and Engineering Company Ltd* [1922] I IR 26 the shareholders passed a resolution authorising the issue of debentures and subsequently the directors passed a resolution to issue the debentures - it was held that the debentures were created on the date of the directors' resolution rather than the date of the shareholders' resolution.

[146.] [1970] 3 All ER 1061; [1970] 2 WLR 158.

[147.] See para **[17.73]**.

[148.] See however *Alan Estates Ltd v WG Stores Ltd* [1981] 2 WLR 892 where the English Court of Appeal held by a majority that when all conditions of an escrow were satisfied, the title which passed under the deed related back so as to operate as between grantor and grantee from the time of the conditional delivery of the instrument.

[149.] See *Esberger v Capital and Counties Bank* [1913] 2 Ch 366.

[150.] Subsequent numbering is the author's.

(ii) unless the prescribed particulars of the charge,

(iii) verified in the prescribed manner,

(iv) are delivered to or received by the Registrar of Companies for registration in manner required by this Act within 21 days after the date of its creation,

(v) but without prejudice to any contract or obligation for repayment of the money thereby secured, and when a charge becomes void under this section, the money secured thereby shall immediately become payable.

When delivering particulars for registration, a registration fee is required by the Companies Registration Office.[151]

Void against the liquidator and any creditor

"Of course the deed is not void to all intents and purposes. It is a perfectly good deed against the company so long as it is a going concern."[152]

[17.57] It should be noted that a registrable charge which is not registered in accordance with the statutory provisions is not void - it is simply void as against the liquidator or any creditor of the company. As it is the company's duty to register the prescribed particulars,[153] the company itself cannot plead that the charge is void due to the absence of registration. This was confirmed by Buckley J in *Independent Automatic Sales Ltd v Knowles & Foster*[154] where he stated:[155]

"The purpose of the section is to enable the liquidator to deal with the assets of the company in the liquidation, in a way which he would not otherwise be able to adopt, for the benefit of the company's creditors ... the rights of the company are wholly unaffected by the section, and consequently, I think on that ground the company is not a proper party to assert that the charge is void for lack of registration. Moreover, ... the Act imposes on the company a statutory duty to register any registrable charge; and consequently *ex hypothesi* where a charge has not been registered, the company is in default of that statutory obligation, and in an action directed to avoiding a charge for non-registration must necessarily plead its own default. That is a position which, it seems to me, the company ought not to be allowed to take up, and it reinforces the view which I have reached, ... that in fact the company is not a proper party to make any such assertion."

Accordingly, an unregistered charge as between the chargor and the chargee is not avoided by s 99.[156] However, as one of the purposes of taking security is to

---

[151.] £25 pursuant to the Companies (Fees) Order, 1997.
[152.] Re Lord Cozens-Hardy MR in *Re Monolithic Building Co, Tacon v The Company* [1915] 1 Ch 643, at 667.
[153.] Companies Act, 1963, s 100.
[154.] [1962] 3 All ER 27.
[155.] *Ibid* at 30.
[156.] See *Re Monolithic Building Co, Tacon v The Company* [1915] 1 Ch 643.

acquire rights of priority against the company's creditors in a liquidation, non-registration of a registrable security will defeat that purpose of taking the security. The consequences for a chargee or its solicitor for failing to register may therefore be calamitous. [157]

[17.58] It should be noted though that an unregistered registrable charge may be enforced prior to the winding up of the chargor and any subsequent liquidator may not seek the return of any assets seized from the chargee's enforcement. In *Mercantile Bank of India Ltd v Chartered Bank of India, Australia and China and Strauss & Co Ltd*[158] letters of hypothecation given by the company to the first defendant were deemed to be floating charges. However, as the first defendant had seized the goods, the subject of the letters, prior to the company's liquidation it was entitled "to the benefit of its security."[159]

REGISTRATION OF JUDGMENT MORTGAGES

[17.59] Section 102(1) of the Companies Act, 1963 states:[160]

> When judgment is recovered against a company and such judgment is subsequently converted into a judgment mortgage affecting any property of the company, the judgment creditor shall cause 2 copies (certified by the Land Registry or the Registry of Deeds, as the case may be, to be correct copies) of the affidavit required for the purpose of registering the judgment as a mortgage to be delivered to the company within 21 days after the date of such registration, and the company shall within 3 days of receipt of such copies deliver one of such copies to the Registrar of Companies for registration in the manner required by this Act. By way of further precaution, the Land Registry, or Registry of Deeds, shall as soon as may be deliver a copy of the said affidavit to the Registrar of Companies.

Although as with the charges required to be registered pursuant to s 99, it is the duty of the company to deliver a copy of the affidavit to the Registrar of Companies, it would be prudent for the judgment creditor to do so as well.[161] *Keane* suggests that failure to file should result in the invalidity of the charge.[162] However, the legislation does not provide for such invalidity and indeed simply sanctions a fine for default.[163]

[157.] See *Orion Finance Ltd v Crown Financial Management Ltd* [1994] 2 BCLC 607 and [1996] 2 BCLC 78 at para **[17.33]** above.

[158.] [1937] 1 All ER 231.

[159.] *Ibid* at 241 *per* Porter J.

[160.] This was introduced following the recommendation of the Report of the Company Law Reform Committee 1958, para 154.

[161.] For the procedure see also Power, 'Practice and Procedure in the Companies Registration Office' (The Irish Centre for Commercial Law Studies) 11 December 1997.

[162.] Keane, *Company Law in the Republic of Ireland* (2nd ed) para 23.13 and Courtney, *The Law of Private Companies* (1994) para 15.032 suggest otherwise.

[163.] Companies Act, 1963, s 102(2).

EXTENSION OF TIME FOR REGISTRATION[164]

[17.60] Section 106(1) of the Companies Act, 1963 provides that where the court is satisfied that:[165]

    (i)   the omission to register a charge within 21 days of its creation,

    (ii)   or that the omission or mis-statement of any particular with respect to any such charge was accidental, or due to inadvertence[166] or to some other sufficient cause,[167]

    (iii)   or is not of a nature to prejudice the position of creditors or shareholders of the company,

    (iv)   or that on other grounds it is just and equitable to grant relief,[168]

    (v)   the court may, on the application of the company or any person interested, order that the time for registration be extended or that the omission or mis-statement be rectified and on such terms and conditions as seem to the court just and expedient.

An application to court[169] arises usually through the failure to complete the particulars of the Form 47 correctly, such as omitting a date under the verification signature.[170] The error is often quite trivial but the Registrar of Companies does not permit any latitude in this regard due to the statutory requirement of the prescribed particulars to be delivered,[171] and the fact that the Registrar's certificate of charge is "conclusive evidence" that the requirements as to registration have been complied with.[172] The applicant for an extension should set out the circumstances giving rise to the application and not simply state that the failure to register was "due to inadvertence."[173]

[164.] See also McCormack, 'Extension of Time for Registration of Company Charges' (1986) JBL 282.

[165.] The numbering is the author's; Ussher, *Company Law in Ireland* (1986) p 464 makes the pertinent point that, "It is strange that section 106 is drafted disjunctively. In view of the fact that the policy behind the requirement that charges be registered is that of warning prospective creditors, one would have thought that the avoidance of prejudice to them should in the drafting have been made paramount. Though in practice the courts in their exercise of this discretion go some way towards making good this deficiency, they do chiefly for the benefit of secured creditors."

[166.] *Re Cork Electric Tranways and Lighting Co Ltd* (1902) 36 ILTR 187.

[167.] "Some other sufficient cause" includes ignorance of the requirement to register (the solicitor having advised the debentureholder that registration was unnecessary) - see in *Re S Abrahams & Sons* [1902] 1 Ch 695.

[168.] For an example of this see *Re Chantry House Developments plc* [1990] BCLC 813 and for a criticism of this decision see (1991) JIBFL 38.

[169.] For an outline of the historical development of such applications, see the judgment of Lord Brightman in *Victoria Housing Estates Ltd v Ashpurton Estates Ltd* [1982] 3 All ER 665.

[170.] See however Keane, *Company Law in the Republic of Ireland* (2nd ed) para 23.05 - "The surprising number of applications to the court for such extensions indicates that there is a laxity in complying with the time limit"; it is submitted that this is not the primary reason for such applications.

[171.] Companies Act, 1963, s 99(1), the Companies (Forms) Order, 1964 SI 45/1964.

[172.] Companies Act, 1963, s 104; see para **[17.71]** below.

[173.] See *Re Kris Cruisers Ltd* [1949] 1 Ch 138.

In *Re Telomatic Ltd, Barclays Bank Ltd v Cyprus Popular Bank Ltd*[174] one of the reasons why the court refused the application for late registration was that there was no evidence as to the circumstances as to why the charge was omitted to be registered; nor was there any evidence that the company's solicitors omitted to register the charge accidentally or inadvertently.

Not to prejudice creditors

[17.61] The consequences of a court granting an extension of time for registration is that, "the charge becomes a valid charge *ab initio* from the date of registration subject to such conditions as the court may impose when it extends the time".[175] Accordingly, as Kenny J has stated:[176]

> "... the court should not extend the time for registration of a charge against a company's property unless there is evidence that a petition for the winding up of the company has not been presented and that the members are not contemplating a resolution for its winding up."

In *Re Telford Motors Ltd; Doody v Mercantile Credit Co of Ireland Ltd*[177] Hamilton J granted an order extending time for registration after notice of a meeting to consider winding up the company had been circulated; but on a subsequent application by the liquidator Hamilton J held the charge to be void against the liquidator.

[17.62] When the courts grant an order under this section for an extension of time they do so typically with a proviso to the effect that the order is to be without prejudice to the rights, if any, of parties acquired prior to the registration of the charge.[178] As Lord Brightman pointed out,[179] the reason for this proviso is that typically applications for extension of time, whether by the chargor or chargee, are made *ex parte* and the chargor's creditors would not have notice of the application. The approach of the courts[180] in considering whether to grant an

---

174. [1993] BCC 404.
175. Costello J in *Re Clarets Ltd (In Receivership): Spain v McCann and Stanchart Bank (Ireland) Ltd* [1978] ILRM 215 at 217.
176. *Re International Retail Ltd* High Court, unrep, 19 September 1974; see also *Victoria Housing Estates Ltd v Ashpurton Estates Ltd* [1982] 3 All ER 665; but see Dixon J in *Re O'Carroll Kent Ltd* (1955) 89 ILTR 72 at 74 - "the fact that a winding-up was in contemplation was not ... a matter which called for provision ... in the making of the order ... If the company were to be wound up, it would be open to the liquidator, if he were of the opinion that his interests had been prejudiced by the extension of time, to take such proceedings as would be appropriate."
177. High Court, unrep, 27 January 1978 Hamilton J - see MacCann, *A Casebook on Company Law* (1991) Butterworths para 11.80
178. See *Re O'Carroll Kent Ltd* (1955) 89 ILTR 72.
179. In *Victoria Housing Estates Ltd v Ashpurton Estates Ltd* [1982] 3 All ER 665 at 670.
180. Section 404 of the English Companies Act 1985 (prior to its amendment in 1989) is equivalent to s 106 of the Companies Act 1963.

order for an extension of time is set out in the judgment of Millett J in *Re Barrow Borough Transport Ltd*[181] where he said:[182]

> "It is well established that, while the company is a going concern and its business is conducted by the directors, unsecured creditors cannot complain of the granting of an extension of time under s 404 and in granting an extension the court will not insert any proviso to protect their rights. This is because ... an unsecured creditor cannot intervene to prevent payment being made to the lender whose charge is not registered, nor can he prevent the creation of a new charge duly registered to take the place of the unregistered charge. However, once the company is in liq the situation changes radically, because existing unsecured creditors become interested in all the assets of the company ... The insertion of the usual proviso to protect the accrued rights of creditors would enure for their benefit and would make any order extending the time for registration futile. Consequently it became an established practice that the court would not make an order extending the time for registration once liquidation had supervened, save in very special circumstances which would justify the exclusion of the usual proviso."

[17.63] It has been held in New Zealand that the requirement to submit details of the company's financial position[183] when applying for late registration would not be required where the charge had already been registered in the Land Registry.[184] Notice to the public by such registration was deemed to be sufficient. However, at least in Ireland such registration would not result in a note of the charge appearing in Stubbs Gazette,[185] widely read by financial institutions, and therefore might not be sufficient notice.

[17.64] It should be noted from Millett J's judgment that the proviso is not designed to protect unsecured creditors for as *Gough*[186] points out:

> "An unsecured creditor relying on the register to disclose charges must inevitably accept and be alert to the possibility that charges may subsequently be registered."

The usual proviso protecting creditors will not be granted by the courts where such creditors are officers of the company whose duty it is to register particulars of the charge. In *Re Fablehill Ltd*[187] the company executed a charge in favour of its bankers whose solicitors failed to register the charge. Two years later the

---

[181.] [1989] BCLC 653.
[182.] *Ibid* at 656; see also the similar remarks of Dillon LJ in *R v Registrar of Companies, ex p Central Bank of India* [1985] BCLC 465 at 471.
[183.] As specifically set out in *Re Dalgety and Co Ltd* [1928] NZLR 731.
[184.] *Re Jack Harris Ltd* [1977] 1 NZLR 141.
[185.] Published by Dun and Bradstreet Ltd.
[186.] Gough, *Company Charges* (2nd ed, 1996) p 773.
[187.] [1991] BCLC 830.

company executed a charge in favour of its directors. In granting the bank's application to have its charge registered out of time, Vinelott J stated,[188]

> "... it would be plainly inequitable to include in an order extending time for registration a proviso protecting the rights of directors who, when they learned that the company had failed in its duty to register the bank's charge, took no steps to remedy the company's breach of duty by applying to register the charge out of time, but created and registered a charge in their own favour."

[17.65] A court will not grant an extension of time where to do so with the usual proviso preserving the rights of intervening creditors would either be futile or unjustified.[189] In the matter of *Farm Fresh Frozen Foods Ltd (in liq)*,[190] the company agreed, through an undertaking by its solicitors, to deposit title documents with a bank as security for a loan. The deeds in fact were not delivered until the day a provisional liquidator was appointed to the company. The court refused the bank's application for an extension of time pursuant to s 106. The bank's failure to perfect its security in a timely manner was highlighted in the judgment of Keane J:[191]

> "The only question that remains is as to whether the time for registration should be extended under s 106 of the Act. It is acknowledged that no useful purpose would be served by making such an order if it included the usual saver for the rights of parties acquired prior to the date of actual registration. I have no doubt that there would be no justification for making such an order in the present case. The bank were entirely free in the present case to stipulate the terms on which they advanced money to the company. They could well have refused to make the advance until the documents of title were deposited with them. Equally, they could have refused to make the advance until such time as the agreement to deposit the title deeds contained in the letter of 29 September 1977 had been accepted for registration ... The Bank chose none of these courses; and to register the charge at this stage without preserving the rights of intervening creditors would be entirely unjustified, having regard to the mischief which the registration sections of the Act are designed to avoid."

[17.66] However, even where liquidation is imminent, or indeed has already commenced, there may be exceptional circumstances where an extension of time is granted, particularly where unsecured creditors will not be affected but the failure to grant an order would affect priorities as between creditors.[192]

---

188. *Ibid* at 841.
189. For examples of courts refusing to grant an extension of time because of the imminence of liquidation see *Re Resinoid and Mica Products Ltd* [1982] 3 All ER 677 and *Re Barrow Borough Transport Ltd* [1989] BCLC 653; where the company is already dissolved see *Re Telomatic Ltd. Barclays Bank Ltd v Cyprus Popular Bank Ltd* [1993] BCC 404.
190. [1980] ILRM 131.
191. *Ibid* at 136.
192. See *Re RM Arnold & Co Ltd* [1984] BCLC 535 and *Re John Bateson & Co Ltd* [1985] BCLC 259 where, although an extension was not granted, Harman J explained his decision in *Re RM Arnold & Co Ltd*; for a discourse on the Australian approach to the relevance of insolvency see (1992) 13 Co Law 230.

[17.67] The intervening rights of creditors which are protected by the usual proviso are rights which are acquired between the expiration of the 21 day period within which registration should have taken place and the order for extension of time. This principle can be seen from *Watson v Duff Morgan & Vermont (Holdings) Ltd*.[193] In that case, the company created a first floating charge in favour of the plaintiff and a second floating charge in favour of the defendant on the same day. The second charge was registered but not the first. The first chargee obtained an order of extension. Following the company's liquidation, the court held that the plaintiff's charge ranked in priority to the defendant's as the defendant's rights, protected by the usual proviso, had not been acquired on the expiration of the 21 day period (when the first charge should have been registered), but prior to that date namely, on the execution of the second charge.

Delay in seeking late registration

[17.68] The danger of delaying in seeking an extension of time for registration can be seen from the facts of *Victoria Housing Estates Ltd v Ashpurton Estates Ltd*.[194] The plaintiff appointed a receiver and manager over the chargor's properties pursuant to a charge. The following month it was discovered that the particulars of the charge had not been registered. Fearing an application for an extension of time would precipitate a liquidation, the plaintiff held off applying for an extension until notice convening a meeting to consider winding up had been issued. The Court of Appeal refused the plaintiff's application for an extension of time. Lord Brightman in giving judgment of the court said:[195]

> "... we think that, when an unregistered chargee discovers his mistake, he should apply without delay for an extension of time if he desires to register; and the court when asked to exercise its discretion, should look askance at a chargee who deliberately defers his application in order to see which way the wind is going to blow."

This judgment was applied in *Re Telomatic Ltd, Barclays Bank Ltd v Cyprus Popular Bank Ltd*.[196] In that case, Barclays Bank discovered nine months after the creation of the charge that it had not been registered under the Companies Act. They first sought to take another charge, and then another and then another. Only then they did apply for late registration. One of the reasons why the Court refused late registration was the long delay in making the application and that it was made only after other remedies had failed.

[193.] [1974] 1 All ER 794.
[194.] [1982] 3 All ER 665.
[195.] *Ibid* at 677.
[196.] [1993] BCC 404.

[17.69] *Re Braemar Investments Ltd*[197] is an example of where a bank was granted an extension of time after it was misled by its own agents, its solicitors, into believing that registration had been effected properly. The court noted that the time for registration could be extended where "it is just and equitable to grant relief" and that this applied notwithstanding the imminence of liquidation where the bank had acted promptly on discovering its solicitors had failed to register its charge.

Rectification

[17.70] The reference in s 106 of the Companies Act, 1963 *"that the omission or mis-statement be rectified"* does not include the deletion of a whole registration. In *Re CL Nye Ltd*[198] Russell LJ stated:[199]

> "Under that section the court may rectify an omission by adding, or rectifying a mis-statement by correcting. It cannot delete a whole registration."

CERTIFICATE OF REGISTRATION

[17.71] The duty to deliver particulars of charges requiring registration[200] falls on the company creating the charge,[201] although the filing may be carried out by "any person interested" in the charge.[202] The failure to file particulars of charges within the statutory period may result in fines on the company and its officers;[203] in practice it is usual for the chargee's solicitors to file the particulars.[204] This practice has developed because it is essential for the chargee that the charge is duly registered so that its security will not be void against the company's liquidator or creditors.[205] When the particulars of the charge have been checked by the appropriate persons in the Mortgages Section of the Companies Registration Office, the Registrar of Companies issues a certificate certifying that a charge has been created in favour of stipulated person(s) to secure certain monies. The certificate is "conclusive evidence" that the requirements of ss 99 to 112 as to registration have been complied with.[206]

---

197. [1988] BCLC 556.
198. [1970] 3 All ER 1061.
199. *Ibid* at 1073.
200. As required by s 99 of the Companies Act, 1963.
201. It should be noted that where a company acquires property which is subject to a charge (particulars of which are required to be registered) particulars of the charge must be delivered to the Registrar of Companies within 21 days of the acquisition (Companies Act, 1963 s 101).
202. Companies Act, 1963, s 100(1).
203. Companies Act, 1963, s 100(3).
204. In such case the filing fees are recoverable from the company pursuant to s 100(2) of the Companies Act, 1963.
205. Pursuant to s 99(1) of the Companies Act, 1963; it may of course be void or invalid for other reasons, such as fraudulent preference.
206. Companies Act, 1963, s 104.

Undated Charges

[17.72] The statutory conclusiveness of the certificate of registration has given rise to litigation challenging such conclusiveness.[207] However, the judiciary have consistently complied with the wording of the legislation, even where to do so has resulted in condoning or at least permitting sloppiness on the part of those filing the particulars. In *Lombard and Ulster Banking (Ireland) Ltd v Amurec Ltd (in liq)*[208] the company acquired ballroom premises in November 1972. At the closing of the sale, the bank's solicitor took the conveyance (which was undated) and the mortgage (also undated). The mortgage was a mortgage of the ballroom premises to secure moneys advanced to the company to enable it to purchase the premises. The company was unable to pay the stamp duty on the conveyance and it was not until March 1974 that the bank decided to pay the duty, at which stage current dates were inserted in the conveyance and mortgage.[209] Particulars of the mortgage were delivered to the Registrar of Companies who subsequently issued a certificate of registration. Following the company's liquidation, the liquidator claimed that the mortgage was void for non-registration within 21 days of its creation. In giving judgment Hamilton J said:[210]

> "... I have considerable sympathy with the submissions made by [counsel for the liquidator], I am, however, bound by the terms of Section 104 of the Companies Act, 1963... the wording of Section 104 is clear and unambiguous ... I have ... no alternative but to hold that the charge is a valid charge and is not void against the liquidator."

[17.73] In complying strictly with the provisions of s 104, Hamilton J followed the English decisions[211] of *Re Eric Holmes (Property) Ltd (in liq)*[212] and *Re CL Nye Ltd*.[213] In the former case, particulars of two equitable mortgages by deposit of title deeds were delivered to the Registrar of Companies on 11 July with a date of creation given as 23 June, although in fact they were created on 5 June. The company's liquidator contended that the mortgages were void for want of registration within 21 days of their creation. Pennycuick J held that although the particulars delivered to the Registrar were incorrect, once the certificate of

---

[207.] for further reading see an excellent article by O'Riordan and Pearce, 'The Conclusiveness of Certificates of Registration of Company Charges' (1986) Gazette 281; see also Pye, 'The s 104 Certificate of Registration' (1985) 3 ILT 213 and McCormick, 'Conclusiveness in the Registration of Company Charge Procedure' (1989) 10 Co Law 175.

[208.] (1978) 112 ILTR 1.

[209.] This procedure resulted in the evasion/avoidance of penalty stamp duty.

[210.] (1978) 112 ILTR 1 at 5.

[211.] Where s 98(2) of the English Companies Act 1948 (since repealed) is identical to s 104 of the Companies Act, 1963.

[212.] [1965] 2 All ER 333.

[213.] [1970] 3 All ER 1061.

registration had issued it was impossible to take the case out of that section. Pennycuick J observed:[214]

> "It is, I think, possible that there is some lacuna in the Act here, inasmuch as the Act gives, apparently, protection where the certificate is made upon the basis of particulars which are incorrect and might even be fraudulent."

In the latter case, on facts not dissimilar to the facts Hamilton J had to contend with, on the purchase of premises by the company, the bank's solicitor took the executed but undated transfer and charge on 28 February. On 9 March the solicitor reported to the bank that the title was valid and the security was good, whereupon the bank advanced funds to the company. On 3 July the solicitor applied for registration of the charge which he dated 18 June. The Registrar duly issued a certificate of registration. The Court of Appeal reversed the High Court's decision[215] and held that although it considered the charge to have been delivered in escrow on 28 February and to have become effective on 9 March, as the certificate of registration was 'conclusive' the charge was valid and binding on the company's liquidator.

Omission in Form 47 of all property charged

> "... when once the Registrar has given his certificate that the registration was complete, and that the mortgage or charge was created by an instrument, identifying it, in my opinion you have to go to the instrument to see what was actually charged, there being nothing in the statute which says that when once registration has taken place the register shall be the evidence of the extent of the charge."[216]

[17.74] The foregoing statement should be borne in mind by persons inspecting the register in the Companies Registration Office to ascertain prior charges and the extent of the property charged - the register may not disclose the full extent of the property charged. In *National Provincial and Union Bank of England v Charnley*,[217] the company mortgaged leasehold premises together with moveable plant. The particulars filed with the Registrar of Companies referred to the leasehold premises but not to the moveable plant. The certificate of registration was duly issued. The English Court of Appeal held that as the certificate identified the instrument of charge and certified that the mortgage or charge thereby created had been duly registered, it must be understood that the certificate certified the due registration of all the charges created by the instrument (including that over the moveable plant).

[214.] [1965] 2 All ER 333 at 344.
[215.] The High Court had found against the bank on the grounds that the bank's solicitor had misstated the date of the charge and that no man can take advantage of his own wrong.
[216.] Bankes LJ in *National Provincial and Union Bank of England v Charnley* [1924] 1 KB 431 at 444.
[217.] [1924] 1 KB 431.

Amount secured misstated on Form 47

[17.75] In *Re Mechanisations (Eaglescliffe) Ltd*[218] the particulars of a charge delivered to the Registrar of Companies stated the principal sum secured by the charge but omitted to state that the payment of interest on that sum was also secured by the charge. The Registrar duly issued the certificate of registration of charge which stated that the charge secured the principal sum only. The company's liquidator sought a declaration that the charge was void in respect of the interest for want of registration. In applying the Court of Appeal's decision in *National Provincial and Union Bank of England v Charnley*,[219] Buckley J held that the charge was a valid security for the full amount due as the Registrar's certificate was conclusive that the necessary preliminaries for registration had been complied with and the prescribed particulars delivered to the Registrar.

Certificate open to judicial review

[17.76] The line of decisions on the Registrar's certificate indicate that the judiciary are not prepared to review the basis on which the certificate has been given even where the certificate has been issued on a false assumption for example, particulars being submitted within 21 days of the charge's creation. However, in 1984 Mervyn Davies J held in England that the Registrar's decision to register a charge was open to judicial review.[220] The Court of Appeal however would have none of this and, on appeal by the Registrar, held[221] that the Registrar's decision was not open to judicial review.[222]

In that case, the Registrar in finding the particulars to be incorrect returned them to the chargee for correction and, following their correct re-submission by the chargee, he issued a certificate of registration on the basis that they had been correctly submitted in the first instance so as to come within the statutory 21 day period required for registration. The Court of Appeal held that the English equivalent of s 104 precluded evidence being adduced to challenge the correctness of the Registrar's decision to register a charge; and that the Registrar had jurisdiction finally and conclusively to determine any question as to whether or not the requirements as to registration had been complied with.

[218.] [1964] 3 All ER 840.
[219.] [1924] 1 KB 431, see para **[17.74]** above.
[220.] In *R v Registrar of Companies, ex p Esal (Commodities) Ltd (in liq)* [1985] BCLC 84; see also *Insolvency Law & Practice* (1985) Vol 1 p 20.
[221.] In *R v Registrar of Companies, ex p Central Bank of India* [1985] BCLC 465; see also *Insolvency Law & Practice* (1986) Vol 2 p 118.
[222.] Other than by the Attorney General as the section does not bind the Crown.

In Ireland the judiciary have shown a greater willingness to consider a judicial review and it is possible that the Irish courts may not take the same line as the English Court of Appeal if an applicant can demonstrate that the Registrar has clearly acted outside the scope of his authority.[223]

Practical Consequences of Conclusiveness of Certificate[224]

[17.77] The judicial decisions upholding the conclusive nature of the Registrar's certificate issued pursuant to s 104 mean that, once a certificate referring to a mortgage or charge has been issued, that mortgage or charge cannot be challenged for want of registration within 21 days of creation,[225] or because the particulars did not disclose the total amount secured,[226] or because the particulars failed to disclose the extent of the company's property the subject of the mortgage or charge.[227] This results in an element of sloppiness in the preparation of Forms 47 being permissible,[228] unless of course a certified copy of the security is submitted with the form in which case the Mortgages Section of the Companies Registration Office are likely to notice the discrepancy which may result in a refusal to issue the certificate.

[17.78] The conclusiveness of the certificate of registration of charge may help to explain the 12 month delay which typically occurs between the filing of the Form 47 and the issue of the certificate - a delay which is unsatisfactory for practitioners and inexplicable when compared with the position prevailing in Northern Ireland or England. However, the Mortgages Section of the Companies Registration Office are helpful in pointing out any obvious errors or omissions within the 21 day period; hence it is desirable to file the Form 47 as soon as possible after the creation of the charge rather than just prior to the deadline. It must also be said that the resources of the Companies Registration Office appear to be taken up with correcting a surprisingly high number of Forms 47 incorrectly completed.[229]

[223.] For further discussion on the prospect of a judicial review see O'Riordan and Pearce, 'The Conclusiveness of Certificates of Registration of Company Charges' (1986) ILSI Gazette 281.

[224.] See also Gough, *Company Charges* (2nd ed, 1996) Ch 29.

[225.] As in *Lombard and Ulster Banking (Ireland) Ltd v Amurec Ltd (in liq)* (1978) 112 ILTR 1; *Re Eric Holmes (Property) Ltd (in liq)* [1965] 2 All ER 333; and *Re CL Nye Ltd* [1970] 3 All ER 1061.

[226.] As in *Re Mechanisations (Eaglescliffe) Ltd* [1964] 3 All ER 840.

[227.] As in *National Provincial and Union Bank of England v Charnley* [1924] 1 KB 431.

[228.] However, a chargee should ensure that full and correct particulars are submitted to the Registrar of Companies - it has been suggested that third parties would not be fixed with notice of any omissions - see Goode, *Legal Problems of Credit and Security* (2nd ed) p 42.

[229.] "Approx 40% of all Form 47s lodged are returned to the presenter for amendment" - Power, *Practice and Procedure in the Companies Registration Office* (The Irish Centre for Commercial Law Studies) 11 December 1997.

[17.79] It may be possible in certain instances to challenge the conclusiveness of the certificate on the grounds of fraud.[230] It may be also possible for a person to obtain damages against the Registrar of Companies for negligence, either in the issue of a certificate or in failing to transcribe correctly the details of the Form 47 onto the relevant company file.[231]

In an English Court of Appeal decision[232] concerning the Land Registry Lord Denning MR stated:[233]

> "Suppose, now, that a clerk in the registry makes a mistake. He omits to enter a charge: or wrongly gives a clear certificate: with the result that the encumbrancer loses the benefit of it. Who is to suffer for the mistake? Is the incumbrancer to bear the loss without any recourse against anyone? Surely not. The very object of the registration system is to secure him against loss. The system breaks down utterly if he is left to bear the loss himself.
>
> Who, then, is to bear the loss? The negligent clerk can, of course, be made to bear it, if he can be found and is worth the money - which is unlikely. Apart from the clerk himself, there is only one person in law who can be made responsible. It is the Registrar. He must answer for the mistakes of the clerk and make compensation for the loss. He is a public officer and comes within the settled principle of English law that, when an official duty is laid on a public officer, by statute or by common law, then he is personally responsible for seeing that the duty is carried out."[234]

[17.80] It should be noted however that if the mortgage/charge is invalid for any reason (other than for non-registration) the issue of a certificate of registration of charge by the Registrar of Companies does not remedy such invalidity.[235] The certificate just confirms that the mortgage/charge cannot be challenged for want of registration within the required time period.

It should also be noted that although the Registrar of Companies has an obligation on receiving particulars of a charge to enter in the appropriate company register the date of the charge, the amount secured by the charge, short particulars of the property charged, and the persons entitled to the charge,[236] a

---

230. See the remarks of Slade LJ in *R v Registrar of Companies, ex p Central Bank of India* [1985] BCLC 465 at 491 and those of Lord Templeman in *Sun Tai Cheung Credits Ltd v Attorney General of Hong Kong* [1987] 1 WLR 948 at 953; see also McCormick, 'Conclusiveness in the Registration of Company Charge Procedure' (1989) 10 Co Law 175.
231. Although see the Privy Council's decision in *Yuen Kum Yeu v Attorney General for Hong Kong* [1988] AC 175.
232. *Ministry of Housing and Local Government v Sharp* [1970] 2 QB 223.
233. *Ibid* at 265.
234. Lord Denning MR went on to say, "It is not open to the public officer to say: "I get low fees and small pay. It is very hard to make me *personally* responsible." By law he is responsible. He will, of course, if he is wise insure himself against his liability; or get the Government to stand behind him."
235. See the remarks of Slade LJ in *R v Registrar of Companies, ex p Central Bank of India* [1985] BCLC 465 at 490.
236. Companies Act, 1963, s 103(1).

person inspecting the company file[237] should not rely on the accuracy of the particulars filed.[238] He should endeavour to obtain a copy of the mortgage/charge from the company to ascertain the extent of the property charged and the amount secured thereby.

NOTICE[239]

"Is it to be said that, although the Companies Act, 1963, makes provision for the registration of certain particulars regarding charges created by a company, it is obligatory upon a third party dealing with that company to go beyond the particulars which have been recorded in the register in the Companies Office in accordance with the section in order to ascertain whether he may deal safely with the company in the ordinary course of a business transaction between them?"[240]

[17.81] The question as to whether a person who takes a fixed charge from a company is fixed with notice that a prior floating charge exists which prohibits the creation of a charge, to rank *pari passu* with or in priority to the floating charge, is not as easily answered as at first might appear.[241] Generally, the Irish publications on company law give scant reference to it[242] and the English publications do not have a common approach.[243] What appears to be emerging as something of a consensus is that the practice of inserting in the Form 47 notice of the restriction (contained in the debenture) on the creation of further charges does not give rise to constructive notice, as notice of such restriction is not a matter which falls within the prescribed particulars which require to be filed.[244] Notwithstanding this, there must be a significant risk that a court may impute notice to a subsequent chargee in view of the common and prudent practice of having a search carried out in the Companies Registration Office and the standard provision nowadays of such a restrictive clause in a floating charge.[245]

[237.] Any person on payment of a fee may inspect a company's file - Companies Act, 1963 s 103(2).

[238.] See the quotation from Bankes LJ in para **[17.74]** above.

[239.] For a general discussion of actual and constructive notice see Fisher and Lightwood's, *Law of Mortgage* (10th ed) p 461-474; for a full and clear explanation of the different forms of notice, see O'Neill Kiely, *The Principles of Equity as applied in Ireland* (1936) p 15-30.

[240.] Parke J in *Welch v Bowmaker (Ireland) Ltd and the Governor and Company of the Bank of Ireland* [1980] IR 251 at 262.

[241.] "It is an important and presently unresolved question as to what aspects of charges registration gives notice" - Penn, Shea and Arora, *The Law Relating to Domestic Banking* (1987) para 21.23.

[242.] Keane, para 22.22 (2nd ed); *Forde*, para 14.17 (1st ed); Courtney, para 14.046, 14.047 and 14.050 but see *Ussher* for a fuller discussion pp 424 - 429.

[243.] See Gore-Browne: "the issue of constructive notice remains open to argument" para 18.14 (44th ed).

[244.] See Palmer (25th ed) para 13.043, Goode, *Legal Problems of Credit and Security* (2nd ed) p 43 and Gough, *Company Charges* (2nd ed, 1996) p 814; see also Gower who acknowledges this difficulty at p 475 (4th ed) having erased what he stated at p 422 (3rd ed) namely, - "It is submitted that if this is done [filing notice of the restriction], notice is given to all the world so that neither a legal nor an equitable mortgagee can take priority".

[245.] See Farrar, 'Floating Charges and Priorities' (1974) 38 Conv 315 at 319; Penn, Shea and Arora, *The Law Relating to Domestic Banking* para 21.23; Courtney, para 14.047.

[17.82] In 1979 the Supreme Court regarded it as settled law that there is no duty on a bank to examine the terms of a prior debenture created by a company to ascertain whether there is a prohibition on the creation of further charges.[246] The Supreme Court regarded it as "common"[247] in debentures to have such a restriction, yet somehow considered the bank would not be fixed with notice of such prohibition.[248]

[17.83] In considering such a position to be settled law the Supreme Court relied on three English decisions of much earlier origin - decisions handed down at a time when the duty on banks and professional advisers was not as onerous as in modern times.[249] In each case, a company created a floating charge with a restriction on the creation of further charges.[250] Particulars of the creation of the charge but not of the restriction were filed in Companies House. The court held that the subsequent chargee was, by virtue of registration, assumed to have notice of the existence of the debenture creating the floating charge but not of the restriction on the creation of further charges. Indeed the first of those cases[251] was decided on the basis of earlier decisions.[252]

[17.84] In *Welch v Bowmaker (Ireland) Ltd and The Governor and Company of the Bank of Ireland*[253] the company created a debenture in favour of the first defendant which included (or was deemed to have created) a floating charge over certain lands. Short particulars of the charge were filed in the Companies Registration Office. The second defendant took an equitable mortgage over those lands. Henchy J was tempted by the argument of the first defendant that the second defendant should be fixed with constructive notice of the provision in the debenture precluding the creation of further security:

> "Since such a prohibition is more or less common form in modern debentures, there would be much to be said for applying the doctrine of constructive notice

246. Henchy J in *Welch v Bowmaker (Ireland) Ltd and The Governor and Company of the Bank of Ireland* [1980] IR 251 at 256.

247. *Ibid.*

248. It seems in Scotland that actual notice of a prohibition may be presumed where a subsequent chargee has failed to make inquiries the result of which he knew might prejudice his position of being unaware of such a restriction - see Palmer (25th ed) para 13.137.

249. Doubt has been cast on the application of such cases to modern commercial practice - see Lingard, *Bank Security Documents* (3rd ed) para 1.12.

250. *Re Standard Rotary Machine Company Ltd* (1907) 9 LTR 829; *Wilson v Kelland* [1910] 2 Ch 306; *G & T Earle Ltd v Hemsworth RDC* (1928) 44 TLR 605; it might be noted that these decisions also formed the basis for a similar decision of the New Zealand Court of Appeal in *Dempsey and the National Bank of New Zealand Ltd v The Traders' Finance Corporation Ltd* [1933] NZLR 1258.

251. *Re Standard Rotary Machine Company Ltd* (1907) 9 LTR 829.

252. *Re Castell & Brown Ltd* [1898] 1 Ch 315; *Re Valletort Sanitary Steam Laundry Company Ltd. Ward v Valletort Sanitary Steam Laundry Company Ltd* [1903] 2 Ch 654.

253. [1980] IR 251.

to such a situation were not that it is settled law that there is no duty on the bank in a situation such as this to seek out the precise terms of the debenture [he then referred to the earlier English decisions decided in another era][254] Actual or express notice of the prohibition must be shown before the subsequent mortgagee can be said to be deprived of priority". [255]

Henchy J went on to state that any extension of constructive notice so as to put a duty of inquiry on the bank "would need to be made prospectively and, therefore, more properly by statute."

[17.85] Yet six years later the Supreme Court held that since a universal professional practice relied upon by the defendants had inherent defects which ought to have been obvious to any person giving the matter due consideration, the defendants were liable in negligence for not having made appropriate inquiries,[256] notwithstanding that it was not the practice to make such enquiries.

[17.86] In 1978 the Supreme Court[257] in considering a case involving a mortgage to a bank to secure monies advanced and in particular the question of notice stated:[258]

"This difficult branch of the law is well summarised at p 50 of the 27th edition of Snell's *Principles of Equity* (...) where it is stated:

'From this it is clear that a purchaser is affected by notice of an equity in three cases:

(1) Actual notice: where the equity is within his own knowledge;

(2) Constructive notice: where the equity would have come to his own knowledge if proper inquiries had been made; and

(3) Imputed notice: where his agent as such in the course of the transaction has actual or constructive notice of the equity.'"

The Court went on to acknowledge earlier authority that constructive notice does not apply to commercial transactions[259] (although it has been acknowledged in the High Court that, "in commercial, as in other transactions, notice or knowledge will be attributed to a person when he 'wilfully shuts his eyes' or 'puts aside suspicion'").[260] This approach, however, may be sensible in trade where goods are bought and sold but need not necessarily apply to all types of commercial transactions.[261]

[254.] See fn 250.
[255.] [1980] IR 251, at 256.
[256.] *Roche & Roche v Peilow and Peilow* [1985] IR 232.
[257.] In *Bank of Ireland Finance Ltd v Rockfield Ltd* [1979] IR 21.
[258.] *Ibid, per* Kenny J at 37; the other four judges agreed with the judgment of Kenny J.
[259.] *Manchester Trust v Furness* (1895) 2 QB 539 *per* Lindley LJ at 545; see also *Feuer Leather Corp v Frank Johnstone & Sons* (1981) Com LR 251.
[260.] Barton J in *Coveney v Persse Ltd and Gardiner* [1910] 1 IR 194 at 207.
[261.] See for example, *Baden Delvaux v Societe Generale SA* [1983] BCLC and (1984) JBL 147 see also Goode, *Legal Problems of Credit and Security* (2nd ed) p 44.

[17.87] There seems no reason why a person taking security and making a search in the Companies Registration Office on discovering a prior debenture should not ask the prospective chargor for sight of such debenture and thereby take the security in good faith.[262] The test for a purchaser in good faith indicated by the Supreme Court[263] in 1979 could be applied equally here, namely:[264]

> "The question whether a purchaser has acted in good faith necessarily depends on the extent of his knowledge of the relevant circumstances. In earlier times the tendency was to judge a purchaser solely by the facts that had actually come to his knowledge. In the course of time it came to be held in the Court of Chancery that it would be unconscionable for the purchaser to take his stand on the facts that had come to his notice to the exclusion of those which ordinary prudence or circumspection or skill should have called to his attention. When the facts at his command beckoned him to look and inquire further, and he refrained from doing so, equity fixed him with constructive notice of what he would have ascertained if he had pursued the further investigation which a person of reasonable care and skill would have felt proper to make in the circumstances."

[17.88] Thus, in *Cox v Dublin City Distillery Co*[265] a bank which took a pledge of whisky was unable to rely on the pledge as it was shown that the bank was familiar with the prior debentures of the pledgor which prohibited the creation of further security in priority to the floating charge under the debentures.

[17.89] The current law as applied by the Supreme Court in *Welch v Bowmaker (Ireland) Ltd and The Governor and Company of the Bank of Ireland*[266] in permitting a prospective chargee to ignore restrictions which would commonly be found in prior security, yet which he is not actually aware of, appears in the context of their application of other duties to be unduly narrow and it may be dangerous to rely on the continuation of this narrow approach. In *Siebe Gorman & Co Ltd v Barclays Bank Ltd*,[267] particulars of a fixed charge over book debts in favour of the defendant was filed in the Companies Office. However, details of the debenture restricting further charges and requiring the chargor to pay book debt proceeds into an account of the chargee were not filed in the Companies Office. The Court held that the plaintiff was fixed with notice of the charge over the book debts but not of the restrictive provisions. Slade J stated:[268]

[262.] See also Lingard's remarks in *Bank Security Documents* (3rd ed) para 1.9 - "It is odd that notice of the existence of a debenture was held in the old cases not to impose any duty to call for a copy of the document or to involve notice of the contents".

[263.] *Somers v Weir* [1979] IR 94; 113 ILTR 81.

[264.] *Ibid per* Henchy J at 108 and 88 respectively.

[265.] [1906] 1 IR 446.

[266.] [1980] IR 251.

[267.] [1979] 2 LLR 142.

[268.] *Ibid* at 160.

"... I treat constructive notice as embracing any matter which would have come to Siebe Gorman's knowledge if such inquiries and inspections had been made as ought reasonably to have been made by it or would have come to the knowledge of its solicitors if such inquiries and inspections had been made as ought reasonably to have been made by them."

He went on to point out that a third party would not necessarily have expected to find provisions in a mortgage creating a specific charge on future book debts as such a charge would be created without such special restrictive provisions.

Thus, there may be a distinction as between what is normally expected and what would not normally be expected in a prior debenture. Nowadays it is common for restrictive provisions in a floating charge to be filed on the Form 47[269] just as the restrictive provisions on a fixed charge over book debts are also filed to avoid a third party suggesting he had not been put on notice. Indeed it may be negligent to omit such restrictions when preparing a Form 47, if the result is such, as appears from the decisions to date, that a subsequent chargee may obtain priority.

[17.90] A person who submits that the filing of the restrictive provisions does not put subsequent chargees on notice of the restriction may draw comfort from reg 6 of the European Communities (Companies) Regulations, 1973.[270] The first two paragraphs of this regulation state:

(1) In favour of a person dealing with a company in good faith, any transaction entered into by any organ of the company, being its board of directors or any person registered under these regulations as a person authorised to bind the company, shall be deemed to be within the capacity of the company and any limitation of the powers of that board or person, whether imposed by the memorandum or articles of association or otherwise, may not be relied upon as against any person so dealing with the company.

(2) Any such person shall be presumed to have acted in good faith unless the contrary is proved.

 The weakness in relying on this regulation is the uncertainty of the meaning of "good faith".[271] It is submitted that a bank cannot be said "to have acted in good faith" when in preparing to take security it, or its solicitor, fails to carry out a search in the Companies Registration Office and ignores a prior floating charge notwithstanding the almost universal practice of such charge incorporating a

---

269. See for example Gower 4th ed p 475; Palmer (25th ed), para 13.043.

270. SI 163/1973 which gives effect to Council Directive of the European Communities of 9 March, 1968 (68/151/EEC) and became operational on 1 July 1973; for a discussion on the equivalent provision operating in England see Bostin, 'Priority of Charges and the European Communities Act 1972' (1975) 125 NLJ 592.

271. See also the application of this Directive in England as discussed by Farrar, 'Floating Charges and Priorities' (1974) 38 Conv 315.

restriction on the creation of further security ranking *pari passu* with or in priority to it.[272]

PROPERTY OUTSIDE THE STATE

[17.91] Registration is required in respect of mortgages or charges created by companies incorporated in Ireland over the assets categorised in s 99(2) of the Companies Act, 1963 whether or not such assets are situate in Ireland. This applies notwithstanding that further proceedings may be necessary to make the security valid in the country in which the assets are situated.[273] Where it is necessary to register the charge in the country where the assets are situated, there must be delivered to the Registrar of Companies a certificate[274] stating that the charge was presented for registration in the relevant country.[275]

FOREIGN COMPANIES

[17.92] The requirement to file particulars of charges within the category as set out in s 99(2) of the Companies Act, 1963 applies also, by virtue of s 111, to charges on property within the State created by a company incorporated outside the State which "has an established place of business in the State".[276]

[17.93] All companies incorporated outside the State which establish a place of business within the State are required within one month of the establishment of their place of business (within the State) to file with the Registrar of Companies particulars of their constitution, directors and secretary and the names and addresses of persons resident in the State who are authorised to accept service of process and notices on behalf of the company.[277]

[17.94] It should be noted though that particulars of charges created over property in Ireland by a company incorporated outside the State still need to be delivered even where such company has not registered its establishment in the State with the Registrar of Companies. This was decided in *NV Slavenburg's Bank v Intercontinental Natural Resources Ltd.*[278] In that case a company incorporated in Bermuda established a place of business in England. It failed to register its establishment under the English equivalent of s 352. It charged its assets in England but failed to file particulars of the charge. The English court

---

[272.] See also the Supreme Court's test of good faith in *Somers v Weir* [1979] IR 94; 113 ILTR 81, para **[17.87]** above.

[273.] Companies Act, 1963, s 99(4).

[274.] Form 47C.

[275.] Companies Act, 1963, s 99(5).

[276.] For further reading see Courtney, *The Law of Private Companies* (1994) Butterworths, paras 15.042-15.053.

[277.] Companies Act, 1963, s 352(1).

[278.] [1980] 1 All ER 955.

held that the charges were void for want of registration as against the Bermudan liquidator.

The chargee argued before the court that the establishment of the company must first be registered, particularly as the Registrar of Companies would not accept particulars of charges unless the company was first registered (which it was not in this case). But Lloyd J stated:[279]

> "The fallacy in the argument lies in regarding registration of the charge ... as a condition precedent to its validity. It is clear ... that it is delivery of particulars of the charge ... that saves the charge, not its registration.
>
> ... it seems to follow that the bank could have preserved the validity of its charges by delivering particulars within 21 days, despite the unwillingness of the Registrar to register the charge without prior registration of the company."

"An established place of business in the State"

[17.95] The question often arises as to what is an established place of business in the State, for unless a foreign company has an established place of business in the State particulars of its charges, even over assets situate in Ireland, do not need to be filed with the Registrar of Companies. In the English decision of *Re Oriel Ltd*[280] Mervyn Davies J accepted the liquidator's counsel's submission that in deciding whether or not the company had an established place of business in England three questions had to be considered, namely:[281]

> "(1) What are Oriel's objects as shown in its memorandum;
>
> (2) Has Oriel acted in pursuance of those objects, ie has it carried on business;
>
> (3) If yes, whether, in so acting it established a place of business in England, and, if so, where."

He also considered that in deciding whether Oriel had established a place of business in England he:

> "must consider whether Oriel has a habitation or office within England. If it has, one has then to consider whether that habitation or office is a place where the company has carried on some business and that to an extent justifies the expression 'established place of business'".[282]

The Court of Appeal[283] upheld the decision of Mervyn Davies J; in the Court of Appeal Oliver LJ clarified somewhat the meaning of "established" where he said:[284]

---

279. *Ibid* at 963 and 964.
280. [1984] BCLC 241.
281. *Ibid* at 249.
282. *Ibid* at 248.
283. [1985] BCLC 343; [1985] 3 All ER 216.
284. *Ibid* at 347 and 220 respectively.

"... when the word 'established' is used adjectively ... it connotes not only the setting-up of a place of business at a specific location, but a degree of permanence or recognisability as being a location of the company's business, ... The concept, as it seems to me, is of some more or less permanent location, not necessarily owned or even leased by the company, but at least associated with the company and from which habitually or with some degree of regularity business is conducted."

[17.96] This passage of Oliver LJ's judgment was adopted by the court in *Cleveland Museum of Art v Capricorn Art International SA*[285] where the court held that in order to find that a foreign company has an established place of business it is necessary to show that it has some more or less permanent location associated with the company and from which habitually, or with some degree of regularity, business is conducted. In the earlier case of *South India Shipping Corp Ltd v Export-Import Bank of Korea,*[286] the English Court of Appeal held that a company established a place of business if it carried on part of its business activities within the jurisdiction and it was not necessary for those activities to be either a substantial part of or more than incidental to the main objects of the company.

[17.97] For particulars of charges by foreign companies to be filed with the Registrar of Companies, the company must have an established place of business at the time of the creation of the charge. In *Re Alton Corporation*[287] Sir Robert Megarry V-C stated in his judgment:[288]

"... the question whether a charge created by Alton is void against the liquidator depends on whether or not Alton had an established place of business in England when the charge was created; for it is common ground that the question falls to be decided as at the moment when the charge was created, and that the result is not affected by the state of affairs at any other time."

The following year in the English Court of Appeal Oliver LJ stated:[289]

"... the critical question is of course not whether the company carried on a business in England, but whether, at the relevant time or times, it had an established place of business in England."

Other case law indicates that there may be an established place of business where such activity is conducted from a fixed address[290] or, a specific location is readily identifiable in the minds of the public from which it may be deduced that

---

285. [1990] BCLC 546.
286. [1985] 2 All ER 219.
287. [1985] BCLC 27.
288. *Ibid* at 30.
289. *Re Oriel Ltd* [1985] BCLC 343 at 347; [1985] 3 All ER 216 at 220.
290. *Act Dayskib Hercules v Grant Trunk Pacific Railway Co* [1912] 1 KB 222.

some substantial business activity is being carried on.[291] Obviously though, ultimately it may not be possible to determine exactly whether or not a company has an established place of business in the State.[292] Practitioners, no doubt to avoid the possibility of being negligent, will file particulars of charges when in doubt.[293] Any reluctance on the part of the company or its advisers to file will need to be supported by overwhelming evidence that a place of business has not been established.

[17.98] If a company which has an established place of business in the State creates a charge over property in the State, the charge may be avoided by its liquidator or creditors if particulars of the charge are not filed even if at the time of liquidation the company no longer has an established place of business in the State.[294]

Future Property

[17.99] The practitioner should note that the requirement to file particulars relates also to future property and is not confined to charges on property in the State existing at the time the charge was created.[295] This can obviously cause difficulties if a foreign company subsequently acquires property in the State, unknown to the chargee, or indeed if a foreign company subsequently establishes a place of business in the State and future property is thereafter charged.[296]

Procedure for Registration

[17.100] Particulars of charges on property in the State created by a company incorporated outside the State (with an established place of business within the State) should be set out on a Companies Office Form 8E.[297] The same particulars are required as for completing a Companies Office Form 47 pursuant to s 99 of the Companies Act, 1963.[298] The Registrar of Companies is obliged to keep a register of such charges and on the payment of a prescribed fee enter appropriate particulars of the charge on the register.[299] He is then obliged to issue a certificate of registration in respect of such charge, such certificate being

---

[291] *South India Shipping Corp v Export-Import Bank of Korea* [1985] 2 All ER 219; [1985] BCLC 163.
[292] For further consideration of the point see Gill, 'Foreign Companies and Establishing "A Place of Business"' (1989) ILT 264.
[293] See generally Courtney, 'Registration of Charges: Foreign Companies and the Slavenburg File' (1992) 86 ILS Gazette 151; Lingard, *Bank Security Documents* (3rd ed) para 3.28.
[294] See *NV Slavenburg's Bank v Intercontinental Natural Resources Ltd* [1980] 1 All ER 955.
[295] *Ibid.*
[296] See further Boyle, '*Slavenburg* case leads to reform proposals for s 106' (1981) 2 Co Law 218.
[297] See Companies (Forms) Order, 1964 SI 45/1964.
[298] See paras **[17.48]-[17.53]** inclusive above.
[299] Companies Act, 1963, s 103.

conclusive evidence that the requirements as to registration have been complied with.[300] However, where a company has not registered itself pursuant to s 352 of the Companies Act, 1963 as carrying on business in Ireland, the Registrar of Companies will not have a register as such against which to file the particulars of the charge. In such case the Registrar issues a letter acknowledging receipt of the particulars.

Judgment Mortgages

[17.101] The provisions of the Companies Act, 1963[301] as to judgment mortgages apply also to judgment mortgages affecting property in the State of a foreign company which has an established place of business in the State.[302]

[300.] Companies Act, 1963, s 104.
[301.] As set out in s 102, see para **[17.59]** above.
[302.] Companies Act, 1963, s 111.

Chapter 18

Compliance

UNFAIR TERMS REGULATIONS

Facility Letters, Loan Agreements, Mortgages and Charges

[18.01] The European Communities (Unfair Terms in Consumer Contracts) Regulations, 1995[1] apply to any term[2] in an agreement,[3] which has "not been individually negotiated",[4] between a supplier of services and a consumer. The Regulations purport to apply to all such terms and contracts concluded after 31 December 1994.[5]

A term is deemed not to have been individually negotiated "where it has been drafted in advance and the consumer has therefore not been able to influence its substance, particularly in the context of a pre-formulated standard contract".[6] Although there may be some uncertainty as to whether the Regulations do apply to facility letters and loan agreements as they may be individually negotiated, certain terms may nonetheless be caught by the Regulations. A standard set of terms and conditions used by a bank to apply to all loans or facilities of certain categories will be subject to the Regulations.[7] A banker who considers that a

---

1. SI 27/1995 - these regulations give effect to Council Directive No 93/13/EEC of 5 April 1993 on unfair terms in consumer contracts; the Directive seems to have emanated from Gesetz Zur Begelurg des Bechts der Allgemeinen Geschaftsbedingungen (Germany 1977) see Padfield [1995] 5 JIBL 175; the equivalent regulations applying in Northern Ireland are the Unfair Terms in Consumer Contracts Regulations 1994, SI 1994/3159 - these took effect on 1 July 1995.
2. Other than any terms which reflect - (i) mandatory statutory or regulatory provisions of Ireland, or (ii) the provisions or principles of international conventions to which Ireland or the European Community are a party (Sch 1).
3. Certain agreements are excluded by Sch 1.
4. Reg 3(1) of SI 27/1995.
5. Reg 1(2); as they were implemented on 1 February 1995 there is considerable doubt as to whether they apply retrospectively to contracts concluded in January 1995, unless the Directive to which it gave effect is deemed to have had direct application; for a discussion on the possibility of a constitutional challenge to the Regulations see Carney, 'The Unfair Terms in Consumer Contracts Regulations - a Standard Form Constitutional Crisis' (1995) CLP 118; for further criticism see (1995) CLP 50 and (1995) CLP 51.
6. Reg 3(4) of SI 27/1995; *Heron* points out that "almost all retail financial services are supplied ... on the basis of pre-formulated standard contracts" 'The Unfair Terms in Consumer Contracts Regulations - A Guide for Banks' (The Irish Centre for Commercial Law Studies).
7. However Paget's *Law of Banking* (11th ed) Butterworths, p 632 considers "the better view is that the bank" by making a loan does not supply a service. The author respectfully disagrees, *Paget* does acknowledge that "the point is by no means free of doubt"; it might be noted that under the Mergers, Take-Overs and Monopolies (Control) Act, 1978 (which applies *inter alia* to persons engaged for profit in the provision of services coming under common control) it was considered necessary to exclude any service provided by the holder of a banking licence.

contract may have been individually negotiated should be conscious of a catch-all provision in the Regulations to the effect that:[8]

> "The fact that a specific term or any aspect of a term has been individually negotiated shall not exclude the application of this Regulation to the rest of the contract if an overall assessment of the contract indicates that it is nevertheless ... a pre-formulated standard contract".

Furthermore, the onus of proof is on the banker to show that any particular term was individually negotiated.[9]

Commercial facilities will not be caught by the Regulations as they apply only to contracts concluded between a supplier of services *inter alia* and a "consumer"[10]. For the purposes of the Regulations a consumer is "a natural person who is acting for purposes which are outside his business."[11]

Nature of an Unfair Term

[18.02] Any term in a contract concluded with a consumer which is deemed to be unfair will not be binding on the consumer.[12] A contractual term in such a contract is regarded as unfair "if, contrary to the requirements of good faith, it causes a significant imbalance in the parties' rights and obligations under the contract to the detriment of the consumer".[13] A reading of this would indicate that the supplier of services is safe if it acts in good faith. However, the term "good faith" is a misnomer here as the test for assessing good faith requires "particular regard" to:[14]

(1) the strength of the bargaining positions of the parties,

(2) whether the consumer had an inducement to agree to the term,

(3) whether the ... services were ... supplied to the special order of the consumer, and

(4) the extent to which the ... supplier has dealt fairly and equitably with the consumer whose legitimate interests he has to take into account.

Thus, banks will find it more difficult than most to be deemed to be acting in good faith as they will invariably be in a stronger bargaining position than a consumer and unlikely to provide any service to a consumer on the basis of a

---

8. Reg 3(5).
9. Reg 3(6).
10. Reg 3(1).
11. Reg 2; "business" includes "a trade or profession".
12. Reg 6(1); thus as Chesire, Fifoot & Furmston's *Law of Contract* (13th ed) states at p 204 -"the [English equivalent] regulations can be used to attack any term which can be argued to be unfair".
13. Reg 3(2).
14. Reg 3(3) and Schedule 2; these tests are not dissimilar to the test of reasonableness applicable to consumers under the Sale of Goods and Supply of Services Act, 1980 s 40 and the Schedule.

special order. A bank will clearly need to satisfy the test of dealing fairly and equitably with the consumer - a subjective test.[15]

Plain, Intelligible Language

[18.03] Further guidance, if not uncertainty, as to whether a term is unfair can be gleaned from regulations 4 and 9.

Regulation 4 provides that a term shall not of itself be considered unfair "by relation to the definition of the main subject matter of the contract ... in so far as these terms are in plain, intelligible language".

Drafting agreements in "plain, intelligible language" however is not an option but a requirement. The banker has a duty to ensure that terms of a consumer contract "are drafted in plain, intelligible language;"[16] it may be difficult however to find any mortgage complying with this requirement. Any doubt as to the meaning of a term will be given the meaning most favourable to the consumer.[17]

Regulation 9 provides that:

> In determining whether or not the terms of a contract are unfair account shall be taken of all its features and in particular of any information it contains concerning the matters set out in the Annex to the Council Directive and in Schedule 3 to these Regulations.

Schedule 3 sets out "an indicative and non-exhaustive list of terms which may be regarded as unfair".[18] These include:

1. A term which permits the banker to retain monies paid by the consumer where the consumer decides not "to conclude or perform the contract" where there is no corresponding compensation of an equivalent amount from the banker where it is the party cancelling the contract. An example of this would be the forfeiture of an acceptance or commitment fee;

2. Any term which requires a consumer who fails to honour an obligation to pay a disproportionately high sum in compensation - this is probably no different from the common law which does not recognise a contractual compensation amount which is a penalty;[19]

[15.] For a useful analysis of these four tests see Heron, *The Unfair Terms in Consumer Contracts Regulations - A Guide for Banks* (The Irish Centre for Commercial Law Studies) para 15.

[16.] Regulation 5(1).

[17.] Regulation 5(2); see also the *contra proferentum* rule at common law - *Chitty on Contracts* (26th ed) paras 836 and 837; Chesire, Fifoot & Furmston's *Law of Contract* (13th ed) p 169.

[18.] Reg 3(7); according to Chesire, Fifoot & Furmston's *Law of Contract* (13th ed) p 205 this "is not a blacklist" but "rather a grey list in the sense that inclusion on the list raises a strong inference that in most circumstances a clause of this kind should be treated as unfair".

[19.] See Chesire, Fifoot & Furmston's *Law of Contract* (13th ed) pp 634-639; Clark, *Contract Law in Ireland* (3rd ed) pp 468-472.

3. Any term which authorises the banker to terminate the contract on a discretionary basis where the same discretion is not reciprocated;

4. Any term which enables the banker "to terminate a contract of indeterminate duration without reasonable notice except where there are serious grounds for doing so". A typical contract here would be an overdraft facility to be available at what is sometimes described as the pleasure of the bank. Usually though overdraft facilities are provided on an annual basis. There is however a softening of this test by a further provision[20] which specifies that the foregoing test "is without hindrance to terms by which a supplier of financial services reserves the right to terminate unilaterally a contract of indeterminate duration without notice where there is a valid reason, provided that the supplier is required to inform the other contracting party or parties thereof immediately";

5. Any provision whereby the consumer is irrevocably bound to terms with which he had no real opportunity of becoming acquainted before completion of the contract. This is particularly applicable to bankers and would clearly apply where a consumer enters a branch and completes a loan contract at the counter. It is incumbent on a banker to ensure that the customer, being a consumer, has ample opportunity to consider the terms of the agreement and where appropriate to take, or be given the opportunity of taking, independent advice. Although a loan contract will incorporate a cooling off period,[21] a customer may waive the cooling off period.[22] That waiver may be unenforceable, and thus the agreement itself, if the bank is unable to show that the customer had a real opportunity of becoming acquainted with its terms. An agreement and waiver signed at the counter or in the bank when not previously considered by the customer is unlikely to satisfy this test;

6. A provision which enables the banker to alter contractual terms unilaterally "without a valid reason which is specified in the contract". Notwithstanding this, a supplier of financial services is specifically permitted[23] to have the right to alter the rate of interest payable by a consumer. What is also permitted is the alteration of other charges for financial services without notice where "there is a valid reason" provided the consumer is informed at the earliest

---

[20]. Schedule 3, para 2(a).
[21]. To comply with the Consumer Credit Act, 1995, s 50.
[22]. *Ibid* s 50(2).
[23]. Schedule 3, para 2(b).

opportunity and the consumer is free to terminate the contract immediately. Similarly, conditions applying to a contract of indeterminate duration may be altered provided the consumer is given "reasonable notice" and is free to terminate the contract immediately;

7. A term which permits a banker to increase its price without giving the consumer a corresponding right to cancel the contract "if the final price is too high in relation to the price agreed when the contract was concluded". However, a price indexation clause is permitted provided the method by which the prices vary is explicitly described;[24]

8. A term which gives the banker the exclusive right to interpret any term of the contract.

The terms in 4, 6 and 7 above do not apply to:

"transactions in transferable securities, financial instruments and other products or services where the price is linked to fluctuations in a stock exchange quotation or index or a financial market rate that the [banker] does not control; contracts for the purchase or sale of foreign currency, traveller's cheques or international money orders denominated in foreign currency".[25]

It can be expected that the Regulations will prove to be a source of litigation, or at least of much dispute to be resolved by the Ombudsman for Credit Institutions.[26] No doubt a body of case law will, in due course, be built up and will help to give some certainty to the practitioner.[27] In the meantime, the practitioner faces an almost impossible task when requested to advise or confirm that a standard form banking agreement will not contravene the Regulations and can be relied upon by the banker.[28] In most circumstances it would be imprudent for any practitioner to so advise.

[18.04] The Regulations have not left it only to the consumer to run the risk of an unsuccessful defence in the courts to enforcement of a contract. The Director of Consumer Affairs is permitted to apply to the High Court for an order prohibiting the use of a term in a contract which the Court will then adjudge as to whether it is unfair.[29] The Director may appoint authorised officers,[30] who may for the purpose of the court application enter a bank's premises, inspect and take copies from any of the bank's books, documents and records and require

---

[24.] Schedule 3, para 2(d).

[25.] Schedule 3, para 2(c).

[26.] see further para **[1.30]**.

[27.] The equivalent UK regulations have been described as "probably good news for lawyers as the Directive contains little guidance on detail ... these ambiguities may well have to be resolved by litigation" - Reid [1995] 16 Co Law 280.

[28.] See also Heron, *The Unfair Terms in Consumer Contracts Regulations - A Guide for Banks* (The Irish Centre for Commercial Law Studies) para 14.

[29.] Regulation 8; notice of the Director's intention to apply must be published in *Iris Oifigiúil* and in at least two national newspapers.

[30.] Regulation 10(1).

any further information.[31] With this very wide power, and with the resources of the State, the Director therefore is empowered at his discretion to undertake a concerted attack on standard bank documentation.[32]

Guarantees

[18.05] As we have seen a guarantee is a contract.[33] Terms (in a contract) which have not been individually negotiated (ie a standard form contract) between a supplier of services and a consumer are subject to the provisions of the European Communities (Unfair Terms in Consumer Contracts) Regulations, 1995.[34] There is no requirement under the Regulations that the supplier of the service must supply the service to the consumer - thus any contract,[35] involving the supply of a service, which a consumer enters into is caught by the Regulations including a consumer guaranteeing payment or re-payment of moneys to such a supplier. It remains to be seen though, whether the courts would apply the terms to individual directors guaranteeing their company's obligations - it would seem logical that such persons should not receive the benefit of the Regulations as they are not strictly consumers within the meaning of the Regulations.[36] The criteria for establishing whether a term in a guarantee with a consumer is unfair and therefore not binding on the consumer[37] is the same as applies for facility letters.[38] Because of the extensive rights of a guarantor to be discharged unless otherwise agreed,[39] there are many common clauses in guarantees excluding or modifying these rights. Such clauses have been built up over at least two centuries as a result of court decisions discharging a guarantor's obligations under a guarantee.[40] It is difficult therefore to draft a guarantee with the usual exclusions which will not contravene the European Communities (Unfair Terms in Consumer Contracts) Regulations, 1995.[41]

CORPORATE GUARANTEES - SECTION 31

"The provisions are lengthy and complex"[42]

[31.] Regulation 10(4).
[32.] This is the means by which Article 7.2 of the Council Directive 93/13/EEC is implemented.
[33.] See para **[9.02]**.
[34.] Reg 3(1) of SI 27/1995.
[35.] Certain categories of contract are excluded by Schedule 1 of the Regulations.
[36.] See para **[18.01]** above.
[37.] Reg 6(1).
[38.] See para **[18.02]**.
[39.] See Ch 7.
[40.] See Milnes Holden, *The Law and Practice of Banking* Vol 2 (7th ed) paras 19-9 to 19-51.
[41.] SI 27/1995; for a very useful article on its application to specific terms of a guarantee see Breslin, 'Guarantees under Attack' (1996) CLP 243.
[42.] Keane, *Company Law in the Republic of Ireland* (2nd ed) para 29.16.

"one cannot make sense of any given provision without cross-reference to another".[43]

Prohibition on corporate guarantees for a director's indebtedness

[18.06] When preparing to take a guarantee from a company one of the most complex statutory provisions to consider is s 31 of the Companies Act, 1990. Although there is no shortage of written material on the section,[44] it is nonetheless not only complex but also more embracing than may at first appear. Thus any person taking third party security should heed the words of *Courtney*.[45]

> "Acquiring an enforceable security for a lending institution without contravening the provisions of s 31 of the Companies Act, 1990 will be a difficult and hazardous task for any solicitor".

It is hoped that the application of the law on this section may be reformed sooner rather than later.[46]

Under s 31(1)(c) (except as provided by ss 32 to 37), "a company[47] shall not enter into a guarantee (or an indemnity[48]) or provide any security[49] in connection with a loan, quasi-loan[50] or credit transaction[51] made by any other person" for:

1. A director or shadow director of the company;

2. A director or shadow director of its holding company; or

3. For a person connected with a director of the company or of its holding company.

Prohibition on corporate guarantees for a person connected to a director

[18.07] A person is deemed to be connected with a director:

1. If he is[52] -

---

43. Courtney, (1991) ILSI Gazette 262.
44. *Keane, op cit* para 29.16-29.20; Courtney, *The Law of Private Companies* paras 7.098 to 7.164; O'Dea (1989) ILT 237; Courtney (1991) ILSI Gazette 261; Practice Note (1991) ILSI Gazette 420; 'CLE - The Giving and Taking of Security and the Provisions of Section 31 of the Companies Act, 1990', 19 November 1992; Courtney (1994) CLP 17; *Warnock* (1994) CLP 243; Editorial (1995) CLP 2.
45. (1991) ILSI Gazette 266.
46. The Law Society of Ireland has made a formal submission for reform to the Minister for Commerce, Science and Technology (December 1996).
47. The provisions apply only to a company formed and registered under the Companies Acts - see Companies Act, 1963, s 2(1).
48. Companies Act, 1990, s 25(1).
49. This would catch a third party charge.
50. Defined in the Companies Act, 1990, s 25(2).
51. Defined in the Companies Act, 1990, s 25(3).
52. Companies Act, 1990, s 26(1).

(a) that director's spouse, parent, brother, sister or child;[53]

(b) a person acting in his capacity as the trustee of any trust, the principal beneficiaries of which are the director, his spouse or any of his children or any body corporate which he controls; or

(c) a partner of that director[54]

unless that person is also a director of the company; or

2. If it is a body corporate (ie a company wherever incorporated[55]) controlled by a director;[56] or

3. If he/it is the sole member of the company (in the case of a single member company).[57]

Control

[18.08] A director is deemed to control a body corporate[58] if he is, either on his own or, with any of the persons referred to in paragraphs (a), (b) or (c) of s 26(1) above:

"interested[59] in more than one-half of the equity share capital of that body or entitled to exercise or control the exercise of more than one-half of the voting power at any general meeting of that body".

A director will also be deemed to control a body corporate where more than one-half of its voting power is controlled or exercised by another body corporate which itself is controlled by that director.[60]

Shadow Directors

[18.09] The first point to note is that a director includes not only a person appointed to that position but also a shadow director. A shadow director is[61] "a person in accordance with whose directions or instructions the directors of a company are accustomed to act" (unless the directors are accustomed so to act by reason only that they do so on advice[62] given by him in a professional capacity). The comments of the Financial Law Panel's 1994 report on Shadow

---

53. Child and parent includes step-child/parent; adopted child/parent (Companies Act, 1990, s 3(1)) and child/parent born outside of marriage (Status of Children Act, 1987, s 3(1)).
54. "Partner" is not defined in the Act but it is considered to mean a partner within the meaning of the Partnership Act, 1890 rather than a partner in the sense of a co-habitee.
55. Companies Act, 1963, s 2(3).
56. Companies Act, 1990, s 26(2).
57. European Communities (Single-Member Private Ltd Companies) Regulations, 1994 SI 275/1994, reg 12.
58. Companies Act, 1990, s 26(3).
59. For the meaning of interested in shares see Part IV Chapter 1 of the Companies Act, 1990.
60. Companies Act, 1990, s 26(4)(b).
61. Companies Act, 1990 s 27(1).
62. Note - advice in a professional capacity is permitted, whereas directions or instructions are not.

Directorships should be heeded when considering whether a person is a shadow director, namely:

> "... any finding of shadow directorship by the courts will be determined by a view of the overall substance of the relationship of the putative shadow director with the company in question. There is a danger in treating separate aspects of the statutory definition as a checklist without sufficient regard to their context".

In *Re Hydrodam (Corby) Ltd*[63] Millett J considered who might be a shadow director. In the course of his judgment he stated:[64]

> "He lurks in the shadows, sheltering behind others who, he claims, are the only directors of a company to the exclusion of himself. He is not held out as a director by the company. To establish that a defendant is a shadow director of a company it is necessary to allege and prove: (1) who are the directors of the company, whether *de facto* or *de jure*; (2) that the defendant directed those directors how to act in relation to the company or that he was one of the persons who did so; (3) that those directors acted in accordance with such directions; and (4) that they were accustomed so to act. What is needed is, first, a board of directors claiming and purporting to act as such; and, secondly, a pattern of behaviour in which the board did not exercise any discretion or judgment of its own, but acted in accordance with the directions of others".

MacCann points out,[65] "A parent company might be regarded as a 'shadow director' of its subsidiary where the board of the subsidiary is accustomed to act in accordance with the directions or instructions of the parent's board."[66] This though should not result in the individual directors of the parent being shadow directors of the subsidiary.[67]

Cross-Company Guarantees

[18.10] While s 31 may seem to cause a difficulty for cross company guarantees, s 34 enables the possibility of such guarantees. This provides that:

> where a company is a member of a group of companies, consisting of a holding company and its subsidiaries,[68] s 31 shall not prohibit that company from ...

---

63. [1994] BCC 161.

64. *Ibid* at 163.

65. *Butterworth Ireland Companies Acts 1963-1990* (1993) n 4 to s 27.

66. Courtney, *The Law of Private Companies* (1994) para 8.082 contends that as a body corporate is precluded by statute from being a director it is arguable that a body corporate cannot therefore be a shadow director.

67. See *Re Hydrodam (Corby) Ltd* [1994] BCC 161; see also Financial Law Panel, *Shadow Directorships* 1994.

68. It is debatable as to whether the exception can apply only where there is more than one subsidiary in the group; it is arguable that subsidiaries mean subsidiary or subsidiaries see Interpretation Act, 1937 s 11(a).

(b) entering into a guarantee or providing any security in connection with a loan or quasi-loan made by any person to another member of the group;

by reason only that a director of one member of the group is connected with another.

Where a company's shares are held in trust for a beneficiary, the question may arise as to which person the company is a subsidiary of. This can be clarified by establishing whether the beneficiary, although not on the company's share register, exercises sufficient control over the company to make the company a subsidiary of the beneficiary within the meaning of s 155 of the Companies Act, 1963.[69] If it does, then the company is a subsidiary of the beneficiary.

Section 35 provides that s 31 shall not prohibit a company from "entering into a guarantee or providing any security in connection with a loan or quasi-loan made by any person to its holding company". Thus, this section is a complete exemption from a s 31 prohibition for a guarantee by a subsidiary of finance being made available to its holding company but not vice versa.

Evidence of Shareholding

[18.11] Following the implementation of s 31[70] a number of banks requested the borrower's/guarantor's solicitor to provide a certificate, upon completion of a transaction, that s 31 did not apply. Effectively, this was putting the consequences of a breach of s 31 upon the solicitor providing such certificate. Accordingly, the Law Society, through its Commercial and Company Law Committee, issued a practice note[71] recommending solicitors to give such certificates only "where they are absolutely certain as to the nature of the inter-company shareholding" and its effect, "have a clear understanding of the application" of the sections "and have direct access to the share registers of the appropriate companies". The practice in respect of such certificates varies. Some certificates given by solicitors or auditors cite the names of directors and shareholders (and voting rights) of the relevant companies - it is for the lender and its adviser to interpret that information relative to the application of s 31.[72] Other certificates are given by auditors certifying that a company is a subsidiary of another within the meaning of s 155 of the Companies Act, 1963.

Consequences of Breach

[18.12] A transaction entered into in breach of s 31 is voidable by the company[73] (and thus by its liquidator) unless restitution of any money or asset which has

---

[69.] See sub-s (1)(a) as applied by sub-section 3(b)(i).

[70.] 1 February 1991 - SI 10/1991.

[71.] (1991) ILSI Gazette 420.

[72.] See requisitions suggested by Courtney (1991) ILSI Gazette 265.

passed is no longer possible, or the company has been indemnified under s 38(2)(b) for loss or damage suffered by it, or "any rights acquired *bona fide* for value and without actual notice of the contravention by any person other than the person for whom the transaction or arrangement was made would be affected by its avoidance."[74]

An offence is committed by any person who procures a company to enter into a guarantee "knowing or having reasonable cause to believe" that it was a breach of s 31.[75] This can result in a maximum penalty of a fine of up to £10,000 and/or imprisonment for a term of up to three years.[76] The application of this provision can apply to the recipient of a guarantee and arguably its legal advisers as they may be considered to have procured the company to enter into the guarantee.

FINANCIAL ASSISTANCE

Prohibition on Financial Assistance

[18.13] At any time where security is to be taken, whether it be a guarantee, mortgage, charge or pledge, the statutory requirements for the giving of financial assistance must be considered.[77] Section 60(1) of the Companies Act, 1963 provides:

> Subject to subsections (2), (12) and (13) it shall not be lawful for a company[78] to give, whether directly or indirectly, and whether by means of a loan, guarantee, the provision of security[79] or otherwise, any financial assistance[80] for the purpose of or in connection with a purchase or subscription made or to be made by any person of or for any shares in the company, or, where the company is a subsidiary company, in its holding company.

---

73. Companies Act, 1990, s 38(1).
74. On the acquisition of rights without actual notice see *Courtney* (1991) ILSI Gazette 264; see also Courtney, *The Law of Private Companies* paras 7.151-7.155.
75. Companies Act, 1990, s 40(2).
76. *Ibid* s 40(1).
77. For an earlier consideration of the financial assistance requirements see Johnston, 'The Application of Financial Assistance Requirements in Ireland' (1989) JIBFL 111; for further treatment see *Courtney*, paras 12.027 to 12.045; see also *Keane*, paras 15.29-15.37; for a brief historical background see Ussher, *Company Law in Ireland* (1986) p 319.
78. "Company" is defined in s 2(1) of the Companies Act, 1963 as meaning "a company formed and registered under this Act, or an existing company"; "existing company" is defined under the same section as "a company formed and registered in a register kept in the State under the Joint Stock Companies Acts, the Companies Act, 1862, or the Companies (Consolidation) Act, 1908".
79. "A usual way, and maybe the only way, in which a company could give financial assistance by means of the provision of a security in circumstances which would not amount to the giving of financial assistance by means of a loan or guarantee would be by entering into a debenture" [which incorporated a charge] - Fisher J in *Heald v O'Connor* [1971] 2 All ER 1105 at 1109.
80. For the common law meaning of "financial assistance" see Sterling, 'Financial Assistance by a Company for the Purchase of its Shares' (1987) 8 Co Law 99.

Meaning of Financial Assistance

[18.14] It should be noted that the language of this sub-section, particularly the reference to "directly or indirectly" and the words "in connection with" are such as to render s 60 applicable to many transactions which are not at first sight obviously apparent. The words "indirectly" have caught a transaction where a company lent money to a person who deposited the funds with a bank who lent the same amount to a purchaser who used that loan to purchase shares in the company.[81] The judiciary have noted that the words "in connection with" are "of wide import".[82] For example, these words will catch the giving of security by a company months after the actual purchase of shares.[83] Furthermore, the absence of any definition of the term "financial assistance" widens rather than narrows its scope. According to Hoffmann J,[84] "The words [financial assistance] have no technical meaning and their frame of reference is in my judgment the language of ordinary commerce". It is therefore a section which should appear on every practitioner's check list in advising on financing transactions.

[18.15] Examples of where s 60[85] may be applicable include (i) acquisitions, particularly management buy-outs, (ii) financing or re-financing transactions[86] and (iii) transactions whose prime motive is the utilisation of capital allowances.

    (i) A financial institution makes a loan to a company's senior managers to enable them to purchase the company's shares; the loan is secured by a guarantee from the company supported by a mortgage/charge over its assets.[87] A common example, often ignored in practice, is where a company pays the costs incurred by the purchasers or subscribers for its shares. These costs may not be insignificant where an investment may involve complex issues.

[81.] *Selanger United Rubber Estates Ltd v Cradock (No 3)* [1968] 2 All ER 1073.

[82.] Murphy J in *Eccles Hall Ltd v Bank of Nova Scotia, Paramount Enterprises Ltd and O'Keeffe* High Court, unrep, 3 February 1995 p 16 where it was indicated that the wide ambit of the phrase "in connection with" may have resulted in its deletion from the UK legislation in 1981.

[83.] See *Skelton v South Auckland Blue Metals Ltd (in liq)* [1969] NZLR 955 (Supreme Court decision) (the Companies Act, 1955 s 62(1) of New Zealand being virtually identical to the Companies Act, 1963, s 60(13)).

[84.] In *Charterhouse Investment Trust Ltd v Tempest Diesels Ltd* [1986] BCLC 1.

[85.] For general background see Carroll, 'Management Buy-Outs' (1990) The Irish Banking Review (Aut) 3; 'Blank-Leveraged Buy-Outs' (1989) JIBL 353.

[86.] For its application to re-financing, see Popham and Walsh, 'Secured Acquisition Finance: Recurrent Financial Assistance Problems' (1988) JIBFL 500.

[87.] For an example of such a transaction see the factual background in *Re SH & Co (Realisations) 1990 Ltd* [1993] BCLC 1309; for a useful article on the approach to be adopted see Lumsden, 'Financial Assistance Problems in Management Buy-Outs' (1987) JBL 111.

(ii) A not untypical financing transaction might involve a US bank providing funds to a US corporation which utilises the funds to inject additional share capital into its US subsidiary and the Irish company, itself a subsidiary of the US subsidiary, although not receiving any funds gives a guarantee (probably supported by a mortgage/charge over its assets) to the US bank to secure the initial advance.

(iii) A transaction set up principally to diminish a tax liability may involve a financial institution advancing funds to a company which uses the funds to subscribe for additional shares in its subsidiary which in turn uses the funds to purchase further share capital in a subsidiary (of the subsidiary). That subsidiary may then use the additional funds to acquire an asset, anything from stocks, shares or other securities to an aircraft. The obvious security for repayment of the funds advanced is a guarantee from the second subsidiary supported by a charge over the purchased asset.

In *Charterhouse Investment Trust Ltd v Tempest Diesels Ltd*[88] it was held that, on the facts, the surrender of tax losses did not amount to financial assistance. It should be borne in mind that Hoffmann J clearly favoured upholding the transaction[89] - an approach mirrored in Ireland.[90] Whether this judicial approach will continue to be applied is a matter outside the control of the banker or legal practitioner.

The provisions of s 60 may apply where financial assistance is given either to a vendor or a purchaser of shares.[91] It should not apply to a foreign incorporated company which provides assistance for the purchase of shares in its Irish holding company even if the nature of the assistance is a mortgage or charge over its property and assets in Ireland.[92] It would be reasonable to assume that the Irish courts will not apply the legislation to companies incorporated outside their jurisdiction.

Authorised Financial Assistance

[18.16] The financial assistance prohibition is subject to three exceptions namely those provided in sub-ss (2), (12) and (13).[93] Sub-section (2) is an

---

88. [1986] BCLC 1.
89. "One must examine the commercial realities of the transaction and decide whether it can properly be described as the giving of financial assistance by the company, bearing in mind that the section is a penal one and should not be strained to cover transactions which are not fairly within it."
90. *Bank of Ireland Finance Ltd v Rockfield Ltd* [1979] IR 21 see para **[18.23]**; *Lombard and Ulster Banking Ltd v The Governor and Company of the Bank of Ireland and Brookhouse School* High Court, unrep, 2 June 1987, Costello J, see para **[18.25]**.
91. *Armour Hick Northern Ltd v Armour Trust Ltd* [1980] 3 All ER 833.
92. *Arab Bank plc v Mercantile Holdings* [1994] 2 JIBL N-32.
93. Sub-section (13)(b) and (c) cover employees - for a commentary on this see Gallagher (1979) ILSI Gazette (March) 27.

enabling provision - in other words it permits the giving of financial assistance by private companies[94] provided the requirements as laid down in s 60 are complied with.[95]

Sub-section (2) enables such financial assistance to be given if the company passes a special resolution[96] within 12 months prior to the giving of such assistance and:

> the company has forwarded with each notice of the meeting at which the special resolution is to be considered a copy of a statutory declaration which complies with sub-sections (3) and (4) and also delivers, on the same day as such notices are issued, a copy of the declaration to the registrar of companies for registration.

The company should of course have the power under its memorandum and articles of association to enter into the transaction;[97] a subsequent amendment to the memorandum of association will be of no effect.[98] Nor can the special resolution sanctioning the financial assistance be made retrospectively.[99] The procedure under sub-s (2) may not be availed of by any company having a director, secretary or promoter who is the subject of a declaration under s 150 of the Companies Act, 1990.[100] Accordingly, a bank or its adviser relying on compliance with sub-s (2) should ascertain from the Companies Registration Office whether such a declaration has been made in relation to the company giving the financial assistance.[101]

---

94. There is a prohibition (save in a few exceptional circumstances) to the giving of financial assistance by public companies (Companies Act, 1963, s 60(15A) (as inserted by the Companies Amendment Act, 1983 s 3)); see also the European Communities (Public Limited Companies Subsidiaries) Regulations, 1997 (SI 67/1997).

95. For a commentary on the procedure to be complied with see MacCann, 'Section 60 of the Companies Act, 1963; Law and Procedure' (1994) CLP 74.

96. Minorities are protected by subsections (7) and (8) which provide that if all the members entitled to vote do not vote in favour of the special resolution, the transaction shall not be carried out before the expiry of 30 days thereafter or before any court application is disposed of (the holders of not less than 10 per cent in nominal value of the company's share capital or any class thereof being entitled to apply to the court for cancellation of the special resolution).

97. See para **[18.30]**; the financial assistance prohibition is reiterated in regulation 10 of Part I of Table A in the First Schedule to the Companies Act, 1963.

98. See McWilliam J in *Securities Trust Ltd v Associated Properties Ltd* High Court, unrep, 19 November 1980; see also Keane J in *Northern Bank Finance Corporation Ltd v Quinn and Achates Investment Co* [1979] ILRM 221 at 230.

99. See Costello J in *Re Northside Motor Co Ltd* High Court, unrep, 24 July 1985.

100. Companies Act, 1990, s 155(2).

101. Companies Act, 1990, s 150(4) requires the court to furnish the Registrar of Companies with prescribed particulars of the declaration; it may be appropriate to obtain as a condition precedent to the completion of the transaction a certificate from the company secretary to the effect that none of the secretary, the directors nor the promoters have been made the subject of a declaration pursuant to s 150 of the Companies Act, 1990.

Directors' statutory declaration

[18.17] It is critical that a copy of the declaration is delivered to the Registrar of Companies on the same day as the notice convening the meeting is circulated. Late delivery, even by one day, will mean that the procedure must be re-started, otherwise the company may be able to avoid the security or other financial assistance given under the transaction. Although there is English case law to the effect that strict compliance as to the timing of the delivery of the declaration to the Registrar of Companies is not essential, it would be unwise to rely on this decision.[102]

[18.18] The importance of strict compliance was emphasised by the High Court in *Lombard and Ulster Banking Ltd v The Governor and Company of the Bank of Ireland and Brookhouse School*,[103] where Costello J stated:[104]

> "The section makes illegal the granting of financial assistance (as defined) and if exemption for a transaction in breach of subsection (1) is claimed because of the adoption of the procedures laid down in subsection (2) and (3) and (4) then strict compliance is necessary. It is not sufficient to show that all the shareholders had authorised their solicitors to take the necessary steps and that they subsequently ratified what in fact was done. If the procedural requirements were not adopted the transaction is an illegal one, if in fact it involved the granting of financial assistance contrary to subsection (1)".

Form of Declaration

[18.19] Subsection (3) provides that the declaration shall be made by a majority of the directors at a meeting held within 24 days prior to the meeting at which the special resolution is to be passed. The contents of the declaration are regulated by sub-s (4) which reads:

> The statutory declaration shall state -
>
> (a) the form which such assistance is to take;[105]
>
> (b) the persons to whom such assistance is to be given;
>
> (c) the purpose for which the company intends those persons to use such assistance;

---

[102] In *Re NL Electrical, Ghosh v 3i plc* [1994] 1 BCLC 22 Harman J held that the only consequence of failing to deliver the statutory declaration within the statutory time period was a breach by the company of its duty to comply with the statute - it did not render the financial assistance illegal.

[103] High Court, unrep, 2 June 1987 Costello J.

[104] *Ibid* at p 9.

[105] Language such as "the granting of a guarantee supported by a fixed and floating charge over the company's assets in favour of [name of financier]" should be sufficient - see *Re SH & Co (Realisations) 1990 Ltd* [1993] BCLC 1309.

(d) that the declarants have made a full inquiry into the affairs of the company and that, having done so, they have formed the opinion that the company, having carried out the transaction whereby such assistance is to be given, will be able to pay its debts in full as they become due.

In England it has been held that in interpreting the requirements of the equivalent English section the severe consequences of non-compliance had to be kept in mind; thus a borderline case was likely to be decided in favour of compliance.[106]

Directors' Liability

[18.20] A lawyer advising directors making the declaration should point out to them the provisions of sub-s (5) which provide that any director making the declaration "without having reasonable grounds for the opinion that the company having carried out the transaction whereby such assistance is to be given will be able to pay its debts in full as they become due," will be liable to a fine and/or imprisonment.

Furthermore, if the company is wound up within 12 months of the declaration and its debts are not fully provided within a further 12 months, "it shall be presumed until the contrary is shown that the director did not have reasonable grounds for his opinion". This section should focus the minds of the directors and in certain circumstances may be a cause of concern, particularly in the type of financing transactions illustrated in (2) above where the additional injection of funds in the United States may be to support an ailing parent of the Irish company.

Procedure

[18.21] The usual procedure for availing of the statutory declaration exception is that a meeting of the board of directors giving the financial assistance is held at which, assuming both a quorum and a majority of the directors being present, the board resolves that a meeting of the members be called to consider and if thought fit by them to pass a special resolution authorising the financial assistance. The statutory declaration would be sworn by a majority of the directors and a copy then delivered to the members with the notice convening the extraordinary general meeting of the members.[107] Simultaneously, a copy of the declaration is filed in the Companies Registration Office.[108] Where the company or its holding company is being taken over as part of the transaction,

---

[106.] See *Re SH & Co (Realisations) 1990 Ltd* [1993] BCLC 1309 where Mummery J stated at 1318 "In future solicitors responsible for completing such a statutory declaration should err on the side of caution".

[107.] Companies Act, 1963, s 60(2)(b).

[108.] *Ibid.*

the retiring directors will not wish to make the declaration and incur the potential liability. In practice, the directors will appoint the new directors and the directors previously in place will resign. Following delivery of the notice of the extraordinary general meeting (EGM) to the members,[109] the EGM[110] will be held prior to which the members and the auditors will consent in writing to the holding of the meeting at short notice.[111] Ideally all the members or, in the case of corporate bodies, their representatives,[112] will be present and will pass the special resolution authorising the financial assistance. In the absence of all the members, notwithstanding the passing of a special resolution, the financial assistance cannot be carried out before the expiration of 30 days[113] (or if a court application is made not until the application is disposed of[114]).

In practice, the meeting of the directors, the swearing of the statutory declaration, the convening of the EGM, the filing of a copy of the statutory declaration, the consenting to short notice for the convening of the members' meeting, the passing of the special resolution and the execution and delivery of the security documents (under which the financial assistance is given) are completed within a matter of a couple of hours.

A practical problem is that not until the security documents are executed and delivered will the bank make available the facilities to be used for the purchase of shares and thus the shares will not be transferred until the completion of the financial assistance procedure. This means that the members passing the special resolution will be the existing members.[115] However, since there is no personal liability falling on the members for the passing of such a special resolution, the existing members will usually facilitate this procedure.[116]

[109.] All members of the company have the right to receive the notice - Companies Act, 1963, s 60(6).

[110.] Companies Act, 1963, s 60(2), (3) and (6) refer to a meeting of the members; accordingly the procedure under section 141(8) permitting a special resolution to be passed through a written instrument cannot be availed of; in the case of a single member company no meeting is required (see European Communities (Single Member Private Limited Companies) Regulations, 1994 (SI 275/1994), reg 9(1)).

[111.] Companies Act, 1963, s 133(3) and s 141(2); the Act does not require the consent to be in writing but in practice it is given in writing.

[112.] Companies Act, 1963, s 139.

[113.] *Ibid* s 60(7).

[114.] *Ibid*.

[115.] The members who may vote are those persons on the share register (Companies Act, 1963, s 31(2)); a transferee is not entitled to be entered in the register until a properly stamped share transfer is presented to the registrar (Companies Act, 1963, s 81(1)).

[116.] for an outline of this predicament see Lumsden, 'Financial Assistance Problems in Management Buy-outs' [1987] JBL 111 at 116.

Notice of a Breach

[18.22] Although the opening words of s 60 provide that "it shall not be lawful for a company" to carry out certain transactions,[117] the unlawfulness is in practice overridden by sub-s (14) which states:

> Any transaction in breach of this section shall be voidable at the instance of the company against any person (whether a party to the transaction or not) who had notice of the facts which constitute such breach.

The courts have held that if the transaction is to be avoided by the company, the company must prove that the person seeking to uphold the transaction had actual notice and not simply constructive notice of the breach. In *Lombard and Ulster Banking Ltd v The Governor and Company of the Bank of Ireland and Brookhouse School*[118] Costello J held that sub-s (14) means:[119]

> (a) that although a transaction in breach of the section is illegal it is only "voidable", not void, and (b) it is only voidable against a person who had notice of the facts which constituted the breach.

In practice, the person who will seek to avoid a transaction (which contravenes s 60) will be a liquidator of the company, so that the company's unsecured creditors may benefit at the expense of the secured creditor. Hence, the need for every lender and its advisers to be ever mindful of s 60.

[18.23] It seems that the judiciary have utilised sub-s (14) to prevent a company receiving a windfall, or its unsecured creditors obtaining payment of debts due to them, as a result of obtaining financial assistance in breach of the statutory requirements.

In *Bank of Ireland Finance Ltd v Rockfield Ltd*,[120] the bank granted a loan to persons who wished to purchase a hotel. Security for the loan was to be an equitable mortgage by way of deposit of the title deeds to the hotel. The borrowers used the loan to purchase shares in the defendant, the owner of the hotel. McWilliam J in the High Court held that the bank should have had notice of the purpose for which the borrowers intended to use the moneys advanced and therefore the mortgage could be avoided by the defendant. In reply to the bank's contention that, on the authority of Lindley LJ,[121] the doctrine of constructive notice did not apply to commercial transactions, McWilliam J concluded:[122]

[117.] Giving rise in theory to fines or imprisonment on every officer of the company who is in default (Companies Act, 1963, s 60(15)).
[118.] High Court, unrep, 2 June 1987, Costello J.
[119.] *Ibid* at p 10.
[120.] [1979] IR 21.
[121.] In *Manchester Trust v Furness* [1895] 2 QB 539 at 545.
[122.] [1979] IR 21 at 28.

"I fully accept the view expressed by Lindley LJ but it seems to me that there must be some limit to the extent to which a person may fail to accept information available to him or fail to make the inquiries normal in his line of business so as to leave himself in the position that he has no notice of something anyone else in the same line of business would have appreciated".

However, the Supreme Court found "considerable difficulty in understanding what the judge meant by this passage",[123] and unanimously allowed the appeal. The Supreme Court held that the transaction between the bank and the borrowers was the loan of money and that it was not the loan of money for the purpose of buying shares in the defendant company; that the defendant could not invoke sub-s (14) as the defendant had failed to establish that prior to the transaction the bank had actual notice of the facts alleged to constitute a breach of that section.

[18.24] Although there is no legal obligation on a bank (or other lender) to enquire as to how its funds lent to a company will be utilised,[124] the Supreme Court's decision gives judicial approval for a bank to lend money without knowing or even enquiring precisely how the funds are to be utilised. The bank was thus able to avoid the illegality under s 60 by not having actual knowledge of the basic details of the project being financed by them. Although this was a decision of five judges[125] of the Supreme Court it would be unwise to rely upon it in the context that any prudent lender will almost invariably be aware, and should be aware, of how its finance is to be utilised. Nonetheless it is a useful decision to support the validity of security given in contravention of s 60 if the person relying on the security can show that he did not have notice of the facts of the transaction.

[18.25] The decision in fact was applied by Costello J in *Lombard and Ulster Banking Ltd v The Governor and Company of the Bank of Ireland and Brookhouse School.*[126] Although the parties to the transaction understood at the time that the procedure envisaged by s 60 needed to be complied with, Costello J found that there was non-compliance in at least two respects, namely, the statutory declaration was not made at the appropriate time and the resolution passed was not a special one.[127] Costello J held that although it was not shown that s 60 had been complied with, as the evidence showed that the plaintiff had

---

[123.] *Ibid* at 35 per Kenny J (the other four members of the Court agreeing with him).

[124.] See Harman LJ in *Re Introductions Ltd* [1969] 1 All ER 887 at 890.

[125.] O'Higgins CJ, Henchy J, Griffin J and Parke J each of whom agreed with the judgment of Kenny J.

[126.] High Court, unrep, 2 June 1987.

[127.] *Ibid* at p 9.

no knowledge of the failure to comply with s 60, the charge was held to be valid.[128] It thus came down to a question of notice, Costello J stating:[129]

> "if a lender knows that an attempt to validate a prohibited transaction and avoid breaching the section by adopting the procedures set out in subsection (2), (3) and (4) is to be made I do not think he has notice of any breach within the meaning of the subsection unless it can be shown (a) that there was in fact non-compliance with the subsections and (b) that he knew of the facts which resulted in non-compliance."
>
> ... as to the nature of the 'notice', it is not sufficient for the liquidator to show that if Lombard and Ulster had made proper inquiries that they would have ascertained that the company had failed to comply with the subsections. It must be shown that Lombard and Ulster had 'actual notice' of the facts which constituted the breach, that is (a) that they or their officials actually knew that the required procedures were not adopted or that they knew facts from which they *must* have inferred that the company had failed to adopt the required procedures, or (b) that an agent of theirs actually knew of the failure or knew facts from which he must have inferred that a failure had occurred (see *Bank of Ireland v Rockfield*). 'Constructive notice' of the failure is not sufficient for subsection (14)."

[18.26] The Supreme Court's decision in *Bank of Ireland Finance Ltd v Rockfield Ltd*[130] and in particular its interpretation as to "notice" under sub-s (14) was applied also by Murphy J in *Eccles Hall Ltd v Bank of Nova Scotia, Paramount Enterprises Ltd and O'Keeffe*.[131] Murphy J said[132] it was clear from the Supreme Court's judgment that:

> "the word 'notice' as used in that subsection (and indeed in all legislation relating to commercial as distinct from conveyancing matters) is 'actual notice' as opposed to and distinct from 'constructive' notice."

[18.27] The interpretation of notice being actual notice, and the more onerous requirement (for a company or its liquidator) to show actual rather than constructive notice, should not give a false sense of security to banks (or other lenders). The High Court's decision in *Re Northside Motor Company Ltd, Eddison v Allied Irish Banks Ltd*[133] should jolt any bank and its lawyer out of any complacency enjoyed from other court decisions. Essentially in that case moneys were advanced to a shareholder to acquire further shares in a company;

[128.] For a criticism of this decision and the earlier Supreme Court decision see Lynch (1988) 10 DULJ 146.
[129.] High Court, unrep, 2 June 1987 at p 10.
[130.] [1979] IR 21.
[131.] High Court, unrep, 3 February 1995.
[132.] *Ibid* at p 16.
[133.] High Court, unrep, 24 July 1985, Costello J.

the company undertook to guarantee repayment of the advance - a classic and straightforward s 60 transaction. Costello J considered the bank was aware of the non-compliance with s 60 and accordingly the company was entitled to avoid the guarantee.

Transaction Voidable

[18.28] Where compliance with the requirements of s 60 have not been fully carried out it would be wrong for any bank and its lawyer to draw comfort from the fact that, as such a transaction is voidable[134] at the instance of the company only, the shareholders and directors are known to the bank and are unlikely to seek to avoid the transaction or might be estopped from avoiding it having been a party to it or sanctioned it albeit improperly. In the event of the company having a receiver or liquidator appointed to it, the liquidator if not the receiver will see it as his duty (to the company's creditors) to challenge the transaction or at least seek the directions of the court.[135]

Discharge of a Liability

[18.29] Subsection (12) of s 60 provides that:

> Nothing in this section shall be taken to prohibit the payment of a dividend properly declared by a company or the discharge of a liability lawfully incurred by it.[136]

The payment of interest on a debt will not constitute the payment of a dividend.[137] If sub-s (12) is to be utilised, it is important to distinguish between the giving of security to enable a debt due by the company to be discharged, and the giving of security to assist or support the purchase of shares in the company (or in its holding company).[138] The English decision in *Armour Hick Northern Ltd v Armour Trust Ltd*[139] is helpful in clarifying to what extent sub-s (12) may take a transaction outside the requirements of s 60. A company owed £93,000 to its holding company. It was agreed that the company's subsidiary would discharge the debt of £93,000 at the time the holding company sold its shares in the company. The court held that although a repayment of a debt by the company to the holding company when selling the company's shares would not

---

[134.] Companies Act, 1963, s 60(14).

[135.] See the remarks of Harman J in *Re NL Electrical Ltd, Ghosh v 3i plc* [1994] 1 BCLC 22 at 25 (the Irish decisions have invariably resulted from applications for directions by liquidators).

[136.] For a commentary on this sub-section see MacCann, 'Section 60 of the Companies Act, Law and Procedure' (1994) CLP 74.

[137.] See FitzGibbon LJ in *Dale v Martin* (1883-84) 11 LR Ir 371 at 376.

[138.] See *Eccles Hall Ltd v Bank of Nova Scotia, Paramount Enterprises Ltd and O'Keeffe* High Court, unrep, 3 February 1995 Murphy J.

[139.] [1980] 3 All ER 833.

have amounted to "financial assistance" because it would not have altered the financial position except to the extent that a debt due was repaid, the same payment when made by the subsidiary would amount to financial assistance to the holding company for the purpose of or in connection with the share purchase by the purchaser because it was a voluntary payment without which the holding company would not have proceeded with the sale.

CORPORATE CAPACITY

> "In dealing with a limited company, which must act strictly within its constitution, a contracting party must watch his step".[140]

Objects and Powers

[18.30] The type of person availing of significant financing is generally a company incorporated under the Companies Acts.[141] The capacity of any such company to enter into and be bound by its obligations under a contract is dependant upon its objects and powers as set out in its memorandum of association.[142] An agreement entered into by a company involving rights or obligations not permitted by the company's memorandum of association is *ultra vires* and unenforceable against the company (unless clearly incidental to the objects as set out).[143]

A company's objects must be set out in its memorandum of association.[144] However, "one cannot have an object to do every mortal thing one wants because that is to have no object at all."[145]

In practice, clause 2 of a company's memorandum of association will be subdivided into numerous paragraphs, the first few of which will set out the objects (or principal activity) of the company, for example, the sale and distribution of law books. Subsequent to these objects will be the paragraphs denoting the

---

140. Johnston J in *Re MJ Cummins Ltd, Barton v The Governor and Company of the Bank of Ireland* [1939] IR 60 at 70.
141. This and subsequent paragraphs do not deal with companies incorporated by statute, such as the Electricity Supply Board or Bord Na Mona.
142. See *The Ashbury Railway Carriage & Iron Company v Riche* (1875) LR 7 HL 653; *AG v Great Eastern Railway Company* (1880) 5 App Cas 473.
143. Buckley LJ in *Re Horsley & Weight Ltd* [1982] 3 All ER 1045 at 1050; Slade LJ in *Rolled Steel Products (Holdings) Ltd v British Steel Corp* [1984] BCLC 466 at 500; for a thorough review of the case law on the doctrine of *ultra vires* see MacCann, 'The Capacity of the Company' (1992) ILT 79; see also Smith, 'The Constitution of a Company' (1984) 5 Co Law 78 and 123; for further reading see Courtney, *The Law of Private Companies* (1994) paras 6.055 to 6.098; see also Ussher, *Company Law in Ireland* (1986) Ch 4.
144. Companies Act, 1963 s 6(1)(c) as amended by the Companies (Amendment) Act, 1983 Sch para 2; Companies Act, 1963 First Schedule Table B.
145. *Per* Harman LJ in *Re Introductions Ltd, Introductions Ltd v National Provincial Bank Ltd* [1969] 1 All ER 887 at 888.

powers of the company.[146] Such powers can be carried out only for the purpose of fulfilling the objects and cannot be carried out (save where specifically provided otherwise[147]) as ends in themselves.[148]

Powers are not Objects

[18.31] A banker and its lawyer would be well advised not to rely on an independent objects clause as is often found at the end of clause 2 of a company's memorandum of association. This clause will typically read as follows:

> "It is hereby expressly declared that each of the preceding sub-clauses shall be construed independently of and shall be in no way limited by reference to any other sub-clause and that the objects set out in each sub-clause are independent objects of the company".

It should be noted that "such a clause is not capable of elevating into an object of the company that which is in essence a power".[149] However, there is authority that such a clause may in fact elevate a power, which is capable of being an object in itself, to that of an object.[150]

This clause was considered by the English Court of Appeal in *Re Introductions Ltd; Introductions Ltd v National Provincial Bank Ltd*.[151] In that case, the objects clause included a power to borrow or raise money. The company's sole activity was pig-breeding. The company provided the bank, which knew its business, with its memorandum and articles of association which did not empower it to undertake pig-breeding. The memorandum of association contained an independent objects clause as set out above. The Court of Appeal agreed with the High Court judge that a power or an object conferred on a company to borrow cannot mean something in the air, that borrowing is not an end in itself and must be for some purpose of the company. It held that as the bank knew that the borrowing was not for a legitimate purpose of the company, the debentures issued by the company to the bank were unenforceable against the company's liquidator.

[18.32] An earlier illustration of this principle in Ireland can be seen from the decision in *Re MJ Cummins Ltd, Barton v The Governor and Company of the*

[146.] For the distinction between objects and powers see Keane, *Company Law in the Republic of Ireland* (2nd ed) para 5.15; see also Instone, *Powers and Objects* (1978) NLJ 948.

[147.] See for example in *Re Horsley & Weight Ltd* [1982] 3 All ER 1045.

[148.] See Buckley J in *Re David Payne & Co Ltd, Young v David Payne & Co Ltd* [1904] 2 Ch 608 at 612.

[149.] Per Browne-Wilkinson LJ in *Rolled Steel Products (Holdings) Ltd v British Steel Corp* [1984] BCLC 466 at 516.

[150.] *Re Horsley & Weight Ltd* [1982] 3 All ER 1045.

[151.] [1969] 1 All ER 887.

Bank of Ireland.[152] In that case Johnston J held that as the company exercised its general borrowing powers for a purpose, to the bank's knowledge, outside its objects the borrowing was *ultra vires*. Accordingly, the bank was precluded from proving its debt in the liquidation of the company. The legal implications for lenders was stated categorically by Johnston J:[153]

> "When an *ultra vires* act is committed by a borrowing company, on the one hand, and by a lending company, on the other, no debt, common law, equitable or otherwise, is thereby created in favour of the latter as against the former. The theory of the law is that the whole transaction is null and void and can give rise to no legal rights or claims whatever".

[18.33] The following power to guarantee in a company's memorandum of association will be a sufficient power assuming it is being utilised for one of the company's principal objects:

> "To guarantee, support or secure, whether by personal covenant (including any indemnity) or by mortgaging or charging all or any part of the undertaking, property and assets (both present and future) and uncalled capital of the Company, or by indemnity or undertaking, or by any one or more of such methods, the performance of the obligations of, and the repayment or payment of the principal amounts of and premiums, interest and dividends on any securities of, indebtedness or obligation of any person, firm or company including (without prejudice to the generality of the foregoing) any company which is for the time being the Company's holding company or subsidiary as defined in section 155 of the Companies Act, 1963, or another subsidiary as defined by the said section of the Company's holding company or otherwise associated with the Company in business.

The following power which can sometimes be seen in a company's memorandum of association is obviously not as comprehensive:

> "To lend and advance money or give credit to such persons and on such terms as may seem expedient and in particular to customers and others having dealings with the Company and to give guarantees or become security for any such persons."

While in the absence of authority it cannot be said to be insufficient, nonetheless it leaves the practitioner, taking responsibility, uncomfortable and it would be advisable to require that the power be amended along the lines of the first power.

[18.34] An alternative approach used by some is to require all the shareholders to consent to the transaction on foot of the power above. However, it should be borne in mind that a company is a separate legal entity distinct from its

---

[152] [1939] IR 60.
[153] *Ibid* at 70.

members.[154] Approval by its members for the company to enter a transaction which is *ultra vires* its objects clause still leaves a question mark over the binding nature of the transaction on the company,[155] particularly if there is any doubt as to the company's solvency at the time. All doubt can be removed, and it is more preferable for future transactions, if the objects clause in the memorandum of association is amended.[156]

Any person contemplating that the members ratify or authorise a transaction *ultra vires* the company should heed the words of Rigby LJ:[157]

> "What is the meaning of an *ultra vires* contract? It is one which the company has no legal power to carry into effect at all, even although in the opinion of each and every shareholder it is a contract advantageous to the company and to them, and though each individual shareholder, being fully competent to agree for himself, approves of and agree with it".

As the assets and undertaking of a company belong to the company itself, it is not within the power of the members[158] to pass a resolution giving away those assets whether by means of gratuitous guarantee or otherwise.[159]

Ignorance of Incapacity - Section 8

[18.35] Section 8 of the Companies Act, 1963 provides:[160]

> (1) Any act or thing done by a company which if the company had been empowered to do the same would have been lawfully and effectively done, shall, notwithstanding that the company had no power to do such act or thing, be effective in favour of any person relying on such act or thing who is not shown to have been actually aware, at the time when he so relied thereon, that such act or thing was not within the powers of the company.

The classic banking and security law case involving the *ultra vires* principle and s 8 is that of *Northern Bank Finance Corp Ltd v Quinn & Achates Investment Co.*[161] In that case, the bank agreed to make a loan to the first defendant to be secured by a guarantee from the second defendant supported by a mortgage over

---

[154.] In *Re Frederick Inns Ltd* [1991] ILRM 582.
[155.] See *Rosemary Simmons Memorial Housing Association Ltd v United Dominions Trust Ltd* [1987] 1 All ER 281.
[156.] By special resolution pursuant to the Companies Act, 1963, s 10.
[157.] In *Kaye v Croydon Tramways Co* [1898] 1 Ch 358 at 371; see also Keane J in *Northern Bank Finance Corporation Ltd v Quinn & Achates Investment Co* [1979] ILRM 221 see para **[18.35]** below.
[158.] Unless specifically permitted by the objects clause.
[159.] See Carroll J in *Roper v Ward* [1981] ILRM 408 at 415.
[160.] For further reading on this section see Ussher, *Company Law in Ireland* pp 123-128; see also MacCann, 'The Capacity of the Company' (1992) ILT 151.
[161.] [1979] ILRM 221.

certain property. In accordance with the usual practice a copy of the second defendant's memorandum and articles of association was sent to the bank's solicitor so that he could satisfy himself that the company had the appropriate power to give the guarantee and the mortgage. Subsequent to the completion of the security and the advance of the loan, the borrower defaulted and the bank sought recovery from the borrower and the guarantor. The guarantor then contended that its guarantee was *ultra vires* and thus unenforceable. The bank submitted that even if it was *ultra vires* it was protected by s 8 and also by the fact that the company had passed subsequently a shareholder's resolution authorising the transaction.

The company's memorandum of association empowered it -

> "to raise or borrow or secure the payment of money in such manner and on such terms as the directors may deem expedient and in particular ... by mortgage, charge, lien or pledge upon the whole or any part of the undertaking, property, assets and rights of the company ... and generally in any other manner as the directors shall from time to time determine and to guarantee the liabilities of the company ..."

It was accepted that reference to guaranteeing the liabilities of the company were meaningless so it all hinged on whether "secure the payment of money" could be said to encompass a guarantee. Keane J held that in the context in which it appeared these words "could not reasonably be read ... as conferring a power to execute guarantees".

The bank relied also upon a subsequent power in the company's memorandum of association which stated:

> "to do and carry out all such other things as may be deemed by the company to be incidental or conducive to the attainment of the above objects or any of them or calculated to enhance the value of or render profitable any of the company's properties or rights."[162]

Keane J considered that the giving of the guarantee could not be deemed incidental or conducive to the attainment to the company's principal objects, namely to acquire and hold stocks and shares.

The bank then contended that it was protected by s 8 of the Companies Act, 1963. The bank's solicitor could not recall whether he had actually read the company's memorandum of association. Keane J found it probable that he had read them - "it would be surprising if he did not, since it was furnished to him so that he could satisfy himself as to the existence in law of the company and its

---

162. For an example of where such a clause was pleaded successfully to uphold a transaction see *American Home Assurance Co v Tjmond Properties Ltd* [1986] BCLC 181 (New Zealand Court of Appeal); this is known as a "Bell Houses Clause" taking its name from the decision in *Bell Houses Ltd v City Hall Properties Ltd* [1966] 2 All ER 674; see Courtney, *The Law of Private Companies* (1994) para 6.063; see also MacCann, 'The Capacity of the Company' (1992) ILT 79 at 81.

power to enter into the proposed transaction".[163] Keane J held that s 8 protected a person who was not on "actual notice" of the deficiency rather than "constructive notice". However he found that, as the bank's solicitor had read the memorandum of association, the knowledge acquired from the reading was imputed to the bank. The bank were thus on notice of the facts that the guarantee was *ultra vires* the company.[164]

Finally, Keane J held that a subsequent special resolution of the company validating the guarantee was ineffective.[165] Keane J indicated that to decide otherwise would lead to strange consequences for:

> "if the company in the present case originally had power to execute a guarantee and deprived itself of that power by the passing of a subsequent resolution, it could hardly be said that the execution of the guarantee prior thereto was thereby invalidated."[166]

Ignorance of Incapacity - Regulation 6

[18.36] A person who fails to review the memorandum and articles of association of a company with limited liability may nevertheless be protected from his lack of diligence, at least when he is not on actual or constructive notice of any irregularity. Regulation 6 of the European Communities (Companies) Regulations, 1973[167] states:

> (1) In favour of a person dealing with a company[168] in good faith, any transaction entered into by any organ of the company, being its board

---

[163.] [1979] ILRM 221 at 227.

[164.] For a strong criticism of Keane J's decision on the grounds that the judge failed to distinguish between "actual awareness" and "notice" see Ussher, *Company Law in Ireland*; (1986) Sweet & Maxwell pp 124-128; see also *Ussher* [1981] DULJ 76 and MacCann, *The Capacity of the Company* (1992) ILT 151 at 152.

[165.] See *Re MJ Cummins Ltd, Barton v The Governor and Company of the Bank of Ireland* [1939] IR 60 where Johnston J stated (at 69) "it is almost unnecessary to say that a company cannot ratify an act of its own or an act of its directors which is outside and beyond the constitutional powers of the company"; see also *The Ashbury Railway Carriage & Iron Co v Riche* (1875) LR 7 HL 653 and Overend J in *National Agricultural and Industrial Development Association v The Federation of Irish Manufacturers Ltd* [1947] IR 159 at 203; see also Sir Barnes Peacock in *Irvine v The Union Bank of Australia* (1877) 2 App Cas 366 at 374 - "A ratification is in law treated as equivalent to a previous authority, and it follows that, as a general rule, a person or body of persons, not competent to authorise an act, cannot give it validity by ratifying it".

[166.] [1979] ILRM 221 at 230.

[167.] SI 163/1973 - these regulations give effect to the European Communities Council Directive of 9 March, 1968 (68/151/EEC) (the First European Communities Companies Directive); Ussher, *Company Law in Ireland* pp 134-136, believes the effect of this Article was already covered by the Companies Act, 1963, s 8 describing the regulations as a "sorry story" and a "legislative blunder"; see also MacCann, 'The Capacity of the Company' (1992) ILT 151.

[168.] The regulations apply only to companies with limited liability - European Communities (Companies) Regulations, 1973, reg 3.

of directors or any person registered under these regulations as a person authorised to bind the company, shall be deemed to be within the capacity of the company and any limitation of the powers of that board or person, whether imposed by the memorandum or articles of association or otherwise, may not be relied upon as against any person as dealing within the company.

(2)   Any such person shall be presumed to have acted in good faith unless the contrary is proved.

It seems from this regulation that a person (dealing with a company), who declines to review a company's memorandum of association to ascertain that the company has the appropriate capacity to enter into the transaction, or the articles of association to ascertain whether there is a restriction on the directors' ability to complete the transaction, will not encounter a successful defence that the company lacked the capacity or the directors lacked the authority to complete the transaction on behalf of the company.[169]

[18.37] In practice, this regulation is not used to obviate the prudence to make certain basic enquiries and to review the information provided from such enquiries when completing a financing transaction.[170] This is probably due to the uncertainty as to what is meant by good faith.[171] Judicial consideration as to the meaning of "good faith" in the context of the English equivalent to the Regulations was given in *International Sales and Agencies Ltd v Marcus*.[172] In interpreting the English legislation Lawson J, considered Article 9 of the Council Directive[173] (which forms the basis for reg 6 in Ireland) and, stated:[174]

"the test of lack of good faith in somebody entering into obligations with a company will be found either in proof of his actual knowledge that the transaction was *ultra vires* the company or where it can be shown that such a person could not in view of all the circumstances, have been unaware that he was party to a transaction *ultra vires*."[175]

[169.] It is suggested in Keane, *Company Law in the Republic of Ireland* (2nd ed) para 12.05 that even a person who reads but fails to understand the memorandum of association will be protected by this legislation.

[170.] *Keane* states at para 12.05 - "The scope of this regulation and the relationship to s 8 of the Principal Act is not clear".

[171.] See Lord Wilberforce in *Midland Bank Trust Co Ltd v Green* [1981] AC 513 at 528 - "not only absence of notice, but genuine and honest absence of notice"; see also Ussher, 'Questions of Capacity' [1975] Ir Jur 39.

[172.] [1982] 3 All ER 551; for a detailed review of the relevant issues of this decision see Green, 'Dealing in Good Faith with a Company' [1983] JBL 303.

[173.] (68/151/EEC).

[174.] [1982] 3 All ER 551 at 559.

[175.] This test has been described as "a sensible construction, in line with the general view of commentators" - 3 Co Law (1982) 177 at 178.

[18.38] When deciding upon the equivalent provision in the Northern Ireland legislation[176], Gibson LJ, while agreeing with Lawson J, placed a slightly more onerous test in holding that:[177]

> "The test of lack of good faith depends upon proof of actual knowledge that the transaction was *ultra vires* the company or that the person dealing with the company could not have been unaware that he was a party to a transaction *ultra vires*, which amounts to a deliberate closing of one's mind to circumstances which would have pointed to the conclusion of *ultra vires*".

The quandary for a lender and its adviser posed by s 8 and reg 6 have been highlighted in the following passage:[178]

> "A little learning would appear indeed to be a dangerous thing visited with a duty tediously to investigate and construe one of the most notoriously convoluted of modern documents, a company's memorandum of association. Inevitably, the scrupulous outsider with some legal knowledge will, in appropriate circumstances, lose efficiency over other members of the business community to whom questions of capacity are happily obscure and who may therefore proceed unquestionably with their consciences unimpaired".

Can a lender who ignores reviewing a company's memorandum or articles of association, a document publicly filed, be said to be acting in good faith?[179] It may be doubtful where the prudent practice is to review the memorandum and articles of association, a practice which even the rule in *Turquand's* case demands.[180]

Whether to review Objects Clause

[18.39] The outcome of the foregoing decision in conjunction with the protection granted by s 8 and reg 6 raises the question as to whether it is preferable, for a lender,[181] to make finance available and obtain security without reviewing the borrower's/guarantor's/mortgagor's memorandum of association for fear of failing to understand that the company was incapable of entering into the proposed transaction, or that it was being entered into for an *ultra vires*

[176.] Companies (Northern Ireland) Order 1978, article 129.
[177.] In *International Factors (NI) Ltd v Streeve Construction Ltd* [1984] NI 245.
[178.] Ussher, 'Questions of Capacity' [1975] Ir Jur 39 at 46.
[179.] It might be noted that the equivalent provision in England, the European Communities Act 1972, s 9 provides that a party shall not be bound to enquire; the absence of such a provision in the Irish regulations implies that some basic level of enquiry should be carried out.
[180.] See para **[18.49]** below.
[181.] This work does not consider the need for a lender to obtain a banking licence (pursuant to the Central Bank Act, 1971 (as amended)) or a moneylenders licence (pursuant to the Consumer Credit Act, 1995), or as to its corporate capacity to provide finance (see *Simmonds v Heffer* [1983] BCLC 298); it is unconscionable for a borrower to decline to repay a debt on the grounds that the lender lacked the corporate capacity to make the advance - *Re PMPA Garage (Longmile) Ltd* [1992] 1 IR 332.

purpose.[182] This is a question which bankers not unreasonably ask their advisers.[183] In his judgment Keane J set out the rationale for s 8:[184]

> "A great number of transactions are entered into every day by companies, public and private, without any of the parties looking at the memorandum in order to see whether the transaction in question is in fact authorised by the memorandum. I think it probable that, on the occasions when the memorandum is looked at before a transaction is entered into, it is normally because the company's solicitor or a solicitor for a third party wishes to satisfy himself that the proposed transaction is *intra vires* the memorandum. I think it is clear that the section was designed to ensure that, in the first category of cases, persons who had entered into transactions in good faith with the company without ever reading the memorandum and accordingly with no actual knowledge that the transaction was *ultra vires* were not to suffer. I can see no reason in logic or justice why the legislature should have intended to afford the same protection to persons who had actually read the memorandum and simply failed to appreciate the lack of *vires*."

[18.40] This passage might have encouraged a practice for lenders to dispense with the time and cost of reviewing memoranda of association - a process which in practice is time consuming where there is a multitude of companies in a group all of whom are giving cross-guarantees for the indebtedness of other companies within the group. The decision in *Re David Payne & Co Ltd, Young v David Payne & Co Ltd*[185] supports the proposition that provided the company has the power to enter into a transaction one need not enquire as to whether the power is being exercised for one of the company's objects. In that case, it was held that a lender was under no obligation to enquire how its money was to be applied and that a loan made available for an *ultra vires* purpose (unknown to the lender) of the borrower was not irrecoverable. However, it would be a brave, if not foolish, banker or lawyer who, in the absence of judicial authority at the highest level, would ignore the uncomplicated task of reviewing a company's memorandum of association prior to it completing a financing transaction to ensure that the company had the power to borrow money for a purpose falling within its principal objects.[186]

[182.] Ussher, *Company Law in Ireland* (1986) p 126 states - "indeed it may be arguable that an agent such as a solicitor in a conveyancing transaction, acting for an outsider might be under a duty to his principal not to investigate the company's capacity to enter into the proposed transaction, since his consequent awareness of lack of capacity might put into jeopardy what would otherwise have been an advantageous transaction".

[183.] "It would appear to be wiser not to look at the objects clause at all" - MacCann, 'The Capacity of the Company' (1992) ILT 151 at 152.

[184.] [1979] ILRM 221 at 229.

[185.] [1904] 2 Ch 608.

[186.] Indeed the Chief Justice of Australia when reviewing this decision in *Northside Developments Pty Ltd v Registrar-General* (1990) 170 CLR 146 indicated, "the reason why the lender should necessarily be relieved of the responsibility of turning his mind to the powers of the company is not altogether apparent to me".

False comfort should not be obtained from this High Court decision[187] albeit that it was unanimously upheld by the Court of Appeal. Buckley J's decision that a person who lends to a company is not "required to investigate whether the money is borrowed for a proper purpose or an improper purpose"[188] was made on an assumption or basis, which is far removed from the practice of corporate banking today, he said:[189]

> "A corporation, every time it wants to borrow, cannot be called upon by the lender to expose all its affairs, so that the lender can say, 'Before I lend you anything I must investigate how you carry on your business, and I must know how you want the money, and how you apply it, and when you do have it I must see you apply it in the right way. It is perfectly impossible to work out such a principle'."

No judge familiar with corporate banking today could be heard to issue such a statement.

[18.41] The Supreme Court's decision in *Roche and Roche v Peilow and Peilow*[190] should be a constant reminder that the adoption of an accepted practice may not be enough to avert a successful claim for negligence. To avoid reading a company's memorandum of association would run contrary to prudent and current accepted practice,[191] and must therefore be even more likely to result in a successful claim for negligence than the circumstances pertaining to *Roche and Roche v Peilow and Peilow*.[192]

[18.42] The guiding principles for lawyers and bankers on the application of *ultra vires* is perhaps best illustrated by the English Court of Appeal in *Rolled Steel Products (Holdings) Ltd v British Steel Corp*.[193] Very briefly, the plaintiff's memorandum of association empowered it to "lend and advance money or give credit to such persons, firms or companies and on such terms as may seem expedient, and ... to give guarantees or become security for any such persons, firms or companies". The objects clause concluded with a provision that each sub-clause was to be construed independently of other sub-clauses. The plaintiff's articles of association provided that a director who declared his

---

187. *Re David Payne & Co Ltd, Young v David Payne & Co Ltd* [1904] 2 Ch 608.
188. *Ibid* at 613.
189. *Ibid*.
190. [1986] ILRM 189.
191. The practice of reviewing memoranda and articles of association is not generally applied in leasing transactions of under IR£50,000.
192. [1986] ILRM 189.
193. [1984] BCLC 466; for a further review of this decision and its application to guarantees see Lingard, *Bank Security Documents* (3rd ed) paras 4.3 to 4.9; MacCann, 'The Capacity of the Company' (1992) ILT 79 at 86 submits, "this case is not good law and should not be followed in Ireland".

interest in a contract with the company was to be counted towards the quorum at a board meeting and could vote at the meeting. At the meeting, approving the guarantee and debenture, the director with an interest did not declare his interest. The Court of Appeal held:

(a) that the guarantee and debenture had been executed without the plaintiff's authority since the board meeting which had purported to authorise the transaction was inquorate as the interested director had failed to disclose his interest in the transaction and therefore could not be counted in the quorum;

(b) a clear distinction should be drawn between transactions which were beyond the capacity of a company and those which were in excess or an abuse of the power of the directors;

(c) where a particular transaction was capable of being performed only as something incidental to the carrying out of a company's objects, it would not be rendered *ultra vires* merely because the directors in entering into the transaction on behalf of the company did so for purposes other than those set out in the memorandum, unless a person dealing with the company had actual or constructive notice that the directors were exercising their powers for unauthorised purposes;

(d) the relevant clause in the plaintiff's memorandum of association was not a substantive or separate object but was merely designed to confer on the company an ancillary power to give guarantees and grant security.

Therefore, although the plaintiff was apparently capable of entering into the transaction, the power had been exercised for a purpose not authorised by the memorandum of association and the defendant being aware of this could not rely on the ostensible authority of the directors and hold the plaintiff to the transaction.

The case must be considered in the context that (1) at the time the transaction took place s 9 of the English European Communities Act 1972 (somewhat equivalent to the European Communities (Companies) Regulations, 1973[194]) had not become law, (2) in English law at that time there was no statutory equivalent of s 8 of the Companies Act, 1963 and (3) the rule in *Turquand's case*[195] was not pleaded.

[194.] SI 163/1973; see para **[18.36]** above.
[195.] *Royal British Bank v Turquand* (1856) 6 El & Bl 327; see para **[18.49]** below.

Principles Applicable

[18.43] Nevertheless, what emerges from the two principal judgments of the Court are principles which need to be borne in mind by practitioners when finalising the completion of corporate guarantees and other security. These principles are:

1. A company (incorporated under the Companies Acts) has the capacity to do only those acts which come within its objects as set out in its memorandum of association or which are reasonably incidental to the attainment or pursuit of those objects.[196]

2. An act which is beyond the corporate capacity of a company cannot be ratified.[197]

3. Even where the objects clause authorises a company to give a guarantee and there is a provision in the memorandum of association requiring each paragraph to be construed as a separate object, such authority is merely a power rather than an object or it can be construed only as a power ancillary to the other objects[198] (an exception to this would be a bank or insurance company which enters into guarantees as part of its business[199]).

4. The directors of a company do not have actual authority from the company to exercise any express or implied power other than for the purposes of the company as set out in its principal objects clause.[200] This absence of authority can be put right if all the shareholders of the company consent to the directors' action.[201]

5. The company's directors have ostensible authority to bind the company to a guarantee which falls within the powers expressly or impliedly conferred on it by its memorandum of association. Accordingly, unless a person is on notice to the contrary, a person dealing in good faith with a company which is giving a guarantee, as

---

[196.] *Per* Slade LJ at 507; see also the House of Lords in *AG v Great Eastern Railway Company* (1880) 5 App Cas 473 thus for example a trading company has an implied power to borrow money for its trade; see in *Re David Payne & Co Ltd. Young v David Payne & Co Ltd* [1904] 2 Ch 608 at 612; see also Buckley LJ *in re Horsley & Weight Ltd* [1982] 3 All ER 1045 at 1050; for further reading on implied powers see Courtney, *The Law of Private Companies* (1994) paras 6.077 to 6.079.

[197.] *Per* Slade LJ at 508.

[198.] *Per* Browne-Wilkinson LJ at 517.

[199.] See para **[9.33]** above.

[200.] *Per* Slade LJ at 507.

[201.] *Per* Slade LJ at 507 and 508; the author doubts the correctness of this proposition - see para **[18.59]** below; see also the comments of MacCann, 'The Capacity of the Company' (1992) ILT 79 at 85.

permitted by its objects clause, is entitled to assume the directors are properly exercising their power for the purposes of the company as set out in its objects clause.[202]

6. A person who has notice (actual or constructive) that a transaction, although within the company's corporate capacity, was entered into in excess of the directors' powers cannot enforce the guarantee and will be accountable as constructive trustee for any funds received from the enforcement of the guarantee.[203]

[18.44] What emerges from these principles is, that for the practitioner to be safe, the guarantor's memorandum of association should be reviewed to establish whether the guarantor has the capacity to give a guarantee and, to understand the purpose for which the guarantee is being given in order to establish whether the power being exercised is in furtherance of one of the company's principal objects.[204] The same principle applies to a company borrowing money or creating security over its present or future assets or undertaking.

CORPORATE AUTHORITY

Articles of Association

[18.45] The practitioner then needs to turn to the company's articles of association. The articles of association set out the rules by which a company is managed internally,[205] or as Carroll J put it:[206]

"They[207] are in effect a contract between the company and its members. When they are registered they bind the company and its members as if they had been sealed and signed by each member and contained covenants on the part of each member to observe all the provisions of the articles".

These provisions will include the authorisation of the board of directors to carry on the company's business, on behalf of the company, within the parameters of the company's memorandum of association. Typically, this authorisation is given by the adoption of reg 80 of Table A.[208] Accordingly, it is the board of directors who decide on behalf of the company whether to implement a banking

---

[202.] *Per* Slade LJ at 507 and 508; see also *Charterbridge Corporation Ltd v Lloyds Bank Ltd* [1969] 2 All ER 1185.

[203.] *Per* Browne-Wilkinson LJ at 517 at 518.

[204.] See also Keane, *Company Law in the Republic of Ireland* (2nd ed) para 12.06.

[205.] Companies Act, 1963, s 11.

[206.] In *Roper v Ward* [1981] ILRM 408 at 412.

[207.] She was referring to the memorandum and articles of association collectively.

[208.] Companies Act, 1963, First Schedule; for a review of different interpretations of reg 80 see Flynn, 'The Power to Direct' [1991] DULJ 101.

transaction and approve the underlying documentation. If a company's articles of association so provide the board may delegate its function to a committee of the board.[209] It appears such a committee may consist of one person.[210] The delegation of a company's borrowing powers is generally given under reg 79 of Table A,[211] which states:

> The directors may exercise all the powers of the company to borrow money, and to mortgage or charge its undertaking, property and uncalled capital, or any part thereof, and subject to section 20 of the Companies (Amendment) Act, 1983 to issue debentures, debenture stock and other securities, whether outright or as security for any debt, liability or obligation of the company or of any third party, so, however, that the amount for the time being remaining undischarged of moneys borrowed or secured by the directors as aforesaid (apart from temporary loans obtained from the company's bankers in the ordinary course of business) shall not at any time, without the previous sanction of the company in general meeting, exceed the nominal amount of the share capital of the company for the time being issued, but nevertheless no lender or other person dealing with the company shall be concerned to see or inquire whether this limit is observed. No debt incurred or security given in excess of such limit shall be invalid or ineffectual except in the case of express notice to the lender or the recipient of the security at the time when the debt was incurred or security given that the limit hereby imposed had been or was thereby exceeded."

[18.46] Usually a company will incorporate this regulation without the restriction. Despite the concluding language of the regulation, it is the practice of lenders to review the borrower's articles of association and to require any restriction to be deleted. The decision of Costello J in *Re Shannonside Holdings (in liq)*[212] has not resulted in any variation of this practice. In that case a company with provisions in its articles of association similar to reg 79 issued a mortgage debenture for an amount in excess of its issued share capital. Subsequent to the directors' meeting authorising the issue, a general meeting of the company was convened and it sanctioned the issue. Costello J found that the debentureholder had no notice of the articles of association and thus the debenture would not be invalidated even if the directors had exceeded their powers. In any event he found that the directors had not exceeded their powers because the members had sanctioned the issue. The fact that the members' meeting was held subsequent to the directors' meeting was considered to be

---

[209.] The articles of association will so provide if reg 105 of Part I of Table A to the Companies Act, 1963, First Schedule is adopted.

[210.] See Astbury J in *Re Fireproof Doors Ltd, Hussey v The Company* [1916] 2 Ch 142 at 149.

[211.] Companies Act, 1963 First Schedule, as amended by the Companies (Amendment) Act, 1983 First Schedule, para 24(c).

[212.] High Court, unrep, 20 May 1993.

irrelevant, as the members' meeting had been held prior to the issue. The fact that the members' meeting was held outside the State, contrary to the company's articles of association,[213] did not invalidate the meeting because the members were free to decide to have meetings wherever they liked and such agreement would be implied even if not expressly agreed. When the directors exceed their borrowing authority, the members may subsequently ratify their action (assuming it does not breach the company's objects clause) even after the borrowing has taken place.[214] In *Kinsela v Russell Kinsela pty (in liq)*[215] Street CJ stated:[216]

> "In a solvent company the proprietary interests of the shareholders entitles them as a general body to be regarded as the company when questions of the duty of directors arise. If, as a general body, they authorise or ratify a particular action of the directors, there can be no challenge to the validity of what the directors have done".

This quotation should not be taken as applying where directors have carried out a transaction on behalf of the company which is *ultra vires* the company.

[18.47] It should be noted that a company may grant, and some do, specific authority under its articles of association for its directors to exercise the company's borrowing powers provided the amount borrowed does not exceed the nominal amount of the company's share capital, unless the company has previously sanctioned a greater amount at a general meeting.[217] In *Re Burke Clancy & Co Ltd*[218] Kenny J left open for future consideration whether a lender could assume that a company passed an appropriate resolution at a general meeting - he said:[219]

> "When articles contain such a provision, it would I think, be prudent for lenders to get proof that such a resolution has been passed by the company at a general meeting."

[18.48] The older case of *Irvine v The Union Bank of Australia*[220] is a useful illustration of the limitations of a ratifying resolution. In that case the company's articles of association stipulated that the directors' power of borrowing on behalf of the company should not exceed one half of the company's paid up capital and for the purpose of securing moneys so borrowed the directors were

---

[213.] Regulation 47 of Part I of Table A, First Schedule to the Companies Act, 1963 provides that all general meetings shall be held in the State.
[214.] *Irvine v The Union Bank of Australia* (1877) 2 App Cas 366; see further para **[18.48]** below.
[215.] [1986] 4 NSWLR 722.
[216.] *Ibid* at 730.
[217.] Companies Act, 1963, First Schedule, Table A, reg 79; for older companies see Companies (Consolidation) Act, 1908 First Schedule Table, reg 73.
[218.] High Court, unrep, 23 May 1974, Kenny J.
[219.] *Ibid* at p 9.
[220.] (1877) 2 App Cas 366.

656

empowered to mortgage or charge the company's assets. It was further provided that the borrowing power could be extended by a vote of the members at a general meeting. The directors arranged for the issue of a letter of credit[221] in excess of the limitation. The members ratified the directors' action but subsequently the directors renewed the letter of credit. The Privy Council held that the limitation on the borrowing and mortgaging power was merely a limitation of the directors' authority (conferred by that article) and that the directors' actions in excess of that authority could be ratified and were so ratified; however such ratification did not authorise a renewal.

Thus, any act carried out by the directors on behalf of the company which is "*intra vires* the company but *ultra vires* the directors", that is outside the directors' power but within the company's capacity, may be ratified subsequently by the company's members. In *Re Burke Clancy & Co Ltd*[222] Kenny J held that the company's approval at its annual general meeting of its accounts, showing borrowings in excess of the directors' authority amounted to a ratification of the unauthorised action of the directors. Kenny J stated unequivocally:[223]

> "It is established law that the members of a company may ratify acts which are outside the powers of the directors but are *intra vires* the company."[224]

Rule in *Turquand's Case*

[18.49] This rule emanates from the decision in *The Royal British Bank v Turquand*.[225] Under this rule persons dealing with a company are assumed to have read the company's memorandum and articles of association, as filed in the Companies Registration Office, and to have ascertained that the proposed transaction is not inconsistent with them.[226] The rule does not require the person to enquire into the regularity as to how the transaction was entered into.[227]

---

[221] Deemed to be a borrowing see (1877) 2 App Cas 366 at 380.

[222] High Court, unrep, 23 May 1974, Kenny J.

[223] *Ibid* at p 7.

[224] Kenny J indicated this was established by the courts' decision in *Irvine v The Union Bank of Australia* (1877) 2 App Cas 366 and *Grant v United Kingdom Switchback Railways Company* (1888) 40 Ch 135.

[225] (1856) 6 El & Bl 327.

[226] For further reading on this rule and its scope see Courtney, *The Law of Private Companies* (1994) paras 6.043 to 6.048; see also McCormack, 'The Indoor Management Rule in Ireland' (1935) ILSI 17.

[227] As explained by Jervis CJ (1856) 6 El & Bl 327 at 332 - "We may now take for granted that the dealings with these companies are not like dealings with other partnerships, and that the parties dealing with them are bound to read the statute and the deed of settlement. But they are not bound to do more. And the party here on reading the deed of settlement would find, not a prohibition from borrowing, but a permission to do so on certain conditions. Finding that the authority might be made complete by a resolution, he would have a right to infer the fact of a resolution authorising that which on the face of the document appeared to be legitimately done".

However, a person cannot rely on the rule when he is on notice that there has been an irregularity.[228]

[18.50] This rule was successfully relied upon in *Ulster Investment Bank Ltd v Euro Estates Ltd and Drumkill Ltd.*[229] In that case, the bank advanced funds to the first defendant on the strength of a guarantee from the second defendant. A directors' meeting of the borrower approving the facility letter and the borrowing was attended by two "B" directors whereas the borrower's articles of association provided that a quorum for a directors' meeting was at least one "A" director and one "B" director. Carroll J held that the bank could rely on the rule in *Turquand's* case; the bank was not obliged to call for copies of the board resolutions or make specific enquiries but was entitled to assume that such authorisations had been properly dealt with in accordance with the company's articles of association. In that case, as in most financing transactions, it was a condition precedent to the advance of funds that copies of the appropriate board resolutions would be furnished to the bank's legal advisers. The question arose as to whether this requirement disentitled the bank from relying on the rule in *Turquand's* case. Carroll J found the bank acted *bona fide* throughout and had no reason to believe that the resolution furnished to them had not been validly passed at a meeting with a quorum present. Furthermore, they were entitled to assume that the affixing of the company's seal to the mortgage was evidence that the mortgage itself had been properly approved by the company.[230]

[18.51] A practitioner who relies on the rule in *Turquand's* case as covering for any lack of attention to detail should heed the words of Slade LJ:[231]

"It is a rule which only applies in favour of persons dealing with the company in good faith. If such persons have notice of the relevant irregularity, they cannot rely on the rule ...

Furthermore, even if persons contracting with a company do not have actual knowledge that an irregularity has occurred, they will be precluded from relying on the rule, if the circumstances were such as to put them on inquiry which they failed duly to make".

A practical example of the application of these words can be seen from the judgments delivered in the High Court of Australia in *Northside Developments Pty Ltd v Registrar General.*[232] In that case, a company guaranteed a loan made

---

[228.] See Slade LJ in *Rolled Steel Products (Holdings) Ltd v British Steel Corp* [1984] BCLC 466 at 497; *AL Underwood Ltd v Bank of Liverpool and Martins Ltd* [1924] 1 KB 775.

[229.] [1982] ILRM 57.

[230.] See also *County of Gloucester Bank v Rudry Merthyr Steam and House Coal Colliery Co* [1895] 1 Ch 629.

[231.] In *Rolled Steel Products (Holdings) Ltd v British Steel Corp* [1984] BCLC 466 at 497.

[232.] (1990) 170 CLR 146.

to a third party, of which the only connection was that it shared a common director. In support of the guarantee it created a mortgage which was sealed without the directors' authority; furthermore it was witnessed by a person who purported to be company secretary. The Supreme Court of New South Wales upheld the security on the basis of the rule in *Turquand's* case. The Australian High Court allowed the appeal on the ground that the mortgagee was put upon enquiry that the mortgage was given to secure an advance to a third party without any indication that the mortgage or advance was for the purpose of the company's business and that the rule in *Turquand's* case did not prevent the company from relying upon the fact that the mortgage was executed without its authority.

Rule in *Turquand's* Case and the Sealing of Documents

[18.52] While there is a view that a person receiving a document executed under the seal of a company need not concern himself with the directors' resolution,[233] Mason CJ set out the limits to that rule:[234]

"The affixing of the seal to an instrument makes the instrument that of the company itself; the affixing of the seal is in that sense a corporate act, having effect similar to a signature by an individual. Thus, it may be said that a contract executed under the common seal evidences the assent of the corporation itself and such a contract is to be distinguished from one made by a director or officer on behalf of the company, that being a contract made by an agent on behalf of the company as principal.

Consequently, it has been held that, if the person dealing with the company receives a document to which the common seal has been affixed in the presence of individuals designated in the articles of association, he is entitled to rely on its formal validity.[235]

In some of the cases it is said that it is enough that the third party relies on the affixing of the seal and the instrument appears to be regularly signed.

However, there is no reason why a third party should be entitled to rely on the formal validity of the instrument and to assume that the seal has been regularly affixed if the very nature of the transaction is such as to put him upon inquiry. If the nature of the transaction is such as to excite a reasonable apprehension that the transaction is entered into for purposes apparently unrelated to the company's business, it will put the person dealing with the company upon inquiry. It is one thing to assume that the common seal has been regularly

---

[233.] See Palles CB in *Cox v Dublin City Distillery (No 2)* [1915] 1 IR 345 at 371-2.
[234.] In *Northside Developments Pty Ltd v Registrar General* (1990) 170 CLR 146.
[235.] In *Re County Life Assurance Co* (1870) LR 5 Ch App 288 (directors not appointed), *County of Gloucester Bank v Rudry Methyr Steam and House Coal Colliery Co* [1895] 1 Ch 629 (no quorum at director's meeting) and *Duck v Tower Galvanizing Co* [1901] 2 KB 314 (no directors appointed).

affixed to an instrument apparently executed for the purposes of the company's business; it is quite another thing to assume that the seal has been regularly affixed when the transaction is apparently entered into otherwise than for those purposes."

[18.53] However, provided there is no suspicion about the transaction once the seal of a company has been affixed to a document and countersigned by a director and the secretary in accordance with the articles of association, a lender is not obliged to make further enquiries to ascertain whether or not the signatories were properly appointed as director and secretary.[236]

Rule in *Turquand's* Case and Lenders

[18.54] The judgments of the Australian High Court in *Northside Developments Pty Ltd v Registrar-General*[237] are useful in considering the operation and non-operation of the rule in *Turquand's* case for lenders taking guarantees. Mason CJ stated:[238]

"What is important is that the principle and the criterion which the rule in *Turquand's* Case presents for application give sufficient protection to innocent lenders and other persons dealing with companies, thereby promoting business convenience and leading to just outcomes. The precise formulation and application of that rule call for a fine balance between competing interests. On the one hand, the rule has been developed to protect and promote business convenience which would be at hazard if persons dealing with companies were under the necessity of investigating their internal proceedings in order to satisfy themselves about the actual authority of officers and the validity of instruments. On the other hand, an overextensive application of the rule may facilitate the commission of fraud and unjustly favour those who deal with companies at the expense of innocent creditors and shareholders who are the victims of unscrupulous persons acting or purporting to act on behalf of companies. Agency principles aside, to hold that a person dealing with a company is put upon inquiry when that company enters into a transaction which appears to be unrelated to the purposes of its business and from which it appears to gain no benefit is, in my opinion, to strike a fair balance between the competing interests. Indeed, there is much to be said for the view that the adoption of such a principle will compel lending institutions to act prudently and by so doing enhance the integrity of commercial transactions and commercial morality.

It is not possible to give specific guidance as to the circumstances in which the nature of a transaction will be such as to put a person dealing with a company upon inquiry. So much depends upon the circumstances of the particular case,

---

[236.] *Re Motor Racing Circuits Ltd*, Supreme Court, unrep, 31 January 1997; (1997) CLP 65.
[237.] (1990) 170 CLR 146.
[238.] *Ibid.*

notably the powers of the company (if relevant), the nature of its business, the apparent relationship of the transaction to that business and the actual or apparent authority of those acting or purporting to act on behalf of the company. Much will also depend upon representations about the transaction made by such persons, for the party dealing with the company may often find protection in the principles of agency or the doctrine of estoppel. In this respect, I should indicate my general agreement with the comments made by Brennan J, in his judgment, ... concerning the position of a creditor who takes a company's guarantee for another's debt."

This then leads to the judgment of Brennan J:[239]

"A creditor will ordinarily be put on inquiry when his debtor offers as security a guarantee given by a third party company whose business is not ordinarily the giving of guarantees, for the execution of guarantees and supporting securities for another's liabilities, not being for the purposes of a company's business nor otherwise for its benefit, is not ordinarily within the authority of the officers or agents of the company. Of course the circumstances may show that the giving of such a guarantee and supporting security (hereafter indifferently described as 'guarantee') is for the company's benefit. For example, it may be for the benefit of solvent companies within a group to guarantee the liabilities of a holding company in order to benefit the guarantor as well as other members of the group. In such a case, provided the creditor has been satisfied that it is such a case, the apparently regular execution of a guarantee and supporting security may be relied on pursuant to the indoor management rule. Of course, the only but important consequence of a creditor being put on inquiry is that, in the event that an apparently regular guarantee turns out not to have been authorised by the guarantor company, the guarantor company may show that it is not bound.

When a creditor is put on inquiry, he cannot rely on the apparent regularity of execution of the instrument of guarantee and the indoor management rule but must be satisfied that the relevant officers and agents of the company had the company's authority to execute an instrument pledging the credit or assets of the company to guarantee another's debts."

Some of the foregoing statement may be taking the level of enquiry too far, such as the creditor having to be satisfied that the guarantee is for the benefit of the guarantor.[240] While there is no clear duty at present in Ireland for a creditor to be satisfied as to the benefit (in contrast to the capacity or authority) when dealing

---

239. *Ibid.*

240. Contrary to McWilliam J's judgment in *Re Metro Investment Trust Ltd* High Court, unrep, 26 May 1977 see para **[18.60]** below; "It is neither reasonable nor necessary that those dealing with a company should be expected to negotiate not only the frequently fraught and difficult issue of how a court might interpret an object's clause, but the question of the purpose of the anticipated transaction as well" - Murray, 'Gratuitous Disposition of Company Assets' [1990] DULJ 26 at 35.

with a corporate guarantor,[241] such duty can arise when dealing with an individual guarantor (or at least a duty to see to it that a guarantor has been independently advised).[242] The approach as set out by Brennan J is useful to bear in mind when taking a guarantee:

> "It is convenient now to state in summary the position of a creditor who takes a company's guarantee for another's debt. If the guarantee is not executed in apparent conformity with the formalities prescribed by the Company's constitution, the guarantee is void. If the guarantee is executed in apparent conformity with those formalities, the validity of the guarantee can be assumed if
>
> (i)   it is executed by officers or agents who would ordinarily be expected to have authority to do so,
>
> (ii) the guarantee is given for the purposes of the company's business or otherwise for the company's benefit, and
>
> (iii) there are no circumstances which put the creditor on inquiry as to the authority of those who executed the guarantee to do so.
>
> If these conditions are not met, the creditor must satisfy himself as to the authority of the persons who executed the guarantee to do so. The inquiry must be made of the appropriate officers of the company.
>
> Where authority to execute the guarantee depends upon an antecedent resolution of the board, a creditor who is put on inquiry must be reasonably satisfied that the resolution was duly passed."

[18.55] Accordingly, in advising on an appropriate practice to be adopted, despite the rule in *Turquand's* case as applied by Carroll J,[243] the current practice of calling for a certified copy of a board resolution should continue[244] - to do otherwise might run the risk of not being seen to be acting *bona fide*. Although the minutes of a meeting of the board of directors are not conclusive evidence of the proceedings at the meeting,[245] obtaining a certified copy of a board resolution will, in the absence of any contrary information known to the recipient, be irrefutable evidence of the "transaction entered into by [the company's] board of directors" within the meaning of reg 6 of the European Communities (Companies) Regulations, 1973.[246] Generally, in practice being the officer in charge of administrative matters, it is the company secretary who provides and signs the certified copy or extract of the minutes. However, the

---

241. However see Commercial Benefit at paras **[18.59]**-**[18.62]** below.
242. See *McMackin v Hibernian Bank Ltd* [1905] 1 IR 296; see para **[8.12]**.
243. In *Ulster Investment Bank Ltd v Euro Estates Ltd and Drumkill Ltd* [1982] ILRM 57 at 65; see also para **[18.50]** above.
244. See also Lingard, *Bank Security Documents* (3rd ed) para 2.1
245. See in *Re Fireproof Doors Ltd. Hussey v The Company* [1916] 2 Ch 142.
246. *TCB Ltd v WA Gray* [1986] 3 CMLR 439.

legislation gives specific comfort to the holder of minutes signed by the chairman of the meeting (at which the resolution was passed) or by the chairman of the succeeding meeting.[247]

The ability to rely on the minutes is supported by Finlay J's decision in *Allied Irish Banks Ltd v Ardmore Studios International (1972) Ltd*.[248] Finlay J held that it was sufficient to rely on a copy of a board resolution, certified by a director and by the company secretary, showing the date of the board resolution and that the borrowing was approved at the meeting. The absence of notice to a third director or any actual minutes of the board meeting[249] were considered by Finlay J to be "classical examples of an irregularity in the internal management of the company".[250]

Evidence of Authorising Directors' Resolution

[18.56] Although the point has not been decided in the Supreme Court, it would seem appropriate to follow the separate decisions of Carroll J and Finlay J for a bank or its advisers not to make specific inquiries as to the attendees of the board meeting; a bank though should obtain a certificate from the chairman or the company secretary showing details of the following from the board meeting:[251]

1. A record of the declaration of interests by any relevant directors, pursuant to s 194 of the Companies Act, 1963 and to the company's articles of association,[252] will avoid what transpired in *Rolled Steel Products (Holdings) Ltd v British Steel Corp*.[253] In that case, it was held that the persons relying on the guarantee were deemed to be on notice that the interested director had not declared his interest in the guarantee and therefore could not be counted in the quorum for the directors' meeting approving the guarantee; accordingly the guarantee was set aside. A director's duty of disclosure under s 194 and the company's articles of association require him to disclose full information as to the type and extent of his interest;[254]

[247.] Companies Act, 1963 s 145(2).

[248.] High Court, unrep, 30 May 1973.

[249.] See also *Re Burke Clancy & Co Ltd* High Court, unrep, 23 May 1974, Kenny J, where the absence of any minute in the minute book did not affect the validity of the borrowing.

[250.] Finlay J followed the decision in *Duck v Tower Galvanising Company Ltd* [1901] 2 KB 314 which held that a company's debenture was validly created notwithstanding that no directors of the company had been appointed and no resolution to issue the debentures had been passed.

[251.] Most companies will adopt reg 89 of Table A, Part I to the Companies Act, 1963, First Schedule in their articles of association, such regulation providing that the directors shall cause minutes to be made of all resolutions of directors and committees of directors.

[252.] Companies Act, 1963, First Schedule, Table A, Part I, reg 83.

[253.] [1984] BCLC 466.

[254.] *Movitex Ltd v Bulfield* [1988] BCLC 104.

2.   That the commercial benefit or otherwise of the transaction was considered and noted;[255]

3.   Approval of the borrowing and the granting of the security;[256] where the security, whether it be a mortgage, charge, debenture or guarantee, is to secure all monies due or to become due, reference should be made to that fact and that it may secure indebtedness under future transactions with the lender;[257]

4.   Authorisation for execution of the facility agreement and the security documents;[258] and

5.   The certificate of the company secretary (or chairman) should conclude with words along the following lines:[259]

> "I certify the foregoing to be a true and correct extract from the minutes of a meeting of the board of directors of [the company] duly convened and held[260] on the [ ] day of [ ] at [ ] and there are no subsisting resolutions to the contrary".

[18.57] When the documents have been executed and delivered to the bank or its solicitor, the recipient should examine the documentation to ascertain that they have been executed by the persons authorised to do so by the board of directors. Where documents are executed under seal by the company it will be necessary to ascertain that the execution is carried out in a manner provided by the company's articles of association.[261] In the case of most companies a document

---

[255.] See para **[18.59]** below.

[256.] Usually specifically provided for in a company's articles of association - reg 79 of Table A, First Schedule to the Companies Act, 1963.

[257.] This should avoid the problems which arose for the security holder in *Bank of Ireland v McCabe* (Supreme Court, unrep, 19 December 1994) (1995) CLP 99; see para **[9.14]** above.

[258.] Security documents are usually executed under seal; most companies adopt, with some modifications Table A of the First Schedule to the Companies Act, 1963 as their articles of association, regulation 115 of which provides that the company's seal "shall be used only by the authority of the directors".

[259.] For specimen minutes see Lingard, *Bank Security Documents* (3rd ed) paras 2.18 and 2.19.

[260.] This statement assumes that notice of the meeting was given to all directors (*Allied Irish Banks Ltd v Ardmore Studios International Ltd* High Court, unrep, 30 May 1973 Finlay J) and a valid quorum was present - any director having an interest in the contract is in some companies (principally public companies) notwithstanding the declaration of his interest, precluded from voting and being counted in a quorum (Companies Act, 1963 First Schedule Table A Part I Reg 84).

[261.] The English decision in *TCB Ltd v WA Gray* [1986] 3 CMLR 439 which held that a debenture under seal countersigned by an unauthorised person was nonetheless valid, should not be relied upon as, unlike the equivalent Irish regulations, the European Communities Act, 1972, s 9 specifically provides that no enquiry is necessary; *Re Motor Racing Circuits Ltd* Supreme Court unrep, 31 January 1997 (1997) CLP 65.

executed under seal "shall be signed by a director and shall be countersigned by the secretary or by a second director or by some other person appointed by the directors for the purpose".[262]

The practice in some jurisdictions is for a bank or its lawyer to see to it that it possesses information which verifies the authority of the signatories to the documents, whether under seal or otherwise.[263] This practice is beginning to be adopted in Ireland for significant transactions. Where a liquidator seeks evidence that the execution of a document under the company's seal was duly authorised by the company's board of directors (in accordance with its articles of association),[264] the presence of the seal on the document should be sufficient to give rise to the presumption[265] that the seal was affixed upon the authority of the directors.[266] But in *Northside Developments Pty Ltd v Registrar General*[267] the Australian High Court held that a mortgage given by a guarantor to secure a loan to an unconnected third party was unenforceable as the seal affixed to the mortgage was done so without the authority of the guarantor's board of directors. Any board resolution ratifying the affixing of the seal would appear to operate only prospectively.[268]

[18.58] Any action carried out by a director or directors without authorisation from the board can be ratified by the board retrospectively provided the three conditions set out by Wright J in *Firth v Staines*[269] are satisfied[270] namely (1) the director whose action is sought to be ratified must have purported to act for the company, (2) at the time the action was carried out the company must have been validly in existence[271] and had the appropriate capacity to enter the transaction and (3) at the time of the ratification the company must have been capable of entering into the transaction. It seems a fourth condition should be added,

---

[262.] This applies where a company incorporates into its articles of association reg 115 of Table A of the First Schedule to the Companies Act, 1963; some companies incorporated prior to the enactment of the Companies Act, 1963 require two directors and the company secretary to sign (companies which incorporate reg 76 of Table A in the First Schedule to the Companies (Consolidation) Act, 1908).

[263.] *Bank of New Zealand v Fiberi Pty Ltd* (1994) 12 ACLC 48.

[264.] Reg 115 of Table A in the First Schedule to the Companies Act, 1963 states that "The seal shall be used only by the authority of the directors".

[265.] Which would be rebutted where the recipient was on notice of an irregularity.

[266.] Palles CB in *Cox v Dublin City Distillery (No 2)* [1915] 1 IR 345 at 371-2; see also Mason CJ in *Northside Developments Pty Ltd v Registrar-General* (1990) 170 CLR 146 at 162.

[267.] (1990) 170 CLR 146.

[268.] *Poignand v NZI Securities Australia Ltd* (1994) 120 ALR 237.

[269.] [1897] 2 QB 70 at 75.

[270.] Approved and applied in the Supreme Court by Kenny J in *Bank of Ireland Finance Ltd v Rockfield Ltd* [1979] IR 21 at 35.

[271.] This strand is not necessary in Ireland by virtue of the Companies Act, 1963, s 37.

namely that the board itself has the requisite authority under the company's articles of association to carry out the action previously done by the director.

COMMERCIAL BENEFIT

"There are to be no cakes and ale except such as are required for the benefit of the company."[272]

[18.59] There is a practice amongst some practitioners to require the members of a company to consent to the giving of a guarantee by the company. Unless there is a concern that a guarantee is not being given for the purpose of the company's business as set out in its principal objects clause,[273] it seems unnecessary for a members' resolution, assuming that the management of the company's business has been delegated to the directors under the company's articles of association.[274] It is for the directors, acting in the course of their duty as directors, to decide whether the guarantee is in the best interests of the company and for its commercial benefit. In *Charterbridge Corporation Ltd v Lloyds Bank Ltd*[275] Pennycuick J stated:[276]

"The proper test ... must be whether an intelligent and honest man in the position of a director of the company concerned, could, in the whole of the existing circumstances, have reasonably believed that the transaction was for the benefit of the company".

If the directors consider that the giving of a guarantee is in the best interests and for the commercial benefit of the company, the minutes of the board meeting should record that fact.

If there is a concern that the guarantee is being given for a purpose other than for the guarantor's business and thus is not for its commercial benefit it seems doubtful whether the members can rectify this difficulty,[277] for the reason that the members of a company are not permitted to give away the company's assets.[278] Neither the directors nor the members can carry out the company's activities otherwise than within the parameters of the company's memorandum of association.

272. *Per* Bowen LJ in *Hutton v West Cork Railway* (1883) 23 Ch D 654 at 673 applied by Murphy J in *Re Kill Inn Motel Ltd (in liq)* High Court, unrep, 16 September 1987.
273. Lingard, *Bank Security Documents* (3rd ed) para 4.2 indicates that a special resolution should be passed where there is a doubt as to whether or not the guarantee is for the commercial benefit of the guarantor; see also Murray, 'Gratuitous Disposition of Company Assets' [1990] DULJ 26 at 40.
274. As in Companies Act, 1963, First Schedule, Table A, reg 80 (and for borrowing reg 79).
275. [1969] 2 All ER 1185.
276. *Ibid* at 1194.
277. Notwithstanding Slade LJ's comments (at fn 201 above) or Lingard's view (at fn 273 above).
278. See *Roper v Ward* [1981] ILRM 408.

If the company is in an uncertain financial position, and the security is likely to be called on, the directors need to bear in mind their potential liability for reckless trading[279] as well as the rights and interests of the general creditors[280] (although the giving of security by an insolvent company should not be *ultra vires*[281]). If the guarantee is being given to support indebtedness being provided to another company which is part of the group of companies to which the guarantor is a member, the directors may well take the view that the finance being made available to a fellow group member benefits all companies in the group including the guarantor.[282] Currently in Ireland there is no distinction between what are described in the United States of America as "up-stream" and "down-stream" guarantees - guarantees by a subsidiary of its parent's obligations and guarantees by a parent of its subsidiary's obligations.[283]

[18.60] In *Re Metro Investment Trust Ltd*[284] a company guaranteed the indebtedness of an associated company. The guarantor had the corporate capacity to give guarantees but its liquidator argued that the guarantee was *ultra vires* on the grounds that the guarantor had received no benefit for giving the guarantee. McWilliam J held that:[285]

> "a third party who enters into a transaction involving a company which has power to enter into that transaction is not concerned to investigate the possibility of the transaction not being for the benefit of the company".

[18.61] However, in *Re PMPA Garage (Longmile) Ltd*[286] Murphy J felt it necessary to consider the commercial benefit point. In that case, a number of companies in the PMPA group guaranteed each other's indebtedness for advances made to them by PMPS. The memorandum of association of the PMPA companies empowered the companies to give guarantees in furtherance of the objects for which they were incorporated. Murphy J acknowledged that a director of a subsidiary is often placed in a dilemma and held that, in discharging

---

[279.] Companies Act, 1963, s 297A.

[280.] See *Re Frederick Inns Ltd* [1991] ILRM 582 and [1994] 1 ILRM 387.

[281.] *John C Parkes & Sons Ltd v Hong Kong and Shanghai Banking Corporation* [1990] ILRM 341.

[282.] See *Re PMPA Garage (Longmile) Ltd* [1992] 1 IR 315 para **[18.61]** below; Lingard, *Bank Security Documents* (3rd ed) para 4.10; see also Instone, *Powers and Objects* (1978) NLJ 948 at 950.

[283.] Other than pursuant to the Companies Act, 1990, s 35; for further reading on international parent-subsidiary guarantees see 'Problems with Inter-Company Guarantees: a Survey' [1986] IFLR (April) 28; [1986] IFLR (September) 26.

[284.] High Court, unrep, 26 May 1977, McWilliam J.

[285.] *Ibid* at p 4.

[286.] [1992] 1 IR 315.

his duties to a company a director is entitled to consider the interests of the group as a whole. He said:[287]

> "In the nature of things companies associated with each other as parent and subsidiary or through common shareholders or who share common management and common titles or logos cannot safely ignore the problems of each other. Even the most independently minded director of any such related company would necessarily recognise that he should and perhaps must protect the interests of the group as a whole or else take steps to secure that the particular company disassociates itself from the group".

Murphy J held that the execution of the guarantees, insofar as it allowed each company to borrow money or enjoy the prospect of borrowing money, had benefited the group as a whole; it was an act in furtherance of the objects of each of the associated companies and accordingly was *intra vires* the powers of those companies.

[18.62] A lawyer, when asked by directors as to what points they should consider when deciding whether a proposed transaction is for the company's benefit, might well bear in mind the words of Bevan LJ in *Hutton v West Cork Railway Company*:[288]

> "Most businesses require liberal dealings. The test there again is not whether it is *bona fide*, but whether, as well as being done *bona fide*, it is done within the ordinary scope of the company's business, and whether it is reasonably incidental to the carrying on of the company's business for the company's benefit."

[287.] *Ibid* at 324.
[288.] (1883) 23 Ch D 654 at 672.

Index

words and phrases (contd)
dishonest, 6.30
document of title, 12.09
equity of redemption, 10.03
exempt security interest, 16.13
family home, 10.60
finance lease, 17.33
financial assistance, 18.14-18.15
fixed plant and machinery, 11.27-11.29
full value, 10.61
good marketable title, 10.90
guarantee, 9.02
guarantee insurance business, 9.40
house, 10.74
in good faith, 5.74
interest, 7.73
interest [in land], 10.60
issue, 17.03
lien, 11.03
machinery, 11.29
moneylender, 7.04
moneylending, 7.04
moneylending agreement, 7.04
mortgage, 10.60, 11.03
mortgage lender, 10.74
mutual, 4.30
not negotiable, 5.48, 5.85
non transferable, 5.49
officer, 13.36

or to the order of a specified person, 5.05
ordinary banking instructions, 3.20
ordinary course of business, 7.32
in the ordinary course of business, 5.51
pay cash or order, 5.05
personal chattels, 11.33
plant, 11.28
pledge, 12.02
present again, 5.24
prospectus, 7.79
public, 7.79
purchaser, 10.61
recognised borrower, 11.44
recognised lender, 11.44
refer to drawer, 5.24
secured creditor, 11.02
stock, 11.42
at the time of, 13.30-13.31
unconscionable conduct, 8.42
undertaking, 13.06
vessel, 17.42
without negligence, 5.75, 5.82
wrongful dishonour of cheque, 5.23

young persons (*see also* **minors**)
opening bank accounts for
    identification procedures, 4.04
security given by
    undue influence, defence of, 8.13